PERENNIALS
for Every Purpose

PERENNIALS
for Every Purpose

Choose the Right Plants for Your Conditions, Your Garden, and Your Taste

Larry Hodgson

RODALE

RODALE

WE INSPIRE AND ENABLE PEOPLE TO IMPROVE
THEIR LIVES AND THE WORLD AROUND THEM

© 2000 by Larry Hodgson
Illustrations © 2000 by Stephanie Osser
Illustrations © 2000 by Allison Mia Starcher

First published 2000
First published in paperback 2003

On the cover: the "flowers within a flower within a flower" of *Astrantia major* (great masterwort). See page 326 to discover how easily this beautiful perennial can fit into your shade garden.

We're always happy to hear from you. For questions or comments concerning the editorial content of this book, please write to:

Rodale Book Readers' Service
33 East Minor Street
Emmaus, PA 18098

Look for other Rodale books wherever books are sold. Or call us at (800) 848-4735.

For more information about Rodale Organic Living magazines and books, visit us at:

www.organicgardening.com

Editor: **Karen Bolesta**

Contributing Editor: **Nancy Ondra**

Researcher: **Heidi A. Stonehill**

Cover and Interior Book Designer: **Nancy Smola Biltcliff**

Layout Designer: **Keith Biery**

Illustrators: **Stephanie Osser and Allison Mia Starcher**

Garden Designers: **Pam Baggett, Beverly Fitts, Joanne Kostecky, Pamela Ruch, and Barbara Wilde**

Cover Photographer: **John Glover (hardcover), David Cavagnaro (paperback)**

Photography Editors: **James A. Gallucci and Lyn Horst**

Copy Editors: **Christine Bucher and Nancy N. Bailey**

Manufacturing Coordinator: **Patrick T. Smith**

Indexer: **Lina Burton**

Editorial Assistance: **Kerrie A. Cadden, Celia Cameron, Sarah Wolfgang Heffner, Susan L. Nickol, and Pamela Ruch**

RODALE ORGANIC LIVING BOOKS

Executive Editor: **Margot Schupf**

Art Director: **Patricia Field**

Content Assembly Manager: **Robert V. Anderson Jr.**

Copy Manager: **Nancy N. Bailey**

Editorial Assistant: **Sara Sellar**

Library of Congress Cataloging-in-Publication Data

Hodgson, Larry.
    Perennials for every purpose : choose the plants you need for your conditions, your garden, and your taste / Larry Hodgson.
        p.   cm.
    Includes bibliographical references (p.   ) and index.
    ISBN 0–87596–823–6 hardcover
    ISBN 0–87596–893–7 paperback
    1. Perennials.   I. Title.
SB434 .H64   2000
635.9'32—dc21   99–00696

Distributed to the book trade by St. Martin's Press

| 4 | 6 | 8 | 10 | 9 | 7 | 5 | | hardcover |
| 2 | 4 | 6 | 8 | 10 | 9 | 7 | 5 | 3 | paperback |

RODALE
ORGANIC GARDENING STARTS HERE!

Here at Rodale, we've been gardening organically for more than 50 years—ever since my grandfather J. I. Rodale learned about composting and decided that healthy living starts with healthy soil. In 1940 J. I. started the Rodale Organic Farm to test his theories, and today the nonprofit Rodale Institute Experimental Farm is still at the forefront of organic gardening and farming research. In 1942 J. I. founded *Organic Gardening* magazine to share his discoveries with gardeners everywhere. His son, my father, Robert Rodale, headed *Organic Gardening* until 1990, and today a fourth generation of Rodales is growing up with the magazine. Over the years we've shown millions of readers how to grow bountiful crops and beautiful flowers using nature's own techniques.

In this book, you'll find the latest organic methods and the best gardening advice. We know—because all our authors and editors are passionate about gardening! We feel strongly that our gardens should be safe for our children, pets, and the birds and butterflies that add beauty and delight to our lives and landscapes. Our gardens should provide us with fresh, flavorful vegetables, delightful herbs, and gorgeous flowers. And they should be a pleasure to work in as well as to view.

Sharing the secrets of safe, successful gardening is why we publish books. So come visit us at the Rodale Institute Experimental Farm, where you can tour the gardens every day—we're open year-round. And use this book to create your best garden ever.

Happy gardening!

Maria Rodale

Maria Rodale
Rodale Organic Gardening Books

CONTENTS

Part 2: *Choosing the Best Perennials*
page 66

A Letter from Larry

"As someone who finds both peace and joy
in gardening as well as beauty in the results,
I feel there is no greater pleasure than
being surrounded by abundant blooms."

Dear Reader,

I confess: I'm a plantaholic! Think of a plant, any plant—I've probably grown it. Every summer, huge boxes of plants find their way to my doorstep. I also grow hundreds of varieties of plants from seed each year. I've tested well over 3,000 species and cultivars of perennials alone!

Since 1983, when I gave up my day job, I've made my living strictly from my passion for plants. I list my profession as "garden writer" but that includes more than writing newspaper columns, magazine articles, books, and copy for seed catalogs. I also lecture, translate French and English horticultural texts, and talk about plants on television and radio.

My father, a self-taught gardener, passed his knowledge of gardening on to me, and what I didn't learn from him, I picked up on my own. In fact, I'm proud to say I've killed more plants than just about anyone I know. Stubborn as I am, I rarely give up on a plant until I've learned its secrets. And the secrets are what I deliver to you in this book.

The Truth and Nothing But . . .
You may notice that I see things differently from other authors of books about perennials.

Some writers make all perennials sound like winners, but I think gardeners should know whether a perennial has a flaw or two. Let's be honest here: There are plants that are so-so at best and others that are real dogs. Wouldn't you like to know that *before* you buy them?

Other perennials, such as delphiniums, are prima donnas: They do perform, but only if you give them star treatment. I've offered a lot of advice on more than 700 perennials. Some give you great value for your money, some are weeds, and some need special care—and you'll learn which is which by reading this book.

I believe in using the easiest possible gardening techniques and choosing plants that are well adapted not only to your needs but also to your growing conditions so your garden can take care of itself. And if your garden can almost take care of itself, that means—if you're a plantaholic like me—you can cut down on lawn and add more gardens.

An Encyclopedia with a Purpose
I've organized this book in a rather unique way to match my rather unique point of view. Most perennial books list plants in alphabetical order,

which is fine but unhelpful. Instead, I've grouped plants together based on special features, such as ease, use, and location. For example, if you want perennials that will bloom for years with little effort on your part, check my selection of "No-Care Perennials" beginning on page 188. If you have a shady area on the north side of your house, check my choices in "Perennials That Bloom in the Shade," starting on page 316. This organization makes it simpler for you to choose plants according to your needs.

In each plant entry, I've summarized the plant's "vital statistics" right at the start for quick reference. You'll also find interesting extra information in the entries. For example, in the *Mertensia* entry on page 332, you'll find "Smart Substitutes": plants that, like bluebells, have blue flowers and early-spring bloom but will thrive in sites where bluebells won't, such as a sunnier, warmer locale. Many of the perennials I've chosen also have close relatives, and I've described them in "Kissing Cousins" boxes.

Because I've traveled to gardens worldwide, I've included another special feature called "Around the World," which gives you a glimpse of the fantastic plants I've seen. I love telling people about plants. That's why you'll find tables at the ends of some chapters—I had so much to say that I had to cram more plant descriptions in these tables because they wouldn't all fit on the plant entry pages.

Writing *Perennials for Every Purpose* was an absolute thrill for me, and I hope you'll find it invaluable when planning and planting your perennial gardens.

Plants for Every Garden

Another special benefit of *Perennials for Every Purpose* is its emphasis on both cold-hardy and heat-tolerant plants. Gardeners in cold-winter areas will appreciate my experience testing plants under rather novel conditions. You see, I live in the heart of French Quebec, in USDA Hardiness Zone 3—a much colder climate than most other garden writers live in. My book offers a unique perspective on adapting plants to northern growing conditions.

And for gardeners in warmer zones, I've also included new and exciting information about the heat tolerance of perennials. As a result of extensive research by the American Horticultural Society, there is now a heat zone map that divides North America into zones based on the intensity of summer heat (you'll find the map on page 502)—often the limiting factor in choosing perennials for warm, humid areas.

Armed with the facts on *both* the cold-hardiness and heat-tolerance of perennials, plus my recommendations on the best plants for any purpose, you should enjoy success with every new perennial you plant. As someone who finds both peace and joy in gardening as well as beauty in the results, I feel there is no greater pleasure than being surrounded by abundant blooms.

Larry Hodgson

PART 1

PERENNIAL GARDENING MADE EASY

If you're just starting to garden with perennials, you'll need to learn some basics before you jump into planting your garden. And even if you're a fairly experienced gardener and know your way around a shovel, a quick refresher on gardening techniques is never a bad idea. This section is just what it purports to be—an introduction to growing perennials the easy way.

There are, of course, all sorts of ways to grow perennials, but many require intensive labor and lots of time. I've been gardening practically all my life, and I've found many ways to eliminate extraneous and time-consuming tasks that don't give much in the way of results. Instead, I'll show you the simplest, fastest ways to get things done. While I can't guarantee that your perennials will grow and thrive on their own, you'll discover enough easy tricks and done-in-a-snap techniques that you can start your perennial garden without a sore back and a handful of blisters. You can practically put your garden on cruise control. What? You never thought of perennials as low-maintenance plants? Read the chapters that follow, and you may completely change your mind!

GETTING YOUR
Garden Started

Don't let the thought of perennial gardening scare you! You don't have to plan, prepare, and plant a perennial garden all in one spring. Of course, you *can* go whole hog, rip out a huge section of lawn, and install a perennial garden over a single weekend. But I hope you have the proper medication for blistered hands and aching muscles. Instead, do what's doable: Break up the tasks, spreading them over a full year or even several years, and create your garden a bit more slowly. It won't be nearly as hard on your back—or your pocketbook.

It's time to get down to the nitty-gritty. For a healthy, easy-to-manage perennial garden over the long term, you must start off right.

◄ Want breathtaking hellebore blossoms like these in your garden? It's easy to do if you start with well-prepared soil and pick the right site.

Step by Step to the Perfect Garden

Here's my foolproof guide to creating your ideal perennial garden. I'm not promising that it will look like Versailles—but it *will* be the garden you want, and it will look as good as you want it to. I promise!

Pick a spot . . . any spot. You can grow perennials just about anywhere. But, to make life easier, why not start with an area of bright, sunny lawn far from any trees or large shrubs? You can be reasonably sure that such an area already has at least moderately good soil, and that it doesn't have many difficult woody roots to deal with. And, a wider variety of perennials will grow in sun than in shade.

Draw up a plan. It doesn't have to be sophisticated or complex, just sufficient to give you an idea of what you want to do. Go out and measure the future garden, then try sketching it on graph paper using proportional spacing: Four squares could represent a square foot (0.093 m^2), or much more or much less, depending on what you're trying to condense on paper and the size of the squares. You can plan the whole yard if you want, or just the flower garden: It's up to you.

When you have your garden mapped, draw irregular patches to represent plants. Now color the patches in shades that please you. Next, choose plants that match the color, height, and bloom season you're looking for and print their names in the appropriate patches. If your plan is for a big garden, decide just how much of the plan you want to carry out in a single year. I repeat: You don't have to (and probably shouldn't) try to do the whole thing at once. Instead, plan to assemble it in stages over several years, starting with the most visible spots and gradually filling in.

Prepare your plant list. From the plan, you can now calculate how many plants of each type you'll need. Start by listing the plants you want on a sheet of paper, then estimate how many you'll need to fill your plan. I estimate that each medium-sized perennial will need at least a square foot (0.093 m²) of space at maturity, larger plants will need much more, and smaller ones somewhat less space. To be sure, check each plant's description in Part 2, starting on page 66, for its eventual spread.

Plan ahead for an approximate planting date. In most areas, early spring is the best time to plant a perennial garden, but fall (or winter in warm-winter areas) is the best time to prepare it. Usually, as a gardener, you're in less of a hurry in fall than in spring and besides, letting the soil settle for a few months makes the garden easier to plant and allows the soil amendments time to do their job. You can prepare *and* plant the garden in the spring or in the fall, but make sure

you leave yourself lots of time if you intend do both in the same season. If you buy all your plants in pots, you can even plant them in midsummer, but be prepared to sweat!

Trace the plan on the lawn. Get out your measuring tape for this! Use stakes hammered into the ground with string drawn taut between them for straight lines. For more rounded edges, use an old hose to determine the border or trace its outline with bonemeal, sand, or a few cups of flour from the kitchen. If the plan doesn't look as good in the garden as it did on paper, now is the time to make adjustments—before you do any digging.

Get the grass out. Once you're satisfied with the garden's shape, it's time to remove the grass (or whatever else was growing there). You'll see how on page 11. It's especially important to remove any perennial weeds by carefully digging

Preparing the soil for a planting of sun-loving perennials like this garden that features irises, sedum, and heucheras is relatively simple: Just clear off the sod, dig in some compost, and you'll be ready to plant.

Larry's Planning Secret

Can't get a handle on what's in bloom when? Try my trick of covering your finished plan with three sheets of tracing paper. Draw the patches representing late bloomers on the bottom sheet, summer bloomers and everbloomers on the middle one, and spring bloomers on the top sheet. (Make sure you label each sheet so you know which is which.) Then look at the sheets separately to see if there is a reasonable amount of bloom and enough of the right colors in each season, correcting the plan if necessary.

them out. Just cultivating the soil is likely to break them into little pieces, each one of which will sprout into a new weed!

Prepare the soil. See page 9 for more details on how to amend and loosen the soil. If you prepare the garden ahead of time (in fall for spring planting, for example), you can even take the time to have the amended soil analyzed. Remember. Preparing the soil in a new garden can take some time. Digging up and amending even a small garden can take up most of a weekend, so be sure to take that into account.

Get the plants you need. If this is your first perennial garden, it's easiest to buy your plants. If you already have perennial beds, of course, you can count on being able to divide or move plants and save a few dollars.

If you're going to grow some of your perennials from seed, start early—as much as a year ahead. And if you're ordering plants by mail,

that will also take some advance planning. Order in winter for spring delivery, and in early summer for fall planting. Most people, though, just shuffle off to the nearest nursery at planting season with a list of what they want, keeping their fingers crossed that all the plants are in stock—and then making lots of substitutions because the plants rarely are.

Test the waters. Trace the planting areas on the soil with bonemeal, flour, or sand, then place the plants, still in their pots, in the appropriate spots. If you want to make changes, remember that now is the time to do so. Once they're planted, many perennials resent being moved.

Don't panic over the garden's temporarily barren look: Perennials take time to fill in—sometimes two or three years—so it's normal to have considerable gaps between the plants at first. If you want a fuller look the first year, interplant with annuals in a similar color range. And

If you're planning a new perennial bed, be sure to experiment with size and layout before you start to dig. Just place your potted plants in a pleasing arrangement, then sprinkle a line of flour on the grass to outline the bed shape.

you may also have out-and-out holes in the garden: plants that you were not able to find or that will only be available later in the season. Plan on filling these spaces in with annuals, too.

Plant, plant, plant. Dig an individual hole for each plant (more details on this on page 12), taking special care not to dig too deeply. Then pop your plant in, fill the hole with soil, and water well.

Mulch your bed. A final touch is to cover the soil between the plants with a 2- to 3-inch (5- to 8-cm) layer of organic mulch. This will not only make the garden look nice, but it also helps the plants grow better and keeps out weeds. You'll find more on mulching on page 60.

Well, that's my method for a perfect perennial garden. Now let's get down to basics and see how it's done.

How to Pick the Right Spot

Some perennials are naturally forgiving. Put them in a bit too much shade, or give them a little less moisture than they'd like, and they'll still do fairly well. Others are quite specific, as in "Give me perfect drainage or I'm outta here!" But no matter how picky or how tolerant certain

perennials can be, all of them grow (and flower) best when you try to meet their needs.

In Part 2, starting on page 66, you'll find descriptions of more than 150 genera of perennials with the specifics of what they need. All you have to do is look at what conditions *you* have available, and when the two match, your plants should thrive. But that means you have to know your own gardening space. You can begin by determining whether your garden is in sun, light shade, partial shade, or full shade.

Sun or Shade?

Full sun can mean a lot of things, but in the garden, it means direct sun for most of the day. In most cases, six hours of direct sun is close enough. Most "full-sun plants" can also cope with light shade, that is, about four to six hours of sun. Even perennials that like full sun probably wouldn't mind some protection from full sun in the middle of the day when it's hottest, especially in warm-summer areas.

Partial shade is not quite so easy to define. It can mean sunlight filtering through overhead trees for much of the day, or from two to four hours of direct sun—perhaps only in the morning or the afternoon—followed by deep shade for the rest of the day.

Even deep-shade areas can receive some direct sun—up to two hours a day—but they often receive none at all. You'll be most likely to have deep shade on the north side of your home or wall. Sometimes these areas are so deeply shaded that only mosses and ferns will thrive. But all is not lost: You'll find examples of plants than can cope with deep shade on page 316.

You'll probably find that your garden has both sun and varying intensities of shade, so make sure you choose plants accordingly.

Many woodland wildflowers need shady, moist conditions to look their best. These trilliums are thriving in a shady spot under trees, edged by low-growing sweet woodruff (*Galium odoratum*).

Wet or Dry?

The level of humidity in the soil can also determine whether your plants thrive—or even survive. Some soils remain evenly moist most of the time, except during severe droughts, and this will suit plants listed as liking moist soils just fine. In fact, *most* plants will do best in evenly moist soils. If you want to grow a wide range of perennials and your soil tends to be dry, put down a thick mulch (this helps keep soil more moist) and consider installing an irrigation system.

"Evenly moist" does not mean wet. Spots where water collects after a rainfall or at snowmelt in spring are said to be poorly drained. Only a few perennials (see "Water-Loving Perennials" starting on page 270) actually tolerate having their roots sit in water for any length of time, and even these will do just as well or better in evenly moist soil. So good drainage is important for most plants. If you have a wet spot in your yard, consider installing a raised bed or berm. Raising the garden just 12 inches (30 cm) above a poorly drained spot is usually enough to solve the problem.

Some plants, though, want more than good drainage, they want *perfect* drainage (most of these plants are found in "Drought-Resistant Perennials," starting on page 242). These plants originate in arid climates or grow among loose rocks in the wild. Any accumulation of moisture in the soil, even if the water sinks right in without puddling, is too much for them. Unless you already know you have sandy, perfectly drained soil, you would do better to choose from the many moisture-tolerant perennials instead.

Rich or Poor?

You can usually tell if your soil is poor almost at a glance. When it's dry, it will probably be stony, heavy, and pale. It will even smell dusty! Rich soils remain dark brown and contain lots of fibrous material, have a fluffier texture, and smell like a rainy day in spring. However, a complete

Annuals like white alyssum and blue salvia are great choices for filling the gaps between perennials in a garden. Here, they make a lovely combination with pink-flowered catmint (*Nepeta* x *faassenii*) and yellow *Heliopsis helianthoides* 'Summer Sun'.

soil test (see "Acidic or Alkaline?" below) is much more dependable then your senses in determining whether a soil is rich, average, or poor.

You'll be relieved to discover that there are a surprising number of perennials that do best in ordinary or even poor soils. You may want to grow these plants during the first years after you've made your garden, since the soil is still on the poor side.

As you add more and more organic matter, your soil will become richer and richer, and your original plants may no longer be suitable. Don't worry! Most perennials flower best in rich soils, so there will be plenty of plants you can use to replace the poor-soil lovers.

Acidic or Alkaline?

All materials are either alkaline, acidic, or neutral. This applies to soils as well. You can measure the acidity or alkalinity of soil by using the pH scale. It runs from 1 to 14, with 1 being impossibly acidic, 14 unbearably alkaline, and 7 neutral. Most perennials are adapted to slightly acid soils, normally between pH 6.0 and 6.9. For garden purposes, then, a soil pH of about 6.5 is ideal because the vast majority of plants will thrive in it.

There are many soil pH test kits on the market, but reading them is sometimes difficult, and translating the results into the proper treatment is even more complicated. It's better to have your soil professionally tested, ideally every four or five years. You'll obtain a more precise reading and exact specifications on how much lime or sulfur to add to correct your pH imbalance. Ask your county extension agent or local garden center if they do pH tests and what you'll need to do. And be sure to tell them you want organic recommendations with your test results.

When you get the test results, you can apply the recommended amount of ground limestone or sulfur to your soil. Work these amendments into the soil if you apply them in spring or summer. But if you apply them in fall or winter, you can simply spread them evenly over the soil surface because plants are dormant then and won't be harmed by any excess concentration. Just let rain and snow work them into the ground over the winter.

If your soil is only slightly acidic or alkaline, it might be enough to add finished compost, which tends to neutralize both acidity and alkalinity. You can apply it anytime, since it won't harm your plants.

Preparing the Site

Now it's time to get down to the nitty-gritty. For a healthy, easy-to-manage perennial garden over the long term, you must start off right. Mistakes made now are hard to correct once the plants are in place, and if you decide to skimp on preparations, you might have to live with your errors for a long time to come.

If possible, work in your garden when the soil is slightly moist, but not soaking wet. Moist soil will make your work easier (wet soil is heavy!); working with soggy soil, especially clay, can destroy its texture, turning it into something resembling cement. One reason preparing the garden in the fall is such a good idea is that soils in many climates tend to remain soggy for weeks in the spring but are much more workable in the fall. If the soil is dry at planting time, on the other hand, water it well two or three days before beginning.

Improving the Soil

You can garden in just about any soil, but the results can be disappointing in heavy clay or pure sand. Clay soils are heavy, drain poorly, and often stay wet and cold for long periods in the spring, which delays planting. Water may puddle up on them, drowning sensitive plants, and roots have a hard time pushing into them. On the other hand, clay soils are often very rich—when you can get them to release their nutrients.

Sand is just the opposite. Water drains right through it, so plants often suffer from a lack of water only a few days after a heavy downpour. And it doesn't hold many nutrients, so it is often very poor.

To test which kind of soil you have, dig up a handful of slightly moist soil, squeeze it in your palm, then open your hand. Garden-quality soil will hold its shape for a few seconds before falling apart. Clay will form a solid lump and stay put. And sand will fall apart immediately, not sticking together at all.

Curiously, the solution to both heavy clay soils and excessively sandy soils is to add plenty of organic material. Compost, leaf mold, decayed manure, chopped leaves, shredded bark, and peat moss are just a few of the organic materials you can use to convert clay or sandy soils into rich garden soil. Just use whatever is most widely available and least expensive in your area.

Heavy clay is the hardest to convert. If you really want to improve it, add 6 to 8 inches (15 to 20 cm) of organic material and work it into the soil to a depth of 12 inches (30 cm). Be forewarned—digging down 12 inches (30 cm) into clay soil is hard labor! With sandy soils, 3 to 4 inches (8 to 10 cm) of organic matter dug in to a depth of 6 to 8 inches (15 to 20 cm) is usually sufficient—and it's *much* easier to do. In both cases, it's important to keep adding 2 to 3 inches (5 to 8 cm) of organic matter every year.

Reworking Old Gardens

If you're simply converting a vegetable garden into a flower garden or an annual garden into a perennial bed, you may not need to do much work at all. This is especially true if the original garden was relatively weed-free and the plants were doing well.

You might want to carry out a pH test as a safeguard (see "Acidic or Alkaline?" on the opposite page), or you can just skip the test (the previous plants were doing well, so why bother?), and dig or pull out any perennial weeds and cultivate the soil. Don't try to hoe or cultivate weeds into submission: They'll simply sprout anew . . . and in greater quantities than ever!

Next, spread a thick layer of organic matter such as compost, well-rotted manure, or peat moss, 3 to 4 inches (8 to 10 cm) deep if possible. (You can rarely go overboard with organic matter!) With a shovel, garden fork, or tiller, turn over the soil to a depth of 5 to 6 inches (13 to 15 cm) or more, then rake it to smooth it a bit. Job done: On to planting!

SITE PROBLEMS

Where's the best place to put your perennials? If you really look at your yard, you'll find that various gardens around your property don't share the same conditions. One end of the garden can be growing in shade while the other is in sun. Or the back of the garden under an overhanging roof may get almost no rain, while the soil in the front part is always soaked. Here are a few typical site problems, with suggestions on how to correct them.

CONDITIONS	SOLUTIONS
Shady conditions	Choose shade-tolerant plants. (See "Perennials That Bloom in the Shade" on page 316 and "Perennials for Fabulous Foliage" on page 346 for suggestions.) Open up wooded areas by removing some lower branches. Consult an arborist to see whether some upper branches can also be removed to increase the light below.
Root competition	Water more often or add an irrigation system. Consider using especially tough plants, such as groundcovers. Add large planters of tender perennials to the site for more interest.
Fast-draining soils (including sand)	Add plenty of organic material to the soil. Choose drought-resistant plants. Consider installing irrigation. If your soil is extremely sandy, try raised beds filled with a good topsoil and compost mixture.
Heavy clay soil	Add plenty of organic material to your soil and double-dig your beds for better drainage. Grow your plants in raised beds. See "Improving the Soil" on page 9 for more suggestions.
Poor soil	Add abundant organic material and long-lasting organic fertilizers. Apply foliar sprays in midseason to perk up yellowing plants. Apply a mulch of grass clippings or shredded leaves annually to add more organic matter. Choose plants adapted to poor soil. (See "Soil Preference" under the individual plant descriptions in Part 2.)
Wet soil	Choose plants that tolerate moist soil (see "Water-Loving Perennials" on page 270). Create a bog or water garden to take advantage of your site conditions. Grow plants in raised beds to create drier conditions. Improve drainage by adding soil amendments or by installing a drainage system.
Dry soil	Add plenty of organic matter. Mulch heavily. Choose drought-resistant plants. Consider installing irrigation.
"Rain shadow" effects	Add plenty of organic matter and mulch heavily to combat the drought-causing effects of roof overhangs and nearby walls. Consider an irrigation system. Choose drought-tolerant or drought-resistant plants.
Poor air circulation	Choose disease-resistant plants. Thin plants occasionally. Allow more space between plants than usual. Consider removing lower branches on overhanging trees.
Windy conditions	Plant a living windbreak of shrubs, evergreens, or perennial grasses. Add a fence to your garden plans.
Slopes and hillsides	Plant a combination of groundcovers and perennials that have spreading root systems. Use erosion-control mats (made of burlap, wool mat, or paper). Cover the mats with mulch until plants are established.

Starting from Scratch the Traditional Way

Most perennial gardens are started from scratch. There are two ways of handling this: The traditional method is slow and requires a considerable amount of elbow grease; the fast-and-easy method requires more money but little time and effort. You choose!

To prepare a perennial bed by the traditional method, start by removing whatever was growing in the spot before. If that was lawn or field, cut out sections of sod with a sharp shovel and dig under them to remove them. Try to remove only the uppermost layer of soil with the sod, about 1 to 2 inches (2.5 to 5 cm) thick because the richest soil is near the surface and you want to keep it.

Next, go through the planting area with a garden fork and dig any weed roots out of the soil. Then cover the soil with at least 3 to 4 inches (8 to 10 cm) of compost or another organic material. Use more if the soil is heavy clay. Using a shovel or rotary tiller, turn the soil over to a depth of 8 to 12 inches (20 to 30 cm), mixing it well.

A big drawback to the traditional method is that turning the soil over has exposed hundreds of weed seeds that were lying dormant. You need to mulch traditionally prepared gardens heavily after you plant them, or your new garden will soon be weed heaven!

My Fast-and-Easy Method

This method allows me to prepare a medium-sized garden in less than an hour, with no back-

When preparing a new bed, use a spade to slice off the top 1 to 2 inches (2.5 to 5 cm) of sod. Any deeper and you'll remove too much rich, nutrient-filled soil.

breaking work. And it's the only method that gives me a truly weed-free garden to start with.

Start by saving up old newspapers for a few weeks, then order an appropriate amount of top-quality soil. I find that buying a soil and compost mix gives me top-quality soil that has been heated enough by natural methods to destroy any lingering weed roots or seeds. Mushroom compost (leftover soil from mushroom growing) is also excellent. Ask your county agent where you can get organic, weed-free soil in your area.

The day before the soil arrives, mow the area if it's a lawn or meadow, or cut back all stems and branches to the ground if it's a former woodlot. There is no need to pick up debris (lawn clippings, branches, dead leaves, etc.). Let it all decompose where it lies.

Now cover the entire area with a layer of newspaper, at least five to ten pages thick. Make

Turn any site into a usable garden almost overnight by overlapping layers of newspaper and adding topsoil. The newspaper acts as a temporary weed barrier until plants and mulch are in place.

sure the newspapers overlap completely at the edges. If the day is windy, soak the newspaper in a bucket of water first to keep it from blowing away. To finish, cover the newspaper with a thick layer of top-quality soil. A full foot (30 cm) is best, but in areas where there are underlying roots of trees or shrubs that you want to preserve, 8 inches (20 cm) is the maximum.

Planting Perennials

If you've ever planted anything, from tomatoes to trees, planting perennials will hold no surprises for you. The techniques for planting a perennial are essentially identical to the ones you use for planting any other plant.

From Pot to Plot

If you're planting perennials purchased in pots or grew your own from seed in individual pots, push any mulch to one side and dig a hole the same depth as the rootball is tall and about twice as wide.

Don't pull the plant from its pot or you may yank off part of the rootball. Instead, turn the plant upside down, slipping your fingers around its base and supporting the rootball with the palm of your hand. Tap sharply on the pot with your palm to loosen it, then remove it and place the rootball in the planting hole.

If the plant's crown (the area where the roots meet the stems) is somewhat below ground level, take the plant out of the hole and add more soil to the bottom. If the crown is above ground level, dig a bit deeper. Now half-fill the hole with soil and water well. Finish filling the hole, firm the soil around the roots, and water thoroughly a second time.

If there are a few roots circling the bottom of the pot, spread them out before planting. If the plant is severely potbound, with *many* roots circling the pot, score the rootball with a knife, running it down about ¼ inch (6 mm) deep on all

To remove a perennial from its pot, hold the bottom of the plant pot, tip it over, and slide out the plant, supporting the rootball with the palm of your hand.

four sides. This will ensure that a fresh crop of new roots grows out in all directions.

When planting perennials growing in peat or fiber pots (often the case when they have fragile roots that shouldn't be disturbed), *don't* remove the pot. Just plant the perennial, pot and all. If the pot rises above the ground, though, cut that part off. Exposed to the air, it could act as a wick, absorbing water from the root zone and causing the plant to dry out.

Bareroot Planting

You may have received bareroot plants through the mail, or you may be transplanting perennials or have dozens of divisions to plant. The technique is almost the same as planting potted perennials, although judging the exact planting depth is not quite as easy.

If your perennial is severely rootbound, score the rootball about ¼ inch (6 mm) deep on all four sides to stimulate new root growth.

First, prepare a planting hole wide enough, since bareroot plants generally have a larger root spread than potted plants. Set the plant in the hole, adjusting its height if necessary by adding or removing soil.

Build a small cone of soil in the center of the hole and place the plant on this cone so the roots can hang down. Spread the roots out and half-fill the hole with soil, tamping it down firmly. Water well, then finish filling the hole, firm the soil around the roots, and water thoroughly a second time.

In dry climates or on slopes where water runs off quickly, build a ring of soil around the plant. (I refer to it as a "donut.") In the future, when you water, fill the donut with water, and you can be sure it will drain to the roots of the plant and not end up watering something else.

After You Plant

To finish any planting, bareroot or from pots, mulch abundantly and insert a plant label next to each new plant. For the next few weeks, water newly planted perennials whenever their soil has become nearly dry.

Of course, before you can start planting, you need to have plants. And selecting your plants is what the next chapter is all about.

Don't let poor soil drainage thwart your dreams of a perennial garden. Just build up a raised bed, and edge it with a sturdy, attractive material like fieldstone that matches the style or color of your house.

PICKING THE PERFECT
Perennials

The secret to easy perennial gardening is simple enough: Prepare the growing area thoroughly, then pick plants that are naturally tough and well adapted to your conditions . . . and plant lots of them! In fact, if you choose the right perennials, you'll scarcely have any work to do at all. Good basic care is all your plants will need.

I can't imagine gardening without perennial catalogs on hand. They are often a gold mine of information, and they carry all the choicest plants I hear other gardeners getting excited about.

◄This purple coneflower (*Echinacea purpurea*) is a good example of a nearly perfect perennial: It's easy to care for, tolerating both heat and drought. The large, pincushion-like flower centers attract a wide array of garden-friendly birds and butterflies. And this perennial beauty blooms for weeks on end!

10 Things to Look For in a Perennial

What exactly are you looking for in a perennial? The right color is probably the first thing that comes to mind, but it's not the most important, since most perennials are available in a wide range of shades. What you *really* should be looking for, if you want ease of care and a garden that is always attractive, are perennials that meet my ten criteria for a perfect perennial:

1. The plant should be adapted to a wide range of general conditions (sun and shade, rain and drought, heat and cold, etc.).

2. It should be well adapted to local conditions that can be limiting factors in your choice of perennials (extremely cold winters or hot summers, particularly dry or humid air, etc.)

3. It should be long-lived.

4. It should be quick to establish. (Who wants to wait five years for results?)

5. It should be naturally resistant to insects and diseases.

6. It should grow more strongly than most weeds, yet not strongly enough to *become* a weed.

7. It should need little in the way of pruning, staking, division, and other fussy maintenance tasks.

8. It should remain attractive over a long period.

9. It should be easy to propagate.

10. It should be widely available.

Sounds great, doesn't it? If there were such a plant, it would truly be the perfect perennial. But it doesn't exist. In fact, some of our criteria contradict each other. For example, criterion number 3, long-lived, and number 4, quick to establish, are almost never found in the same plant. Generally speaking, perennials that are long-lived are very slow to establish, while those that reach perfection in the first season are almost always short-lived perennials that scarcely survive longer than a biennial.

Generally, the best you can do is find perennials that share seven out of ten of the desirable traits. With plants that have seven out of ten good qualities, you'll be in for an easy, beautiful ride. Plants with at least five good traits can also be quite useful. Less than that, though, and you'll probably be in for a lot of work . . . and more than a bit of disappointment.

How to Know What You're Looking For

The worst error any gardener can make is to buy plants without thinking, as when you go to a nursery and pick a plant because "it was the perfect shade of pink and just looked so adorable in its little pot that I couldn't resist." Trust me—looking good in a nursery pot is *not*

a major criterion in picking a perennial. Instead, research your choices before you buy.

Read over the chapters in Part 2, "Choosing the Best Perennials," that specially suit your needs, such as "Perennials That Bloom in the Shade" on page 316 if your garden is shady or "Perennials for Birds & Butterflies" on page 448 if your goal is to attract more wildlife to your garden. Make lists of the plants that suit you and your growing conditions. Then compare them to the "10 Things to Look For in a Perennial" criteria on page 15, pick out the ones that suit you, and order your plants by mail or head to the garden center, detailed list in hand.

This doesn't mean you can never buy perennials on a whim, but if there's a plant you don't know and just can't resist buying, try to find out more about it at the nursery. (Ask around: If it's a good nursery, at least one of the salespeople will be an expert on perennials.) And when you do bring it home, read all about it in Part 2 in this book *before* you plant it, not after it's comfortably installed in a totally inappropriate spot.

While there's no such thing as a perfect perennial, lady's-mantle (*Alchemilla mollis*) comes close. It has long-lasting, attractive foliage and gorgeous chartreuse flowers, and it grows well in sun or shade. Many hybrid *Geranium* cultivars, including 'Nimbus', are also long-blooming, adaptable garden plants.

To get the best from 'Prairie Night' bee balm and other perennials that suffer from leaf diseases like powdery mildew, choose your planting site carefully. The plants will be healthier if they're out in the open, where air can circulate freely around them.

"Think Twice" Perennials

I call perennials with really major flaws—flaws that can override their best qualities and even make you wonder why you ever planted them in the first place—"think twice" perennials. But some of the plants that fall into this category are very popular with gardeners and are featured in many nurseries and catalogs, so they're impossible to ignore. In Part 2, "Choosing the Best Perennials," beginning on page 66, they've been given the **Think Twice** logo, indicating that you should give buying them a second thought.

Often, "think twice" plants are particularly subject to disease or insects or are highly invasive. For example, garden phlox (*Phlox paniculata*) and bee balm (*Monarda didyma*) are both gorgeous garden plants with an unfortunate susceptibility to mildew. But the news isn't all bad—both have cultivars that are disease-resistant; you just have to know to look for them. And highly invasive plants can often be perfectly controlled just by planting them inside a root barrier . . . but you should know that *before* you plant them in your garden! In other words, *think twice* before you buy because you do have a choice between easy plants and difficult ones.

Regional Differences

Criterion number 2 in our list of "10 Things to Look For in a Perennial" is: "It should be well adapted to local conditions that can be limiting factors in your choice of perennials." This is a critical part of choosing a perennial because each area is different, and you need to know your local climate before you can garden with success.

For example, I live in frigid USDA Plant Hardiness Zone 3, where winters are long and cold and there are days on end when no one even expects the car to start. I often have success with plants rated hardy to Zones 6 and (occasionally) 7. Why? Because I have tremendous snow cover. Since snow stays at about the freezing point at all times, I have a thick, relatively warm blanket over my plants that keeps off the worst of winter cold and can help plants survive beyond their usual range. Plus, the snow cover lasts until well into April; by the time the snow has gone and my perennials have started to sprout, there is simply no danger of frost anymore. You can't say that for a lot of places *much* farther south!

COPING WITH REGIONAL DIFFERENCES

Here are a few factors than can influence how you garden in your region . . . and just what you can grow. If in doubt about your plant selections, remember that you can't go wrong selecting perennials that are native to your area.

CONDITIONS	SOLUTIONS
Hot, humid summers	Most perennials will prefer more shade than is usually recommended. Good air circulation will be important. If you need to water, do it in the morning, rather than in the evening, to avoid disease problems. Choose plants according to your AHS Heat Zone rating.
Hot, dry summers	Choose mostly drought-resistant perennials. Mulch abundantly. Avoid spacing plants too closely so they won't compete for moisture. Plant in light shade conditions. Consider installing drip irrigation.
Frequent droughts	Proceed as for "Hot, dry summers." Be sure to water your new perennials while they are getting established.
Cool summers	Avoid applying mulch until the ground has thoroughly warmed up. Flowering seasons may be condensed (spring bloomers will mingle with summer bloomers; summer bloomers with fall bloomers, etc.). Many plants will actually bloom for longer periods in cool-summer areas!
Frigid winters	Stick closely to your USDA Plant Hardiness Zone rating. Winter protection will be an important factor. Don't fertilize your plants after they stop active growth in late summer. Mulch your beds with several inches of chopped leaves in the fall after the ground has frozen. And try to site beds in areas where they're protected from chilling, drying winter winds.
Abundant, reliable snow cover	You can often choose plants 1, 2, or even 3 zones higher than yours because snow insulates the ground. Winter protection, such as pine boughs or a thick layer of mulch, will be important.
Late frosts are common	Apply winter protection and don't be too quick to remove it. Throw snow (where available) onto gardens in winter. Choose later-emerging plants and avoid those that consistently suffer frost damage.
Early frosts are common	Choose fall-blooming plants carefully, picking those recommended for early in the season. Plant frost-sensitive plants on slopes where they are less likely to suffer damage—in front of a south-facing stone wall or on a protected slope.
Winter temperatures are variable	Repeated freezing and thawing episodes can cause newly planted perennials to heave out of the ground. Mulch with several inches of chopped leaves after the ground has frozen to maintain a more constant soil temperature. Use an additional layer of evergreen boughs as insurance.
Rainy climates	Pay extra attention to good drainage. Add organic matter to your beds to improve drainage. Avoid plants known for disease susceptibility.

Figuring Out Plant Names

It wasn't too long ago that if you so much as muttered a botanical name, your friends might label you a "plant nut." But times have changed, and botanical names are being used more widely. Just check mail-order catalogs: You'll find Latin names galore. If you're not up to speed yet on understanding and using botanical names for plants, read on. I'll do my best to guide you through the hows and whys of botanical nomenclature. In this book, I list plants by both common and botanical name. You can choose to use only the common name if you wish, but I recommend that you try to learn the botanical name as well.

Why bother with botanical names? One good reason is that common names for plants vary so much. One person's creeping Charlie is another's ground ivy. Other gardeners know the same plant as gill-over-the-ground, alehoof, cat's-foot, runaway robin, and field balm. But there's only one botanical name for this plant: *Glechoma hederacea.*

Of course, if you *did* mention creeping Charlie to someone, they might well think you were talking about a very different plant: *Lysimachia nummularia* (a.k.a. creeping Jenny, creeping loosestrife, wandering Sally, and moneywort). There's even a houseplant, *Pilea nummularifolia,* that's called creeping Charlie.

Botanical Latin

Botanical names are composed of two parts. The first word in the name is the **genus** name. Many plants can share one genus name, just as many people can share the same family name. Genus names are always capitalized, and they're usually written in italics or underlined. *Hemerocallis* (daylily) is one example of a genus name.

The second word in a botanical name is the **species** name. It serves to identify individual plants. For example, *Hemerocallis citrina* and *Hemerocallis fulva* are both daylilies, but *H. citrina* (citron daylily) has lemony yellow flowers and

Using botanical names helps keep things clear when it comes to buying perennials. For example, both of these perennials are commonly known as coneflowers. However, if you want a purple coneflower, be sure to ask for *Echinacea purpurea*. If it's an orange coneflower you're after, request *Rudbeckia fulgida*.

H. fulva (tawny daylily) has tawny orange blooms. Species names are also underlined or written in italic, but they're not capitalized.

You'll notice that botanical names are always in Latin or latinized Greek: When Carolus Linnaeus developed this system of two-part names in the late eighteenth century, both languages were still in use by students of biology and botany. After Linnaeus developed his system, scientists soon found the need to separate some species into **varieties** or subspecies. For example, some specimens of *H. fulva* found in Japan had a more tubular flower than usual. Botanists didn't consider this difference significant enough to create a new species, so they added a third name instead—the variety name. The new plant became known as *H. fulva* var. *longituba* ("var." stands for "variety," of course) to distinguish it from *H. fulva*.

How about Hybrids?

You'll also notice the occasional use of a multiplication sign (✕) in botanical names. These indicate a hybrid that has achieved species status. *Astilbe* ✕ *arendsii*, for example, is a **hybrid species** that resulted from crosses between *A. chinensis*

var. *davidii* and other astilbes. 'Amethyst', 'Cattleya', 'Erica', and 'Fanal' astilbes are some popular cultivars of this hybrid species.

You'll also occasionally see an ✕ in front of a genus name, as in ✕ *Solidaster luteus*. This indicates a **hybrid genus**, resulting when two different genera (the plural of genus) are crossed together. In this case, an aster (*Aster ptarmicoides*) was crossed with a goldenrod (*Solidago canadensis*), resulting in a plant intermediate between the two. (By the way, you don't need to worry about pronouncing the ✕. It's silent.)

Beyond Latin

When Linnaeus created his naming system, he couldn't have imagined how the modern plant breeding industry would develop. Plant breeders deliberately look for mutations or plants with special characteristics that stand out from the natural form of a plant. They also crossbreed different kinds of perennials to try to create new plants, called hybrids. These days, they're even using genetic engineering to cook up new plants. These manmade plants are called cultivated varieties or **cultivars**. Cultivar names are

If you have your heart set on a specific cultivar of perennial, it pays to be a mail-order-catalog sleuth. Newly developed cultivars or cultivars with unusual colors, like this 'Dawn to Dusk' catmint, may only be available from a few mail-order nurseries.

written in single quotes, as in *Hemerocallis fulva* 'Kwanso'.

Many great cultivars that we grow were developed in Europe. This can create some name confusion because German horticulturists, for example, give their cultivars German names. But some of our nurseries prefer to translate those names into English. So, you may see one nursery offering *Oenothera fruticosa* 'Fyrverkeri', while another offers *Oenothera fruticosa* 'Fireworks'. Would you guess that they're the same plant? They are! I've listed alternate cultivar names in parentheses.

Buying Perennials

In most areas, especially near urban centers, there is no lack of nurseries selling perennials. During the spring season, department stores, hardware stores, supermarkets, public markets, and even "mom and pop" shops get into the act. And there are dozens of mail-order sources. So where should you go for your plants?

Any Old Place

If you have a good eye for healthy plants, you can buy perennials anywhere. Nonspecialist sources—the department store and supermarket gang—are often (but not always) cheaper, although the selection is usually considerably more restricted than in most nurseries. On the other hand, they rarely know plants and you can't ask them questions with any expectation of a reasonable response. Worse yet, their plants can be in poor shape, as they often don't know how to care for them properly.

Garden Centers and Local Nurseries

Garden centers and nurseries usually have a wide selection and a knowledgeable staff. You can obtain almost all the perennials that grow in your climate from a local nursery, although the nursery may not have every cultivar you're looking for.

Although retail nurseries are really set up for impulse purchases, I give them my orders ahead

Top Perennials from Not-So-Knowledgeable Stores

You can get real perennial bargains in nonspecialist stores (department stores, supermarkets, etc.), especially when they use plants priced ridiculously low to draw you into their store. But you can also get some real turkeys. Since you won't be able to count on the staff to help you, you'll need to know what to look for. Here are a few hints.

■ Avoid plants that look yellowed or wilted or have lots of yellow lower leaves: They have probably been mishandled.

■ Look for plants with labels; otherwise you're never really sure what you're getting.

■ Check the hardiness zone and the growing conditions before you buy: A plant is only a bargain if you can grow it!

■ Check for insects (they tend to hide under the leaves).

■ Sniff at the soil. If it smells like a forest on a rainy day, all is well; if it smells like a rotten potato, the root system or crown may be dying.

■ If there are only a few healthy-looking plants mixed in with a lot of sickly ones, avoid them: They are probably suffering from the same problem, but it hasn't yet become obvious.

■ Don't buy a sickly plant, thinking you can nurse it back to health—you probably can't.

■ And most important of all: Find out when they expect a new shipment and *get there on delivery day*. Even department stores selling plants very cheaply buy quality plants; the problem is that the plants go downhill quickly in the store due to poor treatment. If you get there before the store has had a chance to harm the plants, you'll be buying nursery-quality plants at bargain-basement prices.

of time (in late winter, for example, for planting in May). I know I'll get the number of plants I want as well as the right varieties. By ordering early, I get the first choice over other customers.

Nurseries give a better guarantee on perennials than do department stores and their ilk. They don't always have a written policy, but most nurseries will guarantee perennials through the plant's first summer and some over the winter as well.

Mail-Order Catalogs

Then you have plant catalogs. Some are generalist garden catalogs, selling everything from seeds to fertilizer, with a few perennials thrown in. Others specialize in perennials, and some even specialize in a single type of perennial, such as hostas, irises, grasses, or some other specific category of plants.

The advantage of the nurseries producing mail-order catalogs is that they are generally true specialists in their field, often offering rare plants or choice cultivars of more common perennials, plants that you can rarely find locally.

I can't imagine gardening without perennial catalogs on hand. They are often a gold mine of information, and they carry all the choicest plants I hear other gardeners getting excited about; but be careful when ordering a perennial just because you've seen a color photo of it in a catalog or magazine and it just looks fabulous. Such photos often catch a plant at its very peak or in a special lighting situation that you're just not going to see in your garden. Of course, the photo will give you an idea of the plant's outline and an approximation of its color, but it won't always look that good in your garden.

Besides mail-order catalogs that sell plants, there is also a wide range of seed catalogs that carry perennial seeds. Not as many cultivars are offered by seed as in plant catalogs, since many don't come true from seed, but often rare and unusual species perennials are offered, and the prices are unbeatable. But you'll also have to grow the plant from a seedling, and that can take a year or more.

It's easiest to order plants from within your own country because no special permits are

Just Say No

Not all perennials are perfect little angels. Some of them are nasty weeds or poor performers, or they have exceedingly annoying habits. And growing some of them can have negative consequences on the environment. That doesn't mean you won't find these plants for sale in many nurseries. On the contrary, some of them are extremely popular. But I've found, often from bitter experience, that the following plants are just not garden-worthy. Grow them if you must, but be aware that you may well rue the day you ever put them in your plant cart.

Tops for invasiveness on my list are goutweed (*Aegopodium podagraria*), 'Ravenswing' cow parsley (*Anthriscus sylvestris* 'Ravenswing'), common milkweed (*Asclepias syriaca*), creeping and Korean bellflowers (*Campanula rapunculoides, C. takesimana*), fireweed (*Epilobium angustifolium*), Japanese knotweed (*Polygonum cuspidatum*), lesser knotweed (*Persicaria campanulata*, also called *Polygonum campanulatum*), Jerusalem artichoke (*Helianthus tuberosus*), tawny daylily (*Hemerocallis fulva*), plume poppies (*Macleaya* spp.), sensitive fern (*Onoclea sensibilis*), Chi-nese lantern (*Physalis alkekengi*), creeping buttercups (*Ranunculus repens*), goldmoss stonecrop (*Sedum acre*), valerians (*Valeriana* spp.), and creeping speedwell (*Veronica filiformus*).

Perennials to avoid for other reasons are the purple loosestrifes (*Lythrum salicaria* and *L. virgatum*), which have escaped from cultivation in much of North America and taken over waterways and other wetlands, outcompeting native plants; it's illegal to plant them in many areas. And just say no to lady's slipper orchids (*Cypripedium* spp.), which are often wild-collected and eventually die outside their native habitats.

With perennials, you'll find plenty of plants that offer more than just flowers. Sea hollies (*Eryngium* spp.) have unusual spiny leaflike structures called bracts that persist all season. You can even cut them and use them for long-lasting dried flower arrangements.

required. But it's also relatively straightforward for Americans to order plants from Canada and vice versa: At the time this is being written, import forms are no longer required for perennials, although you do have to pay for a "phytosanitary certificate," which usually costs an extra $25. Seed orders, however, cross international borders with no trouble, no paperwork, and no special fees. Use a credit card or pay by money order in the currency of the country you're buying from.

Beyond Flowers

As gardeners, we tend to be so heavily into flowers that we forget perennials can have other attributes such as an attractive silhouette, beautiful leaves, gorgeous fall colors, the ability to attract butterflies or hummingbirds to the garden, showy seedpods or berries, and so on. In fact, if you choose plants solely on the basis of showy flowers, you may end up with a garden of "one-season wonders." Once the flowers fade, you'll find yourself looking for someplace to hide them!

Showy Fruits and Seedpods

Besides the colorful berries of plants like baneberries (*Actaea* spp.) and ornamental strawberries (*Fragaria* spp.), there's a wide range of perennials with attractive seedheads. Seedheads range from the fluffy, flowerlike tufts of adonises and common pasque flower to pods that open to reveal brilliantly colored seeds like blackberry lily and stinking iris (*Iris foetidissima*) to the inflated blackish purple pods of baptisias, and the star-shaped capsules (perfect for drying) of gas plant (*Dictamnus albus*).

There are also perennials that bear "extended flowers" like sea hollies (*Eryngium* spp.), globe thistles (*Echinops* spp.), and most grasses. In these species, the flower just seems to go on and on—until you realize that the real blooms faded weeks ago, and what you're looking at is a cluster of maturing seedheads!

Perennials with Year-Round Interest

Ornamental grasses are the stars among perennials where winter interest is concerned. Many of them are tall, rising well above even deep snow. Other perennials that add year-round interest where they aren't buried in snow include yuccas, aloes, agaves, astilbes, epimediums, hellebores, lavenders, liriopes, mondo grasses (*Ophiopogon* spp.), and sedums.

There's one important thing to remember, though: *Don't* cut these perennials back in the fall, or you'll miss out on the winter show!

Designing YOUR DREAM GARDEN

Conventional wisdom says that you should design your garden, then choose the plants for it. But when you love plants as much as I do, you should pick your plants first, *then* create a design that makes them look good together. This makes especially good sense when you're planting perennials with a purpose: Choose the perennials that suit your purpose, then put them together to make your dream garden.

When you design a perennial garden, imagine that you're decorating your living room. If the colors you pick will work there, they'll work in your garden, too.

◄ When you combine perennials to create a garden, remember to add some annuals and shrubs, too. Here, orange coneflowers (*Rudbeckia fulgida*) look sensational with the blue flower clusters of bluebeard (*Caryopteris* x *clandonensis*), a small shrub that's a great addition to a perennial border.

Basics and Beyond

Although I've planted thousands of perennials in my yard, I'm not an expert on garden design. However, I've picked up a few notions about design during my years of gardening, and I'll share these basics with you here. If I can do it, you can, too! The elements you'll work with are color, texture, and form, and I'll give you some simple guidelines for using them to create pleasing gardens.

Once I've covered the basics, I'll turn things over to the pros: At the end of the chapter, you'll find seven garden designs created by experienced designers. You can copy or adapt these designs for your yard, or use them as inspiration while designing gardens of your own.

Color and Texture

Two of the most important elements in designing a garden are color and texture. If you can get these two elements to click, you're sure to have a beautiful garden. There's a lot of theory about how to combine colors and textures to create pleasing combinations, but remember—it's *theory*, not law. The color police are not going to arrest you!

Most of us do a fine job choosing colors for our homes. Designing a garden isn't that different. The first color choice—green—is made for you. It's hard to make a major mistake when you have that underlying color pulling your design together.

Keep in mind that your garden is *your* garden. Don't think for a minute that you have to follow anyone else's color schemes. If you combine colors in a way that seems pleasing to you, you'll be satisfied, and that's what really counts.

Cool and Warm

When you're thinking about garden design, it's helpful to separate colors into two groups: warm colors and cool colors. Red, orange,

Red-hot colors really liven up a suburban landscape. Plant exuberant red, fuchsia, and yellow perennials in masses to create a garden that's positively electric!

and yellow are warm colors. They give a design more excitement and passion. Also, these colors make the garden seem closer. You might want to use warm colors to make a large garden appear more intimate or to attract attention to a distant part of the garden.

Green, blue, and violet are cool colors. They make the garden seem cooler, calmer, and more peaceful. Cool colors also seem farther away. To make a small garden seem larger, use a lot of cool colors. Cool colors will also make an unwanted view less distracting, since they'll make it seem more distant and unobtrusive.

You can plant a garden that's all warm colors, all cool colors, or a mix of both. If you mix cool and warm colors, remember that warm colors dominate. If you want a garden where warm and cool balance, plant more cool-colored perennials. A few spot plantings of warm colors in a sea of blue and green are enough.

When you mix warm and cool colors, don't put the cool colors in the background, or they'll

Are Blue Flowers *Really* Blue?

When I first started gardening, I wondered if I didn't suffer from some sort of color blindness. All those flowers I saw labeled as blue looked distinctly violet or purple to me. I've since realized that there's nothing wrong with my eyes; it's more a sort of wishful thinking on the part of gardeners. You see, blue is such a rare color in flowers that we've gone a bit overboard in our descriptions and started to see "blues" where there aren't any. A lot of flowers appear blue from a distance, but up close they're probably purple.

There *are* a few true blue flowers, at least to my eye. Forget-me-nots (*Myosotis* spp.) are a true pale blue. And some delphiniums are blue (although if you look hard, you'll see that they have a purplish tinge). Some Siberian iris cultivars are true blue. Perennial flax (*Linum perenne*) is a clear sky blue. Blue corydalis (*Corydalis flexuosa*) is bluer than blue, as is that coveted prima donna, the Himalayan blue poppy (*Meconopsis betonicifolia*).

get lost. Plant cool-colored perennials in front, with the warm-colored ones behind.

Single-Color Gardens

Perhaps the easiest garden to design is a single-color garden. You can create a white garden, a yellow garden, a red garden—they're all winning ideas. Choose a color that you like, and use it in various shades and tints. Choose perennials with different sizes, textures, and shapes, all in various shades of the same color, and you can have both variety and harmony at the same time.

Of course, your garden won't truly be one color because it will have a background of green foliage, and there are many shades and tints of green, too. Green leaves can range from nearly black to blue-green to chartreuse to gray or silver. And that's not counting all the variegated foliage! You can even design a green garden just using foliage. It's fun to create striking and beautiful effects with foliage, especially in shade gardens where foliage is a key factor.

Combining Colors

If you want to create a garden with more than one color, you can use a color wheel to help decide which colors look good together. On the color wheel, each color is flanked by two other colors. You can move beyond a single-color garden by choosing three colors that appear side by side on the wheel.

The colors on a classic color wheel are red, orange, yellow, green, blue, and violet. Colors that oppose each other on the wheel, such as violet and yellow, create striking combinations.

Plant perennials in bold patches of color, like these yellow rudbeckias and goldenrods and the purple asters, to create an eye-catching border.

If you like violet, for example, you could create an interesting garden using violet flowers with blue-violet or red-violet shades. Or go one step further and combine a primary color with the two secondary colors that are closest together on the wheel: orange with yellow and red, for example.

Complementary Colors

Colors that are direct opposites on the color wheel are called complementary colors, and they make very vibrant combinations. Yellow and violet are complementary colors, and so are blue and orange. If these combinations strike you as too jarring, you can use tints of the main hue to prevent a clash, such as pink to soften a vibrant red. Or use white flowers or gray or silver foliage between colors that seem too strong. They'll tend to soften the blow.

Multicolor Mixes

Garden designers might call a garden of mixed colors a "polychromatic scheme," but I just call it a mixed-color garden. It can include all the colors in the rainbow. Although considered daring from a design point of view, most home gardens are color mixes, and many of them work very well indeed. A garden with many different colors often creates a light, lively atmosphere, making it a fun place to be—and that's what many people want for their garden.

I'll admit, sometimes I've created a garden of mixed colors just by randomly planting perennials in a bed. When the bed fills in, sometimes I get a rather pleasing meadow garden look, but at other times, I'm not satisfied because many of the individual colors and plants seem lost in the crowd. So now I stick with a technique that usually gives great results.

I group plants together to create spots of color, then I mix the *spots* together rather than sprinkling individual colors throughout the same garden. How many plants make up a "spot" of color? That varies. When you're planting small perennials like violets, you may need 15 or more to create enough color impact. But with sizable plants like garden phlox (*Phlox paniculata*), 3 plants may be enough. And some perennials are large and imposing enough to stand alone (see "Perennials and Grasses for Dramatic Impact" on page 416 for examples).

Texture

Although we tend to think of color as the mainstay in garden design, texture is just as important. In fact, Japanese gardens often have nothing but shades and tints of green—yet we find them pleasing and harmonious because of the careful choice of textures.

There are three basic textures: fine, medium, and coarse. Plants fit a texture category based on their leaf size and density and their flower placement. For example, bear's breeches (*Acanthus mollis*), with its large, striking leaves, is bold, while peony foliage is medium, and the feathery leaves of artemisias put them in the fine category.

When you create a garden, using a relatively even mix of fine and medium leaves with an accent of larger, bolder leaves is often the safest way to go. You can also design a striking garden using a single texture accented by a contrasting texture every now and then. One classic texture combination is fine-textured ferns with coarse-leaved hostas.

Fine textures tend to have the same effect as cool colors: They're calming and make the garden seem farther away. Coarse textures are almost as exciting and visually stimulating as warm colors and, like them, draw the garden closer. When you're combining textures, you can use the same technique of using "spots" of texture instead of just mixing textures randomly.

Featuring Plant Form

All plants have a natural form: Some plants are vertical, others are spreading, and still others are rounded, open, or prostrate. If a garden mixes too many forms, it can appear chaotic, but *repeating* a limited number of forms can create a very pleasing garden.

Working with form can be more subtle than color or texture. You can create gardens with gradual changes in form, where low plants melt into spreading ones that in turn give way to vertical shapes. You can also use dramatic contrasts in form, planting a rounded perennial like

'Autumn Joy' sedum right next to a vase-shaped perennial like Russian sage (*Perovskia atriplicifolia*). The typical British perennial border is a classic mixture of tall, spiky background plants (verticality with a vengeance!) with rounded plants in the middle and prostrate plants as an edging.

The Form of Flowers

Plants have an overall form or shape, and individual flowers or flower heads have a form as well. Large, bold peonies contrast with airy baby's breath blossoms, for example. There are also bell-shaped flowers, upright spikes of flowers, and daisylike blooms. My wife always complains there

Rich leaf colors and textures will keep this combination of 'Frances Williams' hosta, Japanese painted fern, and 'Deutschland' astilbe exciting all season long.

are too many "daisies" (rudbeckias, purple coneflowers, and perennial sunflowers) in our garden. She's right . . . and I'm trying to do better!

How to Handle Height

The rule of thumb concerning plant height is so simple that most gardeners follow it instinctively: Short plants go in the front of the garden, medium-sized plants in the middle, and tall plants in the back. The deeper the garden, the more varied a range of heights you can use.

This rule is perfect for very formal gardens, but if you're planning a casual garden, don't hesitate to break the rule occasionally. A few tall plants in the middle of the garden, some medium-sized ones in the front and, every now and again, a low-growing plant inching back into the bed will be more natural looking.

The Role of Repetition

Whether you're thinking about color, texture, form, or height, keep in mind that too much variety randomly tossed together can turn a garden into a total hodgepodge. The way to turn a random mix of plants into a pretty garden is through repetition. Even in a small garden, try to repeat at least three groups of the same plant, or at least the same color or texture, in different parts of the garden. You'll often find even the most unlikely plants suddenly gel perfectly!

Flowers of a Feather Bloom Together

Probably one of the most difficult things to plan for when designing a garden is getting bloom times to coincide. Although perennials can be roughly grouped into spring, summer, and fall bloomers, the actual time when a plant blooms varies from year to year, depending on the growing conditions and the weather. You just don't get guarantees on flowering time from Mother Nature.

The longer the growing season, the more difficult it is to coordinate bloom periods. In the Deep South, where Christmas rose (*Helleborus niger*) really *can* bloom at Christmas, each season is stretched to its maximum. The spring flowering season often lasts four months or more. By contrast, in my USDA Zone 3 garden, where spring barely lasts a month, you'll see spring and summer bloomers mingling. This makes it much easier to ensure nonstop color.

Stagger Bloom Times for Best Results

The secret to a perennial garden that always looks good is to stagger bloom times: Combine plants with different flowering seasons so that there's always *something* in bloom in the garden. One thing that can help is including some everbloomers— perennials that bloom for eight weeks or more— in your design. To learn which perennials will bloom nearly forever, turn to page 68.

Staggering bloom times fits well with my "spots of color" technique. A single perennial blooming on its own might have little impact in the garden, but three or more densely flowered patches of the same plant create the impression that there's color everywhere in the garden. By having at least three different perennials in bloom in three different spots at any given time, you can have that "in full bloom" effect right through the growing season.

Of course, to do so, you'll need to know when different perennials bloom. You'll find that out in the individual descriptions in Part 2. Once you've planted your garden, you may find that there's a "hole" in it—a particular time of year when there's nearly nothing in bloom. If this happens, take a stroll through your neighborhood at that time of year and see what's blooming in your neighbors' yards. Come fall, order a few of those plants and work them into your garden.

Finally, if you can't guarantee flowering perennials throughout the season, you *can* count on attractive foliage at all times, so don't hesitate to get some of the color for your garden from foliage. Many of the perennials that have particularly attractive foliage even when not in bloom are found in the chapters "Perennials for Fabulous Foliage" on page 346, "Groundcover Perennials" on page 373, and "Perennials and Grasses for Dramatic Impact" on page 416.

Beyond Perennials: Branching Out

Perennial gardens can include other plants besides perennials, and adding some annuals, bulbs, and shrubs to your perennial garden can stretch its season of color and interest. For ex-

ample, while there are perennials that flower in spring, spring bulbs are the true stars of the early spring and midspring gardens. Annuals add consistent color that can tide your garden over if there are periods when perennials aren't at their best, such as during the high heat of midsummer. And shrubs will give your garden some form and interest through the winter.

Bulbs for Spring Color

From the earliest snowdrops and winter crocuses to May-blooming tulips, not to mention summer-flowering alliums and fall-blooming crocus and colchicums, bulbs ensure color when there is little else around. Spring bulbs are a perfect match for perennials because they produce their foliage in the spring when many perennials are dormant. As spring gives way to summer, the bulb foliage dies back, while the perennials sprout the new season's growth.

Because of this, you can plant bulbs and perennials quite literally in the same space. Just plant the bulbs deeply in the fall (check the bulb package to confirm the planting depth, as it does

If standard foundation shrubs border your house, dress them up by planting a few types of colorful perennials that have a long season of interest, such as astilbes, lady's-mantles, and salvias.

Bright pink annual impatiens make a colorful edging and fill a gap in this perennial bed that features pink-flowered garden phlox and feathery astilbe plumes.

vary), then plant shallow-rooted perennials literally on top. The bulbs will come up right through the perennials—especially low-growing ones like ajugas and lamiums.

I like to plant rings of early bulbs around slow-to-sprout plants like hibiscus and balloonflower. I've found that the bulbs serve as markers so I don't accidentally dig up the slow sprouters when I'm working in the garden preparing beds during the spring.

Adding Annuals

Annuals and perennials make a great combination, as long as you give the annuals enough room to spread without crowding the perennials. Planting patches of annuals through a bed of perennials can ensure that "always-in-bloom" look. A ratio of about one annual to five perennials works well.

Annuals also work well as edging plants for a perennial border. It's a job they do marvelously, and if the front edge of the garden—which is the first thing that catches people's attention when they enter the garden—appears to be in full bloom through the summer, the rest of the garden will seem all that much more attractive.

Shrubs to Anchor the Scene

Shrubs are excellent backgrounds for perennial beds, "anchoring" the garden to its landscape much better than perennials alone could ever do. Many shrubs bloom in the spring or late summer—two times of year when perennials are rather weak—so the marriage is a good one. Just make sure that each shrub has its own space.

One effective combination is shrubs with perennial groundcovers. You can let the groundcover creep under the shrubs and create a living carpet that's beautiful and easy to care for.

Of course, not all shrubs belong strictly in the background of the mixed border. Short, dense shrubs, including dwarf conifers, look great in the middle or even the front of the garden as well. Shrubs come in a wide range of forms, textures, and foliage colors, so it's easy to create beautiful combinations of perennials and shrubs. And, of course, many shrubs have beautiful blooms and colorful fruit as well.

The 10 Commandments of Perennial Design

Now that you know the basics of garden design, you can see that there are unlimited possibilities for designing and planting perennial gardens. But before you start, read my list of important lessons learned from years of gardening and designing. My "ten commandments" are some of the best practical advice I can give you, based on some of my own worst mistakes.

1. Leave room for future growth. Don't cram a new garden with perennials, or they'll have no room to spread over time. And you'll end up having to dig some up and move them. Instead, fill in with temporary plants such as annuals for the first couple of years.

2. Change your garden whenever you feel like it. It's a gardener's prerogative to change his (or her!) mind. Once you have a garden design, even one that's been prepared by a professional designer, feel free to change it. After all, it's your garden! Even professional landscapers change plans as they work.

3. Stagger your planting. Don't plant perennials in straight lines because it looks unnatural and static, except when you're planting an edging for a small rectangular or square garden.

4. Don't go with the flow. Be wary of following gardening fads too closely. True, hot pink may be the "hot" trend, but are you sure you'll be able to live with it ten years from now? Experiment with the latest trends using annuals, but make sure your perennial choices are ones you can live with for a long time.

5. Rein in the spreaders. If you plant a potentially invasive perennial in a flower bed, *always* plant it inside a root barrier. Nothing's harder than trying to dig out an aggressive spreader.

6. Don't be boring. Avoid mirror-image plantings on either side of a walkway or door. They may work in truly formal settings, but they often make for a boring garden.

7. Don't neglect your babies. Remember that all newly planted perennials need extra care for the first year after planting.

8. Show your plants, not your stakes. Stake perennials as discreetly as possible or use stakes that blend in with the plants' foliage. Nothing ruins a nice garden like a forest of ugly stakes.

9. Make big beds. If you're planning a perennial border, make it as wide as you can: Remember, perennials need space to grow! There's nothing more frustrating than having to divide perennials just a year or two after planting them.

10. Don't always follow the rules. Don't follow any design rule too precisely. All rules are meant to be broken, even mine!

Garden Designs with a Purpose

Despite the guidelines I've given, you still may feel a little short on confidence about garden design. Sometimes the way to boost your confidence is to borrow some ideas from experienced garden designers. With that in mind, I've included seven perennial garden designs created by professionals especially for home gardeners like you.

Look over the designs on the next several pages and see how the designers combine color and texture, use repetition, and choose plants that have different seasons of interest. You may find a design that's just perfect for your yard or one that inspires you to take the plunge and design a garden of your own. Good luck, have fun, and don't go overboard on the daisies!

A SULTRY SUMMER BORDER FOR SUN

It can be a challenge to keep a full-sun perennial border in flower right through the steamy days of July and August. Garden designer Pam Baggett rose to the task by picking perennials that are heat-tolerant and perennials with long-lasting foliage, such as Russian sage, sedums, and tradescantia. Pam favors sultry colors, as you can see in this late summer view of the garden, where tall bee balm, butterfly weed, and purple coneflower are in full bloom. This butterfly-attracting border also features the rich colors of daylilies and lilac sage. When fall arrives, count on the tall, smoky purple blooms of 'Rotstrahlbusch' switch grass to turn to seedheads and bleach tan for the winter landscape. This garden will thrive in USDA Plant Hardiness Zones 5 to 7. And if you grow 'Homestead Purple' rose verbena—the least hardy of the plants—as an annual, you can easily extend the hardiness to Zone 4.

Plant List

1 'Blaustrumpf' bee balm (*Monarda* 'Blaustrumpf', also called *M.* 'Blue Stocking') (1 plant)

2 Butterfly weed (*Asclepias tuberosa*) (1 plant)

3 Purple coneflower (*Echinacea purpurea*) (1 plant)

4 'King's Grant' daylily (*Hemerocallis* 'King's Grant') (1 plant)

5 'Gateway' Joe-Pye weed (*Eupatorium fistulosum* 'Gateway') (1 plant)

6 'Purple Rain' lilac sage (*Salvia verticillata* 'Purple Rain') (3 plants)

7 'Filagran' Russian sage (*Perovskia* × *hybrida* 'Filagran') (1 plant)

8 'Matrona' sedum (*Sedum* 'Matrona') (1 plant)

9 'Vera Jameson' sedum (*Sedum* 'Vera Jameson') (3 plants)

10 'Rotstrahlbusch' switch grass (*Panicum virgatum* 'Rotstrahlbusch') (1 plant)

11 'Concord Grape' tradescantia (*Tradescantia* 'Concord Grape') (2 plants)

12 'Homestead Purple' rose verbena (*Verbena canadensis* 'Homestead Purple') (1 plant)

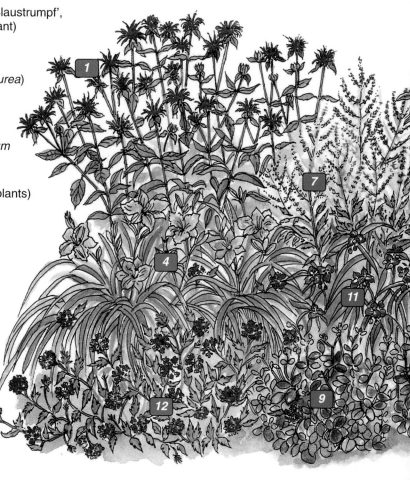

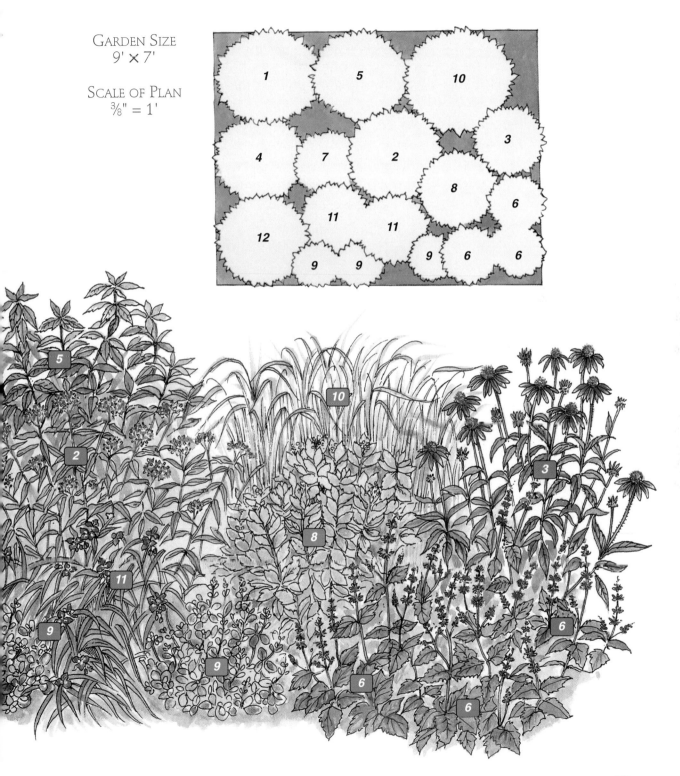

GARDEN SIZE
9' × 7'

SCALE OF PLAN
⅜" = 1'

A GARDEN WITH SEASON-LONG INTEREST

The secret to creating a perennial garden that's full of interest from spring through fall is to combine beautiful bloomers with outstanding foliage plants. Pam Baggett's design features a number of plants that still have something to show off after their blooms have faded, proving that handsome foliage plays a huge role in a garden's success. This garden is shown in midsummer when the peonies are past bloom, the irises are bearing dark brown seedpods, and the switch grass has begun to fade from its original metallic blue. Delicate coreopsis and veronica blooms accent the strong foliage of the chrysanthemum, daylily, and sedum plantings. Pam chose two rather tender perennials for this garden—blue sage and agapanthus. If you live north of Zone 8, you can grow the agapanthus in a large container and overwinter it indoors, or substitute 'Klaus Jelitto' Stokes' aster (*Stokesia laevis* 'Klaus Jelitto') in its place. If you'd prefer a hardier substitute for the blue sage, try mildew-resistant 'David' garden phlox (*Phlox paniculata* 'David'). Plant this garden in moist, well-drained soil and full sun.

Plant List

1 'Peter Pan' agapanthus
   (*Agapanthus* 'Peter Pan') (1 plant)

2 Lesser calamint (*Calamintha nepeta*) (1 plant)

3 Gold-and-silver chrysanthemum
   (*Ajania pacifica*) (1 plant)

4 'Moonbeam' threadleaf coreopsis
   (*Coreopsis verticillata* 'Moonbeam') (3 plants)

5 'Happy Returns' daylily
   (*Hemerocallis* 'Happy Returns') (2 plants)

6 'Silver Edge' Siberian iris
   (*Iris sibirica* 'Silver Edge') (1 plant)

7 'White Swirl' Siberian iris
   (*Iris sibirica* 'White Swirl') (1 plant)

8 Patrinia (*Patrinia scabiosifolia*) (3 plants)

9 'Krinkled White' peony
   (*Paeonia* 'Krinkled White') (1 plant)

10 Blue anise sage
    (*Salvia guaranitica*) (1 plant)

11 'Mediovariegatum' sedum
    (*Sedum alboroseum* 'Mediovariegatum')
    (2 plants)

12 'Heavy Metal' switch grass
    (*Panicum virgatum* 'Heavy Metal') (1 plant)

13 'Sunny Border Blue' veronica
    (*Veronica* 'Sunny Border Blue') (4 plants)

GARDEN SIZE
9' × 8'

SCALE OF PLAN
3/8" = 1'

37

AN ENTRY GARDEN

This inviting entryway garden welcomes guests with vivid color from spring to fall. Designer Barbara Wilde has gathered a collection of perennials that have season-long blooms and great foliage colors and textures. Evergreen boxwood shrubs and tall sunflower stalks form a rich green, leafy backdrop for the bursts of color in this perennial bed. In this midsummer view of the garden, the warm yellow blooms of columbine and yarrow and the bright pink flowers of bee balm graciously usher the visitor to the front door. The drifts of lavender just coming into bloom create a memorable scent when someone brushes by. Rich, plum-colored euphorbia foliage and dense mounds of candytuft leaves keep the bed full and lively through the fall, and the luxurious drifts of lady's mantle provide a groundcover-type edging for this walkway. This garden is hardy at least through Zone 5 and needs full sun; it also requires well-drained soil that has been amended with compost and sand.

Plant List

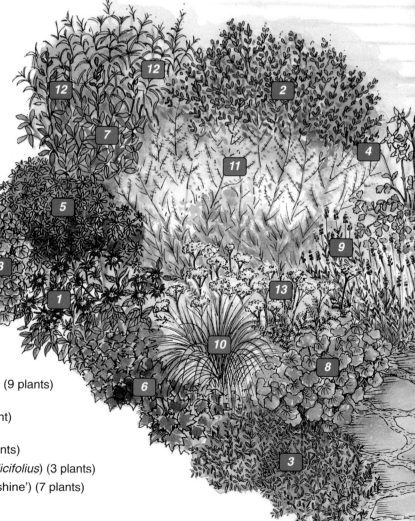

1   'Petite Delight' bee balm (*Monarda* 'Petite Delight') (6 plants)

2   'Arborescens' common boxwood (*Buxus sempervirens* 'Arborescens') (2 shrubs)

3   'Autumn Beauty' evergreen candytuft (*Iberis sempervirens* 'Autumn Beauty') (8 plants)

4   'Yellow Queen' golden columbine (*Aquilegia chrysantha* 'Yellow Queen') (8 plants)

5   'Chameleon' euphorbia (*Euphorbia dulcis* 'Chameleon') (7 plants)

6   'Palace Purple' heuchera (*Heuchera micrantha* 'Palace Purple') (10 plants)

7   Blue false indigo (*Baptisia australis*) (3 plants)

8   Lady's-mantle (*Alchemilla mollis*) (16 plants)

9   'Nana Alba' English lavender (*Lavandula angustifolia* 'Nana Alba') (9 plants)

10   Blue oat grass (*Helictotrichon sempervirens*) (1 plant)

11   'Longin' Russian sage (*Perovskia* × *hybrida* 'Longin') (7 plants)

12   Willowleaf sunflower (*Helianthus salicifolius*) (3 plants)

13   'Moonshine' yarrow (*Achillea* 'Moonshine') (7 plants)

GARDEN SIZE
24' × 14'

SCALE OF PLAN
1" = 5'

A LAYER CAKE GARDEN

This island garden by designer Barbara Wilde provides season-long bloom by using closely spaced "plant partners." These plant partners were carefully chosen according to their bloom time and their overall compatibility, especially with their roots. When the first plant partner's showy blooms are fading, the second partner steps right up and takes over. This August view of the garden, for instance, shows butterfly weed in full bloom at the front of the bed; its plant partner common pasque flower has gone dormant. The butterfly weed plants have grown through the dying foliage of the pasque flower plants and are blooming in brilliant orange to continue the show of color into the fall months. These colorful and harmonious perennial combinations feature plants of varying heights to give a "layer cake" effect. This garden should be planted in full sun and well-drained soil; it's hardy to Zone 5.

Plant List

1. 'Blue Gown' New York aster (*Aster novi-belgii* 'Blue Gown') (3 plants)

2. 'Birch Hybrid' bellflower (*Campanula* 'Birch Hybrid') (5 plants)

3. Great bellflower (*Campanula latifolia* var. *macrantha*) (8 plants); dormant in illustration

4. 'Hello Yellow' yellow blackberry lily (*Belamcanda flabellata* 'Hello Yellow') (8 plants)

5. Blue star (*Amsonia hubrectii*) (2 plants)

6. Butterfly weed (*Asclepias tuberosa*) (7 plants)

7. 'Blue Jay' columbine (*Aquilegia* × *hybrida* 'Blue Jay') (5 plants)

8. 'Purpureus' gas plant (*Dictamnus albus* 'Purpureus') (3 plants); dormant in illustration

9. 'Whirling Butterflies' white gaura (*Gaura lindheimeri* 'Whirling Butterflies') (10 plants)

10. 'Gateway' Joe-Pye weed (*Eupatorium fistulosum* 'Gateway') (1 plant)

11. Leadwort (*Ceratostigma plumbaginoides*) (7 plants)

12. Common pasque flower (*Pulsatilla vulgaris*) (7 plants); dormant in illustration

13. 'Prinzessin Victoria Louise' oriental poppy (*Papaver orientale* 'Prinzessin Victoria Louise') (3 plants); dormant in illustration

14. Northern sea oats (*Chasmanthium latifolium*) (3 plants)

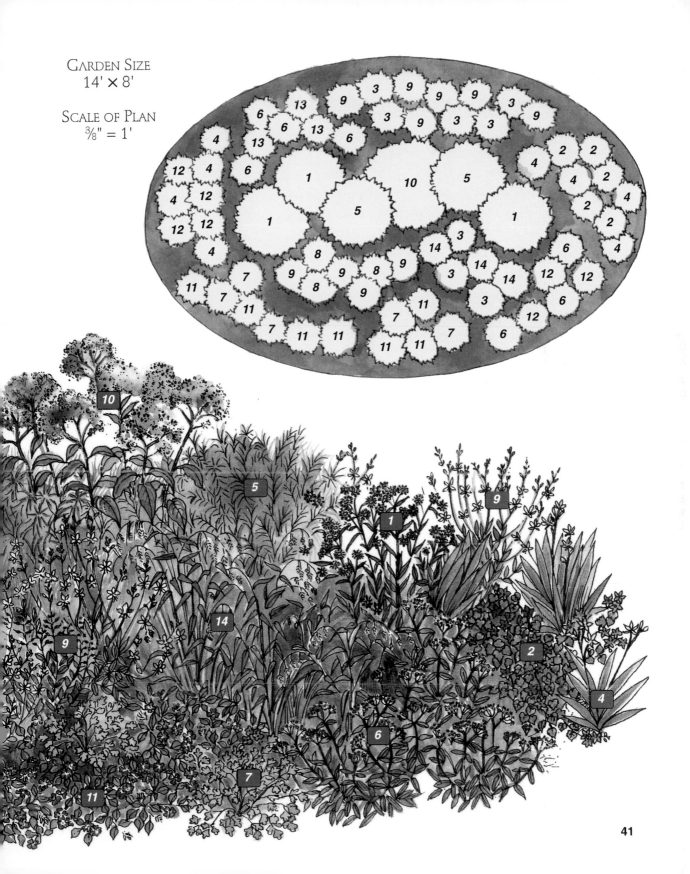

GARDEN SIZE
14' × 8'

SCALE OF PLAN
⅜" = 1'

41

A Shady Foliage Garden

A texture-filled bed can turn a single shade tree into the highlight of your backyard! Designer Beverly Fitts features a 'Heritage' river birch in this garden, shown here in late spring, but you can plant these perennials under any deciduous tree that provides light shade. The nodding flowers of the hellebores will brighten the bed in early spring when the sunlight dapples through the tree; the blooms of Solomon's seal, violets, and irises will continue the color parade through early summer. Enjoy the handsome foliage colors and textures of Christmas ferns, hostas, and lamiums during summer. In winter, the scarlet berries of the irises and the evergreen foliage of the arums and hellebores will add color to your landscape. These plants will thrive in Zones 6 to 8 but will probably successfully establish in Zones 5 to 9. Keep the soil moist with a generous helping of organic matter.

Plant List

1. 'Pictum' Italian arum
(*Arum italicum* 'Pictum') (6 plants)

2. 'Heritage' river birch
(*Betula nigra* 'Heritage') (1 tree)

3. 'Sulphureum' Persian epimedium
(*Epimedium* × *versicolor* 'Sulphureum')
(9 plants)

4. Christmas fern (*Polystichum acrostichoides*) (5 plants)

5. Stinking hellebore
(*Helleborus foetidus*) (8 plants)

6. 'Daybreak' hosta
(*Hosta* 'Daybreak') (1 plant)

7. 'Citrina' stinking iris
(*Iris foetidissima* 'Citrina')
(2 plants)

8. 'Beedham's White' spotted
lamium (*Lamium maculatum*
'Beedham's White') (9 plants)

9. Lenten rose (*Helleborus orientalis*) (6 plants)

10. 'Variegatum' fragrant
Solomon's seal (*Polygonatum odoratum* 'Variegatum') (5 plants)

11. 'Boughton Blue' horned violet
(*Viola cornuta* 'Boughton Blue') (30 plants)

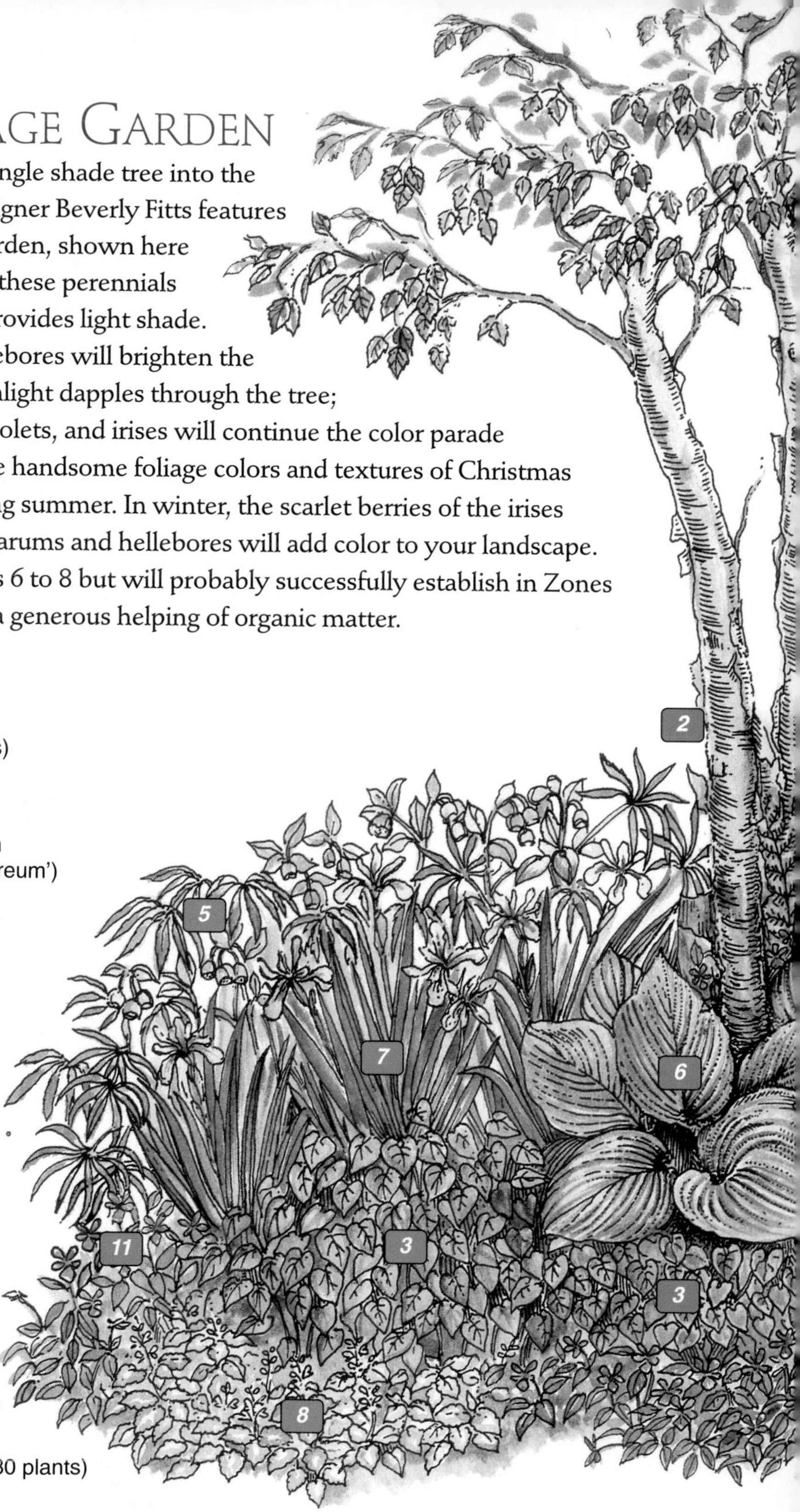

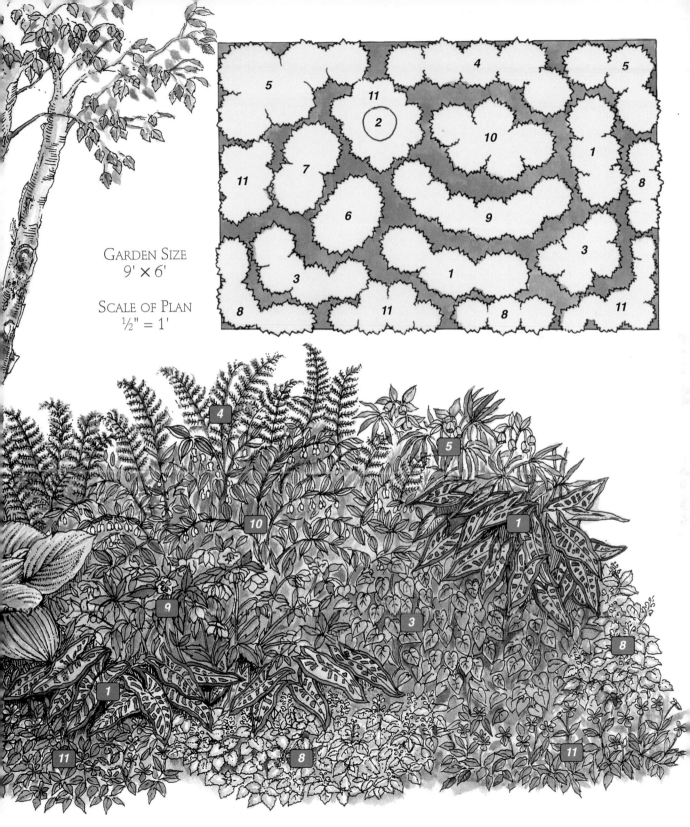

GARDEN SIZE
9' × 6'

SCALE OF PLAN
½" = 1'

A GARDEN WITH MASS APPEAL

A garden doesn't need a dozen different plants to be successful! This plan features only six perennials, planted in large drifts for maximum impact. Designing with large masses of color and texture can be extremely effective, adding a pleasing rhythm to the landscape. This garden by Pam Ruch makes wise use of plants that thrive on neglect (including very little water) in full sun in Zones 5 to 9. It will begin blooming early in the summer with a cloud of blue star, then the purple flower heads of lavender and the tall, white spikes of Adam's-needle provide the color for the next few weeks. The velvety leaves of lamb's-ears contribute an interesting texture throughout the season. Later in the summer, the orange coneflowers contrast handsomely with the gray and green foliage colors of the neighboring past-bloom flowers. In fall, depend on the switch grass to turn a blazing red, complementing the striking yellow-orange blue star foliage and black seedpods of the coneflowers.

Plant List

1   'Bright Edge'
    Adam's-needle (*Yucca
    filamentosa* 'Bright
    Edge) (5 plants)

2   Blue star
    (*Amsonia hubrectii*)
    (8 plants)

3   'Goldsturm' orange
    coneflower (*Rudbeckia
    fulgida* var. *sullivantii*
    'Goldsturm') (12 plants)

4   Fountain grass
    (*Pennisetum alopecuroides*)
    or 'Rotstrahlbusch'
    switch grass (*Panicum
    virgatum* 'Rotstrahlbusch')
    (5 plants)

5   'Big Ears' lamb's-ears
    (*Stachys byzantina*
    'Big Ears', also called
    S. byzantina 'Countess
    Helene von Stein')
    (10 plants)

6   English lavender
    (*Lavandula angustifolia*)
    (11 plants)

GARDEN SIZE
16½' × 10'

SCALE OF PLAN
¼" = 1'

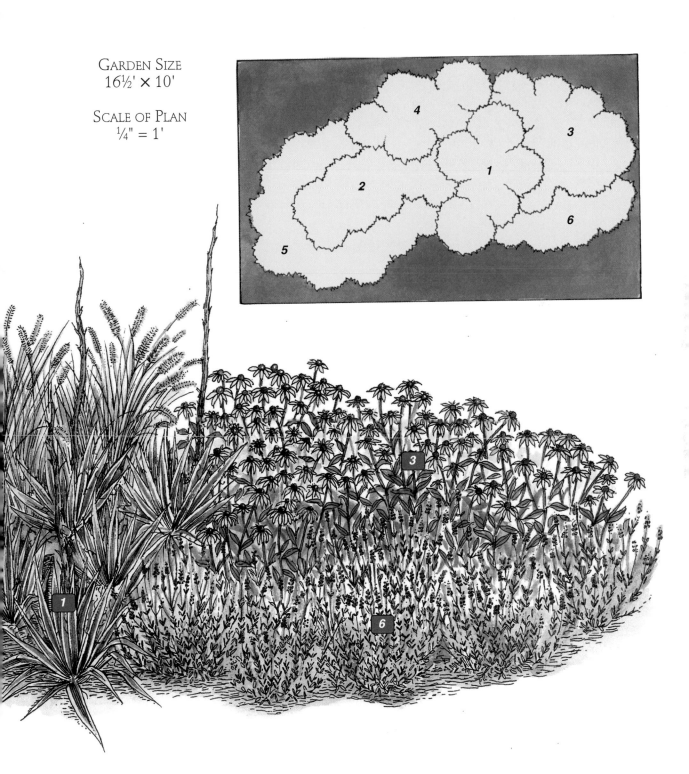

A Garden with a View

A picture-perfect view no matter what the season! Two shrubs with year-round interest serve as anchors for this garden landscape: Winterberry, with its abundant red fruit, brightens the gray days of winter, and as the cold weather gives way to warmer temperatures, the fragrant yellow blooms of witch hazel are a harbinger of spring. A mat of magenta rock cress splashes the garden with color through the showers of April and is followed by lovely May flowers like golden columbine and long-blooming salvia. This late summer view of the garden shows a profusion of soft blue Siberian catmint flowers, but the showstopper has to be 'Lord Baltimore' hibiscus with its brilliant red 10-inch flowers. Bringing the garden full circle into fall is easy-care boltonia with its huge mounds of daisylike flowers. Joanne Kostecky designed this full-sun garden for moist, well-drained soil. Hardy through Zone 5, these plants may thrive as far north as Zone 3.

Plant List

1   'Snowbank' boltonia
    (*Boltonia asteroides* 'Snowbank')
    (3 plants)

2   'Souvenir d'André Chaudron'
    catmint (*Nepeta* 'Souvenir d'André
    Chaudron', also called
    N. 'Blue Beauty') (3 plants)

3   'Yellow Queen' golden
    columbine (*Aquilegia chrysantha*
    'Yellow Queen') (5 plants)

4   'Bengal' rock cress
    (*Aubrieta* × *cultorum* 'Bengal') (5 plants)

5   'Lord Baltimore' common rose
    mallow (*Hibiscus moscheutos*
    'Lord Baltimore') (1 plant)

6   'Mainacht' salvia (*Salvia nemorosa*
    'Mainacht', also called *S. nemorosa*
    'May Night', *S.* × *sylvestris* 'May Night')
    (3 plants)

7   'Winter Red' winterberry
    (*Ilex verticillata* 'Winter Red') (3 shrubs)

8   'Arnold Promise' witch hazel
    (*Hamamelis* × *intermedia*
    'Arnold Promise') (1 shrub)

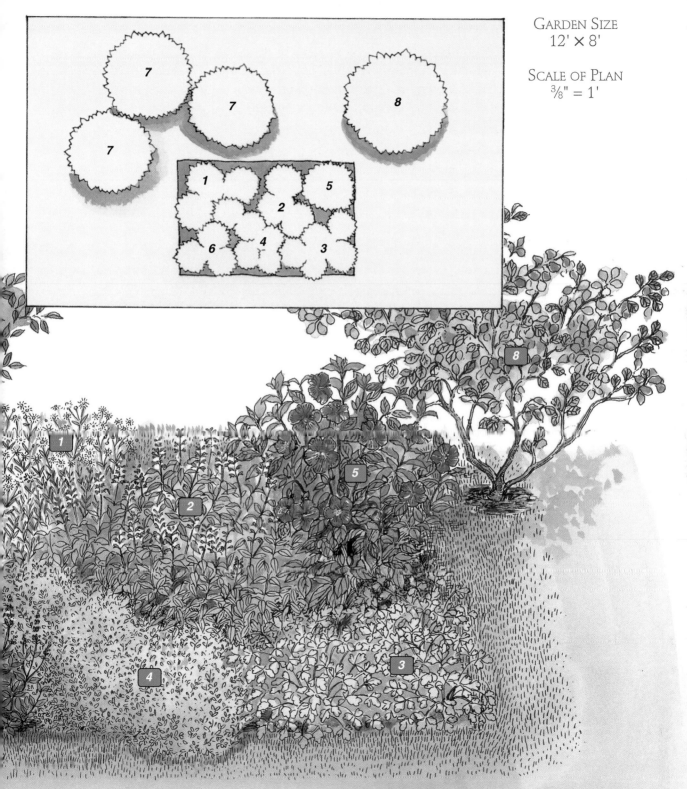

47

KEEPING PLANTS
Alive & Kicking

Buying plants and knowing how (and where) to plant them isn't everything. You also need to know how to keep them healthy. That's what this chapter is all about. Perennials are not wildflowers (at least, they no longer are once they're in our gardens) and need a certain amount of upkeep. Just how much depends on the type of plant: Some need so little looking after they need almost no care. You'll probably find yourself repeating some tasks routinely, while other care methods may only be needed every few years.

Insect damage on perennials isn't quite the same crisis that it is on edibles, since at least you don't have to eat the plants afterward. But that doesn't mean you have to like it—or put up with it!

◄ Some perennials rarely suffer from pest problems but will sulk and die if they're planted in the wrong spot. Torch lilies (*Kniphofia* spp.) will produce knock-'em-dead flower spikes for weeks on end when they're in a sunny bed that's moist in summer and drains well in winter.

Keeping Them in Shape

I'm all for making gardening quick and easy. After all, I want to enjoy my garden, not spend every waking moment delicately staking a single stalk or watering a needy perennial drop by drop. Here you'll find out how I care for my plants—and how I minimize the work involved.

Staking

In the wild, many perennials grow in dense fields or among shrubs where they can take advantage of natural staking. But in the garden, this kind of mutual support is lacking and you may find you'll have to supply it. Furthermore, breeders have often made the situation worse by choosing plants with larger (and heavier) flowers than the stem was really designed to hold.

If you don't think staking plants is fun, you may want to avoid plants that require staking. Two categories of plants are more likely to need support: tall, single-stalked plants, such as delphiniums and taller hollyhocks; and those with multitudes of blooms and weak stems, such as asters, carnations, and chrysanthemums.

If you're allergic to staking, stick with single-flowered varieties or plants with a reputation for being sturdy, like aconites (*Aconitum spp.*) or most single peonies. Personally I don't stake. Any perennial that flops over in *my* garden is instantly turned into a cut flower.

Siting plants correctly can also help. Aconites, for example, can be quite floppy in partial shade, but they stand tall in full sun. Leaving a little more space between plants so they're exposed to wind currents at a younger age can also help, since movement causes their stems to grow thicker and stronger. On the other hand, choose protected spots for those plants you *know* tend to flop.

If you have a perennial with a large flower head, use a single stake to keep the plant from flopping over. Support bushy plants or a group of tall perennials by inserting stakes into the ground and running twine around and between the stakes and flowerstalks.

Don't coddle your plants if you don't want to stake them. Overwatering and using nitrogen-rich fertilizers both tend to stimulate the growth of tall but weak stems. Finally, pinching plants back early in their growth cycle is often used to create denser growth and shorter, more solid stems. You can also avoid staking by planting tall plants behind sturdy plants of medium height, such as shrubs. Sure, they'll lean slightly, but the "support plant" will prevent them from breaking.

If you *do* decide to stake, there are almost endless possibilities—bamboo, wood, plastic, or metal. Inserting stakes early in the season (when the plants are still small) is often recommended so as not to accidentally damage the roots when the plant grows or risk breaking the flowerstalk. But this results in a horde of ugly green poles (at least I hope they're green or some other relatively unobtrusive color) that are visible for weeks on end.

I suggest simply inserting the stake carefully before the plant starts to shoot up to blooming size. Attach the stem to the stake with plant ties, preferably at two or three points along the plant's stem. Fix the ties solidly to the stake but only loosely to the plant: Too tight a hold could lead to chafing or even cut into the stem.

For perennials with numerous stems, use peony rings (metal hoops that are open or have a grill across the tops to support the stems). Or insert several stakes around the plant, then run twine from one stake to the other, forming a barrier around the stems. If you grow several plants together, you can create a maze of stakes with strings running back and forth through the entire section, supporting the whole group.

Deadheading
Although it sounds rather cruel, deadheading is actually painless. It is simply gardening

jargon for removing faded flowers. The main reason for this is aesthetic. However, some perennials, including delphiniums and phlox, will rebloom if you cut the flower stems back promptly.

Deadheading is an absolute necessity in the case of perennials that spread invasively through self-seeding, such as golden marguerite (*Anthemis tinctoria*). If you never let them produce seed, they simply can't spread!

On the downside, deadheading is time-consuming, especially if you insist on removing every faded flower as soon as it appears. Dead-heading also removes flowers that would otherwise dry on the plant and prolong its season of interest. Astilbe and yarrow are just two examples of plants that produce attractive dried flowers you can harvest for indoor use at summer's end.

Never deadhead plants you *want* to self-seed. Columbines, for example, are likely to simply disappear from your garden if you deadhead too fervently, since they constantly renew themselves through self-sown seeds.

Wait until the last flower has faded to dead-head. Then take your pruning shears and nip the stems off just above a set of leaves (in the case of perennials with leafy stems) or cut them to the ground if the stems are bare or nearly leafless.

Cutting Back

With some perennials, it's easier to cut the entire plant back by one-half to one-third than it is to deadhead. This is especially true of perennials with numerous flowering stems and perennials that tend to "fall apart" or collapse in a heap after they bloom, such as golden marguerite, painted daisy (*Tanacetum coccineum*), and spiderworts (*Tradescantia* spp.).

Not only does cutting back remove the faded flowers, it encourages the plants to sprout new, healthier growth and may even stimulate some re-peat bloom. You can cut plants back most quickly with an electric hedge trimmer or string trimmer rather than with pruning shears: *Bzzzz, bzzzz,* and it's over. After being sheared back, they will quickly fill in nicely and may even rebloom.

Many fall-blooming perennials, including the garden mums and boltonias (*Boltonia asteroides)* in this border, will be fuller and less prone to flopping if you cut the plants back by about half in early summer. Other perennials, such as the yellow coreopsis, will rebloom if you shear off the first flush of flowers after they fade.

Watering

How often you have to water will depend on your climate, your soil, and the type of plants you grow. When you do water, though, water thoroughly. Your goal should be to completely soak the rootball, but without wasting water. Superficial waterings that only moisten the upper layer of soil are a waste of time and can actually harm the plant by encouraging it to produce roots only near the surface, where they are in greatest danger of being damaged by drought.

Until you're used to truly deep watering, take a trowel and dig down 3 to 4 inches (8 to 10 cm) into the garden after you think you've watered well. If the soil is still dry at that level, water again. Or leave a rain gauge or straight-sided drinking glass in the garden and check its water level: Usually 1 inch (2.5 cm) of rain will moisten soil about 3 inches (8 cm) deep.

Newly planted perennials are the most dependent on regular watering: Their root systems have not yet developed fully enough to dig deep into the soil and find their own water. Even "drought-resistant" perennials will need extra watering during their first summer. During periods of drought, weekly watering may be necessary to keep even established perennials happy and healthy.

Being Water-Wise

Through careful water management, you can keep your perennials in good health while using very little water. Mulching (see page 60) should be a standard practice everywhere: It keeps the soil cool, which in itself reduces evaporation, and forms a barrier between the soil and the drying effects of wind and sun, further enhancing its water-saving effect. In nature, soil is rarely directly exposed to the elements but is covered with a layer of low-growing plants or decomposing vegetation: Why should things be different in culture?

If you do have to water entire sections of garden as opposed to individual plants, consider using a soaker hose that leaks small amounts of

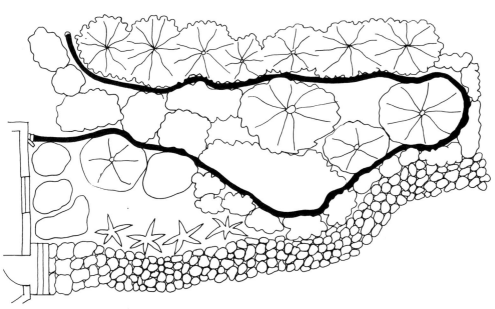

A soaker hose will put water right at the roots, where plants need it most. Watering at soil level also keeps moisture off the foliage, where fungal diseases are apt to take hold.

water over its entire length, moistening the soil and not the air. You can simply run soaker hoses through the garden, in and around the plants, with more loops near needier plants or in drier spots. Then cover them with mulch. They'll be almost invisible under the mulch, and they'll water even more efficiently than when they're exposed to air.

Any new system will require some testing on your part. Try running soaker hoses for two hours, than dig down 3 to 4 inches (8 to 10 cm) to see if that's enough. Because of varying water pressures in different communities and of different irrigation products, it's hard to predict just how long any given system should be operating. Watering at night or early in the morning is most efficient, as less water is lost to evaporation because the sun is not very intense and the air temperature is cooler.

Conquering Pests and Diseases

When you decide to garden, pests and diseases come with the territory. Perennial gardens aren't the worst hit (try growing vegetables and you'll learn what the phrase "constant battle" means!), but they aren't trouble-free. To keep problems at bay as much as possible, try the following:

- **Match your plants** to your garden's conditions. A plant that isn't where it should be may have reduced bloom, stunted growth, and little resistance to pests and diseases.

- **Choose resistant plants** and you'll avoid both work and problems. Pass up the plants that are notoriously susceptible.

- **Check your garden daily** and react to any problem as soon as you see it. Destroying dead or infested leaves can stop or at least slow the problem before it spreads. And never add diseased material to the compost pile—it will only spread the problem.

- **Encourage birds,** toads, and other small predatory creatures to frequent your garden by supplying a wide variety of favorable plants and

conditions. Also avoid toxic pesticides; design or leave hiding spaces for the creatures; and add feeders, nest boxes, and water features.

- **Identify insects** before you destroy them, especially if you can't see them actually chewing on your plants. Most insects are harmless and many, like ladybugs, are beneficial. If in doubt, borrow a book on bugs, check out Internet sites, or take a sample to a garden center or your local Cooperative Extension Service.

- **Yank out weeds** when they're still small, before they have a chance to go to seed.

- **Maintain order** in the garden and never let anything get out of hand. This simple philosophy will help prevent many problems.

Slay the Tiny Pests

Insect damage on perennials isn't quite the crisis it is on edibles, since at least you don't have to eat the plants afterward (if anything is left—yeecch!). But that doesn't mean you have to like it—or put up with it. Here's how to cope with everything from leaf miners on your columbines to slugs on your hostas—organically, of course.

Dry Leaves Mean Less Disease

Another reason that drip systems and soaker hoses are such useful tools is that many plant diseases are spread through water droplets bouncing off infested soil or foliage and landing on susceptible leaves. Since these systems produce no splashing, they can help keep plants disease-free.

If you have no choice but to water from above, water early in the morning. This gives the leaves time to dry off in the sun. If you wait to water late in the day, the foliage can stay moist throughout the night, encouraging the spread of fungal diseases.

In dusty climates, you may still want to hose down your perennials every now and then to keep the leaves clean, even if they are being adequately watered by soaker hoses or drip irrigation. Just make sure you "wash" them early in the morning to prevent disease.

PERENNIAL PESTS

If pests are bugging you and you can see them, glance through the description column and identify who the invader is. If all you see on your plant is damage and there's not a pest in sight, start at the damage column to figure out what's going on. Once you've found the perpetrators, read on to see how to control them or how to live with the damage they've caused.

PEST NAME AND DESCRIPTION	DAMAGE	CONTROLS	LARRY'S HELPFUL HINTS
Aphids They're tiny little round or pear-shaped insects in a wide range of colors: green, pink, purple, red, blue, and black. Aphids are usually wingless.	They damage plants by pumping out the sap, causing the plant to yellow and distort, and often transmit viruses. They look like insect sheep as they "graze," heads down, on your plants.	Spray with water, making sure you hit the undersides of the leaves. Insecticidal soap is also fine. Destroy severely infested leaves.	Hummingbirds love aphids, so placing a vase of red or orange trumpet-shaped cut flowers (the hummingbird's favorite) near infested plants will often enlist their help.
Caterpillars Most gardeners can recognize these fuzzy, creepy-crawly wormlike creatures when they see them. They are the larval stage of moths and butterflies.	Most eat leaves, buds, and flowers, often leaving irregular holes or consuming the foliage entirely. Leafroll caterpillars roll the leaves around themselves, then eat their way through them.	Control by hand-picking or use soap spray when numbers are massive. Bt (*Bacillus thuringiensis*) is helpful if sprayed on leaves and reapplied after rain: Once caterpillars eat the bacteria, they'll quickly lose their appetite and soon die.	Be careful with any type of caterpillar control, especially Bt, if you're trying to attract butterflies to your garden. If you kill caterpillars (butterfly larvae), you've defeated your purpose.
Japanese beetles Japanese beetles are actually very pretty insects with bright metallic green bodies and coppery brown wing covers.	They have a voracious appetite for foliage and flowers, eating small, round holes in leaves and buds. They can do extensive damage in a short time, entirely skeletonizing leaves.	Hand-picking may keep them at bay. Crush them underfoot or drop them into soapy water. Powder plant leaves with diatomaceous earth, reapplying it after every rain.	If you have Japanese beetles, you'll have their larvae (a.k.a. grubs) as well. Grubs feed on grass roots, so apply milky spore (*Bacillus popillus*) to eliminate future generations.

Aphids

Leaf miner damage

PEST NAME AND DESCRIPTION	DAMAGE	CONTROLS	LARRY'S HELPFUL HINTS
Leaf miners Adult leaf miners are rarely recognized: They're tiny black flies. Their pale green offspring are scarcely visible.	The leaf miner offspring burrow white or light green tunnels just under the upper surface of perennial leaves.	Total control of these pests is difficult to impossible. Simply cutting off and destroying infected leaves is the best solution. If infestation is serious, cut the plant back to 2 inches (5 cm) above the ground.	Columbines are tops on the list of host plants, but chrysanthemums, delphiniums, and primroses are popular, too. If you cut your plants back drastically, don't worry—the leaves will grow back and the pests will be gone.
Slugs and snails If they're slimy, tentacled mollusks, they're slugs. If they have shells on their backs, they're snails.	Lower leaves will show holes of irregular size and young plants will be entirely eaten. Both slugs and snails leave a sticky, glistening trail behind as proof of their presence.	Hand-pick and crush the slimers you see. Or leave out bowls of beer—they'll fall in and drown. Trap them under boards left on the ground; visit traps daily and either squish the rascals or drop them in soapy water.	Try putting barriers (like diatomaceous earth) around susceptible plants. If you live in the country, get a duck! Ducks love to eat both slugs and snails.
Spider mites They're tiny eight-legged critters that are essentially invisible to the naked eye. When colonies are large, they can be picked out as moving particles of dust.	They damage plants by piercing tiny holes in the leaves and drinking the sap that leaks out. The plant will become covered with spiderweb-like strands. In dry climates, plants may yellow.	Control is relatively easy: Simply hose down the plant regularly or use insecticidal soap. Repeat weekly.	Spider mites are rarely a problem on perennials in humid or rainy climates because their numbers are small and they do no noticeable damage.
Thrips Under a magnifying glass, they're hyphen-sized insects, either dark in color with double pairs of wings (adults) or pale and wingless (nymphs).	They do damage by scraping plant tissues and drinking the leaking fluids. Leaves will appear silver and will be punctuated with dots of excrement. Flower buds may fail to open or flowers will have brown petals.	Sprays of cold water or insecticidal soap usually work. Or you can use one of the light horticultural oils recommended for the growing season. Deep mulch may prevent adults from emerging in the spring.	You'll never see a thrip (in the singular sense of the word). The word "thrips" is both singular and plural. That said, you may never see a thrips either—they're fast-moving and very small.

Slug

Spider mites and webbing

Chase the Large Varmints

You don't need a magnifying glass to see all your pests! Deer, skunks, raccoons, rabbits, household pets, and rodents (squirrels, mice, voles, gophers, and groundhogs) are also potential trouble-makers in the garden.

Deer are a huge problem in suburban areas, and they're not easy to control. All sorts of home remedies and commercial products, from Irish Spring soap to predator urine, are suggested as means of keeping them at bay, but most have little long-term effectiveness. Repellent sprays are of some help, but they need to be reapplied after each rain. Other than an 8-foot (240-cm) fence, preferably electrified, deer are probably best kept at bay by dogs specifically trained to guard against them. But then you'll need a fence to keep the dogs in! So the battle lines will be expensive to say the least, and the dogs will have to stay outside all the time, which will make them poor pets.

The easiest way to deal with deer is to plant deer-resistant perennials. Deer tend to avoid highly aromatic plants such as artemisias, catmint, salvias, and Russian sage and plants with fuzzy leaves such as lamb's-ears and yarrow. Deer will also head for the hills if your offerings include plants with coarse leaves such as irises, bergenia, yucca, hellebores, and red-hot pokers or plants that are prickly like agave, aloe, or bear's-breeches. Poisonous plants such as foxglove, monkshood, and spurges are also left alone.

Skunks and raccoons are only problems in the perennial garden when they dig up grubs or other insects. They're usually more of a lawn problem than a garden problem. Often, they'll go away on their own when they've finished with the grubs. Replanting parts of the lawn can be a chore but look at it this way—they're helping to keep next year's Japanese beetles under control. Rabbits can be more of a problem (especially if all of your neighbors have cats and you don't). They'll munch on the tender new growth of almost anything. Rabbits, like deer, tend to avoid plants that are tough, aromatic, and poisonous. If you can get your plants past the tender new growth stage, they'll probably survive. Keep a supply of bloodmeal or hot-pepper repellent spray on hand early in the season, though, and apply it as soon as you suspect intruders are visiting your gardens.

Cats will certainly keep the rabbits away, but they can create their own annoyances. They assume that any open spot is a free-range litter box. Although they'll seldom harm established plants, they can do considerable damage to young ones, digging them up almost as fast as

Rabbits love to nibble on tender, young perennial foliage. One way to protect your perennials is to sprinkle blood meal around the plants in spring to repel the bunnies. Once the plants have matured a bit, their foliage won't be as appetizing to rabbits.

Hiding Nature's Mistakes

Many diseases, especially powdery mildew and rust, strike the same plants (like bee balm, hollyhocks, and garden phlox) year after year. These diseases rarely cause permanent harm, but the plants may not look healthy while they are under attack. As a solution to the age-old dilemma of liking a plant even if it's care-intensive, consider planting susceptible species at the back of the garden, where only their flowers are visible. Since you won't see the damage as readily, you may not want to bother treating the plants.

you can plant them. Try using prickly conifer branches as a mulch or keep their favorite spot soaked (cats hate wet feet), and they'll soon go elsewhere. Or, if you have potted plants and you place them strategically (and aesthetically) in newly cultivated areas, cats won't have the room they need to dig comfortably. Dogs also like to dig, and a garden is as good a place as any. Fortunately, they're trainable and, if you can't always stop them from digging, you can usually reach a reasonable agreement with them on where they *shouldn't* dig.

Small rodents won't eat the leaves of your plants, but their presence can be trouble. Moles are strictly carnivores, eating lots of grubs as they tunnel through the soil. But even though plant roots are not in their meal plan, they can harm young plants by disturbing them as they dig. Mice can take advantage of mole holes and devour the newly accessible fleshy roots; your perennials can be left rootless almost overnight. Some rodents, such as voles or meadow mice, make surprise attacks under the snow in winter. The mulch in your perennial bed can provide a cozy home for them. Field mice are active all year round. You can control them by trapping, or you can apply repellents (usually made of predator urine from bobcats or foxes).

Battle the Diseases

Gardeners think plant diseases are mysterious and uncontrollable, since they often strike otherwise healthy perennials, apparently without warning. Actually, before a plant succumbs to a disease, three conditions have to be met. First, the disease-causing organism has to be present. Second, the plant must be susceptible. And third, the environmental conditions (such as temperature and humidity) have to be just right. If any one of these three conditions are not met, the disease won't have a chance.

By the time severe symptoms are apparent, the damage is usually done. To make matters worse, identifying a disease isn't easy: The same symptoms can often be caused by a range of diseases of very different categories, or even just by poor growing conditions. Wind, poor soil, air pollution, excess heat or cold, poor drainage, and drought all can upset a plant's normal functions. The resulting symptoms may mimic a disease or weaken a plant to the point that it becomes susceptible to disease. The first step in disease prevention is making sure that you have each of your plants in its preferred location. It's always easier to move or replace a plant than to battle disease problems year after year.

Fortunately, most perennial diseases only cause temporary visible damage. (Rot, which can kill plants, and many viruses, which won't go away, are the exceptions.) Most perennials recover completely from diseases. But be warned: If your plants have been susceptible to diseases in the past, they probably will be again.

You can prevent diseases from spreading by keeping tools clean, mulching, and watering at ground level. First, dip tools into a solution of one part bleach to four parts water after each use. Second, mulch to prevent water from splashing spores from the ground onto the foliage. The goal is to keep soilborne diseases *on* the ground and *off*

(*continued on page 60*)

PERENNIAL DISEASES

There are a number of diseases that can affect your perennial garden. This brief overview will help you diagnose and treat the most common problems you'll face. Don't despair, however, if you have a plant that's beyond help. All this means is that you'll have an excuse to head to the local nursery and buy more plants to fill in the empty spots in your perennial bed.

DISEASE NAME AND SYMPTOMS	CONTROLS	LARRY'S HELPFUL HINTS
Aster yellows Susceptible plants will yellow, flowers will be stunted and will remain green, and new growth will often be distorted.	The best treatment is to destroy infected plants. Avoid planting susceptible plants in the same spot for several years. Controlling weeds helps to slow the spread of insects that carry the disease.	Aster yellows is not really a virus; it's caused by a little-known organism with characteristics similar to a virus, so it's often labeled as a viral disease.
Downy mildew You'll see fuzzy, cottonlike gray or tan growth under the leaves. The leaves will turn yellow and die back.	Planting fungus-resistant cultivars is the best solution. Space plants and thin out stems to encourage air circulation. Remove and destroy infected leaves.	Downy mildew strikes in humid, rainy weather, especially when days are hot and nights are cool.
Gray mold (botrytis blight) Fungus-infected parts will be covered with a grayish, powdery growth. Shoots will wilt suddenly and fall over, and stem bases will blacken and rot.	Cut back infected parts during the growing season, and destroy foliage of susceptible plants in the fall. Clear mulch from plant crowns in the spring to let the soil dry.	You'll find this mostly on weak or dying foliage and flowers, but it can quickly spread to healthy growth, so keeping a watchful eye may be the best solution.
Leaf spots You won't miss this bacterial disease; leaves have many small brown or purple spots. Heavily spotted leaves may yellow and drop.	Remove infected leaves and slow the spread of the disease with a sulfur-based spray. Spray susceptible plants weekly (starting in the spring) to prevent the disease.	If leaf spots keep coming back, especially for a second year, it's best to remove the plant and replace it with a different species.
Mosaic viruses Mosaic-infected leaves are mottled with yellow, white, and light and dark green spots or streaks. Plants are often stunted.	Once plants are infected, there are no controls; remove and destroy infected plants.	Smokers should wash their hands before pruning or handling plants, since tobacco mosaic virus spreads through contaminated tobacco products.
Powdery mildew Plant leaves are covered with white, powdery masses of spores, then may blacken and die. The disease strikes when the air is moist and the soil is dry.	The best control is to plant fungus-resistant cultivars because the disease tends to come back year after year no matter what treatment is applied.	The disease rarely does permanent damage because it arrives late in the season. Plants have usually had time to store up energy for the following year.

DISEASE NAME AND SYMPTOMS	CONTROLS	LARRY'S HELPFUL HINTS
Rots and wilts The first sign is wilting leaves, but if the soil is moist, rot or wilt is likely. If the plant's roots or crown is soft, soggy, or brown, you have rot. Wilt, on the other hand, may show no outward symptoms, although cutting open a stem may reveal discoloration.	Where rot is visible, cut out the damaged parts with a sharp, sterile knife, and sterilize the remainder with a 10-percent solution of chlorine bleach. Replant in an area with better drainage.	Bacterial rots and wilts come on suddenly and do serious damage. They strike at the roots or the crown of the plant and can quickly kill if not treated.
Rust The symptoms are yellow or pale green spots on the upper surfaces of the leaf and powdery orange spores underneath.	Planting disease-resistant cultivars is the single best prevention. Mulching will help as will watering the plants below the foliage to prevent the leaves from getting wet.	Fungal rust strikes in cool, humid climates or in other areas when the summer is particularly rainy. If you have rust year after year, start choosing perennials with more open growth habits.
Viruses Viruses are very hard to recognize: Sometimes the plant has a mottled appearance with pale or yellow marbling, or its growth can be stunted. Some plants just have a general lack of vigor.	The best prevention for viruses is controlling the insects that carry them, especially aphids. Sterilizing tools with bleach between uses also helps. Otherwise, once a plant is affected, your only recourse is none at all—just dig out the plant and destroy it.	If you suspect a plant has a virus, ask your local Cooperative Extension Service for advice.

Powdery mildew on bee balm leaves

Rust on underside of Jack-in-the-pulpit leaf

the leaves. Third, water plants at ground level if possible for the same reason. You can also reduce the risk of disease by planting plants that you know are susceptible in an area that is open and has frequent breezes to allow for constant air movement. Thinning out crowded stems also helps to improve air circulation. If you're using a fence or hedge as a backdrop for your garden, try, if possible, to make sure there is air movement through it. To prevent a disease from recurring, destroy the foliage and stems of all infected plants in the fall, whether or not the disease seems under control.

Finally, treatments with baking soda spray (1 teaspoon baking soda, ¼ teaspoon liquid soap, and 1 quart of water) and sulfur-based powders or sprays can help in some cases, especially if the disease is recognized early. But even sulfur spray can't remove damage that is already done. You'll have to wait for new, healthy leaves to grow in to hide the damaged ones.

Of course, you can just avoid all the bother to begin with, and avoid diseases altogether, by always buying healthy-looking plants suitable for your site and by choosing cultivars known for their disease resistance. It's not a guarantee, but it does increase your odds.

Keeping Weeds under Control

It is said that nature abhors a vacuum, and you can verify this in your garden: Any open space can and will fill with weeds. Weeds are either annual or perennial, and both kinds can take over in a few short weeks. Annual weeds spread strictly by seed, either germinating when you disturb the soil in a bed or arriving airborne from nearby fields and gardens. They should be controlled immediately because many of them mature and produce seed in only a few weeks.

Perennial weeds can enter the garden as seeds or be spread through invasive underground or aboveground stolons (or runners). In the long run, they are harder to control than annual weeds, especially if their roots mix with the root systems of desirable perennials. Controlling weeds takes work, but there are several ways you can keep the weed population low.

Mulching

Mulching is popular with gardeners with good reason—it excludes weeds from the get-go. Mulches are particularly effective against annual weeds, most of which need light to germinate. If the ground is kept covered, the weeds simply have nowhere to start.

There are two types of mulches. Organic mulches are biodegradable. They decompose over time, enriching the soil as they break down. They can be turned under when they're well on their way to decomposing, or more mulch can simply be layered on top. On one hand, using organic mulches does mean extra work, since they need replacing every year or two in moist climates and every three to five years in drier ones. On the other hand, replacing them regularly doesn't give annual weeds the slightest chance: Just when your mulch begins to turn into the rich soil where weeds get started, you cover up the soil with a fresh layer of mulch. The cheapest organic mulch is chopped leaves. You can either run the leaves through a shredder or spread them on the lawn and chop them up with your lawn mower.

Pine and other evergreen needles are other excellent organic mulches, especially for perennials that like well-drained conditions because they allow greater air circulation to the plant's roots than chopped leaves do. But needles tend to acidify the soil over time, so make sure you do a soil test about every three years.

Inorganic mulches have a much longer life span because they don't decompose readily, so you're not dipping into your wallet every year to replace them. I include large bark chunks with inorganic materials—I know they're really organic and will *eventually* decompose, but they take such a long time to do so! These large chunks can last for five years even in moist climates and last much longer in dry ones. However, they aren't as good at suppressing weeds as are finer mulches, since they leave open spaces for weed seeds to fall through and reach the soil below. As a result, they become weed-ridden rather quickly. Also, care has to be taken not to mix them with the soil when planting—those big chunks of material can interfere with root growth. That means you have to rake them off each time you move or plant something, then rake them back into place when you've finished.

Plastic mulch is definitely inorganic, but it just doesn't hold up well. Plastic mulch *sheets* can become plastic mulch *strips* after just a few windy or stormy days. Decorative stones can be used as mulch, too, but they are best suited to drier climates. They tend to heat up and warm the soil beneath them, keeping it drier, which suits many dry-climate plants just fine. Stone mulches, like large bark chunks, do allow some weeds to grow, and you have to be careful not to mix them into the soil when moving or planting perennials.

Cultivation

Cultivating the soil around perennials is the time-honored way of controlling weeds in most gardens, including the perennial bed. Use a hoe, a cultivator, or another weeding tool (there are probably more tools designed for weeding than for any other kind of garden maintenance!). You simply run the tines or blade under the soil to loosen the soil, and pull the weeds out or cut them off at their base. Always remove any weed or piece of weed that is dislodged because—as you've probably already discovered—any section that's left behind will often reroot. Cultivation also keeps the surface soil loose, making it easier for perennials to form new roots and keeping their roots well aerated.

Pine needles are an attractive summer mulch for perennial gardens, and they're also a good winter mulch for perennials that will rot under a heavy cover.

Cultivation has four drawbacks, however. First, it constantly churns up the soil, exposing new weed seeds to light and allowing them to germinate. Second, it tends to cut into the stems and stolons of perennial weeds, so that instead of eliminating them, it encourages them to proliferate The third flaw is that cultivating the soil to remove weeds often damages the roots of the perennials you want to help. There's a fourth flaw: Repeated cultivation pulverizes the soil, which causes it to compact or erode over time. If you choose to cultivate, do so as shallowly as possible, and avoid working near the base of your perennials.

Hand-Weeding

Hand-weeding is an even more time-honored method of weed control than cultivating, but it

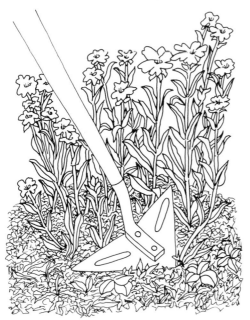
A small-headed winged weeder is a useful culti-
vating tool. Sharpened on all edges, it slices easily
through soil and weeds.

fell into disuse when cultivating tools (hoes,
etc.) became popular. The technique is simple
enough—simply grasp the weed at its base and
pull upward firmly but steadily until it comes
free. If the soil is moist (you could water the
day before), the weed will be easier to uproot.
When the weed is removed, immediately push
the mulch back into place. This will help prevent the weed from resprouting if any part was
left behind.

Off-Season Care

As gardeners in colder areas begin to prepare for
winter, those in mild-winter areas can begin to
prepare for their "supplementary" gardening
season. Plant pots of blooming chrysanthemums
and asters in early fall for bloom until nearly
Christmas. And in December, plant pansies,
forced primroses, and English daisies as well as
cool-season annuals to ensure winter-long color.

But always keep a couple of old blankets and
a few bags of dry fall leaves on hand, even in
USDA Zone 10, for those unusually cold spells
that occur every few winters. That way you can
quickly rush out and protect a few favorite or
particularly frost-sensitive plants.

Keep Watering as Winter Draws Near

Although almost all perennials are fully dormant by late fall and have stopped growing,
they still need water. Not a *lot* of water, but they
shouldn't be allowed to enter the cold season in
a dehydrated state. Once the ground freezes,
though, there's no point in adding water. Hardy
cacti and succulents are the only exceptions—
they actually survive the winter better in a dehydrated condition, so stop watering them by
midfall.

To Clean or Not to Clean?

One of the most furious debates in gardening circles these days concerns fall cleanup. Should you
leave your garden spic-and-span in the fall, removing all dead and dying vegetation and carefully picking up every fallen leaf, or is this
excessive neatness, as some gardeners call it,
actually doing more harm than good?

Those who prefer to clean the garden in the
fall usually do so to help prevent insects and disease the following season. Both, they point out,
tend to overwinter among fallen leaves at the
base of plants. And dead leaves falling from trees
or blowing into the garden can smother perennials and also keep the soil too moist, leading to
rot. They feel that it's better to clean the garden
thoroughly each and every fall.

Those who favor spring cleanup (or no cleanup
at all) refer to Mother Nature as a source of inspiration. Perennials usually have leaves that die back
and cover their tender crown, thus protecting
them from the ravages of winter weather . . . *if*
they're not removed. Leaves not only act as a natural protective mulch but also feed the plants
and improve the soil as they decay. And if
harmful insects and disease spores can hibernate

in plant materials, so can their predators, so by cleaning up, natural controls are lost.

Who's right? Both sides have their points, but studies increasingly show that fall cleanup *does* reduce plant hardiness. Furthermore, there is little evidence that "clean" gardens, with a few exceptions, are any less susceptible to insects or disease. And a buildup of fall leaves, especially if they are finely chopped up, seems to do perennials far more good than harm.

I suggest combining the two approaches. By all means cut back the foliage of disease- and insect-susceptible plants, such as bearded iris, garden phlox, and hollyhocks. In fact, burn or otherwise destroy their leaves: *Don't* add them to the compost bin, or the pests and diseases might show up another season. For other plants, it's probably best to keep the leaves in place in the North and *add* more fall leaves to the garden for increased protection rather than remove them. If they're large leaves, like maple and oak, run them through a leaf shredder or under the lawn mower before applying them to the garden.

In any climate, remove stakes and drain irrigation systems in the late fall or whenever they are no longer in use. Turn off the water to outdoor faucets and drain any hoses. Clean up and sharpen garden tools and store them away carefully.

Why Mulch in Winter?

Many people think you add winter mulch to protect plants from the cold. But unless you supply perennials with artificial heat, the cold will get to them even through the best mulch. What mulch does protect from are harsh, drying winds that can rob frozen plants of their moisture and from the damaging effects of freezing and thawing.

This temperature fluctuation can cause perennials to be thrust out of the soil when freezing nights are succeeded by above-freezing days. This is called frost heave. That's why it's better to apply winter mulches *after* the ground has frozen: You're not trying to warm the plants up with mulch, but you are using the mulch to keep the sun off the soil and thus keep it frozen.

Preparing for the Next Bloom Season
At winter's end, you finally *can* cut any perennial stems still standing upright back to near ground level. And cut back plants like ornamental grasses whose golden foliage looked so good in the winter but now has to be disposed of in order to make room for new leaves.

Don't cut off the leaves of evergreen perennials, unless they have been damaged beyond any chance of recovery by a particularly harsh

Both standard and variegated Japanese pachysandra (*Pachysandra terminalis*) have evergreen foliage that needs no special winter care.

winter. If so, just prune them back to healthy foliage and they'll resprout, although they may not bloom until the following season.

Although it may feel like spring outside in February or March, don't remove the winter mulch from your garden until there is no further danger of frost. While the ground will warm up more quickly if the mulch is removed, giving you earlier bloom, this often pushes perennials into growth too early in the season. Such tender new growth is very frost-sensitive. Instead, by keeping them dormant longer, mulch helps delay their spring growth spurt until a safer time of the year.

Early Spring Checklist

As frost leaves the air and the soil dries out enough to work, you can begin working in earnest in your perennial garden.

- Remove the mulch and put it to one side for now so the ground can warm up. (You can put it back on once the ground is warm.)
- Replant any perennials that have been heaved out of the ground by frost (something that isn't likely to have happened if you mulched properly).
- Divide and transplant perennials as needed.
- Add more organic material to the soil and work it in carefully.

After the First Year

Once your garden has been planted and watered for a year or so and you've moved a few plants around and corrected a few problems, it really will seem to practically take care of itself. You'll mostly find yourself cutting back or dividing a few overgrown plants, renewing the mulch, deadheading, and so on.

Simple Upkeep

Each year is different, though, and care activities will vary. An early spring often leads to drier conditions: Not only will you begin working earlier, but you may also find yourself watering more often. Rainy, cool summers can mean you just watch the plants grow . . . and stake them, if you're into that. In hot, dry summers, watering will become a priority.

It's important to realize that your garden is, in a sense, a living entity in itself, reacting to conditions beyond your control. If you want to have a healthy, happy garden, you simply have to learn to go with the flow, adapting to whatever changes the current season brings.

Time for an Overhaul?

Gardens don't always age gracefully. Maybe you've been a bit negligent and have a severe

Is It Dead or Dormant?

Every year, gardeners anxiously await the first signs of life in their gardens. First the Christmas roses start to bloom, then the earliest bulbs pop out of the ground, then one by one the other perennials start to sprout, some slowly, some seemingly overnight.

But there are always a few plants that make you nervous: Everything else is up. Are they re-ally only dormant, or did the winter cold finish them off? Before you panic, remember that the same plant probably played the same trick on you last year . . . and will next year as well. Some plants are simply slow starters. Make sure you label them well, or you may find you've damaged them by planting other perennials in their place.

On the other hand, some plants really *could* be dead. After all, not all perennials live forever, and spring is as reasonable a time as any to kick the bucket. The only real solution is to wait and see. If nothing has sprouted two months after the last frost date, the plant is almost certainly dead.

And if you just can't stand waiting two months, carefully dig at the base of the plant and check for signs of life: Fresh white roots and pink sprouts shooting upward are signs that it's coming back!

A large container used either as a garden ornament or for a planting of annuals or tender perennials adds an extra-special touch to your garden, especially in a shady spot that doesn't have abundant blooms in the summer.

weed problem you just can't control. Or some of the ornamental plants themselves have gotten out of hand and taken over vast patches of the garden. Or things just didn't turn out the way you wanted. Or you've simply become tired of the effect and want to start fresh: After all, if you can redecorate a room, why not a garden?

First, though, you should seriously consider whether you're ready to redo the entire garden right away or if you prefer to take things more slowly. After all, just as you can create a garden step by step, you can also rebuild a garden piece by piece. If it's a large bed especially, you might want to consider a five-year plan, starting with the most offending part.

Overhauling a garden pretty much means starting from scratch. You might want to dig out and keep a few prized plants, but if the problem involves persistent weeds like goutweed or horsetail, remember than keeping any part of the rootball of a desirable plant could result in introducing a piece of the unwanted one into the new garden. In that case, try taking cuttings if the plant can be reproduced that way, but leave the roots where they are.

My fast-and-easy method (see page 11) for starting a flower bed is also the easiest way of restarting one. Cover the entire area with a thick layer of newspaper to smooth the original plants, then cover that with an even thicker layer of good soil. And this time, be more careful in your choice of plants!

Coping with Maturing Sites

If you didn't already know this, you'll learn it quickly enough: Gardens inevitably become shadier as they mature. The small shrubs you put in the background turn into big shrubs, and the small trees turn into big ones.

Unless you have a special attachment to a plant for sentimental reasons—say, a peony that has been in your family for generations—try not to get overly sentimental about plants. If you don't have a sunny spot where you can replant them or someone to give them to, they're simply going to have to go. Dig them out and find replacements.

Consult the chapters "Perennials That Bloom in the Shade" on page 316, "Perennials for Fabulous Foliage" on page 346, and "Groundcover Perennials" on page 373. You'll find there are a surprising number of shade-tolerant perennials. In fact, you just might like your shade garden better than your sunny garden.

PART 2

CHOOSING THE BEST PERENNIALS

How many perennials are there in the world? Tens of thousands of them—and that can be mind-boggling for even an experienced gardener. How do you know which plants to choose? Larry to the rescue! In this part of the book, I've divided perennials into categories that are specifically designed to help you use perennials to bring out the best in your garden. The perennials I've chosen are the best of the best, at least in terms of performance. You can count on these plants to give results—I know because I've grown most of them in my own garden.

To start, decide what kind of garden you want to create. Then turn to the chapter that best addresses your purpose. For example, does your garden need more color in spring? Turn to "Spring-Blooming Perennials" on page 108. Do you want all-season interest that changes through the seasons? Mix plants from the spring-, summer-, and fall-blooming categories with a selection from "No-Care Perennials" on page 188, and you'll be well on your way. If you want more punch from your perennials, forget the skimpy little ones and try "Perennials and Grasses for Dramatic Impact" on page 416. Perennial gardening has never been easier!

Everblooming PERENNIALS

Every gardener I know wants to be rewarded with beds that brim with blooms all season long. It's the least our perennials can do for us in exchange for the hours of labor we put in digging and planting. To get the most bloom for the least work, choose perennials that look great and show off their stuff for weeks—even months—on end. I call these terrific plants everbloomers, and they have the flower power to encourage a weary gardener onward. When gardeners talk about everblooming perennials, they mean those with a blooming season of at least eight weeks. In the flowering scheme of things, two months is a very long time, covering much of the summer—even *all* of the summer in areas with short growing seasons.

◀ Be sure your garden includes some long-blooming perennials such as this 'Goldsturm' orange coneflower (*Rudbeckia fulgida* var. *sullivantii* 'Goldsturm') to guarantee lively and abundant color from summer through fall.

Bloom You Can Count On

Most everblooming perennials don't know when to quit. Once they get started, they just keep blooming and blooming and blooming. Often they're still blooming so late in the season that their flowers don't have time to produce seed, but they still won't stop. From a strictly Darwinian point of view, most of these plants wouldn't stand a snowball's chance in hell of surviving in the wild—too much of their energy goes into producing "useless" flowers. Gardeners make sure that everbloomers survive by propagating them, something these plants aren't so good at doing on their own.

Plants That Need a Pinch

Some everbloomers need encouragement to keep producing new flowers. You can keep these perennials blooming if you deadhead (pinch off the flowers as they fade) regularly. The reason is easy to understand: When seed production begins, most plants release hormones that cause them to stop blooming and concentrate all their energy on producing seeds. By deadheading, you remove the flowers before this message goes out, so the plants keep blooming. In the plant entry pages for each everbloomer, I'll mention whether deadheading is necessary to stimulate constant bloom or whether you should use another technique to keep the plants looking tidy all season long.

"Seedless" Everbloomers

Perennials can also be everblooming if they have sterile flowers: 'Rosenschleier' baby's-breath (*Gypsophila* 'Rosenschleier', also called G. 'Rosy Veil') is an example. Because these plants don't form seeds,

"Ann Folkard' geranium (*Geranium* 'Ann Folkard') will see this garden through the summer, while earlier and later bloomers come and go. Providing early summer contrast are tall purple foxglove, yellow yarrow, and the large globes of star of Persia (*Allium christophii*).

the "stop blooming" message is never sent and the plants just keep on blooming. There are also some hybrid perennials that don't seem to know they're supposed to stop blooming once seed production is underway. It's as if their "stop blooming" message comes through in half a dozen different languages at once and just isn't understood, so the plants simply keep on flowering. When you plant everbloomers like these, you'll get a long season of flowering even if you don't deadhead.

Everbloomers without Flowers?

Some everblooming perennials are fakers: They have long-lasting seedheads that are virtually indistinguishable from their flowers. Plants such as globe thistles (*Echinops* spp.) may produce true flowers for a short time, but who can tell since their seedheads are nearly the same color and remain on the plants for months? You might consider that cheating, but I give these perennials full credit in the everblooming department for looking good for so long.

I could scarcely discuss everblooming perennials without mentioning a whole other world of perennials that look good even when not in bloom, thanks to their attractive form, shape, or foliage color. These include many graceful ornamental grasses such as miscanthus (*Miscanthus sinensis*) and fountain grasses (*Pennisetum* spp.), and tall perennials such as Russian sage (*Perovskia atriplicifolia*) and Joe-Pye weed (*Eupatorium fistulosum*). They'll add color and interest and lend an architectural accent from spring through fall. To find out more about them, check "Low-Care Perennials" on page 210 and "Perennials & Grasses for Dramatic Impact" on page 416.

The Everbloomer Advantage

The advantage of planting long-blooming perennials is obvious—you can count on everbloomers to add color to your garden throughout most of the flowering season. Long bloomers such as salvias (*Salvia* spp.) and yarrows (*Achillea* spp.)

give a certain stability to the flower garden, guaranteeing a minimum of bloom at all times. Use them abundantly, tossing in your favorite shorter-season perennials as you please.

Filling the Spring Gap

Everbloomers usually don't start flowering until late spring, and many wait until summer is well underway before they begin. So it's best to interplant everbloomers with spring-blooming bulbs like crocuses and daffodils. There's also a wonderful group of perennials that flower in early spring to midspring; they're natural choices for planting with everbloomers. I love spring bloomers such as columbines (*Aquilegia* spp.) and baptisias (*Baptisia* spp.), especially interplanted with everbloomers. I enjoy their spring blooms to the fullest, and trust in my everbloomers to take over when the spring flowers fade.

Deep Carpets of Blooms

Many everblooming perennials make great groundcovers. After all, most people want groundcovers that create a carpet of color all season long, and everbloomers certainly fill the bill. They may be a bit taller or take longer to establish themselves than standard groundcovers such as ajugas (*Ajuga* spp.), but their nonstop bloom often compensates for those flaws. And there's no rule saying groundcovers must be short, so if you want a deep-pile carpet of flowers, you can use even the tallest everbloomers: Imagine a swath of 3-foot (90-cm) 'Coronation Gold' yarrow (*Achillea* 'Coronation Gold') in full bloom as a groundcover!

Don't Let Them Bore You

As with many annuals, the constant bloom of everbloomers can leave your garden a bit static. If you appreciate movement and change, make sure no more than half of the plants in any mixed border are annuals or everblooming perennials.

Everblooming Evolution

The everbloomers I've featured in this chapter are the tip of an evolving iceberg. Nonstop bloom over a long season is a desirable trait that plant breeders are pursuing with fervor. They cross spring-, summer-, and fall-flowering species together to produce plants that bloom in all three seasons.

If it still seems unlikely to you that you'll see *your* favorite perennial (with its dramatic but short-lived bloom) as an everbloomer, remember that, barely a century ago, all roses were strictly seasonal bloomers, mostly in early summer. Many modern roses are in nearly constant bloom from summer right through fall. And more and better everbloomers are certainly on their way.

No Kidding: Bloom All Season Long

Do you really want nonstop, season-long bloom, from the last frost date in spring to the first frosts in fall? Then plant some annuals. Really! Many annuals (marigolds and petunias, for example) will bloom for six months and even up to ten months in mild climates. Since there's no law saying you can't plant annuals and perennials together, take advantage of the nonstop bloom of annuals to add some truly durable color to your garden.

11 More Everbloomers

To widen your selection of everblooming perennials, check out these great plants, too:

Achillea

Yarrow

Tall or small, yarrows are easy to identify: Their flat-topped clusters of tiny flowers and feathery leaves are a dead giveaway. If in doubt, crush a leaf—many types of yarrow have a spicy odor. Fast-growing yarrows quickly form dense mounds of lacy leaves with flower heads that often rise well above the foliage.

Plant Profile

ACHILLEA
uh-KILL-ee-uh

- **Bloom Color:** Brick, lavender, pink, red, salmon, white, or yellow

- **Bloom Time:** Late spring to early fall

- **Length of Bloom:** 3 months or more

- **Height:** Varies by species; see individual listings

- **Spread:** Varies by species; see individual listings

- **Garden Uses:** Cut flower garden, groundcover, herb garden, mass planting, meadow garden, mixed border; attracts butterflies and beneficial insects

- **Light Preference:** Full sun

- **Soil Preference:** Average to poor, well-drained to dry, slightly acid soil

- **Best Way to Propagate:** Divide in spring or fall; take basal cuttings in spring

- **USDA Plant Hardiness Zones:** Varies by species; see individual listings

- **AHS Heat Zones:** Varies by species; see individual listings

Growing Tips

Although yarrows grow well in just about any type of soil, taller types tend to flop over in soils that are rich or overly moist. If your yarrows sprawl, don't stake them; just harvest the fallen stems as cut flowers, then transplant the clumps to a drier, less fertile site in fall or spring.

After two or three years, the centers of the yarrow clumps tend to die out. When this happens, divide and replant the clumps in spring or fall, or dig out and discard the center and fill the hole with fresh soil. The plants will spread to fill the opening.

Good Neighbors

Dependable and adaptable, yarrows combine well with other sun-loving plants that don't require rich soil, including alliums, gayfeathers (*Liatris* spp.), globe thistles (*Echinops* spp.), penstemons, and purple coneflowers (*Echinacea* spp.). Yellow-flowered yarrows look great with blue, purple, or violet companions such as catmints (*Nepeta* spp.), *Geranium* 'Johnson's Blue', and many salvias.

Problems and Solutions

Yarrows have a reputation for weediness, which they don't necessarily merit. Most are well behaved, and the few exceptions are easy to control. Just plant them inside a root barrier, such as a bottomless bucket sunk in the soil. All yarrows can spread by seed, so it's a good idea to deadhead them.

Diseases such as powdery mildew, rust, and stem rot occasionally cause stems to turn brown, especially when plants don't receive full sun. The plants won't die, so just prune out any diseased stems.

Top Performer

Achillea millefolium (common yarrow): Common yarrow forms a ground-hugging mat of dark green, fernlike foliage topped by upright stalks of clustered flowers. Each flower looks like a tiny daisy. In the wild, common yarrow generally produces off-white flowers, but in gardens, you'll find white and all shades of orange, pink, purple, red, and yellow. In rich soil, plant common yarrow inside a root barrier.

Common yarrows grown from seed will usually vary in height and flower color. If you want a specific color, height, or form, buy vegetatively propagated plants. There are three cultivars I particularly like for their long flowering season and sturdy stems: 'Cerise Queen' (cherry red), 'Fire King' (bright red blooms, grayish leaves), and 'Lilac Beauty' (pale purple). 'Summer Pastels' blooms in mixed pastel colors. It's the one exception to the "don't grow common yarrow from seed" rule; in fact, growing 'Summer Pastels' from seed will give you the widest possible color range. Height: 1 to 3 feet (30 to 90 cm). Spread: 1 to 5 feet or more (30 to 150 cm). USDA Plant Hardiness Zones 1 to 9; AHS Heat Zones 10 to 1.

'Summer Pastels' common yarrow (*Achillea millefolium* 'Summer Pastels')

More Recommended Yarrows

Achillea 'Coronation Gold': The flat-headed, golden flower clusters of 'Coronation Gold' yarrow stand firmly upright, without staking, over gray-green, aromatic leaves. Height: 2 to 4 feet (60 to 120 cm). Spread: 3 feet (90 cm). USDA Plant Hardiness Zones 2 to 9; AHS Heat Zones 9 to 1.

A. filipendulina (fernleaf yarrow): Several sturdy cultivars are popular. All have dark green, deeply cut leaves and flat, broad flower heads. 'Cloth of Gold' has pure yellow flowers. 'Gold Plate' has mustard yellow flower heads up to 6 inches (15 cm) across. Height: 3 to 5 feet (90 to 150 cm). Spread: 18 to 36 inches (45 to 90 cm). USDA Plant Hardiness Zones 2 to 9; AHS Heat Zones 9 to 1.

A. 'Moonshine': 'Moonshine' yarrow has silvery foliage and flat-topped flower heads. It tends to be more susceptible to disease than most yarrows—it's not a good choice for hot, humid climates. (For these areas, 'Anthea', derived from 'Moonshine', is a better choice.) Height: 18 to 24 inches (45 to 60 cm). Spread: 1 foot (30 cm). USDA Plant Hardiness Zones 2 to 9; AHS Heat Zones 9 to 2.

Kissing Cousins

If you like deeply cut, ferny foliage and bright yellow flowers, you'll like common tansy (*Tanacetum vulgare*), a relative of yarrow (*Achillea* spp.). Look for this plant in your nursery's herb section because it's grown for its deliciously scented foliage. My favorite is fernleaf tansy (*T. vulgare* var. *crispum*) with triply cut, bright green leaves. It spreads quickly, so plant it inside a root barrier. The only drawback is that it rarely blooms. Height: 2 to 4 feet (60 to 100 cm). Spread: 18 inches (45 cm). USDA Plant Hardiness Zones 3 to 8; AHS Heat Zones 12 to 1.

Campanula

Bellflower

When I think of bellflowers, I always think of their bell- or cup-shaped flowers and of the color blue. That's not to say there aren't other colors in the bellflower palette, but blue is the rule; other colors are exceptions. Bellflower leaves may be rounded, triangular, or lance-shaped, often with some shallow toothing along the margins. While they share similar flower forms, colors, and leaf traits, bellflowers vary widely in habit, ranging from creeping groundcovers to mound-forming edging plants to tall plants best suited to the back of a bed or border.

Plant Profile

CAMPANULA
kam-PAN-yew-luh

- **Bloom Color:** Blue, lavender, pink, purple, violet, or white

- **Bloom Time:** Varies by species; see individual listings

- **Length of Bloom:** 2 months or more

- **Height:** Varies by species; see individual listings

- **Spread:** Varies by species; see individual listings

- **Garden Uses:** Container planting, cut flower garden, edging, groundcover, mass planting, mixed border, rock garden, wall planting; at the back of beds or borders, on slopes

- **Light Preference:** Full sun to light shade

- **Soil Preference:** Average, well-drained soil

- **Best Way to Propagate:** Sow seeds in spring; divide or take cuttings in spring or fall

- **USDA Plant Hardiness Zones:** Varies by species; see individual listings

- **AHS Heat Zones:** 7 to 1

Growing Tips

Bellflowers are generally easy to grow and long-lived. They perform best in cool-summer areas, although partial shade and a deep organic mulch can help them bloom almost as well where summers are warm.

Bellflowers grow readily from seed sown indoors in late winter or outdoors in the spring. (Don't cover the seed, since many species need light to germinate.) In fact, bellflowers' willingness to self-sow occasionally makes them weedy, so don't hesitate to deadhead them after a flush of bloom. The taller types are easy enough to deadhead: Just cut individual stalks back to below the lowest flower. On low-growing types, it's much easier to cut the whole plant back. To tell the truth, I actually take the lawn mower to my Carpathian harebell (*Campanula carpatica*) if it starts looking ragged in midsummer. Chopped close to the ground, the plants rapidly resprout and soon start blooming all over again.

Good Neighbors

Low-growing border and rock garden bellflowers like Carpathian harebell need small companions that won't overpower them. In borders, try 'Moonbeam' threadleaf coreopsis (*Coreopsis verticillata* 'Moonbeam'); lily leek (*Allium moly*), a summer-flowering bulb; or dwarf goldenrods, such as *Solidago sphacelata* 'Golden Fleece'. In rock gardens, mix bellflowers with thymes, candytufts (*Iberis* spp.), pinks (*Dianthus* spp.), and other low-growing plants.

Yarrows, baby's-breath, and smaller varieties of shrub roses look good with the taller bellflowers. Milky bellflower (*C. lactiflora*) is also a good match for peonies—its summer blooms take over just as the last peony flower fades.

Problems and Solutions

Taller bellflowers tend to flop, especially in hot-summer areas. If staking isn't your thing, either plant bellflowers behind shrubby plants that can hold them up or prune them back when they keel over (they make great cut flowers). Or choose dwarf cultivars with sturdier stems. Diseases and insects are rarely a problem, but slugs and snails can chew holes in the foliage.

Top Performer

Campanula carpatica (Carpathian harebell): The triangular, toothed, dark green leaves of Carpathian harebell make it a wonderful choice as an edging plant. Each plant forms a rounded mass of leaves often nearly covered with upturned, bell-shaped flowers up to 2 inches (5 cm) across. Carpathian harebell blooms from early summer through fall, especially if pruned back in midsummer. Popular cultivars include 'Blaue Clips' (also called 'Blue Clips' and 'Blue Chips'), with blue flowers, and 'Weisse Clips' (also called 'White Clips' and 'White Chips'), with white flowers. Height: 6 to 12 inches (15 to 30 cm). Spread: 12 inches (30 cm). USDA Plant Hardiness Zones 2 to 9; AHS Heat Zones 7 to 1.

More Recommended Bellflowers

Campanula lactiflora (milky bellflower): This is one of the tallest bellflowers, and it makes a great choice for the back of a flower border. Each clump produces hundreds of upward-facing bell-shaped, 1-inch (2.5-cm) flowers in terminal clusters from early summer through fall. Flowers are usually milky white (which is how this plant got its name) to light blue, although purple and pink cultivars are also available. Milky bellflower definitely prefers constant moisture (but not waterlogged soil), and partial shade is a must in hot-summer areas. Height: 36 to 60 inches (90 to 150 cm). Spread: 12 to 36 inches (30 to 90 cm). USDA Plant Hardiness Zones 4 to 9; AHS Heat Zones 7 to 1.

Campanula is a vast genus that contains nearly 300 species. I've only included the longest-blooming types here; for other bellflowers, see "Summer-Blooming Perennials," starting on page 134.

Carpathian harebell
(*Campanula carpatica*)

Kissing Cousins

Platycodon grandiflorus (balloon flower): From early to late summer, this bellflower relative produces bluish purple (occasionally white or pink), balloonlike buds that open into 2- to 3-inch (5- to 7.5-cm) star-shaped flowers. As a child, I got a kick out of "popping" the unopened flowers: Press on the sides of a bud and it bursts open with a soft popping sound. You can plant this dependable perennial and ignore it because it will live forever! It dislikes being bothered, so only dig it up to divide it. Height: 24 to 30 inches (60 to 75 cm). Spread: 24 inches (60 cm). USDA Plant Hardiness Zones 2 to 10; AHS Heat Zones 11 to 1.

Centranthus

Red valerian, Jupiter's beard

The flower clusters of red valerian provide double delight: They're wonderfully fragrant, and they attract plenty of foraging butterflies. The plants form rounded mounds of thick stems and blue-green leaves. Although quite dense and upright in poor or average soils, red valerian may flop when growing in rich soil. The leaves are about 4 inches (10 cm) long, smooth-edged (although sometimes lightly toothed at the base), and attached directly to the stem. They give off a medicinal odor when crushed.

Plant Profile

CENTRANTHUS
sen-TRAN-thus

- **Bloom Color:** Pink, rosy red, or white

- **Bloom Time:** Late spring to midfall

- **Length of Bloom:** 3 to 4 months

- **Height:** 2 to 3 feet (60 to 90 cm)

- **Spread:** 2 to 3 feet (60 to 90 cm)

- **Garden Uses:** Container planting, cut flower garden, edging, meadow garden, mixed border, rock garden, wall planting; on slopes; attracts butterflies

- **Light Preference:** Full sun or light shade

- **Soil Preference:** Average, well-drained, alkaline or neutral soil

- **Best Way to Propagate:** Sow seeds or take basal cuttings in spring or early summer

- **USDA Plant Hardiness Zones:** 3 to 9

- **AHS Heat Zones:** 8 to 5

Growing Tips

Just how everblooming red valerian is depends on your climate and the care you give the plants. In cool-summer areas, red valerian blooms right through the summer all on its own. Where summers are hot, though, it tends to bloom heavily in late spring, then only sparsely in summer. To stimulate better summer bloom, pinch off whole flower heads. Go one step further and prune the whole plant back to 6 inches (15 cm) from its base after it blooms, and it will often reward you with a second major burst of color in late summer or fall. If you don't deadhead, red valerian produces fuzzy seedheads much like those of dandelions, although smaller in size. Although red valerian is quite drought-resistant, it will only bloom nonstop if kept at least slightly moist at all times. It lasts a week or so as a cut flower.

Red valerian grows easily from seed, often blooming the first year if you start it indoors two months before the last frost. Sow seeds indoors in peat pots (the plants dislike root disturbance) and just barely cover them with soil mix; thin to one seedling per pot. Or sow directly outdoors in early spring, when the soil is still cool. Don't worry about late frosts, as the seedlings are quite hardy. If you find a plant of a color you particularly like, multiply it by rooting basal cuttings in spring because red valerian rarely comes true from seed. Individual clumps take three years to reach full size, and they're not particularly long-lived, so start new plants every four to five years. Don't bother trying to divide or move established plants: They dislike disturbance and are more likely to die than to recover.

Think Twice: Red valerian has a reputation for being weedy, but how it reacts in your garden depends on its growing conditions.

It loves neutral or alkaline soils, especially if they're on the dry side, and can become a nuisance there if you let it go to seed. It can literally take over limestone-based rock gardens and walls. In acid or slightly acid soils, on the other hand, or in somewhat moister conditions, red valerian is much better behaved. If you're at all worried about it spreading, simply deadhead to prevent any seed formation—red valerian doesn't spread from its base, only through its fluffy seeds.

Good Neighbors

Red valerian's loose, open form and tendency to self-sow make it a better choice for cottage-type gardens than formal plantings. Plant the red variety with softer colored, equally aggressive companions, such as 'White Swan' purple coneflower (*Echinacea purpurea* 'White Swan'), yarrows, or pale cultivars of golden marguerite (*Anthemis tinctoria*), such as 'Moonlight'; then let white cosmos self-sow to fill in any gaps. Or try for a striking combination by alternating red valerian with patches of deep purple-flowering plants such as 'Blue Wonder' catmint (*Nepeta* × *faassenii* 'Blue Wonder').

Problems and Solutions

Red valerian is highly resistant to pests and disease.

Top Performer

Centranthus ruber (red valerian): Of course, red valerian is my top performer; it's the only species of *Centranthus* offered in catalogs and at nurseries. Plants grown from seed produce a range of flower colors from rosy red and pink through white. Nurseries usually produce this plant from seed, so buy it in bloom if you want a specific shade. Or, sow some seed yourself and once the plants come into bloom, you can dig up or pull out plants you don't like. 'Albus', a pure white cultivar, usually comes true from seed, but plants sold as 'Coccineus' (theoretically red in color) and 'Roseus' (which should be pink), are likely to bloom in a wide range of shades.

Red valerian
(*Centranthus ruber*)

Around the World with *Centranthus*

Although native to the Mediterranean, red valerian has traveled well and is a garden escapee throughout the world where summers are not too hot. I've seen it growing on castle walls in Normandy, reddening the white cliffs of Dover in England, and even growing wild on sea cliffs in California and as far afield as Australia and South Africa.

Coreopsis

Tickseed

The pretty, daisylike blooms of coreopsis will brighten up any sunny garden. There are more than 100 species (some are annuals), so you're sure to find a coreopsis that suits your garden. The common name "tickseed" comes from their insect-shaped seeds. If you allow the plants to go to seed, they'll attract lots of seed-eating birds such as goldfinches.

Plant Profile

COREOPSIS
core-ee-OP-sis

- ■ **Bloom Color:** Pink or yellow
- ■ **Bloom Time:** Early summer to midfall
- ■ **Length of Bloom:** 3 months or more
- ■ **Height:** Varies by species; see individual listings
- ■ **Spread:** Varies by species; see individual listings
- ■ **Garden Uses:** Container planting, cut flower garden, edging, groundcover, mass planting, meadow garden, mixed border; at the back of beds or borders; attracts butterflies and birds
- ■ **Light Preference:** Full sun to light shade
- ■ **Soil Preference:** Average to poor, well-drained soil
- ■ **Best Way to Propagate:** Sow seed in spring or fall; can also be propagated by dividing in spring or fall or taking tip cuttings in early summer
- ■ **USDA Plant Hardiness Zones:** 3 to 9
- ■ **AHS Heat Zones:** Varies by species; see individual listings

Growing Tips

All coreopsis are easy to grow—they're good choices for beginning gardeners who want fast results. Most grow rapidly from seed, but individual plants rarely last more than three or four years, so allow some to go to seed or divide your plants every two years.

Coreopsis flower abundantly all summer if you deadhead them regularly. Rather than pinch out the faded flowers one by one, I run a string trimmer or hedge trimmer over the top of my plants and lop all the flowers off at once. You'll lose a few fresh blooms but the plants will return to full bloom in only two weeks.

Good Neighbors

Large-flowered coreopsis (*Coreopsis grandiflora*) and lanceleaf coreopsis (*C. lanceolata*) are perfect for a cottage garden because of their gently mounded shape and their tendency to self-sow. Combine them with purple coneflower (*Echinacea purpurea*), Shasta daisy (*Leucanthemum* × *superbum*), and rudbeckias for a colorful display.

Threadleaf coreopsis (*C. verticillata*), especially the cultivar 'Moonbeam', and pink coreopsis are among the rare plants that look good with just about anything—anything, that is, that won't smother their feathery foliage. Try surrounding them with taller blue- or purple-flowered perennials, such as anise hyssop (*Agastache foeniculum*), bellflowers (*Campanula* spp.), Siberian iris (*Iris sibirica*), and spike gayfeather (*Liatris spicata*).

Problems and Solutions

Large-flowered coreopsis and lanceleaf coreopsis are susceptible to a wide range of diseases and also various insects, but none cause particularly serious problems. Threadleaf coreopsis and pink coreopsis are less susceptible to pests and diseases.

In places where water puddles after a rain or when snow melts, all types of coreopsis may rot, with stems turning brown and mushy and dying back. To prevent rot, plant coreopsis in a well-drained spot.

Top Performer

Coreopsis verticillata (threadleaf coreopsis): One of the best-loved perennials, threadleaf coreopsis produces open clumps of upright stems with very narrow leaves divided into almost needlelike segments, giving the plant a lacy, see-through appearance. The bright yellow flowers bloom from early summer to midfall. Expect plants to last for five or six years or more, but take a few divisions from the edge of the clump after a year or two, just in case. Mark this plant's place in the garden, since it is very slow to sprout in spring. 'Moonbeam', with pale yellow flowers, is the most popular cultivar—it's on many gardeners' lists of top-ten perennials. Height: 18 to 36 inches (45 to 90 cm). Spread: 1 to 3 feet (30 to 90 cm). USDA Plant Hardiness Zones 3 to 9; AHS Heat Zones 9 to 1.

More Recommended Coreopsis

Coreopsis grandiflora (large-flowered coreopsis) and *C. lanceolata* (lanceleaf coreopsis): These species are nearly identical; plants have single, semi-double, or double flowers from early summer to mid-fall. They often bloom themselves to death, producing flowers well into autumn instead of preparing for winter. To help them survive, prune them back every few weeks beginning in mid-September *C. grandiflora* 'Early Sunrise' is a semi-double yellow available from seed. *C. lanceolata* 'Goldfink' is a compact cultivar with single yellow flowers with an orange center. Height: 18 to 36 inches (45 to 90 cm). Spread: 12 to 36 inches (30 to 90 cm). USDA Plant Hardiness Zones 3 to 9; AHS Heat Zones 9 to 4.

C. rosea (pink coreopsis): In a genus known for its yellow flowers, pink coreopsis is the exception, with rose-pink flowers and a yellow center. It has a mounding form but spreads vigorously, so plant it in a root barrier, such as a bottomless bucket sunk into the soil. Height: 9 to 18 inches (23 to 45 cm). Spread: indefinite unless controlled. USDA Plant Hardiness Zones 3 to 9; AHS Heat Zones 8 to 1.

Threadleaf coreopsis (*Coreopsis verticillata*)

Smart Substitutes

For a touch of whimsy in a dry-soil garden, try calliopsis (*Coreopsis tinctoria*). This fast-growing, long-blooming annual species of coreopsis has deeply cut leaves. It's often included in wildflower seed mixtures because of its summer-long storm of yellow daisylike blooms. It will grow well just about anywhere the first year, but I find it only self-sows with any vigor in poor, dry soils where it fills in nicely around young perennials. Height: 24 to 36 inches (30 to 90 cm). Spread: 12 inches (30 cm).

Dianthus

Pink, carnation

Pinks have flowers with fringed petals that look like they've been trimmed with pinking shears—hence their common name. The flowers often have a sweet, spicy, or spicy-sweet fragrance, depending on the species—and this genus includes more than 300. Most are low-growing, clump-forming plants with narrow, sword-shaped, green or gray-green leaves.

Plant Profile

DIANTHUS
dye-AN-thus

- **Bloom Color:** Pink, red, and white; occasionally yellow
- **Bloom Time:** Varies by species; see individual listings
- **Length of Bloom:** 2 months or more
- **Height:** 4 to 18 inches (10 to 45 cm)
- **Spread:** 8 to 18 inches (20 to 45 cm)
- **Garden Uses:** Container planting, cut flower garden, edging, groundcover, herb garden, mass planting, mixed border, rock garden, wall planting; attracts butterflies
- **Light Preference:** Full sun to light shade
- **Soil Preference:** Average, well-drained, somewhat alkaline soil
- **Best Way to Propagate:** Divide or sow seeds in spring; can also be propagated by taking stem cuttings in summer
- **USDA Plant Hardiness Zones:** 3 to 9
- **AHS Heat Zones:** Varies by species; see individual listings

Growing Tips

Pinks are ideal for rock gardens and wall plantings; they're also wonderful edging plants and groundcovers, especially since their foliage (which is usually evergreen) is attractive even when they're not in bloom. Pinks do, however, tend to be short-lived, so it's wise to divide, sow, or take cuttings of all types every two years.

Pinks aren't natural everbloomers. Most bloom in spring or early summer, with a main flowering season lasting up to eight weeks. The ones I've recommended here will rebloom throughout the summer and even into fall if deadheaded regularly. Many pinks bear their flowers above the foliage, so just pull out the hedge trimmer or a string trimmer and chop the faded blooms back!

Good Neighbors

Low-growing pinks combine well with other spreading plants for a low border or a rock garden. The deep green foliage of mother-of-thyme (*Thymus serpyllum*) and the long-lasting blooms of bloody cranesbill (*Geranium sanguineum*) and Carpathian harebell (*Campanula carpatica*) contrast well with the gray-green foliage of many pinks. Pinks also combine well with purple-foliaged heucheras and with silver-leaved plants such as lamb's-ears (*Stachys byzantina*).

Problems and Solutions

Rust and other leaf diseases can cause spots to appear on the leaves, especially in humid climates. Planting pinks in well-ventilated areas or keeping them well spaced will help prevent problems.

Top Performer

Dianthus gratianopolitanus (Cheddar pink): This popular pink forms low, dense mounds of gray- or blue-green leaves, with many small, fragrant, single or double flowers in red, white, or pink. Cheddar pink is good for a rock garden or wall planting. 'Bath's Pink' has fringed, soft pink, single flowers with a deep rose center. 'Tiny Rubies' bears very fragrant, rose pink, double flowers. Height: 6 to 12 inches (15 to 30 cm). Spread: 12 inches (30 cm). USDA Plant Hardiness Zones 3 to 9; AHS Heat Zones 9 to 1.

More Recommended Pinks

While you'll probably have great results with any pinks you plant, I recommend these cultivars because they're widely available, very adaptable, and long-flowering (if deadheaded). All of these cultivars will grow in USDA Plant Hardiness Zones 3 to 9.

Dianthus × *allwoodii* (Allwood pink, modern pink): Compact Allwood pink has gray-green leaves and produces at least two scented, usually double, flowers per stem. 'Doris' bears fragrant, salmon-pink flowers with a rose pink circle and rose-pink markings at the center. 'Frosty Fire' has fringed, deep ruby red blooms. 'Loveliness' (also called 'Rainbow Loveliness Mix') offers highly fragrant, heavily fringed flowers in pink, rose, or white. Height: 12 to 20 inches (30 to 50 cm). Spread: 12 to 18 inches (30 to 45 cm). AHS Heat Zones 8 to 1.

D. deltoides (maiden pink): In sites where it's happy, maiden pink spreads to form a low mat of grasslike, green or purplish green leaves. It produces small red, pink, white, or bicolor flowers in late spring through early summer, and it will rebloom if you shear it back after the first burst of bloom. Maiden pink prefers distinctly alkaline soils and requires excellent drainage. 'Zing Rose' has bright scarlet flowers. Height: 6 to 12 inches (15 to 30 cm). Spread: 12 inches (30 cm). AHS Heat Zones 10 to 1.

D. plumarius (cottage pink, grass pink): Cottage pink forms clumps of blue or grayish, grasslike leaves topped with spicy-smelling fragrant single or double flowers. It resembles Cheddar pink but is usually bigger, with larger and deeply fringed flowers. It prefers alkaline soils but will tolerate some acidity. 'Inchmery' bears highly fragrant, fringed flowers that open shell pink and age to pale pink. Height: 10 to 18 inches (25 to 45 cm). Spread: 12 inches (30 cm). AHS Heat Zones 9 to 1.

'Tiny Rubies' Cheddar pink (*Dianthus gratianopolitanus* 'Tiny Rubies')

Kissing Cousins

Soapworts (*Saponaria* spp.) are closely related to pinks (*Dianthus* spp.) and several *Saponaria* species are very worthwhile perennials. Bouncing Bet (*S. officinalis*) long ago escaped from gardens just about everywhere in North America and is now a common wildflower. Although attractive and long-blooming, bouncing bet spreads aggressively, so always plant it inside a root barrier. A less invasive close cousin is rock soapwort (*S. ocymoides*): it's a perfectly well-behaved creeping rock garden plant with tiny spring flowers of pink, rose, or white. Height for rock soapwort: 4 to 8 inches (10 to 20 cm). Spread: 18 inches (45 cm). USDA Plant Hardiness Zones: 3 to 8; AHS Heat Zones 9 to 1.

Geranium

Hardy geranium, cranesbill

Most hardy geraniums have deeply cut foliage and cup-shaped or starlike, five-petaled flowers, as well as long, pointed seedpods. (The shape of the seedpods is why geraniums are also called cranesbills.) Many also have colorful fall foliage. As can be expected in a genus of well over 250 species, hardy geraniums range greatly in size, hardiness, blooming season, and flower color. Some hardy geraniums form low mounds and make great edging plants or groundcovers. Others are taller and better suited to the middle or back of the mixed border; still others have sprawling stems that weave among other perennials.

Plant Profile

GERANIUM
juh-RANE-ee-um

- **Bloom Color:** Blue, magenta, pink, purple, red, or white

- **Bloom Time:** Varies by species; see individual listings

- **Length of Bloom:** 2 months or more

- **Height:** Varies by species; see individual listings

- **Spread:** Varies by species; see individual listings

- **Garden Uses:** Container planting, edging, groundcover, mass planting, mixed border, rock garden, wall planting, woodland garden; on slopes, in wet areas

- **Light Preference:** Full sun to partial shade

- **Soil Preference:** Humus-rich, moist, well-drained soil

- **Best Way to Propagate:** Divide or take stem cuttings in spring

- **USDA Plant Hardiness Zones:** Varies by species; see individual listings

- **AHS Heat Zones:** Varies by species; see individual listings

Growing Tips

Hardy geraniums are easy to grow and adapt to a wide range of conditions, although they generally do best in areas with cool or mild summers. Provide some protection from midday sun in hot-summer climates. You can leave hardy geraniums in place for many years, only dividing them when they start to decline from overcrowding.

Not all hardy geraniums are everblooming, so stick to those described below if long bloom is your main criteria. Even some of the "everblooming" hardy geraniums tend to peter out in midsummer if left to their own devices. Prune them back harshly, though, and they'll be up and blooming again in no time. Pruning also cures another common flaw: a tendency to flop in summer. Some hardy geraniums are evergreen or semievergreen, though, so don't cut back their foliage in the fall.

Good Neighbors

Choose perennial companions that like the moist, humus-rich soil and semi-shade that suits hardy geraniums. The spiky foliage of Siberian iris (*Iris sibirica*) contrasts well with the mounding forms of hardy geraniums; so do upright pink or purple bloomers, such as delphiniums, gayfeathers (*Liatris* spp.), or milky bellflower (*Campanula lactiflora*). Ornamental grasses that can take shade and moist conditions, such as golden variegated hakone grass (*Hakonechloa macra* 'Aureola') and sedges (*Carex* spp.), are good companions.

Problems and Solutions

Rust can be a problem on hardy geraniums, causing leaves to turn pale with powdery orange spots on the undersides. Remove and destroy infested leaves, or cut plants back severely. Slugs will feast on young plants. For solutions to slug problems, see page 55.

Top Performer

Geranium 'Ann Folkard': This hardy geranium is among the first geraniums to bloom in my garden and the last to stop flowering. The vivid magenta flowers are set off by golden yellow new leaves and apple green mature foliage. I love the way its long stems ramble among my other perennials. Height: 2 feet (60 cm). Spread: 4 feet (120 cm). USDA Zones 5 to 9; AHS Heat Zones 9 to 3.

More Recommended Hardy Geraniums

Geranium ✕ *cantabrigiense* (Cambridge geranium): This groundcover geranium blooms in midspring to late summer. The foliage is semievergreen, and the plants need no deadheading. 'Biokovo' has white flowers tinged with pink; 'Cambridge' has bright pink flowers. Height: 6 to 12 inches (15 to 30 cm). Spread: 8 to 12 inches (20 to 30 cm). USDA Plant Hardiness Zones 4 to 9; AHS Heat Zones 8 to 2.

G. cinereum (grayleaf geranium): This plant forms a dense groundcover with gray-green foliage; from midspring to early fall it has pink flowers. Give it excellent drainage, especially in winter. 'Ballerina' has lilac pink blooms with purple veins; 'Lawrence Flatman' is deep pink with dark veins. Height: 4 to 6 inches (10 to 15 cm). Spread: 12 inches (30 cm). USDA Plant Hardiness Zones 4 to 9; AHS Heat Zones 9 to 5.

G. clarkei (Clarke's geranium): An abundant bloomer from late spring to mid- or late summer, Clarke's geranium prefers a cool or semi-shady spot. 'Kashmir Purple' is deep purple with mauve highlights. 'Kashmir White' has large white flowers with pale violet veins. Height: 2 feet (60 cm). Spread: 2 feet (60 cm). USDA Plant Hardiness Zones 3 to 9; AHS Heat Zones 8 to 5.

G. 'Johnson's Blue': In cool-summer areas, 'Johnson's Blue' is vigorous and has large, lavender-blue flowers from midspring to mid-summer or late summer, but it tends to grow and bloom weakly elsewhere. It doesn't need deadheading, but prune it back harshly in midsummer. Height: 1 to 2 feet (30 to 60 cm). Spread: 2 feet (60 cm). USDA Plant Hardiness Zones 3 to 9; AHS Heat Zones 8 to 1.

'Ann Folkard' geranium (*Geranium* 'Ann Folkard')

Larry's Garden Notes

The plants many people call geraniums really aren't geraniums, botanically speaking. There are hardy geraniums (*Geranium* spp.) and tender "geraniums" (*Pelargonium* spp.) and the two just aren't the same thing. Native to South Africa, pelargoniums tend to be thick-stemmed, somewhat shrubby plants with dense umbels of flowers. They're only hardy in USDA Zones 9 and 10, so as a result, almost all North American gardeners grow them as annuals. To avoid confusion, be sure to call these geraniums "zonal geraniums" or "pelargoniums" to avoid confusing them with hardy geraniums.

Gypsophila

Baby's-breath

If you've ever bought cut flowers, you know baby's-breath. It's the light, frothy "filler" with tiny white or pink flowers that's used to set off the more expensive blooms in the arrangement (and to give you the impression you've gotten your money's worth). You can also get your money's worth and more by growing baby's-breath yourself: It's easy to grow and blooms abundantly. It's also very long-lived, so you can plant it today and still enjoy it 20 years from now.

Plant Profile

GYPSOPHILA
jipp-SOFF-ill-uh

■ **Bloom Color:** Pink or white

■ **Bloom Time:** Early summer to early fall

■ **Length of Bloom:** 2½ months

■ **Height:** Varies by species; see individual listings

■ **Spread:** Varies by species; see individual listings

■ **Garden Uses:** Container planting, cut flower garden, edging, mass planting, meadow garden, mixed border, rock garden; at the back of beds or borders, on slopes

■ **Light Preference:** Full sun

■ **Soil Preference:** Average, well-drained, neutral to alkaline soil

■ **Best Way to Propagate:** Sow seed or divide in spring or fall

■ **USDA Plant Hardiness Zones:** 3 to 9

■ **AHS Heat Zones:** Varies by species; see individual listings

Growing Tips

Baby's-breath is a plant-it-and-forget-it perennial, but make sure to site it in a well-drained spot: It won't tolerate wet soil, especially in winter. Baby's-breath dislikes root disturbance. Either sow it directly where you want it to grow or plant young plants, and then leave it alone. Although you can divide baby's-breath, its long, fleshy roots are hard to handle and break easily. Growing it from seed or from stem cuttings is much easier.

Tall cultivars like 'Bristol Fairy' do tend to flop, but it's hard to hide plant stakes or wire rings among the plants' see-through foliage. For support, try planting them among taller perennials or shrubs, or else stick twiggy branches here and there as the flowering stems form. Or plant dwarf types: They need no staking at all!

For repeat bloom and to prevent plants from self-sowing, cut off the flowerstalks of single-flowered varieties before they go to seed. I don't consider this "deadheading" (which always implies *work*), but rather "harvesting." Hang the cut stems upside down to dry for a few weeks, and then use them in indoor flower arrangements. Double-flowered cultivars are essentially sterile, so even without dead-heading, they'll bloom nonstop all summer.

Good Neighbors

Baby's-breath serves just as beautifully as a filler plant in your garden as it does in cut flower arrangements. Plant it with spring-flowering bulbs and perennials that lose their leaves in summer, such as oriental poppy (*Papaver orientale*) and common bleeding heart (*Dicentra spectabilis*), so it can fill any gaps. It also works wonderfully with most tall, sun-loving perennials and shrubs. Gayfeathers (*Liatris* spp.), irises of all kinds, purple coneflower (*Echinacea purpurea*), rudbeckias, salvias, shrub roses, and sunflowers (*Helianthus* spp.) are just a few of the plants that baby's-breath will set off nicely. The only plants that baby's-breath doesn't combine well with are those with similarly delicate forms or foliage, such as ornamental grasses or statice (*Limonium* spp.).

Problems and Solutions
Baby's-breath has no major pest or disease problems.

Top Performer
Gypsophila paniculata (common baby's-breath): The grasslike, bluish green leaves of common baby's-breath are nothing to write home about, but once the plants start blooming, the masses of ¼-inch (6-mm) white or pink flowers scattered throughout the maze of thin stems are more than impressive. Common baby's-breath blooms from early summer through fall. Popular cultivars include 'Bristol Fairy', which has double white flowers, and is somewhat less cold-hardy (to USDA Zone 4) than other cultivars. 'Pink Fairy' has double pink flowers and grows up to 2 feet (60 cm) tall; 'Viette's Dwarf' has double pink flowers on an even more compact plant. Height: 2 to 4 feet (60 to 120 cm). Spread: 3 feet (90 cm). USDA Plant Hardiness Zones 3 to 9; AHS Heat Zones 9 to 1.

More Recommended Baby's-Breaths
Gypsophila repens (creeping baby's-breath): As its name suggests, creeping baby's-breath is a low, spreading plant that forms an open, airy mat. It has small gray-green leaves and clusters of ¼-inch (6-mm) pink or white flowers from early summer through fall. Creeping baby's-breath is an excellent choice for an edging plant and for rock gardens as well as for walls, where the stems will cascade gracefully. Height: 4 to 6 inches (10 to 15 cm). Spread: 1 to 2 feet (30 to 60 cm). USDA Plant Hardiness Zones 3 to 9; AHS Heat Zones 7 to 1.

G. 'Rosenschleier' (also called G. 'Rosy Veil'): This hybrid between common and creeping baby's-breath is bushy and spreading. From midsummer to late summer, it produces double white flowers that age to pale pink. Height: 2 to 4 feet (60 to 120 cm). Spread: 3 to 4 feet (90 to 120 cm). USDA Plant Hardiness Zones 3 to 9; AHS Heat Zones 7 to 1.

Common baby's-breath
(*Gypsophila paniculata*)

Smart Substitutes

Love the idea of using baby's-breath as a filler plant in your garden but not ready for something quite so permanent? Try annual baby's-breath (*Gypsophila elegans*), which grows 12 to 18 inches (30 to 45 cm) tall and comes in white, pink, and rose-colored forms. It couldn't be easier to grow: Just toss some seeds on the ground in a open spot, rake them in, and water. Within five weeks, you'll have flowers. Since annual baby's-breath dies after blooming, you'll need to sow seed every two weeks for a continuous supply of cut flowers.

Malva

Mallow

When you grow mallows, their lovely cup-shaped blossoms will grace your garden nonstop all summer, and you'll never have to deadhead the plants. Each five-petaled mallow flower lasts only a day or so but is quickly replaced by others. These shrubby, fast-growing perennials generally have slightly hairy, maple-shaped leaves that vary in form, even on the same plant.

Plant Profile

MALVA
MAL-vuh

- **Bloom Color:** Pink or white; more rarely blue or mauve

- **Bloom Time:** Early summer to fall

- **Length of Bloom:** 3 months or more

- **Height:** Varies by species; see individual listings

- **Spread:** Varies by species; see individual listings

- **Garden Uses:** Herb garden, meadow garden, mixed border; at the back of beds or borders

- **Light Preference:** Full sun

- **Soil Preference:** Average, well-drained, slightly acid to alkaline soil

- **Best Way to Propagate:** Sow seed in spring or fall; can also be propagated by dividing in spring or fall or by taking tip cuttings in spring

- **USDA Plant Hardiness Zones:** 3 to 9

- **AHS Heat Zones:** 8 to 1

Growing Tips

Most mallows come true from seed, and produce seed prolifically. To multiply your mallows, sow seed indoors or out, in spring or fall. Just barely cover the seed with soil. It will sprout quickly and, even if sown as late as early summer, the seedlings will bloom the first year. Mallows are so easy to grow from seed that there's no need to consider dividing them or even to bother moving plants if you decide to change your garden layout: Just sow new seed, and you'll have mallows as big and beautiful as the originals in a flash!

Hardiness isn't a concern with mallows—if they don't survive the winter where you live, just treat them as self-sowing annuals. Newly sprouted mallows often don't start to bloom until midsummer, whereas those that survive the winter bloom as early as late spring. If you want be sure your mallows overwinter, shear them back in late summer to force them to produce new stems: Otherwise they often bloom themselves to death.

All mallows grow best in cool-summer areas, tending toward weaker growth and lackluster bloom where summers are hot. They are quite drought-tolerant once established.

On the down side, mallows are short-lived, often acting as biennials or even annuals, and they self-sow prolifically, to the point where some varieties are considered noxious weeds, even by lax gardeners. They're not particularly aggressive in a garden setting where taller plants can shade them out, but if you plant mallow, you can be sure that any empty space in a sunny spot will soon have its resident mallow. If you like plants that stay put, avoid them. If, on the other hand, you like cottage-type gardens where plants are allowed a bit of freedom, you'll enjoy mallow's free-spirited nature.

Good Neighbors

Cottage-garden favorites, mallows pair well with a variety of other vigorous perennials in a casual setting. Try them with summer favorites such as coreopsis, foxgloves (*Digitalis* spp.), garden phlox (*Phlox paniculata*), and poppies (*Papaver* spp.), and fall-bloomers such as boltonia (*Boltonia asteroides*) and goldenrods (*Solidago* spp.). They likewise go well with self-sowing annuals such as cleomes, cosmos, and larkspurs (*Consolida* spp.), thus ensuring an everchanging display.

Problems and Solutions

Besides their habit of going astray (they're easy to yank out if they do wander), mallows are host to just about every insect and disease under the sun, although most cause few visible problems and you can usually ignore them when they strike. Japanese beetles, however, feast on mallows, leaving behind mere skeletons of leaves and flowers. To control these voracious beetles, see page 54.

Top Performer

Malva alcea (hollyhock mallow): Bushy hollyhock mallow blooms abundantly from summer through fall. The flowers are pink or white and about 2 inches (5 cm) wide, with well-separated petals like a pinwheel, each with a notch at the tip. The most common cultivar is 'Fastigiata', which is more narrowly upright than the species and less likely to sprawl. Height: 2 to 4 feet (60 to 120 cm). Spread: 18 inches (45 cm). USDA Plant Hardiness Zones 3 to 9; AHS Heat Zones 8 to 1.

More Recommended Mallows

M. moschata (musk mallow): Musk mallow is very similar to hollyhock mallow but with more deeply cut, almost fernlike leaves. Its flowers are pink, although 'Alba', with white flowers, is also common. Musk mallow blooms from summer through fall. Height: 2 to 3 feet (60 to 90 cm). Spread: 18 inches (45 cm). USDA Plant Hardiness Zones 3 to 9; AHS Heat Zones 8 to 1.

Hollyhock mallow
(*Malva alcea*)

Kissing Cousins

If you'd like to grow a perennial that looks like a giant mallow, try tree mallow (*Lavatera thuringiaca*). It's very like a *Malva*, except that its leaves are less deeply lobed and its stems are woody at the base. Tree mallow generally bears soft pink flowers from summer through fall, although hybrid forms show white, purplish, or bicolor flowers. Height: 4 to 7 feet (120 to 213 cm). Spread: 4 to 5 feet (120 to 150 cm). USDA Plant Hardiness Zones 4 to 9 for the species or 6 to 9 for hybrids; AHS Heat Zones 10 to 1.

Nepeta

Catmint

If you think the name "catmint" sounds suspiciously like "catnip," you're right. Catnip (*Nepeta cataria*) is the perennial that is a cat's favorite plaything, but catnip has too few ornamental qualities to be a flower garden candidate (and even fewer when your neighbor's cat has scratched it to death!). The name cat*mint* refers to the other plants in this vast genus, some of which are not only very ornamental but also bloom abundantly over a long period.

Plant Profile

NEPETA
NEP-uh-tuh

- ■ **Bloom Color:** Blue, lavender, pink, or white
- ■ **Bloom Time:** Early summer to early fall
- ■ **Length of Bloom:** 2½ months
- ■ **Height:** Varies by species; see individual listings
- ■ **Spread:** Varies by species; see individual listings
- ■ **Garden Uses:** Container planting, edging, groundcover, mass planting, mixed border, rock garden, wall planting, woodland garden; along paths, on slopes
- ■ **Light Preference:** Full sun to partial shade
- ■ **Soil Preference:** Average, well-drained soil
- ■ **Best Way to Propagate:** Divide in spring or take tip cuttings in summer
- ■ **USDA Plant Hardiness Zones:** 3 to 9
- ■ **AHS Heat Zones:** 8 to 1

Growing Tips

You'll sometimes find four or five distinctly different catmints sold under the same name. If possible, buy your catmints from a reliable source so you'll get exactly what you want.

Sterile catmint hybrids can bloom throughout the entire summer and well into fall, but they will bloom more heavily if you deadhead the plants after each major flowering period. For catmints that produce seed, deadheading is usually a must for rebloom. You can shear back the entire plant to half its size, and it will quickly grow back and bloom again. Shearing is especially useful for some of the taller varieties or those growing in too-rich soil, as they tend to flop in midsummer. By cutting your catmints down to size, you'll get both new flowers and fresh, sturdy, dense growth!

Catmints are edging plants extraordinaire: dense, mound-forming, spreading plants with gray-green, scalloped, aromatic leaves and four-sided stems. Their two-lipped, tubular flowers are numerous but small, usually about ¼ inch (6 mm) long. They bloom in whorls on narrow spikes at the tips of the stems and sometimes almost cover the foliage.

Some catmints grow rapidly from seed and can become quite weedy. Most ornamental varieties are sterile, so this is not a problem, but if you choose a fertile one, watch out! Deadheading will prevent self-sowing.

Catmints make terrific container plants, but remember that any plant grown in a pot is more likely to suffer winter damage than one grown in the ground. If you live in a cold area, either start your container plants from cuttings in the spring and consider them expendable, or replant the plants you want to save in the garden each fall.

Good Neighbors

Low-growing catmints work well as border plants in the front of other substantial plants, such as peonies and roses. Pair catmints with red flowers, such as red valerian (*Centranthus ruber*), 'Gardenview Scarlet' bee balm (*Monarda didyma* 'Gardenview Scarlet') or *Crocosmia* 'Lucifer', a summer bulb, for an eye-catching combination.

Problems and Solutions

Although ornamental catmints are not as attractive to cats as common catnip (*N. cataria*), they still have appeal, especially when the leaves or stems are broken, releasing the aroma into the air. Since you'll probably damage a few leaves when you plant catmint, cover each plant with a dome of chicken wire as a cat barrier. After a few days, remove the barriers, and cats will leave your plants alone.

Other than felines, catmints have few enemies. In fact, rodents, rabbits, and even deer avoid them, so planting them as an edging plant may just keep a few of your garden's enemies at bay.

Top Performer

Nepeta × *faassenii* (Faassen's catmint): By far the most popular species, Faassen's catmint is sterile, so it doesn't need deadheading. The early summer to early fall flowers are lavender to violet blue; there are also white-flowered cultivars. Leaves are gray-green and about 1 inch (2.5 cm) long. Popular cultivars include 'Blue Wonder', a compact form with dark blue flowers, and bright blue 'Dropmore', which is taller and has larger leaves and flowers. Height: 1 to 2 feet (30 to 60 cm). Spread: 12 to 18 inches (30 to 45 cm). USDA Plant Hardiness Zones 3 to 9; AHS Heat Zones 8 to 1.

More Recommended Catmints

Nepeta 'Six Hills Giant': This catmint is often listed as a *N.* × *faassenii* cultivar but is much taller and has greener foliage than Faassen's catmint. 'Six Hills Giant' produces 9- to 12-inch- (20- to 30-cm) tall spikes of dark violet flowers from midsummer to fall. Height: 3 to 4 feet (90 to 120 cm). Spread: 2 feet (60 cm). USDA Plant Hardiness Zones 3 to 9; AHS Heat Zones 8 to 1.

Faassen's catmint (*Nepeta* × *faassenii*)

Kissing Cousins

Large-flowered calamint (*Calamintha grandiflora*) and other calamints are usually reserved for the herb garden (brew their leaves for a delicious herbal tea!), but they also look great in the flower garden. Large-flowered calamint has felted, green, mint-scented leaves on upright stems and long-lasting spikes of pink flowers from early to late summer. It's drought-tolerant, does best in full sun to partial shade, and can grow in alkaline soil. Plant it inside a root barrier. 'Variegata', with white marbled leaves, is the most popular cultivar. Height: 2 to 3 feet (60 to 90 cm). Spread: 18 to 24 inches (45 to 60 cm). USDA Plant Hardiness Zones 3 to 9; AHS Heat Zones 8 to 1.

Oenothera

Evening primrose, sundrops

Sun-loving evening primroses have satiny, paper-thin, poppylike flowers that add cheer to any sunny garden. Each flower lasts only a day or so, but they're produced over a long season. All plants in the genus *Oenothera* are commonly called evening primroses, even though this name really applies to only those species whose flowers open in late afternoon and fade before morning. The other common name for the genus, sundrops, applies to both night bloomers and day bloomers, and the latter are far more popular for gardens. Evening-flowering species, though, are often highly fragrant, so don't cross them off your list!

Plant Profile

OENOTHERA
ee-no-THEER-uh

- **Bloom Color:** Pink, white, or yellow
- **Bloom Time:** Varies by species, usually early to late summer
- **Length of Bloom:** 2 months
- **Height:** 6 to 24 inches (15 to 60 cm)
- **Spread:** 1 to 2 feet (30 to 60 cm)
- **Garden Uses:** Container planting, edging, groundcover, mass planting, meadow garden, mixed border, rock garden, wall planting; along paths, on slopes
- **Light Preference:** Full sun to light shade
- **Soil Preference:** Average, well-drained soil
- **Best Way to Propagate:** Divide in spring or fall
- **USDA Plant Hardiness Zones:** Varies by species; see individual listings
- **AHS Heat Zones:** Varies by species; see individual listings

Growing Tips

Evening primroses are easy to grow in full sun and well-drained soil. Most are quite drought-tolerant once they're established, and they can tolerate poor soil and salty conditions. Wet conditions, though, especially in winter, can be fatal. All species are easy to grow from seed. Sow seed indoors early, without covering, because the seed needs light to germinate. Plants generally bloom the first year. In many climates (especially south of USDA Zone 5), they'll even bloom their first year from seed sown directly in the garden in early spring. Named cultivars won't come true from seed, so propagate them by taking cuttings or dividing.

Good Neighbors

Plant evening primroses with equally vigorous and drought-tolerant neighbors: Catmints (*Nepeta* spp.), blue false indigo (*Baptisia australis*), and some of the lower-growing ornamental grasses make attractive and stalwart companions. Showy evening primrose (*Oenothera speciosa*) is so vigorous that it often crowds out even the toughest companions. Try it surrounding plantings of tough-as-nails ornamental grasses such as fountain grass (*Pennisetum alopecuroides*) or blue oat grass (*Helictotrichon sempervirens*) or as an underplanting around sun-loving shrubs such as butterfly bushes (*Buddleia* spp.) or viburnums (*Viburnum* spp.). Showy evening primrose is also a good groundcover used alone in infertile soils and on hard-to-manage roadside banks.

Problems and Solutions

Root rot is a problem in wet soils, and it causes plants to first wilt, then die, so provide perfect drainage to prevent the problem.

Top Performer

Oenothera fruticosa (common sundrops):
Common sundrops have lance-shaped
leaves and upright, clumping stems topped
with clusters of bright yellow, day-
blooming flowers from early to late
summer. They spread slowly and may
need division if not planted inside a root
barrier. 'Fyrverkeri' ('Fireworks') is the most
widely available cultivar, but I find it
blooms over a shorter season (about six
weeks) than other cultivars. 'Illumination'
and 'Sonnenwende' ('Summer Solstice')
have a longer blooming period. Both have
red-tinged foliage; 'Illumination' is more
mound-shaped. Height: 18 to 24 inches (45
to 60 cm). Spread: 1 to 2 feet (30 to 60 cm).
USDA Plant Hardiness Zones 3 to 9; AHS
Heat Zones 8 to 1.

Common sundrops
(*Oenothera fruticosa*)

More Recommended Evening Primroses

Oenothera macrocarpa (Ozark sundrops): Also called *O. missouriensis*,
these sprawling plants produce long, narrow, velvety leaves and
yellow, fragrant flowers with a crepe-paper-like texture. The huge
blooms, up to 5 inches (13 cm) in diameter, open in the afternoon
from early summer to early fall. If you don't deadhead, you'll be rewarded with curious winged seedpods. Although Ozark sundrops
prefer full sun, partial shade is best in hot-summer areas; good
drainage is a must everywhere. Height: 6 to 12 inches (15 to 30 cm).
Spread: 1 foot (30 cm). USDA Plant Hardiness Zones 4 to 9; AHS
Heat Zones 8 to 1.

▌ **Think Twice:** *O. speciosa* (showy evening primrose): Showy it is,
but this evening primrose can be weedy due to its aggressive underground stems. Despite its name, showy evening primrose is a day
bloomer, with 1- to 2-inch (2.5- to 5-cm) blooms that are pink, white,
or white fading to pink. In poor or average soil, its stems are upright,
and the plant remains relatively compact. In rich or heavily fertilized
soil, it tends to flop and spread. (Plants sold as *O. berlandieri*, or Mexican evening primrose, are probably shorter varieties of this species.
One popular cultivar is 'Siskiyou', with large pink flowers.) Height: 1
to 2 feet (30 to 60 cm). Spread: unlimited unless controlled. USDA
Plant Hardiness Zones 5 to 9; AHS Heat Zones 8 to 3.

Around the World with *Oenothera*

Although they look pretty
in gardens, evening primroses
(*Oenothera* spp.) are opportunistic
plants that, thanks to their abundant production of long-lived
seeds, willingly leave the confines
of the garden to explore (and
invade!) their surroundings. I've
seen common evening primrose
(*O. biennis*), a pretty biennial
species, throughout Europe, especially in and around seashores.
And common sundrops (*O. fruticosa*) grow wild in Europe, Asia,
Australia, New Zealand, and even
South Africa—all, one assumes,
from plants originally brought over
to decorate somebody's garden.

Rudbeckia

Rudbeckia, coneflower

With their bright yellow petals and dark brown, cone-shaped centers, rudbeckias are almost unmistakable. Various species are native throughout North America, and one or another occurs in almost any sunny location. Rudbeckias make excellent, long-lasting cut flowers and bloom profusely. In summer, their flowers attract butterflies, and in late fall and winter, the seeds attract hosts of hungry birds.

Plant Profile

RUDBECKIA
rood-BECK-ee-uh

- **Bloom Color:** Yellow
- **Bloom Time:** Summer to midfall
- **Length of Bloom:** 3 months
- **Height:** Varies by species; see individual listings
- **Spread:** Varies by species; see individual listings
- **Garden Uses:** Container planting, cut flower garden, hedge, mass planting, meadow garden, mixed border, specimen plant; at the back of beds and borders; attracts butterflies and seed-eating birds
- **Light Preference:** Full sun to light shade
- **Soil Preference:** Average, well-drained soil
- **Best Way to Propagate:** Divide in spring or fall; for short-lived species, sow seeds in spring or fall
- **USDA Plant Hardiness Zones:** Varies by species; see individual listings
- **AHS Heat Zones:** Varies by species; see individual listings

Growing Tips

Most rudbeckias hail from dry meadows and do best in similar conditions—well-drained, dry, not overly rich soil in full sun. All grow well in partial shade, although they may bloom a bit less than in full sun and may need staking. Removing some of the flowers helps stimulate continued bloom, so don't hesitate to harvest cut flowers with a heavy hand.

Division is the method of choice for propagating long-lived rudbeckia species, while short-lived species grow quickly from seed. You can sow the seed indoors for earlier bloom, but many will bloom the first year even from seed sown directly in the garden. Don't cover the seed; it needs light to germinate.

Good Neighbors

A mainstay of mid- to late-season gardens, rudbeckias make a strong statement planted in a mass or as part of a meadow garden. For a garden to attract butterflies and birds, try planting rudbeckias with other meadow plants, such as New England aster (*Aster novae-angliae*), purple coneflower (*Echinacea purpurea*), garden phlox (*Phlox paniculata*), goldenrods (*Solidago* spp.), and ornamental grasses. Orange (*Rudbeckia fulgida* var. *sullivantii*) is effective in mass plantings. For interest throughout the fall and early winter, combine it with masses of Russian sage (*Perovskia atriplicifolia*), 'Herbstfreude' sedum (*Sedum* 'Herbstfreude', also called *S.* 'Autumn Joy'), and ornamental grasses, such as switch grass (*Panicum virgatum* 'Haense Herms' or 'Squaw') and fountain grass (*Pennisetum alopecuroides*).

Problems and Solutions

Some rudbeckias have few pest and disease problems, while others have more than their fair share; see individual listings for details.

Top Performer

Rudbeckia fulgida (orange coneflower): The flowers of this popular species sport yellow petals surrounding a purplish brown central cone. The midsummer-to-late-fall flowers bloom above a mound of dark green, slightly hairy foliage. Orange coneflower is a truly permanent perennial, requiring little more than deadheading to remain in top shape. You don't even need to divide it unless you want to propagate it. This sturdy plant also seems pest- and disease-free. It does spread, although not aggressively, by creeping underground stems. The most popular type sold is 'Goldsturm' orange coneflower (*R. fulgida* var. *sullivantii* 'Goldsturm'), which blooms very abundantly and is shorter than the species—it only grows up to 24 inches (60 cm) tall. 'Goldsturm' doesn't come completely true from seed, yet many nurseries have grown plants from seed, so you're never quite sure you've bought the real thing. Even so, 'Goldsturm' and its variants are great plants—in fact, I'm not alone in considering this plant one of the best perennials of all time. Height: 24 to 42 inches (60 to 105 cm). Spread: 1 to 2 feet (30 to 60 cm). USDA Plant Hardiness Zones 3 to 9; AHS Heat Zones 9 to 1.

More Recommended Coneflowers

Rudbeckia hirta (black-eyed Susan, gloriosa daisy): Originally native to the Midwest, black-eyed Susan's bright yellow flowers with the dark brown or black "eye" are now a common feature in meadows everywhere from early summer to late fall. In cool-summer areas, you can expect some strains to last four or five years, while the same plants are scarcely more than annuals in hot-summer areas. Black-eyed Susan is one tough plant and often comes through the most horrendous climatic conditions unscathed, but it is prone to aphids, sawflies, and powdery mildew. There are hordes of single or double cultivars in sizes ranging from nearly ground-hugging to well over knee-high. Unlike other rudbeckias, most named cultivars of this species were *designed* to come true from seed, so there is little reason to divide plants unless you come across one you especially like and want to maintain. Height: 8 to 36 inches (20 to 90 cm). Spread: 1 to 2 feet (30 to 60 cm). USDA Plant Hardiness Zones 4 to 9; AHS Heat Zones 7 to 1.

'Goldsturm' orange coneflower (*Rudbeckia fulgida* var. *sullivantii* 'Goldsturm')

Kissing Cousins

Mexican hat (*Ratibida columnifera*), also called prairie coneflower, is a rudbeckia look-alike. It does have distinctly different leaves (deeply cut and almost fernlike) and its flowers have much more prominent cones. The narrow, upright, brown cones are up to 2 inches (5 cm) long and are surrounded by downward-arching petals. Each flower does indeed look like a sombrero! The flowers are single or semi-double, and the petals range from yellow to mahogany red, sometimes bicolored. Plants bloom from midsummer to fall. Height: 2 to 3 feet (60 to 90 cm). Spread: 18 to 24 inches (45 to 60 cm). USDA Plant Hardiness Zones: 3 to 9; AHS Heat Zones: 7 to 1.

Scabiosa

Pincushion flower, scabious

It's odd that a top-performing, long-blooming plant like pincushion flower isn't more popular. While its ground-hugging rosettes of narrow leaves are nothing to write home about, the dome-shaped flower heads are pretty and bloom over a very long season. In the proper frost-free climate (USDA Zone 10), in fact, some pincushion flowers can bloom all year long.

Plant Profile

SCABIOSA
scab-ee-OH-suh

- **Bloom Color:** Blue, lavender, pink, white, or yellow
- **Bloom Time:** Early summer to early or midfall
- **Length of Bloom:** 3 months or more
- **Height:** Varies by species; see individual listings
- **Spread:** Varies by species; see individual listings
- **Garden Uses:** Container planting, cut flower garden, edging, mass planting, mixed border, rock garden, wall planting; attracts butterflies
- **Light Preference:** Full sun
- **Soil Preference:** Rich, well-drained, evenly moist soil
- **Best Way to Propagate:** Sow seed in spring; for named cultivars, take basal cuttings or divide in spring
- **USDA Plant Hardiness Zones:** Varies by species; see individual listings
- **AHS Heat Zones:** Varies by species; see individual listings

Growing Tips

Most pincushion flowers are easy to grow, especially in cool-summer climates. They perform well in average garden soil and appreciate full sun. Their flowerstalks are sturdy but may need staking in windy spots. Deadheading will help keep them in bloom for a long time.

It's easy to grow pincushion flower from seed started indoors or out and just barely covered, but if you want to grow a particular cultivar, buy plants and propagate them by division. You can divide established plants every three or four years or remove some of the secondary stems that appear at the base and root them as cuttings.

Good Neighbors

Mix pincushion flower with other summer bloomers in the perennial border: Coreopsis, daylilies, and sunflower heliopsis (*Heliopsis helianthoides*) will all complement its informal look. For an eye-catching combination of butterfly-attracting flowers, try using 'Butterfly Blue' small scabious (*Scabiosa columbaria* 'Butterfly Blue') with anise hyssop (*Agastache foeniculum*), lily leek (*Allium moly*), 'Nanho Blue' butterfly bush (*Buddleia davidii* 'Nanho Blue'), and a generous planting of butterfly weed (*Asclepias tuberosa*).

Problems and Solutions

Pincushion flower doesn't have any major disease or insect problems. If you sow seeds outdoors, patrol for slugs, which may devour young seedlings.

FUN FACTS

I suspect that pincushion flower has long suffered from the negative connotation of its alternate common name of scabious. The name actually derives from the plant's history—it was once used to *treat* scabies and other causes of itching. (It's no longer considered a medicinal plant.)

Top Performer

Scabiosa columbaria (small scabious):
This plant produces finely cut, gray-
green foliage and dome-shaped flowers
up to 3 inches (7.5 cm) across in a wide
range of colors: blue, lavender, pink, or
white. Few people grow the plain
species anymore: All eyes are on the
two stars of the scabious parade, 'Butterfly Blue' and 'Pink Mist'. Both are
dwarf types growing to about 1 foot
(30 cm) high with 2-inch (5-cm)
blooms, and both pump out flowers
nonstop from late spring or early
summer until hard frost. 'Butterfly
Blue' produces lavender-blue flowers
and 'Pink Mist' has pale pink blooms.
Both are top performers, although I
find that 'Butterfly Blue' outdoes 'Pink Mist' in number of flowers.
Height: 1 to 2 feet (30 to 60 cm). Spread: 1 foot (30 cm). USDA Plant
Hardiness Zones 3 to 9; AHS Heat Zones 8 to 1.

'Butterfly Blue' scabious (*Scabiosa columbaria* 'Butterfly Blue')

More Recommended Pincushion Flowers

Scabiosa caucasica (pincushion flower). Thanks to the influence of its
newly popular cousins, 'Butterfly Blue' and 'Pink Mist' scabious
(*S. columbaria* cultivars), this Victorian favorite is being rediscovered
by a new generation of romantic gardeners. Pretty pincushion
flower is larger than small scabious but otherwise very similar. From
early summer to early fall, its sturdy stems carry blooms in various
shades of blue and lavender as well as white. Popular cultivars include 'Fama', with dark lavender-blue flowers with an off-white
center, and House Hybrids (also called Isaac House Hybrids), with
flowers in various shades of white and blue. Height: 18 to 24 inches
(45 to 60 cm). Spread: 18 inches (45 cm). USDA Plant Hardiness
Zones 3 to 9; AHS Heat Zones 9 to 1.

   S. ochroleuca (yellow scabious): The oddball in a genus known for
its blue and white flowers, yellow scabious produces masses of
creamy yellow flowers from early summer to early fall over gray-
green, feltlike foliage. It is much shorter-lived than other species, so
let it self-sow; it comes true from seed. Height: 2 to 3 feet (60 to 90
cm). Spread: 2 feet (60 cm). USDA Plant Hardiness Zones 4 to 9;
AHS Heat Zones 9 to 1.

Kissing Cousins

Cephalaria gigantea (Tatarian
cephalaria): This kissing cousin
looks much like yellow scabious
(*S. ochroleuca*), both in flower and
in leaf, but its size is a dead giveaway. Put this coarse-looking giant
at the back of the garden and give
it lots of room, then enjoy the show
from early summer to early fall. The
primrose yellow, dome-shaped
flowers come in a shade of yellow
that seems to go with everything.
Start Tatarian cephalaria from seed
every two or three years (it will self-
sow) or divide it because it's not
long-lived. Pinch the stems in late
spring and you'll be able to keep
them below 6 feet (180 cm) tall!
Height: 5 to 8 feet (150 to 240 cm).
Spread: 4 to 5 feet (120 to 150 cm).
USDA Plant Hardiness Zones 3 to
9; AHS Heat Zones 8 to 1.

Tradescantia

Tradescantia, widow's tears

Most tradescantias are creeping tropical plants grown as hanging plants indoors or as groundcover in frost-free climates. But a few hardy types native to North America have become popular garden plants in temperate climates the world over. The hardy species are grasslike plants with upright or reclining stems and arching foliage. The stems are topped with clusters of three-petaled flowers in a wide range of colors. Though each flower lasts only one day, the plants produce a succession of blooms over a long period of time.

Plant Profile

TRADESCANTIA
trad-es-KANT-ee-uh

- Bloom Color: Blue, magenta, pink, purple, red, and white
- Bloom Time: Early summer to early fall
- Length of Bloom: 3 months
- Height: 1 to 2 feet (30 to 60 cm)
- Spread: 18 to 36 inches (45 to 90 cm)
- Garden Uses: Edging, groundcover, mass planting, meadow garden, mixed border, rock garden, wall planting, woodland garden; on slopes, in wet areas
- Light Preference: Full sun to partial shade
- Soil Preference: Rich, moist, well-drained soil
- Best Way to Propagate: Divide in spring or fall
- USDA Plant Hardiness Zones: 4 to 9
- AHS Heat Zones: 9 to 1

Growing Tips

Tradescantias grow and flower best in full sun and cool, moist, but well-drained soils. People often grow tradescantias in partial shade because their garden doesn't offer a site that combines full sun with moisture and cool temperatures. They'll also tolerate boggy conditions, but they bloom more abundantly when they have good drainage.

Tradescantias spread in all directions, but they rarely become weedy. Other plants will check their spread, and it's easy to pull out any plantlets that overstep their boundaries. In hot-summer climates, tradescantias can spread naturally by seed and become a bit invasive, so be sure to cut all flowerstalks back after the last blooms fade.

In hot weather, tradescantias tend to collapse into a ragged mess that can scarcely be called decorative. Pruning them back by half after a heavy period of flowering helps prevent this from happening and also stimulates rebloom—consider this mid-season cleanup a necessary task.

Good Neighbors

Tradescantias tolerate partial shade and prefer evenly moist situations, so pair them with other perennials that like those conditions, such as ferns, hostas, and drumstick primrose (*Primula denticulata*). Keep in mind, however, that tradescantia tends to look ragged in the hottest

FUN FACTS

Tradescantia is also called widow's tears because of the unusual behavior of its flower petals. Unlike most petals, which turn brown or drop off as they age, tradescantia flower petals turn into into a clear liquid that looks like teardrops.

summer weeks, so pair them with plants that shine in the heat. Try 'Southern Belle' common rose mallow (*Hibiscus moscheutos* 'Southern Belle') with an underplanting of white-flowered tradescantia, or match 'Desdemona' bigleaf ligularia (*Ligularia dentata* 'Desdemona') with a purple-flowered one. Or surround the glossy, tropical-looking foliage of 'Bressingham Ruby' bergenia (*Bergenia* 'Bressingham Ruby') with a ruby-red tradescantia such as 'Carmine Glow' (*Tradescantia* 'Carmine Glow').

Problems and Solutions

Besides "midsummer meltdown," tradescantia is occasionally subject to various leaf diseases and insects, but it rarely suffers serious problems.

Recommended Tradescantia

Tradescantia Andersoniana Group hybrids: Tradescantia is one of those perennials where the botanical naming is something of a mess. The Andersoniana Group includes virtually all of the tradescantias on the market: Any tradescantia you're growing probably belongs to this group, no matter what botanical name appears on its label! However, you may find some of these hybrids labeled as *T.* × *andersoniana* or *T. virginiana* hybrids.

There are innumerable cultivars, many with short flowering seasons. A few that bloom nonstop through summer if they get ample moisture and aren't exposed to excessive heat are 'Carmine Glow' with deep carmine flowers and 'Red Cloud' with rosy red flowers.

'Snowcap', with huge, pure white flowers up to 3 inches (7.5 cm) in diameter, is the first to bloom in my garden. 'Innocence' is one of the most persistent bloomers among white-flowered tradescantias; it's a clump-former that needs partial shade for good growth.

'J. C. Weguelin' is a vigorous grower with large china blue flowers. 'Purple Passion' has velvety purple, semidouble flowers on very vigorous, compact plants. 'Purple Profusion' offers purple flowers over a particularly long season; it has narrower leaves than most other cultivars, and the sturdy stems are less subject to collapse. 'Zwanenburg Blue' has huge deep blue flowers over purple-veined foliage on mound-shaped plants.

'Snowcap' tradescantia hybrid (*Tradescantia* 'Snowcap')

Kissing Cousins

Tradescantias (*Tradescantia* spp.) have lots of tropical relatives. My favorite, purple-leaved setcreasea (*Tradescantia pallida* 'Purpurea', also called 'Purple Heart') can be grown as an annual groundcover. Space rooted cuttings 1 foot (30 cm) apart in a partially to deeply shaded spot, and they'll spread quickly. The clumps of deep reddish purple leaves and magenta flowers make a bold statement in a border or rock garden. Just remember to take cuttings in fall to use in next year's outdoor garden. Height: 8 to 12 inches (20 to 30 cm). Spread: 16 inches (40 cm). USDA Plant Hardiness Zones 8 to 11; AHS Heat Zones 12 to 1.

Verbena

Verbena, vervain

While verbenas aren't terribly hardy, they're very popular because of their versatility and long bloom. Verbenas range from upright to mat-forming, but nearly all species have four-sided stems and clusters or spikes of funnel-shaped flowers. Brazilian vervain (*Verbena bonariensis*) and rose verbena (*V. canadensis*) are among the hardiest of the ornamental verbenas, but even so they can barely survive cold winters and are often grown as annuals.

Plant Profile

VERBENA
ver-BEAN-uh

- Bloom Color: Pink, purple, red, or white

- Bloom Time: Early summer to midfall

- Length of Bloom: 4 months

- Height: Varies by species; see individual listings

- Spread: Varies by species; see individual listings

- Garden Uses: Container planting, edging, groundcover, mass planting, meadow garden, mixed border, rock garden, wall planting; attracts butterflies

- Light Preference: Full sun or light shade

- Soil Preference: Fertile, well-drained soil

- Best Way to Propagate: Take stem cuttings in spring; sow seed in spring or fall

- USDA Plant Hardiness Zones: Varies by species; see individual listings

- AHS Heat Zones: Varies by species; see individual listings

Growing Tips

Brazilian vervain and rose verbena both love hot, humid summers and tolerate drought quite well. Excellent drainage is a must. (Their intolerance of wet winter conditions often causes more losses than their lack of cold-hardiness.) Winter protection is a good idea almost everywhere if you intend to grow verbenas as perennials, or since both verbenas grow readily from seed and bloom the first year, treat them as self-seeding annuals even in areas where they are hardy.

Good Neighbors

Brazilian vervain has a tall, airy form, that works in the front, middle, or back of the border. Its purple flower heads look great coming up between smaller mounding plants such as 'Moonbeam' threadleaf coreopsis (*Coreopsis verticillata* 'Moonbeam'), common baby's-breath (*Gypsophila paniculata*), and Shasta daisy (*Leucanthemum* × *superbum*, also called *Chrysanthemum* × *superbum*). Pair it with blue star (*Amsonia hubrectii*) for a show that will last through fall. Combine it with butterfly weed (*Asclepias tuberosa*) and dwarf asters to attract butterflies.

Problems and Solutions

Both Brazilian vervain and rose verbena are susceptible to powdery mildew, so avoid moist conditions and provide good air circulation. If a powdery white coating does appear, cut the plants back harshly.

Spider mites can infest the growing tips, so apply insecticidal soap if you notice damaged foliage and webbing.

Top Performer

Verbena canadensis (rose verbena): Rose verbena is a creeping perennial that bears deeply lobed, green leaves that hide the stems from view. The species produces clusters of purple flowers from early summer or mid-summer to midfall; cultivars are available in shades of red, pink, and white.

Rose verbena needs winter protection in most areas, although many gardeners allow it to self-seed to replace any plants that die. Trying to decide the true hardiness is difficult. Some experts suggest USDA Zone 8, yet others say Zone 4. I've found that it is definitely not hardy in Zone 4, although it does self-sow there and might give the appearance of being hardy. On the other hand, gardeners in Zone 6 seem to have little trouble with it, so I've decided to use that zone here. Rose verbena can be very weedy when it self-sows heavily, especially in the hot, humid climates where it does so well.

'Homestead Purple' is a popular cultivar, producing its dark purple flowers early in the season and late into the fall. Height: 6 to 18 inches (15 to 45 cm). Spread: 18 to 36 inches (45 to 90 cm). USDA Plant Hardiness Zones 6 to 9; AHS Heat Zones 12 to 1.

More Recommended Verbenas

Think Twice: *Verbena bonariensis* (Brazilian vervain): Brazilian vervain was an overnight star of perennial gardens, and now it's hard to find a garden that doesn't feature it! This verbena starts out as a clump of narrow, dense leaves but quickly switches to a stiffly upright, very open plant whose rare leaves are scarcely noticeable along its wiry, hairy stems. The 2- to 4-inch (5 to 10 cm) clusters of small purple flowers appear at the end of each stem.

On its own, this plant is tall and ungainly. But when planted in a mass or interplanted in large groups among other plants, it is simply stunning. In rich or humid soils, Brazilian vervain tends to flop, so prune it harshly in spring to promote shorter, denser branches.

Brazilian vervain self-sows profusely. In USDA Zone 8 and south, it's becoming a significant weed problem. If you garden in these warm regions, be sure to deadhead your Brazilian vervain thoroughly to prevent self-sowing. Height: 4 feet (120 cm) in poor, dry soil; up to 6 feet (180 cm) in rich, moist conditions. Spread: 1 to 3 feet (30 to 90 cm). USDA Plant Hardiness Zones 7 to 9; AHS Heat Zones 10 to 1.

Rose verbena
(*Verbena canadensis*)

Larry's Garden Notes

The species name "*canadensis*" in rose verbena (*Verbena canadensis*) has nothing, or at least very little, to do with Canada. Rose verbena is native to points much further south, from Virginia to Florida, and west to Colorado. Back in the eighteenth century when Linnaeus began the botanical name system we use today, there still wasn't much of a distinction between Canada and America (nor, for that matter, Virginia), and names like "*canadensis*," "*americana*," or "*virginiana*" were often handed out in ways that now seem to be incorrect.

Veronica

Veronica, speedwell

You can always count on veronicas for a long-lasting, bright display in your garden. From late spring right through summer, there are always a few veronicas in bloom. Veronicas are a highly varied group of perennials, ranging from ground-hugging creepers to upright, clumping plants. All bear small flowers, usually in shades of purple or blue, although there are pink, red, and white-flowered cultivars. The flowers are generally grouped together in narrow spikes.

Plant Profile

VERONICA
ver-ON-ih-kuh

- **Bloom Color:** Blue, pink, purple, red, and white

- **Bloom Time:** Varies by species; see individual listings

- **Length of Bloom:** 2 months or more

- **Height:** Varies by species; see individual listings

- **Spread:** Varies by species; see individual listings

- **Garden Uses:** Container planting, cut flower garden, edging, groundcover, mass planting, mixed border, rock garden, wall planting, wildflower meadow; along paths, on slopes

- **Light Preference:** Full sun to partial shade

- **Soil Preference:** Rich, well-drained soil

- **Best Way to Propagate:** Divide in spring or fall; take stem cuttings in summer

- **USDA Plant Hardiness Zones:** Varies by species; see individual listings

- **AHS Heat Zones:** Varies by species; see individual listings

Growing Tips

Veronicas are easy-to-grow plants adapted to a wide variety of conditions. The taller-growing ones form dense clumps and are well behaved. Keep your eye on the low-growing, groundcover types, however, because they spread in all directions. Plant them in spots where you can contain their growth. Some veronicas are out-and-out weeds, but the ones I've chosen are easy to control.

Veronicas are easy to propagate by division or stem cuttings. The longest-blooming veronicas perform best if you prune them back after a period of heavy flowering. This also prevents the plants from flopping over in hot, humid weather.

Good Neighbors

Low, spreading veronicas are excellent choices for edging plants and combine well with plants of almost any form and color. Contrast the taller clump-forming veronicas with 'Moonshine' yarrow (*Achillea* 'Moonshine'), butterfly weed (*Asclepias tuberosa*), coreopsis, and 'Goldsturm' orange coneflower (*Rudbeckia fulgida* var. *sullivantii* 'Goldsturm').

Problems and Solutions

Some veronicas suffer from pest or disease problems, notably powdery mildew, but they're rarely serious.

Top Performer

⭐ **Larry's Favorite:** *Veronica* 'Goodness Grows': This veronica is a beautiful, low-growing edging or rock garden plant that also makes an excellent groundcover. It produces upright spikes of rich blue flowers over a mass of green foliage. In my garden, this plant starts blooming in late spring and is still in bloom in early fall. Height: 10 to 12 inches

(25 to 30 cm). Spread: 12 to 18 inches (30 to 45 cm) or more. USDA Plant Hardiness Zones 3 to 9; AHS Heat Zones 8 to 1.

More Recommended Veronicas

Veronica longifolia (long-leaf speedwell): This clump-forming, upright grower is a dependable anchor plant for the middle of a perennial border. Its 12-inch (30-cm) flower spikes are densely covered in deep blue blossoms from midspring to midsummer, with some rebloom until fall.

Long-leaf speedwell looks best planted in clusters of three to five plants. Staking may be necessary in hot climates or in rich soil. It's less drought-tolerant than other veronicas, so keep it at least slightly moist at all times. Deadhead to promote continuous bloom. Height: 12 to 30 inches (30 to 75 cm). Spread: 18 to 24 inches (45 to 60 cm). USDA Plant Hardiness Zones 3 to 9; AHS Heat Zones 8 to 3.

V. spicata (spike speedwell): Spike speedwell is the most popular veronica. This species now includes woolly speedwell (*V. incana*, now known as *V. spicata* subsp. *incana*). Most hybrids now contain the genes of both and come in all sizes, with leaves ranging in color from pure green to diverse shades of gray. All are great edging plants, with mats of dense foliage at the base and narrow upright spikes of blue, pink, purple, red, or white flowers. They can bloom almost constantly throughout the summer if deadheaded. All spike speedwells need good drainage, especially in hot-summer climates. Height: 8 to 24 inches (20 to 60 cm). Spread: 1 to 2 feet (30 to 60 cm). USDA Plant Hardiness Zones 3 to 9; AHS Heat Zones 8 to 1.

V. 'Sunny Border Blue': The dense, compact mounds of crinkled, glossy, bright green leaves are a wonderful feature of 'Sunny Border Blue'. Short spikes of violet blue flowers top the upright stems from midsummer to early fall. Height: 18 to 24 inches (45 to 60 cm). Spread: 12 to 18 inches (30 to 45 cm). USDA Plant Hardiness Zones 4 to 9; AHS Heat Zones 8 to 1.

You'll find many veronicas offered under more than one name. To get the right veronica, choose by *cultivar* name; different nurseries may list various cultivars as belonging to different species, but a veronica cultivar under any other botanical name looks just as great.

'Goodness Grows' veronica (*Veronica* 'Goodness Grows')

Kissing Cousins

Culver's root (*Veronicastrum virginicum*) used to be part of the genus *Veronica* (it was known as *Veronica virginica*), and its flowers look a lot like *Veronica* flowers— narrow spikes of white (occasionally pale blue or pink) flowers. Culver's root is, however, a much taller, distinctly vertical plant, with straight, upright stems and narrow, pointed leaves. It's a lovely accent plant or a good choice for the back of a flower border: You can't help being impressed by its majestic appearance. Height: 4 to 6 feet (120 to 180 cm). Spread: 3 to 4 feet (90 to 120 cm). USDA Plant Hardiness Zones 3 to 9; AHS Heat Zones 9 to 1.

Larry's Last Look: Everbloomers

Here are a few more of my favorite everblooming perennials. I could go on for page after page about their fabulous performance. The combination of long bloom and fabulous color and texture makes these plants essential for the gardener who craves excitement in a perennial bed.

COMMON AND BOTANICAL NAMES	ZONES AND EXPOSURES	BLOOM COLOR AND TIME	DESCRIPTION
❂ Ferny corydalis *Corydalis cheilanthifolia*	Hardiness Zones 3–9 Heat Zones 8–4 Full sun	Yellow flowers in spring	Not an everbloomer, but when not in bloom, its deeply cut blue-gray leaves give it a fernlike appearance. Good choice for colder areas, but be warned— it can be weedy. Height: 9–12 inches (23–30 cm). Spread: 10 inches (25 cm).
Sweet William *Dianthus barbatus*	Hardiness Zones 4–10 Heat Zones 9–1 Sun	Red, purple, pink, white, or bicolor flowers in late spring to early summer	Quintessential cottage garden plant. Self-sows freely. Originally a biennial. Modern strains bloom from seed the first year and are sold as annuals. Likely to survive for years in the garden. Height: 12–20 inches (30–50 cm). Spread: 12 inches (30 cm).
China pink *Dianthus chinensis*	Hardiness Zones 7–10 Heat Zones 10–6 Sun	Red, pink, white, or bicolor flowers in summer	This is sold as an annual but often acts like a perennial, coming back for up to 4 or 5 years. A more upright plant than most pinks, with rather broad green leaves. Height: 6–30 inches (15–75 cm). Spread: 12 inches (30 cm).
Endress's geranium *Geranium endressii*	Hardiness Zones 3–9 Heat Zones 8–5 Sun to partial shade	Pink flowers in early summer to fall	Glossy evergreen foliage. Good drainage is a must. Prune in midsummer for continued bloom. Height: 12–18 inches (30–45 cm). Spread: 1–2 feet (30–60 cm).

Sweet William
(*Dianthus barbatus*)

'Telstar' China pink
(*Dianthus chinensis* 'Telstar')

COMMON AND BOTANICAL NAMES	ZONES AND EXPOSURES	BLOOM COLOR AND TIME	DESCRIPTION
Siberian catnip *Nepeta sibirica*	Hardiness Zones 3–9 Heat Zones 8–1 Sun	Violet flowers in early to late summer	Lightly scented foliage and spike flowers. Deadhead to prevent it from becoming invasive. Height: 2–3 feet (60–90 cm). Spread: 18–24 inches (45–60 cm).
'Goldquelle' cutleaf coneflower *Rudbeckia laciniata* 'Goldquelle', also known as 'Gold Fountain' or 'Gold Drop'	Hardiness Zones 3–9 Heat Zones 9–1 Sun	Yellow flowers in midsummer to late fall	Double flowers on a compact, disease- and pest-resistant, clump-forming plant. Height: 30–40 inches (75–100 cm). Spread: 18–24 inches (45–60 cm).
Giant coneflower *Rudbeckia maxima*	Hardiness Zones 4–9 Heat Zones 9–2 Full sun	Gold flowers in midsummer to late fall	An eye-catching perennial that produces 2-foot-long (60-cm) powder blue leaves and flowers that can reach 5 inches (13 cm) wide. Height: 5-9 feet (150–270 cm). Spread: 2–3 feet (60–90 cm).
Blue anise sage *Salvia guaranitica*	Hardiness Zones 7–10 Heat Zones 12–8 Sun to light shade	Deep blue flowers in early summer through fall	Long, narrow, tubular flowers in whorls on tall spikes. Dark green leaves. Height: 4–6 feet (120–180 cm). Spread: 4–5 feet (120–150 cm).
Meadow sage *Salvia pratensis*	Hardiness Zones 3–9 Heat Zones 9–1 Sun to light shade	Blue, purple, pink, or white flowers in early to late summer	Low mounds of large, rough-textured leaves topped with branching spikes of flowers. Deadhead for repeat bloom; take cuttings annually because this plant is often short-lived. Height: 1–3 feet (30–90 cm). Spread: 18–36 inches (45–90 cm).
Hungarian speedwell *Veronica austriaca* subsp. *teucrium*	Hardiness Zones 3–9 Heat Zones 8–1 Sun to light shade	Blue flowers in midspring to midsummer	This spreading species has short spikes of bright blue flowers. Cut it back after its main flush of bloom from midspring to midsummer to stimulate rebloom. Height: 1–2 feet (30–60 cm). Spread: 1–2 feet (30–60 cm).

Endress's geranium (*Geranium endressii*)

Hungarian speedwell (*Veronica austriaca* subsp. *teucrium*)

Spring-Blooming PERENNIALS

If your garden still looks brown and barren when the grass starts greening up in the spring, this chapter is for you. It's a treasure trove of early-season perennials that will bring your garden to life as soon as spring touches the air. I group spring-blooming perennials into two categories: the short ones and the tall ones. That may sound silly, but it's a useful split. Almost all short spring bloomers flower in early spring, while the tall ones generally bloom toward the end of spring or even in early summer in colder regions.

◄ Sprinkle groupings of early bloomers like these polyantha primroses (*Primula* × *polyantha*) throughout the garden, not just in the front of beds. That way you'll have gardens brimming with color even when most of your perennials are still dormant.

The First Blooms of Spring

Short spring-blooming perennials are up and at it in late winter and early spring, often with the crocuses, snowdrops, and other early bulbs. Most of these perennials are genetically programmed to produce massive numbers of blooms: Pollinators are in short supply at this time of year, so the best strategy for getting bees and flies to visit is to put out so many blooms they simply can't be missed. These low-growing perennials, such as rock cresses (*Arabis* spp.) and primroses (*Primula* spp.), bloom their heads off for about two or three weeks, then take a break until the following spring.

Short Is Smart

It's no accident that early spring perennials are short. For one thing, they don't have to reach for the sky because most of their taller competitors are still either dormant or just beginning to sprout. The sky-high annuals and perennials of midsummer, with their dense leaves that block light and moisture, are months away.

Another reason early bloomers creep, crawl, and cluster close to the ground is that many are alpine plants: They're native to mountaintops and alpine meadows. It's a world of harsh, drying winds and freezing cold nights. Staying low to the ground helps plants survive those cold conditions and take advantage of nearby rocks, which absorb heat during the day and then give it off at night.

Spring Decorating with Spring Bloomers

Low-growing spring bloomers, especially those like moss phlox (*Phlox subulata*) that have attractive, long-lasting foliage, are excellent edging plants. But don't limit their use to the front of beds and borders. With early spring bloomers, you can break the "short plants in the front, tall plants in the back" landscaping rule with impunity.

Caucasian leopard's bane (*Doronicum orientale*) mixes it up beautifully with forget-me-nots (*Myosotis* spp.) in the springtime. It's a lovely but strictly cool-weather pairing. Neither will persist once the temperature rises.

That's because most perennials are still dormant, so your early bloomers will be easy to see no matter where they are in the garden.

Don't hesitate to plant early bloomers throughout the garden, wherever the mood strikes you. Try for splotches of color, not just in front but throughout the garden. We're so starved for color after a long gray or white winter that any patch of bloom will look marvelous. Place a few early spring-flowering perennials here and there, occasionally repeating the same plant in the same color to create a theme.

Twixt Spring and Summer

The tall spring bloomers in this chapter, such as Italian bugloss (*Anchusa azurea*), bloom at the cusp of spring and summer. These perennials are more popular than the early spring bloomers, but it takes thought and planning to use them well. Their foliage is rarely attractive after they finish blooming, and it stands out all too obviously when it's at the front of the garden.

The secret with late spring-blooming perennials is to plant them toward the middle or even the back of the garden and, again, to think in terms of "patches of color." Plant them in clumps of modest size, never in huge masses that will be hard to hide. Don't worry if they seem a bit short for planting near the back: The spring garden is rather two-dimensional. The late spring bloomers will stand out nicely while they flower, and then their foliage will be hidden from sight as later-blooming perennials take over.

Special Care for Spring Bloomers

Many early spring bloomers maintain a fairly decent appearance throughout the growing season. But other plants tend to collapse, and some become quite barren in the center. To remedy this, trim them back harshly after they bloom and their centers will fill in quite nicely after a few weeks.

Low-growing spring bloomers generally adapt perfectly well to moderate competition from surrounding plants as long as their crowns aren't completely covered by neighboring foliage and their roots aren't overrun by invasive competitors. These short plants do most of their photosynthesis in spring anyway, so the shady conditions that develop as their taller neighbors grow during the summer aren't a problem.

Cover-Ups for Fading Spring Flowers

Several spring-flowering perennials, such as wood anemone (*Anemone nemorosa*), common bleeding heart (*Dicentra spectabilis*), bluebells (*Mertensia* spp.), and oriental poppy (*Papaver orientale*)—not to mention almost all spring bulbs—lose not only their flowers but also their foliage once they finish blooming. It doesn't mean the plants are in trouble. The following spring your early bloomers, which showed no sign of life all summer, fall, and winter, will sprout again.

To fill the space left by spring bloomers gone dormant, plant some cover-up plants nearby. Cover-up plants are perennials with spreading branches and leaves that will reach out over the fading spring beauties and hide them. Obviously, you'll have to match the needs of your spring bloomers with those of their cover-ups. You wouldn't want to plant a shade- and moisture-loving groundcover like astilbe to hide the foliage of sun-loving oriental poppy, for example. But baby's-breath (*Gypsophila paniculata*) would be a great companion because it will thrive in sun and well-drained soil, just as oriental poppies do.

Hostas are wonderful cover-ups and perfect complements for early spring bloomers. The heavy, hide-all hosta foliage doesn't start to spread until late enough in the season for spring bloomers to have finished their show. Other great perennials that don't start to spread until spring bloomers are about to give up the ghost include boltonia (*Boltonia asteroides*), Russian sage (*Perovskia atriplicifolia*), small Solomon's seal (*Polygonatum biflorum*), some tall daylilies, and many ornamental grasses. Creeping or mounding-type annual flowers such as petunias, Madagascar periwinkle (*Catharanthus roseus*), and verbenas also work well as cover-ups for dormant perennials.

Label It or Lose It

Here's a word of caution when it comes to spring-blooming perennials: *Always* carefully label any spring bloomers that go dormant and lose their foliage in summer. Like spring-flowering bulbs, they're essentially invisible in summer and often also in fall and winter. It's all too easy to forget where they are and accidentally dig them up when you decide to tuck some new acquisitions into a bed or border. A permanent label sticking out of a seemingly barren part of the garden will act as a stop sign: Don't dig here!

I haven't found the perfect labels yet. I use standard plastic labels because they're inexpensive, but I don't like them very much. They become brittle and break after a few years in the garden. If I had the cash, I'd use those snazzy metal labels with reinforced edges, but in the balance, I'm always more tempted to spend my gardening money on more plants, not fancy labels!

14 More Spring Bloomers

If you're looking for an even wider range of spring-blooming perennials, try some from this list, too. Many of them are beautiful woodland wildflowers that provide spring bloom for shade. Others are perennials that at least start their bloom season during the spring in most climates; some continue blooming into summer.

Anchusa

Bugloss

If you're looking for a bold blue statement for your garden in late spring, you'll find it with bugloss. Forget the washed-out blues of forget-me-nots (*Myosotis* spp.): Bugloss flowers have a rich, brilliant, in-your-face blue that almost seems to sparkle. The flower stems are rolled like the fiddlehead of a fern at first. As they unfurl, the flowers open in succession up the stalk.

Plant Profile

ANCHUSA
an-KOO-suh

- ■ **Bloom Color:** Blue

- ■ **Bloom Time:** Late spring to early summer; some repeat bloom in summer

- ■ **Length of Bloom:** 4 or 5 weeks

- ■ **Height:** 18 to 60 inches (45 to 150 cm)

- ■ **Spread:** 1 to 2 feet (30 to 60 cm)

- ■ **Garden Uses:** Cut flower garden, groundcover, seasonal hedge, mass planting, mixed border, specimen plant, wall planting, wildflower meadow, woodland garden; at the back of beds and borders; on slopes

- ■ **Light Preference:** Full sun to light shade

- ■ **Soil Preference:** Average, moist but well-drained soil

- ■ **Best Way to Propagate:** Sow seed in spring, summer, or fall; for named cultivars, divide or take root cuttings in spring

- ■ **USDA Plant Hardiness Zones:** 3 to 10

- ■ **AHS Heat Zones:** 8 to 1

Growing Tips

Although Italian bugloss (*Anchusa azurea*) is very easy to grow, adapting to almost any soil that isn't either constantly wet or bone-dry, it's not necessarily long-lived. Some gardeners (especially those in AHS Heat Zones 10 to 8) grow it as a biennial, but even in cool-summer areas the plants rarely live more than four years. Since Italian bugloss self-sows (a bit too readily, in fact) and comes relatively true from seed, you can let it maintain itself. Simply allow a few seedlings to sprout each year and yank out any extras. (Before you try this, read the warning below.) Self-sown plants usually sprout in summer and bloom the following year. You can also start the seed indoors in late winter and expect blooms the first year.

Over two or three years, self-sown seedlings of cultivars tend to revert to the ordinary species form. If you want to maintain a cultivar's traits, divide it every year or two, or take root cuttings in spring.

Blue is such a rare color in the garden that you may well be able to forgive Italian bugloss for its major flaw: It needs staking. In rich soil, especially, the plants tend to shoot for the sky, then flop over—and it's not a pretty sight when they go down. Planting them in deeply worked soil so their roots can anchor more firmly will help. Elsewhere, either stake the plants or plant them among sturdy perennials like yarrow or among shrubs that can support them. Dwarf cultivars rarely need staking.

❢ **Think Twice:** Italian bugloss is a Eurasian plant that has escaped from gardens in many parts of the world and become a bothersome weed that competes with native perennials. To keep it from becoming weedy in your yard, you'll probably want to deadhead it as soon as it finishes blooming to prevent seed formation. Deadheading can also stimulate reblooming, so Italian bugloss may continue flowering right through the summer, especially in areas with cool summers. Regularly deadheaded plants tend to be longer-lived, lasting four or five years instead of two or three—another benefit.

Good Neighbors

Add Italian bugloss to a mixed planting of pastel shades of common yarrow (*Achillea millefolium*) for interest and texture early in the season. Or for a vibrant but short-lived color contrast, combine Italian bugloss with oriental poppies (*Papaver orientale*). A planting of Ozark sundrops (*Oenothera macrocarpa*) or Shasta daisy (*Leucanthemum* × *superbum*) in the foreground will extend the period of interest.

Problems and Solutions

In poorly drained soil, Italian bugloss may languish or die due to crown rot. To prevent crown rot, plant Italian bugloss in a well-drained spot.

Top Performer

Anchusa azurea, also called *A. italica* (Italian bugloss): Italian bugloss is a tall, imposing perennial with long, coarsely hairy leaves and multiple flowerstalks. Because of its size, it looks best at the back of the garden, but many of the hybrids are more compact, so you can use them in a variety of sites. Italian bugloss is a wonderful choice for meadow gardens and for plantings at the edge of woodlands. I give it extra brownie points because it blooms through that often barren period between late spring and early summer.

There are many fine cultivars of Italian bugloss. 'Dropmore' (deep blue) and 'Opal' (azure blue) reach up to 4 feet (120 cm) tall and tend to flop. Better choices include 'Loddon Royalist' (gentian blue) and 'Royal Blue' (deep blue), which only grow about 3 feet (90 cm) tall. Both may still require staking in rich soil. 'Little John' has dark blue flowers and reaches only 18 inches (45 cm) tall so it doesn't need staking.

A caution: Some nurseries do propagate Italian bugloss by seed, so you may buy a particular cultivar and later discover it's something quite different than what you expected.

'Loddon Royalist' Italian bugloss
(*Anchusa azurea* 'Loddon Royalist')

Larry's Garden Notes

Italian bugloss (*Anchusa azurea*) was a favorite in this country in the early part of the twentieth century, and many of the selections from that time period are still offered by seed catalogs today. ('Dropmore' dates from 1905.) The dainty sprays of blue flowers work well in sweet old-fashioned nosegays. I find that heirloom varieties, although they can be lanky and untidy in the garden, are wonderfully charming. Besides, growing old cultivars is a great way to keep a part of our garden history alive.

Anemone

Anemone, windflower

Spring-blooming anemones add color and charm to rock gardens and woodland gardens. The genus *Anemone* includes species that bloom at nearly all times of the year. The spring-flowering anemones I describe here grow from creeping roots called rhizomes. For more later-blooming anemones, see page 168.

Plant Profile

ANEMONE
uh-NEM-oh-nee

- **Bloom Color:** Blue, pink, purple, white, or yellow
- **Bloom Time:** Varies by species; see individual listings
- **Length of Bloom:** 2 to 4 weeks
- **Height:** Varies by species; see individual listings
- **Spread:** Varies by species; see individual listings
- **Garden Uses:** Cut flower garden, groundcover, mass planting, rock garden, woodland garden
- **Light Preference:** Varies by species; see individual listings
- **Soil Preference:** Rich, moist but well-drained, slightly acid soil
- **Best Way to Propagate:** Divide in summer or fall; sow seed in spring or fall
- **USDA Plant Hardiness Zones:** Varies by species; see individual listings
- **AHS Heat Zones:** Varies by species; see individual listings

Growing Tips

These early-flowering anemones are generally shade-tolerant plants. They prefer acid soil and—as suits plants that tend to grow in the woods—fertile, humus-rich, loamy soil. To propagate, divide clumps after blooming or in fall, although you can also grow anemones from seed. Remove the fuzzy outer coat from the seed before sowing it outdoors in spring or fall. Barely cover the seeds with soil.

Anemone rhizomes fork as they grow, creeping in all directions. You may find this charming at first, but if you haven't thought ahead, you may find their invasive nature annoying. Either plant these anemones in parts of your garden where their spreading tendencies will do no harm, or control them by planting them inside a root barrier, such as a bottomless bucket sunk into the soil.

Good Neighbors

Wood anemone (*Anemone nemorosa*) and snowdrop anemone (*A. sylvestris*) look great planted in masses under spring-blooming trees or with spring bulbs. Or use their crisp white flowers to accentuate the colors of other early bloomers, such as wild columbine (*Aquilegia canadensis*), and common bleeding heart (*Dicentra spectabilis*).

Problems and Solutions

Anemones may wilt and then die off because of root rot in very moist soil, so avoid boggy soil. Other than root rot, anemones have few pest problems.

FUN FACT

If you shop for wood anemones in the fall, you may find them offered as dormant rhizomes. The rhizomes look so thin and lifeless that buying them is disconcerting. However, just trust in nature (but ask for a guarantee from the nursery). Plant the rhizomes 1 inch (2.5 cm) deep in humus-rich, moist, well-drained soil in partial shade, and they'll sprout as if by magic in spring.

Top Performer

Think Twice: *Anemone nemorosa* (wood anemone): This European native produces short, upright stems, each with a single flower at the tip. Although each star-shaped flower is only 1½ inches (4 cm) wide, the plants slowly form extensive colonies even in deep shade. The dark green, deeply cut foliage contrasts nicely with the flowers.

Wood anemone grows best under deciduous trees and shrubs. In summer, when trees leaf out and cast shade, wood anemone goes dormant. It can also grow in more open areas, although it prefers some protection from full sun. To increase your supply of plants, divide wood anemone after the leaves fade in summer or even when it's in full bloom, as long as you replant it without delay.

The natural form of wood anemone has white flowers, and there are several nice cultivars as well. 'Alba' has single white flowers, whereas 'Flore Plena' (also called 'Alba Plena') has double or semi-double white flowers. 'Lychette' grows 10 to 20 inches (25 to 50 cm) tall and has larger-than-usual, single white flowers.

Blue cultivars include lavender-blue 'Robinsoniana' and deeper lavender-blue 'Allenii'. 'Rosea' is the most common of the pinks. There is confusion about the naming of wood anemone cultivars, so I suggest buying blooming plants of the color you want, without putting too much trust in the label. Height: 6 to 12 inches (15 to 30 cm). Spread: 6 to 8 inches (15 to 20 cm). USDA Plant Hardiness Zones 3 to 9; AHS Heat Zones 8 to 1.

More Recommended Anemones

Think Twice: *Anemone sylvestris* (snowdrop anemone): Snowdrop anemone offers deeply cut, light green leaves and pure white, cup-shaped flowers that are scented and slightly nodding. It's a good companion for spring bulbs because it comes into its own just in time to hide yellowing bulb foliage. The fluffy white seedheads that follow the blooms are an added attraction.

The problem with snowdrop anemone is that it spreads like wildfire in loose soil and moist conditions, so plant it inside a root barrier. Height: 10 to 18 inches (20 to 45 cm). Spread: 1 to 2 feet (30 to 60 cm). USDA Plant Hardiness Zones 4 to 9; AHS Heat Zones 9 to 1.

Wood anemone
(*Anemone nemorosa*)

Kissing Cousins

Common pasque flower (*Pulsatilla vernalis*) is a popular rock garden perennial that's often listed as an anemone (*A. pulsatilla*). Its 2- to 4-inch (5- to 10-cm), urn-shaped flowers, purple with bright yellow centers, have numerous pollen-laden stamens. The pasque flower is cold-hardy to USDA Zone 2 if you mulch it heavily through the winter. Height: 6 to 12 inches (15 to 30 cm). Spread: 10 to 12 inches (25 to 30 cm). USDA Plant Hardiness Zones 3 to 8. AHS Heat Zones 8 to 1.

Arabis

Rock cress

If there's any plant that truly covers itself with bloom, it's rock cress. For weeks at a time, starting in early spring, its foliage completely disappears under a carpet of small, four-petaled, highly perfumed flowers. Afterward it makes a very acceptable foliage plant, with dense evergreen growth usually covering the stems almost to their base.

Plant Profile

ARABIS
AR-uh-biss

- **Bloom Color:** White or pink

- **Bloom Time:** Early spring

- **Length of Bloom:** 3 or 4 weeks

- **Height:** Varies by species; see individual listings

- **Spread:** 12 to 18 inches (30 to 45 cm)

- **Garden Uses:** Container planting, edging, groundcover, mass planting, rock garden, wall planting; along paths, on slopes; attracts butterflies

- **Light Preference:** Full sun or very light shade

- **Soil Preference:** Average to poor soil; needs excellent drainage

- **Best Way to Propagate:** Divide plants in spring; can also be propagated by taking stem cuttings or sowing seeds in spring

- **USDA Plant Hardiness Zones:** Varies by species; see individual listings

- **AHS Heat Zones:** Varies by species; see individual listings

Growing Tips

Rock cresses start out as mounds of foliage, then their stems begin to creep out in all directions and root as they go. They can spread almost without limit under the right conditions. They're not really invasive but may bear watching in the rock garden. In perennial borders, taller plants cast some shade to keep these sun lovers nicely in check.

Poor drainage can be fatal to rock cresses, especially in humid-summer areas. Try tucking a mulch of fine gravel around the base of the plants and anywhere their stems touch the ground: This helps ensure better drainage and aeration under humid conditions.

Rock cresses tend to fall apart after blooming, especially in hot-summer climates, losing most of their leaves to reveal a stringy mass of stems. If this happens, take out your hedge trimmer or string trimmer and chop the plants back to about 6 inches (15 cm) from their base. They will quickly resprout and fill in nicely. And while division is the fast-and-easy way to propagate rock cresses, if you prune your plants, you'll have an endless supply of potential cuttings.

Good Neighbors

In the wild, rock cress grows on rocks and cliffs, so it looks right at home in the rock garden or planted in walls. It needs companions that are adapted to similar conditions, such as sedums, hens-and-chicks (*Sempervivum* spp.), and woolly thyme (*Thymus pseudolanuginosus*). Rock cress is a great low-growing groundcover for sunny, well-drained spots; try it as an edging, too.

Problems and Solutions

Although not particularly susceptible to insects and disease, rock cress is sometimes subject to aphids and downy mildew. For control information, refer to pages 54 and 58.

Top Performer

Arabis caucasica, also called *A. albida* (wall rock cress): Wall rock cress is the most common species for gardens. It's native to the Mediterranean and has succulent, gray-felted leaves.

Most cultivars have single white flowers in early spring. 'Schneeball' (also called 'Snowball') is particularly lush and grows only 4 to 6 inches (10 to 15 cm) tall. 'Flore Plena' (also called 'Plena'), with sterile, double white flowers, is a truly top choice because of its long-lasting flowers. 'Compinkie' is the most common pink form. 'Variegata' has white flowers, with leaves striped with creamy yellow; it looks great even when not in bloom. This cultivar may lose its variegation; if you want to prevent this, pinch out any all-green or all-white stems that appear. Height: 4 to 12 inches (10 to 30 cm). Spread: 12 to 18 inches (30 to 45 cm). USDA Plant Hardiness Zones 3 to 9; AHS Heat Zones 8 to 1.

Variegated wall rock cress (*Arabis caucasica* 'Variegata')

More Recommended Rock Cresses

Arabis blepharophylla (fringed rock cress): A California native, fringed rock cress has red to pink flowers and is less hardy than other species. 'Frühlingszauber' (also called 'Spring Charm'), with slightly fragrant, rosy pink flowers on compact plants, is the most popular cultivar. Height: 4 to 12 inches (10 to 30 cm). Spread: 12 to 18 inches (30 to 45 cm). USDA Plant Hardiness Zones 5 to 9; AHS Heat Zones 8 to 5.

A. ferdinandi-coburgi (Ferdinand's rock cress): This rock cress is similar to wall rock cress but has narrower, greener leaves and a denser habit. It's native to Bulgaria, and the variegated cultivars are the most popular. 'Variegata', perhaps the nicest variegated rock cress, has leaves splashed with white in summer and tinged pink in winter. 'Old Gold' has yellow-and-green variegation. (*A. procurrens,* from southern Europe, is similar to Ferdinand's rock cress, and many experts consider them to be the same plant.) Height: 4 to 6 inches (10 to 15 cm). Spread: 12 to 18 inches (30 to 45 cm). USDA Plant Hardiness Zones 3 to 9; AHS Heat Zones 8 to 3.

Kissing Cousins

The genus *Aubrieta* is so similar to *Arabis* that the two are both called rock cress. Many gardeners can't tell them apart. Most people simply go by color: Both *Arabis* and *Aubrieta* can have white or pink flowers, but only *Aubrieta* has blue, lilac, purple, red, or deep rose ones. *Aubrieta* is somewhat more fickle than *Arabis*—it especially dislikes summer heat and grows best in AHS Heat Zones 5 to 1. Although most *Aubrieta* plants sold are actually hybrids, they're often labeled as *A. deltoidea*.

Aurinia

Basket-of-gold

There's no mistaking the bright yellow flower clusters of basket-of-gold. This low-growing spring bloomer is related to rock cresses (*Arabis* spp. and *Aubrieta* spp.), but while *Arabis* is practically indistinguishable from *Aubrieta*, old-fashioned basket-of-gold is instantly recognizable. Basket-of-gold bears dense clusters of golden flowers and its stems tend to form thick clumps rather than sprawling mats. Basket-of-gold leaves are distinctly silver-gray—the handsome foliage makes basket-of-gold a garden asset all summer, even when it's not in bloom.

Plant Profile

AURINIA
aw-RIN-ee-uh

- ■ **Bloom Color:** Yellow
- ■ **Bloom Time:** Midspring to early summer
- ■ **Length of Bloom:** 4 to 6 weeks
- ■ **Height:** 8 to 12 inches (20 to 30 cm)
- ■ **Spread:** 1 to 2 feet (30 to 60 cm)
- ■ **Garden Uses:** Container planting, edging, groundcover, mass planting, rock garden, wall planting; along paths, on slopes; attracts butterflies
- ■ **Light Preference:** Full sun or light shade
- ■ **Soil Preference:** Average to poor soil; needs excellent drainage
- ■ **Best Way to Propagate:** Divide in fall or take stem cuttings in summer; can also be propagated by sowing seed in spring
- ■ **USDA Plant Hardiness Zones:** 3 to 9
- ■ **AHS Heat Zones:** 8 to 1

Growing Tips

There are two secrets to success when you are growing basket-of-gold: ample sunlight and good drainage. Although it will tolerate light shade in hot-summer climates, basket-of-gold does best in full sun elsewhere. And whether it is placed in full sun or light shade, basket-of-gold simply will not stand having wet feet. If your climate is humid, try placing a ½-inch (1.25-cm) layer of fine gravel at the base of the plant and under its stems to ensure it never sits in dampness.

Basket-of-gold looks best (and lives longer) if you chop it back annually after blooming, even in cool-summer areas. In hot-summer climates, you may need to treat it as a biennial, starting it from seed or cuttings in the summer and planting young plants outdoors in early fall for bloom the following spring. Like many other perennials originating in mountain areas, basket-of-gold often dies back during the heat of summer, but unlike them, it doesn't always come back.

You can grow some cultivars from seed, but fall division or summer stem cuttings are the fastest means of reproducing basket-of-gold—and the only methods of maintaining some of the choice cultivars.

FUN FACTS

Besides changing *Alyssum saxatile* to *Aurinia saxatilis*, taxonomists have also reclassified the popular self-sowing annual sweet alyssum (once known as *Alyssum maritimum*) in a new genus—*Lobularia*—labeling it *Lobularia maritima*.

What's the reason for these changes? The leaf hairs—those tiny hairs that cover plant leaves—just aren't the same. And we couldn't let plants with radically different leaf hairs share the same genus, could we?

Good Neighbors

A rock-garden standard, basket-of-gold thrives in rock crevices or on steep slopes. Combine it with other rock-garden dwellers, preferably those that will take up the slack in the hot weather when basket-of-gold starts to look shabby. Try planting drifts of basket-of-gold in a rock garden, on a slope, or at the top of a retaining wall. These sites provide the excellent drainage this perennial needs. Good neighbor candidates include plants that would enhance rather than compete with the shock of gold flowers: Sedums, thymes, and euphorbias are good choices. Myrtle euphorbia (*Euphorbia myrsinites*) or purple-leaved *E. dulcis* would be interesting choices, as would thrifts (*Armeria* spp.).

'Citrina' basket-of-gold
(*Aurinia saxatilis* 'Citrina')

Problems and Solutions

Basket-of-gold has no major pest or disease problems. In hot weather it may look sick—as if the plant were just collapsing—but this is due to heat stress. The cure is simply to prune the plant back a bit, and it will recover when temperatures cool down.

Top Performer

Aurinia saxatilis (basket-of-gold): *A. saxatilis* is the only *Aurinia* species commonly sold. If the name doesn't ring a bell, you probably know this plant by its old botanical name, *Alyssum saxatile*, which is still on many nursery labels. 'Compacta', perhaps the most common variety, has denser growth than the species, and it usually comes true from seed. 'Citrina', with lemon-yellow bloom, and 'Sunny Border Apricot', with apricot-yellow flowers, are also popular, and their softer colors work into a planting scheme more easily than the almost overbearing yellow of the species. They look great in my garden combined with deep violet and blue rock cresses (*Aubrieta* spp.). 'Dudley Neville Variegated' has apricot-yellow flowers; its leaves have cream-colored margins. To maintain the variegation, prune out any all-green or all-cream stems.

Kissing Cousins

Mountain alyssum (*Alyssum montanum*) is a true perennial *Alyssum* from the mountains of Europe. It's hardier than basket-of-gold, with smaller but still silvery leaves, a shorter, denser habit, and fragrant, bright lemon-yellow flowers from midspring to early summer. Care for it as you would basket-of-gold. 'Mountain Gold' is more compact and blooms more heavily than the species. Height: 6 to 8 inches (15 to 20 cm). Spread: 1 foot (30 cm). USDA Plant Hardiness Zones 2 to 9; AHS Heat Zones 7 to 1.

Iberis

Candytuft

Candytufts derive their name from the sweet perfume of the flowers of the annual species of candytuft (*Iberis amara*). With perennial candytufts, you'll just have to settle for a long blooming season, sparkling white flowers, a drop-dead-gorgeous growth habit, and shiny evergreen foliage! Perennial candytufts form dense, creeping mounds of narrow, dark green leaves that look like they've been dipped in wax. In spring, thousands of four-petaled flowers in terminal clusters cover the plants. The show can last well over two months.

Plant Profile

IBERIS
eye-BEER-iss

- ■ **Bloom Color:** White
- ■ **Bloom Time:** Early spring to early summer
- ■ **Length of Bloom:** 8 weeks or more
- ■ **Height:** Varies by species; see individual listings
- ■ **Spread:** Varies by species; see individual listings
- ■ **Garden Uses:** Container planting, cut flower garden, edging, groundcover, mass planting, rock garden, wall planting; along paths, on slopes; attracts butterflies
- ■ **Light Preference:** Full sun to partial shade
- ■ **Soil Preference:** Average, well-drained soil
- ■ **Best Way to Propagate:** Sow seed or divide in spring or fall; take stem cuttings in spring or summer
- ■ **USDA Plant Hardiness Zones:** Varies by species; see individual listings
- ■ **AHS Heat Zones:** Varies by species; see individual listings

Growing Tips

Candytufts are easy to grow in any well-drained soil. The plants will bloom in partial shade, but full sun is best for abundant flowering. Although very hardy, candytufts can suffer if exposed directly to icy winds, so a winter mulch of evergreen branches is wise in cold-winter areas without dependable snow cover. If your plants suffer winter damage, trim off the dead branches and they will likely sprout anew.

To keep candytufts compact, don't hesitate to prune them back every year or two in spring; otherwise, they'll eventually become quite bare in the middle. If you're in the habit of pruning your perennials back in the fall, don't touch these: Fall pruning won't kill the plants, but it will eliminate spring bloom. Shearing the plants after they bloom will promote growth of fresh foliage.

Candytuft cultivars don't come true from seed (although the plants produced from seed are usually nice-looking enough). If you want to propagate specific cultivars, you'll have to divide or take stem cuttings.

Good Neighbors

Candytufts look great all year long, forming a spic-and-span edging around a flower garden or draping beautifully over rock gardens and walls. Try them with a combination of other low-growing perennials, such as wall rock cress (*Arabis caucasica*), basket-of-gold (*Aurinia saxatilis*), Cheddar pink (*Dianthus gratianopolitanus*), and hens-and-chicks (*Sempervivum* spp.).

Problems and Solutions

Besides a bit of mulch to prevent winter damage, candytufts need little special attention. They are sometimes subject to a disease called clubroot, which causes stunted growth. To help prevent this, never plant candytufts where you've been growing any cabbage relative (including broccoli, brussels sprouts, cauliflower, and kohlrabi) for the last four years.

Top Performer

Iberis sempervirens (evergreen candytuft, edging candytuft): This is the old-fashioned favorite most

Evergreen candytuft
(*Iberis sempervirens*)

perennial gardeners know and grow. There are many cultivars, all with glistening white flowers in early spring or midspring to early summer. Some may take on a pinkish tinge as they fade, especially in cooler climates. Evergreen candytuft has always tended to rebloom in the fall, and some cultivars faithfully bloom a second time, although not as heavily as in spring nor over as long a time. But who can complain about four weeks of fall flowers?

I should mention, though, that reblooming candytufts often form less dense plants and are less tolerant of summer heat, tending to succumb to crown rot. 'Autumn Snow' is one that I find reblooms reliably, with snow-white flowers that are larger than most. 'Weisser Zwerg' (also called 'Little Gem') is the daintiest of the dwarf types, forming tidy mounds to 8 inches (20 cm) tall. 'Snowflake' is one of the most common cultivars, with larger flowers in larger clusters over a long period of time. In my garden, it blooms sporadically throughout the summer and fall. Height: 5 to 12 inches (13 to 30 cm). Spread: 1 to 3 feet (30 to 90 cm). USDA Plant Hardiness Zones 3 to 9; AHS Heat Zones 9 to 5.

More Recommended Candytufts

Iberis saxatilis (rock candytuft): Rock candytuft is a particularly compact plant that forms mounds of small evergreen leaves and masses of flowers from midspring to early summer. The white blooms turn pinkish as they age. Rock candytuft is very much like evergreen candytuft, although better adapted to cold weather. Height: 3 to 6 inches (8 to 15 cm). Spread: 6 to 36 inches (15 to 90 cm). USDA Plant Hardiness Zones 2 to 9; AHS Heat Zones 9 to 1.

Larry's Garden Notes

Don't hesitate to try evergreen candytuft (*Iberis sempervirens*) as a cut flower. Sure, the stems are shorter than many traditional cut flowers, but it makes a nice little posy bouquet. And it can last for weeks to boot! The numerous tiny blooms and creeping stems provide an attractive contrast to other spring cut flowers, such as tulips, which are heavier, denser, and more upright. By harvesting stems for cut flowers, you'll also be pruning back the plant, which will prevent it from getting too scraggly.

Iris

Iris, flag

It would take an entire book to cover all the irises, so I've selected two of the best and most popular ones to describe here: bearded irises (*Iris* bearded hybrids) and crested iris (*I. cristata*). The extremely wide color range of irises is reflected in their name: Iris is the Greek goddess of the rainbow. For other irises, see page 284.

Plant Profile

IRIS
EYE-ris

- **Bloom Color:** Blue, bronze, orange, pink, purple, white, and yellow

- **Bloom Time:** Late spring to early summer

- **Length of Bloom:** 2 weeks

- **Height:** Varies by species; see individual listings

- **Spread:** Varies by species; see individual listings

- **Garden Uses:** Cut flower garden, mixed border, rock garden, specimen plant, woodland garden; at the back of beds and borders

- **Light Preference:** Varies by species; see individual listings

- **Soil Preference:** Humus-rich, well-drained soil

- **Best Way to Propagate:** Divide in early spring or after flowering

- **USDA Plant Hardiness Zones:** Varies by species; see individual listings

- **AHS Heat Zones:** Varies by species; see individual listings

Growing Tips

Bearded and crested irises prefer well-drained soil of just about any type, although taller irises tend to flop over in excessively rich soils. These irises are highly subject to rot if grown under wet conditions. Bearded iris thrives in full sun, while crested iris prefer partial shade.

Bearded and crested irises both grow from a horizontal rhizome—a sort of fattened, creeping stem with leaves at one end and roots underneath. Each year new rhizomes form at the tip of those from the previous year; eventually the old rhizomes die.

Though generations of iris lovers insist you can divide them only after they bloom in late summer or early fall, you can also divide them in early spring, while they're still dormant. Cut back any leafy growth by half, then carefully dig up the rhizomes and discard any with obvious signs of insects or disease. Separate the clumps into segments, each with a fan of healthy leaves, and replant the divisions. In sandy or loamy soil, just barely cover the rhizomes; in heavy clay soil, leave their surfaces partially exposed. Space the rhizomes about 1 foot (30 cm) apart, with their fans pointing *away* from the center of the clump so they spread outward.

Good Neighbors

The dramatic bearded irises don't need to share the spotlight with anything else, so use them as focal points of the spring and early summer garden. Carry on the show with later-blooming companions such as *Geranium* 'Johnson's Blue', Russian sage (*Perovskia atriplicifolia*), and moss phlox (*Phlox subulata*) for a full season of interest.

Crested iris looks best along a wooded path with other shade lovers, such as wild columbine (*Aquilegia canadensis*), fringed bleeding heart (*Dicentra eximia*), and Christmas fern (*Polystichum acrostichoides*).

Problems and Solutions

Other than crown rot, crested irises aren't subject to pests and diseases, other than occasional slug damage. On bearded irises, also watch out for iris borer (particularly east of the Rockies) and soft rot: Both damage the rhizomes. Remove all foliage in the fall and yellowed leaves during the growing season to control both problems.

Top Performer

Iris Bearded Hybrids (bearded iris): All irises bear complex flowers made up of three standards (petals), usually upright in the center of the flower, and ringed by three falls (petal-like structures called sepals), extending outward. The standards and falls can be the same or different colors. Bearded irises get their name from the fuzzy "beard" at the base of their falls.

Bearded irises are classified according to height (and bloom since shorter irises tend to bloom earlier). The main categories include:

- Miniature dwarf bearded irises: 4 to 10 inches (10 to 25 cm)
- Standard dwarf bearded irises: 10 to 15 inches (25 to 38 cm)
- Intermediate bearded irises: 15 to 28 inches (38 to 71 cm)
- Border bearded irises: 16 to 27 inches (40 to 68 cm)
- Tall bearded irises: over 28 inches (71 cm)

Border bearded irises are similar in flower and blooming period to tall beardeds; they make a very nice alternative because they don't need staking and have better insect and disease resistance. Height: 4 to 40 inches (10 to 100 cm). Spread: 10 to 24 inches (25 to 60 cm). USDA Plant Hardiness Zones 3 to 10; AHS Heat Zones 9 to 1.

More Recommended Irises

Iris cristata (crested iris): In early to midspring, this species has small, blue flowers, each bearing a yellow "crest" at the base of the falls. Crested iris prefers partial shade with some sun each day; good drainage is a must. You can also find crested iris cultivars with white or purple flowers. Height: 3 to 10 inches (8 to 25 cm). Spread: 12 to 15 inches (30 to 38 cm). USDA Plant Hardiness Zones 4 to 9; AHS Heat Zones 10 to 1.

Iris Bearded Hybrid

Larry's Garden Notes

Generations of gardeners have neatly trimmed back the sword-shaped foliage of their irises after blooming, cutting the leaves at right angles about 6 inches (15 cm) from the rhizome to create a flat-topped fan. The whys and wherefores have been lost in the mists of time (ask someone who does it, and he will probably say it helps to control disease or insects as often as he will say it helps the plant grow better). All you have to know is that you *don't* have to do this! In fact, the longer the leaf, the more the iris can store up energy for next year's blooming.

Papaver

Poppy

If you're looking for vibrant choices for spring color, turn to oriental poppies (*Papaver orientale*). Oriental poppies have crepe-paper-like flowers with dark, shiny black splotches at their base, plus black stamens in the center of the flower. There's a vast array of cultivars, and for every pastel pink or white cultivar, you'll find half-a-dozen fire-engine reds or shocking oranges to choose from.

Plant Profile

PAPAVER
pa-PAH-ver

- ■ **Bloom Color:** Orange, pink, red, or white
- ■ **Bloom Time:** Late spring to early summer
- ■ **Length of Bloom:** 2 weeks
- ■ **Height:** 18 to 48 inches (45 to 120 cm)
- ■ **Spread:** 2 feet (60 cm)
- ■ **Garden Uses:** Cut flower garden, mixed border, specimen plant; at the back of beds and borders
- ■ **Light Preference:** Full sun or partial shade
- ■ **Soil Preference:** Moderately rich, well-drained soil
- ■ **Best Way to Propagate:** Sow seed in spring; can also be propagated by taking root cuttings or dividing plants in midsummer to late summer
- ■ **USDA Plant Hardiness Zones:** 2 to 9
- ■ **AHS Heat Zones:** 9 to 1

Growing Tips

Oriental poppies are not plants for the Deep South. It's not that the heat gets to them—they're dormant in the summer. Rather, oriental poppies need a period of winter chill at 40°F (4°C) or colder to do well; otherwise they just die out.

Although their hairy flowerstalks look very sturdy, oriental poppies often flop over under the weight of their huge flowers, especially after a heavy rain. Planting them in full sun helps prevent flopping, but your best bet is to choose short-stemmed cultivars with modest-sized blooms. Of course, you *can* stake oriental poppies but it's hard to do unobtrusively.

If your poppies keel over, bring them indoors as cut flowers. They can last more than a week if you plunge the cut ends into boiling water for 30 seconds to stop their milky sap from gumming up the stem.

Several oriental poppy cultivars come true from seed, so starting seeds yourself is an inexpensive way to get lots of poppies with moderately little effort. Sow the seed directly in your garden in spring or indoors in peat pots in late winter, and do not cover the seed. Oriental poppy seed germinates best at cool temperatures, around 55°F (13°C). You can also carefully dig and move self-sown seedlings, but only when they're very young; poppies don't like to be transplanted once their long taproot has formed.

To propagate cultivars that don't come true from seed, make divisions in late summer when plants are dormant, or take 3- to 4-inch (8- to 10-cm) root cuttings. Since oriental poppies resent disturbance, wait until the plants are overcrowded, after four to six years, then dig them up carefully for division.

Another easy way to multiply oriental poppies is simply to move them: You'll inevitably leave a few broken roots behind as you dig them up, and these root fragments will produce new plants with no encouragement from you.

Good Neighbors

Striking in bloom but unattractive shortly afterward, oriental poppies combine best with later-blooming plants that will fill the space as the season progresses. Boltonia (*Boltonia asteroides*), common baby's-breath (*Gypsophila paniculata*), and Russian sage (*Perovskia atriplicifolia*) are all good candidates. While in bloom, bright orange-red poppies make striking contrasts to the deep purples of delphiniums, Siberian iris (*Iris sibirica*), or 'Mainacht' salvia (*Salvia* × *sylvestris* 'Mainacht', also called 'May Night'). Add gray-green 'Powis Castle' artemisia (*Artemisia* 'Powis Castle') to temper the mix.

Problems and Solutions

Oriental poppy is not particularly subject to pests and diseases and is often drought- and heat-resistant.

Top Performer

Papaver orientale (oriental poppy): Oriental poppy is by far the largest of the better-known poppies, with huge crepe-paper-textured flowers that are 4 to 6 inches (10 to 25 cm) across on the smallest cultivars and up to a whopping 11 inches (28 cm) in diameter on some of the largest. Oriental poppies produce sharply pointed, hairy leaves and although the leaves look quite prickly, they're actually soft to the touch. The leaves fade away in midsummer, then sprout anew in the fall, last all winter, and grow again the following spring.

There are well over 100 cultivars of oriental poppy on the market, although you'd be lucky to find more than half a dozen in any one nursery. There are lots of color choices as well as cultivars with fringed petals, bicolor flowers, and double flowers.

I've noted just a few cultivars that do well in my garden (i.e., that don't tend to flop over). All of these cultivars are about 2 feet (60 cm) tall, except as noted.

'Allegro' is a very compact poppy, only 18 to 20 inches (45 to 50 cm) tall, with huge scarlet flowers with black splotches; it's available from seed. 'Brilliant' has fiery red flowers. 'Perry's White' has white petals with a black center and blotches.

Pizzicato hybrids are seed-grown strains in striking mixed colors (including orange, pink, red, salmon, and white) with dark blotches on the petals; its 20-inch (50-cm) stems are sturdy and wind-resistant. The dark-centered scarlet blooms of 'Turkenlouis' (also called 'Turkish Delight') offer exotically fringed petals.

Oriental poppy
(*Papaver orientale*)

Larry's Garden Notes

Bees don't see the dark splotches at the base of oriental poppy flowers as being black. Instead they see brilliant ultraviolet, a color that they particularly love but that our eyes can't see at all. Bees hone straight in to the center of the flower where the "black" is and ignore the brilliant red flowers we find so striking.

Phlox

Phlox

Think of phlox, and you may picture beautiful sweeps of tall garden phlox (*Phlox paniculata*). But instead, imagine a low-growing carpet of foliage covered with lovely five-petaled flowers. Spring-blooming phlox are creepers, not tall border plants. Some are ground huggers that form dense, trailing mats, molding themselves over and around rocks and other obstacles. Taller species have stems that trail at the base yet are distinctly upright at the tips. Phlox foliage also varies by species, from pointed and needlelike to broad and rounded.

Plant Profile

PHLOX
FLOCKS

- **Bloom Color:** Lavender-blue, lilac, mauve, pink, purple, red, and white

- **Bloom Time:** Varies by species; see individual listings

- **Length of Bloom:** 2 or 3 weeks

- **Height:** 6 to 15 inches (15 to 38 cm)

- **Spread:** Varies by species; see individual listings

- **Garden Uses:** Container planting, edging, groundcover, mass planting

- **Light Preference:** Varies by species; see individual listings

- **Soil Preference:** Average, very well drained, slightly acid to alkaline soil

- **Best Way to Propagate:** Divide or layer plants in early summer; can also be propagated by taking cuttings in late fall

- **USDA Plant Hardiness Zones:** 2 to 9

- **AHS Heat Zones:** 8 to 1

Growing Tips

Spring-flowering phlox need perfect drainage. Otherwise, they may suffer from rot in cold, wet weather. These shallow-rooted plants may require summer watering as well, especially in full-sun sites. Because the stems root where they touch the soil, it's easy to multiply creeping phlox: Just dig up rooted sections as needed.

Shearing spring-blooming phlox back after bloom helps keep them full. After a few years, the centers may die out: Dig the clumps and divide them, or cut out the dead sections and add fresh soil.

Good Neighbors

Moss phlox (*Phlox subulata*) tolerates very sandy soil and looks great planted on sunny slopes. Plant it around yuccas for contrast.

Woodland phlox (*P. divaricata*) and creeping phlox (*P. stolonifera*) are nice choices for shade gardens. Combine them with other native plants, such as Virginia bluebells (*Mertensia virginica*), Solomon's seals (*Polygonatum* spp.), trilliums, and violets. Use the red flowers of wild columbine (*Aquilegia canadensis*) for an interesting contrast.

Problems and Solutions

Spider mites can damage phlox foliage, especially in hot, dry weather; spray plants regularly with water. Downy mildew can be a problem, notably with moss phlox (*P. subulata*); plant phlox in a sunny, well-drained site, and shear plants back occasionally.

Top Performer

Phlox subulata (moss phlox, moss pink, ground pink): Moss phlox are covered with blooms in spring, with some rebloom in other seasons.

After the flowers fade, you'll see dense mats of shiny, prickly, needle-like leaves on semi-woody stems. In warm areas, the foliage is evergreen and in colder areas, it's semievergreen. Here are a few of the many cultivars you'll find in large garden centers and nurseries: 'Blue Emerald', lilac-blue; 'Maiden's Blush', pink with a red eye; 'Ronsdorfer Schöne' ('Beauty of Ronsdorf'), rosy red and compact; 'Snowflake', white and compact; and 'Tamanonagalei' (also called 'Candy Stripe'), rose-pink edged in white. Height: 6 to 9 inches (15 to 23 cm). Spread: 1 to 3 feet (30 to 90 cm). USDA Plant Hardiness Zones 2 to 9; AHS Heat Zones 8 to 1.

Moss phlox (*Phlox subulata*)

More Recommended Phlox

Phlox divaricata (woodland phlox, wild blue phlox, wild sweet William): This phlox prefers shady conditions, especially in summer; plants may bloom more heavily with direct morning sun. Woodland phlox looks nothing like moss phlox (*P. subulata*), as it has distinctly broad, dark green leaves. The scented, midspring-to-early-summer flowers are similar to moss phlox flowers, with the same notches at the petal tips, but woodland phlox flowers have narrower petals.

Woodland phlox produces two different types of stems: non-blooming ones that creep and root as they grow and blooming stems that grow upright. Lavender-blue is the main flower color, although there are white and pink selections. 'Dirigo Ice', with pale blue flowers on compact plants, and 'Fuller's White', with a heavy spring flush of pure white blooms, are two common cultivars. Height: 8 to 15 inches (20 to 38 cm). Spread: indefinite. USDA Plant Hardiness Zones 3 to 9; AHS Heat Zones 8 to 1.

P. stolonifera (creeping phlox): The most shade-tolerant of the phlox, this species nevertheless prefers partial shade over full shade. Creeping phlox is upright, dense, and mounding in habit.

'Blue Ridge', with light blue flowers, and 'Sherwood Purple', with fragrant, purple-blue blooms, are two popular cultivars. Height: 6 to 12 inches (15 to 30 cm). Spread: indefinite. USDA Plant Hardiness Zones 2 to 9; AHS Heat Zones 8 to 1.

Larry's Garden Notes

Although creeping phlox are widely used in rock gardens, few gardeners seem to realize their potential as groundcovers. True, they won't stand much foot traffic (and, in fact, you wouldn't want to walk barefoot through the prickly foliage of moss phlox!), but otherwise they're perfect subjects where a low growing carpeting plant is required. Just plant them in appropriate conditions (well-drained soil and partial shade) 10 to 12 inches (25 to 30 cm) apart, and they'll quickly fill in. I like to run the lawn mower over mine once each spring, just after bloom, to thicken up the plants.

Primula

Primrose

It's no wonder primroses are inseparable from spring in our minds. Not only are they among the first perennials to bloom—some even flower in late winter—but their very name implies earliness: *Primula* derives from the Latin word for "early." Most primroses produce a ground-hugging rosette of greenery, and their rounded flowers have five petals each. Their leaves range from thick, smooth, and waxy to narrow, hairy, and toothed. Some species bear one flower per stem while others have dome-shaped or rounded clusters of flowers on each stem.

Plant Profile

PRIMULA
PRIM-you-luh

- **Bloom Color:** Almost any color

- **Bloom Time:** Varies by species; see individual listings

- **Length of Bloom:** 3 or 4 weeks or more

- **Height:** Varies by species; see individual listings

- **Spread:** Varies by species; see individual listings

- **Garden Uses:** Container planting, edging, mass planting, rock garden, wall planting, woodland garden; along paths, on slopes, in wet areas

- **Light Preference:** Partial shade (full sun in cool climates)

- **Soil Preference:** Humus-rich, moist but well-drained soil

- **Best Way to Propagate:** Divide in early summer, after flowering

- **USDA Plant Hardiness Zones:** Varies by species; see individual listings

- **AHS Heat Zones:** Varies by species; see individual listings

Growing Tips

Primroses have common cultural needs, namely moist soil and cool growing conditions. They thrive in full sun in cool-summer areas but usually need partial shade elsewhere. And while they generally need moist soil, most also require good drainage. The main exceptions are Japanese primrose (*Primula japonica*) and, to a lesser degree, drumstick primrose (*P. denticulata*): Both will do well in almost waterlogged soil. Although cold-hardiness varies from plant to plant, a winter mulch is wise almost everywhere to help primroses survive the winter. Gardeners in AHS Heat Zones 12 to 9 have trouble growing many primroses, not because of heat but because the plants need winter chill.

Division is the ideal way to propagate primroses and the only way to maintain specific cultivars. You can also grow primroses from seed, but their need for temperatures between 40° and 50°F (4° to 10°C) during the long period between sowing and the first blooms makes starting plants indoors impractical for most of us.

Good Neighbors

Suitable primrose companions for a moist, partly shaded spot include astilbes, ferns, hostas, Japanese iris (*Iris ensata*), forget-me-nots (*Myosotis* spp.), and pulmonarias. Drumstick primrose (*P. denticulata*) and Japanese primrose (*P. japonica*) are suitable for wetland plantings; try them with marsh marigold (*Caltha palustris*), yellow flag (*Iris pseudacorus*), and cardinal flower (*Lobelia cardinalis*).

Problems and Solutions

Spider mites can be a real plague, especially if you grow primroses in full sun in a hot climate. Infested plants have yellowing stippling on the leaves, and in serious cases, leaves turn brown. To keep spider mites in check, spray plants regularly with water.

Top Performer

Primula × *polyantha* (polyantha primrose): Once upon a time, there were individual wild species of European primroses, such as the fragrant, deep yellow cowslip (*P. veris*) and the lemon-yellow English primrose (*P. vulgaris*). Today, though, these and other primrose species sold commercially are probably all hybrids, and I prefer to lump them together under name *P.* × *polyantha*. This varied group shares wrinkled, tongue-shaped leaves and stemless or stemmed flowers, borne either singly or in clumps. They bloom abundantly in early to late spring and sometimes again, much more lightly, in the fall. Most gardeners grow unnamed plants from popular seed strains such as Pacific Giant Hybrids, with large flowers in the full range of colors, and Cowichan Hybrids, in solid colors (no yellow eye) and with reddish leaves. Height: 6 to 12 inches (15 to 30 cm). Spread: 8 to 9 inches (20 to 23 cm). USDA Plant Hardiness Zones 3 to 9; AHS Heat Zones 8 to 6.

Warm-climate gardeners can either try the polyantha primroses (*P.* × *polyantha*) to see if they'll survive the heat, or treat primroses as annuals, planting them in the fall each year for winter or spring bloom.

More Recommended Primroses

Primula denticulata (drumstick primrose): With drumstick primrose, the name says it all: These plants produce a ball of small blue, lilac, pink, or white flowers on a thick, upright stem. The spoon-shaped leaves emerge at the same time as the flowers (in late winter to early spring) and eventually reach 1 foot (30 cm) long. This species grows well from seed, often producing plants that are variable in color. 'Alba', with white flowers, usually reproduces true. Height: 8 to 12 inches (20 to 30 cm). Spread: 8 to 10 inches (20 to 25 cm). USDA Plant Hardiness Zones 3 to 9; AHS Heat Zones 8 to 1.

    P. japonica (Japanese primrose): Think of this as a late-blooming, giant version of drumstick primrose. It comes in a similar color range, but instead of just one ball of flowers per stem, it produces a series of open clusters, one atop the other. In areas where snow cover is abundant, Japanese primrose will grow as far north as USDA Zone 3, well beyond its usual limit. Height: 12 to 30 inches (30 to 75 cm). Spread: 12 to 30 inches (30 to 75 cm). USDA Plant Hardiness Zones 5 to 9; AHS Heat Zones 8 to 1.

Larry's Last Look: Spring Bloomers

There are a lot of other spring bloomers that are worth a peek even though I wasn't able to cover them in the previous pages. With flowers and leaves that burst with color, these early bloomers can rejuvenate the dormant garden and reinvigorate the soul. And don't just plant one or two of these and leave it at that—plant a whole gardenful for a spring full of bloom!

COMMON AND BOTANICAL NAME	ZONES AND EXPOSURES	BLOOM COLOR AND TIME	DESCRIPTION
Meadow anemone *Anemone canadensis,* also called *A. pennsylvanica*	Hardiness Zones 2–9 Heat Zones 8–1 Partial shade	White flowers in midspring to early summer	Cup-shaped flowers and deeply cut, light green leaves. Likes moist growing conditions and does not go dormant in summer. Makes a great groundcover for partially shaded areas and wet areas but can be highly invasive. Makes a good companion for spring bulbs. Height: 1–2 feet (30–60 cm). Spread: indefinite.
Stinking iris *Iris foetidissima*	Hardiness Zones 6–9 Heat Zones 9–5 Shade	Purple flowers in early summer	Grown for its colorful seedpods that split open in fall to reveal rows of brilliant scarlet seeds. Leaves are evergreen. Some cultivars have yellow flowers and variegated leaves. Height: 18–24 inches (45–60 cm). Spread: 18 inches (45 cm).
Sweet iris *Iris pallida*	Hardiness Zones 4–9 Heat Zones 9–1 Sun to partial shade	Lavender-blue flowers in late spring to early summer	Fragrant, large-flowered iris with flat fans of swordlike leaves. Resistant to insects and disease. Rhizomes used to make orris, a fixative for perfumes and potpourri. Height: 24–36 inches (60–90 cm). Spread: 24 inches (60 cm).
Roof iris *Iris tectorum*	Hardiness Zones 4–9 Heat Zones 9–3 Partial shade to full sun	Violet-blue flowers in early summer	Large-flowered iris with wide, glossy foliage. Long ago it was planted along the peak of thatched roofs, where its thick rhizomes swelled up to prevent water from entering. Height: 12–18 inches (30–45 cm). Spread: 18 inches (45 cm).
'Spring Delight' phlox *Phlox* 'Spring Delight'	Hardiness Zones 3–9 Heat Zones 8–1 Partial shade	Rose-pink flowers in late spring to early summer	Vigorous, upright plant with broad leaves and clusters of flowers. Makes a great cut flower. Height: 15–20 inches (38–50 cm). Spread: 1 foot (30 cm).
Variegated creeping phlox *Phlox × procumbens* 'Variegata'	Hardiness Zones 3–9 Heat Zones 8–1 Sun to light shade	Mauve-pink flowers in mid-spring to late spring	The flowers are a pretty pink color, but no one grows it for its flowers. Instead, check out the foliage. It's beautifully striped in white and is the plant's main claim to fame. Open growth habit. Height: 9–12 inches (23–30 cm). Spread: 1 foot (30 cm).

COMMON AND BOTANICAL NAME	ZONES AND EXPOSURES	BLOOM COLOR AND TIME	DESCRIPTION
Auricula primrose *Primula auricula*	Hardiness Zones 2–9 Heat Zones 8–1 Partial shade	Flowers with a wide color range bloom in early to late spring	Rosettes of thick evergreen leaves with clusters of highly fragrant flowers, often with a cream or yellow eye. Good for cold-climate gardens and more drought-resistant than some primroses. Prefers neutral or somewhat alkaline soil. Height: 4–8 inches (10–29 cm). Spread: 6–8 inches (15–20 cm).
Siebold primrose *Primula sieboldii*	Hardiness Zones 4–9 Heat Zones 8–1 Partial shade	Purple, white, pink, or rose flowers in late spring to early summer	Low rosettes of downy, heart-shaped leaves topped off by large clusters of flowers, both deeply scalloped along the edges. Likes moist conditions in spring but goes dormant in the summer in many climates. Tolerates full sun if soil remains moist at all times. Height: 4–9 inches (10–23 cm). Spread: 6–8 inches (15–20 cm).
Cowslip *Primula veris*	Hardiness Zones 3–8 Heat Zones 8–1 Partial shade	Yellow flowers in early spring to midspring	This is an old-fashioned cottage garden perennial with nodding, fragrant, tubular flowers. Very delicate, with elongated oval leaves. Height and spread: 10 inches (25 cm).
Vial's primrose *Primula vialii*	Hardiness Zones 4–9 Heat Zones 8–3 Partial shade	Violet flowers fading to pink flowers in late spring to mid-summer	Unusual spike-flowered primrose that thrives in bright, cool woodlands where it often reseeds. The flowers open slowly from the bottom of the spike to the top. Height: 1–2 feet (30–60 cm). Spread: 8–12 inches (20–30 cm).

'Variegata' sweet iris
(*Iris pallida* 'Variegata')

Siebold primrose
(*Primula sieboldii*)

Summer-Blooming
PERENNIALS

After the mad spring rush to clean up the garden, sow seeds, plant new perennials, and divide overgrown plants, it's nice to have a bit of a midterm break. For most gardeners, summer coincides with hot, often humid weather that makes working in the garden an uncomfortable effort, if not an out-and-out pain. Personally, I prefer to sit in the shade with a cold drink during the summer heat and just watch my garden grow. Of course, it *is* a major help that many perennials collaborate with our anticipated summer rest by blooming their heads off at this time of the year. In fact, so many perennials are summer bloomers that the term "summer-blooming perennials" can seem redundant.

◄The rich blues and purples of belladonna delphinium (*Delphinium* x *belladonna*) really stand up to the strong light of summer.

Easy-Care Summer Gardens

With the major exception of watering, there's not terribly much to do in the summer garden. And if watering has become more of a chore than you'd like, it may be time to install some automatic drip irrigation. (I explain how on page 52.)

Summer maintenance for perennials involves a bit of deadheading (sometimes too much for my taste), some staking, and a little pruning. I try to take care of these duties in the cooler morning hours; the garden always seems more peaceful then anyway.

It's nice to know that weeds, which are so aggressive in spring and early summer, slow down and stop growing (or at least spread less quickly) when the heat sets in. As long as you've mulched carefully in the spring and pulled any young weeds as they appeared, you won't need to toil over weeding perennial gardens during the summer. In fact, at my house, the major gardening occupation during the hot months is making beautiful bouquets from all those summer-blooming flowers.

Midsummer Meltdown

In a perfect world, all summer-blooming perennials would bloom nonstop from early to late summer. But in reality, most gardens have a distinct downtime between midsummer and late summer, a period when there's a lot more greenery than flowers in the flower beds. I call this doldrum period midsummer meltdown.

Why does it happen? There's a combination of factors. Flowers don't last as long in hot conditions as they do in cooler weather.

Get maximum impact from a large planting of snowy white 'Mt. Fuji' garden phlox (*Phlox paniculata* 'Mt. Fuji'). This summer-blooming perennial will last through the hot days of midsummer and may bloom well into fall if sheared back after the first blooms fade.

So even though your plants may still be producing flowers, the blossoms don't have much staying power.

Heat also takes its toll on the flowers that do remain on plants. They may be smaller, with floppy petals that make your garden look tired. Plus, in midsummer, many perennials flop over and need to be trimmed back. Of course, they'll soon be back in bloom, but until they are, your gardens can look awkward, full of bare stems rising out of what was once a sea of flowers.

Powdery mildew can run rampant in midsummer, particularly in hot, humid climates; it turns the foliage of susceptible plants moldy gray. The only solution is to cut the plants back.

If midsummer meltdown hits your garden, you may wonder why you worked so hard in the spring. A midsummer border full of floppy, mildew-ridden, flowerless perennials can look quite alarming. Remember, it's only temporary!

How to Prevent Meltdown

If you plan your garden right, you can minimize midsummer meltdown. Maybe you can't beat it entirely, but you *can* make it less painful.

The secrets for success are including a wide variety of perennials in your borders, cutting plants back after bloom to promote reflowering, and tucking in some annuals to add season-long interest.

Mix It Up

Successful summer gardening starts at the planning stage, and the key is including a variety of perennials. If you base your garden on two or three plants, and one suffers during hot spells, all is lost. But if you plant 20 different types of perennials, there are bound to be several in bloom to take your mind off those that aren't.

Plant plenty of perennials that bloom in midsummer as well as several everbloomers (see "Everblooming Perennials" on page 68). Also investigate improved cultivars. Each year, nurseries carry new cultivars with sturdier stems or a dwarf habit that are less prone to flop over in the heat. And disease-resistant cultivars can make powdery mildew a thing of the past. Sure, it's wonderful to grow the old bee balm that Grandma loved in that hidden back corner. But in the front yard or anywhere that appearance counts, replace it with a no-nonsense modern cultivar that neither flops nor turns powdery gray at the drop of a pin.

Do Some Sensible Shearing

It's hard to take shears to your plants during the growing season, but the benefits are worth it. Shearing stimulates the growth of fresh foliage and may give more flowers. Bee balm, delphiniums, and phlox especially benefit from this treatment. Check the "Growing Tips" in each entry to learn which perennials take a midseason shearing.

Add a Dash of Annual Color

Include some annuals such as cosmos and zinnias in the garden. Even in a classic perennial border, a patch of annuals won't detract when the rest of the garden is flowering, and it will help if the perennials get the midsummer blues.

More Summertime Tricks

Sometimes your garden doesn't seem at its best in summer, even if it's not in the grip of meltdown. Try these techniques for more gusto.

Check Your Color Combos

If your garden looks pale in summer, check your color scheme. You may need to add more "heat" to your color palette. Pastel shades that look great in spring and fall may be washed out in the harsh light of summer. But rich colors like royal blue, magenta, and deep purple all stand up to strong light, and showy colors like red, orange, and yellow really shine under the bright sun.

Try a Foliar Feed

A midsummer nutrient boost can also liven up tired borders. Give your perennials a shot of foliar fertilizer; the extra nutrients will perk some plants right up.

Take a Pinch Here and There

To extend the early summer bloom show into midsummer, trick your early summer bloomers into delaying their flowering period. Pinch back every second delphinium, for example, just as it starts to shoot up in spring. The plant will bloom with a two- to three-week delay, filling the midsummer flower gap. This technique may result in more flowerstalks than normal.

Postpone Your Garden Parties

Take my advice. If you live in a climate renowned for its summer "dog days," don't invite anyone, least of all the garden club, to your home in midsummer. Even if you've worked on creating plantings that look better in midsummer each year, your garden still won't be at its best. Plus, it's too hot to enjoy being outside. The best times for garden parties are spring, early summer, and early fall, when temperatures are moderate and your garden looks fresh and overflowing with bloom.

18 More Summer Bloomers

There's a dazzling choice of perennials that bloom sometime between the end of spring and the beginning of the fall blooming season (which actually starts a full month before fall officially begins). Here's a heaping handful of other great summer bloomers for your garden.

Achillea (Yarrow) 72	*Kniphofia* (Torch lily) .466
Campanula (Bellflower) 74	*Liatris* (Gayfeather) . .230
Coreopsis (Coreopsis) 78	*Monarda* (Bee balm) .470
	Nepeta (Catmint) 90
Dianthus (Pink) 82	*Rudbeckia* (Rudbeckia) 94
Digitalis (Foxglove) . .224	
Echinacea (Purple coneflower) . .458	*Salvia* (Salvia) 96
	Scabiosa (Pincushion flower) . . .98
Geranium (Hardy geranium) . . .228	*Sedum* (Sedum) 182
Gypsophila (Baby's-breath) 86	*Verbena* (Verbena) . .102
	Veronica (Veronica) . .104

Anthemis

Chamomile, marguerite

Chamomiles have delightful daisylike flowers, which is why they're also called marguerites: Marguerite is the French word for daisy. Chamomile flowers have a yellow center surrounded by orange, yellow, or white petals. The foliage is deeply cut and fernlike, often emitting a medicinal scent when crushed. The plants have either an upright or a mounding habit.

Plant Profile

ANTHEMIS
AN-them-iss

- **Bloom Color:** Orange, white, or yellow

- **Bloom Time:** Early summer to early fall

- **Length of Bloom:** 10 to 12 weeks

- **Height:** Varies by species; see individual listings

- **Spread:** 12 to 24 inches (30 to 60 cm)

- **Garden Uses:** Container planting, cut flower garden, edging, mass planting, meadow garden, mixed border, rock garden, wall planting; attracts butterflies

- **Light Preference:** Full sun or partial shade

- **Soil Preference:** Average, well-drained, somewhat alkaline soil

- **Best Way to Propagate:** Sow seed in spring; for named cultivars, divide or take stem cuttings in spring

- **USDA Plant Hardiness Zones:** 3 to 9

- **AHS Heat Zones:** Varies by species; see individual listings

Growing Tips

Chamomiles are easy-to-grow perennials but are rather short-lived. Divide them at least every two or three years, or let them go to seed; otherwise they may disappear from your garden. In hot, humid-summer climates, buy established plants in pots and plant them outdoors in early spring so they can bloom until midsummer; after that, they aren't likely to survive.

Chamomile flowers bloom nonstop right into fall if you deadhead the plants regularly. You may need to stake plants growing in rich soil (where they tend to produce abundant foliage and floppy stems) or in windy spots. They actually bloom more abundantly in poor to average soil, and they're very tolerant of dry conditions.

Think Twice: Many cultivars of golden marguerite (*Anthemis tinctoria*) and St. John's chamomile (*A. sancti-johannis*) come true from seed. In fact, these two plants can become weedy if you let them self-sow freely. I recommend deadheading all but one or two flowerstalks; then after the petals drop, cover the seedheads with a paper bag tied closed at the base so you can collect the seed without it escaping. Seed sprouts rapidly under average conditions, either indoors or out.

Good Neighbors

Chamomiles' ferny foliage contrasts well with plants that have more substantial foliage, such as mountain bluet (*Centaurea montana*), 'Husker Red' foxglove penstemon (*Penstemon digitalis* 'Husker Red'), and garden phlox (*Phlox paniculata*).

Golden marguerite (*A. tinctoria*) looks wonderful in a wildlife-friendly meadow planting with butterfly weed (*Asclepias tuberosa*), New England aster (*Aster novae-angliae*), coreopsis, purple cone-flower (*Echinacea purpurea*), rudbeckias, and little bluestem (*Schizachyrium scoparium*). In a border, try planting golden marguerite with peach-leaved bellflower (*Campanula persicifolia*), Faassen's catmint (*Nepeta* × *faassenii*), and 'David' garden phlox

Problems and Solutions
Chamomiles suffer from powdery mildew; to avoid this, site them in spots with good air circulation.

Top Performer
Anthemis tinctoria (golden marguerite, golden chamomile): Golden marguerite bears gold-yellow flowers from 1½ to 2½ inches (4 to 6.5 cm) across; some cultivars have orange or white blooms. Plants bloom from early summer to early fall. The dark green leaves are covered underneath with fuzzy white hair. The leaves form a dense clump with smaller leaves along the upright flower stems.

Common cultivars are 'E. C. Buxton', with white flowers; 'Beauty of Grallagh', with gold-orange flowers; 'Grallagh Gold', with pale yellow blooms; 'Kelwayi', with bright yellow flowers; and 'Moonlight', with pale yellow flowers. Height: 18 to 36 inches (45 to 90 cm). Spread: 1 to 2 feet (30 to 60 cm). USDA Plant Hardiness Zones 3 to 9; AHS Heat Zones 8 to 3.

More Recommended Chamomiles
Anthemis marschalliana, also called *A. biebersteiniana* (Marschall chamomile): This is a smaller, mound-forming plant with silvery foliage covered in soft white hairs. The 1- to 2-inch (2.5- to 5-cm)-diameter golden daisies begin in early summer, and plants will rebloom throughout the summer if deadheaded. Marschall chamomile does best in full sun and extremely well-drained soil. Height: 12 to 15 inches (30 to 38 cm). Spread: 1 to 2 feet (30 to 60 cm). USDA Plant Hardiness Zones 3 to 9; AHS Heat Zones 9 to 7.

A. sancti-johannis (St. John's chamomile): It's hard to tell St. John's chamomile apart from golden marguerite. The true St. John's chamomile, however, has shorter flowerstalks than golden marguerite, gray-green rather than green leaves, and orange-yellow instead of yellow flowers. It blooms from early summer to early fall. Height: 18 to 24 inches (45 to 60 cm). Spread: 12 to 18 inches (30 to 45 cm). USDA Plant Hardiness Zones 3 to 9; AHS Heat Zones 9 to 1.

The cheerful yellow daisies of golden marguerite (*Anthemis tinctoria*) bloom so abundantly and for so long, that the plant can suffer from exhaustion and disappear after a couple of years. After the majority of the blooms are spent, cut the plant back to encourage fresh new growth of the lacy, aromatic foliage.

Aster

Aster

You thought perennial asters were strictly fall bloomers? Not by a long shot. In fact, among the some 600-odd species of asters, you'll find many spring and summer bloomers. Most asters are bushy plants that often form dense clumps, but they vary widely in flower size and color, leaf size and shape, plant height, and bloom time. Aster flowers generally look like small daisies, with a similar yellow center but with much more numerous petals, and they're often produced in clusters at the tips of the stems.

Plant Profile

ASTER
AS-ter

- **Bloom Color:** Blue, lavender, pink, purple, red, or white

- **Bloom Time:** Variable, late spring through fall

- **Length of Bloom:** Varies by species

- **Height:** Varies by species; see individual listings

- **Spread:** Varies by species; see individual listings

- **Garden Uses:** Cut flower garden, edging, mass planting, meadow garden, mixed border, rock garden, woodland garden; attracts butterflies

- **Light Preference:** Full sun

- **Soil Preference:** Average to fertile, moist but well-drained soil

- **Best Way to Propagate:** Divide in spring or fall

- **USDA Plant Hardiness Zones:** Varies by species; see individual listings

- **AHS Heat Zones:** 8 to 1

Growing Tips

Provide asters with abundant moisture during the growing season, yet good drainage at all times. They especially dislike soggy winter conditions, which can cause crown rot. Deadheading can encourage some summer asters to rebloom, often keeping them in flower well into fall. Taller species and cultivars may require staking.

Generally speaking, asters grow vigorously into ever-widening clumps that weaken or die out in the center. It's best to divide them every two years or so. Just remove and replant healthy clumps of stems from the outer ring of growth and bury the aging center elsewhere in your garden. (Don't add it to the compost pile, as it can carry disease organisms that could later spread to other asters.)

Some asters grow readily from seed, but only the species come true. You can sow seed of species asters directly in the garden in early spring, when the soil is still cool, or in late autumn.

Good Neighbors

Contrast the bright blooms of Frikart's aster (*Aster* × *frikartii*) with the globular seedheads of globe thistle (*Echinops ritro*), the robust foliage and interesting pods of blue false indigo (*Baptisia australis*), or the stiff flower spikes of torch lilies (*Kniphofia* spp.). Other good companions for the later-blooming summer asters are hybrid Japanese anemone (*Anemone* × *hybrida*) and early-blooming goldenrod cultivars, such as 'Crown of Rays' (*Solidago* 'Crown of Rays') or 'Golden Fleece' (*Solidago sphacelata* 'Golden Fleece'), which will carry the garden into fall.

Problems and Solutions

Powdery mildew is the bane of aster lovers everywhere. Mildew symptoms tend to show up late in the season, so at least it affects many summer bloomers *after* they bloom, but the powder-covered leaves are never a pleasant sight. Powdery mildew mainly attacks crowded plants, so plant them in a spot with good air circulation and divide them frequently. You can also thin out thick clumps, removing half or more of the stems. Once the disease does show up, there's little you can do. Of course, you can plant only disease-resistant cultivars and thus avoid the problem altogether.

Rust, which causes leaves to turn pale and powdery orange spots to appear on leaf undersides, can also be a problem under the same conditions. Prevent it with the same techniques.

Frikart's aster
(*Aster* × *frikartii*)

Top Performer

Aster × *frikartii* (Frikart's aster): I've given this aster top billing for its long blooming season and good mildew resistance. It's a bushy, spreading perennial that's nearly covered by 2- to 3-inch (5- to 7-cm)-wide lavender flowers from midsummer until frost (with deadheading)—even through the winter in milder climates. Excellent winter drainage is a must.

Two fine cultivars of Frikart's aster are lavender-blue 'Mönch' and deeper lavender-blue 'Wunder von Stäfa' ('Wonder of Staffa'). Height: 2 to 3 feet (60 to 90 cm). Spread: 30 to 36 inches (75 to 90 cm). USDA Plant Hardiness Zones 4 to 9; AHS Heat Zones 8 to 1.

More Recommended Asters

⭐ **Larry's Favorite:** *Aster ptarmicoides* (upland white aster): I like this aster not only for its midsummer bloom, but also because it's very cold-hardy and needs minimal care. The clustered flowers are white with greenish yellow centers and appear from early to late summer. In full sun, upland white aster forms a nice low clump of long, narrow leaves with flower stems held well above. You can leave it undisturbed for years. The only cloud on this aster's horizon is powdery mildew. But the plant will finish blooming by the time the leaves are infected, so I just cut it back to the ground after flowering. Height: 12 to 16 inches (30 to 40 cm). Spread: 1 foot (30 cm). USDA Plant Hardiness Zones 2 to 9; AHS Heat Zones 8 to 1.

Kissing Cousins

Japanese aster (*Kalimeris pinnatifida*, also called *Asteromoea mongolica*) is an aster look-alike, but it's much easier to grow than most asters. It produces an upright, open plant with clusters of 1-inch (2.5-cm) white flowers with yellow centers from early summer to fall. It grows in full sun or partial shade, rarely needs dividing, staking, deadheading, or, indeed, any attention at all. Height: 24 to 36 inches (60 to 90 cm). Spread: 18 to 24 inches (45 to 60 cm). USDA Plant Hardiness Zones 3 to 9; AHS Heat Zones 8 to 1.

Begonia

Begonia

Most gardeners have a hard time believing a begonia can be hardy, but seeing is believing, and where hardy begonia (*Begonia grandis*) is happy, it will spread rapidly and last for years. The plants bear arching sprays of pale pink flowers from early summer in mild-winter areas (considerably later in colder ones) and continue until frost. Their leaves and seed capsules are pretty, too, giving the plants long-season interest.

Plant Profile

BEGONIA
bih-GOAN-yuh

- Bloom Color: Pink or white
- Bloom Time: Early or late summer to fall
- Length of Bloom: 8 weeks or more
- Height: 8 to 24 inches (20 to 60 cm)
- Spread: 1 foot (30 cm)
- Garden Uses: Container planting, edging, groundcover, mass planting, mixed border, rock garden, woodland garden
- Light Preference: Partial to fairly deep shade
- Soil Preference: Humus-rich, moist but well-drained soil
- Best Way to Propagate: Plant bulbils (small bulbs) in fall; can also be propagated by taking cuttings from spring through fall
- USDA Plant Hardiness Zones: 7 to 10 (5 or 6 with ample winter protection)
- AHS Heat Zones: 9 to 6

Growing Tips

There are literally thousands of begonias you can grow as houseplants and hundreds as annual bedding plants. Many of these species also make great perennials in frost-free climates (USDA Zones 10 to 11), but only *Begonia grandis* can qualify as "hardy begonia."

As long as you plant hardy begonia in the right conditions, it requires basically no care once established. In most cases, a partially shaded to deeply shaded spot with moist, humus-rich soil is ideal. In northern parts of its range, hardy begonia can tolerate sun if you keep it moist. In fact, sun will help speed up the flowering process—hardy begonias growing in deep shade are very slow to get started in spring.

Hardy begonia sprouts from underground storage stems called tubers. The aboveground parts of hardy begonia will turn to mush at the first frost, but as long as the tubers don't freeze, the plants will sprout again in the spring. Fortunately for the tuber, it receives a certain amount of frost protection just from being underground. In areas where the ground *does* freeze, you can help out the tubers by applying a deep mulch of chopped leaves.

Hardy begonia reproduces on its own through small bulbs (called bulbils) that develop at the leaf axils and drop to the ground in the fall. Thanks to these bulbils, multiplying hardy begonia is a snap: Just dig up and move the young plants that sprout on their own each spring, as you need them. You could also take stem cuttings, but I wouldn't recommend bothering with it unless you're a northern gardener like me. Even though I garden in USDA Zone 3, where temperatures remain below freezing from November to April, I've gotten hardy begonia to survive winter by covering it with a huge pile of fall leaves, which Mother Nature topped with 6 feet (180 cm) of insulating snow. But I've decided it's easier to take stem cuttings in the fall, grow hardy begonia as a houseplant over the winter, and replant it outside in spring. The plants also bloom earlier in the season than they do when they resprout after overwintering outside.

Good Neighbors

Slow-sprouting hardy begonia (*Begonia grandis*) makes an ideal follow-up plant for perennials that bloom early but go dormant in the heat, such as daffodils, common bleeding heart (*Dicentra spectabilis*), and Virginia bluebells (*Mertensia virginica*). Because it stands so well on its own and blooms late, hardy begonia's contrasting flowers seem almost superfluous. In shade and moist, well-drained soil, hardy begonia will provide a lush, tropical-looking groundcover. Appropriate companions include plants that thrive in the same conditions, such as northern maidenhair fern (*Adiantum pedatum*), European wild ginger (*Asarum europaeum*), Lenten rose (*Helleborus* × *hybridus*), and woodland phlox (*Phlox divaricata*).

Problems and Solutions

Hardy begonia doesn't have any serious pest or disease problems.

Top Performer

Begonia grandis, also known as *B. evansiana* or *B. grandis* subsp. *evansiana* (hardy begonia): Hardy begonias produce lopsided heart-shaped leaves that are green above and reddish below and lightly hairy. Red stems and petioles add to the plant's charm. The winged seed capsules are pretty, too: They're light green at first but later become tinged with pink. Pale pink is the normal flower color, but you may also come across 'Alba', with white flowers.

Hardy begonia
(*Begonia grandis*)

Around the World with Begonias

Once, on the island of Martinique in the West Indies, I came across what could only be described as a "valley of begonias." Knee-high, with dark green, shiny leaves and sprays of mostly rose pink flowers, *Begonia nitida*, a tropical cousin of the hardy begonia, arched out of every nook and cranny, from the forest floor to the tops of rocks. Although the plants were taller than the hardy begonia (*B. grandis*) I grew back home, the effect was similar. I hope some day to find some seed of *B. nitida* so the two can finally meet!

Belamcanda

Blackberry lily

Blackberry lily is an iris relative that begins the season as a rather nondescript, flat fan of long, sword-shaped leaves (it reminds me of a gladiolus, but the leaves are narrower). But in early or midsummer—even late summer in colder regions—blackberry lily bursts forth with a series of tall flowerstalks bearing flat, 2-inch (5-cm), star-shaped flowers. Each flower lasts only a day, but a succession of blossoms opens over a period of several weeks.

Plant Profile

BELAMCANDA
bell-am-CAN-duh

- **Bloom Color:** Usually orange, but also pink, purple, red, white, or yellow
- **Bloom Time:** Early, midsummer, or late summer
- **Length of Bloom:** 3 or 4 weeks
- **Height:** 2 to 4 feet (60 to 120 cm)
- **Spread:** 2 feet (60 cm)
- **Garden Uses:** Cut flower garden, meadow garden, mixed border; at the back of beds and borders
- **Light Preference:** Full sun
- **Soil Preference:** Poor to rich, well-drained soil
- **Best Way to Propagate:** Divide or sow seed in spring
- **USDA Plant Hardiness Zones:** 5 to 9
- **AHS Heat Zones:** 9 to 5

Growing Tips

Blackberry lilies tolerate a wide range of soil conditions, but staking is always a must, especially where they grow in rich, moist soil.

Blackberry lilies spread slowly from the base by creeping underground rhizomes, eventually creating a large clump of well-spaced clusters. To propagate, divide clumps in early spring. Plant them with their rhizomes about 1 inch (2.5 cm) deep in USDA Zones 7 to 10, and up to 3 inches (8 cm) deep in colder areas for added frost protection. Blackberry lilies also grow readily from seed sown indoors in late winter or outdoors in spring. The plants usually bloom the second year, although an early start indoors can sometimes bring flowers the first year.

You can grow blackberry lilies well north of their usual range: They thrived for years in my USDA Zone 3 garden with no more than a heavy mulch of dead leaves in the fall and the usual thick layer of snow. But I'll warn you—their performance in cold regions can be disappointing because the flowers come so late in the season that the seedpods don't always mature. I only saw the seedpods twice in ten years, when spring arrived early and fall frost was late.

Good Neighbors

Orange flowers always make a strong impact, and those of blackberry lily are no exception. Use the plants in small doses where the orange will play well against blue or purple neighbors, such as peach-leaved bellflower (*Campanula persicifolia*), 'Blaustrumpf' bee balm (*Monarda* 'Blaustrumpf', also called *M.* 'Blue Stocking'), Siberian catnip (*Nepeta sibirica*), or 'Butterfly Blue' scabious (*Scabiosa columbaria* 'Butterfly Blue').

Blackberry lily is top-heavy and sometimes flops, so position a bushy plant in front to hide the stakes, such as a low-growing catmint (*Nepeta* spp.), a dwarf aster, or a dwarf cultivar of common baby's-breath, such as 'Viette's Dwarf' (*Gypsophila paniculata* 'Viette's Dwarf').

Problems and Solutions

Iris borer can cause leaves to wilt and die back. Removing dead or dying leaves promptly and cutting all the foliage back in fall can help prevent problems.

Top Performer

Belamcanda chinensis (blackberry lily): The species form has orange flowers with red spots, but there are hybrids in pink, purple, red, white, and yellow, with or without spots. Plants bloom in early, midsummer, or late summer. The flowers fade to rounded green seed capsules, which then open to reveal clusters of large, round, shiny black seeds that look for all the world like a blackberry—thus giving the plant its name. The open seed capsules remain attractive through the fall and into early winter. Blackberry lily can reach 4 feet (120 cm) in moist, rich soil but may be only about 2 feet (60 cm) tall in poor, dry soil. 'Freckle Face' is a dwarf cultivar with pale orange flowers spotted with red; it's only 12 to 15 inches (30 to 38 cm) tall. Height: 2 to 4 feet (60 to 120 cm). Spread: 2 feet (60 cm). USDA Plant Hardiness Zones 5 to 9; AHS Heat Zones 9 to 5.

More Recommended Blackberry Lilies

Belamcanda flabellata (yellow blackberry lily): This species has unspotted yellow flowers. The most widely available cultivar is 'Hello Yellow', which may also be sold as *B. chinensis* 'Hello Yellow' in a few catalogs. Height: 2 feet (60 cm). Spread: 18 inches (45 cm). USDA Plant Hardiness Zones 5 to 9; AHS Heat Zones 9 to 5.

Blackberry lily
(*Belamcanda chinensis*)

Kissing Cousins

Candy lily (× *Pardancanda norrisii*) is so similar to blackberry lily that I can't tell them apart. It's the result of a cross between blackberry lily and an obscure plant known as vesper iris (*Pardanthopsis dichotoma*). Candy lily comes in a wide range of colors (orange, pink, purple, red, white, and yellow), with or without spots—but then, so do modern blackberry lilies. Candy lily's other traits are also identical to those of blackberry lily. I can't help wondering: Is candy lily really just another blackberry lily?

Campanula

Bellflower

With bellflowers, your choices range from low creepers to "Harvey-get-the-ladder-I-want-to-pick-some-flowers" giants. All bellflowers have bell- or cup-shaped flowers, mostly in shades of blue. In this section, I've described the most popular midsummer bloomers. Look for longer-season bellflowers on page 74 and the low-growing types on page 378.

Plant Profile

CAMPANULA
kam-PAN-yew-luh

- **Bloom Color:** Blue, purple, pink, or white

- **Bloom Time:** Summer

- **Length of Bloom:** 3 or 4 weeks or more

- **Height:** Varies by species; see individual listings

- **Spread:** Varies by species; see individual listings

- **Garden Uses:** Container planting, cut flower garden, edging, groundcover, mass planting, mixed border, rock garden, wall planting; at the back of beds and borders; on slopes

- **Light Preference:** Full sun to light shade

- **Soil Preference:** Average, well-drained soil

- **Best Way to Propagate:** Sow seed in spring; for cultivars, take stem cuttings or divide in spring or fall

- **USDA Plant Hardiness Zones:** 3 to 9

- **AHS Heat Zones:** 8 to 1

Growing Tips

Long-lived bellflowers are garden staples in cooler regions and also do quite well where summers are warm, especially if you give them partial shade and a deep organic mulch like chopped leaves.

Some of the taller types need staking, although some shorter hybrids are making staking a thing of the past. The problem is that the tall bellflowers are usually much more attractive than their better-behaved brothers. So, beauty or discipline: The choice is yours.

Start bellflowers from seed sown in spring, indoors or out. Don't cover it, as many species need light to germinate. Propagate the cultivars by division, as they rarely come true from seed. You'll have no trouble finding material to propagate: Several of the bellflowers described here spread like wildfire! Deadheading helps keep the plants neat and may encourage some repeat bloom.

Good Neighbors

Peach-leaved bellflower (*Campanula persicifolia*) has a nicely mounded form that makes almost any companion look good. Try planting it with mulleins (*Verbascum* spp.), oriental poppy (*Papaver orientale*), or shrub roses. Add some seeds of annual love-in-a-mist (*Nigella damascena*) for an interesting combination both in flower and later in the season when the seedpods form.

Great bellflower (*C. latifolia*), a tall but comparatively neat bellflower, makes an interesting partner to 'Powis Castle' artemisia, sea holly (*Eryngium maritimum*), or white gaura (*Gaura lindheimeri*).

Problems and Solutions

Slugs and snails can chew large holes in the foliage; they are especially harmful to young plants. See page 55 for controls.

Top Performer

Campanula persicifolia (peach-leaved bell-flower): Peach-leaved bellflower is attractive and easy to grow. The plant forms a mound of long, narrow, leathery, evergreen leaves that do vaguely resemble peach leaves. The sturdy, nearly leafless flower-stalks rise well above the leaves and bear broad cup-shaped flowers in blue, pink, or white from early summer to midsummer—even well into fall if deadheaded.

This bellflower spreads by offsets and can self-sow, so deadhead it to prevent seed production and to stimulate repeat bloom.

There are many cultivars to choose from. 'Chettle Charm' has creamy white flowers edged in lavender, and 'Telham Beauty' is a striking pale china blue. Height: 1 to 3 feet (30 to 90 cm). Spread: 1 to 2 feet (30 to 60 cm). USDA Plant Hardiness Zones 3 to 9; AHS Heat Zones 8 to 1.

Peach-leaved bellflower
(*Campanula persicifolia*)

More Recommended Bellflowers

Campanula glomerata (clustered bellflower): Clustered bellflower spreads to form an open clump of broad, wavy, slightly hairy leaves and solidly upright stems bearing smaller leaves. Tight clusters of long-lasting violet-blue flowers top each stem in early summer.

This bellflower does best in full sun in cool-summer areas, and in light shade elsewhere. Clustered bellflower tends to spread, so plant it inside a root barrier or divide it regularly. There are many cultivars in all shades of blue, purple, and white. Height: 5 to 30 inches (13 to 75 cm). Spread: 1 to 2 feet (30 to 60 cm). USDA Plant Hardiness Zones 3 to 9; AHS Heat Zones 8 to 1.

Think Twice: *C. latifolia* (great bellflower): Great bellflower is one of the tallest bellflowers, so plant it toward the back of the garden. It produces a wide rosette of large coarse leaves that become progressively smaller along the upright flowerstalks. The purplish blue flowers are about 2 to 3 inches (5 to 8 cm) long and appear singly along the flowerstalks, starting at the bottom, from early summer to midsummer. It spreads aggressively, so plant it inside a root barrier. Deadhead to prevent it from spreading by seed. Plants may need staking. Height: 4 to 5 feet (120 to 150 cm). Spread: 3 feet (90 cm). USDA Plant Hardiness Zones 3 to 9; AHS Heat Zones 8 to 1.

Kissing Cousins

Bellflowers have lots of relatives, and many of them make very attractive garden flowers. My favorites, though, are the ladybells, and particularly lilyleaf ladybells (*Adenophora lilifolia*). Throughout much of the summer, it produces upright stalks of nodding, bell-shaped light blue (sometimes white) flowers. It will grow just about everywhere, but it can be a bit invasive if you let its roots ramble and its flowers go to seed. Height: 30 inches (75 cm). Spread: 1 foot (30 cm). USDA Plant Hardiness Zones: 3 to 9, AHS Heat Zones: 8 to 1.

Delphinium

Delphinium

A classic cottage-garden plant, delphiniums are renowned for their tall, stately spires of showy flowers. You'll find delphiniums in cool-summer gardens around the globe. They produce large, deeply cut, hand-shaped leaves on long leaf stalks that radiate from upright stems. At the stem tops, the flowers take over, creating dense spires of color. Although delphinium flowers are traditionally blue, they also come in many other shades. The flowers are complex, with broad petals surrounding an often contrasting center called a "bee," along with a back-facing, nectar-filled projection that attracts butterflies and hummingbirds.

Plant Profile

DELPHINIUM
dell-FIN-ee-um

- **Bloom Color:** Blue, lavender, magenta, pink, purple, red, or white

- **Bloom Time:** Varies by species; see individual listings

- **Length of Bloom:** 3 or 4 weeks or more

- **Height:** Varies by species; see individual listings

- **Spread:** Varies by species; see individual listings

- **Garden Uses:** Cut flower garden, edging, mass planting, meadow garden, mixed border, specimen plant; at the back of beds and borders; attracts butterflies and hummingbirds

- **Light Preference:** Full sun to light shade

- **Soil Preference:** Rich, moist but well-drained soil

- **Best Way to Propagate:** Sow seed in spring; take basal cuttings or divide in spring

- **USDA Plant Hardiness Zones:** Varies by species; see individual listings

- **AHS Heat Zones:** 7 to 1

Growing Tips

Think Twice: Pretty as they are, delphiniums are high-maintenance plants, constantly needing pruning, staking, deadheading, and disease controls. If "low care" is your game, delphiniums may not be for you. Delphiniums grow well in most rich, moist, well-drained soils but do best in alkaline ones. Delphiniums are heavy feeders, so add lots of compost or manure as you plant and side-dress annually with organic fertilizers such as bloodmeal or bonemeal. Be sure to set the crowns at or above soil level or crown rot may ensue.

To stimulate rebloom, cut flowerstalks back to just above the foliage after bloom. When fresh stems appear at the base of the plant, prune off the old stems entirely and let the young growth take over.

Delphiniums are short-lived perennials that need replacing every three or four years. Starting delphiniums from seed is the most popular method for propagating replacements. (Many strains come true from seed.) The seeds need total darkness and a one- to two-week cold treatment before they'll germinate. Started indoors in midwinter, new plants will often bloom the first year. You can also sow seeds outdoors in late summer for bloom the following season. You can also propagate delphiniums by carefully dividing and replanting them or by taking cuttings from the base of healthy new stems in spring.

Warning: All parts of delphiniums—from the seeds to the leaves to the flowers—are toxic, so do not grow this plant in areas where young children can get at them.

Good Neighbors

No cottage garden is complete without delphiniums' showy vertical spikes. Combine them with mounded perennials and other cottage-garden favorites, such as bellflowers (*Campanula* spp.), common baby's-breath (*Gypsophila paniculata*), hardy geraniums (*Geranium* spp.), lilies, oriental poppy (*Papaver orientale*), and shrub roses.

Problems and Solutions

Powdery mildew can be a major problem, especially in crowded conditions. Pruning out some growth can increase air circulation and help prevent or delay the infection. Also, water from below to avoid wetting the foliage.

Several other diseases can trouble delphiniums. If you've had problems with diseased delphiniums in the past, wait at least four years before replanting them where the infected plants grew.

Delphiniums also have insect pest problems: leaf miners, stem borers, and various caterpillars that eat leaves or flowers. You can control these pests manually by removing infested leaves or stems. Finally, spider mites can also be a problem; see page 55 to learn how to control them.

Recommended Delphiniums

Think Twice: *Delphinium* × *belladonna* (belladonna delphinium): This hybrid produces a major center spike surrounded by a few dozen shorter stems, all blooming at once from early summer to midsummer. Blue is the main color in this group, but flowers can also be pink, white, and all shades of purple. Height: 3 to 4 feet (90 to 120 cm). Spread: 18 inches (45 cm). USDA Plant Hardiness Zones 3 to 7; AHS Heat Zones 7 to 3.

Think Twice: *D.* × *elatum* (hybrid delphinium): Hybrid delphinium, with its huge spikes of flowers that seem to reach for the sky, is what most people picture when they think of delphiniums. Each plant tends to produce a single tall flower stem with small secondary stems "filling in" to create a massive display in early summer to midsummer. The flower color range is quite complete—including even a few yellows and greens—but blues and purples still dominate. Height: variable, between 15 to 84 inches (38 to 213 cm). Spread: 2 to 3 feet (60 to 90 cm). USDA Plant Hardiness Zones 2 to 7; AHS Heat Zones 7 to 3.

'Blue Bird' belladonna delphinium (*Delphinium* × *belladonna* 'Blue Bird')

Larry's Garden Notes

Call me cruel, but I can't single out any delphinium as a Top Performer: They all have too many pitfalls. I've labeled both of the species I recommend with my "Think Twice" warning. Sure they're pretty, but they need constant attention, so you need to "think twice" about whether you really want to put that much energy into them.

Leucanthemum

Daisy, chrysanthemum

There are many plants that masquerade under the name "daisy," but in North America, the name goes hand in hand with the yellow-centered white blooms of Shasta daisy (*Leucanthemum* × *superbum*) and oxeye daisy (*L. vulgare*). The flattened surface of the white petals makes a perfect resting platform for feeding butterflies, and the flower centers are actually composed of hundreds of tiny yellow flowers that are perfect for butterflies to feed from.

Plant Profile

LEUCANTHEMUM
lew-CAN-thuh-mum

- **Bloom Color:** White
- **Bloom Time:** Varies by species
- **Length of Bloom:** 4 weeks or more
- **Height:** Varies by species; see individual listings
- **Spread:** 12 to 18 inches (30 to 45 cm)
- **Garden Uses:** Cut flower garden, edging, groundcover, mass planting, meadow garden, mixed border; attracts butterflies
- **Light Preference:** Full sun to partial shade
- **Soil Preference:** Fertile, moist but well-drained soil
- **Best Way to Propagate:** Divide or sow seed in spring or fall
- **USDA Plant Hardiness Zones:** Varies by species; see individual listings
- **AHS Heat Zones:** Varies by species; see indiviual listings

Growing Tips

Shasta daisy and oxeye daisy have similar needs. Though they prefer fertile, moist soil, they'll grow in just about any well-drained situation and will tolerate some drought. Both are relatively short-lived perennials that appreciate division every three or four years, although the oxeye daisy will maintain itself if you don't make a habit of removing the offsets. Both willingly self-sow (except double-flowered cultivars, some of which are sterile), but deadheading is wise because the blooms don't always come true from seed. To propagate those that do come true, sow seed indoors in late winter, just barely covering it. The resulting seedlings will bloom the first year if you sow early enough.

Good Neighbors

Familiar and companionable, these daisies deserve a place in every flower garden. Try a combination of Shasta daisies (*Leucanthemum* × *superbum*) with 'Coronation Gold' yarrow (*Achillea* 'Coronation Gold'), Siberian iris (*Iris sibirica*), 'Six Hills Giant' catmint (*Nepeta* 'Six Hills Giant'), and 'Herbstfreude' sedum (*Sedum* 'Herbstfreude', also called *S.* 'Autumn Joy') for a season of color and interest.

Use oxeye daisy in the front of an informal mixed border. It tends to move around: Older plants die out as new plants and seedlings become established. Or try it in a meadow garden with other informal plants, such as butterfly weed (*Asclepias tuberosa*), coreopsis, purple coneflower (*Echinacea purpurea*), and rudbeckias.

Problems and Solutions

Shasta daisies and oxeye daisies may have an occasional insect and disease problem, but if they do, the effects will be so minor you probably won't even notice.

Top Performer

Leucanthemum × *superbum*, also called
Chrysanthemum × *superbum* (Shasta daisy):
Luther Burbank, the American plantsman,
developed this plant in 1890. He crossed two
obscure European daisies and came up with
a larger, more vigorous plant that became an
instant hit. Subsequent breeders have improved this species too, so if you haven't
grown Shasta daisy for a while, you should
take a second look.

Shasta daisy forms rosettes of coarsely
toothed, dark green, spoon-shaped leaves.
Wiry flower-bearing stems with smaller
leaves arise from the rosette. You can choose
from dwarf to giant varieties with single,
double, and semi-double varieties and often
a much longer blooming period. Many
modern cultivars bloom nonstop from early
summer until fall if you faithfully remove their faded flowers. Among
the better everbloomers are 'Aglaia', a particularly hardy type with
double flowers, 'Esther Read', the most common of the double
daisies, and 'Marconi', available from seed. Dwarf 'Snow Lady' grows
only 12 to 15 inches (30 to 38 cm) tall and comes into bloom in as
little as 11 weeks from seed. Height: 8 to 48 inches (20 to 120 cm).
Spread: 1 to 2 feet (30 to 60 cm). USDA Plant Hardiness Zones 4 to 9;
AHS Heat Zones 8 to 5.

More Recommended Daisies

Leucanthemum vulgare, also called *Chrysanthemum leucanthemum* (oxeye
daisy): Though cursed as a weed when it sprouts where it's not
wanted, oxeye daisy is a lovely flower that looks right at home in
many gardens. Oxeye daisy is very similar to the Shasta daisy, but
smaller. There is a difference in care, though. Oxeye daisy is a
tougher and longer-lived plant that can be invasive, so plant it inside
a root barrier, such as a bottomless bucket sunk into the soil.

Oxeye daisy adapts just as well to warm winter climates as arctic
ones. Plants flower mainly in early summer to midsummer but they
will rebloom if you deadhead them. 'Maikönigen' (also called 'May
Queen') is particularly free-flowering. Height: 12 to 18 inches (30 to
45 cm). Spread: 8 to 12 inches (20 to 30 cm). USDA Plant Hardiness
Zones 1 to 9; AHS Heat Zones 8 to 1.

'Becky' Shasta daisy
(*Leucanthemum* × *superbum* 'Becky')

Around the World with Daisies

Farmers may consider the
oxeye daisy (*Leucanthemum
vulgare*) a weed, but is there anything more beautiful than a vast field
full of their beautiful yellow-eyed
flowers in early summer? Oxeye
daisy mixes effortlessly with other
sun-loving wildflowers, creating a
beautiful floral tableau that even the
best garden designers never seem
to be able to reproduce. Introduced
accidentally from Eurasia to North
America in shipments of grain seeds
generations ago, oxeye daisy has
made itself so at home throughout
all of temperate North America that
you'd have a hard time convincing
anyone it isn't a native. Look for it in
a field near you!

Linum

Flax

I can close my eyes and still imagine them: the seemingly endless summer fields of sky blue flax I've seen on my European travels. But those summer fields are common flax (*Linum usitatissimum*), an annual species that provides both fiber for linen and seeds for linseed oil. I've yet to see a field of the ornamental species of flax (wouldn't that be a lovely sight?), but they do brighten up our gardens for weeks in summer.

Plant Profile

LINUM
LIE-num

- **Bloom Color:** Blue, white, and yellow
- **Bloom Time:** Varies by species; see individual listings
- **Length of Bloom:** 4 to 6 weeks or more
- **Height:** 6 to 24 inches (15 to 60 cm)
- **Spread:** 12 to 18 inches (30 to 45 cm)
- **Garden Uses:** Edging, mass planting, meadow garden, mixed border, rock garden, wall planting
- **Light Preference:** Full sun
- **Soil Preference:** Average, well-drained soil
- **Best Way to Propagate:** Sow seed in spring or fall; take stem cuttings in summer
- **USDA Plant Hardiness Zones:** 3 to 9
- **AHS Heat Zones:** Varies by species; see individual listings

Growing Tips

All flax are quite drought- and heat-resistant, although they bloom better when the soil is at least slightly moist during their flowering period. They tend to bloom from late spring or early summer through midsummer. Many species will rebloom until fall if you deadhead them regularly or prune them back to half their height whenever there's a lull in their blooming.

Don't bother thinking about dividing flax; they produce long taproots that are hard to dig up and easily damaged. Sowing seed is the most popular way of multiplying most flax: Golden flax (*L. flavum*) aside, the seeds sprout and grow quickly. In fact, flax self-sow readily without becoming weedy. If you've purchased or collected seed, sow it directly in your garden in late fall or early spring (cover it lightly) or start it in peat pots indoors six to eight weeks before the last frost.

Good Neighbors

With its fountainlike sprays of cool blue flowers, perennial flax (*L. perenne*) looks best where it's not too crowded. A grouping of perennial flax makes a graceful accent when surrounded by a low-growing groundcover, such as thyme or red-stemmed lady's-mantle (*Alchemilla erythropoda*). Or try a cool grouping of perennial flax with Siberian iris (*Iris sibirica*) and lamb's-ears (*Stachys byzantina*).

FUN FACTS

Winter hardiness always stirs up debate among flax lovers. I've listed the hardiness zones where I've seen them survive *under dry conditions*. If you garden in USDA Zone 6 or north, or if your conditions aren't quite what the plants prefer, I recommend that you apply a light winter mulch like pine needles or conifer branches—if you're lucky, your flax plants will make it through winter just fine.

Golden flax (*L. flavum*) makes a good companion for deep blue flowers, such as lupines (*Lupinus* spp.) and 'Purple Rain' lilac sage (*Salvia verticillata* 'Purple Rain').

Problems and Solutions

Flax are not bothered by insects and disease but are subject to rot in overly wet conditions, so plant flax in well-drained soil.

Top Performer

Linum perenne (perennial flax): By far the most popular ornamental species, perennial flax produces a bushy, broom-shaped plant bearing sky blue, cup-shaped, ¾-inch (2-cm) flowers beginning in late spring or early summer to midsummer or late summer. Each flower lasts only a day, but they're produced in such enormous quantities that you'd never know they were so short lived. Perennial flax can rebloom over much of the summer if you cut it back regularly. It's not a long-lived perennial—it lives three or four years at the most—but it self-sows readily.

Cultivars tend to be more compact than the species: blue 'Saphir' ('Sapphire') and white 'Diamant' ('White Diamond') both reach only 1 foot (30 cm). They self-sow relatively true at first but become taller as years go by, so propagate them by taking stem cuttings instead. Height: 8 to 24 inches (20 to 60 cm). Spread: 2 feet (60 cm). USDA Plant Hardiness Zones 3 to 9; AHS Heat Zones 8 to 5.

More Recommended Flax

Linum flavum (golden flax): Besides blooming in a strikingly different color (golden yellow) than perennial flax, golden flax is a bushier, almost mounding plant. Its flowers are about 1 inch (2.5 cm) in diameter and appear mainly from early summer to midsummer in dense clusters at the end of the stems.

Golden flax is long-lived and slow to establish. Don't expect much of a show for the first two years. After that, it will continue on for a decade or more. Golden flax doesn't self-sow well; stem cuttings are the best way to multiply it. 'Compactum' is roughly half the size of the species and makes a good edging plant. Height: 6 to 24 inches (15 to 60 cm). Spread: 12 to 18 inches (30 to 45 cm). USDA Plant Hardiness Zones 3 to 9; AHS Heat Zones 7 to 5.

Perennial flax
(*Linum perenne*)

Larry's Garden Notes

You might think that you're doing something wrong when your so-called perennial flax dies out after just a couple of years (and if your flax has wet feet, you *are* doing something wrong). But the fact is that *Linum perenne* produces such abundant numbers of flowers and seeds and so little chlorophyll-producing foliage that it's surprising that it has the strength to return at all! If you get into the habit of starting a few of those seeds every year, you won't be without its delicate good looks for a single season.

Lychnis

Campion

If you like color, you'll like campions! They bloom in bright, almost startling shades that just can't help but draw your attention. But other than those eye-popping colors, there is little else the members of this highly variable genus have in common. What you *can* say about campions without too much danger of being proven wrong is that they have simple leaves and flowers with five petals, each with a notch cut into its tip.

Plant Profile

LYCHNIS
LICK-nis

- **Bloom Color:** Magenta, pink, red, scarlet, or white

- **Bloom Time:** Varies by species

- **Length of Bloom:** 3 or 4 weeks or more

- **Height:** Varies by species; see individual listings

- **Spread:** 10 to 18 inches (25 to 45 cm)

- **Garden Uses:** Cut flower garden, mass planting, meadow garden, mixed border; at the back of beds and borders; attracts hummingbirds

- **Light Preference:** Full sun or partial shade

- **Soil Preference:** Fertile, moist but well-drained soil

- **Best Way to Propagate:** Divide plants in spring or fall

- **USDA Plant Hardiness Zones:** Varies by species; see individual listings

- **AHS Heat Zones:** Varies by species; see individual listings

Growing Tips

Campions are highly adaptable, growing just about everywhere except in deep shade; and while they prefer moist soils to dry ones, they are subject to rot if the drainage is less than perfect. Also, campions are short-lived, so learning to maintain them is a must. For the species, that's not a problem: They self-seed with abandon. Many cultivars also come fairly true from seed, but keep a close eye on their offspring and weed out any that don't conform. You can also sow seed indoors in late winter (give it a two-week cold treatment) or directly in the garden in early spring or in late fall.

Deadheading can help some campions to bloom for a longer period or to flower a second time later in the summer. But deadheading isn't always enough: Some look just plain ratty after they bloom. Shear them back harshly and, if they don't flower a second time, at least they'll look fuller and bushier when they grow back.

Good Neighbors

The bright orange-red blooms of Maltese cross (*Lychnis chalcedonica*) can be very exciting in the back of the border with shades of purple, such as 'Six Hills Giant' catmint (*Nepeta* 'Six Hills Giant') and lavender mist (*Thalictrum rochebrunianum*).

Rose campion (*L. coronaria*), with its silver-gray foliage and shocking magenta flowers, is so eye-catching that it's best to pair it with grays, greens, and whites. Safe companions include lady's-mantle (*Alchemilla mollis*), lamb's-ears (*Stachys byzantina*), and white-flowered pinks (*Dianthus* spp.).

Moisture-loving Haage campion (*L.* × *haageana*) would add excitement to a planting of soft blue forget-me-nots (*Myosotis* spp.) in the front of a border.

Problems and Solutions

Campions can suffer from disease woes (including leaf spots, rust, and root rot), but you can prevent most of these by supplying the proper growing conditions: lots of sun and moist soil with good drainage. Prune off leaves and stems that do show symptoms like spots, red patches, or soft, water-soaked areas.

Top Performer

Lychnis chalcedonica (Maltese cross): Maltese cross is the one long-lived campion, surviving a decade or more even without division. Shear the whole plant back to 1 foot (30 cm) high after it blooms, and it may bloom again in early fall. If seeing your garden in flames is too much for you, try the softer rose-pink 'Rosea' or the absolutely sedate 'Alba', with white flowers. Height: 2 to 4 feet (60 to 120 cm). Spread: 12 to 18 inches (30 to 45 cm). USDA Plant Hardiness Zones 3 to 9; AHS Heat Zones 8 to 1.

More Recommended Campions

Lychnis coronaria (rose campion, mullein pink): Color hazard warning: This plant's shocking magenta to brilliant red flowers may be dangerous to your garden's color scheme. The foliage is covered with soft white down so it appears gray. The 1-inch (2.5-cm) flowers bloom singly on long, branched stalks from late spring through early summer.

This plant acts more like a biennial than a perennial but self-sows abundantly. If you enjoy the leaves but not the color of the species, try 'Alba', with white flowers, 'Angel Blush', with white flowers flushed pink, or 'Oculata', white with a pink eye. Height: 18 to 36 inches (45 to 90 cm). Spread: 12 to 18 inches (30 to 45 cm). USDA Plant Hardiness Zones 3 to 9; AHS Heat Zones 8 to 1.

L. × *haageana* (Haage campion): This hybrid species offers 2-inch (5-cm), orange-red blooms that are deeply lobed at the tips, with toothed margins. Plants bloom from early summer to midsummer, with some repeat bloom, especially in cool-summer climates. Haage campion needs abundant moisture and full sun to do well. In hot-summer areas, it tends to go dormant after blooming but returns the following spring. It's short-lived, so plan to replace it every two or three years; it usually comes true from seed. Height: 10 to 18 inches (25 to 45 cm). Spread: 1 foot (30 cm). USDA Plant Hardiness Zones 5 to 7; AHS Heat Zones 8 to 6.

Blooming in midsummer, this old-fashioned favorite, Maltese cross (*Lychnis chalcedonica*), produces small, flaming scarlet flowers. Its intense color simply sparkles against lush green foliage. Plant Maltese cross in a mixed border in moist, well-drained soil.

Penstemon

Penstemon, beardtongue

From their humble beginnings as American wildflowers, penstemons have become stars in Europe and are finally gaining acceptance back at home. Penstemons have tubular flowers generally held on upright spikes. Most are bright reds and blues, but there's a wide variety of other colors. The flower tubes expand at the tip to form two upper lobes and three lower ones. (Some species are not distinctly lobed, having only an upper and a lower lip.) Other than sharing similar flower forms, penstemons are extremely variable, ranging from tiny shrublike creepers to upright leafy clumpers.

Plant Profile

PENSTEMON
PEN-steh-mon

- **Bloom Color:** Almost every color, although yellow is rare

- **Bloom Time:** Varies by species; see individual listings

- **Length of Bloom:** 3 or 4 weeks or more

- **Height:** Varies by species; see individual listings

- **Spread:** Varies by species; see individual listings

- **Garden Uses:** Container planting, cut flower garden, edging, groundcover, mass planting, mixed border, rock garden, wall planting; attracts hummingbirds

- **Light Preference:** Full sun to partial shade

- **Soil Preference:** Average, very well-drained, even dry soil

- **Best Way to Propagate:** Stem cuttings in summer or fall

- **USDA Plant Hardiness Zones:** Varies by species; see individual listings

- **AHS Heat Zones:** Varies by species; see individual listings

Growing Tips

Generally speaking, the penstemons that are native to eastern North America are most amenable to gardens, while the western species don't seem to adapt well beyond their native ranges. The different species vary widely in their needs, but most penstemons demand perfectly drained soil and share a distinct dislike for winter wet. That means a thick but well-aerated fall mulch is important for most species in all but the warmest climates.

Most penstemons are short-lived, often disappearing from the garden for no apparent reason after two or three years, but it's easy to multiply almost all types by stem cuttings. Overwinter the young plants in a coldframe or a cool basement if you're not sure they'll survive the winter. You can also sow seed indoors (do not cover) and provide a two-week cold period, then germinate at 55° to 65°F (13° to 18°C).

Good Neighbors

Tall-growing penstemons look great rising above plants with mounded shapes: Try cushion spurge (*Euphorbia polychroma*, also called *E. epithymoides*), hardy geraniums (*Geranium* spp.), and common baby's-breath (*Gypsophila paniculata*) as well as midsized ornamental grasses. 'Husker Red' foxglove penstemon (*Penstemon digitalis* 'Husker Red') echoes the bronzy purple foliage of plants such as 'Palace Purple' heuchera (*Heuchera micrantha* var. *diversifolia* 'Palace Purple').

Use the diminutive dwarf hairy beardtongue (*P. hirsutus* 'Pygmaeus') to accent wall rock cress (*Arabis caucasica*), sedums, and other rock-garden favorites.

Problems and Solutions

As mentioned above, penstemons do tend to die off for no good reason, but they're not prone to insect or disease problems.

Top Performer

Penstemon digitalis 'Husker Red' ('Husker Red' foxglove penstemon): This cultivar of foxglove penstemon has pale pink flowers and deep purple foliage. The plants generally keep their color throughout the summer if you grow them in full sun, although they may turn green in hot-summer areas.

'Husker Red' is surprisingly adaptable for a penstemon: It even tolerates moderately moist soil as long it drains well. Height: 2 to 3 feet (60 to 90 cm). Spread: 12 to 18 inches (30 to 45 cm). USDA Plant Hardiness Zones 3 to 9; AHS Heat Zones 8 to 1.

More Recommended Penstemons

Penstemon barbatus, also called *Chelone barbata* (common beardtongue): The species produces a low mound of somewhat bluish, narrow leaves topped off from late spring to midsummer by thin spires of pink to red, two-lipped flowers. Cultivars tend to have greener leaves and to be particularly long-blooming. They include scarlet-red 'Coccineus', clear pink 'Elfin Pink', and clear purple 'Prairie Dusk'. All do well over a wide range of conditions, but they insist on perfect drainage and at least a short period of near-freezing winter temperatures. Height: 1 to 3 feet (30 to 90 cm). Spread: 12 to 18 inches (30 to 45 cm). USDA Plant Hardiness Zones 2 to 9; AHS Heat Zones 9 to 1.

P. hirsutus 'Pygmaeus' (dwarf hairy beardtongue): This attractive selection of hairy beardtongue is a low-growing alternative to 'Husker Red' foxglove penstemon (*P. digitalis* 'Husker Red'). Its creeping stems of maroon-tipped leaves bear the soft lavender flowers with white throats from early summer through early fall. Dwarf hairy beardtongue won't tolerate competition from taller plants (it's too small to defend itself). Height: 4 inches (10 cm). Spread: 6 inches (15 cm). USDA Plant Hardiness Zones 3 to 9; AHS Heat Zones 9 to 1.

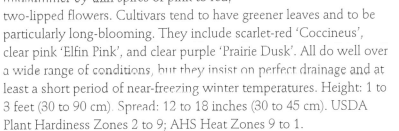

'Husker Red' foxglove penstemon (*Penstemon digitalis* 'Husker Red') seemed to zoom out of nowhere in the mid-1990s to become an overnight sensation. And with good reason—the striking purple foliage livens up the scene long after the blooms have faded.

Persicaria

Fleeceflower, knotweed

I must admit it took me a while to warm up to fleeceflowers. Some of the pink-blooming ornamental species looked so much like a nasty weed called lady's thumb *(Polygonum persicaria)* that I needed some convincing. I started with the clump-forming types, and when they turned out to be as attractive as they were harmless, I tried the creeping species, which were just as nice and not at all hard to control. Some characteristics the plants in this genus share include stems that are swollen at the leaf nodes (the "knot" in "knotweed") and clustered flowers that often resemble bottlebrushes.

Plant Profile

PERSICARIA
per-sih-CARE-ee-uh

- **Bloom Color:** Pink, red, or white

- **Bloom Time:** Early summer to midsummer or late summer

- **Length of Bloom:** 4 or 5 weeks or more

- **Height:** Varies by species; see individual listings

- **Spread:** Varies by species; see individual listings

- **Garden Uses:** Container planting, edging, groundcover, mass planting, mixed border, rock garden, specimen plant, wall planting, woodland garden; on paths, on slopes, in wet areas

- **Light Preference:** Full sun to moderate shade

- **Soil Preference:** Average, well-drained soil

- **Best Way to Propagate:** Divide plants in spring or fall

- **USDA Plant Hardiness Zones:** 3 to 9

- **AHS Heat Zones:** Varies by species; see individual listings

Growing Tips

Fleeceflowers are very adaptable, growing equally well in rich or poor soil that's moderately dry to moist or even wet. Some shade is helpful in hot-summer areas, as these plants appreciate cool conditions. In fact, they generally do best in woodland gardens or near a water garden.

Spring or fall division is the most common means of propagating fleeceflowers, although stem cuttings are just as easy. You can also grow fleeceflowers from seed.

Many creeping fleeceflowers spread quickly, so plant them within a root barrier (such as a bottomless bucket sunk into the soil) or give them lots of room to spread.

Good Neighbors

Combine taller fleeceflowers with hostas, rodgersias, and ornamental grasses for a bold planting with good textural contrast. Low-growing Himalayan fleeceflower (*Persicaria affinis*) forms a vigorous flowering carpet that would add interest to a mounding groundcover such as lady's-mantle (*Alchemilla mollis*) or bloody cranesbill (*Geranium sanguineum*). The interesting foliage of 'Painter's Palette' fleeceflower (*P. filiformis* 'Painter's Palette') makes a strong statement on its own and would be a good choice for planting as a groundcover around a shrub border.

Problems and Solutions

Fleeceflowers don't suffer from any serious pest or disease problems.

Top Performer

Larry's Favorite: *Persicaria filiformis* 'Painter's Palette', also called *Tovara virginiana* 'Painter's Palette' and *Polygonum virginanum* 'Painter's

Palette' ('Painter's Palette' fleeceflower):
When I first saw this plant, I thought I'd
died and gone to plant heaven! It forms a
dense dome of large, oval, pointed green
leaves that are heavily and irregularly marbled with cream. Each leaf bears a large V-
shaped marking that is deep maroon on the
green part of the leaf and bright rose over
a variegated section. The narrow, late-
summer flowerstalks are insignificant, so
ignore them or cut them off.

'Painter's Palette' takes its sweet time in
sprouting: Each spring I gnaw my nails to the
bone thinking it's died, but it's come back
faithfully in my USDA Zone 3 garden for
years. Height: 2 to 3 feet (60 to 90 cm).
Spread: 2 feet (60 cm). USDA Plant Hardiness Zones 3 to 9; AHS Heat Zones 9 to 1.

'Painter's Palette' fleeceflower
(*Persicaria filiformis*
'Painter's Palette')

More Recommended Fleeceflowers

Persicaria affinis (Himalayan fleeceflower): This superb semievergreen
groundcover forms a low, dense, spreading mat of creeping stems.
The upright, leathery leaves are dark green in summer and rusty red in
fall. At each stem tip is a narrow "bottlebrush" consisting of thousands
of tiny pink, red, or white flowers. The flowers mature to pink or red
seedheads that remain on the plant for most of the summer.

Popular cultivars include 'Darjeeling Red', with rose-pink
flowers changing to russet-red and brilliant red leaves in fall, and
'Superba' (also called 'Dimity'), with taller red spikes that turn
pink as they age and larger leaves turning bronze in fall . Height: 9
to 18 inches (23 to 45 cm). Spread: 1 to 2 feet (30 to 60 cm).
USDA Plant Hardiness Zones 3 to 9; AHS Heat Zones 8 to 1.

P. bistorta (snakeweed): This is a deservedly popular fleeceflower
in spite of its uninspiring common name. It forms dense clumps of
arching, shiny green leaves that turn bright red in the fall. Snakeweed puts on its best show in early summer through midsummer,
though, when it produces thick, bottlebrush-shaped spikes of pink
flowers well above the foliage, with sporadic rebloom until early
fall. 'Superba', with larger flowers, is the most widely available
cultivar. Height: 18 to 30 inches (45 to 75 cm). Spread: 24 to 30
inches (60 to 75 cm). USDA Plant Hardiness Zones 3 to 9; AHS
Heat Zones 8 to 1.

Larry's Garden Notes

When the genus *Polygonum* (the
former name for fleeceflowers) was
broken up, most species went into
the genus *Persicaria*; others were
reassigned to *Fallopia*. Japanese
knotweed (formerly *Polygonum
cuspidatum*, now *Fallopia japonica*)
is sold as an ornamental, but it's
among the most invasive plants
I've ever dealt with. I hope for your
garden's sake, you just say no!

Phlox

Phlox

It's hard to imagine a perennial border without at least a few tall summer-blooming phlox. These clump-forming perennials are a staple of summer gardens, with their dense clusters of five-petaled, delightfully fragrant flowers and narrow, pointed leaves. Summer phlox have a distinctly upright growth habit, and their leaves are usually dark green. The flowers appear in summer and, in many cases, keep on blooming until fall. The color range is vast and increases yearly.

Plant Profile

PHLOX FLOCKS

- **Bloom Color:** Blue, mauve-purple, pink, red, salmon-orange, and white
- **Bloom Time:** Midsummer to early fall
- **Length of Bloom:** 6 weeks or more
- **Height:** Varies by species; see individual listings
- **Spread:** 24 to 30 inches (60 to 75 cm)
- **Garden Uses:** Cut flower garden, mass planting, meadow garden, mixed border; at the back of beds and borders; attracts butterflies and hummingbirds
- **Light Preference:** Full sun to partial shade
- **Soil Preference:** Moderately humus-rich, well-drained soil
- **Best Way to Propagate:** Divide in spring; take stem cuttings in summer
- **USDA Plant Hardiness Zones:** 3 to 9
- **AHS Heat Zones:** 8 to 1

Growing Tips

Summer phlox adapt well to most sunny sites with good drainage, although they grow and flower best in rich, evenly moist soil. In hot-summer areas, an organic mulch will help keep the roots cool, and light shade may be necessary to prevent flowers from bleaching. (On the down side, partial shade also tends to produce floppier growth, so you may need to stake the stems.)

Divide the clumps when their centers begin to weaken or die out, usually every three years or so. It's also easy to propagate phlox from cuttings taken from nonflowering stems. Growing phlox from seed is usually disappointing, as even the most colorful cultivars tend to produce plain pink-flowered offspring.

Many phlox hold up well for much of the summer, but if they do start to die out in the center and flop over, shear them back by half; they'll often perk up and bloom well into fall.

Good Neighbors

Summer phlox bloom right through the midsummer meltdown that hits so many perennial borders, so don't hesitate to plant them abundantly. The more brilliant colors of garden phlox (*Phlox paniculata*) combine well with early-blooming goldenrods, such as 'Crown of Rays' (*Solidago* 'Crown of Rays') and 'Golden Fleece' (*Solidago sphacelata* 'Golden Fleece'). Try white 'David' garden phlox with 'Lucifer' crocosmia and 'Mainacht' salvia (*Salvia* × *sylvestris* 'Mainacht', also called *S.* × *sylvestris* 'May Night') backed by a planting of sunflower heliopsis (*Heliopsis helianthoides*).

Early-blooming wild sweet William (*P. maculata*) pairs well with a wide variety of other summer bloomers—yellow daylilies, globe thistle (*Echinops ritro*), and yarrows (*Achillea* spp.), just to name a few.

Problems and Solutions

Mildew is so common in summer-blooming phlox, especially garden phlox, that many people believe you simply can't have one without the other. I used to plant phlox at the back of the border where I could see the flowers but not the foliage. If a "just close your eyes and pretend it isn't happening" attitude is not your cup of tea, try planting phlox in windy sites (where air circulates abundantly) and watering only from below to help minimize mildew.

Top Performer

Phlox paniculata (garden phlox, summer phlox): This is *the* summer phlox in most gardens. It offers the widest color range of any perennial phlox—just about every color but true blue, pure orange, green, yellow, and black are available, and I'll bet we'll have all of the above within a few decades (except black, I hope).

The most important piece of advice I can offer about garden phlox is to choose *only* mildew-resistant cultivars, such as those listed here. 'Bright Eyes' produces purplish foliage, especially in spring, and baby pink flowers with a rose eye; it reblooms well. Pure white 'David' is perhaps the most mildew-resistant garden phlox of all. 'Düsterlohe' blooms in a brilliant shade of deep violet, while the flowers of 'Eva Cullum' are clear pink with a dark eye.

'Norah Leigh' is a variegated garden phlox with pale lilac-purple flowers. Plant cultivars in partial shade or their leaves can burn. Height: 2 to 4 feet (60 to 120 cm). Spread: 24 to 30 inches (60 to 75 cm). USDA Plant Hardiness Zones 3 to 9; AHS Heat Zones 8 to 1.

More Recommended Phlox

Phlox maculata (wild sweet William, meadow phlox): Wild sweet William is similar to garden phlox (*P. paniculata*), although it's some-what shorter and has narrower, thicker leaves. It's more resistant to powdery mildew than is garden phlox. Among the cultivars, I like 'Alpha', a classic pink; 'Miss Lingard', pure white with a pink eye; 'Natascha', a stunning pink and white bicolor; and 'Omega', white with a lilac eye. Height: 2 to 3 feet (60 to 90 cm). Spread: 2 feet (60 cm). USDA Plant Hardiness Zones 3 to 9; AHS Heat Zones 8 to 1.

'Eva Cullum' garden phlox
(*Phlox paniculata* 'Eva Cullum')

Larry's Garden Notes

"Know your enemy," it is said. In the case of garden phlox (*Phlox paniculata*), enemy #1 is powdery mildew. It's a fungus that absorbs nutrients, feeding on the plant's surface cells and causing leaves to yellow. When the leaves drop, the fungal spores drop, too, to infect next year's plants when conditions are right. It thrives in high humidity, but not when leaf surfaces are actually wet. Plants in shade are usually affected more than those in sun, and the more you fertilize, the worse the problem is likely to be.

Polemonium

Jacob's ladder, Greek valerian

With Jacob's ladder, you get two plants in one: It's most noticeable in its role as a flowering plant in early summer, but when Jacob's ladder finishes blooming, the foliage takes over. As the name suggests, the dark to medium-green leaves really do look like an old-fashioned ladder, with a single center rail and rungs extending out on either side. The leaves arch out from the base of the plant, making it look quite like a fern (visitors to my garden usually ask me what kind of fern it is).

Plant Profile

POLEMONIUM
po-leh-MOW-nee-um

- ■ **Bloom Color:** Blue, pink, or white

- ■ **Bloom Time:** Varies by species; see individual listings

- ■ **Length of Bloom:** 2 or 3 weeks

- ■ **Height:** Varies by species; see individual listings

- ■ **Spread:** 12 to 18 inches (30 to 45 cm)

- ■ **Garden Uses:** Edging, groundcover, mass planting, meadow garden, mixed border, rock garden, woodland garden

- ■ **Light Preference:** Full sun to moderate shade

- ■ **Soil Preference:** Moderately humus-rich, moist but well-drained soil

- ■ **Best Way to Propagate:** Divide in spring or fall; take stem cuttings in summer

- ■ **USDA Plant Hardiness Zones:** 2 to 9

- ■ **AHS Heat Zones:** Varies by species; see individual listings

Growing Tips

Jacob's ladders prefer cool, moist conditions, so mulch them heavily. In cool-summer climates, full sun is best; elsewhere, they do better in partial shade. Extra watering may be necessary in summer, but good drainage is a must in winter.

Although sometimes short-lived, Jacob's ladders are easy to grow and often self-sow, ensuring that you'll always have some on hand. In fact, they can be overly prolific in producing seed, so it's wise to shear most flowering stems back to the base after bloom. This will improve the plant's appearance as well, as the flowerless stems detract from its late-summer duties as a fern imitator. Leave one or two flower stems in place if you want some seed. (Cultivars don't come true from seed, so always remove their flower stems after they finish blooming.)

The easiest way to multiply Jacob's ladder is to dig up the self-sown seedlings, which always seem to be present. For cultivars, though, dividing or taking stem cuttings are the techniques of choice.

Good Neighbors

Jacob's ladders combine well with columbines (*Aquilegia* spp.), epimediums, hellebores (*Helleborus* spp.), and hostas. Adding yellow-flowered goldenstar (*Chrysogonum virginianum*) as a foreground cover would offer a nice contrast in early summer. To extend the flowering season, include late-blooming azure monkshood (*Aconitum carmichaelii*).

Problems and Solutions

Occasional outbreaks of leaf diseases may cause white, brown, or orange spots or a dusty white coating on leaves. They're rarely serious enough to require treatment. Brown leaf tips are usually a sign of a lack of water: Keep the soil at least slightly moist in summer.

Top Performer

Polemonium caeruleum (Jacob's ladder, Greek valerian): The most common species for gardens, this Jacob's ladder produces a mound of ladder-like leaves topped by tall, leafy flowering stems. The flowers bloom in loose, sometimes drooping, clusters in late spring or early summer and often through to midsummer.

Light to deep blue are the most common flower shades. White (in the cultivar 'Album') is also available and, I think, nicer than the blues. The cultivar 'Brise D'Anjou' will stop you dead in your tracks. Its beautiful green leaves are neatly lined with a band of white, as if hand-painted. It looks so good in leaf that you'll be forgiven if you find the blue flowers a distinctly secondary attribute. Height: 18 to 24 inches (45 to 60 cm). Spread: 12 to 18 inches (30 to 45 cm). USDA Plant Hardiness Zones 2 to 9; AHS Heat Zones 9 to 1.

More Recommended Jacob's Ladders

Polemonium foliosissimum (leafy polemonium): This plant resembles a taller version of Jacob's ladder with stronger, more upright stems and larger, brighter lavender-blue flowers with yellow or yellow-orange anthers. Leafy polemonium blooms from late spring to early summer, and often through to midsummer. Less inclined to self-sow, it is very long-lived. Height: 24 to 30 inches (60 to 75 cm). Spread: 12 to 18 inches (30 to 45 cm). USDA Plant Hardiness Zones 2 to 9; AHS Heat Zones 7 to 1.

P. reptans (creeping polemonium): "Creeping," is a misnomer, as this plant doesn't really creep but rather has stems that spread outward, giving it a mounded shape. Creeping polemonium blooms from midspring to early summer. Its flowers droop more than those of common Jacob's ladder (*P. caeruleum*) but otherwise it's very similar. It tolerates shade better than the other species and makes a top-notch groundcover for a open woodland garden or a partly shaded rock garden. 'Blue Pearl', with an abundance of bright blue flowers, is the usual cultivar, but 'Album', with white flowers, and 'Pink Beauty', with pale pink ones, are also very elegant. Height: 8 to 18 inches (20 to 45 cm). Spread: 12 to 18 inches (30 to 45 cm). USDA Plant Hardiness Zones 2 to 9; AHS Heat Zones 8 to 1.

The sky blue flowers of Jacob's ladder (*Polemonium caeruleum*) last for several weeks in late spring and summer. Where the soil is moist and the summers are not too hot and dry, the ferny foliage will remain dense and tidy long after the flowers have faded.

Fall-Blooming PERENNIALS

Beginning gardeners often forget to include fall-blooming perennials in their first garden schemes. In the rush to fill flowerbeds with color, beginners tend to buy whatever's in bloom—and during the spring planting season, that tends to be early bloomers. But gardeners quickly learn the value of fall bloomers like asters and goldenrods. It usually takes only one flowerless fall to inspire them to return to the nursery looking for something that will keep their gardens colorful in September and beyond.

◄Fall bloomers, such as depend able 'Herbstfreude' sedum (*Sedum* 'Herbstfreude', also called *Sedum* 'Autumn Joy'), can afford to bloom generously They've been storing solar energy all summer long.

Figuring Out Fall Bloomers

When you think of it, fall is an odd time of year for plants to bloom. In the fall, most plants and animals are slowing down, getting ready for the upcoming hard times of winter. Going against the flow is this group of oddballs, the fall-blooming perennials.

These sturdy plants have to perform three jobs at once: Produce flowers, develop seed, and prepare for winter. Early frosts can happen without warning, often while fall-flowering perennials are in full bloom. Some are cold-resistant enough to survive without losing a petal, but often, early frosts kill blooms before plants produce seeds.

So what's the advantage to blooming in the fall? For one thing, fall-blooming flowers like heleniums and sedums face much less competition for pollinators. In fact, many fall-blooming perennials are practically mobbed by insects desperately looking for a source of food (pollen and nectar). So plants that dare to wait until fall to bloom are practically guaranteed to be well pollinated.

Fall bloomers have another advantage: They've saved up a maximum amount of solar energy by the time they bloom. Unlike spring and summer bloomers that are still trying to absorb energy while they bloom, autumn bloomers have energy to spare. So they can often afford to bloom generously, confident that they have enough put away for a rainy day.

A Pinch in Time Makes Plants Fine

Many fall-blooming perennials (especially chrysanthemums and asters) spend the summer getting taller and taller until they flop over under the weight of their flower buds. You can prevent this by staking the plants, but pinching gives even better results. As the plants begin to shoot up in late spring, pinch them back to a few inches from the ground. This will *not* delay blooming, but it does stimulate the plants

With good planning, fall can be the most colorful season of the year. Here, late blooming sedums, asters, and chrysanthemums provide an abundance of brilliant color for chilly autumn days.

to produce more stems. The stems will be shorter, so the plants will be bushier.

Each pinched stem will sprout at least two shoots. And as these shoots elongate, you can pinch them back again. The beautiful "cushion mums" of fall aren't a natural phenomenon. Left alone, they'd be tall, lanky plants and their flowers would end up flopping over. So if you want abundantly colorful, compact mounds of fall flowers, be sure to keep up with the summer pinching.

Of course, you'll eventually have to stop pinching or you'll remove the still invisible flower buds of the fall flowers. The cutoff date varies from region to region and, to a certain degree, from cultivar to cultivar. However, you can use the following general guidelines with great results:

- Northern gardens (above 50 degrees north latitude): Don't pinch after July 15

- Mid-latitude gardens (between 35 and 50 degrees north latitude): Don't pinch after August 1

- Southern gardens (below 35 degrees north latitude): Don't pinch after August 15

Making the Most of Fall Bloomers

Using fall-blooming perennials does present a problem for gardeners—what to do with them until they bloom? Most fall bloomers are tall plants that stand out from the crowd—the crowd of lower-growing spring- and summer-blooming perennials, that is. But few of them are very attractive without flowers. It can be a challenge to disguise their ho-hum foliage through the summer.

Keep Them in the Background
One solution is to plant ungainly fall bloomers in the back of the garden, where their not-so-nice foliage remains relatively unnoticed. When they finally bloom, all eyes are drawn to their flowers, not to their foliage.

Try Some Short Selections
I like to grow dwarf or medium-height cultivars of the tall fall-flowering perennials. These used to be quite rare, but they are becoming more and more widely available all the time. A few of my favorites are 'Purple Dome' New England aster (*Aster novae-angliae* 'Purple Dome'), dwarf violet

boltonia (*Boltonia asteroides* var. *latisquama* 'Nana'), and 'Golden Fleece' dwarf goldenrod (*Solidago sphacelata* 'Golden Fleece').

Make Modest Plantings
Add fall flowers in modest quantities to your regular mixed border or perennial garden. Many, such as boltonia and sunflowers (*Helianthus* spp.), are tall, spreading plants with substantial foliage and masses of flowers, so you don't need to follow the usual rule of planting them in groups of three or five: A single plant offers plenty of impact.

The "Instant" Fall Garden
One popular method of fall gardening is to replace fading annuals with full-grown, fully blooming chrysanthemums and asters in early fall: Dig holes here and there in the garden, and plop in a pot of blooming mums or asters for instant color. According to this philosophy, the fall-blooming perennials are expendable and can be treated like annuals—in the spring, just pull them out, fill the spot with annuals, and toss the faded fall bloomers into the compost pile.

Producing Potted Fall Bloomers
I can see why this technique is appealing. But I'm sure many gardeners are like me and can't imagine tossing a healthy plant into the compost simply because it won't bloom for another 10 or 11 months. For those gardeners, I suggest my own scheme for producing fall bloomers without buying them at the garden center.

Each spring, just pot up divisions of fast-growing mums, asters, goldenrods, heleniums, and other fall bloomers. (Don't try this with perennials that don't tolerate or recover quickly from frequent division, such as fall anemones and sedums). Stick the pots in an out-of-the-way part of your yard or garden all summer.

When the perennials begin to bloom, plant them in a more visible bed, replacing a dead or dying annual. Leave them there through fall and winter. In spring, dig them up again and move them back out into their less visible spot for the spring and summer, dividing them if necessary.

Overwintering Potted Fall Bloomers
As fall comes to an end, plant your potted perennials in the garden. Potted perennials are less hardy than the same plants grown in the ground. So remove them from their pots and plant them in their new permanent homes in the garden. Or sink them, pots and all, into the ground so their roots will be buffered against the cold. In spring, plant them in a garden or reuse them as container plants.

Potted Possibilities
Keep in mind that fall-blooming perennials make great container plants, too. Just gather a collection of attractive containers for cachepots. Stick the plastic-potted fall bloomers into the cachepots and place them here and there on your patio, balcony, terrace, or wherever you have containers of annuals that are fading away. Or, place the containers directly in a flowerbed, on top of a faded annual, perhaps. There's no law against it!

12 More Fall Bloomers
Here's an even dozen perennials that will also add to the fall show in your garden.

Aconitum (Aconite) 192		Eupatorium (Joe-Pye weed) 426	
Begonia (Begonia) ..142		Hibiscus (Hibiscus) ..432	
Ceratostigma (Plumbago) 382		Kirengeshoma (Kirengeshoma) 434	
Chelone (Turtlehead) 280		Lavatera (Tree mallow) 89	
Cimicifuga (Cimicifuga) 330		Perovskia (Russian sage) 440	
Coreopsis (Tickseed) 78		Rudbeckia (Rudbeckia) 94	

Anemone

Anemone, windflower

With anemones, you have your choice of spring, summer, or fall bloomers, but be sure to try some that bloom in fall. Fall-blooming anemones are native throughout Asia, but they're inevitably called Chinese or Japanese anemones. These anemones form clumps of dark green, slightly hairy, deeply cut or lobed leaves. As the season draws to a close, graceful, branching, upright stems appear, bearing smaller leaves and then round buds. These buds open to large, cup-shaped flowers with a satiny texture and a contrasting green buttonlike center surrounded by a ring of fluffy yellow anthers.

Plant Profile

ANEMONE
uh-NEM-oh-nee

■ **Bloom Color:** Pink, purple, red, or white

■ **Bloom Time:** Late summer to late fall

■ **Length of Bloom:** 5 weeks or more

■ **Height:** 18 to 60 inches (45 to 150 cm)

■ **Spread:** 18 to 24 inches (45 to 60 cm)

■ **Garden Uses:** Cut flower garden, groundcover, mass planting, mixed border, wildflower meadow, woodland garden; at the back of beds and borders

■ **Light Preference:** Full sun to partial shade

■ **Soil Preference:** Fertile, humus-rich, moist but well-drained soil

■ **Best Way to Propagate:** Divide or take root cuttings in early spring

■ **USDA Plant Hardiness Zones:** Varies by species; see individual listings

■ **AHS Heat Zones:** 9 to 3

Growing Tips

Fall-blooming anemones are easy to grow in the right conditions. Though they can tolerate full sun in cool climates and in beds with moist soil, elsewhere they need protection from the summer sun. Semi-shady sites, with some bright sun early in the day, are best.

Chinese and Japanese anemones prefer good drainage at all times, but particularly in the winter, so avoid spots where water accumulates during the winter months. Mulch and anemones are a perfect match. Mulching is especially important in colder climates, as it helps give the plants a bit of extra cold protection.

If your area has short summers, choose anemones that bloom in early fall. It's disappointing to see anemone flowerstalks shoot up in the fall, forming dozens of flower buds that then never open because they've been cut down by frost. For example, Chinese anemone (*Anemone hupehensis*) tends to bloom earlier than Japanese or hybrid anemone (*A.* × *hybrida*, also called *A.* × *elegans*) and so may be a better choice in borderline climates.

It's not easy to grow anemones from seed. You'll have better results if you divide them in very early spring or just dig out the young plants that develop near the originals. You can also take 3- to 4-inch (8- to 10-cm) root cuttings at the same season. Chinese and Japanese anemones don't *need* division: You can leave them alone for decades.

Warning: All anemones are poisonous if ingested, so be particularly careful to keep them out of reach of young children.

Good Neighbors

They're slow to get started in spring, so late-blooming anemones hide the yellowing foliage of tulips and daffodils beautifully.

Plant them in light deciduous shade with other fall bloomers and with plants that will provide interest throughout the growing season. They contrast well with black snakeroot (*Cimicifuga racemosa*), epimediums, ferns, hostas, and fall-blooming asters and goldenrods (*Solidago* spp.).

Problems and Solutions

Fall-blooming anemones are sturdy plants with no particular pest or disease problems.

Top Performer

Anemone hupehensis (Chinese anemone): Chinese anemone has toothed, three-lobed leaves. Flowers are pink, purple, or white and appear in late summer to early fall. Popular cultivars include 'Praecox', with carmine-pink blooms; 'Prinz Heinrich' (also called 'Prince Henry') with deep pink semi-double flowers; and 'September Charm', with single rose-pink flowers. Height: 24 to 38 inches (60 to 100 cm). Spread: 18 to 24 inches (45 to 60 cm). USDA Plant Hardiness Zones 4 to 9; AHS Heat Zones 9 to 3.

More Recommended Anemones

Anemone × *hybrida*, also called *A.* × *elegans* (Japanese anemone or hybrid anemone): This hybrid species is similar to its parent, *A. hupehensis* var. *japonica* (also called Japanese anemone), although it's generally taller and later-blooming, with flowers up to 4 inches (10 cm) across. Hybrid anemones—particularly the older cultivars—often need staking. The old standard, and still the most popular of all fall anemones, is 'Honorine Jobert' with pure white blooms. Other popular cultivars include 'Königin Charlotte' (also called 'Queen Charlotte'), which has slightly fringed, semi-double pink flowers; deep rose-red 'Pamina', which reaches only 2 to 3 feet (60 to 90 cm) tall; and 'Whirlwind', with semi-double white flowers that bloom in early fall. Height: 2 to 5 feet (24 to 150 cm). Spread: 18 to 24 inches (45 to 60 cm). USDA Plant Hardiness Zones 5 to 9; AHS Heat Zones 9 to 3.

'Honorine Jobert' Japanese anemone (*Anemone* × *hybrida* 'Honorine Jobert')

Larry's Garden Notes

The name for the genus *Anemone* comes from anemos, the Greek word for wind. Tall, fall-blooming Chinese anemone (*Anemone hupenhensis*) and Japanese anemone (*A.* x *hybrida*), however, are not well suited for windy environments because strong wind can bend or break their flowerstalks. Although they may not be wind-worthy, Chinese and Japanese anemones will make sturdy and stunning massed plantings if planted in humus-rich, moist soils.

Aster

Aster, Michaelmas daisy

There are asters that bloom at almost any time during the growing season, but for many gardeners the only true aster is a fall aster. In North America, fall-blooming asters are common wildflowers in fields and glades. Pretty as they are, the flowers of wild asters are often tiny, so new gardeners are often surprised by the large flowers and bright colors of garden asters. The flowers range in size from less than ½ inch (1.25 cm) to more than 2 inches (5 cm) in diameter and come in many colors. There are also double and semi-double cultivars.

Plant Profile

ASTER
AS-ter

- **Bloom Color:** Blue, pink, purple, red, or white
- **Bloom Time:** Late summer to late fall
- **Length of Bloom:** 4 or 5 weeks or more
- **Height:** Varies by species; see individual listings
- **Spread:** Varies by species; see individual listings
- **Garden Uses:** Cut flower garden, edging, hedge, meadow garden, mixed border, woodland garden; at the back of beds and borders; attracts butterflies
- **Light Preference:** Full sun to light shade
- **Soil Preference:** Average, moist but well-drained soil
- **Best Way to Propagate:** Divide in early spring; sow seed in early spring or late fall
- **USDA Plant Hardiness Zones:** Varies by species; see individual listings
- **AHS Heat Zones:** 8 to 1

Growing Tips

Asters grow fast and furious, producing ever-widening clumps that weaken or die out in the center and need dividing every two or three years. Dig them up, and remove and replant healthy sections from the outside of the clump.

Sow aster seed directly in the garden in early spring or in late autumn. After your seed-grown plants have bloomed the first time, select the healthiest and most attractive ones and compost the others. Established asters self-sow freely, but their offspring are often less attractive than the originals. It's best to deadhead your plants severely, cutting off the top several inches of growth after bloom.

Asters survive summer drought fairly well, but if you want good fall bloom, make sure their soil remains fairly moist from August on.

Pinching or shearing asters in the spring or early summer will yield bushier, more free-flowering plants in fall. Taller asters often need staking, especially in windy locations.

Good Neighbors

Pair tall aster cultivars with other stately late-season bloomers such as sunflowers (*Helianthus* spp.) and 'Fireworks' rough-stemmed goldenrod (*Solidago rugosa* 'Fireworks'). Shorter asters mix well with boltonia (*Boltonia asteroides*), goldenrods—particularly 'Golden Fleece' dwarf goldenrod (*Solidago sphacelata* 'Golden Fleece') and 'Crown of Rays' goldenrod (*S.* 'Crown of Rays')—and ornamental grasses.

Problems and Solutions

The main problem affecting asters is powdery mildew. The first line of defense is to plant disease-resistant cultivars. Leaving plenty of space between plants and dividing frequently, plus being careful to water only the roots and not the foliage, will also help prevent the dreaded white coating from appearing on the leaves of your plants.

Top Performers

Aster novi-belgii, also called *A.* × *dumosus* (New York aster): This lovely aster has smooth leaves and forms compact mounds covered with flowers. Widely available cultivars include 'Ernest Ballard', with large, reddish pink, semi-double flowers, 30 to 36 inches (75 to 90 cm); 'Patricia Ballard', semi-double rose pink, 30 to 36 inches (75 to 90 cm); and 'Winston Churchill', red, 2 to 3 feet (60 to 90 cm).

Many experts consider *A.* × *dumosus* to be the same species as New York aster, but to me, there's a rather distinct line of low-growing, dome-shaped hybrid asters, and some of them are quite popular. The plants bloom rather early, in late summer to late fall. Two examples are 'Jenny', which has red flowers and grows 12 to 15 inches (30 to 38 cm) tall, and 'Professor Anton Kippenberg', with bright blue, semi-double flowers on plants 12 to 16 inches (30 to 40 cm) tall. Height: 1 to 5 feet (30 to 150 cm). Spread: 18 to 36 inches (45 to 90 cm). USDA Plant Hardiness Zones 4 to 9; AHS Heat Zones 8 to 1.

More Recommended Fall Asters

Aster novae-angliae (New England aster): The original New England aster is a tall plant—to 6 feet (180 cm)—and usually bears deep violet-purple flowers from late summer or early fall to late fall. Its cultivars come in blues, lavenders, pinks, purples, and reds. Most modern cultivars are considerably smaller plants, often less than 4 feet (120 cm) tall. Among the more popular cultivars are 'Andenken an Alma Pötschke' (also called 'Alma Pötschke'), with large, bright pink blooms; 'Harrington's Pink', salmon-pink blooms; and 'Purple Dome' (also known as *A.* × *dumosus* 'Purple Dome'), a dwarf, late-flowering type with deep blue flowers, only 18 to 24 inches (45 to 60 cm) tall. Height: 18 inches to 6 feet (90 to 180 cm). Spread: 18 to 36 inches (45 to 90 cm). USDA Plant Hardiness Zones 3 to 9; AHS Heat Zones 8 to 1.

New York aster
(*Aster novi-belgii*)

Kissing Cousins

Although it's not a true aster, hairy golden aster (*Chrysopsis villosa*, syn. *Heterotheca villosa*) has a somewhat asterlike growth habit, with hairy gray-green leaves and yellow asterlike flowers. This tough plant takes summer droughts and fall rains in stride. Height: 48 to 60 inches (120 to 150 cm). Spread: 24 inches (60 cm). USDA Plant Hardiness Zones 3 to 9; AHS Heat Zones 12 to 1.

Boltonia

Boltonia

This late-summer beauty makes me think of a big aster that's been crossed with baby's-breath. Boltonia produces thin, branching, interlaced stems with narrow, lance-shaped, blue-green leaves, giving it the appearance of an open, airy shrub. At the end of the gardening season, each stem is topped with small but numerous daisylike, yellow-centered, pink, purple, or white blooms, each ¾ to 1 inch (2 to 2.5 cm) wide. Tall though it may be, don't expect boltonia to block out unwanted views: This plant is strictly see-through.

Plant Profile

BOLTONIA
bowl-TOE-nee-uh

- **Bloom Color:** Pink, purple, or white
- **Bloom Time:** Late summer to midfall
- **Length of Bloom:** 6 weeks or more
- **Height:** 2 to 5 feet (60 to 150 cm)
- **Spread:** 3 to 4 feet (90 to 120 cm)
- **Garden Uses:** Cut flower garden, hedge, mass planting, meadow garden, mixed border, specimen plant; at the back of beds and borders; attracts butterflies
- **Light Preference:** Full sun to light shade
- **Soil Preference:** Average, well-drained soil
- **Best Way to Propagate:** Divide plants in spring or fall
- **USDA Plant Hardiness Zones:** 3 to 9
- **AHS Heat Zones:** 9 to 1

Growing Tips

Boltonia is certainly not hard to grow. It thrives in most well-drained soils and takes sun or partial shade, although full sun is necessary to keep plants from flopping. In very dry, poor soil, boltonia will be considerably smaller than otherwise; it can also grow much bigger than normal when planted in rich, moist soil. In either case, it blooms up a storm!

Leave boltonia stems standing even after it finishes blooming. Its airy, dried stems add interest to the winter garden. It looks especially good rising majestically through a layer of fluffy white snow.

Boltonia can self-sow, but the cultivars don't come true from seed, so pull out and compost self-sown seedlings. Boltonia clumps divide at their base, so you can split them every three or four years if you need a few more plants. If you need plenty, take stem cuttings in the summer.

Boltonia is quite well behaved in most gardens. The species, which are rarely grown, usually require staking, but the cultivars are quite sturdy and only need staking if you grow them in shade or in very rich soil. In very loose soil, boltonia tends to spread through somewhat invasive offsets. If you're worried about this, plant it inside a root barrier, such as a bottomless bucket sunk into the soil.

This wonderful plant has one flaw: It's a terrible space hog. If you have a small garden, just don't plant boltonia. It will overwhelm the site and neighboring plants.

Good Neighbors

With its bounty of daisylike flowers in late summer and autumn, boltonia (*Boltonia asteroides*) can stand on its own in a natural-looking garden. Try combining it with ornamental grasses, such as red switch grass (*Panicum virgatum* 'Haense Herms') or fountain grass (*Pennisetum alopecuroides*), and with summer-blooming perennials, such as coreopsis, hardy geraniums, and Faassen's catmint (*Nepeta* × *faassenii*). Or combine boltonia with other late bloomers, such as Japanese anemone (*Anemone* × *hybrida*), New England aster (*Aster novae-angliae*), and goldenrods (*Solidago* spp.). Pair pink-flowered boltonia cultivars with the grayish green foliage of Russian sage (*Perovskia atriplicifolia*) or 'Powis Castle' artemisia.

'Snowbank' boltonia
(*Boltonia asteroides* 'Snowbank')

Problems and Solutions

Gardeners enjoy growing boltonia because it doesn't suffer from pest or disease problems. Notably, it seems nearly immune to powdery mildew, the bane of its cousin, the aster.

Top Performer

Boltonia asteroides (boltonia, white boltonia): Here it is, folks: The one and only species currently grown. Actually, gardeners almost never grow the species itself, as it tends to be a bit too massive for use in most home gardens, but its cultivars are great garden plants. 'Pink Beauty' has pale lilac-pink flowers on 5-foot (150-cm) stems, with a fairly open habit. Yes, I confess: This one sometimes needs staking.

'Snowbank' is the cultivar everyone is talking about. It grows only 3 to 4 feet (90 to 120 cm) tall, so it's much sturdier and rarely requires staking. And it is incredibly floriferous: Just *try* to count all the flowers!

And, yes, Virginia, there *is* a boltonia for smaller gardens—well, at least for medium-sized gardens. Dwarf violet boltonia (*B. asteroides* var. *latisquama* 'Nana') is a real midget compared to the others: only 2 to 3 feet (60 to 90 cm) tall, with larger purple to rosy lilac flowers.

Around the World with Boltonia

I've always admired boltonia as a pretty wildflower, fine for field and forest, but I'd never thought of it as a candidate for my garden until I saw it one fall day at Garden in the Woods in Framingham, Massachusetts. An early frost had hit a few days before so I expected it would have spelled the end for many flowers. As I walked the paths, I was amazed by the beauty of the gardens in full fall regalia. And then I came across a stupendous giant covered with starry white flowers: a wild boltonia at its finest. You can guess what I ordered for my garden the following spring—and I wasn't disappointed!

Chrysanthemum
Chrysanthemum

Chrysanthemum is a large and varied genus that's been the subject of much debate among botanists. The two *Chrysanthemum* species that I describe here are very popular fall perennials. They have cut leaves and daisylike flowers with a yellow center. Through plant breeding, their flowers have become more complex—there are double, semi-double, and fringed types—but strip away a few petals and they're still daisies deep down inside.

Plant Profile

CHRYSANTHEMUM
kris-AN-thuh-mum

- **Bloom Color:** Bronze, lavender, orange, pink, purple, red, white, and yellow

- **Bloom Time:** Late summer to late fall

- **Length of Bloom:** 4 weeks or more

- **Height:** 1 to 3 feet (30 to 90 cm)

- **Spread:** 2 to 3 feet (60 to 90 cm)

- **Garden Uses:** Container planting, cut flower garden, edging, mass planting, mixed border, specimen plant; at the back of beds and borders; attracts butterflies

- **Light Preference:** Full sun

- **Soil Preference:** Humus-rich, moist but well-drained soil

- **Best Way to Propagate:** Divide or take stem cuttings in spring

- **USDA Plant Hardiness Zones:** Varies by species; see individual listings

- **AHS Heat Zones:** 9 to 2

Growing Tips

These late-blooming beauties appreciate full sun and rich, well-drained soil. Pinching them or shearing them back in the spring and summer will help them remain more compact, but be sure to stop pinching before the plants form flower buds (see page 166 for guidelines on when to stop).

Fall chrysanthemums are mounding plants that tend to die out in the center after a few years. To keep them healthy, divide them frequently—every two years or so—discarding the woody center. Pinched at the right season, chrysanthemums are dense, sturdy plants; if you don't prune them in spring, or if you grow them in partial shade, many cultivars will need staking. Mulch them well: They have shallow roots and won't tolerate drying out.

It's easy to multiply chrysanthemums by dividing them or taking stem cuttings in the spring. You can also grow them from seed, although they rarely come true. If you still wish to try, buy seed of hybrid lines that have been tested for good results. Sow indoors in late winter, and don't cover the seed; it needs light to germinate.

If you live in USDA Zones 3 to 5, do *not* clean up your chrysanthemums in the fall. Their dead stems and leaves serve as natural winter protection; removing them can leave you with dead plants. Wait until spring before you cut the old stems off at their base.

Good Neighbors

Available in a wide variety of colors, chrysanthemums are a mainstay of the fall garden. Combine them with asters, 'Herbstfreude' sedum (*Sedum* 'Herbstfreude', also called *S*. 'Autumn Joy'), and ornamental grasses. Or, for a showy season finale, mass them in front of a shrub border or a grouping of plants with interesting textures, such as Russian sage (*Perovskia atriplicifolia*) or yuccas.

Problems and Solutions

In the garden, chrysanthemums rarely have any major problems.

Top Performer

⭐ **Larry's Favorite:** *Chrysanthemum zawadskii* var. *latilobum*, also called *Dendranthema zawadskii*: This chrysanthemum, with its dark green, deeply cut leaves and daisylike blooms with yellow centers, gets my vote as the most trouble-free of its genus. It can stay in the same spot for years, forming a clump that steadily enlarges over time. This chrysanthemum blooms very profusely for a long period, from midsummer or late summer to early fall. You can prune it back hard in early summer to create a denser plant with more flowers, and that's about the only maintenance it needs. Plus, it has delightfully fragrant blooms, an unusual trait for a chrysanthemum.

Popular cultivars include 'Clara Curtis', deep pink; 'Duchess of Edinburgh', muted red; and 'Mary Stoker', butter yellow with a pink tinge. Height: 2 to 3 feet (60 to 90 cm). Spread: 2 to 3 feet (60 to 90 cm). USDA Plant Hardiness Zones 3 to 9; AHS Heat Zones 9 to 2.

More Recommended Chrysanthemums

🛑 **Think Twice:** *Chrysanthemum* × *morifolium,* also called *Dendranthema* × *grandiflorum* (chrysanthemum, garden mum): The Chinese began breeding this plant well over 2,000 years ago, and there are thousands of cultivars. Many produce complex flowers, though these are mostly tender "florist mums." Old-fashioned pompoms in bronze, lavender, orange, pink, purple, red, white, yellow, or bicolors are standard, although some single and semi-double cultivars exist. These chrysanthemums cover themselves with bloom for weeks at a time, from late summer to late fall. Most garden mums are sold by color, without a cultivar name, so there's no use listing choices here; all are well adapted over a wide range of conditions. In USDA Zones 3 and 4, though, where garden mums are theoretically not hardy, you still can grow them—if you choose very carefully. I suggest either the Minn Hybrids (USDA Zone 4) or the Morden (USDA Zone 3). Height: 1 to 3 feet (30 to 90 cm). Spread: 2 to 3 feet (60 to 90 cm). USDA Plant Hardiness Zones 5 to 9; AHS Heat Zones 9 to 2.

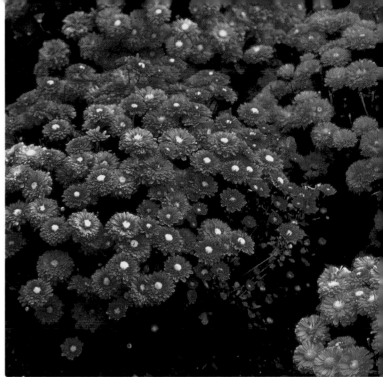

Chrysanthemum
(*Chrysanthemum* × *morifolium*)

Larry's Garden Notes

The florist mums you receive as gifts throughout the year are simply sophisticated versions of the garden mum (*Chrysanthemum* × *morifolium*). If you prune florist mums back harshly after they finish flowering and plant them outside in full sun in well-drained soil, there's a good chance they will bloom again in fall, if frost doesn't kill them first. In USDA Zones 7 to 9, florist mums may even survive the winter to become permanent plants in your garden, but don't count on this in colder zones: When these beauties were developed, cold hardiness was often bred right out of them.

Helianthus

Sunflower

While annual sunflowers are a favorite theme of paintings and T-shirts (not to mention gardens), perennial sunflowers are not nearly as well known. Like the annual species *Helianthus annuus*, perennial sunflowers are generally tall plants, although many cultivars are more reasonably sized. They're not as stiffly upright as annual sunflowers—they grow in clumps and branch readily. Most produce dark green, heart-shaped or lance-shaped leaves that are often roughly textured. All perennial sunflowers bloom late in the season, with daisylike yellow flowers that are much smaller than those of annual sunflowers.

Plant Profile

HELIANTHUS
hee-lee-AN-thus

- **Bloom Color:** Yellow

- **Bloom Time:** Late summer to late fall

- **Length of Bloom:** 4 weeks or more

- **Height:** Varies by species; see individual listings

- **Spread:** 2 to 3 feet (60 to 90 cm)

- **Garden Uses:** Cut flower garden, hedge, meadow garden, mixed border, specimen plant; at the back of beds and borders; in wet areas; attracts birds and butterflies

- **Light Preference:** Full sun

- **Soil Preference:** Average, moist but well-drained soil

- **Best Way to Propagate:** Divide in spring or fall; take stem cuttings in early summer

- **USDA Plant Hardiness Zones:** Varies by species; see individual listings

- **AHS Heat Zones:** Varies by species; see individual listings

Growing Tips

As long as you supply perennial sunflowers with lots of sun, they'll tolerate just about any kind of soil, from rich and well aerated to poor and compacted. They don't tolerate dry soil very well, though, so keep them well watered. Feed sunflowers heavily with compost or bloodmeal if you want more flowers than leaves, particularly from plants growing in poor soil. They often need staking, especially if you don't grow them in full sun.

The best way to propagate perennial sunflowers is to divide plants every three or four years or to take stem cuttings. It's hard to buy seed for perennial sunflowers (many hybrids, in fact, don't produce any seed at all), and the cultivars don't come true from seed.

Good Neighbors

Planted in a mass, tall perennial sunflowers provide a nice green backdrop for a perennial border throughout the summer. The willowy stems and attractive, fine-textured foliage of willowleaf sunflower (*Helianthus salicifolius*) can be such an asset that the yellow flowers that appear in late summer seem like a bonus. Combine this and other tall perennial sunflowers with asters, boltonia (*Boltonia asteroides*), goldenrods (*Solidago* spp.), and tall ornamental grasses such as red switch grass (*Panicum virgatum* 'Haense Herms').

Warning: There is one sunflower I *don't* recommend: the Jerusalem artichoke (*Helianthus tuberosus*). It's an invasive weedy plant that's almost impossible to control (its tuberous roots quickly creep under any root barrier you can think of) and its small, yellow, daisy-like blooms, while pretty enough, pale in comparison to those of the more decorative sunflowers. Keep it out of your flower garden!

Problems and Solutions

Powdery mildew sometimes shows up on aging clumps of sunflowers in areas where air circulation is poor. Divide the plants and place them in a breezier spot, and the problem should resolve itself.

Top Performer

Helianthus × *multiflorus* (perennial sunflower, also called many-flowered sunflower): Once upon a time, many years ago, somebody got the crazy idea of crossing the annual sunflower we all know and love with the perennial thin-leaved sunflower (*H. decapetalus*). And would you believe that it not only worked but also resulted in the most popular perennial sunflower of all, *H.* × *multiflorus*?

There are lots of very nice cultivars with single, semi-double, or double flowers in late summer to midfall. Try 'Capenoch Star', with single, lemon-yellow flowers on 4-foot (120-cm) stems; and 'Loddon Gold', with fully double, bright yellow blooms on stems that reach up to 6 feet (180 cm) tall. Height: 4 to 6 feet (120 to 180 cm). Spread: 2 to 3 feet (60 to 90 cm). USDA Plant Hardiness Zones 3 to 9; AHS Heat Zones 9 to 5.

More Recommended Perennial Sunflowers

⭐ **Larry's Favorite:** *Helianthus salicifolius* (willowleaf sunflower): Feeling despondent about not being able to get a close look at your garden's flowers from your second-floor bedroom window? Plant willowleaf sunflower and flowers will greet you in the morning. Some authorities suggest it reaches a modest 7 feet (210 cm), but I suspect their plants must be starving: In my backyard, willowleaf sunflower grows to about 10 feet (300 cm) tall. The plant produces hordes of single, bright yellow flowers in early to midfall, but until then it will knock you out with its beautiful foliage. In short season areas, leaves may be all you get since the plant doesn't always have time to bloom. Many experts give a rating of USDA Zone 5 for this sunflower, but my plants thrive in Zone 3, so I've compromised with a Zone 4 rating. Height: 5 to 10 feet (150 to 300 cm). Spread: 2 to 3 feet (60 to 90 cm). USDA Plant Hardiness Zones 4 to 9; AHS Heat Zones 9 to 6.

'Loddon Gold' perennial sunflower (*Helianthus* × *multiflorus* 'Loddon Gold')

Kissing Cousins

False sunflower (*Heliopsis helianthoides*) isn't a true sunflower, but who cares? I treat this perennial (which is also called sunflower heliopsis) like the other sunflowers in my garden and no one is the wiser. It's an upright, clump-forming perennial that blooms up a storm, often for a whopping 12 weeks. Choice cultivars include 'Goldgefieder' ('Golden Plume'), 'Goldgrünherz' ('Goldgreenheart'), and 'Sommersonne' ('Summer Sun'). Height: 24 to 72 inches (60 to 180 cm). Spread: 24 to 48 inches (60 to 120 cm). USDA Plant Hardiness Zones 3 to 9; AHS Heat Zones 10 to 1.

Physostegia

Obedient plant, false dragonhead

Many, many moons ago, my great-aunt demonstrated the most striking feature of obedient plant to a group of amazed children (including me). The tiny tubular pink or white flowers on the four-sided narrow spikes are moveable: You can push them to the left or to the right, and they'll stay put. So you can nudge all the flowers to one side of the stalk, turning it into a sort of mini-foxglove, or create a spiral—or even a double spiral—pattern. We kids were entranced for an entire afternoon by these delightful flowers.

Plant Profile

PHYSOSTEGIA
fie-so-STEE-gee-uh

- Bloom Color: Pink or white
- Bloom Time: Midsummer or late summer to early or midfall
- Length of Bloom: 5 weeks or more
- Height: 18 to 48 inches (45 to 120 cm)
- Spread: 2 to 3 feet (60 to 90 cm)
- Garden Uses: Cut flower garden, mass planting, meadow garden, mixed border, woodland garden; at the back of beds and borders; in wet areas
- Light Preference: Full sun to partial shade
- Soil Preference: Rich or poor, wet or dry soil
- Best Way to Propagate: Divide in spring or fall; sow seed in spring
- USDA Plant Hardiness Zones: 3 to 9
- AHS Heat Zones: 8 to 1

Growing Tips

Obedient plant borders are certainly not difficult to grow. Clumps growing in sun prefer moist soil, while drier soil is fine in partially shaded sites. You may need to stake plants growing in rich soil or in excessive shade. If so, consider replacing your floppy plant with a shorter, sturdier cultivar next year.

So much for the good news; now for the bad: This plant is a no-torious spreader, quick to take over if not immediately slapped on the wrist. In fact, I always call it the *disobedient plant*, and experienced gardeners catch the joke without explanation, a sure sign that I'm not the only one who has occasionally let this plant get out of hand. I still grow it, but within a root barrier, and suggest you do the same.

There's always lots of material to divide if you want to multiply your obedient plant. You can also grow it from seed, although the cultivars (and who grows anything else these days?) don't come true.

Besides using the plant as a source of cut flowers, a stem of dried seed capsules looks rather like a stalk of wheat and is a nice addition to dried arrangements. Just harvest the stems when the capsules are still firmly closed and hang them upside down to dry.

Good Neighbors

In evenly moist soil, obedient plant can be quite tall, up to 4 feet (120 cm). Other plants that thrive in similar conditions are the logical choices for companion plants. 'Gateway' Joe-Pye weed (*Eupatorium fistulosum* 'Gateway'), common sneezeweed (*Helenium autumnale*), mildew-resistant bee balms (*Monarda* spp.), and 'Purple Mist' lavender mist (*Thalictrum rochebrunianum*) would all thrive under these conditions.

For a particularly attractive grouping, combine white-flowered obedient plant (*P. virginiana* 'Alba') with purple coneflower (*Echinacea purpurea*) and 'Raspberry Wine' bee balm (*Monarda* 'Raspberry Wine'). Or try planting 'Vivid' obedient plant with its color echo grapeleaf anemone (*Anemone tomentosa*) or with cloudlike 'Snowbank' boltonia (*Boltonia asteroides* 'Snowbank').

Problems and Solutions
Obedient plant has no significant pest or disease problems.

Top Performer
Think Twice: *Physostegia virginiana* (obedient plant): There are about a dozen species in the genus *Physostegia*, but only *P. virginiana* commonly appears in gardens. The plant grows straight up and down, with erect, square stems adorned with narrow, lance-shaped dark green leaves. Fortunately it grows in large clumps, as the individual stems are not very impressive; but in a pack, they create quite a nice effect.

Obedient plant comes in a surprising number of cultivars for a plant that, at first impression, doesn't seem to offer a lot of potential for variety. 'Alba' has pure white flowers on 18- to 24-inch (45- to 60-cm) stems and is perhaps the earliest bloomer, starting almost a month before many of the others. 'Bouquet Rose' is probably the most common cultivar. Its bright pink blooms appear in late summer on 3- to 4-foot (90- to 120-cm) plants, but the stems tend to flop.

'Summer Snow' is another white cultivar and also rather early (midsummer), producing 30-inch (75-cm) plants. It is less invasive than many others. The pink flowers of 'Variegata' take a definite backseat to the striking foliage, which is highly variegated with white. Its 3-foot (90-cm)-tall clumps are less invasive than those of most obedient plants.

'Vivid' is a real charmer and my favorite. It produces rosy pink flowers on a compact plant—2 to 3 feet (60 to 90 cm) tall—that almost never flops.

Spires of obedient plant (*Physostegia virginiana*) make an equally colorful statement whether viewed outdoors in the perennial border or indoors in a vase. Contrary to its name, obedient plant is an exuberant grower; pull out renegade plants regularly to keep plantings in check.

Sedum

Sedum, stonecrop

The genus *Sedum* contains hundreds of species, from tiny groundcovers to upright plants like the universally popular 'Herbstfreude', or 'Autumn Joy', sedum. Here I describe a select group of sedums that bloom in late summer and fall. Many people call these sedums "border stonecrops" to distinguish them from the dwarf species. They share a number of traits, including especially thick stems, comparatively large leaves, and late-season bloom. It also happens that botanists have renamed this very group, the border stonecrops, putting them in the genus *Hylotelephium*.

Plant Profile

SEDUM
SEE-dum

- **Bloom Color:** Pink, purple, red, white, or yellow
- **Bloom Time:** Late summer to late fall
- **Length of Bloom:** 6 weeks or more
- **Height:** 4 to 24 inches (10 to 60 cm)
- **Spread:** 12 to 18 inches (30 to 45 cm)
- **Garden Uses:** Cut flower garden, container planting, edging, groundcover, mass planting, meadow garden, mixed border, rock garden, specimen plant, wall planting; on slopes; attracts butterflies
- **Light Preference:** Full sun to partial shade
- **Soil Preference:** Average, well-drained soil
- **Best Way to Propagate:** Divide in spring; take stem cuttings in summer
- **USDA Plant Hardiness Zones:** 3 to 9
- **AHS Heat Zones:** Varies by species; see individual listings

Growing Tips

Unlike most succulent-leaved plants, fall-blooming sedums can tolerate rainy climates and partly shady spots. But fall sedums do thrive in well-drained soil and full sun: The taller ones, in fact, will tend to flop if they don't get full sun and good drainage.

In hot-summer areas, or when sun is lacking, some fall sedums tend to grow taller than they really should, resulting in weaker stems. Try pruning the plants back by half in early July: This will lead to shorter stems that shouldn't topple.

Sedums don't really need division, at least not for many years. If you want to multiply your plants, stem cuttings are the way to go.

Good Neighbors

There is such variety in the late-blooming sedums that choices for companions are practically unlimited. Try masses of 'Herbstfreude' sedum with blue star (*Amsonia hubrectii*), rudbeckias, and low-growing ornamental grasses or with the silver grays of 'Powis Castle' artemisia or Russian sage (*Perovskia atriplicifolia*).

Use the low-growing, darker-leaved 'Vera Jameson' sedum (*S.* 'Vera Jameson') as an edging plant, along with the fine-textured foliage of sea thrift (*Armeria maritima*) and pinks (*Dianthus* spp.).

Problems and Solutions

Fall sedums are generally free of insect and disease problems.

Top Performer

Sedum 'Herbstfreude', now *Hylotelephium* 'Herbstfreude', also called 'Autumn Joy' ('Herbstfreude' sedum): The thick stems of this hybrid carry broad, gray-green leaves. By late summer, the tops of the stems are totally hidden by huge, 6-inch (16-cm), cauliflower-shaped clusters of densely packed, pale whitish green flower buds that turn bright pink then deep red from late summer to late fall. Height: 18 to 24 inches (45 to 60 cm). Spread: 18 to 24 inches (45 to 60 cm). USDA Plant Hardiness Zones 3 to 9; AHS Heat Zones 12 to 1.

More Recommended Sedums

Sedum spectabile, now *Hylotelephium spectabile* (showy stonecrop): Showy stonecrop produces thick, upright or slightly spreading stems with abundant, rounded, 3-inch (8-cm), blue-green leaves. Dense, dome-shaped clusters of pink flowers bloom from late summer to midfall, turning maroon as they dry on the stalk. Cultivars include 'Brilliant', deep pink and perhaps the most widely available; 'Carmen', particularly nice, with carmine-pink flowers; and 'Iceberg', somewhat more compact than most, with white flowers. Height: 18 to 24 inches (45 to 60 cm). Spread: 18 to 24 inches (45 to 60 cm). USDA Plant Hardiness Zones 3 to 9; AHS Heat Zones 12 to 1.

S. *telephium*, now *H. telephium* (orpine): Very similar to showy stonecrop, this plant has narrower leaves and creamy white flowers. It's best known for its purple-leaved cultivar, *S. telephium* subsp. *maximum* 'Atropurpureum'; it forms upright clumps of maroon-purple leaves and has loose clusters of rose-pink flowers. S. 'Mohrchen' now *H.* 'Mohrchen': 'Mohrchen' is similar to *S. telephium* subsp. *maximum* 'Atropurpureum', but its leaves are purple only at first, tending to become greener as they mature. Height: 18 to 24 inches (45 to 60 cm). Spread: 12 to 18 inches (30 to 45 cm). USDA Plant Hardiness Zones 3 to 9; AHS Heat Zones 9 to 1.

S. 'Vera Jameson', now *H.* 'Vera Jameson' ('Vera Jameson' sedum): This beautiful hybrid is a compact, arching plant with mahogany-red leaves and dusty pink flowers from late summer to midfall. Height: 9 to 12 inches (20 to 30 cm). Spread: 12 to 18 inches (30 to 45 cm). USDA Plant Hardiness Zones 3 to 9; AHS Heat Zones 9 to 1.

'Herbstfreude' sedum (*Sedum* 'Herbstfreude'; also called *Sedum* 'Autumn Joy')

Larry's Garden Notes

With sedums (*Sedum* spp.), propagation is so easy that it makes a gratifying "how to" plant for introducing a child or a novice gardener to cuttings. You don't need rooting hormones or any special growing medium—all you need is an all-purpose potting mix. Just cut a growing tip before it starts to develop flower buds, poke it into a little pot filled with potting mix, and keep it moist. Before long, you'll notice it beginning to elongate. Pinch off the top so it will branch, and you've got your new plant!

Solidago

Goldenrod

Goldenrods can be tiny, ground-hugging herbs or near giants, but most garden goldenrods take a middle road. The genus *Solidago* has 130 species, most native to North America. Almost all commonly grown goldenrods have feathery, branching clusters of bright yellow flowers. The plants have a relatively woody base and simple leaves that are toothed and often narrow and lance-shaped.

Plant Profile

SOLIDAGO
sole-ih-DAY-go

- **Bloom Color:** Yellow

- **Bloom Time:** Late summer to midfall

- **Length of Bloom:** 5 weeks or more

- **Height:** Varies by species; see individual listings

- **Spread:** Varies by species; see individual listings

- **Garden Uses:** Cut flower garden, edging, hedge, meadow garden, mixed border, woodland garden; at the back of beds and borders; attracts butterflies

- **Light Preference:** Full sun to partial shade

- **Soil Preference:** Average, moist but well-drained soil

- **Best Way to Propagate:** Divide in spring; take stem cuttings in early summer

- **USDA Plant Hardiness Zones:** Varies by species; see individual listings

- **AHS Heat Zones:** 9 to 1

Growing Tips

The key to enjoying goldenrod, rather than fighting it, is to grow the right kinds. Canada goldenrod (*S. canadensis*) spreads quickly to become a pest, but its numerous hybrids often faithfully re-create the feathery golden plumes of the species on clump-forming, non-invasive plants. Just to be on the safe side, deadhead goldenrods after they bloom so there's no danger they'll self-sow. Taller golden-rods may require staking, especially in partial shade.

To propagate ornamental goldenrod, rely on division or stem cut-tings—most cultivars and hybrids don't come true from seed. Hybrids and garden types form dense clumps that tend to die back in the center over time. If this happens, remove healthy young sections from the outer ring when you divide the plants and discard the woody core.

Good Neighbors

Pair the taller goldenrods, such as hybrid Canada goldenrods (*S. canadensis* hybrids), with showy plants such as tall asters and purple coneflower (*Echinacea purpurea*). Try 'Fireworks' rough-stemmed gold-enrod (*S. rugosa* 'Fireworks') in front of boltonia (*Boltonia asteroides*) or Joe-Pye weed (*Eupatorium fistulosum*) for a season finale.

'Golden Fleece' dwarf goldenrod (*S. sphacelata* 'Golden Fleece') is much easier to place because of its compact size. Pair it with 'Purple Dome' New England aster (*Aster novae-angliae* 'Purple Dome') with a background of Russian sage (*Perovskia atriplicifolia*) for interest late in the season.

Problems and Solutions

Powdery mildew is a common problem for goldenrods, causing gray patches on leaves. A site with full sun, good drainage, and ample air movement reduces the chance of disease development. You can also divide or thin out dense clumps to increase air circulation. The same techniques also help reduce rust, which causes bronze spots on stems and leaf undersides.

Where goldenrods grow wild, domesticated goldenrods are sometimes infested with goldenrod gall, which shows up as a smooth, spindle-shaped swelling on the flower stems. Caused by a tiny insect, the gall is actually harmless.

Top Performer

Solidago canadensis hybrids (hybrid Canada goldenrod): These hybrids offer the bright yellow, plumelike clusters of Canada goldenrod on shorter, denser, and—most important—noninvasive plants. They also start to bloom as early as midsummer.

The hybrid 'Crown of Rays' (also called 'Strahlenkrone') has bright yellow plumes reaching 15 to 24 inches (38 to 60 cm) tall. 'Golden Thumb' (also called 'Queenie') is only 1 foot (30 cm) tall, with yellow flowers. 'Golden Wings' bears deep yellow flowers on sturdy 5- to 6-foot (150- to 180-cm) stems that generally require no staking. Height: 1 to 6 feet (30 to 180 cm). Spread: 1 to 3 feet (30 to 90 cm). USDA Plant Hardiness Zones 3 to 9; AHS Heat Zones 9 to 1.

More Recommended Goldenrods

Solidago rugosa (rough-stemmed goldenrod): This hairy-stemmed, late-blooming plant offers large, open clusters of yellow flowers in midfall to late fall on arching stems. It produces some creeping roots, but it is not as invasive as Canada goldenrod; plant it inside a root barrier. Compact 'Fireworks' is becoming very popular. Height: 3 to 5 feet (90 to 150 cm). Spread: 2 to 3 feet (60 to 90 cm). USDA Plant Hardiness Zones 3 to 9; AHS Heat Zones 9 to 1.

S. sphacelata (dwarf goldenrod): The species is rarely grown, but its cultivar, 'Golden Fleece', is a popular choice for gardens. It's very different from other goldenrods, forming a ground-hugging mound of rounded leaves topped off with branching wands of little golden flowers from late summer to midfall. Height: 18 to 24 inches (45 to 60 cm). Spread: 12 to 18 inches (30 to 45 cm). USDA Plant Hardiness Zones 5 to 9; AHS Heat Zones 9 to 1.

'Golden Wings' hybrid Canada goldenrod (*Solidago canadensis* 'Golden Wings')

Around the World with Goldenrods

Goldenrods are among the most popular fall flowers in Europe. They're at the top of the list of flowers for yellow color-theme gardens (you should see the one at Sissinghurst Castle: It's like they painted heaven in brilliant yellow!) but are also used abundantly in mixed perennial borders. And European gardeners don't limit themselves to the fall bloomers, either: They also select many of the earlier blooming species like European goldenrod (*Solidago virgaurea*) so that the goldenrod season starts as early as midsummer.

LARRY'S LAST LOOK: FALL BLOOMERS

Gardeners often have a hard time finding enough fall bloomers, but I've found dozens that fit the bill. I couldn't squeeze them all into the previous pages, so the extras are highlighted here in condensed form. So after the summer perennials have faded, look for these chilly-weather bloomers.

COMMON AND BOTANICAL NAME	ZONES AND EXPOSURES	BLOOM COLOR AND TIME	DESCRIPTION
Grapeleaf anemone *Anemone tomentosa*	Hardiness Zones 4–9 Heat Zones 8–3 Sun to partial shade	White to pale pink flowers in midsummer to early fall	Vigorous plant produces new plantlets on long runners; give it lots of space. A star of the fall garden. Height: 2–3 feet (60–90 cm). Spread: 18–24 inches (45–60 cm).
Heath aster *Aster ericoides,* also called *A. multiflorus*	Hardiness Zones 3–9 Heat Zones 8–5 Sun	White, pink, blue, or lavender flowers in midsummer through midfall	Attractive aster with bushy, mounding habit and tiny needlelike leaves. In bloom, this aster has hundreds of tiny, star-shaped flowers. Height: 30–48 inches (75–120 cm). Spread: 2 feet (60 cm).
Tatarian aster *Aster tataricus*	Hardiness Zones 4–9 Heat Zones 8–1 Sun to light shade	Blue to purple flowers in midfall to very late fall	A large, sturdy aster with dense clusters of huge lance-shaped leaves on short stems and clusters of daisylike flowers on tall stems. An excellent selection for long-season gardens because it continues blooming into late fall. Height: 5–7 feet (150–213 cm). Spread: 3 feet (90 cm).
Weyrich chrysanthemum *Chrysanthemum weyrichii,* syn. *Dendranthema weyrichii*	Hardiness Zones 3–8 Heat Zones 9–1 Sun	Light pink flowers in midfall to late fall	Charming low-growing plant that spreads through underground runners to make a great groundcover. Bears shiny green leaves and 1–2-inch (2.5–5 cm) daisylike flowers. Height: 8–12 inches (20–30 cm). Spread: 18 inches (45 cm).
Orange sneezeweed *Helenium hoopesii*	Hardiness Zones 3–9 Heat Zones 8–1 Sun to light shade	Yellow flowers with orange centers in early summer to late summer	Blooms for 8 weeks or more in summer. Often needs staking. Height: 2–3 feet (60–90 cm). Spread: 18–24 inches (45–60 cm).
Nippon daisy *Nipponanthemum nipponicum,* also called *Chrysanthemum nipponicum*	Hardiness Zones 5–9 Heat Zones 10–6 Sun	White flowers with yellow centers in midfall to late fall	A tall dome of dark green leaves on thick stems topped by white daisies. Needs a great deal of heat and a long, frost-free fall season. Prune in spring and pinch in midsummer. A good seaside plant because it can tolerate salt spray. Height: 1–3 feet (30–90 cm). Spread: 2–3 feet (60–90 cm).

COMMON AND BOTANICAL NAME	ZONES AND EXPOSURES	BLOOM COLOR AND TIME	DESCRIPTION
Sedum *Sedum alboroseum,* also called *Hylotelephium erythrostictum*	Hardiness Zones 3–9 Heat Zones 8–1 Sun	Creamy white-pink flowers in late summer to late fall	Has glaucous sea green leaves and dense clusters of creamy white flowers with a pinkish tinge, but the species is rarely grown. The cultivar 'Mediovariegatum' is popular; it has creamy yellow leaves with a gray-green edge and pink flowers. Height: 12–18 inches (30–45 cm). Spread: 1 foot (30 cm).
'Ruby Glow' sedum *Sedum* 'Ruby Glow', also called *Hylotelephium* 'Ruby Glow'	Hardiness Zones 3–9 Heat Zones 8–1 Sun	Ruby red flowers in late summer to midfall	Low-growing perennial that bears upright, somewhat spreading, succulent stems of purple-gray foliage. Flowers bloom in 2-inch (5-cm)-wide clusters and attract hordes of butterflies. Height: 1 foot (30 cm). Spread: 1 foot (30 cm).
October daphne *Sedum sieboldii,* also called *Hylotelephium sieboldii*	Hardiness Zones 5–9 Heat Zones 8–1 Sun to light shade	Dusty pink flowers in late fall	Creeping, blue-gray-stemmed perennial covered with rounded leaves and flat clusters of flowers. Looks great in a rock garden or a hanging basket. Height: 6–8 inches (15–20 cm). Spread: 18–24 inches (45–60 cm).
European goldenrod *Solidago virgaurea*	Hardiness Zones 3–9 Heat Zones 9–1 Sun	Gold flowers in midsummer to late summer	Noninvasive perennial produces upright, dense flower spikes. Starts to bloom as early as midsummer rather than fall, like other goldenrods. Most cultivars listed under this name are actually hybrid forms of Canada goldenrod (*S. canadensis*). Height: 10–36 inches (25–90 cm). Spread: 18 inches (45 cm).

Nippon daisy
(*Nipponanthemum nipponicum*)

'Ruby Glow' sedum
(*Sedum* 'Ruby Glow')

No-Care PERENNIALS

What makes a plant a no-care perennial? To me, the top requirement for a no-care perennial is longevity. Remember, most perennials aren't forever. They die out after 5 to 10 years (and some don't even live that long). To avoid losing a choice plant, then, gardeners have to divide them or take cuttings from time to time, as insurance. But no-care perennials, like daylilies and peonies, are as long-lived as many trees and shrubs, without any fussing or special care on your part. The proof of the pudding is that you can still find many of these perennials around abandoned farmhouses 70 or more years after they were first planted. Now that's staying power.

◄ The nodding flowers of hellebores (*Helleborus* spp.) grace the spring landscape dependably year after year. These no-care perennials thrive in partial shade and make great groundcovers under trees and shrubs.

The Joy of No-Care Perennials

I can't deny it: No-care perennials are my absolute favorites. It's not that I don't enjoy puttering over plants, but it's such a relief to have a few flowers in the garden that don't need my attention—ever—so I can invest my efforts in the ones that do. With most other garden plants, even on those quiet weekends when I just want to relax and do nothing, I get this nagging feeling that I really ought to be in the garden. When I feel that way, I just think of my gas plant (*Dictamnus albus*), growing all on its own where I planted it ten years ago, or of that nameless hosta that I haven't even touched since I moved to this house. Suddenly, I'm at peace. So, take off the pressure, kick off your shoes, and truly *enjoy* your garden: That's what no-care perennials are for!

Caring for No-Care Perennials

I've made no-care perennials sound like perfect plants, but I must admit that the term "no-care" is a *slight* exaggeration. All garden plants require some care at least occasionally—but in many cases, once you plant a no-care perennial, you can forget it. The plant will slowly establish itself, and once it reaches maturity, it will bloom for years and years without any fuss.

The Basics of No-Care

No-care perennials get along fine with only light feedings, such as an occasional topdressing with compost. In fact, they'll still bloom heavily even if you never feed them at all. They may need a bit of weeding now and then (or mulch them heavily and you'll avoid even that maintenance).

Western bleeding heart (*Dicentra formosa* 'Alba') adds lacy texture and elegant long-blooming flower clusters to the garden. Just plant it in rich, moist soil where it will get at least a half day of sun, and it will grace your garden for years with no special care needed.

The only other cares that benefit no-care perennials are an occasional cleanup to remove dead leaves and faded flowerstalks and a bit of watering the first year, until they've settled in.

Pests? No Problem!

No-care perennials are relatively immune to insects and disease. Not that an occasional pest can't nibble on a leaf every now and then, but the damage is slight and the plant always fully recovers. Certain no-care perennials are vulnerable to specific problems. For example, hostas can really suffer from the ravages of slugs and snails. To learn whether a no-care perennial is susceptible to any problems, check the "Problems and Solutions" section of each entry in this chapter.

Perennials That Require Patience

There's a lot to be said for perennials that grow quickly. They rapidly fill space in the garden and please you by flowering the first year you plant them. By the second year, many perennials are at their prime. Of course, they may well go quickly

downhill after that because plants that grow quickly are usually short-lived.

No-care perennials, on the contrary, are total busts when it comes to speed. Most barely move at all the first year and many bloom only lightly, if at all, in the second. Some start to look fairly good in the third year, but many take five years to establish themselves and up to ten to reach their prime.

Small Is Best

If you could buy mature, blooming-size no-care perennials and pop them into your garden, you wouldn't need to worry about their slow growth. But buying large no-care perennials isn't always possible. Many of them produce long taproots, which makes them very difficult to transplant. In most cases, it's best to buy no-care perennials as young plants and plant them where you want them to grow permanently.

A Worthwhile Investment

It takes resolve to buy a no-care perennial at a nursery. You have to ignore the rows of full-to-the-brim containers and abundant flowers of other perennials and pick out the scrawniest plants in the store. No-care perennials are slow growers, so they don't fill out. Young potted plants may only have one or two stems and a half-dozen leaves.

And wait till you see the price. Most no-care perennials are more expensive than other perennials, often considerably so, and the reason is simple. Faster-growing perennials are ready for sale in one growing season, meaning big bucks with little effort for the nurseryman. No-cares may require three or more years of culture before they're ready for sale, so you're paying for those extra years of care. But think of how many years of pleasure they'll give you, and I bet you'll decide that no-care perennials are worth the price.

No-Care Plants for Low-Maintenance Gardens

I often watch homeowners struggle with their professionally planned "low-maintenance gardens" that include landscape fabrics as weed barriers and stone or bark mulches for a tidy finish. Even with mulch on top of it, weeds quickly invade the landscape fabric and the homeowners have to spend time trying to pull them out. Plus, the plants are usually fast-growing perennials because they look good right away. After all, the new garden has to be beautiful or the client (you!) may not want to pay.

Landscapers believe that the landscape fabric will keep those fast-growing perennials in check. It certainly does; it usually kills them within three or four years by preventing them from thriving. Low maintenance, my foot!

My advice is, if you want a low-maintenance garden, plan it yourself. Have it feature the no-care perennials I recommend, as well as some of the low-care perennials listed in "Drought-Resistant Perennials" on page 242. Include some easy-care shrubs and small trees, too. Plant the perennials at their recommended spacing and

mulch with one of the biodegradable mulches described on page 60, *not* landscape fabric. Pile on more mulch annually to keep weed seeds from germinating.

And don't expect instant results: That low-maintenance bed will look pretty barren at first, but it will fill in gradually over time. By the time the plants are mature (three to five years), your low-maintenance garden will require only the most minimal efforts. The only upkeep tasks you'll need to worry about are spreading fresh mulch as the old disappears and watering during the worst of droughts.

Good Neighbors for No-Care Perennials

Because many no-care perennials are slow growers, it's smart to interplant them with fast-growing but short-lived perennials, such as sweet rocket (*Hesperis matronalis*) and musk mallow (*Malva moschata*). Biennials like Canterbury bells (*Campanula medium*) and self-sowing annuals like cosmos (*Cosmos bipinnatus*) also make good neighbors. By the time the slow no-cares are in their prime, the fast-growing perennials will be dying out. And the shade cast by the no-care perennials will keep the biennials and annuals under control, allowing the no-cares to take their rightful place as kings of the garden.

7 More No-Care Perennials

A few no-care perennials have other qualities of note, so I've tucked them into other chapters. When you're looking for long-lasting perennials that are easy to care for, try these, too:

Aconitum

Aconite, monkshood, wolf's bane

Aconites look a bit like delphiniums, but as garden performers, aconites have delphiniums beat. Not only are they pest- and disease-resistant, they bloom for as long as two months. Aconites have hooded blossoms at the top of tall, starkly upright bloom stalks. Aconite leaves are dark green and look like fingers radiating from a hand, and the leaf edges are deeply cut. This distinctive foliage makes the plants attractive even when they're not in bloom.

Plant Profile

ACONITUM
ack-oh-NEYE-tum

- **Bloom Color:** Blue, pink, or white
- **Bloom Time:** Midsummer to late fall
- **Length of Bloom:** 2 months
- **Height:** 3 feet (90 cm) or taller
- **Spread:** 1 to 3 feet (30 to 90 cm)
- **Garden Uses:** Cut flower garden, meadow garden, mixed border, woodland garden
- **Light Preference:** Full sun to light shade
- **Soil Preference:** Humus-rich, moist but well-drained soil
- **Best Way to Propagate:** Divide in spring or fall
- **USDA Plant Hardiness Zones:** Varies by species; see individual listings
- **AHS Heat Zones:** 8 to 3

Growing Tips

Aconites are outstanding plants under the right conditions, but may disappoint you if you plant them in the wrong place. They actually grow better in light shade than in full sun, especially in the southern parts of their range, although they can be spectacular in sunny spots as long as you keep the soil quite moist. Aconites have sturdy stems, so only the tallest types need staking. Give them too much shade or plant them in a windy spot, though, and even the strongest-stemmed aconites can flop over.

You can plant aconite seed at any time, but don't expect fabulous results—germination is often slow and irregular. Your best bet for propagating these plants is division. While they never need dividing to stay vigorous, the carrotlike or tuberous roots respond better to division than those of most no-care perennials; you can expect to see plants bloom as soon as two or three years after being divided.

Good Neighbors

When choosing neighbors, select perennials that thrive in the same cool, moist, partly shaded conditions that aconites love. Good choices include astilbes, ligularias (*Ligularia* spp.), primroses, pulmonarias (*Pulmonaria* spp.), and globeflowers (*Trollius* spp.) as well as hellebores (*Helleborus* spp.), ferns, and forget-me-nots (*Myosotis* spp.).

Warning: Always wash your hands after working with aconites to avoid ingesting any of their toxic sap. If ingested in even small amounts, the plant can cause death by cardiac or respiratory failure. And although it acts more rapidly when ingested, it can also be absorbed through the skin. (In fact, it's not a bad idea to wear gloves to protect your hands.) And remember to keep children and pets away from this plant.

Problems and Solutions

Aconites are highly resistant to diseases and pests.

Top Performer

⭐ **Larry's Favorite:** *Aconitum septentrionale* 'Ivorine' (ivory monkshood): This selection is the shortest and earliest-blooming monkshood that's readily available. It begins blooming as early as late spring and continues into midsummer. Featuring ivory white flowers on short spikes, it seems to do better in shade than other aconites. Best of all, it never needs staking. Height: 2 to 3 feet (60 to 90 cm). Spread: 1 foot (30 cm). USDA Plant Hardiness Zones 1 to 9; AHS Heat Zones 8 to 3.

Ivory monkshood
(*Aconitum septentrionale* 'Ivorine')

More Recommended Aconites

Aconitum × *cammarum*, also called *A.* × *bicolor* (bicolor monkshood): This popular hybrid sports blue-and-white flowers from midsummer to late summer. You may see it growing around old homes, a sign of long-standing popularity. Height: 3 to 4 feet (90 to 120 cm). Spread: 2 feet (60 cm). USDA Plant Hardiness Zones 2 to 7; AHS Heat Zones 8 to 3.

A. carmichaelii (azure monkshood): This late-blooming aconite offers larger, paler blue flowers and less deeply divided leaves than other species. It blooms from late summer through fall. There are several cultivars of various colors, including the intense blue 'Arendsii' (also called *A.* × *arendsii*), which may require staking. Height: 4 to 6 feet (120 to 180 cm). Spread: 3 feet (90 cm). USDA Plant Hardiness Zones 2 to 9; AHS Heat Zones 8 to 3.

A. henryi 'Spark's Variety' ('Spark's Variety' autumn monkshood): Another tall, late-summer-to-fall bloomer, this selection produces deep blue flowers. Like most late-blooming aconites, it may require staking. Height: 4 to 6 feet (120 to 180 cm). Spread: 2 feet (60 cm). USDA Plant Hardiness Zones 2 to 9; AHS Heat Zones 8 to 3.

A. napellus (common monkshood, garden monkshood): The mid-summer to late-summer flowers of this common species are generally blue or purple, but there are also pink, white, and reddish cultivars. It's more heat-tolerant than other aconites, so it's the best choice for the South. Height: 3 to 4 feet (90 to 120 cm). Spread: 1 foot (30 cm). USDA Plant Hardiness Zones 2 to 9; AHS Heat Zones 8 to 3.

Larry's Garden Notes

Aconites (*Aconitum* spp.) have been popular garden plants for a long time. Some of the common names give witness to their hooded blooms—monkshood, helmet flower, turk's cap, friar's cap, and soldier's cap—but they've also been called wolf's bane since the roots were used to poison wolves. Various species grow wild throughout the Northern Hemisphere. You may spot cultivated varieties growing in or near old gardens, often in places that have been abandoned for more than a century.

Baptisia

Baptisia, wild indigo, false indigo

Baptisias have something to offer in all seasons. In early spring, they add interest with their thick, asparagus-like stalks; later their flowers appear. Their dense, cloverlike blue-green leaves on sturdy stems look great throughout summer and their often colorful seedpods are the finishing touch through summer and fall. If you love lupines, but you don't have time to cater to their every little need, baptisias are the perfect substitute. They produce tall, lupinelike spikes of pea-shaped flowers, but unlike lupines, baptisias are long-lived, and aphids don't devour them.

Plant Profile

BAPTISIA
bap-TEEZ-ee-uh

- **Bloom Color:** Blue, purple, or white
- **Bloom Time:** Late spring to early summer
- **Length of Bloom:** 3 or 4 weeks
- **Height:** 3 to 4 feet (90 to 120 cm)
- **Spread:** 3 to 4 feet (90 to 120 cm)
- **Garden Uses:** Cut flower garden, hedge, mass planting, meadow garden, mixed border, specimen plant; at the back of beds or borders
- **Light Preference:** Full sun to partial shade
- **Soil Preference:** Average, well-drained, cool soil
- **Best Way to Propagate:** Sow seed in late summer, as soon as it matures
- **USDA Plant Hardiness Zones:** Varies by species; see individual listings
- **AHS Heat Zones:** 9 to 1

Growing Tips

Slow and steady wins the race, said Aesop, and baptisias are definitely more tortoises than hares. Although they may bloom lightly in their second year, baptisias take at least five years to reach their full, thick, shrublike appearance.

The only maintenance that baptisias need is to have their frost-blackened leaves cut back in fall or spring. Baptisias form dense, impenetrable clumps that no weed could ever work its way into. And these plants even supply their own fertilizer: They're legumes, so they develop colonies of nitrogen-fixing bacteria on their roots. How's that for making your life easier?

In some climates, baptisias may need staking if you grow them in partial shade. If you know your plants tend to flop, try placing a peony ring or other support over the clump in early spring.

Baptisias really only have one drawback: They're darn slow to multiply. I'm a truly patient guy, but even I find it hard to wait for baptisia seedlings to mature. If you want to try, soak the hard seeds overnight in tepid water, then carefully chip them with a sharp knife before sowing them ¼ inch (6 mm) deep indoors in peat pots. Or sow them outside in fall; they'll sprout the following spring. It's best to sow them where you want them to grow, as even young seedlings quickly form taproots and are hard to move without risking injury to the plant.

You can propagate cultivars by dividing the thick, long taproots, but don't expect the mother plant to forgive you easily for uprooting her. The only time I tried this, mine moped for two full years before agreeing to bloom (lightly). If I ever need new baptisias again, I'll head straight to the garden center and buy them.

Good Neighbors

Early in the season, combine the blue spikes of blue false indigo (*Baptisia australis*) with contrasting orange-red oriental poppy (*Papaver orientale*), or echo the blue with bearded irises. Good choices for foreground plantings include lady's-mantle (*Alchemilla mollis*), fringed bleeding heart (*Dicentra eximia*), and hardy geraniums.

With their sturdy gray-green foliage that remains handsome all season long, baptisias look beautiful as a backdrop for midsized, later-blooming plants, such as asters and coreopsis.

Problems and Solutions

Baptisias are not subject to any serious disease or insect problems.

Top Performer

⭐**Larry's Favorite:** *Baptisia australis* (blue false indigo): How can I help but like blue false indigo best? It's rock-hardy yet survives the heat of Deep South summers (at least to AHS Heat Zone 9) without complaint, making this one of the most widely adaptable of all perennials. The 10- to 12-inch (25- to 30-cm) flower spikes range in color from light blue to deepest indigo and last about four weeks, from late spring to early summer. 'Purple Smoke', a natural hybrid of blue false indigo and white false indigo (*B. alba*), has beautiful gray-blue flowers. Height: 3 to 4 feet (90 to 120 cm). Spread: 3 to 4 feet (90 to 120 cm). USDA Plant Hardiness Zones 2 to 9; AHS Heat Zones 9 to 1.

More Recommended Baptisias

Baptisia alba (white false indigo): White false indigo looks much like blue false indigo, except that its flowers are white instead of blue. *B. pendula*, which is also called *B. alba* 'Pendula', may or may not be a separate species, but it's virtually identical to white false indigo. It has one unique characteristic: Its seedpods droop rather than remain erect. Western white false indigo (*B. lactea*, also called *B. leucantha*) is also almost identical to white false indigo. Height: 3 to 4 feet (90 to 120 cm). Spread: 3 feet (90 cm). USDA Plant Hardiness Zones 4 to 9; AHS Heat Zones 9 to 1.

Blue false indigo
(*Baptisia australis*)

Kissing Cousins

False lupines, or bush peas (*Thermopsis* spp.), are similar to baptisias—just their seed capsules and yellow flowers are different. *Thermopsis caroliniana*, also called *T. villosa* (Carolina lupine), is a bushy plant with bluish green leaves. Height: 30 to 48 inches (75 to120 cm). Spread: 36 to 48 inches (90 to 120 cm). USDA Plant Hardiness Zones 3 to 9; AHS Heat Zones 10 to 1.

T. lupinoides, or *T. lanceolata* (lanceleaf thermopsis, lanceleaf false lupine): This dwarf species is ideal for colder climates. Height: 8 to 12 inches (20 to 30 cm). Spread: 12 to 18 inches (30 to 45 cm). USDA Plant Hardiness Zones 1 to 9; AHS Heat Zones 7 to 1.

Dicentra

Bleeding heart

The flowers of bleeding hearts are unmistakable, for they really are heart-shaped.
The two outer petals are rounded at the tops and splayed at the tips. The flowers
also have inner petals that just barely protrude through the outer shell. The flowers
are borne on leafless stems over deeply cut, fernlike foliage. There are two distinct
types: the taller, larger, spring-blooming, common bleeding heart (*Dicentra spectabilis*)
and the various dwarf species that bloom later and throughout much of the summer.

Plant Profile

DICENTRA
dye-SEN-truh

- **Bloom Color:** Pink, red, or white

- **Bloom Time:** Varies by species; see individual listings

- **Length of Bloom:** Varies by species; see individual listings

- **Height:** Varies by species; see individual listings

- **Spread:** Varies by species; see individual listings

- **Garden Uses:** Cut flower garden, edging, meadow garden, mixed border; attracts birds, butterflies, and hummingbirds

- **Light Preference:** Full sun to partial shade

- **Soil Preference:** Humus-rich, moist but well-drained soil

- **Best Way to Propagate:** Divide or take root cuttings in spring or fall

- **USDA Plant Hardiness Zones:** Varies by species; see individual listings

- **AHS Heat Zones:** Varies by species; see individual listings

Growing Tips

All bleeding hearts prefer rich, moist soil and rather cool conditions. In
cool-summer areas, you can grow the ones described here in full sun as
long as you keep their soil evenly moist. In hot-summer areas, though,
plant them in partial shade or in a spot that gets morning sun and afternoon shade. The dwarf species even do quite well in deep shade.

Multiplying the dwarf bleeding hearts is not a problem: You can
lift the plants out of the ground and divide them in early spring or
fall every three or four years. Many will also self-sow, although the
offspring of hybrids will not come true.

Common bleeding heart (*Dicentra spectabilis*) comes true from
seed. It's best to sow the seed immediately after it ripens, directly
into the garden where it will germinate rapidly.

Common bleeding heart is a typical no-care perennial, preferring
to be left alone. You can dig it up and divide it, but it will take several years for the divisions to get established as well as for the
mother plant to recover. Other options include taking stem cuttings
in early summer, just after the flowers have faded, or taking root cuttings in spring or fall.

Good Neighbors

Bleeding hearts add beautiful color and texture to plantings of ferns,
hostas, epimediums, and pulmonarias.

Fringed bleeding heart (*D. eximia*) and western bleeding heart
(*D. formosa*) also combine well with the same companions as
common bleeding heart. They'll also pair nicely with other low-
growers that thrive in moist soil and partial shade, such as Siberian
bugloss (*Brunnera macrophylla*) and Allegheny foamflower (*Tiarella
cordifolia*).

Problems and Solutions
Bleeding hearts have no major problems.

Top Performer

⭐ **Larry's Favorite:** *Dicentra spectabilis* (common bleeding heart): Common bleeding heart's tall, arching stems with dangling, pink, heart-shaped flowers, set off by fernlike foliage, create a charming display from late spring to early summer. Keep the soil moist and cool if you want the foliage to last. If the soil gets hot or dry, the foliage will yellow and is best cut back. 'Alba', with pure white flowers, is just as charming as the species. Height: 18 to 36 inches (45 to 90 cm). Spread: 2 to 4 feet (60 to 120 cm). USDA Plant Hardiness Zones 1 to 9; AHS Heat Zones 9 to 1.

Common bleeding heart
(*Dicentra spectabilis*)

More Recommended Bleeding Hearts

The following plants are all in the "dwarf bleeding heart" category—smaller plants that don't go summer dormant and that bloom all summer in most cases.

Dicentra eximia (fringed bleeding heart): This species forms dense mounds of deeply cut, fernlike, gray-green leaves topped off by branching stems of rosy pink flowers. It's an early summer bloomer in the wild, but most cultivars will keep on blooming through much of the summer as long as you keep the soil moist. Fringed bleeding heart is more heat-resistant than the western bleeding heart (*D. formosa*) so it's a better choice for hot-summer areas; otherwise, the species are basically identical. 'Alba' has white flowers. Height: 8 to 18 inches (20 to 45 cm). Spread: 12 to 18 inches (30 to 45 cm). USDA Plant Hardiness Zones 2 to 9; AHS Heat Zones 8 to 1.

D. hybrids (hybrid dwarf bleeding heart): Many dwarf cultivars are hybrids of *D. eximia* and *D. formosa*. They tend to bloom more abundantly over a longer period of time, from early summer well into fall. Some of the most popular cultivars are ruby-red 'Adrian Bloom'; 'Bacchanal', with stunning, deep wine-red flowers; rosy red 'Bountiful'; 'Langtrees', which has white flowers touched with coral; pink 'Luxuriant'; and rose-red 'Zestful'. Height: 8 to 18 inches (20 to 45 cm). Spread: 12 to 18 inches (30 to 45 cm). USDA Plant Hardiness Zones 2 to 9; AHS Heat Zones 9 to 1.

Larry's Garden Notes

When I was a kid, we used to called common bleeding heart (*Dicentra spectablis*) "naked lady in a bath." Just turn the flower upside down and pull down the two pink petals to reveal what vaguely resembles a pale female figure in a bathtub. Quite a titillating experience—if you're 6 years old.

Dictamnus

Gas plant, dittany

The gas plant is an especially handsome perennial. Its spikes of lemon-scented white flowers are highly attractive in their own right, and the flowers mature to form curious star-shaped seedpods that are fun to add to dried flower arrangements. Better yet, the entire plant takes on the form of a dense shrub, with leathery-textured, glossy green leaves much like the leaves of ash trees. You can even plant gas plant in rows to form a compact hedge, but it will die to the ground each winter.

Plant Profile

DICTAMNUS
dik-TAM-nus

- **Bloom Color:** White or pink
- **Bloom Time:** Early summer
- **Length of Bloom:** 1 month
- **Height:** 2 to 3 feet (60 to 90 cm)
- **Spread:** 2 feet (60 cm)
- **Garden Uses:** Hedge, mass planting, mixed border, specimen plant
- **Light Preference:** Full sun to light shade
- **Soil Preference:** Moderately rich, well-drained soil
- **Best Way to Propagate:** Sow seed outside in fall
- **USDA Hardiness Zones:** 3 to 9
- **AHS Heat Zones:** 8 to 1

Growing Tips

One of the very best of the no-care perennials, gas plant has never received the popularity it merits. The reason becomes quite obvious when you see it at a nursery; it is simply so awkward-looking in a pot that many customers never give it a chance. The reason for this half-dead appearance is that the poor plant has deep taproots that simply cannot stand being confined in a pot.

Since it hates being transplanted, even when young, a gas plant barely grows at all the first year and only a bit more the second. By the third year, you can expect the first few flowers. From the fifth year on, though, it becomes one of the most attractive plants in your garden.

As weak and spindly as potted gas plants may be, they are usually already several years old when sold and therefore comparatively expensive. If you're patient, try growing them from seed. Although you can start the seed indoors, you'll have better results by sowing it directly outdoors where you want to see it bloom. Fall sowing is best, as the seeds need a period of cold to sprout. About one-quarter of the seeds will germinate the first spring, about another quarter the following year, and the rest over the next two or three years, if they germinate at all. And don't expect to see any flowers for the first four or five years.

FUN FACTS

The common name for this plant comes from the lemon-scented volatile gas that the leaves give off when they are rubbed. On a hot, windless evening, try holding a match to its flowers. The accumulated gas quickly ignites, causing a rapid-fire series of low-temperature sparks that don't even harm the petals.

If you feel tempted to divide an established gas plant, resist the urge! Divisions often die, and the mother plant may be so shocked that it refuses to bloom for years. If you want to try anyway, leave the mother plant in its place and carefully brush away the soil on the least visible side, removing one or two of the woody, carrot-like roots. Cut the roots into short sections, and lay them in moist potting soil to sprout—just don't expect rapid results.

Warning: The deliciously fragrant volatile oil that covers the entire plant can cause an allergic skin rash in some people, but only if the affected body part is exposed to sun. The moral of the story? Either wear gloves and long sleeves when you handle a gas plant (and you'll probably only have to touch it at planting time!), or work on it after dark.

Good Neighbors

Since gas plants don't like having their roots disturbed, the best neighbors may be flowering shrubs and rosebushes because you're less likely to move these more permanent plantings. But as long as you can remember not to disturb your gas plants when digging nearby plants to divide or transplant, don't be shy about combining gas plant with Siberian iris (*Iris sibirica*), bee balm (*Monarda didyma*), or daylilies for a pleasing color display in the garden.

Problems and Solutions

Gas plant is not bothered by pests or diseases.

Top Performer

Dictamnus albus (gas plant): There's really no choice when it comes to the "top performer" with *Dictamnus* because it's generally known as a one-species genus. *D. albus* has white flowers in early summer. The cultivar 'Purpureus', with its deep-purple-veined pink flowers in early summer, is deservedly far more popular than the species.

Though it may take a few years for gas plant (*Dictamnus albus*) to reach its full potential, it's well worth the wait. Left undisturbed, it will reward you—eventually—with imposing clumps of glossy green foliage and magnificent spires of blooms.

Helleborus

Hellebore

Hellebores are about the earliest of all perennials to bloom, and their flowers last and last. They may stay in bloom for three months or more if you have a long, cool spring. Hellebores are totally trouble-free once established. Most live just about forever, but they're very slow to get started. Usually evergreen, hellebore leaves are toothed along the edges and divided into broad or fingerlike lobes or leaflets. There are two categories of hellebores: those with noticeable stems, and those whose leaves and flowers rise directly from the ground.

Plant Profile

HELLEBORUS
hell-uh-BORE-us

- Bloom Color: Green, pink, purple, red, yellow, or white

- Bloom Time: Late winter to midspring

- Length of Bloom: 8 to 12 weeks or more

- Height: 8 to 24 inches (20 to 60 cm)

- Spread: 10 to 18 inches (25 to 45 cm)

- Garden Uses: Edging, groundcover, mass planting, mixed border, rock garden, woodland garden; alongside paths, on slopes

- Light Preference: Partial to full shade

- Soil Preference: Humus-rich, moist but well-drained soil

- Best Way to Propagate: Divide in spring or sow fresh seed when ripe

- USDA Plant Hardiness Zones: 4 to 9

- AHS Heat Zones: 8 to 1

Growing Tips

In most gardens, hellebores put on their best show in partial shade in rich, humusy, well-drained soil that is moist in spring. They are surprisingly tolerant of summer drought but will absolutely not tolerate wet feet at any time of the year. The best advice I can give you about hellebore culture is to plant 'em and ignore 'em.

If you want to propagate a specific cultivar, you'll have to dig the plant up after it blooms and carefully divide it into sections, each with several roots and some dormant buds. Multiplying by seed is less stressful on the plant, but it's not fast: Expect to wait two or three years for the first flowers and seven or eight years for a nice, thick clump. If you buy packaged seed, I recommend sowing it in summer in a neglected part of the garden where you won't be digging or planting for the next few years. It may take seedlings several years to appear.

I advocate the no-brainer method for multiplying hellebores: Just let them do what comes naturally. They self-sow modestly, with young plants appearing mostly near the bases of established plants. Carefully dig and transplant these seedlings while they're still small.

Good Neighbors

Hellebores in bloom never fail to make an impact, even when planted alone. To add to the impact, use them as groundcovers under deciduous trees and shrubs with attractive winter silhouettes or colors that help highlight the hellebores below them, such as Siberian dogwood (*Cornus alba* 'Sibirica'), witch hazels (*Hamamelis* spp.), or winterberry (*Ilex verticillata*), for example.

Warning: Hellebores are poisonous. Do not consume any part of these plants, and warn your children not to touch them. Some people even develop rashes if they come into contact with the sap, so for safety's sake, wear gloves when handling them.

Problems and Solutions

Hellebores aren't troubled by pests or diseases.

Top Performer

Helleborus × *hybridus* (hybrid hellebore): Most modern hellebores, and especially any labeled *H. orientalis* (Lenten rose), are actually hybrids. Hybrid hellebore is very close to the true Lenten rose, with some added "blood" from other species, but it has a far wider range of flower colors than any of its parents. The flowers can be drooping or nearly upright, deeply cupped or nearly flat, and single or double.

While true cultivars are generally quite expensive, so-called "red," "pink," and "purple" hellebores, as well as some other colors, are available as "strains." Seed strains generally produce plants that fall into the described color range, although you'll never be sure of the exact shade you'll get. Height: 16 to 24 inches (40 to 60 cm). Spread: 12 to 18 inches (30 to 45 cm). USDA Plant Hardiness Zones 4 to 9; AHS Heat Zones 8 to 1.

More Recommended Hellebores

Helleborus foetidus (stinking hellebore, bearsfoot hellebore): Although its name may give you pause, stinking hellebore's flowers are actually not heavily scented. Personally, I haven't noticed any scent at all. The foliage does release a slightly unpleasant marigold-like scent when crushed.

Stinking hellebore produces leathery, dark green leaves, each with 4 to 11 narrow leaflets, on thick, upright stems. Its clustered, cup-shaped, drooping, green flowers open in late winter or early spring and last until late spring or early summer. Unlike the other long-lasting species, stinking hellebore plants often disappear for no apparent reason after five or six years. Fortunately, they self-sow abundantly and usually flower in their second year, so you won't need to replant. Height: 18 to 24 inches (45 to 60 cm). Spread: 18 inches (45 cm). USDA Plant Hardiness Zones 4 to 9; AHS Heat Zones 8 to 1.

Hybrid hellebore
(*Helleborus* x *orientalis*)

Larry's Garden Notes

One reason hellebore flowers last so long is that their broad, rounded "petals" aren't really petals at all. They're sepals, which are sturdy, petal-like plant parts that surround the true petals, which are very small and wispy.

If you shop for hellebores at a nursery, be forewarned: They look so awful in a pot that you'll be reluctant to pay the apparently exorbitant price on the label. The secret behind their high cost, of course, is that they take so long to produce, and they'll take just as long to really amount to anything in your garden. But once established, they're well worth the price you pay.

Hemerocallis

Daylily

The ever-popular daylily needs little in the way of introduction: It's a favorite in most gardens. Unlike true lilies, daylilies don't have leaves all the way up their stems—their foliage grows in a fan from the plant's base. Daylilies eventually form dense clumps of long, grasslike leaves that arch at the tips, making them quite attractive even without blooms. During the summer, they produce stems of multiple trumpet-shaped flowers, usually held well above the foliage. The flowers come in a wide range of shapes, sizes, and colors.

Plant Profile

HEMEROCALLIS
hem-er-oh-CAL-iss

- **Bloom Color:** Lavender, orange, pink, purple, red, salmon, yellow, or near white

- **Bloom Time:** Varies by species; see individual listings

- **Length of Bloom:** 4 weeks or more

- **Height:** 10 to 72 inches (25 to 180 cm)

- **Spread:** 1 to 5 feet (30 to 150 cm)

- **Garden Uses:** Container planting, forest edge garden, mass planting, wall planting; on slopes; attracts butterflies and hummingbirds

- **Light Preference:** Full sun to partial shade

- **Soil Preference:** Humus-rich, well-drained soil

- **Best Way to Propagate:** Divide in early spring or fall

- **USDA Plant Hardiness Zones:** Varies by cultivar, but usually 3 to 9

- **AHS Heat Zones:** Varies by cultivar, but usually 12 to 1

Growing Tips

The fact that daylilies are so popular should clue you in that they're easy to grow; in fact, they'll grow in just about any well-drained soil and almost as well in partial shade as in full sun. Furthermore, they have thick roots that store water, making them highly drought-resistant once established. For maximum bloom, however, plant them in light, humusy soil where they'll receive afternoon sun with some midday shade, and keep them slightly moist at all times.

Meticulous gardeners insist on deadheading their daylilies daily to remove the faded flowers, but that's a lot of work for little results. Unless the garden club is coming over for tea, try to ignore the dried petals (they often drop off on their own after a few days anyway).

Hybrid daylilies don't come true from seed, so the best way to propagate hybrids is to divide them, ideally in early spring or fall.

Although there are relatively few daylily species, there are literally thousands of cultivars: some 40,000 of them, with nearly 1,000 new introductions each year. Daylily cultivars are often classified according to their traits, including:

- Flower color
- Bloom time: extra-early, early, early midseason, midseason, late midseason, late, very late, and reblooming
- Height in bloom: dwarf , from 6 to 12 inches (15 to 30 cm); low, from 1 to 2 feet (30 to 60 cm); medium, from 2 to 3 feet (60 to 90 cm); and tall, over 3 feet (90 cm)
- Foliage type: evergreen, semievergreen (which can stay green year-round in warm-winter climates but dies back in cold-winter climates), or deciduous.

Years ago, the rule of thumb was that evergreen and semievergreen daylilies did better in the heat of the South but were not hardy enough for the cool North, and vice versa for the deciduous daylilies. To be safe, if you live in either an extremely cold climate or an extremely hot one, ask a local daylily expert which cultivars are the most appropriate for your area.

Good Neighbors

Carefree daylilies are an excellent choice for covering a hard-to-mow bank. In a border, plant them between bulbs and perennials that go dormant in summer, such as oriental poppy (*Papaver orientale*). Or combine them with some complementary summer hues and textures, such as peach-leaved bellflower (*Campanula persicifolia*), red valerian (*Centranthus ruber*), or veronicas.

Problems and Solutions

Daylilies sometimes have problems with Japanese beetles, slugs, and leaf spot, but these tough plants usually overcome the problems on their own.

Recommended Daylilies

Hemerocallis hybrids: It's almost impossible to write a description that would adequately cover the myriad varieties of modern daylilies. They come in a wide range of colors and flower forms, plus different blooming seasons and heights. One approach to choosing daylilies is to look for cultivars that have won a prize from the American Daylily Society. The most prestigious award is the Stout Silver Medal, usually abbreviated as ST in catalogs. Winners of an Award of Merit (AM) or a Lenington All-American Award (LEN), among others, are also good choices.

New hybrids can be extremely expensive, so look for plants that have been on the market for ten years or so. They'll still be "new" as far as your neighbors are concerned, but they'll be much less costly than the latest releases. There's not much use suggesting specific cultivars in this fast-changing genus: Check out your local nursery or favorite mail-order source and choose for yourself.

'Charles Johnston' daylily (*Hemerocallis* 'Charles Johnston')

Larry's Garden Notes

Two terms you should know when you're shopping for hybrid daylilies are "tetraploid" and "reblooming." Tetraploid refers to plants that have double the usual number of chromosomes. Tetraploids tend to have thicker, larger flowers in brighter colors and are often more vigorous than regular daylilies. Reblooming (or recurrent) simply means the daylily will bloom more than once during the season.

Hosta

Hosta, plantain lily, funkia

Hostas are perhaps the perfect no-care shade plants, with dense leaves covering the ground from late spring through fall and stalks of narrow, lilylike flowers. For most hostas, foliage is the key to their beauty. The leaves can be lance-shaped, heart-shaped, or oval, with smooth or wavy edges, and may have a quilted or puckered texture. The leaves come in all shades of green and many cultivars have beautifully variegated foliage.

Plant Profile

HOSTA
HOSS-tuh

- **Bloom Color:** Mauve, purple, or white

- **Bloom Time:** Varies by species; see individual listings

- **Length of Bloom:** 3 or 4 weeks

- **Height of foliage:** Varies by species; see individual listings

- **Spread:** Varies by species; see individual listings

- **Garden Uses:** Container planting, edging, groundcover, mass planting, mixed border, specimen plant, woodland garden; attracts hummingbirds

- **Light Preference:** Full sun to full shade

- **Soil Preference:** Humus-rich, moist but well-drained soil

- **Best Way to Propagate:** Divide in spring or fall

- **USDA Plant Hardiness Zones:** 3 to 9

- **AHS Heat Zones:** 8 to 1

Growing Tips

In cool-summer areas, most hostas will grow in full sun all day without complaint as long as you keep the soil moist. Hostas will also tolerate deep shade in any climate, but they'll grow more slowly and less vigorously. If in doubt, plant hostas in light shade: Nearly all cultivars will do well in light shade no matter what your climate.

The main means of hosta multiplication is division. The best time to divide hostas is in early spring, before their buds are starting to show, or in late fall. Hostas take so long to reach maturity and so long to recuperate from division that it's almost a shame to bother a well-established clump. If you have one you absolutely must propagate, simply choose the least visible side and, with a sharp shovel, cut out a pie-shaped wedge from near the center out to the edge of the rootball. If you fill in the hole with fresh soil, the plant will appear unscathed the following growing season, even if you removed as much as one-quarter of the plant. Why, you ask? Because the leaves will spread while the plant is *slowly* filling in the bare spot with new shoots. The wedge you removed will provide several new plants that can be cut apart.

Good Neighbors

Hostas mix well with more upright shade lovers, such as ferns, small Solomon's seal (*Polygonatum biflorum*), or meadow rues (*Thalictrum* spp.). Plant early-spring bulbs or very early-blooming perennials, such as wood anemone (*Anemone nemorosa*) or primroses (*Primula* spp.), nearby to add interest while you're waiting for your hostas to emerge.

Problems and Solutions

Though hostas are easy, no-care plants, they do have a major flaw: They're extremely susceptible to slug and snail damage. You'll find suggestions on slug and snail control on page 55. To avoid severe slug problems, plant only hostas recommended as slug-resistant, usually those with especially thick or waxy foliage.

Recommended Hostas

Hosta hybrids: Almost all hostas grown in gardens are hybrids. Hybrid hostas are a vast and varied group, and I couldn't possibly describe all the hostas available on the market. Just check out your favorite nursery or mail-order source and choose according to your needs.

Here are a few hybrid hostas that are particularly pest-resistant, a factor often neglected but of enormous importance if you're looking for no-care perennials. In all the descriptions, the height is that of the foliage, not the flower stems.

'Golden Tiara' hosta
(*Hosta* 'Golden Tiara')

'Big Daddy' is a fast-growing cultivar that produces huge, deep blue leaves that are heavily quilted. It has white flowers that bloom in midsummer. Height: 3 feet (90 cm). Spread: 40 inches (100 cm).

'Gold Edger' produces neat, dense, fast-growing mounds of gold to chartreuse heart-shaped leaves topped by masses of lavender flowers in midsummer. It prefers at least some sun. Height: 10 inches (25 cm). Spread: 1 foot (30 cm).

'Hadspen Blue' is slow-growing and has wide, thick, deep blue-green leaves with an almost corrugated texture and lavender flowers that bloom in late summer. Height: 1 foot (30 cm). Spread: 16 inches (40 cm).

'Krossa Regal' is a highly rated blue-green hosta with an upright vase shape and lavender flowers in late summer. Height: 30 inches (75 cm). Spread: 28 inches (70 cm).

'Love Pat' boasts heavy, upright mounds of puckered, thick, gray-green leaves. It's a prolific bloomer, with pale lavender flowers in early summer. Height: 22 inches (56 cm). Spread: 18 inches (45 cm).

'Sum and Substance' is one of the largest hostas, with golden to chartreuse leaves that form a huge mound eventually spreading to more than 6 feet (180 cm) in diameter. It produces pale lavender flowers in late summer, and its color is better when it gets some sun. Height: 30 inches (75 cm). Spread: 5 feet (150 cm).

Larry's Garden Notes

If possible, buy your hostas (*Hosta* spp.) from a nursery that has a display garden featuring mature specimens. Otherwise, it's very hard to imagine how a scrawny little thing with only a few leaves will look when it reaches maturity. Even though some hostas fill in quickly enough in pots to offer a semblance of what they will look like in your garden, you really need to see specimens that are four, five or, better yet, ten years old to get a fair portrait of the plant's potential.

Paeonia

Peony

This classic garden plant traveled to North America with immigrants from Eurasia who wanted a living souvenir of their old homelands. As a result, you can often find peonies around old homes, sometimes long abandoned. In fact, of all the no-care perennials, peonies are perhaps the most permanent. Once well established, they can live practically forever. There are two major groups of peonies: garden peonies and tree peonies. Garden peonies die to the ground each fall and sprout anew each spring, while tree peonies are actually shrubs with woody stems.

Plant Profile

PAEONIA
pay-OHN-ee-uh

- **Bloom Color:** Pink, red, salmon, white, and yellow
- **Bloom Time:** Varies by species; see individual listings
- **Length of Bloom:** 2 weeks
- **Height:** 30 to 48 inches (75 to 120 cm)
- **Spread:** 30 to 36 inches (75 to 90 cm)
- **Garden Uses:** Cut flower garden, hedge, mixed border, specimen plant, woodland garden; at the back of beds or borders
- **Light Preference:** Full sun or light shade
- **Soil Preference:** Fertile, moist but well-drained, deep soil
- **Best Way to Propagate:** Propagating peonies yourself is not recommended
- **USDA Plant Hardiness Zones:** 2 to 9
- **AHS Heat Zones:** 9 or 8 to 1

Growing Tips

Peonies have long, thick roots that reach deep into the ground and therefore require deep soil. They prefer fertile, humus-rich soil with good drainage but will tolerate average soil. Peonies flower most abundantly in full sun and more modestly in partial shade.

Garden peonies definitely prefer cool conditions. In mild-winter areas, don't bother planting bareroot plants: They rarely thrive. And look for established early-flowering and single or Japanese-flowered cultivars because they tend to do better with less of a winter chill.

If you have a peony you would like to transplant or divide, the best advice I can give you is: Don't do it! Peonies hate being disturbed. The easiest way to grow peonies is to buy nursery plants, since dividing a peony is a daunting task. Most plants available commercially are sold dormant in the spring or early fall as short sections of crown with one or more swollen buds and long tuberous roots. (It's odd: Peonies do best if planted in the fall, yet commercial sources mostly sell them in the spring. Go figure!)

Plant the rhizomes with the root or roots pointing downward. If you live in a cold-winter region, set the buds 1½ to 2 inches (4 to 5 cm) below the surface of the soil; gardeners in warm-winter areas should set the buds 1 inch (2.5 cm) deep. If you buy potted peonies, scrape away a bit of soil to see where the stem bases are: These correspond to the buds. Never plant peony buds any deeper than 3 inches (7.5 cm) or the stems will "come up blind," as my father used to say: that is, produce only foliage and no flowers.

The most annoying thing about peonies has to be their need for staking. If your plants tend to flop, support them with peony rings (metal hoops attached to three or four legs) to prevent this. I never stake peonies because I don't grow the double-flowered ones, and single peonies almost never require staking.

Good Neighbors

Peonies take center stage during their relatively brief bloom time, so surround them with supporting players that will complement them rather than compete for attention. Good choices include columbines (*Aquilegia* spp.), peach-leaved bellflower (*Campanula persicifolia*), and 'Johnson's Blue' hardy geranium. Plants with spiky blooms or foliage, such as foxgloves (*Digitalis* spp.) and Siberian iris (*Iris sibirica*), can offer a nice contrast.

Problems and Solutions

Peonies are subject to gray mold (botrytis blight). It causes flower buds to blacken and die and may lead to leaf and stem spotting. In serious cases, the stems wilt and collapse. To prevent it, cut back and destroy peony stems in fall and treat shoots with an organic fungicide like sulfur in spring, before the disease strikes.

Top Performer

Paeonia hybrids: This group includes most plants labeled *Paeonia lactiflora* and *P. officinalis.* These peonies sprout sturdy upright stems in spring. The stems bear handsome, deeply cut, glossy foliage with narrow, sometimes lobed leaflets. The leaves have a distinctly reddish tinge as they emerge, then they turn dark green. Large rounded buds appear at the tips of the stems and open to reveal large, often sweet-smelling flowers. In the fall, the stems and leaves turn deep red—it's quite spectacular in some cultivars—then die back.

When you shop for peonies, rather than checking for particular species, I suggest you look for plants that are early, midseason, or late flowering: Planting a few from each category can extend the bloom season from midspring to late spring into early summer.

All kinds of colors and color combinations are possible, mostly in shades of cream, magenta, pink, and red. The single, semi-double, or double flowers usually measure from 4 to 6 inches (10 to 15 cm) in diameter, but there are some reaching up to 10 inches (25 cm)!

'Festiva Maxima' peony
(*Paeonia* 'Festiva Maxima')

Around the World with Peonies

The gorgeous tree peony, or mountain peony (*P. suffruticosa*), is a true shrub. It has thick, woody branches and dinner-plate-size flowers. I'd wondered why we call it a "tree peony" because I hadn't seen one taller than 5 feet (150 cm). But in Europe I found centenarian tree peonies about 8 feet (240 cm) tall—with no sign of stopping!

Try tree peonies in a site protected from the strongest winds in USDA Hardiness Zones 4 to 8. These shrubs are just as permanent as herbaceous peonies . . . and dislike being moved just as much. Find a spot you don't intend to change for the next three centuries, and plant them there.

LARRY'S LAST LOOK: NO-CARES

No-care perennials should be at the top of every gardener's wish list, so I've chosen a few more of my favorites that are worth their no-fuss, no-muss reputation. No-cares may start off slowly in the garden and look a tad scrawny for the first few years, but once they're established, you may as well climb into a hammock for a little R & R.

COMMON AND BOTANICAL NAME	ZONES AND EXPOSURES	BLOOM COLOR AND TIME	DESCRIPTION
Western bleeding heart *Dicentra formosa*	Hardiness Zones 2–9 Heat Zones 8–1 Light shade to shade	Pink or white flowers in early summer to early fall	This bleeding heart has cherry red flowers and blue-gray foliage and adapts nicely to drier soils. It may, however, go summer dormant in very dry conditions. Keep it well watered for blooms into early fall. Height: 9–18 inches (23–45 cm). Spread: 12–18 inches (30–45 cm).
Christmas rose *Helleborus niger*	Hardiness Zones 3–9 Heat Zones 8–1 Light shade to shade	White with pink or green flowers that bloom in late fall, winter, or early spring through late winter	Despite its name, this perennial usually waits until January to pop its white flowers through a light snow covering. The plant is picky about where it will grow. For success, think "open deciduous woodland with lots of leaf litter." Height: 10–18 inches (25–45 cm). Spread: 12–16 inches (30–40 cm).
Purple hellebore *Helleborus purpurascens*	Hardiness Zones 5–9 Heat Zones 8–1 Light shade	Purple flowers with greenish tinge that bloom in early winter or early spring to midspring or late spring	The most commonly available of the deciduous hellebores, and one of the easiest to grow. The plant eventually forms a low carpet of foliage. Height: 8–12 inches (20–30 cm). Spread: 10–16 inches (25–40 cm).

Western bleeding heart
(*Dicentra formosa*)

Citron daylily
(*Hemerocallis citrina*)

COMMON AND BOTANICAL NAME	ZONES AND EXPOSURES	BLOOM COLOR AND TIME	DESCRIPTION
Citron daylily *Hemerocallis citrina*	Hardiness Zones 3–9 Heat Zones 12–1 Sun to light shade	Lemon yellow flowers in midsummer	Renowned for its lemon yellow, highly fragrant, nocturnal flowers (dozens per stem). Forms a dense clump of dark green deciduous leaves. Height: 3–4 feet (90–120 cm). Spread: 2 feet (60 cm).
Middendorf daylily *Hemerocallis middendorffii*	Hardiness Zones 3–9 Heat Zones 12–1 Sun to light shade	Orange-yellow flowers in midsummer	Compact, nonspreading daylily with cup-shaped, fragrant flowers held well above the foliage. Particularly tolerant of shade and moist soils. Height: 24–30 inches (60–75 cm). Spread: 2 feet (60 cm).
'Inniswood' hosta *Hosta* 'Inniswood'	Hardiness Zones 3–9 Heat Zones 9–2 Light shade	Lavender flowers in midsummer	Dynamic plant with its bright yellow, heart-shaped leaves edged in green and lavender flowers. Height: 22 inches (56 cm). Spread: 4 feet (120 cm).
'Invincible' hosta *Hosta* 'Invincible'	Hardiness Zones 3–9 Heat Zones 9–2 Light shade	Blue flowers in midsummer	The name says it all—slugs and other pests just don't like this glossy, dense, all-green hosta with large, fragrant, blue flowers. Sun-tolerant. Height: 10 inches (25 cm). Spread: 1 foot (30 cm).
Fragrant hosta *Hosta plantaginea*	Hardiness Zones 3–9 Heat Zones 9–2 Sun to light shade	White flowers in late summer to early fall	The only hosta grown for its flowers rather than foliage. The highly scented huge trumpets grow up to 4–5 inches (10–13 cm) long. Heat-tolerant but not pest-resistant. Height: 24–30 inches (60–75 cm). Spread: 2 feet (60 cm).
⚑ Fernleaf peony *Paeonia tenuifolia*	Hardiness Zones 2–9 Heat Zones 8–1 Sun to light shade	Red flowers in early spring	Stands out because of its gorgeous fernlike leaves. Terribly expensive and a slow grower but a choice plant for the plant person who must have everything. Height: 12–18 inches (30–45 cm). Spread: 12–18 inches (30–45 cm).

Fragrant hosta
(*Hosta plantaginea*)

Fernleaf peony
(*Paeonia tenuifolia*)

Low-Care PERENNIALS

Reliable low-care perennials can be the foundation of a great perennial garden, especially if your goal is a garden that practically takes care of itself. By my definition, low-care perennials are perennials that require very little maintenance. My low-care favorites have a tough-as-nails attitude. Once they're established, these plants can live without extra watering during a drier-than-usual summer; in fact, they usually come through the worst weather disasters relatively unscathed. Plus, low-care perennials have few, if any, problems with disease or insects. If problems do occur, they're unlikely to be severe enough to require treatment. What else can I say, except don't you wish all perennials were this easy?

Top Picks

◀ Sea thrift (*Armeria maritima*) and many other low-care perennials are tough plants that can take difficult sites. Since it's native to seaside sites, sea thrift is salt-tolerant, so it's a great choice for planting along walkways where someone might spread de-icing salt in winter.

Low-Care Considerations

The main difference between *low-care* perennials and *no-care* perennials (the ones I described in "No-Care Perennials" on page 188) is that low-care perennials *will* eventually need division to stay vigorous. While truly no-care perennials like daylilies and hostas will live 20, 30, or 40 years—or more—without either dying out or spreading too much, low-care perennials will need to be divided after about 7 or 8 years in the garden. Otherwise they may die out or get too big.

Low-care perennials are also more likely to reach beyond their limits, mostly through self-seeding (few of them spread by invasive roots). They're not space hogs, determined to take over your garden, but they may occasionally overstep their bounds. Either be prepared to pull out a few unwanted seedlings, or plant these low-care perennials in informal settings where it won't matter if they self-sow and spread.

Unlike many other perennials, low-care perennials don't usually suffer from the "donut-hole" syndrome—where the plants grow outward nicely, but the center dies out, leaving a big hole. As low-cares age, their clumps get wider and wider, but they won't die back in the center. You may need to divide low-care plants because they're starting to take over too much garden space, but you don't have to do so as a matter of course just to keep them looking healthy.

In exchange for their slightly greater care needs, low-care perennials have a major advantage over no-care perennials: They grow faster. While no-care perennials may take four, five, or even six years to settle in and finally put on a show, low-care perennials generally look quite presentable in their first year and very handsome by their second. By the third year, they'll be in their prime, and they'll stay that way for four years or more after that.

Low-care perennials don't need dividing often, but when they do, it can take some time and strength to separate their large rootballs into sections. Use a sharp knife to cut through the tough roots.

Dividing and Conquering

By the time low-care perennials need dividing, they'll have had years to grow and fill out. So dividing them can be a considerable project. They'll need an out-and-out overhaul, and that involves digging up the entire plant and splitting it into parts.

This kind of operation is always a shock to the plant, so deciding the best time to undertake it is important. Here are some guidelines.

If you live in a cold climate (USDA Zones 1 to 4), or if you're dealing with plants that are borderline hardy in your region, stick to early spring. That way, the divisions will have the longest possible time to produce new roots and to settle in before facing the rigors of winter.

If you're dividing a perennial that blooms in the spring, divide it immediately after it flowers.

The plants usually slow their growth at this time, and some even go summer dormant.

If you're not limited by either of the first two guidelines, try to divide the plant at a time of the year when it isn't actively growing. Early spring, late summer, or early fall are usually the best periods for division.

Getting Prepared for "D-Day"

Once you've decided when to divide a low-care perennial, it's best to prepare the plant in advance. A day or two before the "operation," water the plant well. This will help reduce transplanting shock. Watering in advance also makes the procedure easier on *you* because the soil will be easier to dig if it isn't hard and dry.

When you water, it's also a good idea to cut off any upright stems 4 to 6 inches (10 to 15 cm) above the ground. This won't hurt the plant, and it will make it easier to see what you're doing while you dig and to separate the plant into pieces afterward.

Digging In for Division

If possible, dig and divide the plant on a cloudy day, or early in the evening, as the less time its roots spend exposed to dry air, the better it will recuperate. Use a garden fork or shovel to cut through roots and soil in a circle a few inches (4 to 8 cm) from the outer edge of the plant clump.

Once you've cut a complete circle, the next step is to lift the rootball up and out of the soil. (If the perennial is very large, you may need a helper for this step.) Before you try to lift the rootball, spread a tarp or a large sheet of heavy plastic nearby. Then, using tools for leverage, try to pull or push the rootball out of the hole. Cut right through any deep taproots as evenly as possible to free the rootball. Once the rootball is up and out of the soil, place it on the tarp or plastic sheet.

If the rootball is too big and heavy to lift, rock the rootball to one side and, folding the leading half of the plastic or tarp into pleats, slip it underneath. Then rock the rootball to the other side and try to pull the pleated section out from underneath. It may take a few tries, but you should be able to center the rootball on the tarp. Then gather the sheet together and lift it out of the hole carefully.

Pulling the Pieces Apart

Wash the soil away from the top of the exposed rootball. You'll notice that the rootball is probably composed of intermingled roots of various sizes topped by many individual crowns. You can usually see where one crown begins and the next ends because each crown will have its own series of roots. Try pulling the rootball in half with your hands. If that works, then pull each half apart again. Larger divisions usually recuperate more quickly than smaller ones, so only make as many divisions as you need. Even if you want lots of divisions, you may want to keep one large multicrowned division for immediate replanting in the original planting hole. You can then divide the rest into pieces that have three or four crowns each.

Some rootballs are too tough and woody to pull apart easily. In that case, try using a shovel to cut the rootball into quarters from top to bottom. If you want lots of individual divisions, you can then use a sharp knife to divide tough roots into individual plants. Try cutting along any obvious natural divisions. If there aren't any, just cut blindly: Perennials are inherently tough and will almost always survive division.

Some perennials will have a woody center that doesn't produce much topgrowth: This can simply be discarded. Also remove and compost any dead parts or tough, woody sections as well as any small pieces that result from the dividing process.

Replanting the Right Way

Now replant all the divisions you want to keep into freshly amended soil, water well, and cover the base of the new plants with mulch. Water the newly planted divisions regularly for the first few weeks. If you can't replant them immediately, cover the sections in damp burlap and keep them moist and out of the sun.

If you have too many plants for your own needs, pot up the surplus in good soil, water them well, and offer them to neighbors or friends or to a local charity's plant sale. Keep them out of full sun because they've lost a lot of roots and will quickly shrivel up if exposed to sun and heat.

Large divisions will recover quickly and may well bloom the same summer. Smaller divisions ought to recover rapidly enough to bloom the following year. If you divide all the way to individual crowns, you may have to wait several years for your new divisions to mature to blooming size.

15 More Low-Care Choices

I'm pleased to say that there's a nice list of low-care perennials that also serve other purposes, such as blooming in shade or attracting butterflies. Here are 15 multipurpose perennials that meet my definition of a low-care plant:

Actaea (Baneberry) . .320	*Gaura* (Gaura) 430
Aruncus (Goat's beard) 420	*Kirengeshoma* (Kirengeshoma) 434
Astilbe (Astilbe) 324	*Kniphofia* (Torch lily) 466
Cimicifuga (Cimicifuga) 330	*Perovskia* (Russian sage) 440
Echinacea (Purple coneflower) . .458	*Rheum* (Rhubarb) . . .442
Echinops (Globe thistle) 254	*Veronicastrum* (Culver's root) 105
Epimedium (Epimedium) 390	*Yucca* (Yucca) 268
Fryngium (Sea holly) . .256	

Acanthus

Bear's breeches

The best reason to grow bear's breeches is for its fabulous foliage. Its flowers are very nice, too, but you can't depend on them to bloom faithfully in all climates. To avoid disappointment, learn to appreciate this perennial for its dense rosettes of arching, deeply cut, shiny dark green leaves. Bear's breeches flowers are strange-looking at first sight, probably due to the funereal purple shade of the spiny hooded bracts (leaflike structures) that surround the white to pale pink flowers.

Plant Profile

ACANTHUS
uh-KAN-thus

- **Bloom Color:** Pink and purple or white and purple

- **Bloom Time:** Late spring to midsummer

- **Length of Bloom:** 3 or 4 weeks

- **Height:** 30 to 60 inches (75 to 150 cm)

- **Spread:** 2 to 3 feet (60 to 90 cm)

- **Garden Uses:** Container planting, cut flower garden, groundcover, mass planting, mixed border, seasonal hedge, specimen plant, woodland garden; at the back of beds and borders

- **Light Preference:** Full sun to partial shade

- **Soil Preference:** Average, well-drained soil

- **Best Way to Propagate:** Take root cuttings in spring or fall; sow seeds in summer

- **USDA Plant Hardiness Zones:** Varies by species; see individual listings

- **AHS Heat Zones:** Varies by species; see individual listings

Growing Tips

For bear's breeches to be truly low-care, you have to plant them inside a root barrier, such as a bottomless bucket sunk into the soil. Otherwise, they can be aggressive, sending up new sprouts from their long underground shoots. A root barrier will keep them under control, and then they'll need practically no care.

Although regarded as shade plants, bear's breeches actually prefer at least some sun. In deep shade, they will never bloom, and even the foliage won't be at its best. Partial shade is a good compromise, giving great foliage and some bloom.

While bear's breeches can adapt to a range of soil conditions, they insist on perfect drainage, especially in winter. Keep them moist in spring, though, until after they have finished blooming.

Cold damage is one reason bear's breeches might not bloom each year. This damage usually occurs when warm spring weather stimulates the plant to start growing, then a cold snap hits. The plant can sprout new leaves from its base, but the flower buds are gone for the season. The best solution is to mulch all species heavily in late fall in USDA Zones 3 to 7, and leave the mulch on well into spring until danger of heavy frost is past.

To keep bear's breeches plants looking healthy in hot-summer climates, cut them back harshly after they bloom. In cold-winter climates, leave the foliage standing in fall and wait until new growth begins in spring to cut off damaged leaves.

Bear's breeches hate being moved, so choose the planting site carefully. To multiply them, thrust a shovel into the ground at the base of an established plant in fall to cut through the roots (then remove the shovel). The next spring, baby plants galore will sprout for you to dig and replant.

Good Neighbors

Use bear's breeches as a bold accent in a perennial border. Pair its distinctive form with rounded or open plants, such as white gaura (*Gaura lindheimeri*), hardy geraniums, and peonies.

Problems and Solutions

Bear's breeches are often subject to slug and snail damage, especially in moist climates. Aphids can also feed on the leaves. For suggestions on how to control these pests, see pages 54 and 55.

Top Performer

⭐ **Larry's Favorite:** *Acanthus hungaricus*, also called *A. balcanicus* and *A. longifolius* (Balkan bear's breeches): Although it's the least known of the bear's breeches, this species adapts to a much wider climatic range than any of the others. It also blooms later, so it's more likely to flower every year. If you've never had much success with bear's breeches in the past, Balkan bear's breeches is the one to try. It produces 12- to 18-inch (30- to 45-cm) spikes of white flowers with purple bracts over spineless leaves in midsummer. Although most sources give this plant a hardiness rating of only USDA Zones 7 to 9, it's actually quite popular in USDA Zone 3. Even if you subtract abundant snow cover, that should give you a plant hardy to at least Zone 4. Height: 30 to 60 inches (75 to 150 cm). Spread: 3 feet (90 cm). USDA Plant Hardiness Zones 4 to 9; AHS Heat Zones 9 to 5.

More Recommended Bear's Breeches

Acanthus mollis (common bear's breeches): As the common name suggests, this is the most popular species, but it's also the most difficult, growing well in only a relatively narrow range. Its broad, shiny, deep green leaves are deeply cut, and each lobe ends in a soft spine. The late-spring to early-summer flowers are almost identical to those of Balkan bear's breeches, although they are sometimes tinged with pink. Height: 30 to 60 inches (75 to 150 cm). Spread: 3 feet (90 cm). USDA Plant Hardiness Zones 7 to 9; AHS Heat Zones 12 to 1.

Balkan bear's breeches
(*Acanthus hungaricus*)

Larry's Garden Notes

If you want to try a long shot, you can grow bear's breeches from seed, although the young plants take several years to reach full size. Start the seed outdoors in early spring, where you want them to grow, covering them with ¼ inch (6 mm) of soil. Indoors, plant in peat pots and germinate at 50° to 60°F (10° to 15°C).

Alchemilla

Lady's-mantle

Lady's-mantle looks like an old-fashioned cottage-garden plant, but it's actually a rather recent introduction to perennial gardens. Go ahead and use it in cottage gardens, though: It will fit right in. It has rounded, silvery or yellowish green leaves that are often covered in soft down. The tiny, star-shaped flowers of lady's-mantle are charming, but not spectacular. They're produced in dense to open sprays, but their yellowish green coloring doesn't stand out against the green leaves. They add a soft, billowy look to the plant.

Plant Profile

ALCHEMILLA
al-keh-MILL-uh

- **Bloom Color:** Yellowish green
- **Bloom Time:** Late spring to midsummer
- **Length of Bloom:** 4 or 5 weeks
- **Height:** 6 to 24 inches (15 to 60 cm)
- **Spread:** 1 to 2 feet (30 to 60 cm)
- **Garden Uses:** Container planting, cut flower garden, edging, groundcover, mass planting, mixed border, rock garden, wall planting, woodland garden; along paths, on slopes
- **Light Preference:** Full sun to partial shade
- **Soil Preference:** Fertile, moist but well-drained soil
- **Best Way to Propagate:** Divide or sow seed in spring or fall
- **USDA Plant Hardiness Zones:** Varies by species; see individual listings
- **AHS Heat Zones:** 8 to 1

Growing Tips

Lady's-mantle is easy to grow in almost any garden. Give it full sun and cool growing conditions, and it will tolerate drought and nearly all types of soils. Of course, "cool" and "sun" just may not go together well in your climate, so you'll be happy to know that lady's-mantle also adapts well to light or even moderate shade. It won't tolerate dry conditions in hot-summer areas.

Lady's-mantle requires little care once established. If you need a few extra plants, consider removing sections from the edges or back of the clump and leaving the center intact, rather than digging up a whole thriving clump. You can also multiply lady's-mantle by digging up the numerous seedlings that it will produce by self-sowing.

Lady's-mantle tends to look great from spring through fall in cool-summer areas or when grown in cool shade. It can, however, start to look ratty by midsummer in hot, dry climates or full sun. If so, just cut it back by half and it will look fresh and new a few weeks later.

Good Neighbors

Because the yellowish green flowers of lady's-mantle liven up other colors and clash with none, finding good companions is easy. The best companions are those that thrive in moist, partial shade, where lady's-mantle will be at its best.

FUN FACTS

Lady's-mantle leaves that have downy hairs on their upper surfaces have a curious characteristic: The leaves catch water from rain, overhead watering, or dew, causing it to bead up, much like transparent drops of mercury. The beads roll to and fro as the leaves wave in the wind, or when a person moves them about. Young children will play for hours with a cup of water and a single lady's-mantle leaf!

Upright perennials such as tall astilbes, Siberian iris (*Iris sibirica*), and foxglove penstemon (*Penstemon digitalis*) all make great companions. A time-honored use for lady's-mantle is as a groundcover around roses.

Problems and Solutions

Lady's-mantle grows luxuriantly with nary a problem in most climates, but in areas with hot, humid summers, diseases tend to discolor the foliage of species with downy upper leaves, usually by midsummer or late summer. Either cut the plant back to stimulate fresh, healthier growth, or stick with smooth-leaved lady's-mantles.

Top Performer

Alchemilla mollis (lady's-mantle): This is by far the most popular lady's-mantle and well deserving of its popularity. It produces large leaves—2 to 4 inches (5 to 10 cm) wide— that are more or less rounded, with a slightly lobed edge, and covered in soft, silky hair. The late-spring to midsummer flowers are more yellowish than those of most other lady's-mantles and therefore more striking. Its one flaw is susceptibility to leaf diseases in hot, humid areas. There are several cultivars, but they're similar to the species form. Height: 1 to 2 feet (30 to 60 cm). Spread: 18 to 24 inches (45 to 60 cm). USDA Plant Hardiness Zones 3 to 9; AHS Heat Zones 8 to 1.

Lady's-mantle (*Alchemilla mollis*) is among the most obliging of plants and its airy lime green flowers are quite beautiful in large drifts. After the blooms fade in midsummer, cut the plant back hard. It will put forth a fresh set of bright green leaves, providing an attractive groundcover for the rest of the season.

More Recommended Lady's-Mantles

Alchemilla alpina (mountain lady's-mantle, alpine lady's-mantle): Second in popularity but still not that widely available, mountain lady's-mantle is a much smaller plant than lady's-mantle (*A. mollis*). You'll grow this one more for its attractive foliage than for its green spring flowers. The 2-inch (5-cm) leaves are round and cut right to the center into five to seven toothed lobes. Their texture is smooth and shiny, and they have an intriguing and attractive silver edge, actually due to silver hairs that cover the underside of the leaf and extend beyond the leaf's edge. This plant spreads by runners as well as by seed but is not invasive. Height: 6 to 8 inches (15 to 20 cm). Spread: 1 foot (30 cm). USDA Plant Hardiness Zones 1 to 9; AHS Heat Zones 8 to 1.

Amsonia

Amsonia

Blue is a rare color among flowers, and that makes amsonia an extra-special perennial. Its clustered, star-shaped blooms are a lovely true light blue. Amsonia flowers form dense clumps of thick, rigidly upright stems covered by narrow, lance-shaped, dark green leaves. The leaves turn bright golden yellow in the fall and last a long time, giving this perennial a distinct second period of interest.

Plant Profile

AMSONIA
am-SOWN-ee-uh

- **Bloom Color:** Pale blue
- **Bloom Time:** Late spring to early summer
- **Length of Bloom:** 4 weeks
- **Height:** 1 to 3 feet (30 to 90 cm)
- **Spread:** 2 to 3 feet (60 to 90 cm)
- **Garden Uses:** Cut flower garden, meadow garden, mixed border, seasonal hedge; at the back of beds and borders
- **Light Preference:** Full sun or partial shade
- **Soil Preference:** Average, moist but well-drained soil
- **Best Way to Propagate:** Divide or sow seed in spring
- **USDA Plant Hardiness Zones:** Varies by species; see individual listings
- **AHS Heat Zones:** Varies by species; see individual listings

Growing Tips

Amsonias are easy to grow: Just plant them and ignore them. They prefer full sun and adapt to most soils, including poor ones, as long as they don't dry out completely in summer.

Amsonias rarely, if ever, need any support unless planted in shade. Nor do they seem to care one way or the other about deadheading. If you cut them back harshly after they bloom, though, they will produce new, thicker growth. This pruning can also help promote bushier growth on plants growing in shade, eliminating the need for staking.

Although amsonia produces dense growth (just let any weed *try* to poke its way through!), they never seem to die out in the center. Nor do they ever grow out of bounds: The clumps grow slowly in diameter for first eight or ten years, then stay put. So you don't really have to divide amsonia at all. You *can* divide them if you want more plants, though. It's best to divide the plants when they're dormant so you can better see what you're doing. You can also take stem cuttings or sow seed, although germination can be a bit irregular. For good germination, soak the seed overnight in warm water before sowing, then expose it to temperatures between 55° and 60°F (13° to 15°C) until the seedlings appear (this will take a month or two). Plants will bloom in the second year from sowing.

Good Neighbors

One of the outstanding features of amsonia is the persistent, yellow-orange fall foliage. To show it off, plant it in masses with heavier-textured plants such as 'Goldsturm' orange coneflower (*Rudbeckia fulgida* var. *sullivantii* 'Goldsturm') and 'Herbstfreude' sedum (*Sedum* 'Herbstfreude', also called *S.* 'Autumn Joy').

For seasonal color accents, interplant amsonia with oriental poppies (*Papaver orientale*), or grow it with white gaura (*Gaura lindheimeri*) for touches of soft color all season.

I've also seen this plant used alone as a semiformal summer hedge: It's so full and upright that it makes a great privacy screen.

Problems and Solutions

Amsonia doesn't suffer from any serious problems.

Top Performer

Amsonia hubrectii (blue star, also called Arkansas amsonia): With its very narrow leaves, blue star looks almost feathery when it's not in bloom. The flowers are the typical pale blue clusters of any amsonia. Although listed in many books as hardy only to USDA Zone 6, it grows with no protection other than snow in my Zone 3 garden; I'll bet it's hardy even without snow cover to at least USDA Zone 4. If in doubt, mulch it well. Height: 2 to 3 feet (60 to 90 cm). Spread: 2 to 3 feet (60 to 90 cm). USDA Plant Hardiness Zones 4 to 9; AHS Heat Zones 9 to 3.

More Recommended Amsonias

Amsonia tabernaemontana (willow blue star): This is the species you'll find most often at nurseries. Other than its somewhat broader leaves, this plant is a dead ringer for blue star (*A. hubrectii*). The late-spring to early-summer flowers are said to be darker blue than those of blue star. Most sources suggest that willow blue star is much hardier than amsonia, but I haven't found any great difference there either. A dwarf subspecies, *A. tabernaemontana* var. *montana,* grows no taller than 1 foot (30 cm); use it as an edging plant or in the rock garden. Height: 2 to 3 feet (60 to 90 cm). Spread: 2 to 3 feet (60 to 90 cm). USDA Plant Hardiness Zones 3 to 9; AHS Heat Zones 8 to 4.

Blue star
(*Amsonia hubrectii*)

Larry's Garden Notes

I like to see a pathway lined with a mass of blue star (*Amsonia hubrectii*) because it feels and looks luxuriously soft as you brush by. It's a bit tall for an edging plant and not particularly colorful in summer, but its delightful texture gives it a special appeal. In fact, you often see this plant used in public garden spaces as part of a texture garden. At Longwood Gardens in Pennsylvania, they pair it with *Stachys byzantina* 'Big Ears' for a lush and *very* tactile combination.

Armeria

Sea thrift, sea pink, common thrift

Sea thrifts form mossy cushions of grasslike green leaves, and if it weren't for their flowers, you might mistake them for a lawn grass. Sea thrift blooms, though, couldn't be less grasslike—they're dense, globelike clusters of tiny, colorful flowers. Flowers appear in the spring, but all sea thrifts also rebloom at least occasionally, especially when deadheaded. Many of them bear more than a passing resemblance to garden chives: The main difference is that sea thrifts have flat rather than round leaves, and they don't smell anything like onions!

Plant Profile

ARMERIA
ar-MAIR-ee-uh

- **Bloom Color:** Lilac, pink, red, rose, or white

- **Bloom Time:** Spring to early summer; some rebloom until fall

- **Length of Bloom:** 4 weeks or more

- **Height:** Varies by species; see individual listings

- **Spread:** 6 to 12 inches (15 to 30 cm)

- **Garden Uses:** Container planting, cut flower garden, edging, groundcover, mass planting, rock garden, wall planting; along paths, on slopes

- **Light Preference:** Full sun to light shade

- **Soil Preference:** Average, well-drained soil

- **Best Way to Propagate:** Divide plants or offshoots in spring or fall; sow seed in spring

- **USDA Plant Hardiness Zones:** 4 to 9

- **AHS Heat Zones:** 9 to 4

Growing Tips

As their name suggests, most sea thrifts are native to rocky cliffs near the sea, where they're exposed to cruel winds and periodically doused with salt spray. The end result is tough plants that can take considerable punishment. They tolerate salty conditions not only from ocean spray but also from road salt or naturally salty soil. In my cold-winter climate, where maintenance crews pour road salts onto streets and highways for months in the winter, this plant makes a wonderful grasslike groundcover to replace grasses killed by salt toxicity. (Actually, it makes a wonderful groundcover just about everywhere, but it spreads very slowly, so covering large areas with sea thrift can be an expensive proposition.)

Sea thrifts do best in full sun or very light shade (some protection from afternoon sun is wise in hot-summer areas). They'll grow in just about any kind of soil and usually do best when the soil is not too rich. Excellent drainage is, however, an absolute must: Sea thrifts will not tolerate wet feet.

Over time, sea thrift clumps spread to form an ever-widening mat. It's a slow process, though, so you need not worry about them becoming invasive. You can divide them if you wish, although established plants may suffer from the move. It's much less painful for the plant if you dig up some of the small sideshoots that appear at the outer rim of the mat. You can also dig up the whole plant and divide it into sections, ideally when the plant is dormant in early spring or midfall.

Sea thrifts also grow readily from seed sown indoors or out. Soak the seeds in warm water for half a day or so first, and just barely cover them. If you sow them indoors, place the seed trays in darkness at 60° to 70°F (15° to 21°C). Germination takes from 10 to 20 days.

Good Neighbors

Plants with gray foliage make handsome companions for pink-flowered sea thrifts· Try myrtle euphorbia (*Euphorbia myrsinites*), lavender cotton (*Santolina chamaecyparissus*), or woolly thyme (*Thymus pseudolanuginosus*) as companions in a rock garden.

Sea thrifts provide reliable green grassy foliage long after the flowers fade. Take advantage of this feature by using them to set off other small perennial gems, such as common pasque flower (*Pulsatilla vulgaris*) or dwarf bearded irises (*Iris pumila*).

Problems and Solutions

Sea thrifts have no serious disease or insect problems.

Top Performer

Armeria maritima (sea thrift, common thrift): This is the most popular species, producing flat, extremely narrow leaves and 1- to 1½-inch (2.5- to 4-cm) globes of tiny flowers. Each flower cluster lasts about three weeks but is immediately replaced by others during the main flowering season (midspring to late spring). Most modern cultivars bloom repeatedly if you deadhead them. 'Düsseldorfer Stolz' (also called 'Dusseldorf Pride') reaches only 6 to 8 inches (15 to 20 cm) tall and has wine-red flowers and a good reblooming habit. 'Splendens' has redder flowers and likewise reblooms well. Height: 6 to 12 inches (15 to 30 cm). Spread: 10 to 12 inches (25 to 30 cm). USDA Plant Hardiness Zones 4 to 9; AHS Heat Zones 9 to 4.

More Recommended Sea Thrifts

Armeria alliacea, also called *A. plantaginea* (plantain thrift): This plant has much broader leaves than sea thrift, and its white to pinkish flower heads are more oblong. Plantain thrift is also quite a bit taller, making it more suitable for standard perennial beds or borders. It blooms in late spring to early summer. Plantain sea thrift is the parent of many popular hybrid cultivars, including the popular Bees Hybrids, with a wide range of flower colors—'Bees Ruby', cerise red, is the most popular. The Formosa Hybrids have red, pink, or white flowers. Height: 12 to 18 inches (30 to 45 cm). Spread: 1 foot (30 cm). USDA Plant Hardiness Zones 4 to 9; AHS Heat Zones 9 to 4.

Sea thrift
(*Armeria maritima*)

Larry's Garden Notes

Remember that sea thrift (*Armeria maritima*) is an evergreen, so if you start getting itchy pruning fingers in the fall, fulfill your fantasies on some other plant, not this one. Aggressive fall pruning can destroy the following spring's bloom!

Bergenia

Bergenia, pigsqueak

Bergenia's leaves are its most remarkable feature. They're large, rounded, and leathery, with lightly toothed edges. The plants form rather open rosettes that remind me of giant wax begonias. In the fall, the leaves take on a distinctly reddish or purplish color, which they retain through the winter, making them great choices for adding winter interest. Bergenias also have attractive five-petaled flowers that appear in late winter or early spring on thick, upright stems. They may show some repeat bloom in fall, especially in cool-summer climates.

Plant Profile

BERGENIA
ber-GEEN-ee-uh

- **Bloom Color:** Pink, red, rose, purple, or white
- **Bloom Time:** Late winter or early spring to midspring or late spring
- **Length of Bloom:** 3 weeks or more
- **Height:** 12 to 18 inches (30 to 45 cm)
- **Spread:** 1 to 2 feet (30 to 60 cm)
- **Garden Uses:** Container planting, cut flower garden, edging, groundcover, mixed border, rock garden, wall planting, woodland garden; on slopes, in wet areas
- **Light Preference:** Full sun to partial shade
- **Soil Preference:** Humus-rich, moist but well-drained soil
- **Best Way to Propagate:** Divide or sow seed in spring
- **USDA Plant Hardiness Zones:** Varies by species; see individual listings
- **AHS Heat Zones:** Varies by species; see individual listings

Growing Tips

Bergenias have a reputation for being able to grow just about anywhere, and that reputation is largely well deserved. They seem to grow almost as well in dry gardens as by the water's edge; in full sun (especially in cool-summer areas) to quite dense shade; in soils rich or poor, acid or alkaline; and in climates hot (well, moderately hot) to cold. Of course, bergenia does have its preferences. It will grow more luxuriously in light to moderate shade and in rich, constantly moist soil that is slightly acid to neutral. In deep shade, grow it for its foliage alone because it probably won't bloom. If you grow it in full sun, keep it moist at all times.

Bergenias spread slowly by thick, ground-hugging stems, and division is the best way to multiply your plants. If you don't want to dig up established plantings, simply leave the mother plants in place and cut out a few stems at their base, then dig them out with their share of roots. It's best to do this in spring: Bergenias are very slow-growing and may not have time to establish themselves well from fall divisions. You can also start bergenias from seed, either outdoors early in spring, when the ground is still cold, or indoors eight to ten weeks before the last frost date. Don't cover the fine seed—just water well to settle it in slightly. Indoors, cover the trays in plastic and refrigerate for two weeks, then germinate at 60° to 70°F (15° to 21°C).

Good Neighbors

Create a winter scene by taking advantage of bergenias' attractive foliage: Combine them with groupings of other cold-season standouts, such as red-osier or Tatarian dogwoods (*Cornus stolonifera*, *C. alba*), hellebores, and very early bulbs, including crocuses, winter aconite (*Eranthis hyemalis*), and snowdrops (*Galanthus* spp.).

For interesting contrast during the growing season, pair bergenias with finer-textured plants that thrive in humus-rich, moist soil and partial shade. Good choices include columbines (*Aquilegia* spp.), bleeding hearts (*Dicentra* spp.), ferns, golden variegated hakone grass (*Hakonechloa macra* 'Aureola'), and Solomon's seals (*Polygonatum* spp.).

Problems and Solutions

Slugs and leaf spots may attack leaves, but they rarely cause significant damage.

Top Performer

Bergenia hybrids: Although most bergenias on the market are labeled *B. cordifolia* (heartleaf bergenia), almost all are actually hybrids between the various species. Their leaves are smooth and shiny and their late-winter to midspring flowers range from pure white to deepest carmine red.

Many cultivars are so similar you can scarcely tell them apart, so I suggest choosing according to flower color. Here are just a few that are sufficiently different to be noticeable. 'Baby Doll' is an especially dwarf type, growing to only about 12 to 15 inches (30 to 38 cm) tall, with smaller leaves and soft pink flowers. 'Glockenturm' (also called 'Bell Tower'), with rose-pink flowers, is distinctive for its reliable fall rebloom. 'Silberlicht' (also called 'Silver Light') is one of the rare bi-color bergenias, bearing pinkish white flowers with a red center. Height: 12 to 18 inches (30 to 45 cm). Spread: 1 to 2 feet (30 to 60 cm). USDA Plant Hardiness Zones 3 to 9; AHS Heat Zones 9 to 2.

More Recommended Bergenias

Bergenia ciliata (winter begonia, fringed bergenia): Winter begonia leaves are covered in soft hairs. And unlike the evergreen species, this bergenia goes dormant in the fall. Its late-winter to midspring flowers are very light pink, turning nearly rose as they age. I recommend a winter mulch for your winter begonia if your area doesn't have reliable snow cover. Height: 12 to 15 inches (30 to 38 cm). Spread: 1 foot (30 cm). USDA Plant Hardiness Zones 4 to 9; AHS Heat Zones 8 to 3.

'Baby Doll' bergenia
(*Bergenia* 'Baby Doll')

Larry's Garden Notes

Even though we may never know where some plants get their names, others have relatively obvious histories. The common name "pigsqueak" comes from the sound that's produced when you rub your fingers over the foliage of smooth-leaved bergenias. Your kids or grandkids (or even you!) will get a kick out of trying.

Digitalis

Foxglove

To me, foxgloves look like cathedral spires: Even the shortest ones seem to reach for the sky, with narrow flowerstalks bearing drooping tubular flowers. The flowerstalks arise from ground-hugging rosettes of arching, often beautifully textured, leaves. Although most foxgloves are true perennials, common foxglove (*Digitalis purpurea*), a biennial, is the most widely grown species. That's why many gardeners tend to think of all foxgloves as being strictly two-season wonders. It's well worth discovering the exceptions because they can be long-lived, truly low-care beauties.

Plant Profile

DIGITALIS
dij-uh-TAL-lis

- **Bloom Color:** Cream, pink, purple, red, white, and yellow

- **Bloom Time:** Late spring to midsummer; some repeat bloom

- **Length of Bloom:** 3 or 4 weeks

- **Height:** 2 to 5 feet (60 to 150 cm)

- **Spread:** 1 to 2 feet (30 to 60 cm)

- **Garden Uses:** Cut flower garden, mass planting, wildflower meadow, woodland garden; at the back of beds and borders; attracts hummingbirds

- **Light Preference:** Full sun to partial shade

- **Soil Preference:** Humus-rich, moist but well-drained soil

- **Best Way to Propagate:** Divide or sow seed in spring or fall

- **USDA Plant Hardiness Zones:** Varies by species; see individual listings

- **AHS Heat Zones:** Varies by species; see individual listings

Growing Tips

Foxgloves do best in partial shade; they'll also do okay in full shade if you can ensure the soil will stay constantly moist. Although they don't like drying out, foxgloves won't stand sitting in soggy soil either, so well-drained soil is a must.

Most foxgloves will rebloom if you cut their flower spikes immediately after reblooming. The second flower showing will have shorter spikes with fewer flowers. After the second bloom, let the biennial species go to seed so you'll get self-sown seedlings to carry on. Deadheading perennial species is optional.

It's easy to multiply the truly perennial foxgloves by dividing them in spring or fall. You can also let them self-sow or sow the seed yourself, outdoors, in spring or summer.

Good Neighbors

Mix foxgloves with plants of various shapes, colors, and sizes in a cottage-style garden: peach-leaved bellflower (*Campanula persicifolia*), irises, oriental poppy (*Papaver orientale*), garden phlox (*Phlox paniculata*), and shrub roses are great companions. Foxgloves are useful as accents in the woodland garden because deer don't like them. Pair them with other plants that grow well in partial shade, such as ferns and hostas.

Warning: All foxgloves are extremely poisonous if ingested.

FUN FACTS

Both the common and botanical names of foxglove refer to the supposed resemblance of the flowers to the fingers of a glove with the tips cut off. The "fox" in foxglove actually derives from "folks," as in the wee folks: in other words, fairy gloves.

Problems and Solutions

Slugs love foxglove leaves, so if you have serious slug problems, try one of the control methods suggested on page 55. If leaf diseases discolor the foliage, cut back the ratty leaves; the perennial species will produce a flush of fresh, healthy foliage.

Top Performer

⭐ **Larry's Favorite:** *Digitalis grandiflora*, also called *D. ambigua* or *D. orientalis* (yellow foxglove): Yellow foxglove produces a low rosette of long, narrow, hairy leaves at its base, then less-leafy spikes of yellow trumpet-shaped flowers marked with brown inside. The plants bloom mainly in early summer to midsummer but usually rebloom in fall if you deadhead them. Height: 2 to 3 feet (60 to 90 cm). Spread: 12 to 18 inches (30 to 45 cm). USDA Plant Hardiness Zones 3 to 9; AHS Heat Zones 8 to 1.

Yellow foxglove (*Digitalis grandiflora*) is not only beautiful, but it's also one of toughest and the best-performing members of its clan. Yellow foxglove produces spires of large, yellow trumpet-shaped flowers with lacy brown netting on the inside. Cutting the plant back after the first bloom in early summer often inspires a fall encore.

More Recommended Foxgloves

Digitalis ferruginea (rusty foxglove): This foxglove produces a low rosette of lance-shaped medium-green leaves and spikes of rusty red flowers in late spring to midsummer. It tends to act like a biennial in hot-summer areas but like a perennial in cooler ones. To ensure its "perenniality," meticulously deadhead it before it goes to seed, but let at least one plant self-sow just in case the others do give up the ghost. Height: 4 to 6 feet (120 to 180 cm). Spread: 18 inches (45 cm). USDA Plant Hardiness Zones 4 to 9; AHS Heat Zones 7 to 1.

D. lutea (straw foxglove): Straw foxglove has shiny, smooth leaves and smaller pale yellow flowers. Straw foxglove is also less heat-resistant. Height: 2 to 3 feet (60 to 90 cm). Spread: 1 foot (30 cm). USDA Plant Hardiness Zones 3 to 9; AHS Heat Zones 8 to 1.

D. × *mertonensis* (strawberry foxglove): Strawberry foxglove produces a wide rosette of large, velvety leaves and tall spikes of coppery rose flowers from late spring to midsummer. Although it has a reputation for being short-lived if not divided, I find it totally permanent as long as I cut the flower stems back before they go to seed. Height: 2 to 3 feet (60 to 90 cm). Spread: 2 feet (60 cm). USDA Plant Hardiness Zones 3 to 9; AHS Heat Zones 8 to 1.

Euphorbia

Euphorbia, spurge

Welcome to *Euphorbia*, the largest genus in the plant kingdom. It includes more than 2,000 annuals, biennials, perennials, trees, shrubs, aquatic plants, and succulents: If you want it, *Euphorbia* probably has it! However, only about 30 ornamental perennial species are adapted to temperate climates and of these, only the few described below are commonly available. Most perennial euphorbias are upright or mounding plants that form dense clumps. They have smooth leaves, and the ones I describe have terminal clusters of petal-like leaves called bracts surrounding the tiny flowers.

Plant Profile

EUPHORBIA
you-FOR-bee-uh

- **Bloom Color:** Orange or yellow

- **Bloom Time:** Varies by species; see individual listings

- **Length of Bloom:** 3 or 4 weeks

- **Height:** Varies by species; see individual listings

- **Spread:** Varies by species; see individual listings

- **Garden Uses:** Container planting, edging, groundcover, mixed border, rock garden, seasonal hedge, wall planting; at the back of beds and borders, along paths

- **Light Preference:** Varies by species; see individual listings

- **Soil Preference:** Average, well-drained soil

- **Best Way to Propagate:** Divide or sow seed in spring or fall

- **USDA Plant Hardiness Zones:** Varies by species; see individual listings

- **AHS Heat Zones:** Varies by species; see individual listings

Growing Tips

Euphorbias generally prefer full sun or light shade and poor to ordinary soil that's on the dry side. Most need some protection from midday sun in hot-summer areas. Some euphorbias sprawl after blooming, especially when they're growing in soil that's too fertile or moist. If this happens to your plants, just cut them back by half: They'll soon resprout.

Euphorbias generally prefer to be left alone, but you can lift and divide larger clumps if needed. Taking stem cuttings is a faster way to propagate euphorbias and causes less stress to the mother plant; take cuttings in midsummer, after the plants bloom. Some euphorbias self-sow abundantly (you may want to cut them back after they bloom to keep them from spreading).

Good Neighbors

Neatly mounded, brilliant chartreuse cushion spurge (*Euphorbia polychroma*) provides a striking color accent for spring gardens because most spring-flowering perennials have blue or purple blossoms. Combine it with upright plants such as peach-leaved bellflower (*Campanula persicifolia*) or Jacob's ladder (*Polemonium caeruleum*). The purple-red foliage of 'Chameleon' euphorbia (*E. dulcis* 'Chameleon') contrasts beautifully with silver-gray plants, such as 'Bath's Pink' Cheddar pink (*Dianthus gratianopolitanus* 'Bath's Pink') or English lavender (*Lavandula angustifolia*). Pair the hot red-orange, early-summer bracts of Griffith's spurge (*E. griffithii*) with the soft yellow-green of lady's-mantle (*Alchemilla mollis*), or with blues and purples, such as Siberian iris (*Iris sibirica*).

Warning: All euphorbias have bad-tasting milky sap that can be caustic. Always wear gloves and long sleeves when working with euphorbias because the sap easily works its way into cuts or your mouth, a most disagreeable experience. If you prune euphorbias, wear goggles. Also, don't plant euphorbias near fishponds because rainfall may carry residue from their leaves into the water and poison the fish.

Problems and Solutions

Euphorbias are rarely bothered by pests or diseases. Even deer won't eat them!

Top Performer

Euphorbia polychroma, also called *E. epithymoides* (cushion spurge): Cushion spurge quickly forms a perfect mound of narrow, pale green leaves topped off with long-lasting, glowing chartreuse bracts in early spring. The foliage continues to look great all summer and turns bright red in the fall. Height: 12 to 18 inches (30 to 45 cm). Spread: 18 inches (45 cm). USDA Plant Hardiness Zones 3 to 9; AHS Heat Zones 9 to 4.

Cushion spurge
(*Euphorbia polychroma*)

More Recommended Spurges

Euphorbia dulcis 'Chameleon': 'Chameleon' is a clustering, non-spreading euphorbia with small, thick, oblong, purple leaves topped off with lime green bracts in spring; sometimes these are purple-tinged as well. The leaves tend to become greener as the summer wears on, then they turn deep purple—with flame highlights—again in the fall. Height: 12 to 18 inches (30 to 45 cm). Spread: 15 to 20 inches (30 to 50 cm). USDA Plant Hardiness Zones 4 to 9; AHS Heat Zones 9 to 4.

E. griffithii (Griffith's spurge): A taller, shrublike euphorbia, this species produces thick, reddish stems and medium-green, willow-like leaves that turn bright red in fall. Like many spurges, it looks great even without bloom, but its flowers are spectacular: long-lasting deep red or orange bracts blooming from early to late summer. Plant it inside a root barrier to prevent it from spreading. Although it tolerates dry soil, this euphorbia will be happiest in relatively moist conditions. Height: 20 to 36 inches (50 to 90 cm). Spread: 2 feet (60 cm). USDA Plant Hardiness Zones 3 to 9; AHS Heat Zones 9 to 1.

Around the World with Euphorbias

Euphorbias (*Euphorbia* spp.) are among the plants I most enjoy seeking out when I travel. Because of their characteristic flowers—colorful petal-like bracts surrounding insignificant little blossoms—they're actually quite easy to identify. Along the Mediterranean coast, you'll spot shrubby, mounding euphorbias. In tropical Africa, I've seen spiny succulent tree euphorbias, such as *E. candelabrum*. There's also Mexican flame leaf (*E. pulcherrima*) of Mexico, which has very large bracts. In the Midwest, the native euphorbia is an annual with glistening white flowers called snow on the mountain (*E. marginata*). Euphorbias are one of the plants that make continent-hopping so much fun!

Geranium

Hardy geranium, cranesbill

Every garden needs a few hardy geraniums, and with more than 250 species found all over the Northern Hemisphere, you have plenty to choose from. Hardy geraniums are easy-care plants that offer a long season of interest thanks to their deeply cut, maplelike foliage. And when they're in bloom, their starlike or cup-shaped flowers make them true stars of the garden.

Plant Profile

GERANIUM
jer-ANE-ee-um

- **Bloom Color:** Blue, magenta, pink, purple, red, or white

- **Bloom Time:** Varies by species; see individual listings

- **Length of Bloom:** 2 months or more

- **Height:** Varies by species; see individual listings

- **Spread:** Varies by species; see individual listings

- **Garden Uses:** Container planting, edging, groundcover, mass planting, mixed border, rock garden, wall planting, woodland garden; on slopes, in wet areas

- **Light Preference:** Full sun to partial shade

- **Soil Preference:** Humus-rich, moist, well-drained soil

- **Best Way to Propagate:** Divide or take stem cuttings in spring

- **USDA Plant Hardiness Zones:** 4 to 9

- **AHS Heat Zones:** 8 to 1

Growing Tips

Hardy geraniums grow well just about anywhere as long as they don't suffer extreme drought. For optimum performance, though, hardy geraniums prefer moist, well-drained soil that's rich in organic matter. Full sun to partial shade is perfect for hardy geraniums—they do prefer cool growing conditions. In truly hot climates, plant them in sites that get abundant morning sun but deep afternoon shade. Mulching can also be helpful in areas with hot or dry summers.

Once hardy geraniums are established in your garden, you can ignore them for several years: They need little care other than removing the dead stems in spring. If your plants tend to flop in midsummer, chop them back to about 6 inches (15 cm) from the ground—they'll resprout quickly and look as good as new in no time.

Division is the most popular means of propagating hardy geraniums; spring or fall is the best time. However, if you don't want to bother uprooting a healthy clump, consider taking summer stem cuttings instead.

Problems and Solutions

Rust can be a problem with hardy geraniums, causing leaves to turn pale, with powdery orange spots on the undersides. Remove and destroy infested leaves, or cut plants back severely. Slugs will feast on young plants. For solutions to slug problems, see page 55.

Good Neighbors

Contrast the mounded shapes of hardy geraniums with the upright forms of Siberian iris (*Iris sibirica*) or hybrid lupines (*Lupinus* hybrids). For a low-maintenance garden with season-long interest, combine hardy geraniums with ornamental grasses such as oriental fountain grass (*Pennisetum orientale*) or switch grass (*Panicum virgatum*).

Shade-tolerant mourning widow (*Geranium phaeum*) looks stunning next to golden variegated hakone grass (*Hakonechloa macra* 'Aureola') or a gold-leaved hosta.

Top Performer

Geranium sanguineum (bloody cranesbill): Bloody cranesbill is perhaps the most popular of all geraniums, probably because it's so adaptable, growing equally well in both hot-summer and cold-winter climates. It forms a short, rather spreading mound of rounded, deeply cut leaves that are green for most of the growing season, then turn crimson in the fall. Bloody cranesbill stays compact and makes a great border plant. Flower color ranges from white to pink. 'Album' is the most popular white-flowered cultivar, but I prefer the variety *striatum* (also called 'Lancastriense'). It's shorter and denser than the species, growing only 6 to 8 inches (15 to 20 cm) tall and produces its light pink flowers with darker veins throughout much of the summer if you deadhead it. Height: 9 to 18 inches (23 to 45 cm). Spread: 1 foot (30 cm). USDA Plant Hardiness Zones 3 to 9; AHS Heat Zones 8 to 1.

Bloody cranesbill
(*Geranium sanguineum*)

More Recommended Hardy Geraniums

Geranium phaeum (mourning widow): Deep purple, nearly black flowers give this plant its common name. Mourning widow blooms mainly from late spring to early summer, but it may rebloom if you deadhead it. It grows well even in deep shade. Mourning widow prefers moist soil but tolerates drought. 'Album' has white flowers. Height: 18 to 36 inches (45 to 90 cm). Spread: 24 to 30 inches (60 to 75 cm). USDA Plant Hardiness Zones 4 to 9; AHS Heat Zones 8 to 1.

Think Twice: *G. pratense* (meadow cranesbill): Meadow cranesbill produces tall flower stems over dense clumps of foliage. Bloom occurs from late spring to summer. Prune the plants back harshly after flowering to avoid self-sowing and a tendency to become weedy. 'Mrs. Kendall Clark' has paler blue flowers with translucent veins. Watch out: It spreads! 'Striatum' (also called 'Bicolor') is white with variable blue splotches and streaks. Height: 2 to 4 feet (60 to 120 cm). Spread: 16 to 24 inches (40 to 60 cm). USDA Plant Hardiness Zones 4 to 9; AHS Heat Zones 8 to 1.

Larry's Garden Notes

Don't confuse hardy geraniums (*Geranium* spp.) with the popular container and garden plants that are a mainstay of garden center displays. Those geraniums are tender perennials (properly called zonal geraniums), and they belong to the genus *Pelargonium*. Zonal geraniums are related to true geraniums—one way you can tell is that both types have seedpods that are shaped like the beak of a crane (that's why geraniums are also called cranesbills, by the way). However, zonal geraniums are native to South Africa and won't survive more than a few degrees of frost.

Liatris

Gayfeather, blazing star

Gayfeathers are easy-to-grow perennials with a striking and unusual silhouette and vivid, feathery flowers. They produce dense tufts of narrow, grasslike basal leaves followed by tall, upright flower spikes of rose-purple flowers. The individual flowers are fluffy, with intermingled strands that give the impression they are having a bad hair day. Oddly, while the flower spikes of most plants start blooming from the bottom of the spike, gayfeather flowers start blooming at the top and bloom progressively down the spike.

Plant Profile

LIATRIS
lee-AH-tris

- **Bloom Color:** Lavender, pink, purple, rose, or white
- **Bloom Time:** Midsummer to early autumn
- **Length of Bloom:** 6 to 8 weeks
- **Height:** Varies by species; see individual listings
- **Spread:** 18 to 24 inches (45 to 60 cm)
- **Garden Uses:** Cut flower garden, meadow garden, mixed border, specimen plant; at the back of beds and borders; attracts butterflies
- **Light Preference:** Full sun to light shade
- **Soil Preference:** Average, well-drained soil
- **Best Way to Propagate:** Divide or sow seed in spring
- **USDA Plant Hardiness Zones:** 3 to 9
- **AHS Heat Zones:** Varies by species; see individual listings

Growing Tips

Gayfeathers will grow in full sun or light shade in just about any kind of soil, as long as it's not soaking wet in the spring. In rich soil, gayfeathers grow extra tall and often require staking.

You can plant gayfeathers as you would spring bulbs because they produce tuberous roots or underground stems called corms (they can produce either) or as an herbaceous perennial. In nurseries, you'll find gayfeathers growing in pots in the perennial section, but you'll also find bagged gayfeather corms in the bulbs section.

If you buy gayfeathers as plants, just plant them as you would any other potted perennial. If you buy corms or tuberous roots, plant them about 4 to 6 inches (10 to 15 cm) deep. Once they're established, you can leave gayfeathers alone for years. If you want to multiply them, dig up the roots in the spring and cut them into sections with a sharp knife, making sure each section has at least one "eye," or bud. Dust the cut surfaces with rooting hormone powder (available from garden centers) before replanting. You can also raise gayfeathers from seed. Sow indoors six to eight weeks before the last frost, just barely covering the fine seed, or outdoors in early spring. Seed-grown plants will bloom the following season.

Cut off the flower spikes at the base of the plants when the last blooms have faded to prevent them from going to seed. If the flower spikes mature, the plants will self-sow in open spaces where sun can reach the soil. The plant is not aggressive, however.

Good Neighbors

Because gayfeathers are one of the best butterfly-attracting plants, you may want to use them in a butterfly garden, along with other favorites such as butterfly weed (*Asclepias tuberosa*), Frikart's aster (*Aster × frikartii*), and purple coneflower (*Echinacea purpurea*). Gayfeathers actually prefer poor soil, so they make great meadow garden plants, mixed with others such as coreopsis, rattlesnake master (*Eryngium yuccifolium*), and rudbeckias.

Problems and Solutions

Other than root knot nematode in southern gardens, gayfeather is not particularly subject to pests and diseases. Root knot nematode is usually seen first as simply stunted growth. When the plant is dug up, however, the roots seem to be infested with nodules. Infested plants should be destroyed and that section of garden planted in marigolds. Nematodes will infest the marigold roots but are unable to reproduce in them. The following season, the section will be nematode-free and you'll be able to plant whatever you want there.

Top Performer

Liatris spicata, also called *L. callilepis* (spike gayfeather): Spike gayfeather is the most popular and widely available species and the only one offering much choice in color and height. Native to marshy areas, it should (at least in theory) need moist soil, but it's surprisingly drought-resistant. Cultivars range from 2 to 5 feet (60 to 150 cm) tall and bloom in shades of rose-purple, white, pink, and lavender from midsummer to early fall. The differences between the cultivars are minor. One worth mentioning is 'Kobold' ('Goblin'), a relatively compact selection with multiple spikes of mauve flowers. Height: 2 to 4 feet (60 to 120 cm). Spread: 18 to 24 inches (45 to 60 cm). USDA Plant Hardiness Zones 3 to 9; AHS Heat Zones 9 to 1.

More Recommended Gayfeathers

Liatris scariosa (tall gayfeather): All flowers on each spike of this plant open at the same time during midsummer to early fall. 'September Glory' (deep purple) and 'White Spire' (pure white) are the two common cultivars. Both will grow 3 to 4 feet (90 to 120 cm) tall but need staking to support their heavy flower spikes. Height: 18 to 60 inches (45 to 150 cm). Spread: 18 to 24 inches (45 to 60 cm). USDA Plant Hardiness Zones 3 to 9; AHS Heat Zones 9 to 5.

'Kobold' spike gayfeather (*Liatris spicata* 'Kobold')

Larry's Garden Notes

A final note about my experience with gayfeathers: All 40-odd species of gayfeathers look pretty much alike, so I suggest you start by deciding what height or flower color you want. Then pick plants of whatever species you like that fit your choice of height or color.

Limonium

Statice, sea lavender, perennial statice

What a knockout! A mass of billowing sea lavender blossoms looks just like a cloud—the effect comes from the dozens of arching, wiry stems, each bearing hundreds of tiny flowers. Before those flowers appear in midsummer to late summer, sea lavender is much less impressive. The wide, dark green, pointed leaves form a rather flattened, ordinary rosette. But once it blooms, you'll be glad you had the patience to grow it.

Plant Profile

LIMONIUM
lih-MOAN-ee-um

- **Bloom Color:** Lavender, purple, or white
- **Bloom Time:** Midsummer to late summer
- **Length of Bloom:** 6 weeks or more
- **Height:** Varies by species; see individual listings
- **Spread:** Varies by species; see individual listings
- **Garden Uses:** Cut flower garden, edging, mass planting, mixed border, wildflower meadow
- **Light Preference:** Full sun
- **Soil Preference:** Average, well-drained, sandy soil
- **Best Way to Propagate:** Sow seed in spring
- **USDA Plant Hardiness Zones:** 3 to 9
- **AHS Heat Zones:** 12 to 3

Growing Tips

Sea lavenders were originally seashore plants, so they thrive in tough conditions. They'll grow best in sandy loam, but any well-drained soil, even a very poor or stony one, will do. In wet or heavy soil, they will generally fail to thrive or even die. Since they're quite immune to salt damage, sea lavenders are a great choice for planting along roadsides or in any area where the soil is contaminated by de-icing salts. Full sun is best in most areas, but some cooling afternoon shade is a must in hot-summer areas.

Sea lavenders are *not* fast-growing plants. Seed-grown plants may require three or four years before they bloom, plus three or four more years to reach their maximum size. The quickest way to get results is to buy an established plant. Even then, it may take a year or two to get the first flowers. From then on, they'll bloom more and more heavily for many, many years. Ten-year-old plants are about in their prime!

Once you have beautiful sea lavender plants established, don't try to divide or transplant them. If you disturb the plant's long, thick taproot, you may set the plant back several years or even kill it altogether. If you must dig one out, sacrifice the mother plant: Cut her roots into 3- to 4-inch (8- to 10-cm)

FUN FACTS

Sea lavender used to belong to the genus *Statice*, and that's why its common name is statice. Annual statice, of dried flower fame, was also a member of the genus. However, plant name experts long ago decided to eliminate that genus and scattered its members far and wide. The two common perennial species are now in the genus *Limonium*, and so is common annual statice, under the name *L. sinuatum*.

segments and try them as root cuttings. Sometimes they sprout; sometimes they don't.

Good Neighbors

The airy lavender or white blooms
of sea lavenders can fill the spaces
between more substantial plants,
such as daylilies, bearded irises, and
yuccas. Sea lavenders are also excellent choices for filling the gaps left
by summer-dormant plants, such as
spring bulbs and oriental poppy
(*Papaver orientale*).

Problems and Solutions

With sea lavenders, you only have
to arm yourself with patience, not
pest and disease remedies. Where
they are happy, these tough perennials seem to be immune to all
problems.

Top Performer

Limonium latifolium, also called *L. platyphyllum* or *Statice latifolia*
(sea lavender, wide-leaf sea lavender): This is the most popular
and widely available species, with very broad, hairy leaves and
lavender-blue flowers that bloom from midsummer to late
summer. 'Blue Cloud' has paler blue flowers and 'Violetta' has dark
violet ones. Height: 24 to 30 inches (60 to 75 cm). Spread: 24 to
30 inches (60 to 75 cm). USDA Plant Hardiness Zones 3 to 9;
AHS Heat Zones 12 to 3.

More Recommended Statices

Limonium tataricum, also called *Goniolimon tataricum* and *Statice tatarica*
(German statice, Tatarian statice): This is a similar but smaller
plant, with flowers that look white or pale blue from a distance
but are distinctly pink when seen close up. Compared to *L. latifolium*, German statice leaves are narrower, smaller, and nearly hairless. Height: 10 to 16 inches (25 to 40 cm). Spread: 12 to 16 inches
(30 to 40 cm). USDA Plant Hardiness Zones 3 to 9; AHS Heat
Zones 12 to 3.

Sea lavender
(*Limonium latifolium*)

Larry's Garden Notes

Sea lavenders are top-quality cut
flowers, fresh or dried. For fresh
use, harvest when most flowers
are showing some color. Expect
the stems to remain in bloom for
at least two weeks. For dried
flowers, harvest a bit later, when
all the flowers are fully open.
Hang them upside down, or stick
them upright into a vase.

Lysimachia

Loosestrife

There are two ways to use loosestrifes as low-care perennials. One is to simply plant loosestrifes and let them take over your entire garden, thereby reducing your maintenance to zero—but I don't recommend it! The other way is to plant loosestrifes inside root barriers, where they'll live nearly forever with almost no care. You'll be able to enjoy their cup- or star-shaped, white or yellow flowers with no fear that they'll smother neighboring plants.

Plant Profile

LYSIMACHIA
lie-sih-MAH-kee-uh

- **Bloom Color:** White or yellow

- **Bloom Time:** Varies by species; see individual listings

- **Length of Bloom:** 4 weeks or more

- **Height:** 18 to 36 inches (45 to 90 cm)

- **Spread:** 1 to 3 feet (30 to 90 cm)

- **Garden Uses:** Cut flower garden, groundcover, mass planting, meadow garden, mixed border; seasonal hedge; at the back of beds and borders, in wet areas

- **Light Preference:** Full sun or partial shade

- **Soil Preference:** Fertile, moist or even wet soil

- **Best Way to Propagate:** Divide in spring or fall; sow seed in fall

- **USDA Plant Hardiness Zones:** Varies by species; see individual listings

- **AHS Heat Zones:** 8 to 1

Growing Tips

Think Twice: Loosestrifes can be invasive due to their wide-ranging root systems. New shoots can sprout from the roots 10 feet (3 m) or more from the original clump. But mostly loosestrifes just push forward in dense waves, chasing other garden plants out before them. The good news is that the roots run only a few inches (1 to 10 cm) underground, so all you need is a good root barrier to keep them under control. I use 1-gallon (4-l) or 2-gallon (8-l) pots with the bottoms cut out. Sink the pots into the ground to their rims, with a single division of loosestrife in each one. The plants quickly fill their limited space but will go no farther. Watch for wayward seedlings; prevent these by cutting the plants back after they bloom.

Plant loosestrifes in full sun or partial shade in moist, well-drained soil of any type, although rich soil results in better bloom. They'll also thrive in dry soil as long as they receive some shade.

Propagate loosestrifes by digging out a division with a few roots attached and replant, ideally in spring or fall. Or grow loosestrifes from seed: Toss the seed on freshly turned ground in the fall, without covering it, and it will germinate in spring.

Good Neighbors

Use loosestrifes as groundcovers in areas where natural barriers, such as shrubs, rocks, walls, or sidewalks, can keep them from spreading. Plant them in partly shaded or sunny, moist locations around moisture-tolerant woody plants such as summersweet (*Clethra alnifolia*), winterberry (*Ilex verticillata*), or willows (*Salix* spp.). Or try combining graceful gooseneck loosestrife (*L. clethroides*)—planted inside a root barrier—with hostas, purple coneflowers (*Echinacea purpurea*), and dropwort (*Filipendula vulgaris*). Yellow loosestrife

(*L. punctata*) would complement purple-blooming hardy geraniums (*Geranium* spp.) or Siberian iris (*Iris sibirica*).

Problems and Solutions

Loosestrifes will brush off any occasional insect problems with no help from you.

Top Performer

Think Twice: *Lysimachia clethroides* (gooseneck loosestrife, shepherd's crook): Gooseneck loosestrife has tiny white flowers on thin spikes that arch outward in the middle, then somewhat upward again at the tip, like the neck of a swan. The slightly hairy, broadly lance-shaped leaves take on a beautiful reddish coloration in the fall. This plant loves moist soil and will do best in wet spots, but beware: It will also spread more rapidly in wet soil. In drier conditions, it's much easier to control. I suggest using a root barrier no matter what your situation as well as cutting off all flowers when blooming is finished. Height: 2 to 3 feet (60 to 90 cm). Spread: 3 feet (90 cm). USDA Plant Hardiness Zones 3 to 9; AHS Heat Zones 8 to 1.

The flower spikes of gooseneck loosestrife (*Lysimachia clethroides*) all point in the same direction, creating an effect that's absolutely charming in the garden from late summer into fall. This garden beauty does have a downside though—it spreads quickly, so plant it inside a root barrier.

More Recommended Loosestrifes

Think Twice: *Lysimachia punctata* (yellow loosestrife, whorled loosestrife): This is the fastest-spreading loosestrife, so never plant it without putting it in a root barrier. If you keep it under control, yellow loosestrife is a stunning plant with a long bloom period. The narrow leaves are medium green and the star-shaped flowers are brilliant yellow. They bloom from early to late summer. Yellow loosestrife does best in moist to wet soil in full sun, so plant it in partial shade if your soil is on the dry side. 'Alexander' is a variegated cultivar with white-and-green leaves. It's a little less aggressive than the species, but you should still contain it. Height: 1 to 3 feet (30 to 90 cm). Spread: 1 to 2 feet (30 to 60 cm). USDA Plant Hardiness Zones 2 to 9; AHS Heat Zones 8 to 1.

Pennisetum

Fountain grass

The "fountain" in fountain grass is the arching stalks of bristly, bottlebrush-like flower spikes that appear in late summer. The spikes erupt from the dense, upright mounds of slender, arching bright green leaves. Fountain grasses add pleasant motion to your garden because the leaves and flower spikes move gracefully in the wind. Unlike many ornamental grasses, fountain grass flowers seem to fall apart with the first few days of cold weather. The foliage does offer some winter interest, turning golden brown in the fall and slowly fading to straw color by spring.

Plant Profile

PENNISETUM
pen-ih-SEE-tum

- **Bloom Color:** Black, cream, pink, purple, or white

- **Bloom Time:** Late summer to fall

- **Length of Bloom:** 8 weeks or more

- **Height:** Varies by species; see individual listings

- **Spread:** 24 to 30 inches (60 to 75 cm)

- **Garden Uses:** Container planting, cut flower garden, edging, groundcover, mass planting, mixed border, seasonal hedge, specimen plant; at the back of beds and borders

- **Light Preference:** Full sun

- **Soil Preference:** Fertile, moist but well-drained soil

- **Best Way to Propagate:** Divide or sow seed in spring

- **USDA Plant Hardiness Zones:** Varies by species; see individual listings

- **AHS Heat Zones:** Varies by species; see individual listings

Growing Tips

Fountain grasses can tolerate a wide range of growing conditions as long as they get the full sun and moist, well-drained soil they love so much. They prefer rich, loamy soil but will usually settle for most soil conditions. They will also tolerate light shade, although they will bloom less abundantly.

It's easy to propagate fountain grasses by dividing. Spring is the ideal time, but fall is fine, too, although you'll find it easier to cut the foliage back before you dig. Otherwise, fountain grass can live on its own practically forever without division.

It's easy to grow the species from seed started indoors or out in early spring, but the cultivars will not come true. Fountain grasses can be invasive through self-sown seedlings, especially in moist climates, so it's best to cut back the flower spikes in late fall. Many gardeners simply cut the whole plant back in fall, leaving "winter interest" up to other grasses in the garden. If you do leave the foliage in place for the winter, be sure to cut it back in early spring to make way for the new leaves.

Good Neighbors

To cover a lot of ground, combine masses of fountain grass with other perennials that have multiseason interest: Good choices include blue star (*Amsonia hubrectii*), white gaura (*Gaura lindheimeri*), orange coneflower (*Rudbeckia fulgida*), and 'Herbstfreude' sedum (also called 'Autumn Joy' sedum). In smaller gardens, use plants with contrasting forms as companions, such as spiny bear's breeches (*Acanthus spinosus*), asters, Ozark sundrops (*Oenothera macrocarpa*), or foxglove penstemon (*Penstemon digitalis*).

Problems and Solutions

Fountain grasses have no serious insect or disease problems.

Top Performer

Pennisetum alopecuroides (fountain grass): This common species of fountain grass blooms from late summer to fall. Its flower spikes usually emerge light pink or cream, then darken to reddish brown, although their color varies on plants grown from seed. Popular cultivars include 'Hameln', a hardy earlier-flowering selection; 'Little Bunny', a miniature cultivar ideal for tiny gardens, with silvery plumes just barely rising above 1-foot (30 cm) leaves; and 'Moudry', known as black fountain grass for its nearly black spikes (deadhead to prevent self-sowing). Height: 1 to 3 feet (30 to 90 cm). Spread: 24 to 30 inches (60 to 75 cm). USDA Plant Hardiness Zones 5 to 9; AHS Heat Zones 9 to 1.

Fountain grass
(*Pennisetum alopecuroides*)

More Recommended Fountain Grasses

Pennisetum orientale (oriental fountain grass): An excellent choice for warmer climates, oriental fountain grass is one of the earliest grasses to bloom and also one of the longest lasting. It produces blue-green leaves and rose-pink, late-summer-to-fall flower spikes that fade to light brown. Cut it back in October to prevent self-sowing. Height: 2 to 3 feet (60 to 90 cm). Spread: 24 to 30 inches (60 to 75 cm). USDA Plant Hardiness Zones 6 to 10; AHS Heat Zones 9 to 1.

    P. setaceum, also called *P. ruppelii* (tender fountain grass): This beautiful grass can only be grown as a perennial in frost-free areas. The feathery, arching spikes of pinkish flowers move in the slightest wind. In areas with only light frosts (UDSA Zone 9 and occasionally Zone 8b), the plant will resprout from the base each spring. 'Rubrum', also called 'Cupreum', has deep purple leaves and reddish purple plumes fading to beige. 'Rubrum Dwarf' is similar but only 30 to 60 inches (75 to 90 cm) tall. Height: 3 to 5 feet (90 to 150 cm). Spread: 24 to 30 inches (60 to 75 cm). USDA Plant Hardiness Zones 8b or 9 to 11; AHS Heat Zones 12 to 1.

Larry's Garden Notes

Although they make great cut flowers, fountain grasses don't work well for dried floral arrangements because their seedheads fall apart shortly after ripening. If you'd like to use fountain grass in a wreath or vase and need the seedheads to last longer, harvest and dry them early, then spray them with a ton of hair spray to keep the seedheads intact.

Thalictrum

Meadow rue

You'd be forgiven if you mistook meadow rue foliage for columbines (*Aquilegia* spp.). Their leaves are very similar, with thin stalks and rather wedge-shaped, broadly toothed leaflets. Of course, when meadow rues bloom, you'd never mistake them for columbines because they have large fuzzy flower heads that look like pink powder puffs. Most meadow rues are tall, open plants with airy, open clusters of flowers; their leaves often have a bluish tinge.

Plant Profile

THALICTRUM
thuh-LICK-trum

- **Bloom Color:** Lilac, pink, purple, white, and yellow
- **Bloom Time:** Varies by species; see individual listings
- **Length of Bloom:** Varies by species; see individual listings
- **Height:** Varies by species; see individual listings
- **Spread:** 2 to 4 feet (60 to 120 cm)
- **Garden Uses:** Cut flower garden, mass planting, mixed border, seasonal hedge, specimen plant, wildflower meadow, woodland garden; at the back of beds and borders
- **Light Preference:** Full sun to partial shade
- **Soil Preference:** Humus-rich, moist but well-drained soil
- **Best Way to Propagate:** Divide in spring; sow seed in spring or fall
- **USDA Plant Hardiness Zones:** Varies by species; see individual listings
- **AHS Heat Zones:** 9 to 1

Growing Tips

Think of meadow rues as permanent plants. They don't need dividing unless you want to multiply them, and they don't appreciate being moved. Just plant them and let them take care of themselves: They'll probably still be around when you are long gone!

In cool-summer climates, these adaptable perennials grow well in a sunny site with moist, well-drained soil; elsewhere, they can adjust to drier soil as long as they're in partial shade or dappled sunshine. Although they like rich soil, they'll put up with poor soil.

You can grow meadow rues from seed—fresh seed is best, as packaged seed sometimes needs several cycles of cold and warmth before it will bloom. In either case, sow directly outdoors in late summer or fall. Fresh seed should germinate the first spring and provide the first flowers the following year, but packaged seed can germinate sporadically over several years. Columbine meadow rue (*Thalictrum aquilegifolium*) is the main exception: It germinates readily even from packaged seed and doesn't need cold treatment. Sow it indoors or out in early spring.

For most gardeners, division, although risky, is still the best way of multiplying meadow rues and the *only* way you can multiply cultivars at home. Carefully dig up the plants, ideally in spring, and separate the clumps into individual plants.

Good Neighbors

Pair columbine meadow rue (*Thalictrum aquilegifolium*) with other plants that thrive in partial shade and moist soil, such as lady's-mantle (*Alchemilla mollis*), ferns, and hostas. Tall, refined Yunnan meadow rue (*T. delavayi*) and lavender mist (*T. rochebrunianum*) brighten the back of the border, fronted by other late-summer bloomers, such as Japanese anemone (*Anemone* × *hybrida*) and pink turtlehead (*Chelone lyonii*).

Yellow meadow rue (*T. flavum*) is a beautiful back-drop for the blue flowers of aconites. Plant the foreground with lower-growing plants with strong foliage, such as bergenias and hellebores (*Helleborus* spp.).

Problems and Solutions

Some meadow rues are occasionally subject to leaf diseases, such as powdery mildew and rust, but the outbreaks are rarely severe enough to require treatment.

Top Performer

Thalictrum aquilegifolium (columbine meadow rue): With its blue-green fernlike leaves on relatively compact plants, this old-fashioned favorite produces lilac cotton-candy blooms that last several weeks in the North (much less in the South). There are several cultivars in shades of white through pink and dark purple, as well as seed mixes that will give you variously colored flowers. Height: 3 to 5 feet (90 to 150 cm). Spread: 2 to 3 feet (60 to 90 cm). USDA Plant Hardiness Zones 3 to 9; AHS Heat Zones 9 to 1.

More Recommended Meadow Rues

Thalictrum delavayi (Yunnan meadow rue): Yunnan meadow rue produces an open, airy "shrub" of fine, lacy green foliage, topped off with a veritable cloud of purple or lavender flowers with yellow stamens from early or midsummer to early fall. 'Hewitt's Double', with double lilac flowers, can remain in bloom more than two months; it may need staking. Height: 3 to 6 feet (90 to 180 cm). Spread: 2 to 3 feet (60 to 90 cm). USDA Plant Hardiness Zones 4 to 9; AHS Heat Zones 9 to 1

T. flavum subsp. *glaucum*, also called *T. rugosum* or *T. speciosissimum* (dusty meadow rue): It seems surprising that there should be such a strongly yellow-flowering species in a genus where purples and lavenders dominate, but look closer—the tiny sepals are white or very pale yellow: It is actually the abundant yellow stamens that give this flower its color. Plants bloom from midsummer to late summer or early fall. The species, yellow meadow rue (*T. flavum*), has green leaves, but the plant usually grown is dusty meadow rue, which has beautiful blue-green leaves. Height: 3 to 6 feet (90 to 180 cm). Spread: 2 to 4 feet (60 to 120 cm). USDA Plant Hardiness Zones 4 to 9; AHS Heat Zones 9 to 1.

An old-fashioned favorite, columbine meadow rue (*Thalictrum aquilegifolium*) is charming and relatively carefree. Among the showiest of the meadow rues, it puts forth puffy pink clouds of flowers early in the season and grows as tall as 5 feet (150 cm)—but don't worry, it doesn't need staking!

LARRY'S LAST LOOK: LOW-CARES

Take a gander at some of these other low-care perennials that are just too terrific not to include in this chapter. Low-cares don't scream out for constant attention because they practically take care of themselves. Just do a little dividing every seven years or so, and they'll be good for another 100,000 miles.

COMMON AND BOTANICAL NAME	ZONES AND EXPOSURES	BLOOM COLOR AND TIME	DESCRIPTION
Spiny bear's breeches *Acanthus spinosus*	Hardiness Zones 5–9 Heat Zones 9–1 Sun to partial shade	Purple to green flowers with purple veins, which bloom in late spring to early summer	White spines on the leaves give a distinct thistlelike appearance. Plants form dense clumps. Height: 3–5 feet (90–150 cm). Spread: 3 feet (90 cm).
Pinwheel lady's-mantle *Alchemilla conjuncta*	Hardiness Zones 3–9 Heat Zones 7–1 Sun to partial shade	Yellow-green flowers in early summer to early fall	Spreading perennial with deeply cut leaves that are silvery underneath. Height: 12–18 inches (30–45 cm). Spread: 12–18 inches (30–45 cm).
Red-stemmed lady's-mantle *Alchemilla erythropoda*	Hardiness Zones 3–9 Heat Zones 7–1 Sun to light shade	Yellow-green flowers in spring	A diminutive species featuring small blue-green leaves that are edged in silver. If grown in the sun, it will have reddish flower stems. Height 6–9 inches (15–23 cm). Spread: 1 foot (30 cm).
Spanish thrift *Armeria juniperifolia,* also called *A. caespitosa*	Hardiness Zones 3–9 Heat Zones 7–4 Sun	White, pink, red, or lilac flowers in late spring to early summer	Best grown in a rock garden or container. Has tiny rosettes of awl-shaped dark green leaves and rounded flower heads. Use a thin mulch of fine gravel at its base for good drainage. Height: 2–4 inches (5–10 cm). Spread: 6 inches (15 cm).

Spiny bear's breeches

Common foxglove
(*Digitalis purpurea*)

COMMON AND BOTANICAL NAME	ZONES AND EXPOSURES	BLOOM COLOR AND TIME	DESCRIPTION
Common foxglove *Digitalis purpurea*	Hardiness Zones 3–9 Heat Zones 8–1 Sun to partial shade	White, pale pink, purple, or yellow flowers in late spring to midsummer	Spectacular, easy to grow, but really a biennial. Produces a rosette of wrinkled, downy leaves and a tall spike of pendulous flowers in a range of colors. Many cultivar lines. Height: 30–84 inches (75–213 cm). Spread: 12–30 inches (30–75 cm).
Myrtle euphorbia *Euphorbia myrsinites*	Hardiness Zones 3–9 Heat Zones 8–5 Sun	Chartreuse flowers in spring	Resembles a trailing eucalyptus with its paddle-shaped, blue-green leaves on creeping stems. Prefers well-drained—even dry—conditions. Good for rock gardens. Height: 6–8 inches (15–20 cm). Spread: 12–18 inches (30–45 cm).
Kansas gayfeather *Liatris pycnostachya*	Hardiness Zones 3–9 Heat Zones 9–1 Sun	Purple flowers in midsummer to early fall	This tall species adds height in your garden but does need staking. Prefers steady soil moisture in summer but needs good drainage in springtime. Height: 4–5 feet (120–150 cm). Spread: 2 feet (60 cm).
Loosestrife *Lysimachia ephemerum*	Hardiness Zones 5–9 Heat Zones 9–7 Sun to partial shade	White flowers in late spring to late summer	Well-behaved loosestrife that won't spread. Has clumps of upright stems and pairs of long, narrow, willowlike, blue-green leaves. An absolute delight with its 10–15 inch (25–38 cm) spikes of starry-shaped flowers. Height: 3 feet (90 cm). Spread: 2 feet (60 cm).
Lavender mist *Thalictrum rochebrunianum*	Hardiness Zones 4–9 Heat Zones 9–1 Sun to partial shade	White to purple flowers with yellow stamens, which bloom in late spring to late summer	The tallest of the meadow rues (*Thalictrum* spp.), but it rarely requires staking. Attractive fernlike leaves with huge, billowy clusters of flowers. Height: 4–6 feet (120–180 cm). Spread: 3 feet (90 cm).

Myrtle euphorbia
(*Euphorbia myrsinites*)

Lavender mist
(*Thalictrum rochebrunianum*)

241

Drought-Resistant
PERENNIALS

In their native habitats, drought-resistant perennials are quite capable of surviving the worst droughts. They'll usually do just as well in the dry parts of your yard or garden. Remember, though, that while the perennials I describe in this chapter are all drought-resistant, that doesn't mean they necessarily all like the same growing conditions. Some, such as aloes and agaves, like it hot all the time, while others, such as sea hollies, enjoy hot days and cool nights. In general, dry soils are very poor in organic matter, and drought-resistant plants have had to adapt to cope with both dry conditions and poor soil.

Top Picks

◄ Once established, agapanthus (*Agapanthus* hybrid) is a tough perennial, able to survive even a long period of drought. The stunning clusters of trumpet-shaped flowers may not bloom as profusely in dry years, but the plant will certainly make it through without harm.

Do You Need Drought Resistance?

Does the average gardener need to worry about planting drought-resistant perennials? Only you know your own climate, so you'll have to answer this question yourself. During periods of extreme drought, discouraged by repeated waterings or the wilted appearance of average perennials, you're likely to answer "yes." If such periods are fairly common, you should indeed consider trying drought-resistant plants. On the other hand, if your climate is generally humid with only occasional light droughts, you might find the best solution is to use good, all-around perennials not necessarily grown specifically for their drought resistance, but that can put up with a bit of drought every now and again.

The good news for gardeners is that on the whole, perennials are a fairly drought-resistant group of plants. Once they're well established, perennials can rely on their relatively deep roots to find underground moisture, allowing them to pull through most droughts without serious damage. Perennials may not be as drought-resistant as trees and shrubs—which have much longer roots—but they're much better at surviving dry spells than are lawn grasses, annuals, and vegetables. Also, many perennials slow their growth or even go somewhat dormant during periods of drought. It's a natural response for a plant that wants to survive for several years because occasional drought is a fact of nature. Annuals, on the other hand, usually quickly go to seed and die during a drought, trusting in nature to provide better conditions for the new generation next year.

So what happens if you don't water your perennial garden during a drought? The plants bloom less abundantly, and if the drought is

243

Well-established, drought-tolerant perennials with extensive root systems (*left*) can withstand long dry spells. But newly planted perennials don't have a big root system (*right*). They'll need watering throughout their first year in your garden.

severe, they'll stop flowering altogether. But they recuperate quickly once it rains, and it's business as usual the following year. So if you *don't* choose drought-tolerant perennials, convert an annual garden or a section of lawn into a perennial border to reduce water use.

The Right Time for Tough Plants

There are places where drought-tolerant perennials are the best choice for a trouble-free garden. Try these tough plants under the eaves of the house or under shallow-rooted trees where conditions can be nearly desert-dry much of the time. And drought-resistant perennials are a terrific solution in sites where nearby objects absorb heat and dry the soil (like that little strip of grass between your sidewalk and the street).

New Perennials Can't Take Drought

Newly planted perennials *will* need watering, even if they're classified as drought-resistant. When you first plant a perennial, it hasn't had a chance to spread its roots far and wide in search of moisture. It relies on you to provide consistent waterings so that it can grow both new top-

growth and new roots. It takes most perennials a full calendar year from planting to develop a well-established root system.

Identifying Drought-Tolerant Perennials

When you're shopping for plants, you can often make your own deductions about which perennials are drought-resistant just by observing the plant's stems and leaves. For example, succulents, those cactuslike plants with thick stems or leaves, are quite clearly equipped to resist drought: Those fleshy plant parts store water to help the plant cope with dry conditions. Some other clues to drought tolerance include:

- A waxy coating on the leaves
- Densely hairy leaves
- Silvery, grayish, or bluish foliage
- Narrow leaves
- Prickly leaves

Of course, some drought-tolerant plants don't show any obvious signs of their special adaptability: Aboveground, they just look like any other perennial. Those perennials owe their drought tolerance to their thickened, water-storing roots or tubers; or, they may have very *long* roots that reach deep into the soil for moisture.

Watering Wisdom

Using drought-resistant plants is only one way of conserving water in your garden. Here are a few other suggestions for coping with dry growing conditions.

Mulch abundantly. Mulch isn't just for weed control: It keeps soil cool and moist as well.

Don't crowd your plantings. Dense plantings need more water because there are more thirsty roots to "feed"; open plantings give individual plants a greater share of the supply of soil moisture.

Use the water nature supplies. Catch and store rainwater from rooftops in a rain barrel. Or capture the water that runs off your driveway by providing shallow irrigation channels that direct water to the lawn or garden rather than to the street, where it becomes stormwater runoff and doesn't benefit anyone. Then use the stored water as needed. You'll often find Nature does supply all the water you could ever need!

Water wisely. If you have to water, do it with care. Apply water slowly over a long period of time so it sinks in rather than evaporating. Never sprinkle your garden lightly: If the water doesn't sink in, most of it will just be lost to evaporation from the soil and leaf surfaces and will never help your plants at all. If possible, apply water at ground level rather than as a spray, so less will be lost to evaporation. Using some type of drip irrigation is best: It supplies water slowly, at ground level, and really soaks the soil.

Live and learn. If one or two plants in your garden just can't tolerate the drought, move them and replace them with others.

Chill out. Most people are poor judges of watering needs and tend to water far more than plants really require. If a plant is generally recommended for your climate and has done well in the past, it probably won't need watering. Just learn to trust Mother Nature: She usually comes through!

Dealing with Desert Conditions

If you live in the arid regions of the southwestern United States and Mexico, drought-resistant plants may have to be the mainstay of your gardens. If so, you may not be satisfied with my choices of drought-tolerant perennials because not all of them are adapted to grow well in the Southwest. I've limited myself to drought-tolerant perennials that can survive in colder climates as well, even when it comes to succulents. So if there's more sagebrush than lilac in your immediate environment, you'll probably want to consult some books about plants especially suited for hot, dry climates. I've included a few of my favorites in the reading list on page 480.

14 More Drought Fighters

Filling the dry beds and odd spots around your yard with colorful perennials is easy with the drought-resistant plants I've described in this chapter. Try these other perennials and ornamental grasses that can tough out dry spells, too:

Agapanthus

Agapanthus, African lily

For a striking show in a container or in the garden, try agapanthus. This tough perennial produces dense, fountainlike clumps of long, thick, arching, dark green, strap-shaped leaves. Shooting up from the foliage are thick, leafless stalks that each bear a single globelike cluster of 30 or more trumpet-shaped, blue, purple, or white flowers. The bloom clusters tower 1 foot (30 cm) or so above the leaves, and in full sun and well-drained soil, they can last more than two months.

Plant Profile

AGAPANTHUS
ag-uh-PAN-thus

■ **Bloom Color:** Blue, purple, or white

■ **Bloom Time:** Early summer to early fall

■ **Length of Bloom:** 8 to 10 weeks or more

■ **Height:** 1 to 4 feet (30 to 120 cm)

■ **Spread:** 1 to 3 feet (30 to 90 cm)

■ **Garden Uses:** Container planting, cut flower garden, edging, groundcover, mass planting, mixed border, seasonal hedge, specimen plant, woodland garden; at the back of beds and borders; attracts butterflies

■ **Light Preference:** Full sun to partial shade

■ **Soil Preference:** Average, well-drained soil

■ **Best Way to Propagate:** Divide after flowering

■ **USDA Plant Hardiness Zones:** Varies by species

■ **AHS Heat Zones:** 12 to 3

Growing Tips

Agapanthus are resilient, grow-them-almost-anywhere plants. They prefer slightly moist soil at all times, but established plants can sail through prolonged droughts without showing any sign of stress. They'll adapt to a wide range of soil conditions as long as the site isn't constantly wet. Full sun is best, but agapanthus also thrive in partial shade. They can be either evergreen or deciduous, depending on the species and the climate. They flower anytime from late spring to late summer, again depending on type and climate.

Some species of agapanthus aren't hardy enough for northern gardens, although the hardiest types survive quite well in USDA Zones 6 and 7 when they're planted in well-drained soil and mulched well during winter. Fortunately, agapanthus are easy to grow in containers in any climate. Come winter, you can bring them indoors and treat them as houseplants (give them bright light and occasional waterings during their stay indoors). Or, if you have a cold basement or root cellar, store agapanthus in their pots or bareroot without water, using peat, perlite, or vermiculite.

Dividing an agapanthus planted outdoors can be a daunting task and is best accomplished with the help of a burly neighbor or two. For detailed directions on dividing large agapanthus, turn to page 212. Fortunately, you don't have to divide them often. As long as they're thriving, just let them grow—they'll form large clumps. (Division *is* the best and fastest method of multiplying them, though, and it is the only way of ensuring that a particularly nice plant comes true).

When they're growing in containers, agapanthus will often tell you it's time to repot them by splitting the pot open with their massive roots. Though it's tempting to repot them into much larger containers so you won't have to repot again for a long time, don't do it! Agapanthus bloom better when their roots are crowded. If you're dividing them at the same time, plant them in containers only slightly larger than the rootball of each division.

Despite rumors to the contrary, agapanthus are easy to grow from seed. Start them indoors or, in frost-free climates, outdoors, and just lightly cover the seeds. Germination is irregular, taking from 20 to 90 days. Seedlings should bloom in their second or third year.

Good Neighbors

Try planting agapanthus in large containers with a low-growing all-season plant such as creeping zinnia (*Sanvitalia procumbens*) or 'Limelight' licorice plant (*Helichrysum petiolare* 'Limelight').

In an ideal site, agapanthus may successfully overwinter outdoors. Use it as a focal point surrounded by neighbors such as lady's-mantle (*Alchemilla mollis*), evergreen candytuft (*Iberis sempervirens*), or yellow scabious (*Scabiosa ochroleuca*).

Problems and Solutions

Agapanthus are not particularly subject to insects or diseases.

Top Performer

Agapanthus hybrids: Most agapanthus are sold as *A. africanus* or *A. umbellatus*, but technically speaking, they're almost always hybrids with *A. praecox* subsp. *orientalis*. There are dozens of named cultivars, but few of them are widely available. Instead, most agapanthus are sold by flower color, usually blue or white. For permanent plantings in colder climates, the Headbourne Hybrids are the best choice. They're usually available in shades of blue, but they are variable because many of them are seed-grown. There are also several dwarf hybrids that are good for planting in borders in mild-winter areas or in containers in cold regions. They include 'Peter Pan', with narrow leaves and pale blue flowers. There are also white-flowered dwarfs and the striking variegated 'Tinkerbell', which has narrow leaves lined in white. It's grown primarily for its foliage—it rarely blooms.

Agapanthus (*Agapanthus* hybrid) is an easy perennial to grow in a container or, where winters are mild, right in the garden. Originally from southern Africa, agapanthus lends an exotic touch to the garden or patio with its long flowerstalk and abundant flowers.

Agave

Agave, century plant

No perennial makes a more dramatic statement than a gigantic agave in an entry garden. Native to arid regions of the New World tropics and subtropics, agaves have tremendously tough, spiny leaves. The plants may take ten years or more to bloom, but when they finally do, they provide a fantastic floral show that lasts several months, with each plant producing a tall, treelike, usually branched cluster of hundreds of bell-shaped or tubular flowers.

Plant Profile

AGAVE
a-GAH-vee

- **Bloom Color:** Green, white, or yellow
- **Bloom Time:** Spring through fall
- **Length of Bloom:** Varies by species; see individual listings
- **Height:** Varies by species; see individual listings
- **Spread:** Varies by species; see individual listings
- **Garden Uses:** Container planting, hedge, rock garden, specimen plant; on slopes
- **Light Preference:** Full sun
- **Soil Preference:** Average, well-drained soil
- **Best Way to Propagate:** Remove and replant offsets or sow seed at any time
- **USDA Plant Hardiness Zones:** Varies by species; see individual listings
- **AHS Heat Zones:** 12 to 5

Growing Tips

Where they're hardy, plant agaves in full sun and any kind of soil. Perfect drainage is a must: They will not stand wet soil for more than a few days. Established plants are extremely drought-resistant, shriveling but remaining alive up to a year without rain. Even when watered regularly, agaves are very slow-growing, taking at least five years from seed to near full height.

In colder climates, treat agaves as container plants or houseplants. Bring them outdoors in the summer to decorate terraces and balconies, or sink their pots into the garden and then bring them back indoors in the fall. In winter, keep them growing in a brightly lit spot indoors by watering them when they're nearly dry, or let them dry out and go dormant, then place them in the dark in a cool basement or a root cellar.

Be forewarned that some types of agaves will grow to monstrous sizes if you let them. Keeping them in small pots and not fertilizing them at all will help keep them under control for decades.

Most agaves eventually produce offsets at their base or on short runners. You can cut these off and root them as separate plants. All agaves will grow from seed sown indoors or out, although variegated forms don't come true from seed.

Warning: Agave leaves are every bit as wicked as they look. For the safety of all garden visitors, you should cut the daggerlike points off the tips of the leaves.

Good Neighbors

Where they're hardy, agaves are perfect choices for dry-soil gardens or rock gardens, sharing the scene with other drought-resistant plants. In containers, agaves look and perform best when combined with other succulents, such as sedums and hens-and-chicks (*Sempervivum tectorum*).

Problems and Solutions

In and near their native areas (the southwestern United States and Mexico), agaves are subject to various insects and diseases but rarely suffer serious damage. Elsewhere, they have few problems. Keep in mind that it's normal for these plants to die after they produce flowers, but the offsets they've produced should survive and continue to grow.

Top Performer

Agave americana (century plant, American aloe): A giant of a plant, this popular species produces blue-green leaves up to 6 feet (1.8 m) long, usually bending downward at the middle, with hooked spines along the edges and a vicious straight spine at the tip. When it blooms, it produces a branched flowerstalk that can stretch from 15 to 40 feet (4.5 to 12 m) tall! The flowers are greenish yellow. In very dry conditions, the century plant is very hardy, surviving winter in protected spots of USDA Zone 7 with little difficulty. Unfortunately, the combination of cold and humidity can be fatal, so grow it outdoors only in USDA Zones 9 to 11. There are several variegated cultivars with white or yellow stripes or bands on the leaves. Height: 3 to 6 feet (90 to 180 cm), or 15 to 40 feet (4.5 to 12 m) when in bloom. Spread: to 10 feet (3 m). USDA Plant Hardiness Zones 9 to 11; AHS Heat Zones 12 to 5.

More Recommended Agaves

Agave victoriae-reginae (Queen agave): A smaller agave of distinctly manageable size, Queen agave forms a dense, rounded rosette of stiff, thick, dark green leaves about 6 inches (15 cm) long marked with thin white lines. The leaf terminates abruptly in a short, blunt spine. It can take decades to produce its giant flowerstalk of dense yellow flowers, usually in late spring to fall. Queen agave produces neither offsets nor bulbils, so you can multiply it only from seed. Height: rosette, 1 to 2 feet (30 to 60 cm); flowerstalk, 13 to 15 feet (3.9 to 4.5 m). Spread: 20 inches (50 cm). USDA Plant Hardiness Zones 10 to 11; AHS Heat Zones 12 to 5.

Century plant
(*Agave americana*)

Larry's Garden Notes

Agaves (*Agave* spp.) are also called century plants because people used to believe that the plants would only bloom once every 100 years. Smaller agaves can bloom in as few as 5 to 10 years, although some of the larger species may take up to 20 or 40 years to bloom. Agaves planted in containers may never bloom and are sometimes handed down from one generation to the next as living family heirlooms.

Aloe

Aloe

If you live in Florida or mild-winter parts of the Southwest, you'll be able to enjoy growing aloes in your garden and watching the hummingbirds that come to feed at their blossoms. If you garden farther north, you can enjoy growing these drought-hardy succulents in containers, or you can treat them as annuals and replant each year. Aloes form rosettes of fleshy blue-green leaves; the leaves snap off readily and ooze sticky sap.

Plant Profile

ALOE

AL-oh (common pronunciation)

A-low-ee (botanical pronunciation)

- **Bloom Color:** Orange, pink, red, or yellow
- **Bloom Time:** Varies by species; see individual listings
- **Length of Bloom:** 4 weeks or more
- **Height:** Varies by species; see individual listings
- **Spread:** 8 to 24 inches (20 to 60 cm)
- **Garden Uses:** Container planting, edging, mass planting, mixed border, rock garden, wall planting; at the back of beds and borders, on slopes; attracts hummingbirds
- **Light Preference:** Full sun to light shade
- **Soil Preference:** Average, well-drained soil
- **Best Way to Propagate:** Divide or take cuttings at any time
- **USDA Plant Hardiness Zones:** 9 to 11
- **AHS Heat Zones:** 12 to 3

Growing Tips

Aloes grow in most well-drained soils, or in practically no soil at all, since they will root into rock crevices with only a handful of earth. Watering established plants outdoors is unnecessary. Where frost is a danger, plant aloes in protected spots, out of cold winds.

For many gardeners, growing aloes in containers is a must. Bring the plants outdoors for a dose of summer sun, then move them back inside for the winter. Place them in a sunny window at room temperature—they can tolerate temperatures down to 50°F (10°C)—and water them only when their soil is nearly dry to the touch.

Some aloes don't produce noticeable stems. The best way to propagate these types is by dividing the offsets that form around the edges of the plant. You can do this at any time of year, but spring is preferable. For aloes with noticeable stems, you can take stem cuttings as well as divide them.

Good Neighbors

Sink potted aloes into the ground in an herb garden or plant them there in warm climates, where their exotically different foliage adds considerable drama. Position them where they'll rise above a carpet of low-growing herbs such as mother-of-thyme (*Thymus serpyllum*) or prostrate rosemary (*Rosmarinus officinalis* 'Prostratus').

Problems and Solutions

Aloes have no particular pest and disease problems, although mealybugs can be a problem in-

> ### FUN FACTS
>
> **The sap of medicinal aloe (***Aloe vera***)** has been used at least since biblical times as an ointment for healing wounds. To treat a minor wound, scrape, insect bite, or burn at home, disinfect the wound, then cut a leaf of aloe open and delicately apply the clear sap to the wounded area.

doors. Mealybugs look like pieces of cotton fluff and can be found anywhere on the plant, but especially in the little cracks and crevices you just can't reach. Spray with a solution of insecticidal soap weekly for a month, following label instructions carefully and lightly coating the entire plant.

Top Choice

Aloe vera, also called *A. barbadensis* (medicinal aloe): This is the best-known species because of its medicinal uses and its tough nature. Plants are fan-shaped with fresh green leaves spotted with white; they have light spines along the edges. They produce many offsets. More mature plants produce rosettes of stiffer, blue-green leaves with less spotting. Adult forms planted outdoors flower abundantly, with dense spikes of tubular yellow flowers atop 3 foot (90 cm) stalks in spring and summer. Height: 6 to 48 inches (15 to 120 cm). Spread: 4 to 12 inches (10 to 30 cm). USDA Plant Hardiness Zones 9 to 11; AHS Heat Zones 12 to 3.

More Recommended Aloes

Aloe brevifolia: A dwarf species, *A. brevifolia* forms a dense, stemless rosette of thick, generally triangular, blue-green leaves up to 2½ inches (6.5 cm) long. The leaves bear little white teeth along the edges and in a single line on the underside. *A. brevifolia* produces offsets quite freely. It bears dense spikes of pale scarlet flowers in early spring. Height: 3 to 18 inches (7.5 to 45 cm). Spread: 3 inches (7.5 cm). USDA Plant Hardiness Zones 9 to 11; AHS Heat Zones 12 to 3.

A. variegata (partridge breast aloe): A stemless aloe, this species produces an elongated rosette of short, triangular leaves spotted and banded with white. The leaves are edged with tiny teeth. The 1-foot (30 cm) flowerstalk produces tubular pink flowers in spring. Partridge breast aloe usually only produces offsets if the main rosette is wounded. To propagate, cut a stem near the base and break off five or six lower leaves to expose the bare stem, then root the stem. Offsets will soon form at the base and can be removed and rooted when they have five or six leaves. Height: 1 foot (30 cm). Spread: 20 inches (50 cm). USDA Plant Hardiness Zones 9 to 11; AHS Heat Zones 12 to 3.

Medicinal aloe
(*Aloe vera*)

Larry's Garden Notes

People have used the sap of the medicinal aloe (*Aloe vera*) since Biblical times as an ointment for healing wounds (it was even used for embalming Egyptian mummies!). Commercial growers now raise medicinal aloe on a large scale, and the sap is used in everything from beauty creams to shampoos.

Delosperma

Hardy ice plant

Ice plants fascinate gardeners with their daisylike flowers that bloom in incredibly bright colors. For the most part, though, these South African natives have been difficult for North American gardeners to grow due to their lack of winter-hardiness. But in the early 1980s, plant explorers discovered hardy ice plants above the frost line on South African mountains. The two species widely available so far are both low-growing, mat-forming groundcovers or rock garden plants.

Plant Profile

DELOSPERMA
deh-loh-SPUR-muh

- **Bloom Color:** Purple and yellow
- **Bloom Time:** Varies by species; see individual listings
- **Length of Bloom:** 4 to 6 weeks
- **Height:** 2 to 6 inches (5 to 15 cm)
- **Spread:** 1 to 3 feet (30 to 90 cm)
- **Garden Uses:** Edging, groundcover, mass planting, rock garden, wall planting; along paths, on slopes
- **Light Preference:** Full sun
- **Soil Preference:** Average, very well-drained soil
- **Best Way to Propagate:** Take stem cuttings or divide from spring through fall
- **USDA Plant Hardiness Zones:** Varies by species; see individual listings
- **AHS Heat Zones:** 12 to 1

Growing Tips

Hardy ice plants are strictly for very sunny, very well-drained sites. They won't tolerate moist soil for long and need little if any watering once they're established (which happens very quickly, within weeks of being planted).

You only need to buy one ice plant because they're very prolific, spreading well the first year and rooting into the ground as they creep. They're a snap to multiply from stem cuttings or divisions at just about any season. They also grow rapidly and easily from seed (you can buy it or collect your own). Just sow it indoors on top of moist growing mix, and place the container in darkness at room temperature until germination occurs. Then expose the seedlings to the brightest light possible. They'll bloom the first year from seed if sown 10 to 12 weeks before the last frost date.

Good Neighbors

The low-growing succulent foliage of hardy ice plants is an interesting addition to a rock garden. Combine it with contrasting colors and textures. Good companions for orange-yellow hardy ice plant (*Delosperma nubigenum*) include red-and-yellow-flowered wild columbine (*Aquilegia canadensis*), Carpathian harebell (*Campanula carpatica*), and dwarf irises. Pair purple hardy ice plant (*D. cooperi*) with cushion

FUN FACTS

Ice plants get their common name from the crystalline dots on their leaves that sparkle like ice crystals. The common name has carried over to species that have smooth leaves as well. The petals also contain special reflective cells that make the flowers almost seem to glow before our eyes. I always think of neon when I see these flowers.

spurge (*Euphorbia polychroma*) and hens-and-chicks (*Sempervivum tectorum*), or use it as a groundcover around yuccas.

Problems and Solutions
Crown rot is a problem in moist soil, especially as cooler fall temperatures set in. Crown rot causes the stem to rot away just at the base and if you don't react quickly by taking stem cuttings of healthy growth, the whole plant can quickly die. Remember, perfect drainage is a must for these plants!

Top Performer
Delosperma cooperi (purple hardy ice plant): This is the most widely available of the hardy ice plants. It produces cylindrical, shiny, medium green leaves and spreads rapidly, forming a dense shag carpet of intermingled foliage and stems. The 2-inch (5-cm) daisylike flowers are vivid purple-red. It starts blooming in early summer and continues through the first fall frosts in many climates. In fall, its leaves take on a strong red coloration, which they retain until spring (then they turn green again). A light winter mulch of conifer branches can help purple ice plant survive into USDA Zone 5. Perfect drainage is an absolute must, especially in climates with moist or rainy winters. If purple hardy ice plant dies during the winter in your garden (and it may in wet or cold climates), consider growing it as an annual. Height: 6 inches (15 cm). Spread: 1 to 2 feet (30 to 60 cm). USDA Plant Hardiness Zones 6 to 10; AHS Heat Zones 12 to 1.

More Recommended Hardy Ice Plants
Delosperma nubigenum (yellow hardy ice plant): This ice plant is much hardier than purple hardy ice plant and less dependent on perfect drainage, too. Native to the tops of South Africa's coldest mountains, its botanical name means "born of a cloud." It literally does grow in the clouds, which also explains its greater tolerance of humidity. It's much smaller than purple hardy ice plant and has small, fleshy, evergreen leaves that are mint green in summer; the leaf tips turn red in fall and winter. Its bright yellow flowers last four to six weeks, from late spring to early summer. Height: 2 inches (5 cm). Spread: 1 to 3 feet (30 to 90 cm). USDA Plant Hardiness Zones 4 to 9; AHS Heat Zones 12 to 1.

Purple hardy ice plant
(*Delosperma cooperi*)

Kissing Cousins

Orange ice plant (*Lampranthus aurantiacus*), also called bush ice plant, has bright orange flowers from midwinter to spring, and there are cultivars that bloom in various shades of yellow and gold. The three-sided leaves are gray-green and succulent. They're so popular as weed-fighting groundcovers along California roadways that people there just call them highway daisies. Height: 10 to 15 inches (25 to 40 cm). Spread: 2 feet (60 cm) or more. USDA Plant Hardiness Zones 9 to 11; AHS Heat Zones 12 to 1.

Echinops

Globe thistle

Don't let the common name fool you: Globe thistle is *not* invasive like the weedy thistles that curse some gardens. Both the leaves and the flower heads are, however, quite prickly. At the end of each upright stem, globe thistle bears a ball of pointed blue buds that open into blue flowers. The apparently long blooming period of the globe thistle is an illusion. Since the entire flower head is bluish in color, the plant seems to be in blossom from the time the head forms until it develops seeds and dries. But in fact, the tiny, attractive, starlike flowers last only a short while.

Plant Profile

ECHINOPS
ECK-in-ops

- **Bloom Color:** Blue or white

- **Bloom Time:** Early summer to early fall

- **Length of Bloom:** 10 weeks

- **Height:** Varies by species; see individual listings

- **Spread:** Varies by species; see individual listings

- **Garden Uses:** Cut flower garden, mass planting, mixed border, seasonal hedge, specimen plant, wildflower meadow; at the back of beds and borders; attracts butterflies

- **Light Preference:** Full or partial shade

- **Soil Preference:** Average, very well-drained soil

- **Best Way to Propagate:** Take root cuttings or sow seed in spring

- **USDA Plant Hardiness Zones:** 3 to 9

- **AHS Heat Zones:** 12 to 1

Growing Tips

Globe thistles actually do best in poor or average soil and under dry conditions, preferably in full sun. Water them relatively well the first year, that is, every few weeks if it doesn't rain; after that, you can ignore them except during the worst droughts. If not for their habit of losing their lower leaves (something you can easily conceal by planting mounding plants at the base), globe thistles would be just about perfect.

Think of globe thistles as permanent: They don't like to be disturbed once they're established. To propagate globe thistles, carefully dig out the offsets that form at the base of older plants and replant them elsewhere in the spring. Or, thrust a shovel deep into the ground about 6 inches (15 cm) from the base of an established plant in late fall: This will sever a few roots from which new shoots will sprout the following spring. You can dig up the new sprouts and transplant them. A third option is to dig some thick side roots carefully from the base of the plant in the spring, cut them into 3- to 4-inch (8- to 10-cm) sections, and pot up the root cuttings.

To multiply globe thistles by seed, start the seeds indoors or out, just barely covering them. The seeds sprout irregularly about one to two months later. Unfortunately, the better cultivars do not come true from seed.

Warning: Globe thistle flowers have bristly bracts that can prick you, so wear gloves when you handle them.

Good Neighbors

The metallic blue of globe thistle combines well with many companions. Here's one suggestion: Try 'Taplow Blue' globe thistle (*Echinops ritro* 'Taplow Blue') with milky bellflower (*Campanula lactiflora*) and pastel-flowered garden phlox (*Phlox paniculata*) for a pretty summer show.

Problems and Solutions

Globe thistle is an easy-to-grow plant with few major problems.

Top Performer

Echinops ritro (globe thistle, small globe thistle): Globe thistle seems very prickly, but its leaves are not as fearsome as they look. The deeply cut dark green leaves are generally smooth above and woolly white below, and the tips are more pointed than spiny—only the very tip of the leaf has a true spine. This is the only species offered by most nurseries, although the plants sold may be labeled *E. bannaticus* (see below). The basal leaves can be 1 foot (30 cm) with distinct leaf stems, but the upper leaves, which clasp the stem, are much smaller. It has metallic blue buds and flowers from early summer to early fall. 'Taplow Blue' has steel blue flowers and a silvery cast. 'Veitch's Blue' is darker blue. Height: 2 to 4 feet (60 to 120 cm). Spread: 2 to 3 feet (60 to 90 cm). USDA Plant Hardiness Zones 3 to 9; AHS Heat Zones 12 to 1.

More Recommended Globe Thistles

Echinops bannaticus (globe thistle): This species is very similar to *E. ritro*, and you may find various cultivars linked to either or both species names. 'Blue Globe' (also called 'Blue Ball'), which has deep blue flowers from early summer to early fall, is definitely a cultivar of globe thistle. It's denser and somewhat shorter than other globe thistles, making it a good choice for the middle of the border. Height: 2 to 4 feet (60 to 120 cm). Spread: 2 to 3 feet (60 to 90 cm). USDA Plant Hardiness Zones 3 to 9; AHS Heat Zones 12 to 1.

E. sphaerocephalus (great globe thistle): As you might expect from its name, great globe thistle is taller than the other species I've described and has slightly grayer blue flowers from early summer to early fall. Height: 4 to 7 feet (1.3 to 2.1 m). Spread: 3 to 4 feet (90 to 120 cm). USDA Plant Hardiness Zones 3 to 9; AHS Heat Zones 12 to 1.

'Taplow Blue' globe thistle (*Echinops ritro* 'Taplow Blue')

Kissing Cousins

Cardoon (*Cynara cardunculus*) is a vegetable, but I must slip it in here because it creates such a beautiful effect in the garden. It has huge, deeply cut, prickly, felted, gray-green leaves that form an enormous mound. The bloom, if indeed you ever see it (cardoon isn't very hardy and it won't bloom in its first year), looks just like a giant purple thistle. As an ornamental, cardoon is a drought-tolerant, no-nonsense plant. Height: 6 feet (1.8 m). Spread: 6 feet (1.8 m). USDA Plant Hardiness Zones 6 to 10; AHS Heat Zones 11 to 1.

Eryngium

Sea holly, eryngo

Sea holly flowers look like a Star Wars version of an Elizabethan collar. The cone-shaped or rounded flower heads are surrounded by stiff, incredibly spiny petal-like structures called bracts. The plants grow stiffly upright, with spiny leaves as well as flowers. Their lower leaves are usually green, spiny, and fairly large. The upper ones tend to be smaller and are often silvery or metallic blue, as are the flowers. Sea hollies look like thistles—but they're actually cousins to garden carrots.

Plant Profile

ERYNGIUM
er-IN-gee-um

- Bloom Color: Blue or creamy green
- Bloom Time: Midsummer to late summer
- Length of Bloom: 4 to 8 weeks
- Height: Varies by species; see individual listings
- Spread: 1 to 2 feet (30 to 60 cm)
- Garden Uses: Cut flower garden, mass planting, mixed border, seasonal hedge, specimen plant, wildflower meadow; at the back of beds and borders; attracts butterflies and birds
- Light Preference: Full sun or partial shade
- Soil Preference: Average, very well-drained, even sandy soil
- Best Way to Propagate: Take root cuttings in spring or sow fresh seed in late summer
- USDA Plant Hardiness Zones: Varies by species; see individual listings
- AHS Heat Zones: Varies by species; see individual listings

Growing Tips

As cactus growers like to say, you should grow sea hollies "hard": That is, don't baby them. Well-drained, poor to average, and even sandy soils are perfect, as are hot, sunny conditions that would cause most other plants to wilt. As you'd expect from seashore plants, sea hollies don't mind salty soils—they'll thrive along northern roadways that are treated with de-icing salts. Sea hollies do prefer to contrast their desert hot days with cool nights. In fact, they produce their *very* best colors in northern gardens; the excessive heat of southern climes can cause them to bleach out.

Like other taprooted perennials, sea hollies don't like to be disturbed: Trying to move or divide a plant can be fatal to it. Instead, carefully dig up the offsets that form at their base or remove a few thick outer roots and use them for root cuttings. If you want to start sea hollies from seed, be sure to sow *fresh* seed (that is, straight from the plant into your garden). Seed from packets needs special care. Sow it outside in the fall on the surface of the soil. Indoors, place the trays in the fridge for two or three weeks; then move to room temperature. Prick out any seedlings as they appear (germination can take from 9 to 90 days), then put the trays back in the fridge and repeat. It can take up to three cold treatments to get good germination.

Warning: The petal-like bracts that surround sea holly flowers are beautiful but very sharp, so wear heavy gloves when handling the plants.

Good Neighbors

Place sea hollies in front of a green background (such as a tall ornamental grass or shrub) or pair them with handsome purple great bellflower (*Campanula latifolia*) to complement their silver-gray color. Other good companions include balloonflower (*Platycodon grandiflorus*), garden phlox (*Phlox paniculata*), and pink shrub roses.

Problems and Solutions
Sea hollies are seldom bothered by pests or diseases.

Top Performer
Eryngium alpinum (alpine sea holly, bluetop eryngo): The entire top part of this sea holly really is blue. The plants bear large cone-shaped flower heads in midsummer to late summer. The bracts that surround the flower heads are finely divided, even lacy. The lightly toothed foliage ranges from green and heart-shaped at the base to lobed or featherlike, blue-tinged leaves farther up the stems. Height: 18 to 24 inches (45 to 60 cm). Spread: 1 to 2 feet (30 to 60 cm). USDA Plant Hardiness Zones 4 to 9; AHS Heat Zones 8 to 4.

Alpine sea holly
(*Eryngium alpinum*)

More Recommended Sea Hollies
Eryngium amethystinum (amethyst sea holly): Amethyst sea holly is especially popular with northern growers because it's extremely cold-hardy. It also succeeds better in hot-summer gardens than most other sea hollies. From midsummer to late summer, the plants produce branching stems of small metallic blue flowers with very long, pointed bracts. The flower stems are also blue. Height: 18 to 30 inches (45 to 75 cm). Spread: 18 to 24 inches (45 to 60 cm). USDA Plant Hardiness Zones 2 to 9; AHS Heat Zones 8 to 1.

 E. planum (flat sea holly): Adaptable and widely available, flat sea holly does as well in the South as in the North. It has spineless, scalloped, dark green basal leaves and small but plentiful dark blue flowers with thin, pointed blue bracts from midsummer to late summer. Height: 2 to 3 feet (60 to 90 cm). Spread: 1 to 2 feet (30 to 60 cm). USDA Plant Hardiness Zones 3 to 9; AHS Heat Zones 9 to 1.

Larry's Garden Notes

Sea hollies (*Eryngium* spp.) make great cut flowers. For fresh use, harvest the flowers when they are fully open. For dried flower use, cut them any time from the moment the buds start to swell and the bracts reach their full size to late summer, before they start to lose their blue coloration. They'll dry in a week if hung upside down. For great winter interest, leave the flowers right on the plants—they look stunning under frost or light snow. And seed-eating finches will also take them for a self-serve food counter, extending your garden's usefulness well into winter.

Lavandula

Lavender

Drinking in the aroma of lavender is one of the true delights of perennial gardening. There are several species of lavender, and they vary notably in fragrance, but all produce grayish or silvery evergreen leaves and narrow spikes of flowers, mostly in shades of lavender-blue to purple. If you look closely, you'll also see that lavender has the square stems and two-lipped flowers characteristic of plants in the mint family.

Plant Profile

LAVANDULA
lav-AN-djew-luh

- **Bloom Color:** Lavender-blue, pink, violet, or white

- **Bloom Time:** Late spring to late summer

- **Length of Bloom:** 2 months or more

- **Height:** Varies by species; see individual listings

- **Spread:** Varies by species; see individual listings

- **Garden Uses:** Container planting, cut flower garden, edging, groundcover, mass planting, mixed border, rock garden, specimen plant, wall planting; along paths, on slopes; attracts butterflies

- **Light Preference:** Full sun

- **Soil Preference:** Poor, well-drained soil

- **Best Way to Propagate:** Take stem cuttings in spring or summer

- **USDA Plant Hardiness Zones:** Varies by species; see individual listings

- **AHS Heat Zones:** 12 to 7

Growing Tips

First and foremost, lavenders need full sun. They will bloom poorly, if at all, if they get less than six hours of sun per day. But sun alone won't do: Lavenders also require extremely fast-draining soil. They especially dislike winter wet. When you plant lavenders, remind yourself that poor, sandy, or even stony soils will produce thicker, healthier, longer-lived plants than will humus-rich soil.

Since lavenders tend to be short-lived in many climates, it's smart to always have a few plants coming along to replace any that die. The easiest, fastest way to propagate lavenders is to take green stem cuttings with just a slice of old wood. Start them in spring or summer in cold-winter areas or in spring or fall in mild areas. You can also grow lavenders from seed sown outdoors or indoors in early spring. If you sow indoors, seal the sown seed container in a plastic bag and place it in the refrigerator for four to six weeks; then move it to a relatively cool location—about 55° to 65°F (13° to 18°C)—for germination. Use a strain specifically offered for seed culture because many lavenders don't come true from seed.

Good Neighbors

Lavenders look great with roses! They also pair well with other drought-tolerant plants, including 'Coronation Gold' yarrow (*Achillea* 'Coronation Gold'), butterfly weed (*Asclepias*

FUN FACTS

Lavender has been, and still is, used in treating a long list of ailments, from sore throats and burns to depression and headaches. I suggest drying lavender flowers and tossing them into potpourris, sachets, and pillows: With all those medical uses behind them, how can they help but be good for what ails you? (Besides, if you put lavender in your pillow, it's said you'll have sweet dreams!)

tuberosa), and sea hollies (*Eryngium* spp.), just to name a few.

Problems and Solutions

Lavender has no serious pests, but it is subject to what I call "sudden death syndrome," especially in excessively humid conditions. Seemingly healthy plants just die, sometimes declining for a few weeks beforehand and other times wilting suddenly, in either winter or summer, for no obvious reason.

Top Performer

Lavandula angustifolia, also called *L. officinalis*, *L. spica*, and *L. vera* (English lavender, common lavender): This lavender not only has the scent that comes to mind when we think of lavender, but it also is far more widely adapted to varying growing conditions, and notably cold winters, than any other species. If this is your first attempt with lavender, put all the chances on your side and try English lavender!

English lavender is a densely shrubby plant with narrow, gray-green leaves. The 3- to 4-inch (8- to 10-cm) spikes of whorled flowers are usually lavender to purple, but sometimes white or pink, and bloom from late spring to late summer. 'Hidcote' (also called 'Hidcote Blue') has rich purple flowers over a long season on 16- to 18-inch (40- to 45-cm)-tall plants. 'Munstead' (also called 'Munstead Variety') is a similar but smaller seed-grown strain. It reaches about 1 foot (30 cm) tall. 'Lavender Lady' will reach blooming size the first year from seed if started indoors in midwinter. It produces typical lavender blue flowers on a compact 10-inch (25-cm)-tall plant. Height: 10 to 60 inches (20 to 150 cm). Spread: 1 to 3 feet (30 to 90 cm). USDA Plant Hardiness Zones 5 to 9; AHS Heat Zones 12 to 7.

More Recommended Lavenders

Lavandula latifolia (spike lavender): A close cousin of English lavender (*L. angustifolia*) and almost as hardy, spike lavender has somewhat more silvery, broader leaves, a fuller growth habit, and branching flowerstalks from late spring to late summer. It has a scent all its own, which reminds me more of camphor than lavender. Height: 12 to 18 inches (30 to 45 cm). Spread: 12 to 18 inches (30 to 45 cm). USDA Plant Hardiness Zones 6 to 9; AHS Heat Zones 12 to 7.

'Twickel Purple' English lavender (*Lavandula angustifolia* 'Twickel Purple')

Around the World with Lavender

Although it's called English lavender, *Lavandula angustifolia* is actually native to the Mediterranean. There, it grows abundantly in the hot, dry, alkaline soil. To me, a whiff of lavender always brings back memories of the garrigue (scrubland) in the south of France, where field upon field of lavender blush soft purple during the summer months. On one of those hot, sun-washed days that only Provence can provide, you can roll down the windows of your car as you whisk along the twisting mountain roads and easily imagine the entire world smells of lavender!

Lewisia

Lewisia, bitter root

To see a lewisia is to want one! Lewisia flowers are incredibly charming. The cup-shaped blossoms are often striped and may sport more than one pretty color on their petals. On an established lewisia, the flowers can be so numerous that the plant becomes a solid dome of blooms. Under all those flowers is a rosette of thick, succulent, spoon- or strap-shaped leaves. If you fall for lewisia, keep in mind that it's not just drought-tolerant—it's *drought-requiring* during the summer and won't survive in a wet spot.

Plant Profile

LEWISIA
loo-IHS-ee-uh

- **Bloom Color:** Cream, magenta, orange, pink, purple, red, white, and yellow
- **Bloom Time:** Late spring to midsummer
- **Length of Bloom:** 3 weeks or more
- **Height:** 6 to 10 inches (15 to 25 cm)
- **Spread:** 8 to 10 inches (20 to 25 cm)
- **Garden Uses:** Edging, mass planting, rock garden, wall planting; along paths, on slopes
- **Light Preference:** Full sun to partial shade
- **Soil Preference:** Average, extremely well-drained, even stony soil
- **Best Way to Propagate:** Divide in spring
- **USDA Plant Hardiness Zones:** 4 to 9
- **AHS Heat Zones:** 8 to 3

Growing Tips

Most lewisias can be difficult to grow because they need special growing conditions to thrive. While you can get them to grow well in your garden, it will take some careful preparation. The first and most important key to lewisia survival is perfect drainage—that is, soil that drains extremely rapidly. If your garden soil is average or even top quality, with lots of organic matter, that's a good start, but add lots of crushed rock or coarse sand to improve drainage. When you plant your lewisias, leave the crown a full inch (2.5 cm) above soil level, then mulch up to the crown level with fine gravel or loose rock. This open layer at the base of the crown will provide the air circulation required to prevent crown rot. Without this aboveground drainage layer, your lewisia will probably just rot away, especially in humid conditions. Another solution is to locate lewisias in a rock garden, planting them almost vertically into crevices between rocks, so that gravity will ensure perfect drainage.

Another key to success with lewisias is abundant moisture during the blooming season and dry conditions during the summer. This is usually an easy requirement to meet because most regions are at their most humid in the spring when lewisias bloom and much drier in summer. Where summers are rainy, the perfect drainage described above is an absolute must. Usually lewisias prefer partial shade, but in rainy climates, plant them in full sun, where they'll dry out more quickly after a rainfall.

The final secret to lewisia culture is providing good winter protection while keeping the plants dry. I like to cover my lewisias with conifer branches to protect the plants from drying winter winds and buffer drastic temperature changes while allowing good air circulation. That, plus abundant snow cover, gets them through my USDA Zone 3 winters with no problem at all. (USDA Zone 4 is probably a safer bet where snow cover is not reliable.)

Of course, if all else fails, grow lewisias in containers in a well-drained soil mixture (always with a drainage layer on top), then move them as necessary, from sun in spring to cool shade in summer to a protected spot in winter.

Until you've gotten the hang of lewisias, it's best to start with purchased plants. If your plants produce multiple crowns when they get established, you can divide them, ideally in spring. You can also grow them from seed started indoors 10 to 12 weeks before your last frost date. Sow them on the surface of a moistened mix, then refrigerate for four or five weeks before placing them in light at 50° to 60°F (10° to 15°C) to stimulate germination. If nothing comes up after two months, repeat the refrigeration process.

Common lewisia
(*Lewisia cotyledon*)

Good Neighbors

Plant lewisias with other alpine plants in a rock garden or rock wall. For companions, consider mountain lady's-mantle (*Alchemilla alpina*), mountain sandwort (*Arenaria montana*), rock soapwort (*Saponaria ocymoides*), and hens-and-chicks (*Sempervivum tectorum*).

Problems and Solutions

The only pest or disease problem that troubles lewisias is crown rot, and perfect drainage is the solution. 'Nough said!

Top Performer

Lewisia cotyledon (common lewisia): This is the most widely available species and the only one you're likely to find in local nurseries. There are dozens of cultivars in every imaginable shade of pink, red, purple, magenta, yellow, orange, cream, and white, often with a contrasting stripe or vein. The flowers are 1 to 2 inches (2.5 to 5 cm) in diameter. This species and its hybrids bloom from late spring to midsummer.

Larry's Garden Notes

The name *Lewisia* (used for both the common and botanical names of this terrific perennial) commemorates the explorer, Merriweather Lewis, one of the leaders of the Lewis and Clark expedition (1804–1806). One thing many people don't realize about Lewis and Clark's explorations is that they brought many new plants native to the West back to the settled East.

Opuntia

Prickly pear

Prickly pears are more a curiosity than a typical garden perennial. These spiny, creeping succulents are true cacti: yep, just like the saguaros of the Southwest. And they produce beautiful, cup-shaped yellow flowers. The flowers turn into edible, fig-shaped, spiny green fruits that may turn red or purple as they mature. In the right location, prickly pears can be very attractive, and they certainly draw attention in a garden of leafy foliage.

Plant Profile

OPUNTIA
oh-PUN-tee-uh

- **Bloom Color:** Yellow
- **Bloom Time:** Early summer
- **Length of Bloom:** 3 weeks or more
- **Height:** 6 to 12 inches (15 to 30 cm)
- **Spread:** 1 to 2 feet (30 to 60 cm)
- **Garden Uses:** Container planting, edging, groundcover, mass planting, rock garden, wall planting; on slopes
- **Light Preference:** Full sun
- **Soil Preference:** Average, very well-drained soil
- **Best Way to Propagate:** Take cuttings or sow seeds in spring or summer
- **USDA Plant Hardiness Zones:** 3 to 9
- **AHS Heat Zones:** 12 to 1

Growing Tips

Grow prickly pears in full sun and very well-drained soil. Although many types are adapted to moist or even rainy summers, the fleshy stems, which are called joints, must be able to dry out in the fall in order to become dormant or they won't survive frost. (When the joints go dormant, they become limp and shriveled and may look dead. But don't worry: The joints will simply plump right up again in the spring or early summer.)

In many areas, prickly pears grow best in raised beds or rock gardens in soil that's heavily amended with coarse sand or crushed rock. Cover the soil all around the base of the plants with a 1-inch (2.5-cm) layer of gravel or stones to further improve surface drainage because prickly pears are highly susceptible to crown and stem rot in moist-winter climates.

If you garden north of USDA Zone 7, apply a very light, well-aerated mulch such as pine, hemlock, or other conifer branches as winter protection for your plants.

It's easy to multiply prickly pears through stem cuttings. Just break or knock off a joint and place it in slightly moist sand. You can also divide prickly pears, but given their spiny nature, cuttings are a more popular method. Growing prickly pears from seed is not easy, and the hardy species in particular are very reluctant to sprout. For best results, sow seed indoors in moist growing mix, place the container in the fridge for four

FUN FACTS

I hope you never have to extract prickly pear spines from any part of your body, but if you do, here's an easy way to remove them: Cover the itchy area with masking tape, press lightly, then give a hard yank!

weeks, and then expose the seed to warmth for eight weeks. If nothing comes up, repeat, and repeat yet again if necessary. Eventually you should be able to get some germination.

Good Neighbors

Combine prickly pears with plants that prefer very well-drained, sandy soil, such as sedums and yuccas. Rocks also make great backdrops for these plants.

Problems and Solutions

Most problems with prickly pears, including crown or stem rot and winter damage, are due to overly moist conditions, so think drainage, drainage, and more drainage if you want your plants to be happy.

Prickly pear
(*Opuntia humifusa*)

Top Performer

Opuntia humifusa, also called *O. compressa* (prickly pear): The wild prickly pear found in northeastern North America, this species is comparatively well adapted to cold and moisture, although it still needs good drainage. Authorities differ on the exact identity of this plant, but it's usually sold as *O. humifusa*. Typically this prickly pear produces 2- to 6-inch (5- to 15-cm) flattened joints called pads. The pads are spotted with brownish areoles, which are small, downy cushions armed with tiny, hooked spines called glochids. Glochids break off when touched and work their way into your skin. They're more annoying than truly painful, but you'll quickly learn to enjoy your prickly pears at a distance. The plants may also have a few spines along the edges of the pads, but they are essentially leafless. Their pads or joints are *not* leaves, but sometimes small leaves do form on new growth, only to fall off rather quickly.

    O. humifusa is a creeping type of prickly pear, with relatively upright new growth the first year that bends to the ground in the fall. The early summer flowers are bright yellow and the fruits are red or green.

Larry's Garden Notes

In the wild, prickly pears (*Opuntia* spp.) usually multiply in an unusual way. The joints of the opuntia plant are quite fragile, breaking off at the slightest touch. When an animal passes by, the plant's sharp spines hook on to its legs or body (and that hurts!). The joint comes loose, and the piece of prickly pear travels along with the animal. The unwitting carrier tries to knock the painful guest off and when it finally does so, often at great distances from its original home, the joint falls to the ground and roots, soon forming a new colony.

Phlomis

Phlomis

Phlomis is an oddball group of plants. I'd describe their flower spikes as a floral shish kebab—the upright stalks bear widely spaced pairs of leaves with a rounded ball of flowers at the base of each pair. When the flowers dry up and fall off, they leave behind rounded clusters of spiky green seed capsules. Phlomis plants have four-sided stems and hairy, even fuzzy, heart-shaped or oval leaves that are attractively textured or wrinkled. Most are evergreen in warmer climates; all are deciduous in USDA Zone 7 and north.

Plant Profile

PHLOMIS
FLOH-miss

- **Bloom Color:** Lavender, pink, and yellow

- **Bloom Time:** Varies by species; see individual listings

- **Length of Bloom:** 4 weeks or more

- **Height:** Varies by species; see individual listings

- **Spread:** Varies by species; see individual listings

- **Garden Uses:** Mixed border, seasonal hedge, wildflower meadow; at the back of beds and borders

- **Light Preference:** Full sun to light shade

- **Soil Preference:** Well-drained, light, sandy, infertile soil

- **Best Way to Propagate:** Take stem cuttings in summer or fall

- **USDA Plant Hardiness Zones:** Varies by species; see individual listings

- **AHS Heat Zones:** Varies by species; see individual listings

Growing Tips

With their grayish, hairy leaves and soft flower colors, phlomis look naturally sun-bleached, as if they love heat, sun, and drought—and they do. If your climate is Mediterranean, with hot, dry summers and mild, wettish winters, phlomis will fit right in. You'll find they do best in partial shade under such conditions. But if you live where summers are the slightest bit wet, full sun and perfect drainage are a must. I've found that just placing phlomis in raised beds makes a lot of difference, since this improves drainage considerably. Slopes suit them well, too.

Stem cuttings are the fastest and easiest way to propagate phlomis. You can also divide your plants, and mature plants eventually need to be divided as well. Phlomis also grow readily from seed, blooming the following year. Sow them outdoors in early spring if you wish, just barely covering the fine seed, but you'll probably get better germination indoors. Start seeds eight to ten weeks before the last frost date, and germinate them on the cool side, about 60°F (15°C); they will sprout in a few weeks.

Good Neighbors

Try phlomis with peach-leaved bellflower (*Campanula persicifolia*), red valerian (*Centranthus ruber*), 'Six Hills Giant' catmint (*Nepeta* 'Six Hills Giant'), or 'Prairie Fire' penstemon. To echo the yellow flowers, plant phlomis with lady's-mantle (*Alchemilla mollis*) or 'Moonbeam' threadleaf coreopsis (*Coreopsis verticillata* 'Moonbeam').

Problems and Solutions

Other than crown rot in poorly drained soil, phlomis is usually free of pests and diseases.

Top Performer

Phlomis fruticosa (Jerusalem sage): The
slightly spreading, semi-woody stems
of this species give it a more shrublike
appearance than many of its cousins.
The hairy, yellow stems will overwinter
in warmer climates, as do the attractively wrinkled gray-green leaves. In
northern areas, though, both die to the
ground each year. The curled-up yellow
flower buds form round balls at different heights around the stem and
then open to 1-inch (2.5-cm) golden
yellow flowers. Plants flower from late
winter through late summer in the
South, and early to late summer in the
North. If you cut the plant back by half
after it blooms, it may bloom again; in
fact, it can bloom repeatedly in milder
climates. Height: 2 to 4 feet (60 to 120
cm). Spread: 3 feet (90 cm). USDA
Plant Hardiness Zones 4 to 9; AHS
Heat Zones 9 to 1.

Jerusalem sage
(*Phlomis fruticosa*)

More Recommended Phlomis

Phlomis russeliana (Jerusalem sage): This is the most commonly
available species, although not the most widely adaptable one.
It produces heart-shaped, wrinkled, woolly leaves that are sticky
to the touch. The early- to late-summer flowers are distinctly
hooded and a lovely butter yellow color. It spreads by underground stems called rhizomes, and it can make a nice weed-
suppressing groundcover in a well-drained area. Height: 3 feet
(90 cm). Spread: 2 to 3 feet (60 to 90 cm). USDA Plant Hardiness
Zones 5 to 9; AHS Heat Zones 9 to 3.

    P. tuberosa: Here's a hardier *Phlomis* species that isn't quite as
demanding of perfect drainage. It's a relatively tall plant with
toothed green leaves that are deciduous in all climates. The large
whorled summer flowers are lavender to pink. And like its species
name suggests, the roots have small, rounded, well-spaced tubers
or nodules on them. Height: 4 to 7 feet (1.2 to 2.13 m). Spread:
3 feet (90 cm). USDA Plant Hardiness Zones 3 to 9; AHS Heat
Zones 8 to 3.

Larry's Garden Notes

One of the most common mistakes
beginning gardeners make is to
buy one of this and one of that, with
the end result being a free-for-all.
Well, in the case of Jerusalem sage
(*Phlomis fruticosa*), buying just one
is not a mistake. Oddball, architectural plants like *Phlomis* can be just
what your garden needs to bring it
focus. Follow up its early bloom
with a later focal point like tall, annual flowering tobacco (*Nicotiana
sylvestris*), and you'll have people
stopping all summer to ask, "What
is that tall plant?"

Phormium

Flax lily, New Zealand flax

When they're not in bloom, flax lilies look like broad-leaved ornamental grasses or overgrown Siberian irises (*Iris sibirica*). The clumps of thick, leathery, sword-shaped leaves shoot up vertically and then arch outward. Tall, branching flowerstalks bear tubular red or yellow blooms, but sometimes these are hard to appreciate because the flowerstalks can tower as high as 15 feet (4.5 m) above the leaves! However, flax lilies don't bloom all that often, especially not in containers, and most gardeners grow them strictly for their dramatic foliage.

Plant Profile

PHORMIUM
FORE-mee-uhm

- Bloom Color: Red or yellow

- Bloom Time: Summer

- Length of Bloom: 4 or more weeks

- Height: Varies by species; see individual listings

- Spread: 1 to 3 feet (30 to 90 cm)

- Garden Uses: Container planting, mixed border, specimen plant; at the back of beds and borders

- Light Preference: Full sun to partial shade

- Soil Preference: Average, well-drained soil

- Best Way to Propagate: Divide in spring

- USDA Plant Hardiness Zones: 9 to 10

- AHS Heat Zones: 12 to 1

Growing Tips

"Tough as nails" is a good description for flax lilies. They grow in nearly any kind of soil, from dry to moist and rich to poor. In dry climates, just plant them in deep soil, and water well the first year. They'll find their own water after that, thanks to their long, tough, thick roots. The only care you'll need to provide is pulling off dead leaves, and if the plants ever bloom, cutting back faded flower stems.

The one thing flax lilies won't tolerate is cold. Their leaves can withstand temperatures as low as 15°F (-9°C) for short periods of time, but the roots can't withstand frozen soil. I've sheltered them through winter in USDA Zone 3 under heavy mulch and 4 feet (1.2 m) of snow, but their leaves were killed back to the bases and they took ages to recuperate. So I've switched to growing them in containers, and I move them indoors for the winter. Unless you garden in USDA Zone 8 or south, I recommend growing flax lilies as container plants—they're ideal for dramatic effect on the summer patio or balcony.

When they're outdoors in containers, flax lilies need more watering than in the ground. During their indoor stay, you can store them in a root cellar (tie the leaves together; otherwise they take up a lot of space) or put them on display with your other houseplants in sun or in shade.

Division is the best way to multiply flax lily hybrids (and almost all those sold *are* hybrids). However, even small plants are incredibly hard to separate. Try unpotting them and soaking them in water until the soil falls off, so you can see where to cut. If the rhizomes are too thick to cut with your pruning shears, you may need to saw them apart.

You can also try growing flax lilies from seed, although they may not reproduce true to type. Sow them at any time, just covering the seeds, and keep them at 60° to 65°F (15° to 18°C). Germination is slow and irregular, taking from one to six months.

Good Neighbors

Flax lilies add a wonderful vertical element to container gardens. Accent the foliage colors with everblooming flowers, such as tuberous begonias or verbenas, or with a collection of coleus for foliage interest.

Problems and Solutions

Flax lilies aren't bothered by any pests or diseases. The only thing that will hurt them is cold.

It's the grassy foliage and not the flowers that makes New Zealand flax (*Phormium tenax*) a striking addition to the container garden or warm-zone perennial border. Give it plenty of room though—its leaves alone can reach up to 9 feet (2.7 m) tall, and in rare instances where blooms appear, the flowerstalks can shoot up to 15 feet (4.5 m).

Top Performer

Phormium hybrids: It's not easy to determine whether a flax lily is a hybrid or a variant of New Zealand flax (*P. tenax*) or mountain flax (*P. colensoi*). For the most part, the popular hybrid flax lilies are dwarf or even miniature plants, usually with colorful leaves: red, gold, or green, and striped with white, yellow, pink, red, or all of the above. All the cultivars I know of are excellent: Just pick the one that's the right color and size for your needs. Height: 1 to 3 feet (30 to 90 cm). Spread: 1 to 2 feet (30 to 60 cm). USDA Plant Hardiness Zones 9 to 10; AHS Heat Zones 12 to 1.

More Recommended Flax Lilies

Phormium tenax (New Zealand flax): The giant of the group, this plant bears leaves to 9 feet (2.7 m) long and 5 inches (13 cm) wide at the base. Deep red summer flowers are borne on upright flowerstalks taller than some houses. This species is not as drought-resistant as the hybrids, so keep it somewhat moist at all times. Height (in bloom): 8 to 15 feet (2.4 to 4.5 m). Spread: 2 to 3 feet (60 to 90 cm). USDA Plant Hardiness Zones 9 to 10; AHS Heat Zones 12 to 1.

Yucca

Yucca, Spanish bayonet, Adam's-needle

If you're looking for dramatic, drought-tolerant plants that you can plant right in your garden, yuccas might be the plant for you. These grasslike plants form dense, clumping rosettes of tough, sword-shaped leaves and tall terminal, branching spikes of scented, nodding white or whitish bell-like flowers. Their leaves are often fringed in loose fibers and tipped with a wicked-looking spine.

Plant Profile

YUCCA
YUK-uh

- **Bloom Color:** White or greenish white
- **Bloom Time:** Varies by species; see individual listings
- **Length of Bloom:** 1 month or more
- **Height:** Varies by species; see individual listings
- **Spread:** 2 to 3 feet (60 to 90 cm)
- **Garden Uses:** Container planting, cut flower garden, mixed border, rock garden, seasonal hedge, specimen plant; at the back of beds and borders
- **Light Preference:** Full sun
- **Soil Preference:** Average, well-drained soil
- **Best Way to Propagate:** Separate offsets in spring
- **USDA Plant Hardiness Zones:** Varies by species; see individual listings
- **AHS Heat Zones:** 9 to 1

Growing Tips

Yuccas are no-nonsense plants: They don't give any, and they won't take any. Just plant them in full sun and well-drained soil of any type, even poor or stony. Allow lots of open space around them because you don't want to have to work near these plants. In my opinion, a tough, weed-smothering, drought-tolerant groundcover like delosperma would be the best next-door neighbor for a yucca.

About the only maintenance you'll need to provide for yuccas is pulling off leaves that turn brown and cutting back dead flower stems (wear gloves for this!). In the northern part of their range, you may want to pull the leaves together at the tip and tie them up in the fall to protect the center of the plant from temperature extremes.

Division is unnecessary unless you need new plants or your clump has gotten so big *something* has to be done about it. In this case, put on thick pants, long sleeves, leather gloves, and goggles. You can either cut offsets free at their base and root them, or dig them up with roots intact. Use a very sharp shovel and your strongest pruning shears—maybe even a saw.

You can also grow yuccas from seed, although they can take three or four years to reach garden size and may not bloom for a decade. Sow seeds indoors in late winter or outdoors in spring, just barely covering the seeds, but be patient—the seed can take anywhere from a month to a year to germinate.

Warning: Yucca spines are just as dangerous as they look. Don't plant yuccas along a sidewalk or in any location where someone could brush against them unless you plan to diligently clip off all the leaf spines.

Good Neighbors

Dramatic in leaf and in flower, yuccas can be a welcome change of pace in Northeast gardens. For a deer-resistant garden, use yuccas in a bed of low-growing shrub roses. Yuccas also combine well with drought-tolerant groundcovers, such as bloody cranesbill (*Geranium sanguineum*) or rose verbena (*Verbena canadensis*), on a sunny bank.

Problems and Solutions

Other than occasional leaf spotting (not very visible and needing no treatment), yuccas rarely have pest or disease problems, as long as you grow them in well-drained soil. Crown rot is possible in overly moist conditions.

Top Performer

Yucca filamentosa (Adam's-needle): Adam's-needle has thick, convex, sword-shaped leaves with long, curly threads along the leaf margins. Each leaf ends in a sharp, stout spine. This popular yucca blooms from midsummer to early fall, and the flower stems can range from 4 feet (120 cm) tall to a whopping 12 feet (360 cm) tall. You can grow this species in USDA Zone 4 or even 3, with moderate winter protection (mulch them and tie their leaves together). There are many variegated cultivars, with leaves variously striped and banded with yellow, cream, pink (in full sun), or white. They are similar in appearance and effect, so you don't need to search for a specific cultivar: Just choose one that's readily available. Height: foliage, 2 to 3 feet (60 to 90 cm); flowers, 4 to 12 feet (120 to 360 cm). Spread: 2 to 4 feet (60 to 120 cm). USDA Plant Hardiness Zones 5 to 9; AHS Heat Zones 9 to 1.

More Recommended Yuccas

Yucca glauca (soapweed): The best yucca for cold-climate gardens, soapweed grows as far north as Alberta, Canada, in the wild. It's a somewhat smaller, more refined-looking yucca, with narrower, bluish green leaves with a whitish margin. Soapweed blooms in early summer to midsummer. Height: foliage, 1 to 2 feet (30 to 60 cm); flowers, 3 to 5 feet (90 to 150 cm). Spread: 1 to 2 feet (30 to 60 cm). USDA Plant Hardiness Zones 3 to 9; AHS Heat Zones 9 to 1.

'Golden Sword' Adam's-needle
(*Yucca filamentosa* 'Golden Sword')

Larry's Garden Notes

Young yuccas (*Yucca* spp.) can take several years to reach blooming size, a fact many gardeners accept quite readily. But when the yuccas fail to bloom the year after their first bloom, gardeners begin to wonder what they did wrong. The answer is—nothing!

Yuccas form rosettes of leaves on a very short, usually hidden stem, but each rosette only blooms once. The plant will only bloom again when secondary rosettes have reached blooming size, and that can take a few years. It may take as long as a decade to get a nice clump of yuccas containing enough of both the mature and young rosettes to guarantee yearly bloom.

Water-Loving PERENNIALS

A wet area can be the most fascinating gardening adventure your yard has to offer. For one thing, wet areas are very popular with wildlife, drawing birds, butterflies, toads, frogs, and other fascinating creatures like a magnet. And once you discover the world of water-loving perennials, you'll find that you can create impressive gardens in wet areas, featuring beautiful flowers such as Siberian irises, dramatic foliage plants such as rodgersias, and even oddities like pitcher plants. Plus, wet areas tend to irrigate the rest of the yard, so even if your neighbors arc struggling to protect their gardens from drought, your perennial beds will be taking advantage of all that water right nearby.

Top Picks

◄Have a site that stays moist at all times? Try dramatic umbrella plant (*Darmera peltata*). Planted next to a stream or pond, this plant will positively flourish. The large (really large!) leaves can reach 18 inches (45 cm) in diameter, and the plant spreads where it's happy, so plan ahead before you plant.

How Wet Is Wet?

Let me start by telling you how I define a wet-soil area. It's *not* soil that's underwater all year, but rather it's dry land that isn't *always* dry. Usually, it's easy to tell when your soil is wet: The mud stains on your carpet attest all too well to that. Surface puddles on the soil after a rain are an initial visual clue that you have a wet-soil area. Such puddles should be enough to steer you away from planting perennials that require well-drained soil there. There's also a simple drainage test that's more reliable than just observing your soil on the surface: Dig a hole about 12 inches (30 cm) deep in the suspect area, and fill it with water. Let it sit for an hour, and then check the water level in the hole. If it's still half-full or more, you can be pretty sure that water is not draining from that part of your garden.

Some damp sites are wet simply because they border bodies of water: a river, stream, pond, or lake, for example. Any such area is bound to be damp even if it's rarely, if ever, underwater. Other sites suffer from poor drainage. Usually they are soaking wet or slightly underwater in the spring, then dry up more in the summer. They may fill up again during long bouts of rain. This can be due to a naturally high water table (meaning there is groundwater just under the surface) or to clay soil that drains slowly.

Often damp soils are stagnant—that is, lacking in oxygen—and oxygen is something *most* plants need at root level for healthy growth, but "most" does not mean all. There are plenty of plants, including the perennials I've included in this chapter, that get along fine when oxygen isn't that abundant. Not all "wetland" plants

Moist garden soil can provide the perfect conditions for water-loving perennials like rodgersia (*Rodgersia* spp.). You've probably heard that digging and planting in wet soil will compact the soil, but forest-edge gardens like this one are rich in organic matter, which keeps the soil loose even when it's wet.

tolerate stagnant water. Those that are native to sites near moving water like plenty of oxygen at their roots.

Wet Soil Isn't Always Wet

Don't assume that wet soils always need be wet to support water-loving perennials. In most climates, water is far more abundant in spring than throughout the rest of the year and sites that are very wet in spring can be quite dry at other times. Although there are a few water-loving perennials that insist on damp soil at all times, most are quite well adapted to the typical "wet-in-spring, dry-in-summer" cycle. You'll find, though, that the foliage of these plants looks better if they are kept moist throughout the summer, which may mean watering during dry spells or using drip irrigation.

Creating a Wet-Soil Garden

While it's true that your choice of plants will be somewhat limited when you're planning a wet-soil garden, it may not be as limited as you think. Lots of "standard" perennials, such as

daylilies and Siberian iris (*Iris sibirica*), do just fine in wet areas. So to inspire yourself, check out some water gardens in your area. You may be surprised by the variety of plants that grow well in "marginal" conditions, that is, in the moist soil alongside (but not in) a pond or water garden.

You've probably heard that it isn't wise to work in wet soil, as this can damage the soil structure, rendering it excessively compact. There's certainly truth to that, but, unless they're rich in peat (in which case no amount of pounding will destroy their spongy texture), naturally wet soils already have a heavy structure. A bit of digging isn't going to change that much. The real problem is that wet soil is heavy soil and that *does* make digging awkward. You can therefore build some muscles by putting on your knee-high boots and digging in the mud in the spring. Or you can wait until fall, when the ground is usually drier, to prepare new beds and to plant new perennials.

As you prepare a new wet-soil bed, add lots of organic material such as compost to heavy soils to help loosen them up somewhat. That will make it easier to dig it in future. If your soil is on the peaty side (in which case, it will have an unmistakable spongy texture), there's little need to add organic matter because the soil is naturally humusy.

In both cases, do a soil test to check the soil's pH, then add appropriate amendments. Many wet soils are excessively acid and may need a bit of lime to bring them up to standard.

Making Things Wetter

If I've convinced you not to drain that wet spot in your yard, wonderful! But what if the idea of gardening in damp soil is appealing to you, but you just don't have a soggy spot in your yard? Can you actually create a wetland garden? Sure!

Start by digging out a 1- to 2-foot (30- to 60-cm) hole in the lowest part of your garden, then test it by filling it with water and seeing whether the water drains out rapidly, slowly, or not at all. If the answer is "not at all," you have a wet spot just waiting to be discovered. Simply enlarge the hole to whatever size you need and add a layer of good soil: Your wetland garden is ready.

If the water does drain away in less than an hour, you'll need to help your bog garden along. Dig it out to the desired size and add a 3-inch (8-cm) layer of clay, both on the sides and the bottom, then water well and tamp the clay layer down with your feet. Fill this new waterproof depression with humus-rich soil, then plant water-loving plants. Compacted clay holds water almost as well as cement, so if you now fill the garden with water, it will probably stay there. You've created a wetland garden with little effort or investment.

Artificial wet areas will probably need your help in staying moist, so you'll have to water them every now and then, but if you've reduced the rate of drainage with a clay liner, they won't actually require much more water than the average flower garden.

Tree and Shrub Companions for Soggy Spots

If your damp spot is really too wet, as in "underwater for weeks at a time," consider planting trees and shrubs that will dry things out a bit. Some water-loving trees and shrubs can drain off surface water because of their rapid growth rates and the large amount of water transpired by their huge masses of leaves. They may be so efficient that you'll soon scarcely recall the spot ever was boggy. Red-osier dogwood (*Cornus stolonifera*), poplars (*Populus* spp.), silver maple (*Acer saccharinum*), and willows (*Salix* spp.) are just four widely adaptable trees and shrubs that will improve drainage of damp spots. As they become established, you can enhance them by planting water-loving perennials around them.

If you want to keep your soggy spot soggy, you can instead choose water-loving trees and shrubs that won't change the soil's status quo. Some good choices are arborvitaes (*Thuja* spp.), bald cypress (*Taxodium distichum*), birches (*Betula* spp.), black gum (*Nyssa sylvatica*), summersweet (*Clethra* spp.), pin oak (*Quercus palustris*), and sweet gale (*Myrica gale*).

13 More Water Lovers

Want more water-loving perennials to choose from? Take a look at these moisture-appreciating species featured in other chapters.

Acorus

Sweet flag

Sweet flags look like irises or ornamental grass, but they're actually related to a common houseplant, the philodendron, and to jack-in-the-pulpit (*Arisaema triphyllum*). You'll grow sweet flags strictly for their fans of attractive, sword-shaped leaves because their narrow green to yellow-brown flower spikes barely show, just peeking beyond a flattened stem that could easily be mistaken for yet another leaf. Sweet flags don't bloom every year, at least not in all garden conditions. The blooms can, however, add an interesting touch to flower arrangements.

Plant Profile

ACORUS
A-KOR-uhs

- **Bloom Color:** Green to yellow-brown

- **Bloom Time:** Spring

- **Length of Bloom:** 1 month

- **Height:** Varies by species; see individual listings

- **Spread:** 1 to 2 feet (30 to 60 cm)

- **Garden Uses:** Container planting, edging, groundcover, mixed border, specimen plant, woodland garden; in wet areas

- **Light Preference:** Full sun to partial shade

- **Soil Preference:** Rich, moist or wet soil

- **Best Way to Propagate:** Divide in spring or fall

- **USDA Plant Hardiness Zones:** Varies by species; see individual listings

- **AHS Heat Zones:** Varies by species; see individual listings

Growing Tips

Sweet flags do best in moist, soggy areas, but they'll also grow nicely in well-drained garden soil as long as it never dries out completely. They thrive in full sun to partial shade. They'll spread somewhat where they are happy, but sweet flags are never invasive. Sweet flag (*Acorus calamus*) is deciduous and only requires a bit of cleanup in early spring. Grassy-leaved sweet flag (*A. gramineus*) is evergreen but likewise needs a bit of cleaning upon occasion. Damaged leaves can be cut back at any time.

Division is the only method of propagating sweet flags that I recommend because they're certainly not easy to grow from seed. When the plants start to crowd their beds, dig up a clump in spring or fall, and separate the fans by pulling them apart (it may take some effort) or cut the thick rhizomes into sections, each with at least one growing point, or bud.

Good Neighbors

Use sweet flags as a vertical accent in a grouping of water-loving plants. Plant sweet flags at pond's edge, directly in the shallow water, or in moist conditions. Combine water lilies (*Nymphaea* spp.) and marsh marigold (*Caltha palustris*) with sweet flags in a small, backyard pond. Try grassy-leaved sweet flag (*A. gramineus*) in small-scale tub gardens.

FUN FACTS

Sweet flags have long been confused with all sorts of other plants. Even the common name refers to the long-held belief that they are an iris ("flag" is the old name for iris). To tell a sweet flag from any impostors, though, simply break off or crush a piece of leaf: Sweet flag has a distinctly sweet smell.

Problems and Solutions

Sweet flags don't have any particular insect or disease problems. If your plants turn yellow or die back in the summer, the problem probably isn't a pest or disease—the likely culprit is dry soil. Try watering the plants more often to see if the problem persists.

Top Performer

Acorus calamus (sweet flag): You'll find the variegated selection, 'Variegatus', of this sweet flag offered most often at nurseries or in catalogs. It produces narrow fans of flat, wide, sword-shaped leaves that have broad, creamy white, lengthwise stripes. It blooms in spring, but the flowers aren't noticeable. This plant is prized more for its beautiful foliage than for its flowers. Height: 2 to 3 feet (60 to 90 cm). Spread: 2 feet (60 cm). USDA Plant Hardiness Zones 3 to 9; AHS Heat Zones 12 to 2.

Variegated sweet flag
(*Acorus calamus* 'Variegatus')

More Recommended Sweet Flags

Acorus gramineus (grassy-leaved sweet flag): As its name suggests, grassy-leaved sweet flag is grasslike, with narrow, arching leaves in dense clumps. Try planting it as a groundcover. It's rather slow-growing, but it will tolerate drier soil than other sweet flags. The spring flowers are somewhat more showy than those of *A. calamus* because each spike is surrounded by a leaflike bract, but it's still the foliage that attracts all the attention. The species itself is rarely grown, but some of the cultivars are quite remarkable. 'Ogon' is my favorite, with bright yellow stripes on chartreuse, 8- to 10-inch (20- to 25-cm) foliage—the plant almost seems to glow. 'Variegatus' is about 1 foot (30 cm) tall, with green leaves striped in cream; it tends to bleach out in sun and looks better in partial shade. There are also many miniature cultivars, such as 'Minimus', with dark green leaves only 3 inches (8 cm) high, as well as its golden-leaved brother 'Minimus Aureus'. Height: 3 to 12 inches (8 to 30 cm). Spread: 1 foot (30 cm). USDA Plant Hardiness Zones 5 to 9; AHS Heat Zones 9 to 4.

Kissing Cousins

Think Twice: Common rush (*Juncus effusus*), also called soft rush, has dense clumps of dark green, tubular, leaflike stems and makes a good substitute for a mid-size ornamental grass in a moist site. The flowers appear from early summer until frost. Give common rush partial shade in hot-summer climates, full sun elsewhere, and moist conditions. And plant it within a root barrier: It can be invasive. One cultivar, 'Spiralis', grows in a spiral, twisting pattern. Height: 18 to 30 inches (45 to 75 cm). Spread: 12 to 18 inches (60 to 45 cm). USDA Plant Hardiness Zones 3 to 9; AHS Heat Zones 9 to 1.

Calamagrostis

Reed grass

Reed grass wins high marks not only because of its good looks but also because of its great adaptability. It forms dense clumps of arching, bright green leaves from which rise stiffly upright stalks of feathery flowers. The flowers change in color as they age but can remain on the plant right through the winter. The blooms wave gracefully back and forth in the slightest breeze, adding to the plant's allure.

Plant Profile

CALAMAGROSTIS
kal-ah-mah-GROS-tis

- **Bloom Color:** Beige, gold, green, pink, or silver
- **Bloom Time:** Midsummer through winter
- **Length of Bloom:** 2 to 8 months or more
- **Height:** Varies by species; see individual listings
- **Spread:** 2 to 3 feet (60 to 90 cm)
- **Garden Uses:** Mass planting, mixed border, seasonal hedge, specimen plant, wildflower meadow; in wet areas; at the back of beds and borders
- **Light Preference:** Full sun to partial shade
- **Soil Preference:** Rich, moist soil; tolerates heavy soil
- **Best Way to Propagate:** Divide in spring or fall
- **USDA Plant Hardiness Zones:** Varies by species; see individual listings
- **AHS Heat Zones:** Varies by species; see individual listings

Growing Tips

Although they tolerate partial shade, reed grasses tend to become floppy and bloom less abundantly if you don't give them full sun. They adapt to most soil conditions without complaint and grow taller in moist spots than in dry ones. Reed grasses thrive in cool climates but also do well in hot-summer areas as long as they get good soil moisture and enough winter chill. In mild-winter climates, reed grasses are usually semievergreen, but they die back completely in colder regions. It's best to cut plants back by two-thirds in late winter or early spring to leave room for new growth.

In mild-winter areas such as Zone 8 and above, reed grasses may not bloom at all, so gardeners in such regions grow them strictly for their foliage. If you need extra plants, divide clumps in spring or fall in milder climates. This can be done with little effort, unlike many ornamental grasses that are hard to dig up and even harder to divide. Divide clumps in spring or fall in milder climates. In colder climates, it's best to divide your plants in spring because fall divisions may not have time to settle in well enough to survive colder winters. If you don't need extra plants, you can let your reed grasses grow all on their own for a decade or more, as the clumps tend to stay nicely in place.

Good Neighbors

Use 'Karl Foerster' feather reed grass (*C. × acutiflora* 'Karl Foerster') as a background element in a moist-soil perennial border with other moisture lovers, such as 'Gateway' Joe-Pye weed (*Eupatorium fistulosum* 'Gateway'),

FUN FACTS

Let reed grass flowers dry on their stems, then spray them with hair spray for long-lasting feathery plumes for winter arrangements or as a wreath base.

helenium (*Helenium autumnale*), common rose mallow (*Hibiscus moscheutos*), bigleaf ligularia (*Ligularia dentata*), and bee balm (*Monarda didyma*).

Problems and Solutions
Reed grass is usually insect- and disease-free.

Top Performer
Calamagrostis × *acutiflora* (feather reed grass): Feather reed grass is the hardiest of the reed grasses, and it's also the first to bloom—the flower heads appear in early summer. It has thick clumps of green leaves that reach 18 to 36 inches (45 to 90 cm) tall but are dwarfed by the taller flower stems. One popular cultivar is 'Karl Foerster'—which may or may not be the same as 'Stricta' (and even if they really *are* distinct cultivars, the differences are very slight). The flower heads of 'Karl Foerster' are greenish with purple highlights at first, then they turn pink, followed by silver, finally fading to beige in fall and winter. 'Overdam' is a gorgeous variegated cultivar with white-striped leaves and gold flowers starting in midsummer. It's somewhat more compact than 'Karl Foerster' but not quite as hardy, tolerating temperatures only to USDA Zone 5. Height: 3 to 5 feet (90 to 150 cm). Spread: 2 to 3 feet (60 to 90 cm). USDA Plant Hardiness Zones 4 to 9; AHS Heat Zones 9 to 1.

More Recommended Reed Grasses
Calamagrostis arundinacea (reed grass): This smaller reed grass has arching blue-green foliage. The whole plant turns golden brown in the fall, even in warm climates. Since the plant dies back to the base, you can cut it to the ground in the spring. It usually blooms from late summer into fall. Fall-blooming reed grass (*C. arundinacea* var. *brachytricha*, also called *C. brachytricha*) is a later-blooming variety with arching stems of bottlebrush flowers that start out pink and turn golden brown. Neither the species nor this variety has much winter interest. Both reed grass and fall-blooming reed grass tolerate partial shade better than most grasses. Height: 2 to 3 feet (60 to 90 cm). Spread: 2 feet (60 cm). USDA Plant Hardiness Zones 5 to 9; AHS Heat Zones 9 to 3.

'Karl Foerster' feather reed grass (*Calamagrostis* × *acutiflora* 'Karl Foerster')

Larry's Garden Notes
Reed grasses make wonderful accent plants in the garden. They bloom earlier than most grasses, so they have an extended period of interest. Spaced at intervals, clumps of reed grass can help to unite a garden design; planted in a mass, they make a great living screen.

Caltha

Marsh marigold

The brilliant yellow, buttercup-like flowers of the marsh marigold are a sure sign of spring. Each flower has five petals and numerous stamens, but they're much larger than wild buttercups, measuring up to 2 inches (5 cm) across. Marsh marigolds are related to buttercups, and just as with a buttercup, if you hold a marsh marigold flower under someone's chin, its bright golden coloration will reflect on their skin.

Plant Profile

CALTHA
KAL-thuh

- **Bloom Color:** White or yellow
- **Bloom Time:** Midspring to late spring
- **Length of Bloom:** 3 or 4 weeks
- **Height:** 6 to 24 inches (15 to 60 cm)
- **Spread:** 1 foot (30 cm)
- **Garden Uses:** Edging, mixed border; in wet areas
- **Light Preference:** Full sun to partial shade
- **Soil Preference:** Rich, moist soil
- **Best Way to Propagate:** Divide after blooming or in fall
- **USDA Plant Hardiness Zones:** 2 to 9
- **AHS Heat Zones:** 7 to 3

Growing Tips

Although marsh marigolds often grow with their roots in water in the wild, they do perfectly well in any moist garden soil as well. Ideally, you should plant them in a spot where they receive full spring sun but summer shade. A flowerbed under deciduous trees is a perfect location. Marsh marigolds go dormant after they bloom, but even so, they may not survive if the soil dries out during the summer.

Marsh marigolds are easy to multiply by division; it's best to do this just after the plants bloom, but you can also do it in fall. If you plan to divide your plants in the fall, carefully mark the spot where they're planted so you can find them because they will be dormant at that time.

You can also start marsh marigolds from fresh seed, harvested from the plants in early summer (but keep in mind that cultivars will not come true from seed). Seedlings must have wet conditions, so sow the seed in moist peat and keep it very moist while the seedlings grow. You can also sow seed outdoors, but be sure to sow it in a wet spot. If you're planning to plant in a bed that's only moderately moist, let the young plants become well established before you move them.

Good Neighbors

Marsh marigold is happiest in a bog. It will grow beautifully in water-saturated soil along the sunny border of a backyard pond with other pondside plants. Combine it with Virginia bluebells

FUN FACTS

In many parts of the world, people pick marsh marigold leaves in early spring to eat as a vegetable. The leaves must be cooked before eating because they're toxic when raw. The flower buds can be pickled, too; they're an interesting substitute for capers.

(*Mertensia virginica*) for a blue-and-gold spring show. Spike rush (*Eleocharis montevidensis*), Japanese iris (*Iris ensata*), cardinal flower (*Lobelia cardinalis*), and ferns would offer varied color and interest later in the growing season. You can also plant it in a moist garden bed among a moisture-loving groundcover, such as creeping Jenny (*Lysimachia nummularia*) or water forget-me-not (*Myosotis scorpioides*), once the marsh marigolds die back in summer; the groundcover will fill the gaps.

Problems and Solutions

Marsh marigold has few serious insect or disease problems.

Top Performer

Caltha palustris (marsh marigold): While marsh marigold usually grows about 15 inches (38 cm) tall at most, plants can reach a full 2 feet (60 cm) in very moist conditions. In ideal moist conditions, the plant can grow to 2 feet (60 cm) wide as well. Its shiny green, heart-shaped leaves, from 2 to 7 inches (5 to 18 cm) in diameter, are attractive in their own right, creating an almost tropical effect in the garden. The mounds of leaves grow from a thick crown of fleshy white roots. Once the plant blooms, its moist soil requirements are less critical. 'Flore Pleno' ('Multiplex' and 'Plena' are just a few of the other names it's known by) is a drop-dead-gorgeous cultivar with fully double flowers that last for a week or more. Although this cultivar has been grown in gardens since the seventeenth century, it might take a bit of searching to find it at your local garden center. Your best bet may be a water garden catalog or supplier. Variety *alba* has pure white flowers that seem to glow in contrast to the brilliant green leaves—it may also take a little hunting to find this variety, but it's worth the effort.

Marsh marigold
(*Caltha palustris*)

Around the World with *Caltha*

Travel just about anywhere in the Northern Hemisphere during the spring, and you'll find marsh marigold (*Caltha palustris*). In Holland, it's one of the rare spring-flowering plants, other than skunk cabbage, that decorates the country's beautiful water gardens. If you're visiting Amsterdam, walk or take the subway to Hortus Botanicus, the city's small but beautiful botanical garden, and enjoy the beautiful golden cups of marsh marigold.

Chelone

Turtlehead

Turtleheads get their name from their flowers. Each puffy, tubular flower has a beaklike opening that resembles a turtle with its mouth open. Turtlehead plants have a very tidy, upright habit and dark green, oval, lightly toothed leaves on stiff stems. The flower clusters appear late in the season. Turtleheads are versatile perennials for many purposes: They're great plants for a wet site, they're fall bloomers, they flower in shade, they make a great groundcover, and they require little care. So plant some!

Plant Profile

CHELONE
chee-LOW-nee

- **Bloom Color:** Pink, red, or white
- **Bloom Time:** Late summer to late fall
- **Length of Bloom:** 3 to 6 weeks or more
- **Height:** Varies by species; see individual listings
- **Spread:** Varies by species; see individual listings
- **Garden Uses:** Cut flower garden, mass planting, meadow garden, mixed border, woodland garden; in wet areas
- **Light Preference:** Full sun to full shade
- **Soil Preference:** Humus-rich, moist to wet soil
- **Best Way to Propagate:** Divide in spring or fall
- **USDA Plant Hardiness Zones:** Varies by species; see individual listings
- **AHS Heat Zones:** 9 to 3

Growing Tips

Turtleheads are easy, no-nonsense plants that will put up with just about anything—except hot summers. They will survive in warm-summer climates but must be kept moist at all times. In cool-summer areas, the plants will remain more compact and be more dense. Turtleheads prefer full sun to partial shade and moist to wet conditions. They'll tolerate full shade as long as the foliage canopy is quite high; just cut them back by half in midspring to keep them more compact, or they may flop over. Turtleheads also grow in fairly dry soil through the summer, as long as conditions are moist in the spring. Actually, they grow well in just about any kind of soil, even very acid soil.

Turtleheads form full, thick clumps in three or four years, then usually stay put indefinitely. To propagate, divide them in early spring in cold climates and early fall in warm ones, or take stem cuttings in early summer. It's also a snap to grow them from seed sown indoors or out in early spring; the seedlings will bloom in their second year.

Good Neighbors

Surround turtleheads with low-growing dwarf goat's beard (*Aruncus aethusifolius*) or Bethlehem sage (*Pulmonaria saccharata*) for early-season color and continuing foliage interest. Compatible blooming partners include Chinese astilbe (*Astilbe chinensis*), cimicifugas, and 'Gateway' Joe-Pye weed (*Eupatorium fistulosum* 'Gateway'). Moisture-loving ferns, such as lady ferns (*Athyrium* spp.) and flowering ferns (*Osmunda* spp.), and sedges (*Carex* spp.) would add season-long foliage interest.

Problems and Solutions

Powdery mildew may cause gray patches on leaves in late summer if the soil dries out, so try to maintain steady soil moisture. Otherwise, turtleheads are rarely bothered by insects or diseases.

Top Performer

Chelone glabra (white turtlehead): This is perhaps the best-behaved and most compact of a very good group of plants, but it does prefer cool conditions. The flowers, appearing in late summer to early fall, are white to cream and may have a red or pink tinge. The dark green leaves hug the erect stems. Although attractive, the blooms of white turtlehead don't last as long as those of other turtleheads. The flowers really stand out against the dark foliage, though. Height: 2 to 3 feet (60 to 90 cm). Spread: 24 to 30 inches (60 to 75 cm). USDA Plant Hardiness Zones 2 to 9; AHS Heat Zones 9 to 3.

Pink turtlehead
(*Chelone lyonii*)

More Recommended Turtleheads

Chelone lyonii (pink turtlehead): Each leaf of pink turtlehead has a long leaf stem (petiole), which gives the plants a more open appearance than that of other turtleheads. Despite its name, there are selections of pink turtlehead with distinctly rose and even nearly red flowers from midsummer to early fall. Pink turtlehead is the best choice if your soil is less than moist; it does quite well in average garden soil. 'Hot Lips' is a choice cultivar with rose-pink flowers, red stems, and leaves that start out reddish and change to deep green. Height: 1 to 3 feet (30 to 90 cm). Spread: 18 to 24 inches (45 to 60 cm). USDA Plant Hardiness Zones 3 to 9; AHS Heat Zones 9 to 3.

C. obliqua (rose turtlehead): If you garden in hot-summer areas, this is the best turtlehead to try because it's the most heat-tolerant. Rose turtlehead blooms from late summer well into fall. It also survives cold winters: I've seen it thrive in USDA Zone 3, even without snow cover. 'Alba' is pure white and looks very similar to white turtlehead. 'Praecox Nana' grows only 16 inches (40 cm) tall and blooms earlier than other cultivars, from midsummer to late summer. Height: 2 to 3 feet (30 to 90 cm). Spread: 2 feet (60 cm). USDA Plant Hardiness Zones 3 to 9; AHS Heat Zones 9 to 3.

Around the World with Turtleheads

I'm always surprised (and pleased!) to see one of our native North American wildflowers growing in gardens in other countries. That's the case with turtleheads (*Chelone* spp.). Although North American gardeners are just learning to use them, turtleheads are staple fall flowers in European gardens, notably in Germany and England, where you sometimes see moist woodlands filled with their pink or white flowers in September and October.

Darmera

Umbrella plant

Although the flowers of umbrella plant are nice enough, the leaves really are
the stars of the show. Rounded and shield-shaped, the shiny leaves have
deeply cut edges and measure up to 18 inches (45 cm) across, with leaf stems
that can stretch up to 6 feet (180 cm) tall. The deep green foliage becomes even
more attractive in the fall when it turns coppery red. Umbrella plant is a
knockout if you have the space and the moist soil it demands.

Plant Profile

DARMERA
DAR-mer-uh

- **Bloom Color:** Pink or white

- **Bloom Time:** Late spring to early summer

- **Length of Bloom:** 3 or 4 weeks

- **Height:** 2 to 6 feet (60 to 180 cm)

- **Spread:** 4 to 6 feet (120 to 180 cm)

- **Garden Uses:** Seasonal hedge, specimen plant, woodland garden; in wet areas; at the back of beds and borders

- **Light Preference:** Full sun to partial shade

- **Soil Preference:** Rich, damp to wet, acid soil

- **Best Way to Propagate:** Dig out chunks of underground stems (rhizomes)

- **USDA Plant Hardiness Zones:** 4 to 9

- **AHS Heat Zones:** 9 to 3

Growing Tips

Think Twice: Umbrella plants prefer soil that's at least damp
at all times, and they can even grow with their base in standing
water. They also produce hordes of roots, so you can plant them
to stabilize slopes and banks in wet areas. Those roots also mean
the plants are tough to dig out, and since umbrella plants can be
invasive in favorable conditions, watch out. Don't let them loose
in a small water garden or you may never see it again (the water
garden, that is)!

I planted umbrella plant in a spot where the soil is never more
than moist and found that, though the foliage remains somewhat
dwarfed at about 3 feet (90 cm) tall, at least the plant is much
better behaved. It's hard to imagine a root barrier that would control the umbrella plant if it *really* loved your conditions, although a
culvert turned on its end with the umbrella plant planted inside
would do the trick if you could dig a hole deep enough to bury
the culvert to its rim. (I tried this in a friend's garden, and it
worked perfectly, but lugging that culvert in, not to mention
burying it, was a major chore!)

Umbrella plant likes to stay cool. In most climates, it does best
in partial shade, but where heat is not a problem, full sun seems
best. To propagate it, try digging out chunks of rhizome (underground stems); you'll find them on or near the surface of the soil
where they're easy to get at with a garden trowel. Just replant the
rhizome immediately in another moist spot, at about the same
depth that you found the original rhizome. It's a good thing that
umbrella plant doesn't need to be divided to keep it vigorous—I
shudder to think how you would manage to lift a full-grown plant
to divide it!

Many experts suggest umbrella plant is not terribly hardy, but obviously it doesn't know this, as mine positively thrives in my USDA Zone 3 garden under snow cover. I also know people in snowless Zone 4 who also grow umbrella plant with no problem, so even cold-winter gardeners can grow it.

Good Neighbors

With its mounds of giant glossy leaves, umbrella plant is a dramatic foliage accent for even a small garden. Combine it with contrasting moist-soil inhabitants that are large enough to be visible from a distance. Good candidates include black snakeroot (*Cimicifuga racemosa*), great Solomon's seal (*Polygonatum commutatum*), Japanese primrose (*Primula japonica*), and large ferns, such as ostrich fern (*Matteuccia struthiopteris*) and royal fern (*Osmunda regalis*).

Problems and Solutions

Umbrella plant doesn't suffer from any insect or disease problems.

Top Performer

Darmera peltata, also called *Peltiphyllum peltatum*: Umbrella plant is all alone in its own little genus. While its foliage is the main attraction, it does bear interesting flowers in late spring to early summer. The flowers really do stand out on this plant, not because they're exceptionally gorgeous but because they appear before the foliage. They are, however, still in bloom when the leaves do appear. The dense, rounded clusters of pink (or occasionally white) flowers rise straight up on bristly reddish stalks that can reach 3 to 6 feet (90 to 180 cm) tall. There is a dwarf cultivar, 'Nana', which is ideal for smaller gardens. It grows only 12 to 18 inches (30 to 45 cm) tall.

The leaves of umbrella plant (*Darmera peltata*) are so large that tiny woodland creatures use them as shelter during heavy forest rains. Well, truthfully, that's just conjecture, but you'll be impressed by this perennial's huge, shiny leaves and towering leaf stalks.

Iris

Iris

Gardeners who love irises are lucky: They can grow irises in nearly any soil, wet or dry. Many beautiful irises, including Siberian iris *(Iris sibirica),* grow well in wet conditions. These moisture-loving irises tend to have narrow, almost grasslike leaves and to form distinct clumps. All the wetland irises are beardless irises; that is, they don't have a fuzzy or crested section on their flowers, unlike the popular German or bearded iris *(Iris Bearded Hybrids)*. They also have thin roots, while irises that tolerate dry soil have fleshy roots.

Plant Profile

IRIS
EYE-ris

- **Bloom Color:** Blue, bronze, orange, pink, purple, red, white, or yellow
- **Bloom Time:** Late spring to early summer
- **Length of Bloom:** 2 weeks
- **Height:** Varies by species; see individual listings
- **Spread:** Varies by species; see individual listings
- **Garden Uses:** Cut flower garden, mass planting, meadow garden, mixed border, specimen plant; in wet areas
- **Light Preference:** Full sun to partial shade
- **Soil Preference:** Rich, moist to wet, loamy soil
- **Best Way to Propagate:** Divide in late summer
- **USDA Plant Hardiness Zones:** Varies by species; see individual listings
- **AHS Heat Zones:** 9 to 1

Growing Tips

All wetland irises prefer moist to wet soil. In the wild, many grow with the base of their stems in the water. Wetland irises can grow in ordinary, well-drained garden soil, but they may not grow as tall as in damper conditions. They prefer full sun but will do well in partial shade, especially the Siberian iris *(I. sibirica)*.

Division in the fall is the best way to multiply these irises, but you can divide them in early spring, too. Replant the divisions quickly because their roots dry out rapidly when exposed to the air.

Good Neighbors

Wetland irises combine well with swamp milkweed *(Asclepias incarnata),* marsh marigold *(Caltha palustris),* pink turtlehead *(Chelone lyonii),* and cardinal flower *(Lobelia cardinalis),* which all tolerate wet soils well, providing an attractive solution to a wet area where lawn grass just won't grow.

Although happiest in moist soil, Siberian iris *(I. sibirica)* will adapt well to a variety of conditions. Its attractive, upright foliage and persistent pods make it a good anchor for the perennial border. Combine it with other early-blooming plants, such as columbines *(Aquilegia* spp.), peonies *(Paeonia* spp.), and oriental poppy *(Papaver orientale)*.

Problems and Solutions

Wetland irises seem less susceptible or even immune to the common diseases and insect pests that affect the dry-soil species.

Top Performer

⭐ **Larry's Favorite:** *Iris sibirica* (Siberian iris): Siberian irises are one of the easiest irises to grow. They produce thick clumps of narrow, grasslike leaves and slender stems bearing two to five flowers with flaring to drooping falls and narrow, upright standards from late spring to early summer. Most modern cultivars rebloom quite regularly in the fall. Height: 24 to 40 inches (60 to 100 cm). Spread: 2 feet (60 cm). USDA Plant Hardiness Zones 3 to 9; AHS Heat Zones 9 to 1.

More Recommended Irises

Iris ensata, also called *I. kaempferi* (Japanese iris): Although Japanese irises have a reputation of being hard to grow, there are many tough, no-nonsense garden hybrid Japanese irises that are worth a try. In general, Japanese irises have large flowers—up to 10 inches (25 cm) in diameter—in early summer to midsummer. The flowers may be single or double, and the color range is vast, often with contrasting veins or edges. They produce clumps of graceful, narrow leaves with a distinct midrib. Japanese irises prefer average to moist growing conditions at flowering time and will grow with their roots in water, but they like things drier later in the season. Often sold only by color in nurseries, you'll find named cultivars in specialized catalogs. Height: 2 to 4 feet (60 to 120 cm). Spread: 18 to 24 inches (45 to 60 cm). USDA Plant Hardiness Zones 4 to 9; AHS Heat Zones 9 to 1.

Think Twice: *I. pseudacorus* (yellow flag): This is the iris represented on the French flag as the fleur-de-lis. Having escaped from culture throughout much of the world, it now grows in swamps and slow-moving bodies of water just about everywhere. This wetland iris is capable of growing under quite dry conditions, too. The broad, swordlike leaves form dense clumps and spread wildly in moist conditions. To be smart, plant yellow flag within a root barrier, such as a bottomless bucket sunk into the soil. Yellow flag produces bright yellow flowers from late spring to early summer. The blooms often have brown markings. The variety *bastardii* bears pale yellow blooms. 'Variegata' is grown mostly for its foliage, which is striped with yellow and green in spring, fading to all green in summer. Height: 2 to 4 feet (60 to 120 cm) in dry conditions; up to 7 feet (2.1 m) when grown in water. Spread: 2 feet (60 cm). USDA Plant Hardiness Zones 2 to 9; AHS Heat Zones 9 to 1.

Easy-care Siberian irises (*Iris sibirica*) lend an air of sophistication to perennial borders. Their beardless blooms float atop a mound of foliage that remains attractive long after the flowers have faded. Siberian irises are less prone to soft rot and iris borers than their frilly bearded cousins.

Ligularia

Ligularia, groundsel, golden-ray

Bold and beautiful is the best way to describe ligularias. They form huge masses of large leaves topped by clusters of large, daisylike blooms or narrow spikes densely covered with flowers. Flower color can be bright orange to yellow. Even when you plant ligularias at the back of a flower border, they can dominate the scene with their large leaves and striking flowers. Pair them with equally bold companions for a breathtaking display in moist borders and along the edges of water gardens.

Plant Profile

LIGULARIA
lig-you-LAIR-ee-uh

- **Bloom Color:** Orange or yellow
- **Bloom Time:** Varies by species; see individual listings
- **Length of Bloom:** 3 or 4 weeks
- **Height:** Varies by species; see individual listings
- **Spread:** 2 to 4 feet (60 to 120 cm)
- **Garden Uses:** Cut flower garden, groundcover, mass planting, mixed border, seasonal hedge, specimen plant, woodland garden; at the back of beds and borders, in wet areas
- **Light Preference:** Full sun to partial shade
- **Soil Preference:** Rich, moist to wet, cool soil
- **Best Way to Propagate:** Divide in spring
- **USDA Plant Hardiness Zones:** Varies by species; see individual listings
- **AHS Heat Zones:** 8 to 1

Growing Tips

To grow ligularias well, remember two important words: cool and moist. Ligularias have dramatically broad leaves that are relatively thin. They lose a lot of water by transpiration, so if it's too hot or too dry, the leaves wilt dramatically. Of course, the plant often recovers in the evening, when temperatures drop, but their afternoon "wilted lettuce" look is not an attractive feature.

Ligularias are especially nice near pools and moving water, and they positively glow in bog gardens. In wet, cool conditions they can tolerate full sun, but gardeners in other areas will need to plant their ligularias in partial shade, and especially afternoon shade, simply because shade is cooler.

Where these perennials are happy, just plant them and ignore them. Ligularias are long-lived plants that seldom need division, unless you need more plants or want to control them. Division is, however, the best means of propagating ligularias.

Good Neighbors

Imposing in leaf and in flower, ligularias combine best with foliage plants. Try them with epimediums, moisture-loving ferns, and hostas. The fine-textured foliage of astilbes or dwarf goat's beard (*Aruncus aethusifolius*) also offers a good contrast.

To accentuate the dark leaf undersides of 'Desdemona' bigleaf ligularia (*Ligularia dentata* 'Desdemona'), try surrounding it with black mondo grass (*Ophiopogon planiscapus* 'Nigrescens').

'The Rocket' narrow-spiked ligularia (*L. stenocephala* 'The Rocket') looks striking with moisture-tolerant trees or shrubs, such as winterberry (*Ilex verticillata*) or sweet bay (*Magnolia virginiana*).

Problems and Solutions

Slugs love to feast on ligularia leaves. See page 55 for ideas on coping with this pest. Spring and early summer is the critical time for slug control. If you can manage to get the leaves to maturity before they're nibbled on, you're home free.

Top Performer

Ligularia dentata (bigleaf ligularia): With leaves like these, who needs flowers? Bigleaf ligularia has leathery-looking, round to kidney-shaped leaves that are toothed along the edges. It forms a huge mounding clump of foliage just a few years after planting. Some gardeners grow it simply for its foliage, cutting off the brilliant yellow-orange, daisylike blooms as they appear from midsummer to fall. It's not that their blooms are not attractive, but some gardeners find the startling yellowness of the flowers a bit too overpowering. Two dark-leaved cultivars are the most popular: 'Othello', with leaves that are purple below and green above, and 'Desdemona', with even darker leaves. Height: 3 to 4 feet (90 to 120 cm). Spread: 2 to 4 feet (60 to 120 cm). USDA Plant Hardiness Zones 3 to 9; AHS Heat Zones 8 to 1.

'Desdemona' bigleaf ligularia (*Ligularia dentata* 'Desdemona')

More Recommended Ligularias

Ligularia przewalskii (Shavalski's ligularia): Gorgeous! Purple-black stems bear large deep green leaves that look like fingers radiating from a hand. They are very attractive in their own right, but then the tall, narrow spikes of light yellow flowers come and steal the show from early summer to midsummer. It's a less domineering plant than bigleaf ligularia (*L. dentata*) and a real knockout in a semi-shaded garden (or a cool, sunny, moist one). Height: 4 to 6 feet (1.2 to 1.8 m). Spread: 2 to 4 feet (60 to 120 cm). USDA Plant Hardiness Zones 4 to 9; AHS Heat Zones 8 to 1.

L. stenocephala (narrow-spiked ligularia): This plant is practically identical to Shavalski's ligularia, except that its leaves are more heart-shaped and less deeply cut. It blooms in early summer to midsummer. 'The Rocket' is the most popular cultivar. Height: 4 to 6 feet (1.2 to 1.8 cm). Spread: 2 to 4 feet (60 to 120 cm). USDA Plant Hardiness Zones 4 to 9; AHS Heat Zones 8 to 1.

Kissing Cousins

Leopard plant (*Farfugium japonicum*, also called *Farfugium tussilagineum*) used to be a ligularia. Its botanical name was *Ligularia tussilaginea* or *L. kaempferi*, and you may still find it sold that way. Leopard plant produces shiny, 6- to 10- inch (15- to 25-cm) rounded leaves and the stalks each bear a few daisylike flowers in midfall to late fall. It's not terribly hardy, but it is evergreen, so try growing it in a pot, outside in summer and indoors in winter. Height: 1 to 2 feet (30 to 60 cm). Spread: 18 to 24 inches (45 to 60 cm). USDA Plant Hardiness Zones 7 to 9; AHS Heat Zones 9 to 1.

Lysichiton

Skunk cabbage

Although they're spectacular spring-blooming plants, skunk cabbages aren't included in gardens as often as they deserve to be, perhaps due to their common name. However, the distinctly musky odor of skunk cabbages is only noticeable up close or on a hot, windless spring day when you're standing amidst a large group of the plants—and how often does *that* happen? Just think how much better these plants would seem if we called them "spring callas" (their flowers do look a lot like calla lilies)!

Plant Profile

LYSICHITON
lih-sih-KYE-ton

- **Bloom Color:** White or yellow
- **Bloom Time:** Early spring to midspring
- **Length of Bloom:** 3 or 4 weeks
- **Height:** Varies by species; see individual listings
- **Spread:** 2 to 4 feet (60 to 120 cm)
- **Garden Use:** Specimen plant; in wet areas
- **Light Preference:** Full sun
- **Soil Preference:** Rich, wet soil
- **Best Way to Propagate:** Divide in early spring
- **USDA Plant Hardiness Zones:** 6 to 9
- **AHS Heat Zones:** Varies by species; see individual listings

Growing Tips

Skunk cabbages prefer truly wet soil, especially in spring, and will grow in up to 6 inches (15 cm) of water. They tolerate drier soil in the summer, especially if they're well mulched. Skunk cabbages grow very slowly: Unless you buy a large plant to start, you can expect to wait a year or so for bloom and up to five years for the plant to reach full size. These plants will thrive for decades with no care whatsoever.

You can divide established plants in early spring if you need more plants, but that can mean waiting a long, long time. If you want more plants relatively quickly, buy them! Skunk cabbages will also sprout from fresh seed. Collect seeds from plants growing in a nearby garden when they reach maturity in early to mid-summer, then sow them without delay in constantly moist soil.

Skunk cabbages don't tolerate very hot summers or cold winters, so make sure they're adapted to your climate before you choose them. They'll grow as far north as USDA Zone 3, but only with a very thick winter mulch spread over the clump so the cold won't "leak in" from the sides. At least a light mulch is recommended, even in USDA Zone 5.

The upright-pointing, paddle-shaped leaves of skunk cabbage are quite spectacular, and it would be nice to be able to say that they look great throughout

FUN FACTS

Perhaps the most intriguing feature of the skunk cabbage is its ability to melt snow and ice. The flower buds start to sprout at the end of winter and give off a considerable amount of heat, melting the snow and ice around it. Often the plant is in full bloom in a landscape still white with snow!

the summer, but that's rarely the case. In all but the coolest, moistest conditions, the leaves tend to sulk after the first heat wave and start looking more like wilted lettuce than like firm cabbage foliage. It's best to think of skunk cabbage as a plant with prolonged spring visual interest and one that requires some sort of foliage cover-up from early summer on.

Good Neighbors

Plant skunk cabbage near the edge of a bog garden where you can see the unusual flowers, which look like calla lilies. Choose companions that will provide interest later in the season, such as Japanese iris (*Iris ensata*), perennial lobelias (*Lobelia cardinalis* and *L. siphilitica*), and royal fern (*Osmunda regalis*).

Problems and Solutions

Although their thick, leathery leaves look like they're made of cast iron, skunk cabbages are a favorite with slugs; see page 55 for tricks on how to control these slimy pests.

Top Performer

Lysichiton americanus (yellow skunk cabbage): All skunk cabbages are impressive plants, with large waxy flowers made up of a thick yellow or white sheath around a columnlike cluster of tiny flowers. The leathery, waxy, wavy leaves unfurl to form an attractive dark green rosette. Yellow skunk cabbage has paddle-shaped leaves up to 5 feet (1.2 to 1.5 m) long. Its early spring to midspring flowers are bright yellow and can measure a whopping 1 foot (30 cm) tall and 8 inches (20 cm) across! Height: 3 to 5 feet (90 to 150 cm). Spread: 2 to 4 feet (60 to 120 cm). USDA Plant Hardiness Zones 6 to 9; AHS Heat Zones 9 to 6.

More Recommended Skunk Cabbages

Lysichiton camtschatcensis (white skunk cabbage): White skunk cabbage is very similar to yellow skunk cabbage, but with pure white flowers and smaller leaves. It doesn't merit the name of skunk cabbage at all, as the early spring to midspring flowers actually smell sweet. Height: 2 to 3 feet (60 to 90 cm). Spread: 2 to 3 feet (60 to 90 cm). USDA Plant Hardiness Zones 6 to 9; AHS Heat Zones 9 to 1.

Yellow skunk cabbage (*Lysichiton americanus*)

Kissing Cousins

If you'd like to try growing a skunk cabbage that's not as fussy as *Lysichiton*, try *Symplocarpus foetidus* instead. It's better adapted to survive both cold winters and hot summers. Although it still demands wet soil in hot-summer areas, *Symplocarpus* seems to adapt to average garden soil in cooler climates, at least if you keep it well watered in the spring. Its flowers aren't as pretty, but the two skunk cabbages are similar in foliage. The flowers smell quite strongly of cooked cabbage, and the leaves, when crushed, do have the musky smell usually associated with skunks. Height: 2 to 3 feet (60 to 90 cm). Spread: 2 to 3 feet (60 to 90 cm). USDA Plant Hardiness Zones 2 to 9; AHS Heat Zones 9 to 1.

Myosotis

Forget-me-not

Anyone with an ounce of romance in their heart knows forget-me-nots as the symbol of true love that can never be forgotten. Their clusters of tiny sky blue flowers cover the short, creeping stems for a long period. When the flower-stalks first appear, they're curled like the tail of a scorpion, and they unfurl as the flowers open. The flowers have white or yellow centers, and there are pink and white forms, too. But a true blue flower is such a rare thing, it's almost a shame to grow a forget-me-not of any other color.

Plant Profile

MYOSOTIS
my-uh-SOH-tiss

- **Bloom Color:** Blue, pink, or white

- **Bloom Time:** Varies by species; see individual listings

- **Length of Bloom:** Varies by species; see individual listings

- **Height:** 6 to 8 inches (15 to 20 cm)

- **Spread:** 6 to 8 inches (15 to 20 cm)

- **Garden Uses:** Edging, groundcover, mass planting, mixed border, rock garden, wall planting, wildflower meadow, woodland garden; on slopes, in wet areas

- **Light Preference:** Full sun to partial shade

- **Soil Preference:** Humus-rich, moist to wet soil

- **Best Way to Propagate:** Varies by species; see individual listings

- **USDA Plant Hardiness Zones:** 3 to 9

- **AHS Heat Zones:** Varies by species; see individual listings

Growing Tips

Depending on the species, forget-me-nots prefer wet to somewhat moist growing conditions. They thrive in partial shade but also grow well in full sun as long as the soil remains moist and temperatures are not too hot. Prolonged temperatures higher than 86°F (30°C) can weaken or even kill them. All are easy to grow, making them good plants for beginners. Forget-me-nots tend to fall apart in mid-summer, especially in hot-summer areas: Just prune them back, and they'll resprout nicely.

Check out the individual species for details on propagation, as some are truly perennials, while others are biennials or annuals. However, you really don't need to know *how* to propagate forget-me-nots: They all multiply quite nicely on their own. They never become annoyingly weedy (and they're easy to pull out), but they *do* get around. If you prefer formal plantings, this may not be the plant for you.

Good Neighbors

Forget-me-nots are best in an informal garden, where their tendency to self-sow can be an advantage. Water forget-me-not (*Myosotis scorpioides*), which thives in wet soil, can be a colorful companion for other bog plants such as variegated sweet flag (*Acorus calamus* 'Variegatus'), Japanese iris (*Iris ensata*), or yellow flag (*I. pseudacorus*). Plant garden forget-me-not (*M. sylvatica*) in moist soil in an informal garden area. Suitable companions include astilbes, bergenias, hostas, and yellow primroses (*Primula* spp.). A planting of garden forget-me-not and red tulips can be a wonderful spring sight.

Problems and Solutions

Various leaf diseases are common on forget-me-nots, especially in hot, humid climates. Trim the plants back harshly, and they'll soon produce a flush of clean new growth.

Top Performer

Myosotis scorpioides, also called *M. palustris* (water forget-me-not): This is the most common forget-me-not that's truly perennial. It has narrow, slightly hairy leaves on creeping stems that root as they grow. Water forget-me-not is easy to multiply by division, although you can grow it from seed. It will put up with moist soil, but it prefers things wet and will even grow into a water garden if planted along the edge. There are several cultivars in various shades of blue, pink, and white, all of which tend to rebloom somewhat after the main late-spring-to-early-summer blooming season. My favorite is 'Semperflorens'. It is a typical pale blue forget-me-not, but it simply won't stop blooming from spring right through to early fall. If there's a lull in bloom, just prune it back and it will bloom again. Height: 6 to 8 inches (15 to 20 cm). Spread: 6 to 8 inches (15 to 20 cm). USDA Plant Hardiness Zones 3 to 9; AHS Heat Zones 9 to 1.

More Recommended Forget-Me-Nots

🚩 **Think Twice:** *Myosotis sylvatica* (garden forget-me-not): This plant is a biennial or even an annual, but it self-sows readily and tolerates drier soil. Growing it from seed is the obvious way to go (just sprinkle it on the ground in spring or fall and watch it take off), but you can also "divide" it simply by digging up and moving individual plants. Don't grow this plant if you like plants that stay in one place.

Garden forget-me-not tends to be more of a "one-season wonder" than water forget-me-not, but it will rebloom somewhat, especially if you prune it back after the main late-spring to early-summer display. There are lots of cultivars in various shades of blue, pink, and white as well as dwarf cultivars. 'Victoria Blue' is a choice early bloomer with deeper blue flowers than usual. If you must have a pink forget-me-not, 'Victoria Rose' has true rose-pink flowers. Height: 6 to 8 inches (15 to 20 cm). Spread: 6 to 8 inches (15 to 20 cm). USDA Plant Hardiness Zones 3 to 9; AHS Heat Zones 7 to 1.

Water forget-me-not
(*Myosotis scorpioides*)

Larry's Garden Notes

Legends explaining how the forget-me-not got its name are many and varied, but I have a favorite. A young man goes to the river bank to gather a bouquet of the blue flowers for his beloved, loses his balance, and falls into the rushing water. As the raging current carries him away, he holds up the bunch of flowers and cries, "Forget me not!"

Rodgersia

Rodgersia

A well-established rodgersia could easily pass for a shrub, with its bold, beautifully textured leaves that take on dramatic red and bronze tones in fall. The plants form large clumps that rise up from thick, creeping underground stems. Rodgersias are related to astilbes, and although it's hard to see the similarities when the plants aren't in bloom, the family relationship is very clear when they are in flower. Like astilbes, rodgersias produce fluffy plumes of tiny flowers held well above the foliage.

Growing Tips

Rodgersias adapt well to a wide range of light levels, from full sun to partial shade. However, they prefer cool growing conditions, and since moist soil and cooler, moister conditions are more the norm in shady nooks than in brilliant sun, that's where they often wind up. They tolerate wet soil with ease and are probably at their best planted along the edges of a water garden or in a bog garden. Try to avoid planting in windy spots: Rodgersia leaves are not as solid as they look and damage easily. A winter mulch is wise in cold-winter climates.

Rodgersias can take a few years to get going, but once they're established, they become massive plants that require lots of space. Multiply them by division (get out your pickax—established plants have quite a root system!), or sow seed outdoors in fall or indoors in late winter. (*Note:* Cultivars may not come true from seed.) Unless you need to multiply rodgersias, leave them alone, as they hate being disturbed.

Good Neighbors

Rodgersias make a striking contrast to the straplike foliage of Japanese iris (*Iris ensata*) and yellow flag (*Iris pseudacorus*). Bold ferns, such as ostrich fern (*Matteuccia struthiopteris*) and royal fern (*Osmunda regalis*), also complement the coarse foliage of rodgersia. Choices for underplanting include hostas, forget-me-nots (*Myosotis* spp.), and pulmonarias.

Problems and Solutions

Insects and diseases are rarely a problem on rodgersias.

Top Performer

Rodgersia aesculifolia (fingerleaf rodgersia): This is the giant of the group, a tall plant with large, coarse, toothed leaves divided like the fingers of a hand into five to seven 10-inch (25-cm) leaflets. The leaf stalks, leaf veins, and even flowerstalks are covered in shaggy brown hair. The last of the genus to bloom, fingerleaf rodgersia produces a wide, airy plume of creamy white flowers from midsummer to late summer. Height: 3 to 6 feet (90 to 180 cm). Spread: 3 to 4 feet (90 to 120 cm). USDA Plant Hardiness Zones 4 to 9; AHS Heat Zones 8 to 4.

More Recommended Rodgersias

Rodgersia pinnata (featherleaf rodgersia): Featherleaf rodgersia leaves have five to nine leaflets arranged on either side of a midrib, with one leaflet at the tip, like a feather. The red flowers bloom in early summer to midsummer and make great cut flowers. Some cultivars, such as 'Superba', have attractive bronze leaves, especially in the spring. Height: 3 to 4 feet (90 to 120 cm). Spread: 2 to 4 feet (60 to 120 cm). USDA Plant Hardiness Zones 4 to 9; AHS Heat Zones 8 to 4.

R. podophylla (bronzeleaf rodgersia): Bronzeleaf rodgersia develops the nicest fall color of any of the rodgersias. The creamy white midsummer flower plumes, held up to 2 feet (60 cm) above the foliage, bloom in midsummer to late summer. There are a few cultivars, such as 'Pagode', with a more tiered flower arrangement, and 'Rotlaub', whose leaves retain a bronze tinge right through the summer before turning red in the fall. Height: 3 to 5 feet (90 to 150 cm). Spread: 2 to 4 feet (60 to 120 cm). USDA Plant Hardiness Zones 4 to 9; AHS Heat Zones 8 to 4.

R. sambucifolia (elderberry rodgersia): This rodgersia is usually the hardiest, smallest, and earliest to bloom. Its leaves look much like those of featherleaf rodgersia (*R. pinnata*), but with up to 11 leaflets. Elderberry rodgersia produces flat-topped clusters of white to pink flowers from late spring to early summer. 'Rothaut' (also called 'Red Skin') has bronze leaves and deeper pink blooms. Height: 3 to 4 feet (90 to 120 cm). Spread: 2 to 4 feet (60 to 120 cm). USDA Plant Hardiness Zones 3 to 9; AHS Heat Zones 8 to 4.

Fingerleaf rodgersia
(*Rodgersia aesculifolia*)

Kissing Cousins

Shieldleaf rodgersia (*Astilboides tabularis*, also called *Rodgersia tabularis*) has been reclassified because it has a different leaf structure than rodgersias. And those leaves are its main claim to fame: They're huge—up to 3 feet (90 cm) in diameter—and are pale olive green and round, with slightly lobed edges. Height: 3 to 5 feet (90 to 150 cm). Spread: 2 to 4 feet (60 to 120 cm). USDA Plant Hardiness Zones 4 to 9; AHS Heat Zones 7 to 1.

Sarracenia

Pitcher plant

I have to say it: Pitcher plants are weird. Renowned worldwide as "carnivorous plants," pitcher plants are actually insectivorous—they eat insects and other arthropods, not meat. Pitcher plants *can* be attractive, but that's rarely the main reason for growing them. Most people grow them because they're so different from standard garden plants—or to knock the socks off garden visitors!

Plant Profile

SARRACENIA
sa-ruh-SEH-nee-uh

- **Bloom Color:** Usually red; pink, purple, and yellow possible

- **Bloom Time:** Spring

- **Length of Bloom:** 2 or 3 weeks

- **Height:** Varies by species; see individual listings

- **Spread:** Varies by species; see individual listings

- **Garden Uses:** Container planting, cut flower garden, specimen plant; in wet areas

- **Light Preference:** Full sun to partial shade

- **Soil Preference:** Average, moist to wet, acid soil

- **Best Way to Propagate:** Divide in spring or fall

- **USDA Plant Hardiness Zones:** 2 to 9

- **AHS Heat Zones:** 12 to 1

Growing Tips

Pitcher plants are ideally suited to wet areas. If you have a natural wetland in your garden, you can often simply plant pitcher plants with no special preparation; just make sure there aren't any large or fast-spreading plants in the area that would shade or crowd out the pitcher plants. Otherwise, try planting pitcher plants in a pot of sphagnum moss, and sink the pot into a wet spot in your garden. Just make sure the crown of the plant is above water level.

Pitcher plants often produce two sorts of leaves: flattened, sword-shaped leaves, and hollow, pitcher-shaped leaves that attract and trap insects. The pitchers are varied in color—they can be all green, red, or purple, and they're often attractively marbled with purple, white, or red veins. The pitcher ends in a lid or hood usually designed to keep rainwater out. They may also have pale "fenestrations": translucent yellow or white windows that fool insects into believing this is the way out. The insects eventually become exhausted trying to escape from the inside of the plant and are then digested by the plant. Pitcher plants also produce out-of-this-world flowers. The often scented blooms are nodding and solitary on the upright stems and are made up of five petal-like sepals that hang over long petals that surround the flying-saucer-shaped pistil.

Strike one urban legend: You *shouldn't* feed your pitcher plants hamburger. In fact, you don't need to feed them much of anything. If your plants look a little pale and stretching, and you suspect a nutrient deficiency, spray them with an organic foliar fertilizer like liquid seaweed or fish emulsion at one-fourth the normal strength specified on the label for foliar applications. Old pitchers eventually die; cut them away.

Once you've gotten the hang of pitcher plants, you'll be able to propagate your own. Each plant forms a rosette of leaves rising from a creeping underground stem called a rhizome. The easiest method is to divide and replant the extra rosettes that develop over time. You can also cut the rhizomes into 2-inch (5-cm) sections, and plant them horizontally in moist sphagnum.

Good Neighbors

Grow pitcher plants in a bog garden with other small oddities, such as grassy-leaved sweet flag (*Acorus gramineus*), corkscrew rush (*Juncus effusus* 'Spiralis'), and golden club (*Orontium aquaticum*).

Warning: Some pitcher plants are very rare in the wild and even have protected status as endangered species. Others are not protected but are nevertheless rare enough to deserve some respect. For that reason, never collect pitcher plants yourself from the wild, and before you buy them from a commercial enterprise, ask the salesperson whether the plants were collected in the wild.

Problems and Solutions

Insects and diseases are rarely a problem with pitcher plants. If your plants die, it's probably due to drought or an overdose of fertilizer.

Top Performer

Sarracenia purpurea (common pitcher plant): This is the "beginner's pitcher plant," as it will withstand things that are supposed to be absolute no-nos, like dry soil and alkaline growing conditions. Common pitcher plant is also very hardy—it's the only pitcher plant gardeners in colder zones can grow outdoors. Its pitchers are rather short and fat, lying mostly on their sides, and the "hood" of the pitcher is just a lip surrounding the opening. The pitchers range in color from dark crimson, maroon, or green-veined purple to pure green. Plants produce new pitchers all summer and last over the winter. The spring-to-summer flowers are red. Height: 12 to 18 inches (30 to 45 cm). Spread: 18 to 24 inches (45 to 60 cm). USDA Plant Hardiness Zones 2 to 9; AHS Heat Zones 12 to 1.

Common pitcher plant
(*Sarracenia purpurea*)

Around the World with Pitcher Plant

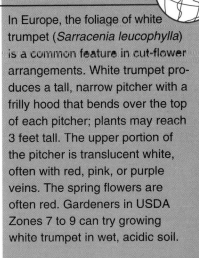

In Europe, the foliage of white trumpet (*Sarracenia leucophylla*) is a common feature in cut-flower arrangements. White trumpet produces a tall, narrow pitcher with a frilly hood that bends over the top of each pitcher; plants may reach 3 feet tall. The upper portion of the pitcher is translucent white, often with red, pink, or purple veins. The spring flowers are often red. Gardeners in USDA Zones 7 to 9 can try growing white trumpet in wet, acidic soil.

PERENNIALS FOR
Cool-Summer CLIMATES

This chapter highlights some rather amazing perennials that aren't terribly common in our North American gardens. These beautiful plants, such as lupines and globeflowers, like it cool even in midsummer. But you can't control the weather, and if you garden in an area with hot summers, you may have to treat cool-season perennials as biennials or annuals (but see my suggestions below for helping cool-loving plants survive the heat). However, there are many areas, such as Maine, Atlantic Canada, and the Pacific Northwest, that rarely see temperatures above 80°F (27°C). For the millions of gardeners in these regions, cool-summer perennials are a terrific choice.

◄ Tall, stately lupines (*Lupinus* hybrids) have dense flower spikes that often sport more than one color on the same bloom spike. Quintessential cottage garden perennials, lupines bloom in late spring in climates with warm, sunny days and cool nights.

Consider Yourself Lucky

I imagine that some gardeners would feel sorry for me, stuck up north in Zone 3. They might assume that I miss out on growing many perennials that just aren't hardy enough to survive my winters. I take the opposite view. While I can't grow tropical plants, I can grow nearly all hardy perennials that other North American gardeners grow, plus I can grow a wonderful group of perennials that only look their best in cool-summer areas like mine. So if you're a gardener with cool summers, be glad!

After all, with only a few exceptions, such as prickly pears (*Opuntia* spp.) and hardy ice plants (*Delosperma* spp.), perennials do fine in cool-summer areas. Winter cold can be a limiting factor for perennials, but almost any perennial will thrive in climates where summer temperatures stay low. In fact, cool summer temperatures tend to extend the blooming seasons of many perennials. Those that normally bloom for four weeks might often stay in top shape a week longer where temperatures never rise much above 70°F (21°C). Humans might prefer more heat, but temperate-climate perennials really don't need it, nor do they like it.

Defining Cool Summer

Gardeners from warmer parts of the North American continent tend to assume that if winters are cold, summers must be, too, but that's not always the case. In USDA Hardiness Zone 3, for instance, temperatures can drop to an incredibly frigid −40°F (−40°C) in winter, but some parts of that zone can have temperatures above 80°F

You never know where Iceland poppies (*Papaver nudicaule*) will pop up in the garden from one year to the next because they self-sow quite readily. In cooler climates, you can move the seedlings in the fall, transplanting them to a more planned site if you prefer. Most will bloom the following spring.

(27°C) for days on end in summer. After all, that's what defines a continental climate, shared by much of the center of this continent: cold winters and hot summers.

Where Are You?

So how can you tell if you live in a hot-summer area? If you have air-conditioning in your home, or know neighbors who do, that's one clue. But if you'd like a more scientific measurement of how hot your climate is, you can consult the American Horticultural Society's (AHS) Heat Zone Map (see page 502).

The Heat Zone Map depicts different zones, determined by the average number of days per year when temperatures exceed 86°F (30°C). You can consider yourself to be in a cool-summer area if you live in Heat Zones 3 or less, and especially in Heat Zones 2 and 1—that is, with an average of fewer than 14 days above 86°F (30°C) per year. You should have no trouble growing any of the plants in this chapter. And those of you who live in Heat Zone 4 may also have some luck with cool-summer perennials,

especially if you carefully choose the coolest possible spots in your garden to plant them.

Much of the Pacific coast of North America, from northern California right up through Alaska, as well as northern New England, Atlantic Canada, eastern Quebec, and the northeastern part of the Great Lakes region, plus the more mountainous regions of the West and all of northern Canada, are in AHS Heat Zones 1 to 3. AHS Heat Zone 4 includes much of the rest of the northern United States, from New England right across the prairies, plus parts of the Appalachians and much of Canada.

Growing Cool-Summer Perennials in Hot-Summer Areas

Even if you don't live in a cool-summer area, you may be able to create cool-summer conditions in certain small pockets in your garden. I like to stretch the limits on what can grow where, so check the entries in this chapter for special tips on how to help your plants adapt to hot-summer areas. And I've suggested, where possible, special species and cultivars that might just be able to thrive a heat zone or so further south. In general, there are a number of things you can do to help keep perennials cool:

Give them a bit more shade. Plants that do best in full sun in cool climates will often adapt to partial shade in hot ones, and those that prefer partial shade may do well in deep shade. And even if you *do* intend to plant them in a more shaded spot than usual, look for an area that gets its shade in the afternoon, when the blazing sun is at its very hottest.

Mulch, mulch, and mulch again. Up to 4 inches (10 cm) of good organic mulch naturally keeps the ground underneath it moister and cooler than usual. Spreading the mulch around the plant's root area can make a huge temperature difference.

Water more. Moist soils are cool soils, so don't be afraid to water more than usual during extreme heat. Of course, don't drown the plants, but keep the soil moist to cool it down.

Plant near bodies of water. Water warms the air during the winter but tends to cool it off during the summer. Even standing water, such as a water garden or swimming pool, can have a cooling effect. Moving water can have a much more dramatic effect—a bubbling brook or rushing stream can dramatically reduce surrounding air temperatures.

Take advantage of natural air currents. Moving air refreshes plants as well as people, so look for spots where breezes naturally blow. Spots where tree and shrub leaves and even branches are constantly on the move are bound to be cooler than the surrounding area.

Take advantage of elevation. Slopes are usually cooler than flat surfaces and hilltops can be a few degrees cooler than valleys, at least if there is some air movement. Not everyone has a mountain in the backyard, of course, but if you do have a choice as to where to grow, try high land over low.

Suiting Garden Style to Your Climate

It's not surprising that standard garden perennials prefer cool summers. The classic perennial border is a gardening style that first developed in Great Britain, where winters are mild and summers are cool.

Compare that to North America, and you'll find a major contrast. The vast majority of the continent suffers from hot, sweltering summers.

Of course, North American gardeners also have a vast selection of native perennials that are better adapted to hot conditions, including beautiful meadow and prairie natives like gayfeathers (*Liatris* spp.), goldenrods (*Solidago* spp.), and heliopsis (*Heliopsis* spp.). Southwest gardeners also have wonderful native perennials, such as agave, penstemon, and yucca. Prompted by the urge to garden no matter *what* the weather, gardeners in hot-summer areas have learned how to work these native perennials into beds and borders, creating their own unique style of perennial gardening.

16 More Cool-Summer Perennials

A wide range of perennials thrives in cool summers, so this list could be awfully long. I'll limit myself to those that are apt to truly shine in cool-summer climates and struggle a bit in hot summers. Here's my list.

Lupinus

Lupine

Most gardeners have no trouble picking a lupine out of a crowd: The tall, dense spikes of blossoms, shaped like those of the pea plant, are a dead giveaway. Most cultivars also have typical lupine leaves—they're shaped like hands, and each "finger" is a narrow leaflet. These cool-summer perennials form beautiful clumps, with several stems arising from a single base. After the flowers fade, flat pea-shaped pods form, positive proof that lupines belong to the pea family.

Plant Profile

LUPINUS
lew-PIE-nus

- **Bloom Color:** Blue, cream, pink, purple, red, white, or yellow

- **Bloom Time:** Late spring to early summer or midsummer

- **Length of Bloom:** 3 to 5 weeks

- **Height:** 16 to 60 inches (40 to 150 cm)

- **Spread:** 1 to 2 feet (30 to 60 cm)

- **Garden Uses:** Cut flower garden, mass planting, meadow garden, mixed border; at the back of beds and borders

- **Light Preference:** Full sun to partial shade

- **Soil Preference:** Rich, slightly acidic, moist, well-drained soil

- **Best Way to Propagate:** Sow seed in early spring

- **USDA Plant Hardiness Zones:** 3 to 9

- **AHS Heat Zones:** 6 to 1

Growing Tips

Certainly among the most desirable of all perennials, lupines would be as widely grown in North America as they are in Europe if they just weren't so picky about their growing conditions. Just being able to grow lupines would be reason enough to move to a cool-summer climate! Not only do lupines thrive in cool climates, but they even self-sow with a vengeance.

In hot-summer areas, it's a very different story. Plants collapse after blooming, hit by the double whammy of powdery mildew and aphids. And the hot temperatures don't give the plants much of a chance to recuperate: They often simply die.

Lupines have taproots, so when you plant them, try to disturb the rootball as little as possible. And look for them in 1-gallon (2-liter) containers: Like other plants with long taproots, lupines don't tolerate life in small pots with any grace.

To keep your lupines going for as long as possible, grow them in a cool spot in rich, constantly moist yet well-drained soil. Although full sun is best for outstanding bloom, you may have to compromise and plant them in partial shade in order to keep them cool and happy. After bloom, or when the flower spikes begin to look ratty, deadhead them to prevent seed production: This can help give the plant more energy. (In cool-summer areas, they may even rebloom in the fall.) If the mildew/aphid combination hits, simply cut them back to the ground and keep your fingers crossed—if the weather isn't too hot, they'll quickly sprout anew.

Sowing seed is generally the easiest way to propagate lupines. Soak or chip the hard seeds first, then sow in early spring, indoors in peat pots or outdoors where they are to grow. Lupines don't like being divided or transplanted.

Good Neighbors

Lupines are a wonderful addition to the late-spring and early-summer garden. Combine them with other perennials that bloom at the same time, such as irises, peonies, oriental poppy (*Papaver orientale*), and hardy geraniums like *G.* × *magnificum* and *G. sanguineum*. Also include later-blooming plants that will carry the garden into midsummer to late summer—Russian sage (*Perovskia atriplicifolia*), garden phlox (*Phlox paniculata*), rudbeckias, and pincushion flowers (*Scabiosa* spp.), to name just a few.

Warning: Lupines contain toxic substances called alkaloids that are poisonous if ingested. Although all parts of the plant are poisonous, the only real danger is that children might mistake the pods for peas or beans and eat them. For safety's sake, pick the pods off as they appear or cut off the entire flowerstalk after the flowers fade.

Problems and Solutions

Aphids and powdery mildew are the banes of lupines' existence, but just prune the plants back to the ground if they begin to look under the weather; they'll quickly sprout healthy new growth. Where lupines fail to thrive, consider replacing them every year or two.

Top Performer

Lupinus hybrids: The most commonly available hybrid lupines are those developed by Yorkshire gardener George Russell. Russell hybrid cultivars have sturdy, upright flowerstalks. They bloom from late spring to early summer or midsummer; colors range from the palest pastels (whites, pinks, blues, and yellows) to the deepest reds and purples. Many cultivars come true from purchased seed, but if you raise them from homegrown seed, you'll soon find yourself with mostly purple shades. Choice dwarf strains that you may see sold as "dwarf Russell lupines" include the Gallery Hybrids, that grow 16 to 18 inches (40 to 45 cm) tall, and the Minarette Hybrids, that reach 18 to 20 inches (45 to 50 cm) tall. Don't search for specific Russell lupine cultivars—just choose plants according to whatever color interests you from among the hundreds available.

Lupine (*Lupinus* hybrid)

Around the World with Lupines

Lupines are more popular in Europe and elsewhere than their native land! The reason, of course, is climatic: They *do* prefer cool summers. In Great Britain, where summers are cool, lupines grow everywhere—from the Royal Botanical Gardens in Edinburgh, to cottage gardens throughout all of the British Isles. And I've seen lupines galore in northern France and Germany, and around Queenstown on the South Island of New Zealand where they line the roadways with their beautiful spires of blue and pink.

Mimulus

Monkey flower

You'll have to look closely to see a monkey's face in one of these velvety flowers. The flowers *are* often covered with spots, so I suppose, like looking at clouds, you can see what you like in them. Monkey flower plants form attractive mounds (or may be spreading) and have hairy stems covered with shiny, toothed, medium green leaves. The flowers are generally funnel-shaped, but with two lips: a small two-lobed upper one and an often much larger lower one with three lobes.

Plant Profile

MIMULUS
MIM-you-luss

- **Bloom Color:** Brown, cream, orange, pink, purple, red, and yellow
- **Bloom Time:** Summer to early fall
- **Length of Bloom:** 6 to 8 weeks or more
- **Height:** 6 to 36 inches (15 to 90 cm)
- **Spread:** 6 to 36 inches (15 to 90 cm)
- **Garden Uses:** Edging, groundcover, mass planting, mixed border, rock garden, woodland garden; in wet areas; attracts hummingbirds
- **Light Preference:** Full sun to partial shade
- **Soil Preference:** Rich, moist, slightly acid soil
- **Best Way to Propagate:** Sow seed in spring
- **USDA Plant Hardiness Zones:** 4 to 9
- **AHS Heat Zones:** 6 to 1

Growing Tips

When I first tried growing monkey flowers, I treated them as annuals because I'd read so many warnings about how tender the plants are. I figured they wouldn't survive their first winter in my Quebec (USDA Zone 3) garden, but they not only survived—they thrived! It's possible this is due to extra protection from snow cover, careful plant placement, and other factors, but even so, many monkey flowers should be able to survive at least to USDA Zone 4 in the right conditions.

The secret to growing monkey flowers is protecting them from heat and drought. Full sun is perfect in cool-summer areas as long as you can ensure plentiful moisture. In warmer areas, partial shade is necessary, even if that means the plants bloom less enthusiastically. The ideal spot for monkey flowers in a hot-summer area would be right next to a cool, refreshing stream in the shade. And a winter mulch can help get them through the winter in almost any climate, cold or mild.

That said, don't expect individual monkey flower plants to be all that long-lived. Two or three years of bloom is about all you can hope for. But plants spread so readily by seed and by underground stems that you will scarcely notice the mother plant has given up the ghost.

Seed is probably the best way to multiply monkey flowers, as most will self-sow where they are happy. Indoors, start seed about 10 to 12 weeks before the last frost. Scatter the seed over the surface of moist potting mix, enclose the pot in a plastic bag, and put the bag in the refrigerator for 3 weeks. Afterward, expose the container to warmth and light: The seeds sprout quickly and will bloom the first season. If you have a plant you particularly like, taking cuttings or dividing plants in spring is the best way to go because even species monkey flowers never come exactly true from seed.

Good Neighbors

Because they're well adapted to very moist soil, monkey flowers make great companions for other plants that can tolerate wet sites. Use them as a colorful accent around bold perennials such as heartleaf bergenia (*Bergenia cordifolia*), large hostas, and bigleaf ligularia (*Ligularia dentata*).

Problems and Solutions

Sad but true: Slugs love monkey flowers. For tips on controlling these pests, see page 55. Also, you can always prune back slug-damaged stems, and the plants will fill in nicely.

Top Performer

Mimulus × *hybridus* (hybrid monkey flower): Hybrid monkey flowers range in color from creamy white to bright yellow to orange or red, often with very heavy mottling and usually a broad face, like common monkey flower (*M. guttatus*). Plants bloom from early summer to early fall. The leaves are usually toothed and rather broad. The easiest way to obtain hybrid monkey flower is from mixed seed strains such as 'Calypso', so even labeled plants bearing the same name can be widely different in shape and color. Height: 6 to 36 inches (15 to 60 cm). Spread: 1 to 3 feet (30 to 90 cm). USDA Plant Hardiness Zones 4 to 9; AHS Heat Zones 6 to 1.

More Recommended Monkey Flowers

Mimulus lewisii (Lewis monkey flower): This species offers pink to rosy red flowers with spotting at the center, produced from early summer to early fall on upright, sticky, hairy stems. It prefers moist soil but seems to tolerate less moist conditions better than other monkey flowers. Height: 18 to 30 inches (45 to 75 cm). Spread: 30 to 36 inches (75 to 90 cm). USDA Plant Hardiness Zones 4 to 9; AHS Heat Zones 6 to 1.

Monkey flower
(*Mimulus* hybrid)

Larry's Garden Notes

Monkey flowers vary widely in height. In dry conditions, they may only reach 1 foot (30 cm) tall, but they can immediately leap to 3 feet (90 cm) when transplanted to a bed with moister soil. Spread also varies depending on soil moisture: In moderately moist soil, monkey flowers stay nice and compact; in wet soil, they tend to run.

Papaver

Poppy

I can't imagine gardening without poppies of some sort: It seems to me that every garden needs at least a few. Iceland poppy (*Papaver nudicaule*) and alpine poppy (*P. alpinum*) are the poppies of choice for cool summers. They produce ground-hugging rosettes of gray-green foliage. The thin but sturdy flowerstalks bear silky-textured, cup-shaped blooms with intriguing clusters of yellow stamens in the center. If summers are not too hot, these poppies will bloom nonstop from late spring until fall; otherwise, they'll bloom until the heat cuts them back.

Plant Profile

PAPAVER
pa-PAH-ver

- **Bloom Color:** Orange, pink, red, salmon, white, or yellow
- **Bloom Time:** Late spring to late summer or early fall
- **Length of Bloom:** 2 months or more
- **Height:** 6 to 18 inches (15 to 45 cm)
- **Spread:** 6 to 12 inches (15 to 30 cm)
- **Garden Uses:** Container planting, cut flower garden, edging, groundcover, mass planting, mixed border, rock garden, wall planting
- **Light Preference:** Full sun
- **Soil Preference:** Moderately rich, well-drained soil
- **Best Way to Propagate:** Sow seed in early spring or fall
- **USDA Plant Hardiness Zones:** Varies by species; see individual listings
- **AHS Heat Zones:** 6 to 1

Growing Tips

Iceland and alpine poppies will grow just about anywhere as annuals, but only cool-summer gardeners can really appreciate how floriferous and long-blooming they are. In cool-summer areas, they'll live for years and bloom practically all season. In hot climates, poppies won't even live through their first summer.

If your summers are only moderately hot, such as those in AHS Heat Zones 7 to 4, these poppies will bloom in spring and early summer, sometimes into midsummer. They'll tend to act as short-lived perennials, blooming for a summer or two before dying out. But they usually self-seed before they go.

To grow long-lived cool-summer poppies, you'll also need very good drainage; they can take dry cold, but not winter wet. In the spring and summer, though, they prefer their soil at least slightly moist, so don't hesitate to water as needed while they're growing. A winter mulch can also help prolong the life of your poppies because they usually depend on snow cover for protection. Where snow cover is lacking, a light and airy winter mulch is wise. I like to use conifer branches: They keep off the cold winds and don't allow any moisture to accumulate.

The easiest way to multiply these poppies is to let them self-sow. Although mature plants hate being moved, you can carefully dig up the young seedlings and transplant them to other spots in your garden. They'll bloom the following spring.

You can also sow purchased seed in the fall or in very early spring for bloom the first year. In colder climates, sow the seed in summer and move the seedlings in the fall. Just sprinkle the seeds over the ground, without covering them.

To keep cool-climate poppies blooming over the summer, deadhead them regularly, leaving a few seedpods to ensure the plants self-sow.

Good Neighbors

Enjoy Iceland poppy (*Papaver nudicaule*) as an accent in a border with ornamental grasses or blue- and purple-flowered perennials, such as blue false indigo (*Baptisia australis*), hardy geraniums, and irises.

Alpine poppy (*P. alpinum*) is also at home in the rock garden with companions such as mountain lady's-mantle (*Alchemilla alpina*), thrifts (*Armeria* spp.), and rock cresses (*Arabis* spp.), to name a few.

Problems and Solutions

Neither of these plants has any particular problems with insects or disease, but you must supply cool conditions and good drainage if you want them to survive.

Top Performer

Papaver nudicaule (Iceland poppy): Iceland poppies produce ground-hugging tufts of light green, hairy, lobed leaves and wiry, hairy, leafless stems of lightly scented, cup-shaped flowers up to 8 inches (20 cm) in diameter. They bloom from late spring through early fall. 'Oregon Rainbows' is a mixed strain that has large flowers, mainly in pastels and bicolors, but it demands cool summers to do well. 'Champagne Bubbles' is the standard Iceland poppy, with 3-inch (8-cm) flowers in the full color range. Height: 10 to 30 inches (25 to 75 cm). Spread: 1 foot (30 cm). USDA Plant Hardiness Zones 1 to 9; AHS Heat Zones 6 to 1.

More Recommended Poppies

Papaver alpinum (alpine poppy): You might think of this species as a miniature Iceland poppy (*P. nudicaule*) for the front of the border or the rock garden. It produces 1- to 1½-inch (2.5- to 4-cm) flowers in white, orange, yellow, pink, and salmon from late spring through late summer. Height: 6 to 8 inches (15 to 20 cm). Spread: 6 to 8 inches (15 to 20 cm). USDA Plant Hardiness Zones 2 to 9; AHS Heat Zones 6 to 1.

Iceland poppy
(*Papaver nudicaule*)

Kissing Cousins

Welsh poppy (*Meconopsis cambrica*) will grow almost everywhere as a self-seeding perennial. It blooms almost nonstop all summer. The blooms are yellow, orange, and scarlet, and there are single and double-flowered forms. The hotter the climate, the more it will act like an annual, but it does well as a perennial into AHS Heat Zone 7. In cooler climates, it will live for years in soil that is well drained and rich in humus. Like most poppies, it produces a basal rosette of bright green, hairy, toothed leaves. Height: 1 to 2 feet (30 to 60 cm). Spread: 1 foot (30 cm). USDA Plant Hardiness Zones 2 to 9; AHS Heat Zones 8 to 1.

Trollius

Globeflower

"Giant, rounded buttercups" is how one of my friends describes globeflowers, and she's perfectly right: The large, usually bright yellow flowers are buttercup-like inside and out. The only major difference (besides size) is that globeflowers tend to remain rounded, opening only into a cup-shaped form—which is why we call them globeflowers. Even the large, dark green leaves, which look like fingers radiating from a hand, are easy to mistake for those of buttercups. But unlike buttercups, which are a rather unruly bunch, globeflowers stay put.

Plant Profile

TROLLIUS
TROH-lee-us

- **Bloom Color:** Cream, orange, or yellow
- **Bloom Time:** Spring
- **Length of Bloom:** 3 or 4 weeks
- **Height:** 20 to 36 inches (50 to 90 cm)
- **Spread:** 12 to 30 inches (30 to 75 cm)
- **Garden Uses:** Container planting, cut flower garden, edging, mixed border, rock garden, specimen plant, wildflower meadow, woodland garden; at the back of beds and borders, in wet areas
- **Light Preference:** Full sun to partial shade
- **Soil Preference:** Rich, moist, even boggy soil
- **Best Way to Propagate:** Divide in spring or early autumn
- **USDA Plant Hardiness Zones:** 3 to 9
- **AHS Heat Zones:** 6 to 1

Growing Tips

Cool and wet: Those are the conditions you need if you want to succeed with globeflowers. They don't appreciate hot summers or drought so keep them at least evenly moist at all times.

In the cool, moist conditions globeflowers prefer, their foliage remains attractive all summer long. Elsewhere, they tend to become tired-looking or yellow by midsummer; just prune them back harshly.

Globeflowers are rather slow off the mark. Don't worry if they don't seem up to potential for the first year or so. They'll eventually grow and fill in. In fact, after five or so years, you might need to divide them, as the clumps tend to get thin in the middle over time. Division is the best way to multiply globeflowers; in fact, it's the only way to propagate the cultivars. The ideal time to divide your plants is just after they've finished blooming. You *can* grow the species from seed, but it's tricky. If you want to try, use fresh seed, and sow it within a few weeks of harvest into wet soil outdoors. It should germinate the following spring.

Good Neighbors

Bright yellow globeflowers complement the blues and purples of spring nicely. For color contrast, plant them with Japanese and Siberian irises (*Iris ensata* and *I. sibirica*), Virginia bluebells (*Mertensia virginica*), and forget-me-nots (*Myosotis* spp.) in a constantly moist site.

Problems and Solutions

Powdery mildew sometimes causes white patches on leaves, especially if the soil is on the dry side. The easiest thing to do is to simply cut the damaged leaves back, and next year, be sure to keep the soil moist.

Top Performer

Trollius × *cultorum* (hybrid globeflower):
There's a wide variety of hybrid globeflower cultivars with yellow, orange,
or cream flowers from midspring to
early summer. Some of my favorites
are 'Cheddar', with creamy white
flowers; 'Earliest of All', with large
golden yellow flowers that are indeed
fairly early; and 'Lemon Queen',
with pale yellow blooms. Height: 2
to 3 feet (60 to 90 cm). Spread: 18 to
36 inches (45 to 90 cm). USDA Plant
Hardiness Zones 3 to 9; AHS Heat
Zones 6 to 1.

More Recommended Globeflowers

Trollius chinensis (Chinese globeflower):
There's not much difference between
this species and the hybrids, but for
what it's worth, it's usually a later-
blooming plant with larger yellow to
orange, globe-shaped flowers in early summer. 'Golden Queen',
with golden orange flowers up to 4 inches (10 cm) in diameter,
belongs here. Height: 2 to 3 feet (60 to 90 cm). Spread: 18 to 36
inches (45 to 90 cm). USDA Plant Hardiness Zones 3 to 9; AHS
Heat Zones 6 to 1.

 T. europaeus (common globeflower): Plants sold under this name
are often actually hybrids, which certainly doesn't make things any
less confusing. In theory, common globeflower blooms earlier
(from early to midspring), with smaller leaves and smaller lemon
yellow or orange blooms. Height: 18 to 24 inches (45 to 60 cm).
Spread: 2 feet (60 cm). USDA Plant Hardiness Zones 3 to 9; AHS
Heat Zones 6 to 1.

 T. pumilus (dwarf globeflower): Now this one *is* different. Dwarf
globeflower is a nice dwarf species for smaller areas, such as a rock
garden or the front of the border. It produces the same yellow,
globe-shaped spring flowers as the others, but they're only 1 inch
(2.5 cm) in diameter. Height: 9 to 12 inches (23 to 30 cm). Spread:
1 foot (30 cm). USDA Plant Hardiness Zones 3 to 9; AHS Heat
Zones 6 to 1.

'Earliest of All' hybrid globeflower
(*Trollius* × *cultorum* 'Earliest of All')

Larry's Garden Notes

Most globeflowers are very
similar in appearance, size, and
behavior, so their division into
species and cultivars may seem
arbitrary—in fact, it is! The differ
ences are so minor that even
botanists get confused. So don't
feel put off by a lot of different
labels on plants that all look alike
to you—just pick out one you find
attractive and grow it!

PERENNIALS THAT
Bloom in the Shade

Shade is no obstacle to a successful perennial garden. I have gardened in both sun and in shade over the years (and in more than my fair share of the latter), and I've learned to love my shade gardens. For one thing, it's cooler to work in a shady garden during the summer. Plus, shade gardens tend to require *less* work than sunny gardens. And if you're worried that your shade gardens will be all greenery and no flowers, read this chapter to learn about great perennials that bloom beautifully in the shade.

◄The delicate flowers of Siberian bugloss (*Brunnera macrophylla*) show that the shade garden can be quietly colorful. As the spring flowers fade, the heart-shaped leaves grow larger and more prominent to keep the plant looking good throughout the summer.

Select Carefully for Success

The secret to gardening in the shade is choosing the right plants. In a shady spot, there's a lot of competition for what little light is available, and plants that have not adapted to shady conditions will quickly lose out to those that have. Most perennials that do well in shade are slow-growing, so they don't need large amounts of light to fuel rapid growth. Shade lovers may not reach blooming size until four or five years after planting seed. Because of this, most shade-blooming perennials require patience when raising them from seed. The seeds will germinate and grow, but you'll have to wait an awfully long time to get blooming plants.

The Many Shades of Shade

Of course, the kind of shade you have will influence your shade garden. Shade can range from very light shade, which won't limit your plant choices much at all, to deep shade, where your plant selection may be limited to foliage perennials and ferns. The plants I've picked for this chapter all cope very well with partial shade, which can mean sunlight filtering through overhead trees for much of the day or about two to four hours of direct sun followed by shade for the rest of the day. Some of these plants even do well in deep shade, or less than two hours of sun a day.

Some parts of your yard are only shady in summer, when deciduous trees are in full leaf. For spots like these, you can plant early-season perennials that sprout early in spring and bloom before the trees leaf out. There's a wide variety of spring-blooming perennials that cope perfectly with seasonal shade.

There's nothing like a shady spot on a hot summer day! This enjoyable outdoor living space features shade-loving, flowering perennials like astilbe and hosta. 'Fanal' hybrid astilbe (*Astilbe* x *arendsii* 'Fanal') flower plumes are a highlight in high summer, while the seersucker hosta (*Hosta sieboldii*) will send up tall stalks of violet blossoms in late summer to keep the woodland garden full of bloom.

Subtle but Beautiful Blooms

Subtle but Beautiful Blooms

I have to admit that shade-tolerant perennials don't bloom as prolifically as sun-loving plants. Plants that grow in full sun can afford to pull out all the stops and try to outbloom all their neighbors. And why not? They can soak up more sun in one month than many shade plants can in a full year.

Shade plants are more discreet. Flowering takes energy and so does producing seeds. Shade plants concentrate their effort on just a few flowerstalks, often condensing many blossoms into just a bit of space.

You'll find that shade even has favorite flower colors: white and very pale shades of yellow and blue. These light colors reflect more light than darker flowers and show up better against the dark background of a shady setting. That means pollinators have an easier time finding these light flowers. And the few darker-flowered shade bloomers usually have special perfumes that can draw pollinators even if their blooms aren't spectacular to the human eye.

Planting a Shady Garden

Starting a perennial garden in an open, sunny area is a straightforward task, but starting a garden under trees is a little trickier. You don't want to disrupt the entire area because that could damage or even kill the trees. Plus, shade plants tend to grow slowly, so your garden can look rather bare for the first few years. You can overcome that problem by filling in with shade-loving annuals or putting your potted houseplants out in the garden for the summer.

Preparing Planting Pockets

Preparing Planting Pockets

Many types of trees, including oak, tulip poplar, ash, and honey locust, have relatively deep roots. It's fairly easy to dig planting pockets for perennials near their base. Just look for an open spot between any large roots and dig carefully. You will probably need to cut through a few smaller roots, so keep a sharp knife handy. Dig a slightly larger planting hole than you would if you were planting in a standard garden bed, and add as much high-quality soil as possible.

Planting over Roots

If your yard has shallow-rooted trees, such as maples, digging will be almost impossible. Instead, cover the area around the base of each tree with sheets of newspaper and 4 inches (10 cm) of a light soil mix that contains lots of compost, then plant in this minigarden. If you're planting a groundcover, set the plants one-third closer together than usual. Groundcovers won't develop as thickly as they would in other areas of the garden because they'll be competing with tree roots. Ideally, you should leave an unplanted ring 6 to 8 feet (180 to 245 cm) in diameter around the tree base, and mulch this ring with 3 inches (7.5 cm) of composted leaves or composted wood. This small perennial-free zone will reduce the competition for water and nutrients.

Be sure to water new perennials planted under trees very well during their first year of growth. If they haven't adapted by the end of the first growing season, their chances of long-term survival are slim. By the second year, the tree will reconquer the planting site. In very dry wooded areas, a permanent irrigation system would be a wise investment, as competition for water will be a constant problem.

More Shade = Less Work

Once your shade garden is established, it often requires less care than a sunny garden. With the exception of gardens planted under trees, shady gardens tend to need less watering than sunnier nooks because the plants grow more slowly and less water is lost to evaporation.

Slow growth also means there is little or no need to fertilize. In shady gardens, most perennials get all the nutrients they need from the yearly crop of tree leaves that fall and decay. Even weeds cause fewer problems in a shady garden; there's less energy to go around, so if you've managed to fill all the space with desirable plants, weeds see no reason to interfere.

Is Shade in Your Future?

Even if your garden isn't shady now, it may well become so in the next 10 years. It's the natural evolution of a home landscape. If you've planted young trees or shrubs, your garden is bound to become shadier and shadier over time. In 20 years those scrawny saplings will be big trees with thousands of leaves soaking up all the solar energy they can grab.

This increase in shadiness can throw a curveball to gardeners who figure they've finished landscaping their yards and don't plan to make any changes. But shade gardens need so much less work than sunny ones that I think it's a welcome change. After all, in 20 years we all may be ready to slow down a bit!

Since a sunny garden doesn't become a shady one overnight, you can go with the flow: As sun-loving plants gradually peter out, replace them with shade-tolerant perennials. That way the evolution from sun to shade won't require any major effort on your part.

14 More Shade Lovers

If you have lots of shady areas to plant, don't limit yourself to the plants listed in this chapter. Most of the perennials I describe in "Perennials for Fabulous Foliage" on page 346 will thrive in shade, too. And if you'd like more flowering perennials for shady sites, try these great plants:

Actaea

Baneberry

Why baneberries aren't more popular is one of the great garden mysteries of all time. They have long-lasting, attractive foliage and bottlebrush-shaped, fuzzy clusters of white flowers in spring, and the flowers mature to strikingly colored, long-lasting berries that remain on the plants well into fall. Plus, they're easy to grow and widely adaptable. They're a great choice for any and all shade gardens. My suggestion? Test-drive them in your garden. I suspect you'll be as enthusiastic as I am about these beautiful plants.

Plant Profile

ACTAEA
ak-TEE-uh

- Bloom Color: White
- Bloom Time: Late spring
- Length of Bloom: 3 to 4 weeks
- Height: 2 to 3 feet (60 to 90 cm)
- Spread: 2 feet (60 cm)
- Garden Uses: Groundcover, mass planting, mixed border, woodland garden; at the back of beds and borders
- Light Preference: Full sun to full shade, depending on species
- Soil Preference: Humus-rich, moist, slightly acid soil
- Best Way to Propagate: Divide in spring or fall
- USDA Plant Hardiness Zones: 2 to 9
- AHS Heat Zones: 8 to 1

Growing Tips

The secret to growing baneberries is providing a cool, moist spot with rich, humusy soil. Sun—or the lack of sun—is irrelevant: They'll grow with equal ease in full sun or full shade (at least in the shade under deciduous trees, where some sunlight appears in the spring). If you live in a cool-summer climate, try baneberries in the perennial border for an outstanding effect with no effort whatsoever. Just make sure you use a good mulch to keep them relatively cool and moist.

When you buy baneberry plants, make sure to seek out plants that are nursery-grown. Baneberries are not rare anywhere, but they do grow in sensitive environments, so wild harvesting can do considerable damage to their native habitats.

Baneberries are long-lived perennials that are slow to establish. They'll grow in a given spot indefinitely, spreading only somewhat slowly at the base. You don't need to divide them to keep them vigorous, but it's the simplest means of propagating baneberries. You can also grow them from seed; just extract the seeds fresh from the berry and plant them 1 inch (2.5 cm) deep in late summer or fall and mulch heavily. They will sprout the following spring and produce lovely flowers within three years.

Good Neighbors

Baneberries make an attractive backdrop for low-growing woodland plants, including Jack-in-the-pulpits (*Arisaema* spp.), Canadian wild ginger (*Asarum canadense*), and small Solomon's seal (*Polygonatum biflorum*). Other appropriate shady-site companions include epimediums and pulmonarias.

Don't limit this beauty to the woodland garden: Baneberry's long season of interest makes it an outstanding choice for the perennial border as well. Brunneras, hellebores (*Helleborus* spp.), and hostas are just a few of the many compatible border companions. Baneberry berries are a handsome addition to fall border plants that are starting to fade to yellow.

Warning: Baneberries are poisonous, and the berries *are* bright and colorful. So don't plant this perennial in areas where young children can get at them, or be sure to pick the berries off yourself and dispose of them. Ingesting as few as six berries may cause illness.

Problems and Solutions

Baneberries are relatively trouble-free plants with few enemies.

Red baneberry
(*Actaea rubra*)

Top Performer

Actaea alba, also called *A. pachypoda* (white baneberry, doll's eyes): The type of baneberry usually sold is the eastern North American form with white flowers in late spring followed by glistening white berries tipped in black and thick, red flowerstalks to show off the berries. It's a stunning plant that every gardener should consider growing. Height: 2 to 3 feet (60 to 90 cm). Spread: 2 feet (60 cm). USDA Plant Hardiness Zones 2 to 9; AHS Heat Zones 8 to 1.

More Recommended Baneberries

Actaea rubra, also called *A. spicata* var. *rubra* (red baneberry): This baneberry blooms with white flowers in late spring. But the later show of brilliant red, shiny berries on thin green stalks is a knockout—the stalks turn red as they mature, creating a glow in the perennial bed. Height: 2 to 3 feet (60 to 90 cm). Spread: 2 feet (60 cm). USDA Plant Hardiness Zones 2 to 9; AHS Heat Zones 8 to 1.

A. spicata (baneberry): This baneberry is native to Europe. It has black berries and green flowerstalks, but I advise looking for forms that have white or red berries because they're more attractive. Height: 2 to 3 feet (60 to 90 cm). Spread: 2 feet (60 cm). USDA Plant Hardiness Zones 2 to 9; AHS Heat Zones 8 to 1.

Larry's Garden Notes

There aren't many perennials that are grown for their ornamental fruit, let alone named for it. With baneberries (*Actaea* spp.), you have your choice of fruit colors— white (*A. alba*), red (*A. rubra*), and black (*A. spicata*, named in this case for flower shape, not fruit color). Although the poisonous berries can be worrisome if you have young children, the very fact that they are poisonous keeps them from being eaten by wildlife. This means that you when you plant baneberries, you're sure to have unusual and long-lasting color in your fall garden.

Arisaema

Jack-in-the-pulpit

Jack-in-the-pulpits are among the more bizarre perennials to try in your shade garden. These tuberous plants produce a single green or mottled stem and just one or two leaves per season. Their claim to fame, though, is their out-of-this-world flower. The actual blooms are tiny and are clustered on a columnlike stalk called a spadix (or Jack) that's surrounded by a leafy sheath called a spathe (or the pulpit). The spathe forms a tube around the base of the spadix, then usually arches up and over the top, forming a hood for Jack's pulpit.

Plant Profile

ARISAEMA
ar-iss-EE-muh

- **Bloom Color:** Green, purple, and white

- **Bloom Time:** Spring

- **Length of Bloom:** 4 or 5 weeks

- **Height:** Varies by species; see individual listings

- **Spread:** Varies by species; see individual listings

- **Garden Uses:** Specimen plant, woodland garden

- **Light Preference:** Sun or light shade to full shade

- **Soil Preference:** Humus-rich, well-drained soil that's moist in spring

- **Best Way to Propagate:** Divide after flowering

- **USDA Plant Hardiness Zones:** Varies by species; see individual listings

- **AHS Heat Zones:** 9 to 1

Growing Tips

Most Jack-in-the-pulpits are spring growers, blooming while the air is still cool and the soil still moist, then going dormant and losing their leaves after their fruit has matured. It's hard to predict what size a Jack-in-the-pulpit will reach. You'll have to try them out to learn exactly how they'll grow in your garden's conditions.

Many types of Jack-in-the-pulpits like moist soil in the spring—their main growing season—then tolerate drought after they go dormant. Both of the species described here (*Arisaema triphyllum* and *A. sikokianum*), though, will appreciate the conditions of a garden bed under a deciduous tree: full sun to dappled sunlight in spring followed by summer shade. They won't mind drought later in the summer. In cool climates, they'll also grow perfectly well in full sun as long as they get enough moisture during their growing season.

You'll find Jack-in-the-pulpits sold in pots in spring and as bare tubers in early spring or fall. Both are fine for garden use, but tubers are often cheaper. Either way, plant the tubers about 4 inches (10 cm) deep.

Jack-in-the-pulpits are rather difficult to propagate. Many produce offsets at the base and can be divided, but the plants may take two to four years to flower; dividing the mother plant also sets it back considerably. For types that don't produce offsets, you'll need to start from seed. Fresh seed is best, so extract your own from a ripe fruit. Wear rubber or plastic gloves because handling the fruit can cause a burning sensation in your fingers. Sow the seed in a container indoors. After germination, which can take a month or so, let the plants grow until they go dormant and dry out before planting them outside. In all honesty, the best way to get new Jack-in-the-pulpits from those that don't produce off-sets is to buy new plants!

Warning: All Jack-in-the-pulpits are poisonous. They contain calcium oxalate, which has needlelike crystals that cause an immediate burning sensation; flushing the affected area with water will help.

Good Neighbors

Plant Jack-in-the-pulpits along a woodland walkway so you can appreciate their unusual flowers and attractive foliage and berries. Combine them with other woodland species, such as baneberries (*Actaea* spp.), epimediums, and crested iris (*Iris cristata*) in the shade of deciduous trees.

Jack-in-the-pulpit
(*Arisaema triphyllum*)

Problems and Solutions

Once you get over the panic caused by seeing your Jack-in-the-pulpit turn yellow and die back after blooming (that's normal!), you'll find it is quite immune to pests and diseases.

Top Performer

Arisaema triphyllum (Jack-in-the-pulpit): The typical wild Jack-in-the-pulpit of eastern North America, this plant is my top choice simply because it's inexpensive, easy to find, and it multiplies abundantly. This species produces two leaves with three (or occasionally five) leaflets. The spring spathes (hoodlike structures) are usually green striped with purple, but they can also be all green or all purple. The plant varies widely in color, size, and hardiness. Height: 1 to 3 feet (30 to 90 cm). Spread: 1 to 2 feet (30 to 60 cm). USDA Plant Hardiness Zones 2 to 9; AHS Heat Zones 9 to 1.

More Recommended Jack-in-the-Pulpits

Arisaema sikokianum (gaudy Jack): The leaves of this Asiatic species, borne two per stalk, are normally plain green with three leaflets, but as plants mature, they often develop silvery markings. The early spring flower is quite unlike the others, with the tip of the white club-shaped spadix emerging completely from the deep purple-brown, funnel-shaped spathe. To top it all off, the spathe ends in an upward projection, like a sail in the wind. Height: 6 to 24 inches (15 to 60 cm). Spread: 20 inches (50 cm). USDA Plant Hardiness Zones 4 to 9; AHS Heat Zones 9 to 1.

Larry's Garden Notes

Did you know that jack-in-the-pulpits (*Arisaema* spp.) often change sexes? In fact, they may go back and forth from one sex to another. Typically, young plants are male and produce only pollen until they build up enough energy to produce a female flower. After they produce seed, they often go back to being male again.

Astilbe

Astilbe, false spirea

Astilbes are a favorite of shade gardeners, and once you've tried growing them, you'll know why. These lovely perennials produce clumps of deeply cut, medium to dark green, fernlike foliage, often with a coppery sheen in spring. The foliage usually remains in fine shape well into fall. Astilbes' individual flowers are tiny, but they're grouped into feathery plumes held well above the plant. Not only are they long-lasting, but they often fade to soft beige, brown, and reddish shades, then remain on the plant until fall.

Plant Profile

ASTILBE
uh-STILL-bee

- **Bloom Color:** Cream, magenta, pink, purple, red, salmon, and white
- **Bloom Time:** Varies by species; see individual listings
- **Length of Bloom:** 4 to 6 weeks
- **Height:** 6 to 48 inches (15 to 120 cm)
- **Spread:** 1 to 3 feet (30 to 90 cm)
- **Garden Uses:** Container planting, cut flower garden, edging, groundcover, mass planting, mixed border, rock garden, woodland garden
- **Light Preference:** Full sun to deep shade
- **Soil Preference:** Average, moist but well-drained soil
- **Best Way to Propagate:** Divide in spring or fall
- **USDA Plant Hardiness Zones:** 4 to 9
- **AHS Heat Zones:** 8 to 2

Growing Tips

Astilbes like things cool and moist. They prefer light to partial shade, but even deep shade will do as long as they enjoy sun for part of the day. They'll also thrive in full sun where the soil stays moist.

Where they're happy, astilbes fill in quickly, forming dense clumps. If they take up too much room, dig them up and separate them. Most astilbes can last six years without being divided. As you divide astilbes, you can cut the thicker roots into 1-inch (2.5-cm) sections and root them, covering them with about 1 inch (2.5 cm) of soil.

Seed is only a good method of multiplying the species, because cultivars will not come true. Either sow seed indoors in late winter or outdoors in spring or autumn. Don't cover the fine seed.

Astilbes almost never need staking and thrive on neglect. Unless your soil is naturally moist, they appreciate regular applications of organic mulch. Although I've listed USDA Zone 4 as the northern limit for astilbe culture, they're a snap to grow in Zones 2 and 3, where snow cover is abundant.

Good Neighbors

Because the bloom times of astilbes vary widely, you can combine different types for a continuously blooming garden. Choose other moisture-loving plants, such as lady's-mantle (*Alchemilla mollis*), Siberian iris (*Iris sibirica*), bigleaf ligularia (*Ligularia dentata*), and meadow rues (*Thalictrum* spp.), for companions.

Problems and Solutions

Astilbe foliage can turn brown along the edges or even die back entirely in dry conditions. The plants will likely sprout again the fol-

lowing year, but this time either make sure
you keep them moist or move them to
more appropriate conditions. Japanese beetles will also munch on the foliage: See page
54 for some possible treatments.

Top Performer

Astilbe × *arendsii* (hybrid astilbe): Some authorities separate *A.* × *arendsii*, *A.* × *hybrida*,
and *A. japonica* hybrids as three different
hybrid species, but I fail to see any major
difference and have lumped them together
here for simplicity. The hybrid astilbe is
available in a wide range of colors, from
white and cream through all shades of pink
and red, plus magenta. Most have green
leaves, but some have attractive bronze foliage instead. 'Amethyst' is an upright cultivar with violet-rose flowers. 'Bressingham
Beauty' is a midseason pink. 'Fanal' is an
early red with dark bronze leaves. 'Weisse
Gloria' (also called 'White Gloria') is a
compact early bloomer. Height: 2 to 4 feet (60 to 120 cm). Spread:
24 to 30 inches (60 to 75 cm). USDA Plant Hardiness Zones 4 to 9;
AHS Heat Zones 8 to 2.

Hybrid astilbe
(*Astilbe* × *arendsii*)

Larry's Garden Notes

If you're the slightest bit patient,
you can fill in an entire bed with
astilbes in relatively short order,
using just one original plant.
Simply grow the plant for one
full season in your garden, then
dig it up and divide it. Even the
smallest section of root will do
as long as it has at least one
eye. You may get nearly a
dozen plants from that one
plant. You can also cut the
longer roots into sections and
root those as well.

More Recommended Astilbes

Astilbe chinensis (Chinese astilbe): Chinese astilbe differs from the hybrid astilbe in its more deeply cut, dense, lacy foliage, late-summer
blooming period, and generally smaller size. Chinese astilbe also
tends to be more drought-tolerant than most. There are some hybrids that maintain a distinct resemblance to Chinese astilbe. 'Finale'
is bright pink. 'Pumila' has rose-purple flowers. Height: 10 to 24
inches (25 to 60 cm). Spread: 1 to 2 feet (30 to 60 cm). USDA Plant
Hardiness Zones 4 to 9; AHS Heat Zones 8 to 2.

A. simplicifolia (star astilbe): In general, these are low-growing,
dense plants with particularly shiny leaves. They produce loose clusters of starlike flowers, often late in the summer, although some hybrids do bloom in midsummer. 'Sprite', with dark bronzy green
leaves and airy shell pink flowers, is the most popular cultivar.
Height: 10 to 18 inches (25 to 45 cm). Spread: 2 feet (60 cm). USDA
Plant Hardiness Zones 4 to 9; AHS Heat Zones 8 to 2.

Astrantia

Masterwort

Masterworts are delicate-looking plants with a tough-as-nails constitution. They form a thick clump of medium green, deeply cut, maplelike leaves that are attractive in their own right, but the blooms are even nicer. The tiny flowers are arranged in a form called an umbel that looks like a small pincushion, and each flowerstalk is topped by an open dome composed of several of these umbels. The umbels are surrounded by a spiky collar of petal-like leaves called bracts. The total effect is that of a very sophisticated Queen-Anne's-lace.

Plant Profile

ASTRANTIA
ah-STRAN-she-uh

- ■ **Bloom Color:** Pink, red, greenish white, or white

- ■ **Bloom Time:** Varies by species; see individual listings

- ■ **Length of Bloom:** 6 to 12 weeks

- ■ **Height:** Varies by species; see individual listings

- ■ **Spread:** 18 to 24 inches (45 to 60 cm)

- ■ **Garden Uses:** Cut flower garden, edging, groundcover, mass planting, mixed border, woodland garden; in wet areas; attracts butterflies

- ■ **Light Preference:** Sun to partial shade

- ■ **Soil Preference:** Moist, humus-rich soil

- ■ **Best Way to Propagate:** Divide in spring or fall

- ■ **USDA Plant Hardiness Zones:** 4 to 9

- ■ **AHS Heat Zones:** 7 to 1

Growing Tips

Masterworts grow well in open woods, filtered sunlight, or sunny spots with afternoon shade. They also appreciate cool conditions, another good reason not to expose them to full sun in most areas. In cool-summer areas, though, full sun is just fine. Like many other woodland natives, masterworts like moist soil. They'll tolerate drier conditions in midsummer, but they are at their best in constantly moist soil. Using an organic mulch to keep the soil both moist *and* cool is a good idea.

Masterworts spread where they are happy, but they aren't aggressive: If there's space available, they simply fill it in. They spread by division from the base, by creeping underground stems, and also by seed. You'll especially appreciate their capacity to fill in empty spaces in woodland gardens where establishing plants is so difficult. Just plant a few masterworts on the outer fringe, where the soil is easier to dig, and let the colony work its way inward.

Of course, masterworts' spreading habit makes multiplication a snap: Just dig up offsets and replant them in early spring or fall. Or you can divide the plant itself into sections. Masterworts grow easily from seed and will often self-sow, but the resulting plants are variable. If you want to stick to a specific color or cultivar, deadhead your plants as they near the end of their flowering season to prevent self-sowing. Or let them self-sow and enjoy the full color palette.

Good Neighbors

Planted in midday shade with ample moisture, white or soft pink masterworts make great mixers. Combine them with other moisture lovers, including aconites (*Aconitum* spp.), lady's-mantle (*Alchemilla mollis*), Siberian bugloss (*Brunnera macrophylla*), hostas, and ferns. For mid-season interest, drop in some Turk's-cap lilies (*Lilium martagon*).

Problems and Solutions

Masterworts are happily untroubled by any major pest or disease problems.

Top Performer

Astrantia major (great masterwort): All the masterworts are wonderful plants, but great masterwort wins—simply because it is the most widely available species.

Great masterwort is a modestly sized plant that forms a thick clump nicely topped off with flowers. The species produces greenish white flowers, surrounded by white bracts often tipped with green, from early to late summer. This is much more attractive than it sounds, but if the green element worries you, many cultivars come in shades of pink or red or have at least a pinkish tinge. 'Rosea' includes various shades of pink and red. 'Rosensymphonie' (also called 'Rose Symphony') is a great choice, with silvery bracts and rosy pink blooms. *A. major* ssp. *involucrata* 'Shaggy' (also called 'Margery Fish') has much longer bracts that are white with green tips; they surround pale pink blooms. 'Sunningdale Variegated' has wide yellow to cream margins around pale green maplelike leaves. The older leaves fade to green in the summer, but new ones just keep on coming. Did I mention it has pink-tinged bracts? Height: 2 to 3 feet (60 to 90 cm). Spread: 18 to 24 inches (45 to 60 cm). USDA Plant Hardiness Zones 4 to 9; AHS Heat Zones 7 to 1.

More Recommended Masterworts

Astrantia carniolica (lesser masterwort): Compared to great masterwort (*A. major*), lesser masterwort has more finely divided leaves and also shorter bracts. The species has greenish white to pink blooms from early to late summer, but 'Rubra', a dark red with silvery highlights, is the most available cultivar. Height: 12 to 18 inches (30 to 45 cm). Spread: 18 to 24 inches (45 to 60 cm). USDA Plant Hardiness Zones 4 to 9; AHS Heat Zones 7 to 1.

Native to the woods' edge in Europe, 'Rubra' great masterwort (*Astrantia major* 'Rubra') will spread at a comfortable rate where it's happy. Masterworts will gracefully fill the spaces in a woodland garden without outcompeting other woodland species.

Brunnera

Brunnera, Siberian bugloss

Here's a perennial that actually makes you wish you had *more* shade. When it first pops out of the ground in the spring, Siberian bugloss (*Brunnera macrophylla*) produces small, oblong, medium green leaves on wispy upright stems that branch into even thinner flowerstalks. The five-petaled blue flowers with yellow centers are miniscule but very abundant, covering the plant so thickly you can barely see the foliage. After flowering slows, the plant produces new heart-shaped leaves, and during the summer, the plant acts as an attractive foliage accent.

Plant Profile

BRUNNERA
BRUN-er-uh

- **Bloom Color:** Blue

- **Bloom Time:** Early to late spring

- **Length of Bloom:** 4 weeks or more

- **Height:** 12 to 18 inches (30 to 45 cm)

- **Spread:** 18 to 24 inches (45 to 60 cm)

- **Garden Uses:** Cut flower garden, edging, groundcover, mass planting, mixed border, specimen plant, woodland garden; in wet areas

- **Light Preference:** Sun to shade

- **Soil Preference:** Rich, evenly moist soil

- **Best Way to Propagate:** Divide in spring or fall

- **USDA Plant Hardiness Zones:** 3 to 9

- **AHS Heat Zones:** 9 to 3

Growing Tips

Siberian bugloss will grow in sun or shade but needs protection from the hot rays of the afternoon sun in summer, at least in hot-summer climates. Like so many shade lovers, it's most at home in cool, evenly moist or even wet soil and will thrive along a stream bed or near a pond. It can tolerate dry soil, too, as long as it's growing in shade, but it will go dormant if a drought persists for more than a few weeks. Mulching is a big help, especially in hot-summer areas, as it keeps the plant cooler. Siberian bugloss does amazingly well in the dense seasonal shade found under many deciduous trees as long as it gets plenty of light in spring. Truly deep shade is not ideal because the plants will tend to produce only foliage or to flower only very lightly.

Plan to multiply your Siberian bugloss plants occasionally because they're short-lived and prone to simply dying out for no particular reason after four or five years. Division is the easiest way to multiply Siberian bugloss, and fall is the best time to do it in all but the coldest climates (try early spring division there). You can also propagate Siberian bugloss by taking root cuttings.

Where it's happy, Siberian bugloss self-sows abundantly, and you can easily move extra plantlets to whatever spot you desire. You can also sow the seed yourself: Simply sprinkle it on the ground outdoors in late summer or fall and rake it in lightly. If you keep it moist, the seed may sprout in the fall or wait until spring, but in either case you will quickly have a small colony of new plants. Indoors, sow the seed in a moist medium, barely covering it, then refrigerate for a month. It will sprout afterward when exposed to normal indoor temperatures.

Good Neighbors

Combine Siberian bugloss with more delicately textured plants such as bleeding hearts (*Dicentra* spp.), ferns, and meadow rues (*Thalictrum* spp.). The bright yellow flowers and low-growing foliage of goldenstar (*Chrysogonum virginianum*) paired with Siberian bugloss's blue blooms would provide a nice spring sight. Or interplant Siberian bugloss with daffodil bulbs for another complementary color combination; the perennial's attractive foliage will help to hide the yellowing bulb foliage.

Problems and Solutions

Siberian bugloss doesn't have any particular insect or disease problems.

Top Performer

Brunnera macrophylla (Siberian bugloss): This is the only commonly grown species. The large 8-inch (20-cm), heart-shaped leaves form a round mound of foliage. Since Siberian bugloss is valuable as a foliage perennial as well as a shade bloomer, consider trying some of the truly lovely variegated cultivars. 'Dawson's White' (also called 'Variegata') is perhaps the most charming, with broad white to cream margins sometimes extending well into the center of the leaf. It is, however, a relatively delicate plant that burns in full sun, rots easily in excess shade, and needs steady moisture to thrive. If you find it just the right amount of partial shade and keep it damp, though, this plant will dazzle you! 'Hadspen Cream' is similar but has narrower creamy white borders and a tougher disposition, although it also prefers steady moisture. Finally, 'Langtrees' (also called 'Aluminum Spot') is totally different from the others, with silver spots just inside the leaf margin. It's a tough plant and will thrive anywhere the nonvariegated forms will grow. None of the variegated forms come true from seed and even root cuttings often result in all-green plants. The variegated forms are quite rare and expensive because you can only raise them slowly, a few plants at a time, through division.

The delicate, bright blue flowers of Siberian bugloss (*Brunnera macrophylla*) illuminate the garden in spring. Nestle it into an evenly moist location and its abundant blooms will be followed by healthy new heart-shaped foliage that will remain ornamental all summer long.

Cimicifuga

Cimicifuga, bugbane, cohosh

Cimicifugas form lacy clumps of deeply cut foliage, and mature plants have enough foliage to create shrublike impact in a shady garden. At summer's end, cimicifugas suddenly send up pencil-thin shoots of dense, fuzzy, white flowers, like rockets shooting for the sky. Although the individual flowers are of the "get out your magnifying glass" variety, the stretched-out bottlebrush look of the flowering spikes is uniquely beautiful.

Plant Profile

CIMICIFUGA
sih-mih-cih-FYU-guh

- **Bloom Color:** White

- **Bloom Time:** Varies by species; see individual listings

- **Length of Bloom:** 4 to 8 weeks

- **Height:** Varies by species; see individual listings

- **Spread:** Varies by species; see individual listings

- **Garden Uses:** Cut flower garden, specimen plant, woodland garden; at the back of beds and borders, in wet areas

- **Light Preference:** Full sun to deep shade

- **Soil Preference:** Humus-rich, moist soil

- **Best Way to Propagate:** Divide in spring or fall

- **USDA Plant Hardiness Zones:** Varies by species; see individual listings

- **AHS Heat Zones:** Varies by species; see individual listings

Growing Tips

"Plant 'em and leave 'em" is the proper attitude to take toward cimicifugas. They're slow-growing, fend-for-themselves perennials that don't need any care—not even staking. Cimicifugas will grow in almost any kind of shade, but they won't flower in the deepest shade. They'll also grow in full sun if conditions are moist. Once established (which can take several years), they'll tolerate drought, but they prefer steady moisture.

Cool conditions give the best results, all the more reason to keep cimicifugas in at least afternoon shade—and to mulch, mulch, mulch. Also, note that cimicifugas need some winter chill. There's not much use trying them if you can't supply them with at least a few weeks of near-freezing temperatures.

Cimicifugas are difficult to multiply. They have long taproots and hate being disturbed, but if you want to propagate your plants, your only choice is to divide them. Dig up established clumps carefully in the fall (early spring in cold-winter areas) and separate the crowns. Don't expect either the mother or children to react very well: You'll have to wait three to five years for either to bloom again.

Good Neighbors

You may want to keep cimicifugas in the background of your garden because a few types have an unpleasant, musky scent. Compatible companions include daylilies, hardy geraniums, hostas, and phlox (*Phlox divaricata* or *P. paniculata*). Dark-leaved cultivars, such as *Cimicifuga ramosa* 'Atropurpurea', look great with other plants that have purple foliage, such as 'Palace Purple' heuchera (*Heuchera micrantha* 'Palace Purple') and 'Husker Red' foxglove penstemon (*Penstemon digitalis* 'Husker Red').

Problems and Solutions

In the right environment, cimicifugas are basically trouble-free!

Top Performer

Cimicifuga racemosa (black snakeroot, black cohosh): Black snakeroot is perhaps the most charming species in this devastatingly charming genus. It's also one of the tallest, with narrow, bottlebrush-like spikes of creamy white flowers, often branching at the base, on wiry, lightly leaved stalks. The bloom time varies from midsummer to late summer or late summer to fall. Height: 6 to 8 feet (180 to 240 cm). Spread: 3 to 4 feet (90 to 120 cm). USDA Plant Hardiness Zones 3 to 9; AHS Heat Zones 8 to 1.

More Recommended Bugbanes

Cimicifuga ramosa (branched bugbane): This species looks very much like black snakeroot, except that branched bugbane has flowerstalks that branch more abundantly. Its bloom time varies from midsummer to late summer or late summer to fall. The dark-leaved cultivars are particularly prized. 'Atropurpurea' produces purple-flushed green leaves, while 'Brunette' bears bronze-purple leaves on smaller plants. The leaves of 'Hillside Black Beauty' are such a dark purple they appear black. Height: 6 to 8 feet (180 to 240 cm). Spread: 3 to 4 feet (90 to 120 cm). USDA Plant Hardiness Zones 3 to 9; AHS Heat Zones 10 to 1.

Think Twice: *C. simplex* (Kamchatka bugbane): Here, the Think Twice logo means you have to consider your local climate before buying the plant. Although hardy to USDA Zone 3, Kamchatka bugbane often blooms so late that even gardeners in Zone 5 scarcely have a chance to see it bloom. It needs a six month frost-free season, at the least, to bloom; seven months is even better. Kamchatka bugbane has lacy green foliage and shorter stems than most bugbanes, often with secondary flower spikes taller than the first. The flowers are, as usual, creamy white, but rather skunklike in scent. 'White Pearl' (also called 'Armleuchter') is the one most often grown. Height: 3 to 4 feet (90 to 120 cm). Spread: 2 to 3 feet (60 to 90 cm). USDA Plant Hardiness Zones 4 to 9; AHS Heat Zones 8 to 1.

Black snakeroot
(*Cimicifuga racemosa*)

Larry's Garden Notes

When you have a large area, a planting of *Cimicifuga* spp. will help draw the eye to a particular spot with its soft wands of white blossoms. Even in a less expansive setting, the arching vertical candles of flowers are perfect against green foliage. And when you plant cimicifugas at the back of a bed or border, its objectionable odor won't be noticeable.

Mertensia

Bluebells

Look quickly or you'll miss them—bluebells pop up in early spring, and their flowers are here and gone all too soon. But bluebells are so beautiful in bloom, most gardeners forgive the brevity of their display. The plants have smooth, blue-green, deeply veined leaves. Soon after the leaves appear, clusters of pink buds form on narrow, arching stalks, then the nodding buds open to display lavender-blue, trumpet-shaped flowers.

Plant Profile

MERTENSIA
mer-TEN-see-uh

- **Bloom Color:** Lavender-blue
- **Bloom Time:** Early spring to midspring
- **Length of Bloom:** 2 to 3 weeks
- **Height:** 18 to 24 inches (45 to 60 cm)
- **Spread:** 1 foot (30 cm)
- **Garden Uses:** Rock garden, woodland garden
- **Light Preference:** Full sun to deep shade
- **Soil Preference:** Fertile, humus-rich soil that's moist in spring
- **Best Way to Propagate:** Sow seed in summer
- **USDA Plant Hardiness Zones:** 3 to 9
- **AHS Heat Zones:** 8 to 1

Growing Tips

Bluebells are masters of seasonal shade. Their life cycle revolves around unfurling their leaves as early as possible in the spring to take advantage of any sun filtering through the branches of over-hanging deciduous trees. After they bloom, though, bluebells quickly bid farewell, turn yellow, and disappear from sight. Their foliage sometimes lasts most of the summer in truly cool-summer areas, but elsewhere, it's already a memory by late June or early July.

Even when dormant, though, bluebells can't withstand hot, dry summer soil. They enjoy cool, mostly moist conditions in their native eastern North American forests, and their fleshy roots won't take the heat and dryness of a full-sun location. So you can grow them easily in full to partial shade, but full sun is only suitable in areas with very cool summers.

Where bluebells are happy, they'll spread on their own, with colonies slowly increasing through offsets and, more quickly, self-seeding. And it's just as well they handle this themselves, as they are *very* reluctant to let humans help them out. The easiest way to do so (and I hesitate to use the word "easy") is by sowing fresh seed in early summer. Do so outdoors: You'll find it too difficult to provide the cool temperatures and winter cold they need inside. Sow them directly on the ground, just covering the seeds, under the same conditions the adult plants like: filtered to full spring sun; summer shade; and cool, moist soil. You can also sow them in flats placed in a shady spot and kept moist. They usually sprout as temperatures become cooler in the fall, go dormant in the winter, then sprout again the following spring. By the time they go dormant the following summer, they'll be large enough to transplant, but don't expect any bloom until their third year of growth at the earliest.

Bluebells dislike transplanting, and it's difficult to divide them without damaging them. Ideally you should only do so when your plants have formed a small colony and you can afford to spare a few. Dig and replant them carefully as they go dormant. I find if I try digging up a clump of about five plants, I'll usually succeed in getting at least the center plants to survive.

Good Neighbors

For a simple but graceful combination, surround a clump of bluebells with wild ginger (*Asarum* spp.) and ferns. For color contrast, add white-flowered fringed bleeding heart (*Dicentra eximia* 'Alba'). Because they go dormant in the heat of summer, it's best to give bluebells neighbors that will fill in for them after they're gone: Late-blooming Japanese anemone (*Anemone* × *hybrida*), hardy begonia (*Begonia grandis*), or common toad lily (*Tricyrtis hirta*) will fill this role nicely. But be sure to leave enough space around each clump of bluebells so they can return, uncrowded, the following spring.

Problems and Solutions

When established in the cool, seasonally shady spots they love, bluebells rarely suffer from any problems.

Top Performer

Mertensia virginica (Virginia bluebells): Virginia bluebells is certainly a top performer among shade-blooming perennials, and it also happens to the only species of bluebells widely available in the United States and Canada. It offers pink buds that open into trumpet-shaped blue flowers borne in one-sided clusters of 5 to 20 flowers in early spring. If you wish, you can grow the white ('Alba') or pink ('Rubra') cultivars—but the blue of the species is the favorite of most gardeners.

Virginia bluebells
(*Mertensia virginica*)

Smart Substitutes

A distant bluebell relative, borage (*Borago officinalis*) is usually considered a culinary herb—its flowers and leaves have a cucumber-like flavor. But borage can replace bluebells in sunnier, warmer locales where bluebells simply won't thrive. A fast-growing, self-sowing annual, it sprouts quickly in the spring and produces star-shaped blue flowers in great abundance throughout the summer. Sow seeds directly in the garden, either in early spring or fall. Height: 12 to 36 inches (30 to 90 cm). Spread: 18 inches (45 cm). USDA Plant Hardiness Zones: annual. AHS Heat Zones 11 to 1.

Polygonatum

Solomon's seal

While Solomon's seals have nice enough flowers, their blooms are not their most striking feature. The tubular, creamy white flowers dangle *under* the stems, so they're easy to miss. No, it's arching stems that make Solomon's seal so interesting. The stems arch outward and slightly down at the tip, and the top half of each is clothed in smooth, medium green, broadly lance-shaped leaves that alternate along the sides. Plus, the entire plant turns bright yellow in fall in a beautiful farewell-to-summer display.

Plant Profile

POLYGONATUM
poe-lig-oh-NAY-tum

- **Bloom Color:** White tipped with green
- **Bloom Time:** Spring to early summer
- **Length of Bloom:** 2 to 3 weeks
- **Height:** Varies by species; see individual listings
- **Spread:** 1 to 2 feet (30 to 60 cm)
- **Garden Uses:** Containers, cut flower garden, edging, groundcover, mass planting, mixed border, rock garden, woodland garden; at the back of beds and borders; in wet areas
- **Light Preference:** Partial to full shade
- **Soil Preference:** Average, moist to somewhat dry soil
- **Best Way to Propagate:** Divide in spring or fall
- **USDA Plant Hardiness Zones:** 3 to 9
- **AHS Heat Zones:** 9 to 1

Growing Tips

Solomon's seals are shade plants extraordinaire. They slowly form huge colonies in even the darkest corners of the garden. Indeed, they'll only tolerate sun in climates with very cool summers.

Provide shade and relatively cool conditions, and you can grow Solomon's seals in just about any soil. They prefer moist conditions and humus-rich soil but will even tolerate dry, stony soil; they'll need thorough watering the first few years to become established.

Solomon's seals never need dividing, and since they're slow-growing, you'll have to wait several years before colonies are big enough to dig and divide for propagation purposes. You can also dig out offsets from around the edges of mature colonies. If you're in a hurry to multiply Solomon's seals, you can dig up the rhizomes (underground stems) each year and divide them, but this doesn't give the mother plant much chance to develop. If you try this approach, you can cut the rhizomes into pieces to produce even more plants, as long as each section has one bud.

Solomon's seals seeds can take up to 18 months to sprout! Harvest the seeds in fall by picking the berries and removing the dark flesh from around the seeds. Plant seed outdoors immediately in a moist, shady spot, just barely covering it.

Good Neighbors

For a successful shade garden, try combining Solomon's seals with Siberian bugloss (*Brunnera macrophylla*), golden scaled male fern (*Dryopteris affinis*), stinking hellebore (*Helleborus foetidus*), and hostas. Solomon's seals also complement more colorful woodland plants, such as bleeding hearts (*Dicentra* spp.) and Allegheny foamflower (*Tiarella cordifolia*).

Problems and Solutions

Slugs can chew holes in the leaves, but the damage is rarely serious; see the control tips on page 55. Other than these slimy pests, Solomon's seals are tough plants with no particular problems.

Top Performer

Polygonatum odoratum (fragrant Solomon's seal): Fragrant Solomon's seal stands out not because of its appearance, but because of the heady, lilylike perfume of its creamy white flowers, tipped with yellow-green. The blooms are borne singly or in pairs from spring to early summer. 'Variegatum', a delicately variegated cultivar, is my real choice for top performer. Its light green leaves are broadly edged in cream, and the result lights up the darkest, shadiest garden like a glowing candle. Height: 18 to 24 inches (45 to 60 cm). Spread: 1 to 2 feet (30 to 60 cm). USDA Plant Hardiness Zones 3 to 9; AHS Heat Zones 9 to 1.

'Variegatum' fragrant Solomon's seal (*Polygonatum odoratum* 'Variegatum')

More Recommended Solomon's Seals

Polygonatum biflorum (small Solomon's seal): Native to the woodlands of eastern North America, this species varies widely in size. The botanical name implies that it produces two flowers per leaf joint, which is usually true, but it can also bear three or four of the greenish white blossoms at each joint from spring to early summer. Height: 1 to 3 feet (30 to 90 cm). Spread: 1 to 2 feet (30 to 60 cm). USDA Plant Hardiness Zones 3 to 9; AHS Heat Zones 9 to 1.

P. × *hybridum* (common Solomon's seal): In the retail nursery trade, this plant is often confused with fragrant Solomon's seal (*P. odoratum*), which is one of its parents, and it is frequently sold as *P. multiflorum*, which is its other parent. The all-green form is about the same as fragrant Solomon's seal, but its variegated cultivar 'Striatum' has white stripes in the leaves (*P. odoratum* 'Variegatum' leaves just have white borders). Common Solomon's seal usually produces clusters of four creamy white, green-tipped blossoms per leaf joint from spring to early summer. Height: 18 to 24 inches (45 to 60 cm). Spread: 1 to 2 feet (30 to 60 cm). USDA Plant Hardiness Zones 3 to 9; AHS Heat Zones 9 to 1.

Kissing Cousins

When it's not blooming or bearing fruit, you can scarcely tell false Solomon's seal (*Smilacina racemosa*) from Solomon's seal (*Polygonatum odoratum*) because their arching stems and smooth, lance-shaped leaves are almost identical. But when the plants bloom, you won't get them confused. False Solomon's seal produces its dense, frothy clusters of white flowers at the ends of the stems. The blooms are followed by clusters of numerous red berries, much different from the occasional blue-black ones of Solomon's seal. Height: 24 to 36 inches (60 to 90 cm). Spread: 36 to 48 inches (90 to 120 cm). USDA Plant Hardiness Zones 3 to 9; AHS Heat Zones 7 to 1.

Pulmonaria

Pulmonaria, lungwort, Bethlehem sage

If you haven't paid attention to pulmonarias in a while, take a second look! These low-growing shade plants have undergone a radical transformation because of plant breeding efforts. In early spring, pulmonarias produce arching clusters of tubular flowers that are usually pink in bud, opening to blue or purple. That hasn't changed, but the leaves sure have. While most pulmonarias used to have fairly ordinary rosettes of hairy green leaves, now there's a range of hybrids with leaves that are spotted or highly marbled with white or silver, giving the plants a much longer season of interest.

Plant Profile

PULMONARIA
puhl-muhn-AIR-ee-uh

- **Bloom Color:** Blue, pink, purple, or white
- **Bloom Time:** Early to late spring
- **Length of Bloom:** 3 or 4 weeks
- **Height:** 10 to 18 inches (25 to 45 cm)
- **Spread:** 1 to 2 feet (30 to 60 cm)
- **Garden Uses:** Edging, groundcover, mass planting, mixed border, rock garden, woodland garden; in wet areas
- **Light Preference:** Full sun to deep shade
- **Soil Preference:** Humus-rich, evenly moist soil
- **Best Way to Propagate:** Divide after flowering or in fall
- **USDA Plant Hardiness Zones:** Varies by species; see individual listings
- **AHS Heat Zones:** 8 to 1

Growing Tips

Pulmonarias will take just about anything you throw at them—from full sun to deep shade, and moist, humusy soils to dry, stony ones—and still bloom abundantly. But if you want their foliage to remain in top shape, you'll have to better meet their need for cool, moist growing conditions. Pulmonarias actually prefer shade to sun, even in cool-summer climates. They prefer partial shade and soil that's evenly moist but not wet, although good drainage is still vital, especially in winter. And because cool temperatures are a must, the combination of shade and a good organic mulch is a definite plus in hot-summer climates.

Pulmonarias spread only slowly through creeping roots and easily stay within bounds. You can leave them in place for years, but dividing overcrowded clumps every five or six years will help maintain abundant bloom.

Division after flowering or in fall is the fast and easy way to multiply pulmonarias, but you can also propagate them through seed, although the cultivars won't come true. Sow indoors in late winter or outdoors in early spring, just barely covering the seed.

Good Neighbors

The interesting spotting on most pulmonaria foliage makes it an ideal candidate for the front of the shade garden border. Choose companions with contrasting forms, such as astilbes, bleeding hearts (*Dicentra* spp.), ferns, and crested iris (*Iris cristata*).

Problems and Solutions

In hot, humid climates, powdery mildew can cause dusty gray patches on some pulmonarias. Try moving them to better-ventilated spots or areas where they get some morning sun to help dry off dew faster because the disease spreads quickly on moist foliage.

Top Performer

Pulmonaria saccharata (Bethlehem sage): Most modern pulmonarias are actually hybrids of several species, but for the sake of convenience I've grouped them under the name *P. saccharata*. Their botanical name means "sugar-coated," and the irregular silvery gray mottling certainly could be mistaken for a sugary frosting. The species produces pink flower buds that open into trumpet-shaped, purple to bluish purple flowers in early to late spring, but the numerous selections now include plants with white and pink flowers. 'Berries and Cream' is my favorite pink-blooming plant, with ruffled leaves that have a silver center and green edges. 'Excalibur' has rosy pink blooms, too, but they pale in comparison to its brilliant silver foliage edged in green. 'Mrs. Moon' is a sentimental favorite; she was the first hybrid pulmonaria I ever grew. Her leaves are heavily spotted in silver and her bright pink buds open to a lovely pale blue. 'Roy Davidson' has baby pink buds opening to pale blue flowers and rather narrow forest green leaves heavily spotted in silver. The foliage of 'Sissinghurst White' is only moderately speckled, but the flowers are white, a rare color among pulmonarias. Height: 10 to 18 inches (25 to 45 cm). Spread: 1 to 2 feet (30 to 60 cm). USDA Plant Hardiness Zones 3 to 9; AHS Heat Zones 8 to 1.

More Recommended Pulmonarias

Pulmonaria angustifolia (blue lungwort): Blue lungwort has the brightest flowers of all pulmonarias. The pink buds open into masses of large, brilliant gentian-blue flowers from early to late spring: They'll knock your socks off. The leaves are long, narrow, and unspotted. This is a good selection in areas where powdery mildew is a problem because this species seems quite resistant to the disease. There aren't many cultivars, but 'Munstead Blue', a large plant with large blue flowers, is a nice choice. Height: 10 to 18 inches (25 to 30 cm). Spread: 1 to 2 feet (30 to 60 cm). USDA Plant Hardiness Zones 2 to 9; AHS Heat Zones 8 to 1.

Bethlehem sage
(*Pulmonaria saccharata*)

Around the World with Pulmonarias

Pulmonaria is certainly not a new kid on my block. In Quebec City, common lungwort (*Pulmonaria officinalis*), a European native, grows everywhere. Most likely it had been grown as a medicinal plant by someone and had escaped from culture long ago. I never saw it as anything but a pretty weed until I saw a planting of longleaf lungwort (*Pulmonaria longifolia*) spotted with brilliant silver in a shady nook at Savill Garden (just a short hike from Queen Elizabeth's summer cottage, Windsor Castle). From then on, I've planted pulmonarias profusely!

Tiarella

Foamflower

Stars of woodland wildflower gardens, foamflowers—especially some of the colorful hybrids—also look great in many shady perennial gardens. Foamflowers are clump-forming perennials with lobed, usually heart-shaped, somewhat hairy leaves, often with a velvety texture. The leaves turn red or yellow in the fall but last through the winter, so foamflowers offer all-season color. In spring they produce upright, airy spikes of small, fuzzy-looking flowers. The flowers are usually white, but they are often pink in bud and may have a pink tinge when they open as well.

Plant Profile

TIARELLA
tee-uh-REL-uh

- **Bloom Color:** Pink or white
- **Bloom Time:** Late spring to midsummer
- **Length of Bloom:** 6 weeks
- **Height:** 6 to 12 inches (15 to 30 cm)
- **Spread:** 1 foot (30 cm)
- **Garden Uses:** Edging, groundcover, mass planting, mixed border, rock garden, woodland garden
- **Light Preference:** Partial to deep shade
- **Soil Preference:** Rich, moist but well-drained, acid soil
- **Best Way to Propagate:** Divide in early spring
- **USDA Plant Hardiness Zones:** 3 to 9
- **AHS Heat Zones:** 7 to 1

Growing Tips

Foamflowers are native to deciduous forests, so they're no strangers to shade. They make a wonderful groundcover even in deep shade and seem to settle into even the most root-infested of forested areas with great ease. But there's dry shade and there's moist shade, and foamflowers prefer the moist kind. In dry shade, foamflowers remain open and scrawny; in moister shade, they fill in nicely and take on a thick, luxuriant appearance. In spite of their love for shade, though, they need good drainage; winter wet, especially, can be fatal.

A carpet of fallen leaves makes for happy foamflowers, but if you can't supply that, they'll do fine in the horticultural equivalent: a yearly application of mulch, about 2 inches (5 cm) deep. Both leaves and mulch help acidify the soil, something foamflowers also appreciate.

Division—ideally in early spring or in fall—is the main way of propagating foamflowers. If possible, try not to bother the main clump, as established foamflowers don't like having their roots disturbed. Just dig up an offset or two and replant elsewhere in moist shade. You can also grow foamflowers from seed sown outdoors immediately after harvest (it ripens in summer) in a shady spot without covering the tiny seeds. Keep the soil moist until germination the following spring. You can also start seed indoors by sowing the seed, then refrigerating the container for several weeks before exposing it to cool temperatures, about 50°F (10°C).

Good Neighbors

Useful as a groundcover, foamflowers look good in and out of bloom planted in masses in the woodland garden. Combine them with astilbes, hellebores (*Helleborus* spp.), hostas, ferns, woodland phlox (*Phlox divaricata*), and other shade-loving plants for a low-care landscape.

Problems and Solutions

Foamflowers are not particularly subject to pests and diseases.

Top Performer

Tiarella cordifolia (Allegheny foamflower): Allegheny foamflower has long, creeping, underground stems that allow it to rapidly spread into new territory. It's not really weedy, as it doesn't push out other plants and besides, in the kind of deep shade it likes, anything green is usually welcome by a gardener. This spreading nature makes for a great groundcover. Its leaves can be all green or velvety and marked with burgundy along the center veins. There's a wide range of hybrid foamflowers, often with attractively cut leaves and dark mottling. I consider all of them good plants, but two of my favorites are 'Skeleton Key', with white flowers and much more deeply cut leaves than the species and a very dark, almost black center; and 'Eco Red Heart' with red-centered, red-veined, heart-shaped leaves and pink flowers. Height: 6 to 12 inches (15 to 30 cm). Spread: 1 foot (30 cm). USDA Plant Hardiness Zones 3 to 9; AHS Heat Zones 7 to 1.

More Recommended Foamflowers

Tiarella cordifolia var. *collina* (Wherry's foamflower): Wherry's foamflower is a variety of Allegheny foamflower that's often sold as *T. wherryi*. The two foamflowers are very similar, but Wherry's foamflower doesn't produce creeping stems—it develops into dense clumps instead. The leaves of this variety are especially velvety and are often marked with dark burgundy. Its flowers tend more toward pink than those of Allegheny foamflower. Height: 6 to 12 inches (15 to 30 cm). Spread: 6 inches (15 cm). USDA Plant Hardiness Zones 3 to 9; AHS Heat Zones 7 to 1.

Allegheny foamflower (*Tiarella cordifolia*)

Kissing Cousins

White foamy bells (× *Heucherella alba*), a cross between *Heuchera* × *brizoides* and *Tiarella cordifolia* var. *collina*, is a lovely plant with leaves much like those of foamflowers (*Tiarella* spp.). The flowers are later blooming and somewhat more substantial. The vigorous plants bloom for a long time, starting in early summer and lasting for eight weeks or more. 'Bridget Bloom', the most common cultivar, has shell pink blooms. 'Rosalie' has purple-centered leaves and deep pink blooms. Height: 12 to 18 inches (30 to 45 cm). Spread: 1 foot (30 cm). USDA Plant Hardiness Zones 3 to 9; AHS Heat Zones 7 to 1.

Trillium

Trillium, wakerobin

The name trillium means "three" and with trilliums, almost every part of the plant comes in threes. Mature plants produce three leaves in spring, then continue on to produce three green petal-like leaves called sepals that arch back to reveal a flower with three large, pointed petals, sitting either just atop the leaves or a short length of stem above them. The flower can be upright, nodding, or drooping. It all sounds deceptively simple, but the effect is often magical.

Plant Profile

TRILLIUM
TRIL-ee-um

- **Bloom Color:** Maroon, pink, deep red, white, or yellow
- **Bloom Time:** Early spring
- **Length of Bloom:** 2 to 3 weeks
- **Height:** Varies by species; see individual listings
- **Spread:** Varies by species; see individual listings
- **Garden Uses:** Mass planting, mixed border, specimen plant, woodland garden
- **Light Preference:** Partial to full shade
- **Soil Preference:** Rich, moist but well-drained, acid soil
- **Best Way to Propagate:** Divide in early spring or fall
- **USDA Plant Hardiness Zones:** Varies by species; see individual listings
- **AHS Heat Zones:** 8 to 1

Growing Tips

Trilliums are native to cool, wooded areas and thrive in crumbly, humus-rich soil like that found in natural woodlands. They'll do best when grown in these same conditions in the home garden, and you can create this environment by mulching your trilliums with chopped leaves or other organic materials. Trilliums are ideal for that shady, undisturbed nook where some leaf litter is already present, but if you're just starting a shade garden and suspect your soil is more litter than leaf, you might want to incorporate plenty of compost: Half soil and half compost is just about right.

Trilliums have underground stems that store energy for the following year's growth and bloom. After blooming, the foliage hangs around for about two months (sometimes longer in cool-summer areas) and brown to reddish fruit may form, but then the plant goes entirely summer-dormant.

Trilliums hate being disturbed and don't need division, ever. You can, however, divide established colonies if you're careful. One method is to carefully dig up a colony in very early spring, just as the leaves start to appear, and separate individual plants for replanting. A second, less risky method is to mark their spot in the spring, then dig up, separate, and replant the rhizomes when they're dormant in fall.

As for growing from seed—well, it *is* done, mostly by Mother Nature. The easiest way is to harvest fresh seed in summer, extracting it from the berries just as the leaves begin to yellow, and to plant it without delay, without cover, outdoors in humusy soil. Some may germinate the first year, others the second or third.

Warning: Although trilliums may seem abundant in woodlands in your area, keep in mind that they are very fragile plants, and they don't adapt well to being transplanted from the wild. Collectors have overharvested trilliums on a massive scale, and wild trilliums have now disappeared from many of their native environments. So never buy a trillium unless you're sure it was nursery-propagated, not wild-collected. The good news is that trilliums are now grown commercially on a large scale, so there's no reason for wild-collecting. Many garden centers now guarantee that they sell only nursery-grown stock, so ask before you buy.

Good Neighbors

Trilliums are choice specimens for a woodland garden. For companions, consider the well-behaved Jack-in-the-pulpit (*Arisaema triphyllum*), crested iris (*Iris cristata*), and other noncompetitive woodland beauties.

Problems and Solutions

Given the right growing conditions, trilliums are seldom bothered by pests or diseases.

Great white trillium
(*Trillium grandiflorum*)

Top Performer

Trillium grandiflorum (great white trillium, snow trillium, white wake-robin): This trillium is the star of any woodland garden, with its large, 2- to 3-inch (5 to 8 cm), slightly nodding blooms held well above smooth, wavy, dark green leaves from early spring to midspring. The waxy and white flowers age to bright pink, then the petals dry up completely. The plant will then likely go entirely dormant within two months. Great white trillium tends to form dense colonies relatively quickly, so it will put on a striking display after only a few years. Height: 12 to 18 inches (30 to 45 cm). Spread: 1 to 2 feet (30 to 60 cm). USDA Plant Hardiness Zones 3 to 9; AHS Heat Zones 8 to 1.

More Recommended Trilliums

Trillium sessile (toad trillium, toadshade): Unlike many other trillium species, toad trillium produces perfectly upright, fragrant flowers that sit right on the top of the whorl of leaves from early spring to midspring. But to be honest, you'll grow this species more for the wonderful maroon and green mottling of its leaves than its narrow, lance-shaped maroon petals. Height: 6 to 12 inches (15 to 30 cm). Spread: 9 to 12 inches (23 to 30 cm). USDA Plant Hardiness Zones 4 to 9; AHS Heat Zones 8 to 1.

Larry's Garden Notes

If you're expecting your small patch of trilliums to multiply itself into a luxuriant groundcover, it will happen (eventually) under ideal conditions because they spread by underground stems called rhizomes. But don't depend on seedlings to increase your trillium patch. Trilliums seed usually takes 2 or more years to germinate, and, depending on the variety, the seedlings can take from 5 to 15 years to flower! The trick is to plant trilliums in sufficient numbers so that they'll make an impact in a relatively short time.

Uvularia

Merrybells, bellwort

Merrybells offer great beauty, but they don't hit you over the head with blazing color to get your attention. You can walk by them without noticing them, but if you stop and look closely, you'll discover that they're absolutely gorgeous. Merrybells produce upright stems that arch at the tip. The lance-shaped leaves are smooth and bright green with distinct veins. In midspring, dangling flowers appear at the joints where the upper leaves meet the stem. The yellow petals unravel from a twisted bud and never quite straighten themselves out.

Plant Profile

UVULARIA
you-view-LAH-ree-uh

- **Bloom Color:** Yellow
- **Bloom Time:** Spring
- **Length of Bloom:** 2 to 3 weeks
- **Height:** Varies by species; see individual listings
- **Spread:** 12 to 18 inches (30 to 45 cm)
- **Garden Uses:** Mass planting, mixed border, woodland garden
- **Light Preference:** Partial to deep shade
- **Soil Preference:** Humus-rich, moist, slightly acid soil
- **Best Way to Propagate:** Divide in fall
- **USDA Plant Hardiness Zones:** 3 to 9
- **AHS Heat Zones:** 9 to 1

Growing Tips

Place these easy-to-grow perennials in cool, moist shade and they'll do wonderfully; they'll also tolerate partial shade. Though merrybells prefer humus-rich soil, they'll tolerate average garden soil as long as you keep them cool and don't let them dry out completely. A good organic mulch is merrybells' best garden friend: Use it abundantly to keep the soil cool, moist, and crumbly.

Where they are happy, merrybells spread readily by creeping underground stems. You couldn't call them weedy, and it's easy to control them by digging out any sections that grow where they're not wanted. But you should keep an eye out in woodland gardens because merrybells can be somewhat aggressive and crowd out more mild-mannered plants. In these spots, consider planting them inside a barrier, such as a bottomless bucket sunk into the soil.

Multiply merrybells by division in fall, removing plants from the outside of the clump. If you need lots of material, you can dig up and divide the entire clump. However, merrybells look so much better when it fills in after a few years that digging it up for division always seems a shame. And division really only is a question of propagation: Merrybells can grow for decades in the same spot without declining in any way.

If you want to grow merrybells from seed, be sure your seed is fresh. Harvest it in late summer and sow it in a moist, shady spot outdoors, just barely covering it. It will sprout the following spring. If all you have is stored seed, just sow it outdoors as described above and wait. One fine spring day the seeds will eventually sprout.

Good Neighbors

Surround merrybells with wild ginger (*Asarum* spp.) to accentuate their early bloom. In a wooded area, add other woodland dwellers, such as baneberries (*Actaea* spp.), ferns, Solomon's seals (*Polygonatum* spp.), and trilliums. Or use clumps of merrybells in the shade border along with bleeding hearts (*Dicentra* spp.), epimediums, hostas, Allegheny foamflower (*Tiarella cordifolia*), and other shade-tolerant plants.

Problems and Solutions

Merrybells have no serious pest or disease problems.

Top Performer

Uvularia grandiflora (large-flowered bellwort, big merrybells): The leaves of large-flowered bellwort are perfoliate, meaning they wrap around the stem at their base. From midspring to early summer, this lovely perennial produces often-dense clusters of bright yellow flowers from 1 to 1½ inches (2.5 to 4 cm) long, with the distinctly twisted petals of all merrybells. The vibrant yellow and larger size of its flowers make this species the most striking of the merrybells. Height: 12 to 30 inches (30 to 75 cm). Spread: 12 to 18 inches (30 to 45 cm). USDA Plant Hardiness Zones 3 to 9; AHS Heat Zones 9 to 1.

More Recommended Bellworts

Uvularia perfoliata (perfoliate bellwort, wood merrybells, strawbell): Consider this a paler, smaller version of large-flowered bellwort. If you don't like strong yellows, the creamy lemon shade of perfoliate bellwort makes it a good choice. Height: 12 to 18 inches (30 to 45 cm). Spread: 12 to 18 inches (30 to 45 cm). USDA Plant Hardiness Zones 3 to 9; AHS Heat Zones 9 to 1.

U. sessilifolia (sessile bellwort, wild oats): This plant has a more open form, partly due to its thinner stems. Its leaves join but do not wrap around the stem at their base. Its flowers are even smaller and paler yellow than those of *U. perfoliata*. Height: 12 to 18 inches (30 to 45 cm). Spread: 12 to 18 inches (30 to 45 cm). USDA Plant Hardiness Zones 3 to 9; AHS Heat Zones 9 to 1.

Large-flowered bellwort (*Uvularia grandiflora*)

Kissing Cousins

🚩 Think Twice: Japanese fairy bells (*Disporum sessile*) are like merrybells (*Uvularia* spp.) with a more branching habit and straight, rather than twisted, bell-shaped flowers. Japanese fairy bells also produce berries, not seed capsules, and they tolerate dry soil. They may wander a bit more, too, so a root barrier is a necessity under many conditions. My top cultivar choice is 'Variegata'. Height: 9 to 24 inches (23 to 60 cm). Spread: 12 to 24 inches (30 to 60 cm). USDA Plant Hardiness Zones 4 to 9; AHS Heat Zones 8 to 1.

Viola

Violet, pansy, viola

Violets and pansies are reliable charmers for cool, shady gardens. Violets are spring bloomers with small flowers, often with well-separated petals arching outward like butterflies; their leaves can be heart-shaped or deeply cut and almost feathery. Pansies are mostly short-lived perennials, and their flowers have broad, rounded petals that often nearly overlap to form a circle. Their leaves are oval or lance-shaped, usually with scalloped margins.

Plant Profile

VIOLA
vy-OH-luh

- **Bloom Color:** Blue, peach, violet, white, and yellow
- **Bloom Time:** Varies by species; see individual listings
- **Length of Bloom:** Varies by species; see individual listings
- **Height:** Varies by species; see individual listings
- **Spread:** Varies by species; see individual listings
- **Garden Uses:** Container planting, edging, groundcover, mass planting, mixed border, rock garden, wall planting, woodland garden
- **Light Preference:** Full sun to deep shade
- **Soil Preference:** Cool, rich, well-drained, moist soil
- **Best Way to Propagate:** Varies by species; see individual listings
- **USDA Plant Hardiness Zones:** Varies by species; see individual listings
- **AHS Heat Zones:** 9 to 7

Growing Tips

Violets and pansies are popular, easy-to-grow perennials that do best in cooler climates—they languish in the heat. In hot-summer areas, they grow best in partially shaded spots or even in deep shade (although they do need some spring sun). In cooler areas, though, they'll easily grow in full sun even in the summer.

Violets and pansies will grow in most soils but prefer rich, moist, well-drained soil with lots of organic matter. In hot climates, mulching is almost essential to keep them alive.

Propagation methods for violets and pansies differ from one species to the next, but you can grow all of them from seed. The seed needs darkness to germinate and cool conditions to do well. Many species also self-sow prolifically. Most true violets grow either in tufts or have creeping stems that root as they grow: Both kinds are easy to multiply by division.

Good Neighbors

Violets and pansies make great groundcovers for moist, shady sites among clump-forming ferns, such as cinnamon fern (*Osmunda cinnamomea*) or Christmas fern (*Polystichum acrostichoides*), or with sturdy wildflowers, such as white baneberry (*Actaea alba*).

Problems and Solutions

Slugs and snails love violets and pansies, and these pests will make

FUN FACTS

Many of the true violets have a curious characteristic: They produce two very different kinds of flowers. Their lovely spring flowers are designed to attract and be pollinated by insects. But during the summer, violets produce hidden flowers that have no petals or just traces of petals. These flowers are called cleistogamous, from the Latin word for "cloistered"—that is, they self-pollinate without ever opening.

short work of the foliage if they're not quickly controlled. A tray of beer for the suds-guzzling mollusks will put a quick end to them, but keep refreshing the tray to catch new waves of the slimy pests. Diseases of various types, such as downy mildew and leaf spots, are occasional problems, but violets and pansies are tough plants: If diseases cause them to die out, they'll usually just sprout up again somewhere else.

Top Performer

Viola corsica, also called *V. bertolonii* (Corsican violet): Corsican violet actually belongs to the pansy group of *Viola*, with rounded flowers about 1 inch (3 cm) across, in a typical deep violet-blue with even darker markings. They bloom over a very long period, from shortly after snowmelt right into fall in cool-summer areas. In hotter climates, you can still expect flowers from spring until at least midsummer. And, contrary to the norm for pansies, Corsican violet is a long-lived plant. And although it's sometimes listed in catalogs as hardy only in USDA Zones 9 and 10, I've found it perfectly hardy in my Zone 3 garden. Height: 8 inches (20 cm). Spread: 1 foot (30 cm). USDA Plant Hardiness Zones 3 to 10; AHS Heat Zones 9 to 7.

More Recommended Violets

⭐ **Larry's Favorite:** *Viola odorata* (sweet violet): Although this violet can be invasive, it has such a sweet, intoxicating yet fleeting scent that I can't help but call it my favorite. Sweet violet has large, toothed, heart-shaped, dark green leaves. It spreads by long runners, moderately under average garden conditions but rapidly in rich, moist soil where it can become annoyingly weedy. It also self-sows quite readily, although mulching can help prevent that. The species has violet-colored, small-petaled flowers, but various single and double cultivars in other colors are also available. They include 'Czar', deep violet; 'White Czar', white; 'Queen Charlotte', dark blue; 'Royal Robe', purple-blue; and 'Rosina', rose-pink. Sweet violets primarily bloom from early to late spring, but many cultivars will rebloom lightly in late fall. Height: 2 to 10 inches (5 to 25 cm). Spread: 6 to 16 inches (15 to 40 cm). USDA Plant Hardiness Zones are variable, usually 5 to 9; AHS Heat Zones 9 to 7.

Sweet violet
(*Viola odorata*)

Larry's Garden Notes

Sweet violet (*Viola odorata*) depends on ants to disperse its seed. Seeds are tipped with tiny oil glands—a delicacy for ants. When the seed capsule is ready to open, the flowerstalks collapse onto the ground, where the seeds tumble out. The ants then carry them home where they can chew off the edible tips in safety, and the cast-off seeds are left to sprout nearby.

PERENNIALS FOR
Fabulous Foliage

Focusing on foliage instead of on flowers may seem like a strange idea, but there are good reasons to grow perennials strictly for their foliage. For one thing, some perennials have absolutely gorgeous foliage. Whether it's color, texture, shape, an intriguing silhouette, or just plain all-around good looks, foliage perennials have plenty to offer. I'm personally fascinated by ferns—their feathery, lacy fronds and subtle differences in color and texture give even cold-climate flowerbeds a touch of tropical spice. Plus, foliage perennials are easy to grow: There are no floppy flower stems to worry about staking and no deadheading to bother with. And because their beauty lies in long-lasting foliage, not short-lived flowers, foliage perennials give your garden a long season of interest.

Top Picks

◄ Distinctive foliage can become a focal point in your garden just as easily as a gorgeous bloom can. The gray and silver leaves of 'Silver Queen' white sage (*Artemisia ludoviciana* 'Silver Queen') are deliciously aromatic and perfectly suited to a walkway and patio garden.

Getting the Most from Foliage

All perennials have foliage, but for gardeners a foliage plant is a plant grown for something other than its flowers. In other words, a foliage plant is the opposite of a flowering plant. Some plants are naturally bloomless. Ferns, for example, never produce flowers of any sort. Most other foliage plants do have flowers, but they're so small that you may never notice them among the foliage.

What's Worth Looking For

For a perennial to be useful as a foliage plant alone, it's not enough for it to have pretty leaves. Strong foliage perennials have leaves that stay looking good all season and aren't prone to turning yellow or withering with age. They're also resistant to leaf diseases. The beauty of phlox flowers allows us to sometimes overlook the white coating of powdery mildew on the leaves, but with foliage plants, nothing less than perfection, in leaf and form, is required throughout the growing season.

Excellent foliage perennials have truly distinctive foliage, which may be due to their color, size, shape, texture, or a combination of all of these factors. They are able to tie together any color scheme in a perennial garden. Alumroot, for example, has foliage with such exotic colors that it could well be a rex begonia; painted fern combines a pleasing texture with interesting and unusual colors. And for soft, strokable foliage you just can't help fondling as you pass by, I don't think anything could beat the silvery, silky leaves of lamb's-ears.

Contrasting foliage textures make for exquisite perennial combinations, as this combination of fringed bleeding heart (*Dicentra eximia*) and Canadian wild ginger (*Asarum canadense*) clearly confirms.

Capitalizing on Color

While all of the factors above are important, having a variety of colors is key to a successful foliage garden. When you stop to think about it, you'll realize that perennial foliage is available in almost all the shades that perennial flowers are. If you don't believe me, read on!

Every shade of green. Leaves are green, right? But green can be dark or light, as with the attractive light green foliage of European wild ginger (*Asarum europaeum*), and it can range from yellowish or bluish to pure green. It's amazing what beauty you can create just by combining different greens of varying leaf shapes and textures. Some shade gardens offer nothing else, and many Japanese gardens basically offer nothing but green during the summer months.

Silver, gray, and white. Some leaves have a coating of white or reflective hairs. The leaf is in fact green, but the outer hairs reflect light in such a way that we see them as gray or silver and sometimes even as white, as with the silky smooth texture of lamb's-ears (*Stachys byzantina*) leaves. Most plants with this kind of coloration

are native to arid climates, rocky cliffs, or sandy beaches. The leaf hairs protect the leaf from the burning sun and help reduce water loss to evaporation.

Blue. Leaves that look blue are usually really green, but their leaf surfaces are coated with a waxy or powdery white substance called bloom. Blue oat grass (*Helictotrichon sempervirens*) is a good example—it's the bloom that makes the leaves look blue to our eyes. Bloom is also common on plants in hot, dry situations. It acts to reflect excess light and to reduce evaporation.

Bronze. Bronze leaves are really dark red or purple. They result when a plant produces an excess of red pigment. Many leaves contain red pigmentation, but it's usually hidden by the dominant green pigmentation of the leaf. When plants produce more than the usual quantity of red pigments, the red pigments combine with the green pigmentation to give the leaf a purplish or reddish tinge, as with 'Bressingham Bronze' small-flowered alumroot (*Heuchera micrantha* 'Bressingham Bronze'). This affects the plant's vigor in a positive way. In fact, red pigments can act like a sunscreen, helping the plant to survive in overly sunny locales.

Spots. White mottling is common in shade plants such as 'Pictum' Italian arum (*Arum italicum* 'Pictum'), and scientists theorize that the mottling provides camouflage against marauding pests. To an insect's eye, the spotting makes the leaf seem riddled with holes from previous insects; hungry pests may move on to a more luscious-looking plant. Many plants use color as guides to pollinating insects. Their leaves often have chevrons or veins pointing the way to hidden flowers. Or the upper leaves may change color to attract pollinators to hard-to-see flowers. In fact, colored leaves that attract insects are called bracts. The most famous bracts are those of the poinsettia: Its bright red "petals" are colored leaves, not petals, and the true flowers are the tiny yellow structures at the center of each cluster of bracts.

Variegation. Every now and then, nature makes a mistake and a plant appears with discolored leaves, usually lacking in the green pigment called chlorophyll. Variegated foliage occurs when just parts of each leaf lack chlorophyll. Lacking any chlorophyll, these parts allow the other pigments in the leaf to show through, resulting in patches of white or cream, or sometimes yellow or pink, on an otherwise normal leaf; a good example of variegation is variegated Japanese sedge (*Carex morrowii* 'Variegata'). Usually variegation occurs as a mutation, but there are some *viruses* that can cause a leaf to have a variegation as it grows.

Keeping Foliage at Its Finest

Taking care of a foliage garden is really fairly simple. If you like, you can occasionally patrol the garden and cut off leaves that seem to be losing their color or vigor, or that were torn by wind or a storm. Or, you can simply let nature take her course and enjoy the various colors and wonderful textures.

If you're growing foliage plants with variegated leaves, keep an eye out for the occasional shoot or offset that's entirely white or entirely green. If you spot any, remove them. The white shoots have no chlorophyll at all, so they can't produce any food supply; they'll just sap the plant's strength. Entirely green growths, on the other hand, have more chlorophyll than the variegated part and often outgrow and outcompete the variegated part. Eventually the green growth takes over, and you'll have lost your lovely variegated plant! Most variegation is stable once the leaf has formed, but some variegated leaves green up as time goes on, especially in hot-summer areas, and completely lose their variegation. In such cases, new growth will still be variegated. Such plants are variegated in the spring and plain green or nearly so in the summer.

14 More Foliage Perennials

There are some terrific foliage perennials described in other chapters, too. To decide whether a perennial qualified as a good foliage perennial, I just asked myself whether I would still grow the plant even if it never flowered. If the answer was yes, I added that plant to this list!

Artemisia

Artemisia, wormwood, sagebrush, mugwort

Artemisias are the most spectacular of the silver-gray foliage plants, producing upright subshrubs, rounded masses, or spreading mats of silver to gray-green foliage that's often deeply cut and feathery. Artemisias' foliage is so beautiful (and often so aromatic) that you won't mind how small and understated the flowers are. Artemisia flowers are often white or yellowish and either hidden among the leaves or borne on silvery spikes.

Plant Profile

ARTEMISIA
ar-teh-MEEZ-ee-uh

■ **Foliage Color:** Silver-gray

■ **Length of Foliage Season:** Spring through fall; spring through summer in hot, humid climates

■ **Height:** Varies by species; see individual listings

■ **Spread:** Varies by species; see individual listings

■ **Garden Uses:** Container planting, cut flower garden, edging, groundcover, mass planting, mixed border, rock garden, seasonal hedge, specimen plant; at the back of beds and borders

■ **Light Preference:** Full sun to partial shade

■ **Soil Preference:** Average, well-drained soil

■ **Best Way to Propagate:** Take cuttings in spring or early summer

■ **USDA Plant Hardiness Zones:** 3 to 8

■ **AHS Heat Zones:** Varies by species; see individual listings

Growing Tips

In the garden, artemisias prefer well-drained soil that's not overly rich. While they can adapt to a variety of climates, many artemisias find the hot, muggy air of the Southeast too stifling. In such conditions, try growing them in an exposed area with lots of air circulation. If they still flop open, or if they lose their lower leaves, prune them back to about 2 inches (5 cm) above the ground and they'll quickly fill in.

Think Twice: Some artemisias are well-behaved plants that stay exactly where you put them, while others are incorrigible wanderers. Always contain the spreading types by planting them in a root barrier at least 18 inches (45 cm) deep.

Artemisias need little care. If they die back in the center after a few years, just divide and replant them. Or dig out the dying center and fill in the resulting hole with soil: The plants will quickly fill in again. And prune them back harshly once a year, ideally in the spring, to leave room for new growth.

To multiply artemisias quickly, take stem cuttings. Or, if you have to divide or move your artemisias for some reason, divide them into as many sections as you want. Growing from seed is another possibility. Cultivars will not come true, however, and some hybrids are sterile, so you'll only be able to grow the species. Sow seed indoors 10 to 12 weeks before the last frost, pressing it into the growing mix without covering it; artemisias need light to germinate. Outdoors, sow in a bright, well-drained spot.

Good Neighbors

Silvers and grays add an appealing softness to stronger colors. Pair artemisias with showy perennials such as asters and purple coneflower (*Echinacea purpurea*) for a drought-tolerant mix. Or combine them with rose verbena (*Verbena canadensis*) and yuccas for an interesting study in contrasts.

Problems and Solutions

Rot is a major problem in moist soil; artemisias just blacken at the base and keel over. Prevent it by planting only in well-drained soil. Rust can cause leaf dieback at the base of the plant in hot, humid weather. Prune affected plants back to the ground when you first notice yellow spots on the lower leaves.

Top Performer

Artemisia ludoviciana (white sage, western mugwort): This is one artemisia you should always plant inside a good root barrier. If you control it from the start, it's a real pussycat. It produces clusters of silvery white flowers in late summer, but these blooms don't really add to the plant's already silvery effect. White sage merits its Top Performer rating because it will grow just about anywhere. 'Silver King' is a very silvery cultivar that turns reddish in fall. 'Silver Queen' is similar but with deeply cut leaf margins. 'Valerie Finnis' is very much like 'Silver King' but only about half the height. Height: 2 to 4 feet (60 to 120 cm). Spread: 24 to 30 inches (60 to 75 cm). USDA Plant Hardiness Zones 3 to 8; AHS Heat Zones 8 to 1.

More Recommended Artemisias

Artemisia schmidtiana (silvermound artemisia): This noninvasive artemisia forms a perfect dome of densely cut, silvery gray, silky-haired leaves with insignificant flowers. Popular in cool-summer areas, it's not nearly as well adapted to hot areas. To prevent plants from falling open from the center in midsummer, prune the plant back to about 2 inches (5 cm) high in early summer. There's considerable controversy as to whether the commonly sold form of this plant is the species (*A. schmidtiana*) or whether it's actually the cultivar 'Nana' or 'Silver Mound'. If you buy a plant labeled with any of these names, you'll likely be getting the same thing. Height: 6 to 12 inches (15 to 30 cm). Spread: 12 to 18 inches (30 to 45 cm). USDA Plant Hardiness Zones 3 to 8; AHS Heat Zones 8 to 3.

'Silver Queen' white sage
(*Artemisia ludoviciana* 'Silver Queen')

Larry's Garden Notes

Although people usually find wormwoods (*Artemisia* spp.) pleasantly scented, their perfumed leaves evolved as a defense mechanism, and insects and animals (even deer) will avoid wormwoods. Dogs and cats dislike some wormwoods, notably silvermound artemisia (*A. schmidtiana*) and southernwood (*A. abrotanum*), so planting them can help keep pets out of your garden. You can even dry the leaves of southernwood and place them in sachets to repel clothes moths.

Arum

Arum, lords and ladies

With its arrow-shaped, dark green leaves featuring prominent cream to gray veins, Italian arum (*Arum italicum*) will stop you in your tracks. In most areas, arum leaves appear in late fall and remain attractive through the winter. The flowers, each composed of an upright yellow stem called a spadix surrounded by a greenish white hood called a spathe, appear in spring. As summer approaches, the leaves and flowers yellow and die back, leaving the spadix, which becomes covered in bright orange-red berries.

Plant Profile

ARUM
AR-um

- **Foliage Color:** Dark green with silver hightlights

- **Length of Foliage Season:** Winter through summer

- **Height:** 12 to 20 inches (30 to 50 cm)

- **Spread:** 12 to 18 inches (30 to 45 cm)

- **Garden Uses:** Container planting, mixed border, specimen plant, woodland garden; in wet areas

- **Light Preference:** Sun or shade

- **Soil Preference:** Humus-rich, moist soil

- **Best Way to Propagate:** Divide in fall

- **USDA Plant Hardiness Zones:** 6 to 9

- **AHS Heat Zones:** 9 to 7

Growing Tips

Although Italian arum (*Arum italicum*) can tolerate full sun in a wet or evenly moist location, especially in cool-summer areas, it prefers partial shade in other types of locations. It will even do perfectly well in deep summer shade, as long as it gets a taste of warm spring sunshine. It thrives in woodland conditions with humus-rich soil and mulch to keep it cool. It needs plenty of moisture from fall through spring so you can enjoy its breathtaking winter foliage. It will even grow in soil that's wet during the spring months as long as the soil dries out a bit more in summer.

You can buy Italian arum as potted plants or as dry tubers. Potted plants can be planted at any time but are usually sold in leaf in the spring at nursery and garden centers. If you start with tubers, fall is the best time to buy them. Plant tubers about 6 inches (15 cm) deep.

Where it's happy, Italian arum multiplies readily, dividing at its base. Once you have a well-established colony, don't hesitate to harvest a few leaves every now and then for a cut-flower arrangement. To propagate Italian arum, mark the location of the plant while it's visible and dig it up in the fall while it is still dormant or just as it is starting to leaf out. You'll need to separate the offsets and plant them. Or start new plants from seed. Harvest the fruits at the end of summer or early in the fall and clean the pulp from the seed, then sow them outdoors. If you purchase seed from a commercial source, sow it indoors in early spring, 10 to 12 weeks before planting outside, and place the seed container in a cool spot—about 55° to 60°F (13° to 15°C). Arum seed can often take up to a year to germinate.

Good Neighbors

Leafless in summer, Italian arum is at its best from fall through winter, after the white-marbled leaves have emerged. (In climates that are cold or have a short growing season, the foliage remains dormant until the end of winter, so the plant has spring interest only.) Combine Italian arum with plants that will fill the summer gap: Suitable companions include astilbes, hardy begonia (*Begonia grandis*), and epimediums.

Problems and Solutions

Slugs can chew ragged holes in Italian arum leaves. To keep slugs from reaching your arums, sprinkle a 2-inch- (5-cm)-wide band of crushed eggshells or natural-grade diatomaceous earth around the plants. Slugs can't cross these jagged (to a slug) barriers, so your plants should be safe. Renew the barriers if heavy rain washes them away.

Recommended Arum

Arum italicum (Italian arum): This is the only arum that is at all popular. The species itself, which has deep green leaves or leaves only slightly mottled with white, is rarely grown. Instead, the cultivar 'Pictum', with heavily marbled foliage, is the commonly grown version described above. It usually comes true from seed.

'Pictum' Italian arum (*Arum italicum* 'Pictum') is a highlight in shade and woodland gardens all year long. Creamy white veins glow along its spear-shaped, dark green leaves in fall and winter. The flowers look rather like those of Jack-in-the-pulpits (*Aricaema* spp.) and appear early in spring, then give way to columns of brilliant red berries by fall.

Asarum

Wild ginger

Wild gingers are strictly foliage plants, but this hasn't stopped them from becoming more and more popular, especially among gardeners in the know. They make perfect carpets of foliage in dark spots, and their heart- or kidney-shaped leaves are either velvety or shiny, depending on the species. Many types also have attractive silver marbling on their leaves. Wild gingers do bloom, but the small maroon-purple to brown flowers lie flat on the ground and are totally hidden by the large leaves.

Plant Profile

ASARUM
uh-SAH-rum

- **Foliage Color:** Light green to dark green

- **Length of Foliage Season:** Varies by species; see individual listings

- **Height:** 4 to 9 inches (10 to 23 cm)

- **Spread:** 8 to 10 inches (20 to 25 cm)

- **Garden Uses:** Edging, groundcover, mass planting, rock garden, woodland garden; on slopes

- **Light Preference:** Partial to deep shade

- **Soil Preference:** Humus-rich, evenly moist, well-drained soil

- **Best Way to Propagate:** Divide in spring or early fall

- **USDA Plant Hardiness Zones:** Varies by species; see individual listings

- **AHS Heat Zones:** Varies by species; see individual listings

Growing Tips

Wild gingers are very tough, yet slow-growing, plants that will do well in moist, cool soil in most shady to partially shady spots. They thrive in deciduous woodlands and even under conifers as long as the soil is only moderately acid.

Simply plant wild gingers and ignore them; they really need no care where they are well adapted. They'll spread slowly but surely through creeping roots yet they aren't invasive. If they ever do overstep their bounds, simply cut away or pull out any offending sections.

Fall is the best time to multiply wild gingers, but you can also do it in the spring. Just dig out a clump with a section of creeping root and a few fibrous roots and move it elsewhere. Although they never *require* division, you can divide them as necessary for propagation purposes.

In many woodland gardens, wild gingers self-sow but just about as slowly as they grow from divisions. For more controlled results and a greater number of plants, harvest the seed in the fall and sow immediately; look for seedlings in spring. Indoors, sow the seed in a moist growing medium, then seal the container in a plastic bag and refrigerate for three or four weeks before exposing it to relatively cool temperatures: 60° to 65°F (15° to 18°C). Seeds germinate in only a week or so, but the plants grow slowly afterward. Plant the seedlings outdoors in a shaded spot after the last frost.

Good Neighbors

Slow to spread but well worth the wait, wild gingers combine beautifully with any and all woodland plants. The native Canadian wild ginger (*Asarum canadense*) is a great companion for bloodroot (*Sanguinaria canadensis*), woodland phlox (*Phlox divaricata*), great white trillium (*Trillium grandiflorum*), and other woodland natives.

Showier evergreen wild gingers make exquisite groundcovers in moist shade. Bleeding hearts (*Dicentra* spp.), ferns, hostas, early spring bulbs, and other shade lovers all make good neighbors in a shady border.

Problems and Solutions

Slugs and snails can trouble young plants; see page 55 for some ideas on how to control them.

Top Performer

Asarum canadense (Canadian wild ginger): All wild gingers are worth growing, but this is the one that gardeners seem to like most. The soft, velvety texture of the light green, heart-shaped, 6-inch (15-cm) leaves is its most attractive point. The leaves are deciduous, which makes this species far more adaptable than others, as it is less susceptible to late frosts and other vagaries of the early spring climate. Height: 4 to 8 inches (10 to 20 cm). Spread: 10 inches (25 cm). USDA Plant Hardiness Zones 3 to 9; AHS Heat Zones 8 to 1.

More Recommended Wild Gingers

Asarum europaeum (European wild ginger): This is probably the second most popular wild ginger, grown mainly for its very shiny, heart-shaped, leathery, evergreen foliage. Due to its slower growth habit, though, it is more expensive than Canadian wild ginger (*A. canadense*), and you'll need to buy more plants to cover the same area. In cold climates, place the plants in a spot with good snow cover; otherwise, the evergreen leaves may be damaged. Height: 5 to 8 inches (13 to 20 cm). Spread: 8 inches (20 cm). USDA Plant Hardiness Zones 3 to 9; AHS Heat Zones 8 to 1.

A. shuttleworthii, also called *Hexastylis shuttleworthii* (mottled wild ginger): This is one of the most handsome native gingers. Found in the Appalachians from Virginia to Alabama, it forms a mat of evergreen heart-shaped leaves like most of the others but beautifully mottled with silver. 'Callaway' has particularly heavy silvery markings. Height: 4 to 9 inches (10 to 23 cm). Spread: 8 inches (20 cm). USDA Plant Hardiness Zones 5 to 9; AHS Heat Zones 9 to 4.

Canadian wild ginger
(*Asarum canadense*)

Larry's Garden Notes

Most North American gardeners will find one species or another of wild gingers (*Asarum* spp.) in forests near their homes, but don't even think of collecting wild plants for your own garden! Wild ginger was so popular as a condiment in the past (the rhizomes made an excellent substitute for true ginger, a tropical plant) that it was seriously over-collected and, in many areas, is still slowly recuperating. Current populations only represent a shadow of its original abundance. So if you find wild ginger in the woods, leave it alone. And before you buy plants, check with your supplier to ensure that they haven't been wild-collected.

Athyrium

Lady fern

Lady ferns have lacy, delicate-looking fronds, and some of the most beautiful cultivated forms are wonderfully colorful. All lady ferns form dense clumps with fronds that arch upward and outward. Over time, they divide at the base, taking on a denser appearance. Lady ferns are potentially evergreen, but in most climates, they turn brown quickly when the first fall frosts strike.

Plant Profile

ATHYRIUM
a-THIH-ree-uhm

■ **Foliage Color:** Green

■ **Length of Foliage Season:** Late spring to fall

■ **Height:** Varies by species; see individual listings

■ **Spread:** Varies by species; see individual listings

■ **Garden Uses:** Container planting, groundcover, mass planting, mixed border, rock garden, specimen plant, woodland garden; in wet areas

■ **Light Preference:** Light to deep shade

■ **Soil Preference:** Humus-rich, moist but well-drained soil

■ **Best Way to Propagate:** Divide in spring or fall

■ **USDA Plant Hardiness Zones:** Varies by species; see individual listings

■ **AHS Heat Zones:** Varies by species; see individual listings

Growing Tips

The delicate appearance of lady ferns belies a tough nature. As long as you don't expose them to prolonged drought and burning sun, they adapt well to most garden conditions, although they *are* most at home in moist, humus-rich, wooded or semi-wooded areas that are sheltered from winds.

Avoid the temptation to clean up your lady ferns in the fall. Wait until spring, when new fronds appear, before removing the old ones. (Those browned, collapsed fronds help to protect the plant's crown from drying winter winds.)

For groundcover use, plant lady ferns densely, as they spread very slowly from clumps that gradually widen at the base. In habitats they really like, though, they can self-sow with abandon, so don't hesitate to pull out unwanted sporelings if this does occur. If you need more lady ferns, simply dig up mature plants in spring and divide them into separate crowns; otherwise, just leave them be.

Good Neighbors

Lady ferns are a natural choice for shade gardens, and they make handsome groundcovers. The yellow-green fronds of lady fern (*Athyrium filix-femina*) add an appealing freshness to a shaded spot, particularly when contrasted with dark green foliage, such as European wild ginger (*Asarum europaeum*) or hellebores (*Helleborus* spp.).

Japanese painted fern (*Athyrium niponicum* 'Pictum') lights up the garden with its silver-tipped, pink-veined fronds. Use it to pick up the color of a pulmonaria or mass it behind an area planted with Allegheny foamflower (*Tiarella cordifolia*) or a dainty cultivar of Chinese astilbe (*Astilbe chinensis*).

Use any of the *Athyrium* around bulbs to hide the spent foliage after the flower fades.

Problems and Solutions

These ferns have few insect or disease problems.

Top Performer

Athyrium niponicum 'Pictum', also called
A. goeringianum 'Pictum' (Japanese painted
fern): All-green *A. niponicum*, the original
species, is rarely offered because all eyes are
on its more colorful cultivar 'Pictum' (also
called 'Metallicum'). The fronds of 'Pictum'
have a shiny, silvery sheen over most of
their surface, with only the edges of the
frond fading to dark olive green. The central
part, from the leaf stalk up into the lower
leaflets, is deep red fading to lavender and
then to silvery gray. Such coloration really
has no equivalent among other ferns, so this
one always stands out from the crowd.

Japanese painted fern
(*Athyrium niponicum* 'Pictum')

Japanese painted fern is a small, compact, slow-growing fern that
is very easy to grow. It actually does better in light shade than in the
darker conditions under which so many other ferns thrive, although
deep shade is acceptable as well. Be aware that it's slow to start in
spring, though. Carefully mark its location, as it totally disappears
from sight in the fall and emerges much later than the surrounding
vegetation. Height: 1 to 2 feet (30 to 60 cm). Spread: 1 foot (30 cm).
USDA Plant Hardiness Zones 3 to 9; AHS Heat Zones 8 to 2.

More Recommended Lady Ferns

Athyrium filix-femina (lady fern): Lady fern is a relatively upright species
with a soft green coloration that nicely brightens up plantings of darker
ferns. Its new leaf stems are often colored dark red, giving it some early
color. It makes an excellent groundcover, and while not a fast grower, it
is much quicker to reach its mature size than its painted cousin.

Crested lady fern (*A. filix-femina* 'Vernoniae Cristata') is much like the
species, except the fronds end in a unique fork, giving the plant a
denser, tasseled appearance. Its leaf stalks tend to retain their shiny red
coloration well into summer. The tatting fern (*A. filix-femina* 'Frizelliae')
is very different from the species. Its leaflets are reduced to mere circles
of green along a thin stalk, giving the frond a narrow, almost necklace-
like appearance. Height: 2 to 4 feet (60 to 120 cm). Spread: 2 feet
(60 cm). USDA Plant Hardiness Zones 2 to 9; AHS Heat Zones 9 to 1.

Larry's Garden Notes

Back in days of yore when people
had no inkling that ferns reproduced by spores, how ferns
spread was a subject of some
debate. For example, people believed that anyone who found fern
seeds could become invisible
(and why not, since ferns don't
bear seeds at all!). The relation-
ships between the different ferns
in European forests were likewise misunderstood. A case in
point is the lady fern (*Athyrium
filix-femina*), which, with its lacy
foliage, was thought to be the
female counterpart of the more
macho-looking male fern
(*Dryopteris filix-mas*). Today we
know that the two aren't even
closely related.

Carex

Sedge

When is a grass not a grass? When it's a sedge! While sedges look very much like grasses, they're actually only distant relatives. Most sedges have long, narrow to relatively broad sword-shaped leaves that arch upward, outward, and then down, usually from a dense central clump. The brownish or greenish spikes of flowers usually aren't showy, but they're a curiosity because there are separate male and female flowers in each spike. And, most importantly, sedges have flower stems that are triangular in cross-section; grasses have round ones.

Plant Profile

CAREX
KAH-recks

- **Foliage Color:** Varies by species; see individual listings

- **Length of Foliage Season:** Evergreen

- **Height:** Varies by species; see individual listings

- **Spread:** Varies by species; see individual listings

- **Garden Uses:** Container gardens, edging, groundcover, mass planting, mixed border, rock garden, specimen plant, woodland garden; in wet areas

- **Light Preference:** Full sun to deep shade

- **Soil Preference:** Humus-rich, moist soil

- **Best Way to Propagate:** Divide at any time

- **USDA Plant Hardiness Zones:** Varies by species; see individual listings

- **AHS Heat Zones:** Varies by species; see individual listings

Growing Tips

Ornamental sedges generally prefer full sun to partial shade (some tolerate deep shade) and evenly moist, sometimes even wet, soil. Many will grow with their roots or even their crowns constantly under water.

Sedges don't need division and will grow for decades all on their own, but dividing them is the simplest way of obtaining more plants of a favorite cultivar. Just dig up the clumps at any time of the year and cut them into sections. Sedges also sprout readily from seed sown in the fall under whatever conditions that species prefers.

Although generally evergreen (or nearly so), their foliage can be a tangled mess of brown and green by spring. If you want to tidy your sedges, chop them back to near ground level in spring to give the newer leaves some growing space; this isn't necessary though.

Good Neighbors

Sedges provide great textural interest with their fine, arching foliage. Use them around the edges of shaded walkways or curving beds, or as accents in the garden.

The foliage of leatherleaf sedge (*Carex buchananii*) stays orange-brown all year, making it an unusual contrast to plants with long-lasting foliage, such as epimediums and hardy geraniums.

Yellow-green Bowles' golden sedge (*C. elata* 'Aurea', also called *C. elata* 'Bowles' Golden') brings a welcome bit of sunlight to the

FUN FACTS

Ever wonder how to tell a sedge from a grass? Find a flowerstalk and roll it between your fingers. Grasses have round stems and will roll as requested. Sedges have triangular stems that won't budge. That's how my dad taught me to tell the difference when I was a kid: "A sedge is a wedge."

shade garden, especially when planted among hellebores (*Helleborus* spp.) or bigleaf ligularia (*Ligularia dentata*).

Problems and Solutions

Sedges are rarely bothered by either pests or diseases.

Top Performer

Carex buchananii (leatherleaf sedge): You either like this plant or you don't. I think it's a great conversation piece in the garden. But my wife calls it "that dead grass thing" and refuses to believe it's alive. You see, leather leaf sedge produces dense, arching, hairlike clumps of *brown* leaves.

Grow this sedge in full sun or partial shade and moist to wet conditions. In cold climates, grow it in a pot and overwinter it indoors. For a similar plant in a smaller size, try *C. comans* 'Bronze': It grows only 9 to 12 inches (23 to 30 cm) tall. Height: 15 to 18 inches (38 to 45 cm). Spread: 12 to 18 inches (30 to 45 cm). USDA Plant Hardiness Zones 6 to 9; AHS Heat Zones 9 to 1.

More Recommended Sedges

Carex elata 'Aurea', also called *C. elata* 'Bowles' Golden' (Bowles' golden sedge): This popular cultivar forms dense hummocks of long, narrow, somewhat arching leaves in bright yellow with only the narrowest green edge. This sedge needs lots of moisture. Light to partial shade is a must in hot climates, and it does reasonably well in full shade. In cooler climates, though, give it at least some sun. Height: 2 to 3 feet (60 to 90 cm). Spread: 3 to 4 feet (90 to 120 cm). USDA Plant Hardiness Zones 5 to 9; AHS Heat Zones 9 to 3.

C. morrowii (Japanese sedge): Japanese sedge offers various variegated cultivars that are true stars among foliage plants. They form dense mounds of flat, arching, semievergreen foliage that looks as soft as a pillow. Japanese sedge does better in partial to deep shade than in full sun, especially in hot-summer areas. Moist soil is a must at all times. 'Variegata' has white-striped leaves, while 'Goldband' has gold instead of white margins. Height: 12 to 18 inches (30 to 45 cm). Spread: 6 to 12 inches (15 to 30 cm). USDA Plant Hardiness Zones 5 to 9; AHS Heat Zones 9 to 3.

Leatherleaf sedge
(*Carex buchananii*)

Around the World with Sedges

You really can go around the world with sedges (*Carex* spp.). Although most common in temperate zones, you can find 1 of the some 2,000 species of sedges just about every place in the world. Except perhaps for a few isolated islands no one has thought to check, there are native sedges everywhere except the Galapagos Islands, the Kerguelen Archipelago near Antarctica, and Antarctica itself. I wouldn't even be surprised to learn that there are sedge seeds dormant under the Antarctic ice waiting for the climate to warm up enough for them to grow.

Dryopteris

Wood fern, shield fern, buckler fern, male fern

Wood ferns are one of the most common kinds of wild ferns, and they add a pleasant "forest grove" ambience to the landscape. They're generally medium-sized and clump-forming (although sometimes creeping) with distinctly triangular fronds. The fronds are typically leathery with stout stalks, and they reach upward and outward from a central crown. Wood ferns fill in gaps without stealing the show from other more colorful perennials. When the latter are not in bloom, wood ferns take over with feathery, lacy fronds.

Plant Profile

DRYOPTERIS
dry-AHP-teh-riss

- **Foliage Color:** Dark green

- **Length of Foliage Season:** Evergreen in most species

- **Height:** Varies by species; see individual listings

- **Spread:** Varies by species; see individual listings

- **Garden Uses:** Container planting, edging, groundcover, mass planting, mixed border, rock garden, specimen plant, woodland garden; on slopes, in wet areas

- **Light Preference:** Full sun to deep shade

- **Soil Preference:** Humus-rich, moist soil

- **Best Way to Propagate:** Divide in spring or fall

- **USDA Plant Hardiness Zones:** Varies by species; see individual listings

- **AHS Heat Zones:** Varies by species; see individual listings

Growing Tips

Wood ferns are generally very easy to grow and less fussy than many other ferns. While they thrive in the deep to partial shade of their natural environments, they'll also adapt to full sun as long as you keep them at least slightly moist. And although they do prefer moist or even wet, humus-rich soil in the wild, they adapt well to average garden soil and even to quite dry conditions once they're established.

Dividing established plants is the easiest way to reproduce wood ferns if you need new plants.

Good Neighbors

Combine wood ferns with other woodland inhabitants, such as Canadian wild ginger (*Asarum canadense*) and large-flowered bellwort (*Uvularia grandiflora*). Or use their long-lasting foliage as contrast to hostas, bluebells (*Mertensia virginica*), pulmonarias, and other shade plants in the garden.

Warning: Although many ferns appear common enough in a localized spot, they can be rare overall, so never collect them from the wild for garden use. Instead, buy them from commercial sources that clearly state that they offer only nursery-grown plants.

Problems and Solutions

Like most ferns, wood ferns are not particularly susceptible to insects or disease.

Top Performer

Dryopteris filix-mas (male fern): Male fern is a stately plant with dark green fronds, often reaching an impressive size where it's happy, yet staying dense and compact when it's more drought-stressed. Male fern is evergreen in most climates, becoming deciduous in only the very coldest regions. There are numerous cultivars, including 'Cristata' with crested segments on either side of the frond. (The tip of the frond is normal.) 'Linearis Polydactyla' is a real oddity; each leaflet is heavily crested, giving the plant an especially fine, lacy appearance. Height: 2 to 5 feet (60 to 150 cm). Spread: 2 feet (60 cm). USDA Plant Hardiness Zones 2 to 9; AHS Heat Zones 8 to 3.

Male fern
(*Dryopteris filix-mas*)

More Recommended Wood Ferns

Dryopteris affinis (golden scaled male fern): This evergreen fern is very similar to male fern in size and form, but with fronds that are even more leathery and stems that are heavily coated with golden scales. There is a host of cultivars in a wide range of sizes. 'Crispa Gracilis' is a dwarf with crested, ruffled fronds, while 'Pinderi' has very narrow fronds to 3 feet (90 cm) tall, giving it a lighter, more elegant look. Height: 2 to 5 feet (60 to 150 cm). Spread: 2 feet (60 cm). USDA Plant Hardiness Zones 4 to 9; AHS Heat Zones 8 to 1.

D. erythrosora (autumn fern): Unlike many ferns, this evergreen species offers seasonal changes, as new fronds appear in coppery red then fade to dark green. Although most numerous in the spring, fresh fronds can still appear into summer. The spores underneath the fronds turn bright red in the fall, adding to the plant's winter appearance. 'Prolifica', with its narrower, slightly curled fronds, has a beautiful shape. It sometimes produces tiny plantlets on the upper surface of the fronds. Height: 1 to 2 feet (30 to 60 cm). Spread: 1 to 2 feet (30 to 60 cm). USDA Plant Hardiness Zones 5 to 9; AHS Heat Zones 9 to 3.

D. marginalis (marginal wood fern): A native of eastern North America, marginal wood fern is among the most evergreen of the wood ferns, often sticking up through the snow to beautify the winter landscape. The rather coarse-textured, thick, and leathery fronds are dark green with an attractive bluish tinge. Height: 18 to 24 inches (45 to 60 cm). Spread: 18 to 24 inches (45 to 60 cm). USDA Plant Hardiness Zones 3 to 9; AHS Heat Zones 8 to 1.

Larry's Garden Notes

Male fern (*Dryopteris filix-mas*) was once believed to have mystical powers. To understand the songs of birds, for example, it was believed one only had to wear a ring of male fern ashes around a finger. You should know, however, that this plant is poisonous—it causes paralysis if ingested in any quantity. So resist the urge to wear its ashes around your finger even if you want to commune with the local bird population.

Festuca

Fescue

While many fescues are popular turfgrasses, they're not the types of fescue I'm talking about. As nice as fescues are in a lawn, there are much more ornamental choices we can grow in the garden. Ornamental fescues are evergreen clump-forming grasses of generally small size, usually with flat, narrow, arching leaves that create a dense, fountainlike tuft of green—or blue!—in the garden. The thin, wheatlike flower clusters are only of minor interest.

Plant Profile

FESTUCA
fes-TOO-kah

- Foliage Color: Green or blue
- Length of Foliage Season: Evergreen
- Height: 6 to 18 inches (15 to 45 cm)
- Spread: 8 to 12 inches (20 to 30 cm)
- Garden Uses: Container planting, edging, groundcover, mass planting, mixed border, rock garden, specimen plant, wall planting; on slopes
- Light Preference: Full sun to partial shade
- Soil Preference: Average to poor, well-drained soil
- Best Way to Propagate: Divide in spring or fall
- USDA Plant Hardiness Zones: 4 to 9
- AHS Heat Zones: 12 to 1

Growing Tips

Ornamental fescues do best in cool, dry climates but adapt well to most garden conditions. They won't tolerate poor drainage, nor will they do well with a combination of extreme heat and high humidity. In Southeast gardens, they can perform poorly; elsewhere, they are true winners in every way. Give them poor to average soil and hold off on the water, and they'll be gorgeous!

Fescues need little care. Just plant them, water them once or twice, and let nature take its course. As the flowers fade, you'll want to deadhead them to prevent self-sowing. If you have heavy garden soil, the centers of your fescues may die out after several years, but this is easily remedied. Just dig up the plants in the spring and divide them into attractive clumps, discarding the centers. Then replant the clumps.

Don't count on much spread from fescues; they tend to form a clump and stay put, scarcely increasing in size after their first summer. For a groundcover effect, therefore, make sure you plant them densely.

The best means of propagation is through division, preferably in spring. To grow fescues from seed, simply rake over a spot in the garden, sow the seed without covering it, then water well. Germination takes about three weeks. However, remember that most ornamental fescues are cultivars and will not come true from seed, so expect a great deal of variability in the offspring.

Good Neighbors

Fescues make a neat edging in front of upright plants such as gas plant (*Dictamnus albus*) and irises. They also blend nicely with other cool colors: Try them with pink or blue hardy geraniums, pink checkerbloom (*Sidalcea malviflora*), and a scattering of light yellow 'Moonbeam' threadleaf coreopsis (*Coreopsis verticillata* 'Moonbeam'). And it almost goes without saying that they're effective in a massed, large-scale planting of shrubs and perennials.

Problems and Solutions

Rust can be a problem on fescues. In some cases, there are just a few orange spots on the lower leaves; other times, the foliage turns almost entirely orange. This rarely harms the plant, but it can spoil its appearance at the end of the season. See page 59 for suggestions on how to control rust.

Top Performer

Festuca cinerea, F. amethystina, F. glauca, or *F. ovina* (blue fescue): A botanist friend tells me there *are* differences among all these species of fescues, but that you'd mostly need a microscope to detect them. Besides, according to him, most plants sold under any one name are probably one of the other species because everyone has trouble telling them apart. So I've decided they're all top performers!

Blue fescues are small, dense clumps of thin bluish or grayish leaves. 'Elijah Blue' is my favorite true blue fescue simply because it really is that color, not gray, and it maintains its color all summer without fading. 'Solling' is a close second: It's a pretty blue-gray, retains its color well, and gets extra brownie points because it almost never blooms. 'Skinner's Blue' isn't quite as blue as the other two (it's more turquoise than anything else) but does better in cold-winter areas, up to USDA Zone 3, where other blue fescues are often short-lived. Beware of plants simply labeled 'Glauca'; that name seems to be used as a cover for any fescue of unknown origin.

More Recommended Fescues

F. mairei (Maire's fescue): This fescue stands out from the crowd because it doesn't have a trace of blue! Instead it is a charming, clump-forming, light *green* fescue about twice the size of the blue forms. Other than color and size, it is a typical ornamental fescue. Height: 24 to 36 inches (60 to 90 cm). Spread: 18 to 24 inches (45 to 60 cm).

'Superba' sheep's fescue (*Festuca amethystina* 'Superba')

Kissing Cousins

Blue oat grass (*Helictotrichon sempervirens*, also called *Avena sempervirens*) looks like a giant blue fescue with slightly broader leaves. It forms a perfect dome of broad, intensely blue leaves topped by stalks of bluish white, early-to-late-summer flowers that turn golden in the fall. Blue oat grass is particularly easy to grow, with evergreen (everblue?) leaves that need no special care other than simply pulling out any brown ones that happen to appear. In care and needs, it's very much the equivalent of blue fescue; in appearance, I'd say it's even nicer. Height: 2 to 3 feet (60 to 90 cm). Spread: 2 feet (60 cm). USDA Plant Hardiness Zones 4 to 9; AHS Heat Zones 8 to 1.

Heuchera

Heuchera, alumroot

Once upon a time, heucheras had plain old green leaves, but nowadays, heuchera foliage is anything *but* green! You'll love growing the spectacular heuchera cultivars I describe below. Heucheras are mounding plants with long-stalked, heart-shaped or rounded, lobed maplelike leaves, usually covered in soft hairs, and tend to be evergreen in most climates. Heuchera flowers—borne on tall, wispy stems—are tiny and inconspicuous, generally in shades of greenish white or yellowish green.

Plant Profile

HEUCHERA
HUE-ker-uh

- **Foliage Color:** Varies by species; see individual listings

- **Length of Foliage Season:** Evergreen in most climates

- **Height:** 1 to 2 feet (30 to 60 cm)

- **Spread:** 12 to 18 inches (30 to 45 cm)

- **Garden Uses:** Container planting, edging, groundcover, mass planting, mixed border, rock garden, specimen plant, woodland garden

- **Light Preference:** Sun to deep shade

- **Soil Preference:** Average, moist but well-drained soil

- **Best Way to Propagate:** Divide in spring or fall

- **USDA Plant Hardiness Zones:** 4 to 9

- **AHS Heat Zones:** 8 to 1

Growing Tips

Heucheras grow in a wide range of conditions, but they do best in light to partial shade. Full sun is fine in cool-summer areas but can cause the plants to bleach out elsewhere. Deep shade is all right in hot climates. Heucheras tolerate some drought but prefer evenly moist conditions. They don't mind ordinary garden soil but do best in rich, humusy soil, and they appreciate some mulch.

Heucheras grow readily from seed, sown indoors eight to ten weeks before the last frost or outdoors in spring or late fall. (Don't cover them because they need light to germinate.) However, most cultivars will not come true from seed, so division is the best method of maintaining them. Dig up overgrown clumps every three or four years, and use the younger, rooted divisions to start new plants.

Besides heucheras grown for their attractive foliage, other species called coral bells are grown for their flowers; see page 464.

Good Neighbors

The mounded form and marbled foliage of heucheras look good in a partly shaded border, paired with bleeding hearts (*Dicentra* spp.), woodland phlox (*Phlox divaricata*), and Allegheny foamflower (*Tiarella cordifolia*). Add hostas and other plants for later interest.

Problems and Solutions

Heucheras have few serious pest or disease problems.

Top Performer

Heuchera americana (American alumroot): In its original form, American alumroot was at best a foliage plant of limited interest for all-season greenery in shady spots. Its heart-shaped or rounded, 4- to

6-inch (10- to 15-cm)-long leaves were rather ordinary, and the tiny, greenish white flowers were very insignificant.

The hybrids are practically different plants. (In fact, they *are* different plants, given the considerable importation of hybrid genes). Though probably not pure *H. americana*, they have enough genes from the latter to have adopted its overall shape, but they've taken on a deep purple to red coloration and a silvery overlay. 'Chocolate Ruffles', with its large ruffled leaves that are deep chocolate brown on top and burgundy underneath, is a stunner. 'Pewter Moon' is bright silver with purple edges and deep purple veins, while 'Velvet Night', with dark plum leaves overlaid with silver veins, is nearly black in color. Height: 1 to 2 feet (30 to 60 cm). Spread: 12 to 18 inches (30 to 45 cm). USDA Plant Hardiness Zones 4 to 9; AHS Heat Zones 8 to 1.

American alumroot (*Heuchera americana*)

More Recommended Alumroots

Heuchera micrantha (small-flowered alumroot): Like American alumroot (*H. americana*), small-flowered alumroot came from humble beginnings. Its heart-shaped, 2- to 3-inch (5- to 8-cm) leaves were simply green in color with a slight silvery overlay, and its late-spring-to-early-summer, yellowish-white flowers had only minimal impact. Then came 'Palace Purple' and the whole alumroot world did a double flip! The leaves are a deep, shiny purple in spring, fading to deeper bronzy brown in summer under hot conditions and are bigger than those of the species. Although sold as *H. micrantha* var. *diversifolia* 'Palace Purple', no one is actually really sure where this plant belongs taxonomically—but everyone knows it was a real trailblazer.

'Palace Purple' had the unfortunate habit of "coming somewhat true from seed." As a result, many growers raised the plant from seed and sold the resulting plants as 'Palace Purple', but the seedlings varied widely in color and form. If you want to grow this plant, insist on the original 'Palace Purple'. Or try *H. micrantha* 'Bressingham Bronze' with crinkly, deep purple leaves that maintain their color throughout the summer. Height: 1 to 2 feet (30 to 60 cm). Spread: 12 to 18 inches (30 to 45 cm). USDA Plant Hardiness Zones 4 to 9; AHS Heat Zones 8 to 1.

Kissing Cousins

Piggyback plant (*Tolmiea menziesii*), a native of the Pacific Northwest, is often used in hanging baskets. Its flowers and spreading, apple green leaves aren't that spectacular. What makes this plant fascinating are the new plantlets that form at the base of each leaf, weighing them down as they grow. I grow piggyback plant outdoors, where it's fun to watch it slowly spread outward, each leaf bending down and rooting into the soil below it. Height: 12 to 24 inches (30 to 60 cm). Spread: 12 to 24 inches (30 to 60 cm). USDA Plant Hardiness Zones 4 to 10; AHS Heat Zones 11 to 1.

Osmunda

Flowering fern, osmunda

Flowering ferns are big, luxuriant plants that add a tropical, back-to-the-dinosaur-era look to the garden. Their deciduous fronds generally have a bright green color in spring and darken to deep green in summer. Flowering ferns look even more tropical after several years of growth because their crown, which is underground in a young plant, gradually rises upward as the plant ages. Eventually, it forms a short, thick, black "trunk" to 1 foot (30 cm) high, much like the tree ferns of the tropics.

Plant Profile

OSMUNDA
ahz-MUN-dah

- **Foliage Color:** Bright green to dark green
- **Length of Foliage Season:** Spring through late summer
- **Height:** Varies by species; see individual listings
- **Spread:** Varies by species; see individual listings
- **Garden Uses:** Groundcover, mixed border, seasonal hedge, specimen plant, woodland garden; at the back of beds and borders, on slopes, in wet areas
- **Light Preference:** Full sun to deep shade
- **Soil Preference:** Humus-rich, moist to wet soil
- **Best Way to Propagate:** Divide in spring or fall
- **USDA Plant Hardiness Zones:** 3 to 10
- **AHS Heat Zones:** Varies by species; see individual listings

Growing Tips

If flowering ferns have one specific need, it's for soil that remains at least slightly moist at all times—preferably evenly moist or even wet. Where they can find soil moisture, they'll grow in just about any condition, from full sun to the deepest shade. And they thrive in out-and-out muddy conditions, such as on the borders of natural ponds and streams. They prefer humus-rich soil and in the wild usually grow under somewhat acid conditions, but they will put up with just about anything (even lime!) if they get their moisture quota.

Although flowering ferns grow over a wide range of conditions, from tropical climates to cold ones, don't be surprised if they do better in cool climates. Even in the wild, flowering ferns are never as large and attractive in hot-summer areas as in cool-summer areas.

The easiest way to multiply flowering ferns is to divide well-established plants once multiple crowns have formed.

Good Neighbors

Flowering ferns are appropriate for moist, shaded locations; streamside or pondside is ideal. Combine them with other moisture-loving plants; ideal candidates include astilbes, marsh marigold (*Caltha palustris*), 'The Rocket' narrow-spiked ligularia (*Ligularia stenocephala* 'The Rocket'), and primroses.

FUN FACTS

The common name "flowering fern" is a contradiction in terms. Ferns never produce flowers; they reproduce by producing spores on special, fertile fronds. With flowering ferns, the fertile fronds are so different from the sterile fronds, both in their clustered shape and reddish-brown color, that they play a role similar to a flower on a plant.

Problems and Solutions

Flowering ferns are not troubled by any significant pest or disease problems.

Top Performer

Osmunda cinnamomea (cinnamon fern): Depending on whose opinion you ask, the cinnamon fern gets its common name either from its fertile fronds, which turn golden brown after a few weeks and look like cinnamon sticks; or from the fuzzy hair that covers the young fiddleheads. White at first, it quickly turns cinnamon-brown.

The first fronds to appear are the fertile (spore-bearing) ones. Strictly upright and narrow with leaflets than never seem to unfurl totally, they are green at first, then turn cinnamon-brown. Then the sterile fronds start to unroll. They too are relatively erect, but they arch outward at the top, creating a stately vaselike pattern, soon overtaking the shorter fertile fronds. These new fronds are typically fernlike, each looking like a tall, green feather. Height: 3 to 5 feet (90 to 150 cm). Spread: 3 feet (90 cm). USDA Plant Hardiness Zones 3 to 10; AHS Heat Zones 9 to 1.

More Recommended Flowering Ferns

Osmunda regalis (royal fern): Although very fernlike in the spring while the reddish to purple stems of its curled-up fiddleheads unravel, it scarcely resembles a fern at all by summer. Each upright, slightly arching frond is divided into secondary stems with well-spaced leaflets, making the plant look for all the world like a shrub, an effect further enhanced by the brownish coloration of the frond stalks. The fertile fronds produce normal divisions and leaflets up to near their summit, then the tips of the fronds change suddenly into narrow, upright clusters of golden brown spore cases. From a distance, you could easily mistake royal fern for a flowering shrub—perhaps a golden brown spirea (*Spiraea* sp.)—even more so because of its quite unfernlike proportions. This is one fern that likes things really wet. It will even grow and thrive with its roots soaking in water much of the time, but it does adapt perfectly to ordinary garden soil as long as you keep it watered. Height: 4 to 6 feet (120 to 180 cm). Spread: 4 feet (120 cm). USDA Plant Hardiness Zones 3 to 10; AHS Heat Zones 9 to 4.

Need a little spice in your perennial bed? Try the dramatic-looking cinnamon fern (*Osmunda cinnamomea*). Its cinnamon-colored fertile fronds last until about midsummer before collapsing; the sterile fronds remain attractive all summer, then turn bright yellow or orange in the fall.

Polystichum

Holly fern

Looking for a small fern to fit a tiny corner of your garden? Holly ferns are a good choice; most are small- to medium-sized plants, ideal for tight spots where larger ferns appear too massive. Holly ferns include mostly clump-forming, evergreen species. Their fronds are shinier and more leathery than those of most other ferns. To distinguish holly ferns from other ferns, look for a dense covering of scales on the frond stalks; most other ferns have no scales or only a light coating.

Plant Profile

POLYSTICHUM
pah-LIH-stih-kum

- **Foliage Color:** Dark green
- **Length of Foliage Season:** Evergreen
- **Height:** Varies by species; see individual listings
- **Spread:** Varies by species; see individual listings
- **Garden Uses:** Container planting, groundcover, mass planting, mixed border, rock garden, specimen plant, wall planting, woodland garden; on slopes
- **Light Preference:** Light to deep shade
- **Soil Preference:** Humus-rich, well-drained soil
- **Best Way to Propagate:** Divide in spring
- **USDA Plant Hardiness Zones:** Varies by species; see individual listings
- **AHS Heat Zones:** Varies by species; see individual listings

Growing Tips

Holly ferns are particularly easy to grow, so they're good choices for the beginning fern grower. They'll grow practically in spite of you! Although, like most ferns, holly ferns prefer cool, moist conditions, they are amazingly adaptable, tolerating even moderate drought once they are established. And unlike most other ferns, holly ferns really don't like soggy soil. They prefer good drainage at all times, making them a good choice for slopes. Just about any type of soil will do, although rich loam is best. Full sun is all right, as long as the soil remains at least slightly moist; otherwise, holly ferns are better off in light to deep shade. The best means of multiplying holly ferns is dividing the multiple crowns in the spring.

Good Neighbors

Evergreen holly ferns can tolerate drier conditions than most ferns, so it's easy to incorporate them into gardens. Native Christmas fern (*Polystichum acrostichoides*) is a good choice for an evergreen groundcover on a steep shady slope. Use it in conjunction with other tough plants, such as hostas and fragrant Solomon's seal (*Polygonatum odoratum*).

Use the tall, neat fronds of soft shield fern (*Polystichum setiferum*) as an accent in the shade garden, complementing Siberian bugloss (*Brunnera macrophylla*), pulmonarias, and other shade lovers.

Problems and Solutions

Holly ferns have few problems with insects or disease.

Top Performer

Polystichum acrostichoides (Christmas fern): This native of eastern North America is one of the most common ferns throughout its range, and it's widely grown in gardens as well. It gets its name from its evergreen fronds, used by the first settlers as a Christmas decoration, and it's still popular with florists as foliage for flower arrangements. It forms a single crown with spreading, dark green, leathery fronds. The fertile fronds are similar to the sterile ones, but the leaflets closest to the tip appear narrower. The fertile fronds usually die back after they release their spores, but the sterile ones remain green through the winter. Christmas fern only occasionally produces offsets and therefore doesn't fill in over time like many other ferns, so you'll need to plant it densely if you want a groundcover effect. Height: 12 to 18 inches (30 to 45 cm). Spread: 1 foot (30 cm). USDA Plant Hardiness Zones 4 to 9; AHS Heat Zones 8 to 1.

Christmas fern
(*Polystichum acrostichoides*)

More Recommended Holly Ferns

Polystichum setiferum (soft shield fern): This is one of the larger holly ferns, but even so it's modest in size compared to the flowering ferns (*Osmunda* spp.). Soft shield fern forms a ground-hugging rosette of deeply cut, semievergreen fronds that are soft to the touch. The fiddlehead is covered with large brown scales and is often slow to unfurl entirely. There are literally hundreds of selections of this fern, with variously twisted, crested, and otherwise mutated fronds. 'Congestum Cristatum', a dwarf form, has dense, overlapping leaflets that are forked at the tip. The fronds of 'Divisilobum' are highly divided, giving them a very lacy appearance. 'Proliferum' is a particularly hardy cultivar that produces baby ferns among its leaflets. 'Rotundatum' has nearly round leaflets. Height: 12 to 30 inches (30 to 75 cm). Spread: 18 inches (45 cm). USDA Plant Hardiness Zones 5 to 9; AHS Heat Zones 9 to 1.

P. tsus-simense (Korean rock fern): This dwarf fern forms neat compact clumps of triangular dark green fronds that often have a purplish cast as they first emerge. One identifying feature is that the fronds have nearly black stems. This slow-growing fern also grows well indoors and is commonly used in terrariums. Height: 6 to 12 inches (15 to 30 cm). Spread: 1 foot (30 cm). USDA Plant Hardiness Zones 6 to 9; AHS Heat Zones 9 to 1.

Kissing Cousins

Northern maidenhair fern (*Adiantum pedatum*) is a delicate-looking deciduous fern, but its soft appearance belies a rather tough nature. Northern maidenhair fern is the only truly cold-hardy type of maidenhair fern. Like most maidenhair ferns, northern maidenhair produces thin, shiny, black stems bearing nearly triangular, soft green, lacy leaflets. Because it's so beautiful, many people have dug wild plants for their gardens, so it's become rare in the wild. Make sure you buy *only* nursery-grown stock. Height: 12 to 24 inches (30 to 60 cm). Spread: 12 to 24 inches (30 to 60 cm). USDA Plant Hardiness Zones 3 to 9; AHS Heat Zones 8 to 1.

Stachys

Lamb's-ears, betony

Lamb's-ears has to be one of the most charming of all perennials. Its soft, furry, silvery, 4-inch (10-cm) leaves really are as soft as lamb's ears, and they're well worth stroking for the sheer pleasure of it. From midsummer on, each major rosette produces a woolly, upright stalk with pink to purple flowers just barely protruding from the silky hairs.

Plant Profile

STACHYS
STAY-kiss

- **Foliage Color:** Silver-gray
- **Length of Foliage Season:** Spring through late summer
- **Height:** 4 to 18 inches (10 to 45 cm)
- **Spread:** 1 foot (30 cm)
- **Garden Uses:** Container planting, cut flower garden, edging, groundcover, mass planting, mixed border, rock garden, specimen plant, woodland garden; along paths, on slopes
- **Light Preference:** Full sun to partial shade
- **Soil Preference:** Average, moist but well-drained soil
- **Best Way to Propagate:** Divide in spring or summer
- **USDA Plant Hardiness Zones:** 3 to 9
- **AHS Heat Zones:** 8 to 1

Growing Tips

Lamb's-ears are no-nonsense, easy-to-grow plants that thrive in full sun to at least partial shade. They have trouble dealing with hot, humid air, but they adapt much better in evenly moist, well-drained soil, so don't hesitate to mulch abundantly and to irrigate as needed. Avoid watering them from above, though, as this can cause spotting or even leaf dieback. If you *must* water from above, do it in the morning so the leaves have time to dry out before nightfall. Beware of overly rich soil, as it tends to encourage lax growth and floppiness. Lamb's-ears do better in poor to average soil.

To keep your plants looking neat and trim and to prevent them from self-sowing, cut off the flowering stems when the last blooms fade. (Some people prefer cutting off the flowering stalks as they form to maintain a pristine silver-carpet appearance.)

Although not weedy, lamb's-ears do produce an abundance of offsets that are easy to divide if you need more plants. They tend to die out in the center after several years. If this happens, cut out the dead sections and replant with young plants from the outer rim of the clump. Lamb's-ears are likewise very easy to reproduce by seed—that is, those that flower. (Some cultivars don't bloom.) Just sow the seed on the surface of the soil, indoors or out, and they'll sprout within two or three weeks.

Good Neighbors

Lamb's-ears' woolly gray leaves are ideal for the front of the border, complementing plants of all kinds. They combine well with either pastel or brightly colored flowers. Use them in formal beds with 'Zagreb' threadleaf coreopsis (*Coreopsis verticillata* 'Zagreb'), irises, salvias, 'Herbstfreude' sedum (*Sedum* 'Herbstfreude', also called

S. 'Autumn Joy'), and others that maintain their good looks all season. Lamb's-ears also look great in less formal gardens, perhaps interplanted with Brazilian vervain (*Verbena bonariensis*). They work well in mass plantings, too, provided they get excellent drainage and the climate is not excessively humid. Repeat the silver color with 'Powis Castle' artemisia (*Artemisia* 'Powis Castle') and pinks (*Dianthus* spp.).

Problems and Solutions

Dieback and various leaf diseases kill or discolor the foliage, and slugs enjoy feeding on fresh new leaves. If the damage is slight, ignore it. The plants fill in quickly on their own. If many leaves are affected, cut the plants back to just 1 inch or so (about 3 cm) from the ground. New growth will appear readily.

Lamb's-ears
(*Stachys byzantina*)

Top Performer

Stachys byzantina, also called *S. lanata*, *S. olympica* (lamb's-ears, woolly betony): This popular species forms a thick, creeping carpet of silver rosettes only 4 to 6 inches (10 to 15 cm) tall, rooting as they spread. Over time they can cover considerable ground, but they really aren't invasive if you deadhead them. 'Cotton Boll' (also called 'Sheila McQueen') is mostly grown as an oddity. Its flowerstalks rise up, look ready to bloom, then produce only white woolly masses where the flowers should be. 'Primrose Heron' is a golden form of the species, with primrose-yellow leaves in spring that turn more silvery-gray as summer goes on. (It seems to be everybody's darling these days, but I find the sickly yellow-green leaves quite ghastly.) 'Silver Carpet' is a popular cultivar that rarely if ever blooms and thus saves you a lot of pruning effort. 'Big Ears' (also called 'Countess Helene von Stein') is like a large-leafed version of 'Silver Carpet', blooming only rarely. The leaves are less densely hairy, so they are more gray-green than silver, but they're also much less subject to leaf damage under humid conditions than the other cultivars.

Smart Substitutes

In climates too hot and humid for lamb's ears, try Swedish ivy (*Plectranthus argenteus*). This silky, silvery-leaved mint relative is only hardy in USDA Zone 10 or possibly to Zone 9 in a protected spot. But it's easy to propagate through cuttings and thrives indoors over the winter in a moderately bright spot. It has a semi-upright, somewhat spreading habit and narrow spikes of purple flowers. I always keep a few pots going to tuck into the garden whenever something dies back.

Groundcover PERENNIALS

A perennial groundcover is one of the most useful kinds of perennials: It reduces maintenance and makes your yard more beautiful in one fell swoop. A groundcover is simply a planting that densely covers a large surface, and it's a great solution for sites where maintaining a flower garden would be difficult, such as on a steep slope. Groundcovers are also a low-maintenance alternative to a monotonous lawn. And groundcovers make a lovely living mulch when planted around shrubs or tall perennials. If you choose the right groundcover for your site, you'll rarely need to care for it other than watering it during severe drought and weeding it occasionally.

◄ If your yard has poor soil and lots of hot, full sun, hybrid sun rose (*Helianthemum* hybrid) will love it! This low-growing, spreading perennial positively thrives in sandy, well-drained soil.

Groundcovers for Minimal Maintenance

The best-known groundcover is lawn grass. We use lawns abundantly to cover the ground around our homes, schools, churches, and businesses (some would even say far *too* abundantly). But lawns need constant mowing, fertilizing, and watering. For all their apparent simplicity, lawns are one of the most labor-intensive areas in the yard—there always seems to be something to do. That's one reason why many homeowners are turning to perennial groundcovers: They just don't require as much maintenance.

In some cases, lawn grass is the best choice for a groundcover. For example, very few groundcovers will tolerate foot traffic as easily as a lawn can, and I can scarcely imagine playing football or golf on anything but grass.

With the right groundcover, though, it's possible to create a lovely green landscape feature with truly minimal upkeep (certainly with little mowing). And you can even enjoy a few flowers now and then, although constant bloom is rarely a major concern where groundcovers are concerned.

Planting Groundcovers on a Budget

One reason lawns are popular is that they're so inexpensive to install. Growing a lawn can be as cheap and simple as buying a bag of seed. Perennial groundcovers, on the other hand, can be an expensive proposition. At a typical spacing of one plant per square foot, covering a large surface can cost hundreds of dollars. That's one reason why fast-spreading groundcovers, such as ajuga (*Ajuga reptans*) and lamiums (*Lamium* spp.), are used so often. You can space

To separate an offset from the main section of your groundcover, just insert a trowel next to the offset and gently lift it from the ground. You can replant it immediately where it's needed.

them widely and still get fast coverage. Also, you can buy them in trays as rooted cuttings at a much lower cost than the individual pots most other perennials are sold in (not all nurseries offer this kind of service, though, so shop around). Many such groundcovers are simply planted at 1-foot (30-cm) intervals, in staggered rows, and allowed to fill in on their own. Or you can direct their growth by moving stems or runners to fill in empty spaces, pegging them into place with a hairpin or a coffee stirrer that has been bent in half.

For even greater savings, buy just a few plants of a spreading groundcover. Plant them where you want to establish your groundcover carpet. Then, take cuttings two or three times per summer and root them, or dig up offsets as they form and transplant them to expand the area you'd like covered. You'll be quite surprised at how quickly they multiply—and how quickly their babies produce babies! Within a year, I'll bet you can cover a space the size of the average swimming pool with cuttings and divisions from just half a dozen plants.

One disadvantage to working with a fast-spreading groundcover like ajuga is that the groundcover may spread too rampantly to suit your plans. If you want more control, try a clump-forming groundcover that won't spread on its own, such as hakone grass (*Hakonechloa macra*) and epimediums. You can still save money on these groundcovers by buying only a few plants, then dividing them regularly—even annually—until you have the coverage you need. Or try to negotiate wholesale prices based on a larger-than-average purchase. If you're talking about buying 50 to 100 pots or more, you should be able to haggle and negotiate the price down a bit. To ensure perfect cover with these plants, use staggered plantings based on the mature spread of the plant. And apply an organic mulch, such as shredded leaves, at least 2 inches (5 cm) thick over any open spaces between plants until they do fill in, or your groundcover area may quickly fill with weeds, defeating your purpose.

Establishing Groundcovers on Slopes

If you're planting a groundcover on a gentle slope, just plant as usual. On steeper slopes, though, watering new groundcovers can be difficult, as any moisture simply flows down the slope without sinking in. To make sure your new plants get the water they need, build up a ring of soil around the edge of each plant, as described on page 13. And consider using irrigation (a soaker hose or drip irrigation), at least to get the plants started. In many naturally dry climates, though, watering slopes remains a problem even once the groundcovers are well established, so you may need to consider using irrigation on a permanent basis.

After You Plant
Most groundcovers benefit from extra watering not only for the first year but also for the second year, especially if they're planted in areas with heavy root competition. And as mentioned above, continue to mulch well with an organic mulch until the planting area has entirely filled in.

Mow Once in Midseason
Some groundcovers, such as lamiums, benefit from being cut back in midsummer, as they can become unshapely and grow higher in some spots and lower in others: You can use a string trimmer or a lawn mower (set at its highest level) to do this. This kind of pruning also tends to stimulate the plant to fill in more rapidly. And evergreen groundcovers that show winter damage, such as burned leaf edges, leafless stems, and dead sections, can likewise be mowed back in early spring to stimulate more abundant fill.

Leave the Leaves
You may wonder what to do about the leaves that fall on groundcovers planted under trees. Unless leaf drop is very heavy, most fall leaves will simply melt into the groundcover and re-quire no cleanup; even large leaves like those of maples (*Acer* spp.) and sycamores (*Platanus* spp.) will eventually work their way to the base of the plant.

If the tree leaves on your groundcovers seem too messy in fall, rake very lightly (you don't want to harm the groundcovers themselves) only in spots where the leaves are most visible, usually near the front of the garden or along paths. Then chop the leaves by using a shredder or by running the lawn mower over them, and spread them back over the groundcover where they came from, watering them in so they quickly disappear. Why put the leaves back? Because by doing so you'll be feeding the groundcover. For most groundcovers, naturally decaying leaf mulch is all the plant food they'll ever need.

"Think Twice" Can Be Nice
🛈 Don't be alarmed (at least not *too* alarmed) by the many *Think Twice* logos in this chapter. Many of them simply indicate that the plant tends to spread—which is just what most groundcovers are supposed to do if you want fast and complete cover. One downside of many groundcovers is that they don't limit their spreading nature to their chosen spots; they end up invading other parts of the garden. This is predictable behavior under the circumstances, and you are probably choosing these plants knowing full well they have this little flaw, but I feel I should at least remind you!

13 More Groundcovers
There are hundreds of groundcover perennials to choose from, so I couldn't include all of them in this chapter or even in this book. But there are some great groundcovers featured in other chapters, so don't overlook them.

Ajuga

Ajuga, bugleweed

Ajugas are one of the most popular and useful perennial groundcovers. They're low-growing, mat-forming plants with spoon-shaped leaves and short, square, upright stems that bear numerous tiny flowers. The species usually has blue to violet flowers and dark green leaves, but there are all sorts of variations among the many cultivars. The leaves are evergreen in most climates, although they do die back somewhat in very cold areas.

Plant Profile

AJUGA
uh-JOO-guh

- **Bloom Color:** Pink, violet-blue, or white

- **Bloom Time:** Late spring to early summer

- **Length of Bloom:** 2 weeks or more

- **Height:** Varies by species; see individual listings

- **Spread:** Varies by species; see individual listings

- **Garden Uses:** Container planting, edging, groundcover, mass planting, mixed border, woodland garden; along paths, on slopes

- **Light Preference:** Full sun to deep shade

- **Soil Preference:** Humus-rich, well-drained, sandy soil

- **Best Way to Propagate:** Divide at any time

- **USDA Plant Hardiness Zones:** 3 to 9

- **AHS Heat Zones:** 9 to 1

Growing Tips

Ajugas are all-purpose groundcovers, thriving in both full sun (in moist soil) and in seasonally deep shade. They also adapt to just about every type of soil, from rich to poor and dry to moist, although they're most prolific in moist, well-drained soil that's relatively rich in humus.

All ajugas spread by creeping roots. *Ajuga reptans* also produces stems that creep along the ground and form plantlets, or offsets, where they touch the ground. You can multiply all species easily by digging up these rooted plantlets. Ajugas are so prolific that there's little need to think of propagating them by seed. Ajugas do self-seed abundantly, however, so if you're worried about them invading your lawn, deadhead them after they bloom.

Good Neighbors

Ajugas come in three speeds: fast, medium, and slow. Use *Ajuga reptans* when you want a weedproof, carefree cover—fast! Plant it under shrubs or trees, or use it in front of equally vigorous companions, such as clump-forming ornamental grasses. Medium-speed Geneva bugleweed (*A. genevensis*) is more neighborly. Try it in the shade garden with turtleheads (*Chelone* spp.), hostas, and other sturdy companions. Upright bugleweed (*A. pyramidalis*) looks great in a lightly shaded rock garden, with bloody cranesbill (*Geranium sanguineum*), small ferns, and other rock garden perennials.

Problems and Solutions

Although generally tough, undemanding plants, ajugas can rot at the base in overly wet spring soil or in areas where they get little air circulation. The plants usually recover fully, but if this is a frequent problem, it's better to combine your ajugas with other groundcovers that can fill in where the ajugas die back.

Top Performer

Ajuga reptans (common ajuga, common bugleweed): This is by far the most common species and the most aggressive as well. Because the stems creep along above the ground, it's difficult to control them with a root barrier: You'll probably find yourself pulling out wayward plants now and then. 'Alba' has green leaves and white flowers in late spring to early summer, while 'Rosea' is similar with pink blooms. There's considerable confusion about names among the purple- to bronze-leaved cultivars: 'Atropurpurea', also called 'Purpurea', is the best known. 'Silver Carpet', with attractive silver-gray leaves highlighted by a thin green margin, is one of several gray-leaved cultivars; 'Multicolor' (also called 'Rainbow' and 'Tricolor') is one of the better-known variegated types, with leaves in a wide range of greens, purples, whites, yellows, and pinks. Height: 6 to 8 inches (15 to 20 cm). Spread: 12 to 18 inches (30 to 45 cm). USDA Plant Hardiness Zones 3 to 9; AHS Heat Zones 9 to 1.

More Recommended Ajugas

Ajuga genevensis (Geneva bugleweed): This species produces a basal rosette of coarse-toothed, hairy, dark green leaves and eventually develops into a thick mat of foliage. Abundant spikes of very upright blue flowers bloom from late spring to early summer. The best known cultivar, 'Pink Beauty', is hardy only to Zone 5. Height: 6 to 8 inches (15 to 20 cm). Spread: 8 to 10 inches (20 to 25 cm). USDA Plant Hardiness Zones 3 to 9; AHS Heat Zones 9 to 1.

A. *pyramidalis* (upright bugleweed): This slow-spreading species produces more rounded leaves than common ajuga (A. *reptans*) and leafy flowerstalks that partly hide the lavender-blue flowers. The most widely available cultivar is 'Metallica Crispa', with wrinkled reddish brown leaves with a metallic sheen. Height: 6 to 10 inches (15 to 25 cm). Spread: 6 to 8 inches (15 to 20 cm). USDA Plant Hardiness Zones 3 to 9; AHS Heat Zones 9 to 1.

Common ajuga
(*Ajuga reptans*)

Larry's Garden Notes

Ajuga (*Ajuga reptans*) is not at its best after flowering, but the plants will reward you with fresh foliage if you cut them back. One easy way to do this is to mow over the entire area, chopping back spent flower spikes along with some of the foliage.

Campanula

Bellflower

Bellflowers are popular, long-lived, easy-to-grow perennials, and the low-growing groundcover types are very much at home in rock gardens, rock walls, raised beds, and containers of all sorts, especially in cool-summer areas. They have attractive, small leaves and bell- or star-shaped flowers, usually in blue or violet shades.

Plant Profile

CAMPANULA
kam-PAN-yew-luh

■ **Bloom Color:** Blue, purple, and white

■ **Bloom Time:** Varies by species; see individual listings

■ **Length of Bloom:** 2 to 3 weeks or more

■ **Height:** Varies by species; see individual listings

■ **Spread:** Varies by species; see individual listings

■ **Garden Uses:** Container planting, edging, groundcover, mass planting, rock garden, specimen plant, wall planting; along paths, on slopes

■ **Light Preference:** Full sun to partial shade

■ **Soil Preference:** Average, well-drained soil

■ **Best Way to Propagate:** Divide in spring or fall

■ **USDA Plant Hardiness Zones:** Varies by species; see individual listings

■ **AHS Heat Zones:** Varies by species; see individual listings

Growing Tips

Average, well-drained soil will suit groundcover bellflowers just fine. Most bellflowers do best in cool-summer areas, but they will also thrive in hot-summer areas in partial shade if you mulch generously.

Division is the easiest way to multiply cultivars, but bellflowers also grow readily from seed sown indoors or out in spring. Don't cover the seeds because many species need light to germinate. You can also grow bellflowers from stem cuttings.

Many bellflowers self-sow somewhat, but not to the point of becoming major pests. To prevent any spread at all, simply deadhead your plants or cut them back harshly after their first flush of bloom. As a bonus, deadheading or cutting back will usually stimulate some repeat bloom.

Good Neighbors

For early color, interplant groundcover bellflowers with spring-blooming bulbs, such as early yellow crocuses or white snowdrops (*Galanthus* spp.). In rock gardens, possible partners include sea thrift (*Armeria maritima*), cushion spurge (*Euphorbia polychroma*, also called *E. epithymoides*), sedums, and hens-and-chicks (*Sempervivum tectorum*). In the flower border, good companions include low-growing neighbors, such as 'Moonbeam' threadleaf coreopsis (*Coreopsis verticillata* 'Moonbeam'), pinks (*Dianthus* spp.), and evergreen candytuft (*Iberis sempervirens*).

Problems and Solutions

Diseases and insects are rarely a problem with bellflowers, but slugs and snails can damage them by munching on the leaves. For suggestions on controlling these pests, see page 55.

Top Performer

Campanula portenschlagiana, also called *C. muralis* (Dalmatian bellflower): Of all the creeping bellflowers, Dalmatian bellflower is probably the best known. It's a low, mounding, mat-forming creeper with toothed, wavy, heart-shaped leaves and stems. Although it won't choke out other plants, it does spread quickly. The violet-blue flowers are bell-shaped and flare open at the tips. They appear most abundantly in late spring but usually rebloom in fall if you cut the plant back after its first flush of bloom. 'Resholt Variety', with larger, darker blue flowers, and 'Alba', with white flowers, are popular cultivars. Height: 4 to 6 inches (10 to 15 cm). Spread: 1 foot (30 cm). USDA Plant Hardiness Zones 4 to 9; AHS Heat Zones 7 to 1.

More Recommended Bellflowers

Campanula garganica, also called *C. elatines* var. *garganica* (Gargano bellflower): This low, creeping plant bears toothed, gray green, nearly evergreen leaves that are oval at the base and heart-shaped on the stems and clustered, flat, star-shaped blue flowers. Although principally a late-spring-to-early-summer bloomer, it generally flowers more lightly until fall in cool climates. It does best in full sun except in hot-summer areas, where it appreciates partial shade. There are several cultivars, but the most striking is 'Dickson's Gold', with impressive gold-green leaves. Height: 3 to 6 inches (8 to 15 cm). Spread: 1 foot (30 cm). USDA Plant Hardiness Zones 4 to 9; AHS Heat Zones 7 to 1.

C. rotundifolia (harebell, bluebell, bluebells-of-Scotland): If you look for the rounded leaves suggested by its botanical epithet, *rotundifolia*, you may be disappointed. Only the rosette leaves are rounded, and they usually disappear by flowering time. The upper leaves, the ones you actually see, are narrow and grasslike. The bell-shaped flowers, usually bright blue in color, are nodding and measure up to 1 inch (2.5 cm) in diameter. They're borne in loose clusters, usually a few at a time, from early summer to early fall. Height: 6 to 12 inches (15 to 30 cm). Spread: 1 foot (30 cm). USDA Plant Hardiness Zones 2 to 9; AHS Heat Zones 7 to 1.

You'll also find an entry on long-blooming bellflowers in "Everblooming Perennials" on page 74. One of those everblooming species, Carpathian harebell (*C. carpatica*), also makes a wonderful groundcover and a great edging plant.

Dalmatian bellflower
(*Campanula portenschlagiana*)

Around the World with *Campanula*

The Scottish may wax poetic over the "bluebells-of-Scotland" (*Campanula rotundifolia*), but they share their bluebells (harebells) with about half the Northern Hemisphere! Of all the plants I've seen in my travels, this species is the most pervasive; it's native to cool rocky areas, grasslands, and open forests all over the globe. I've seen the plant in Scotland, of course, but also in the national parks of western Canada and the United States, in the Alps of Europe, escaped from culture in the Southern Alps of New Zealand, and in many places in the mountains of northeastern North America.

Cerastium

Snow-in-summer, chickweed

You'll grow these charming but rather aggressive groundcovers as much for their silky, silvery foliage as for their brilliant white blooms, which give them their common name of snow-in-summer. They form dense mats of narrow, pointed, silver-gray leaves. They're fully evergreen, though the plants often look a bit ratty in early spring until new growth appears. Each flower has five petals, but the petals are so deeply notched that the flowers appear to have twice that number.

Plant Profile

CERASTIUM
sir-AS-tee-um

- **Bloom Color:** White
- **Bloom Time:** Midspring to late spring
- **Length of Bloom:** 3 to 5 weeks
- **Height:** Varies by species; see individual listings
- **Spread:** Varies by species; see individual listings
- **Garden Uses:** Container planting, edging, groundcover, mass planting, rock garden, specimen plant, wall planting; along paths, on slopes
- **Light Preference:** Full sun to light shade
- **Soil Preference:** Average, well-drained soil
- **Best Way to Propagate:** Divide in spring or fall
- **USDA Plant Hardiness Zones:** 2 to 7
- **AHS Heat Zones:** 7 to 1

Growing Tips

Snow-in-summer are stellar performers in cool-summer areas, where they do best in full sun. In warmer climates, they tend to melt down in summer if you don't prune them back, but otherwise they're a fine choice for partial shade. The high heat and humidity of the Southeast combine to make it a poor home for this plant.

Not particular about soil types, snow-in-summer will grow in all but soggy conditions. They do grow best in very well-drained, poor soil, where they stay more compact and flower more profusely. Rich, moist soil can lead to floppy, less attractive growth and sparser bloom.

Think Twice: Many species root wherever their underground runners reach, often spreading out of their alloted boundaries, and they also self-seed easily. To control the spread by seed, simply mow the plants back after they bloom. Surrounding them with vigorous companions can hold their creeping in check.

Choose your favorite means of propagation: Snow-in-summer are a snap to divide and are easy to root from cuttings, and they self-sow willingly. If you grow them from seed from commercial sources, expect fast germination and growth; just sow seeds indoors in late winter or outdoors in spring.

Good Neighbors

Snow-in-summer are popular as groundcovers for hard-to-reach slopes, which they cover at great speed. They also look great between stepping stones, on flat surfaces, and along paths. Try them under sun-loving shrubs, such as northern bayberry (*Myrica pensylvanica*) or rugosa rose (*Rosa rugosa*), or around clumps of mound-forming ornamental grasses, like fountain grass (*Pennisetum alopecuroides*).

Problems and Solutions

About the only problem you'll encounter is root rot if you plant snow-in-summer in soggy soil; good drainage is important to prevent this disease.

Top Performer

Cerastium tomentosum (snow-in-summer): The most common species, this snow-in-summer can be aggressive if you don't control it. It has somewhat broader, more spoonlike leaves than the other species described here, but otherwise the different silvery species are notoriously difficult to tell apart. Snow-in-summer grows to about 1 foot (30 cm) tall, but most plants sold these days are usually better-behaved, smaller cultivars. All bloom from midspring to late spring. Variety *columnae* is the most dwarf form, growing to about 4 inches (10 cm) tall, with a denser, less aggressive growth habit than the species. 'Silberteppich' (also called 'Silver Carpet') is similar, but it has much whiter leaves and grows to 6 inches (15 cm). 'Yo-Yo', at 10 inches (25 cm) tall, is especially free-flowering. Height: 4 to 12 inches (10 to 30 cm). Spread: 1 to 2 feet (30 to 60 cm). USDA Plant Hardiness Zones 2 to 7; AHS Heat Zones 7 to 1.

More Recommended Snow-in-Summer

Cerastium alpinum subsp. *lanatum* (alpine chickweed): This dense, mat-forming species has no aggressive tendencies, so it's perfect for the rock garden. Plant it more densely than snow-in-summer (*C. tomentosum*) for use as a groundcover in other situations. The silver-gray leaves are densely covered with grayish white hairs, and the midspring to late-spring flowers are just as white as those of snow-in-summer, though smaller. Height: 2 to 4 inches (5 to 10 cm). Spread: 6 to 12 inches (15 to 30 cm). USDA Plant Hardiness Zones 2 to 7; AHS Heat Zones 7 to 1.

    C. biebersteinii (Taurus chickweed): According to the experts, the leaves of this chickweed are longer and narrower than those of snow-in-summer (*C. tomentosum*). In a garden setting, you can scarcely tell the two apart, even when you plant them side by side. Just plant whichever is locally available and don't expect any noticeable difference. Height: 4 to 12 inches (10 to 30 cm). Spread: 1 to 2 feet (30 to 60 cm). USDA Plant Hardiness Zones 2 to 7; AHS Heat Zones 7 to 1.

Snow-in-summer
(*Cerastium tomentosum*)

Larry's Garden Notes

Think about snow-in-summer (*Cerastium tomentosum*) as a problem solver in desperate situations. Rock walls, sandy sunny slopes, and dry, rocky soils may seem inhospitable to most, but not to this robust spreader! And it's no coincidence that this tough, drought-tolerant perennial has hairy leaves—the minute hairs protect the plant by conserving water in the leaves.

Ceratostigma

Plumbago, leadwort

No wonder plumbagos are catching on rapidly as groundcovers—they're tough, easy-to-grow plants. The wiry stems bear bronzy to dark green, 3-inch (8-cm) leaves that turn a pretty red in the fall. From midsummer (earlier in mild-winter areas) into fall, the upper parts of the stems are spotted with clusters of bright blue flowers. In mild-winter climates, the leaves may hang on through the winter but don't hesitate to cut the plant back in spring if it looks worse for wear.

Plant Profile

CERATOSTIGMA
sir-at-oh-STIG-muh

- **Bloom Color:** Blue
- **Bloom Time:** Midsummer to midfall or late fall
- **Length of Bloom:** 2 months or more
- **Height:** Varies by species; see individual listings
- **Spread:** Varies by species; see individual listings
- **Garden Uses:** Container planting, edging, groundcover, mass planting, mixed border, rock garden, specimen plant; along paths, on slopes
- **Light Preference:** Full sun to partial shade
- **Soil Preference:** Humus-rich, well-drained soil
- **Best Way to Propagate:** Divide at any time
- **USDA Plant Hardiness Zones:** Varies by species; see individual listings
- **AHS Heat Zones:** Varies by species; see individual listings

Growing Tips

Plumbagos adapt to a wide range of conditions, doing well in both full sun and partial shade. Although they prefer rich soil with plenty of organic matter, they will also thrive in poor, even stony, soil. One thing they won't tolerate is soggy conditions, especially in winter: Good drainage is a must.

Division is the best way to multiply plumbagos. You can do this any time the ground is not frozen.

Think Twice: Plumbagos spread vigorously by underground stems, and they can be pushy, invading and dominating other plants. Grow them on their own, use a root barrier to keep them under control, or plant them in spots where they're surrounded by trees on all sides: Any of these measures will keep them in check.

Although plumbagos are semievergreen, it's still best to cut them to the ground in fall or spring to stimulate new growth. A winter mulch is wise in USDA Zone 5. Older plants tend to die out in the center over time. The solution is easy: Simply dig out the dead area and fill in the hole with fresh soil. Plumbagos will quickly move back in to fill the gap.

Good Neighbors

Although plumbagos are a beautiful addition to the late-season garden, don't turn these rapid spreaders loose in a formal border. Instead, try them under shrubs, particularly those with late-season color, such as hollies, shrubby cinquefoil (*Potentilla fruticosa*), and shrub roses. Tough perennials such as yuccas and ornamental grasses will also stand up to the competition. Interplanting with spring bulbs will provide color while you're waiting for your plumbagos to emerge. The bright green foliage and deep blue flowers are also pretty for walls and rock gardens and planted along pathways.

Problems and Solutions

Plumbago has no significant problems with insects or diseases.

Top Performer

Ceratostigma plumbaginoides, also called *Plumbago larpentae* (leadwort): Leadwort is the only commonly grown plant in this genus. It can be aggressive if you don't control it from the start, but it's a real pussycat if you plant it within a weed barrier. The main flaw with leadwort as a groundcover is its slow spring start. In the coolest parts of its range, it generally takes until the beginning of summer to start sprouting, and in areas with short-growing seasons, frosts can hit when flowering has barely begun. In warmer climates, though, leadwort begins blooming as early as July and is still in bloom when the first frosts occur several months later. Needless to say, leadwort is a better choice for long-summer areas than short-summer areas. Height: 8 to 12 inches (20 to 30 cm). Spread: 18 inches (45 cm). USDA Plant Hardiness Zones 5 to 9; AHS Heat Zones 9 to 1.

Leadwort
(*Ceratostigma plumbaginoides*)

More Recommended Plumbagos

Ceratostigma willmottianum (Chinese leadwort): This is a taller, shrublike plumbago with smaller leaves. Its flowers are very similar to leadwort (*C. plumbaginoides*), though perhaps slightly more violet than blue, and its leaves are only half the size, with hairy margins. Chinese leadwort blooms for about two months in late summer, but it tends to stop sooner than its more widely grown relative, well before the first frosts. Besides turning red in the fall, Chinese leadwort doesn't offer as much contrast between the blue flowers and fall colors as its cousin. It has upright woody stems, but it dies back in winter in most climates, so prune it to the ground in spring so it can make a fresh start. Height: 2 to 3 feet (60 to 90 cm). Spread: 2 to 3 feet (60 to 90 cm). USDA Plant Hardiness Zones 6 to 9; AHS Heat Zones 9 to 6.

Smart Substitutes

If your soil is too acid for leadwort, try lithodora (*Lithodora diffusa*, also called *Lithospermum diffusum*). The flowers are very similar, although they start earlier in the summer and the hairy, gray-green leaves are evergreen in most climates. It prefers acid conditions and does well in the company of other acid-loving plants such as azaleas and heathers. It needs perfect drainage and relatively poor soil to bloom well. A good winter mulch is advisable in the northern part of its range. Height: 6 to 12 inches (15 to 30 cm). Spread: 12 to 18 inches (30 to 45 cm). USDA Plant Hardiness Zones 5 to 9; AHS Heat Zones 8 to 1.

Chrysogonum

Goldenstar, green and gold

This absolutely charming little plant is more than a simple native wildflower: It also makes a wonderful groundcover. Goldenstar (*Chrysogonum virginianum*) produces a mass of slightly fuzzy, dark green, triangular, lightly toothed leaves. The leaves are evergreen in the South but die back in late fall in the North. Star-shaped golden yellow flowers, 1 to 1½ inches (2.5 to 4 cm) across, start appearing in spring in the South and in early summer in the North. Each flower has five broad rays (petals) that are deeply notched at the tips.

Plant Profile

CHRYSOGONUM
krih-SAW-goh-nuhm

- **Bloom Color:** Yellow

- **Bloom Time:** Late spring to early summer, repeating until fall

- **Length of Bloom:** 4 weeks or more

- **Height:** 4 to 12 inches (10 to 30 cm)

- **Spread:** 12 to 18 inches (30 to 45 cm)

- **Garden Uses:** Container planting, edging, groundcover, mass planting, mixed border, rock garden, specimen plant, wall planting, woodland garden; along paths, on slopes

- **Light Preference:** Full sun to deep shade

- **Soil Preference:** Moist, well-drained soil

- **Best Way to Propagate:** Divide in spring

- **USDA Plant Hardiness Zones:** 4 to 9

- **AHS Heat Zones:** 9 to 2

Growing Tips

Goldenstar (*Chrysogonum virginianum*) needs at least some soil moisture at all times, yet it won't tolerate wet soil. It does seem to appreciate a site sheltered from the harshest winds. Full sun to only light shade are ideal in cool-summer climates; partial shade is best where summers are hot.

Goldenstar's cold-hardiness is excellent wherever snow cover is available, and it absolutely thrives in my USDA Zone 3 garden, coming through the winter with nary a scratch and springing into vigorous growth shortly after snow melt (which is, admittedly, well into May most years). However, where snow cover cannot be guaranteed, goldenstar will probably need some winter protection north of USDA Zone 5: A light mulch of evergreen boughs brings it through the winter in fine shape in a friend's Zone 4 garden in Minnesota.

Digging up one of the plentiful offsets is the easiest way to multiply goldenstar, but you can also snip off some of the unrooted plantlets and treat them like cuttings. Or sow the seed directly outdoors in summer while it's still fresh. You can also collect the seed, store it in your refrigerator, then sow it indoors in late winter. Germination takes place quickly, in about three weeks. In the garden, goldenstar self-sows to a certain degree but without becoming too invasive.

Good Neighbors

A native woodland species, goldenstar is a natural choice for mass planting under the shade of open trees and shrubs. Weave it in and out of groupings of ferns, hostas, and Solomon's seals (*Polygonatum* spp.) for a low-care shade planting. In a more formal, partly shaded garden, combine the gold with blues or purples—such as Siberian iris (*Iris sibirica*) or Jacob's ladders (*Polemonium* spp.)—for an eye-catching early combination.

Problems and Solutions

Slugs, snails, and caterpillars occasionally take chunks out of the leaves but do little lasting damage because the plants quickly produce fresh leaves. Otherwise goldenstar doesn't seem to have many problems.

Top Performer

Chrysogonum virginianum (goldenstar, green and gold): Goldenstar is the only plant in the *Chrysogonum* genus that's grown in gardens, but even if it had competition, it would easily rank as my top performer. Goldenstar flowers profusely at the beginning of the season for four to five weeks, but the plant still keeps on blooming, albeit more lightly, right through the summer in cool-summer areas. In hotter climates, flowering peters out as the temperature rises, especially in sunny or dry sites. And in most climates, goldenstar starts another period of heavy blooming with the return of cooler weather in the fall.

There are several varieties and cultivars that all look very much like the species, but with different habits. *C. virginianum* var. *australe* produces long runners with plantlets at their tips, much like those of a strawberry plant. It spreads particularly rapidly and is a choice groundcover in areas where speed is important. 'Mark Viette' is a selection that was chosen for its more abundant bloom. 'Eco Lacquered Spider' has the longest runners of all and attractive gray-green foliage. 'Springbrook' is a particularly dwarf cultivar, no taller than 8 inches (20 cm) even when in flower. *C. virginianum* var. *virginianum*, with lighter green leaves, tends to flower more freely but produces fewer offsets and few or no runners. 'Allen Bush' is a selection that just doesn't want to stop blooming.

A native woodland wildflower, goldenstar (*Chrysogonum virginianum*) is an ideal choice for the meandering spaces around ferns, hostas, and shrubs in the shade garden. Its starry yellow flowers appear in early spring, often fading away during the hot days of summer; the flowers usually return with a smaller showing in the fall.

Convallaria

Lily-of-the-valley

For such a beloved perennial, lily-of-the-valley is certainly not very imposing. It's a tiny plant, each stem bearing only two or three smooth, dark green, broadly oval leaves unrolling on short stems directly from fast-creeping roots, which are called pips. In spring, the plant produces narrow flowerstalks with tiny, usually white, bell-shaped flowers that are extraordinarily fragrant. Occasionally, some of the flowers develop into green berries that turn brilliant red by fall.

Plant Profile

CONVALLARIA
con-val-AIR-ee-uh

- Bloom Color: Pink or white
- Bloom Time: Midspring to late spring
- Length of Bloom: 2 or 3 weeks
- Height: 6 to 12 inches (15 to 30 cm)
- Spread: 1 foot (30 cm)
- Garden Uses: Container planting, cut flower garden, edging, groundcover, mass planting, rock garden, wall planting, woodland garden; along paths, on slopes, in wet areas
- Light Preference: Full sun to deep shade
- Soil Preference: Rich, moist, well-drained soil
- Best Way to Propagate: Divide in spring or fall
- USDA Plant Hardiness Zones: 1 to 8
- AHS Heat Zones: 9 to 1

Growing Tips

Lily-of-the-valley will grow just about anywhere you plant it, from full sun to deep shade, in rich, moist soil or poor, dry sites. For best results, though, plant it in light to partial shade and well-drained, humus-rich, moist soil. It will do fine in full sun only in humid, cool conditions, and though it will grow well in deep shade, its bloom there leaves a lot to be desired.

In hot or dry conditions, lily-of-the-valley doesn't die, but the leaves quickly yellow, then turn brown, and become tattered at the tips. The plant's effect as a groundcover is totally lost, so if heat and drought are the best you can offer, you'd do best to grow this plant in a out-of-the-way spot where its summer appearance isn't noticeable— or mow it to the ground when the leaves become unattractive. Don't worry that you might kill it by cutting it back so early in the year: Lily-of-the-valley is one of those plants that could probably live through a nuclear attack and still bloom the following year.

Lily-of-the-valley is so easy to grow in so many climates that it can be an out-and-out weed! But in mild-winter climates, lily-of-the-valley tends to form only weak clusters, without spreading. And in areas where it doesn't get at least a few weeks of cold winter weather, they may not even bloom.

The fastest and easiest way to propagate lily-of-the-valley is by dividing the abundant creeping roots in spring or fall. Mulch abundantly the first few years until the

FUN FACTS

You can also force lily-of-the-valley's creeping roots for winter bloom indoors, much as you force spring bulbs. Dig them up in the fall after they've undergone a few hard frosts, and pot up only the thickest roots. Then store them in a cool, bright place—about 65°F (18°C)—until the plants bloom.

plants fill in: After that, lily-of-the-valley can pretty much take care of itself.

Good Neighbors

Dainty in flower but not so dainty in habit, fast-spreading lily-of-the-valley is an ideal plant to use as a dense groundcover under the shade of trees and shrubs. Site it in a moist, well-drained spot where you can enjoy the spring fragrance. Combine only with the toughest of herbaceous plants, such as a large grouping of ferns, and be prepared to divide it frequently.

Warning: Lily-of-the-valley is highly poisonous in all its parts. Even the water in the vases where you've placed the flowers can become toxic! For young children, however, the greatest danger is in the seductively red berries that look just like candy, so cut off the flowerstalks before the berries mature.

Problems and Solutions

Various leaf spots may occur in midsummer to late summer but are rarely pronounced enough to detract from the plant's appearance. A scorched appearance, with leaves browning at the edges or with streaks of brown through the center, is due to dry conditions. This doesn't hurt the plant in the long run, but for great leaves all summer, lily-of-the-valley must be kept moist at all times.

Top Performer

Think Twice: Although it's attractive, lily-of-the-valley (*Convallaria majalis*) is a highly invasive plant in most climates, so plant it within a root barrier to control its spread. It does, however, make a great groundcover under deciduous trees and shrubs and in other places where it can't escape control.

There are a number of very attractive cultivars and varieties. Variety *rosea*, with pink flowers, is particularly nice, as is 'Plena', with double white flowers lasting longer than those of the species. 'Fortin's Giant', reaching up to 15 inches (38 cm) tall, with larger flowers, is also a great cultivar. 'Striata' (also called 'Aureo-variegata', 'Lineata', or 'Variegata') has green leaves with cream to yellow stripes. It needs a fair amount of sun to retain its color.

Lily-of-the-valley
(*Convallaria majalis*)

Around the World with *Convallaria*

Although lily-of-the-valley is popular as an old-fashioned perennial in North America, that's nothing compared to its near cult status in Europe, where it's considered one of the principal harbingers of spring. In many areas, lily-of-the-valley is called mayflower and is the very symbol of the month of May. If you're ever in Paris on the first of May, you'll see flower girls on nearly every corner hawking bouquets of lily-of-the-valley and hear songs on the radio waxing poetic about the beauties of lily-of-the-valley—and the situation is much the same in Germany.

Deschampsia

Hair grass

An ornamental grass may seem like an unlikely choice for a groundcover, but hair grass works beautifully as a groundcover with a difference. These fine-textured ornamental grasses produce dense clumps of very narrow, hairlike leaves. Their thin flower clusters are even lighter and more ethereal than the foliage. You'll especially appreciate their extremely early bloom because most other grasses don't put on much of a show until late summer or fall. The billowy flowers usually appear in late May and are so abundant they almost hide the foliage!

Plant Profile

DESCHAMPSIA
deh-SHAMP-see-uh

- **Bloom Color:** Bronze, gold, green, purple, or silver

- **Bloom Time:** Late spring to midsummer

- **Length of Bloom:** 8 to 10 weeks

- **Height:** Varies by species; see individual listings

- **Spread:** Varies by species; see individual listings

- **Garden Uses:** Container planting, cut flower garden, edging, groundcover, mass planting, meadow garden, mixed border, rock gardens, specimen plant; in wet areas

- **Light Preference:** Full sun to deep shade

- **Soil Preference:** Rich, moist soil

- **Best Way to Propagate:** Divide in spring, summer, or fall

- **USDA Plant Hardiness Zones:** 4 to 9

- **AHS Heat Zones:** 9 to 1

Growing Tips

Hair grasses grow best in moist, rich soil and light to partial shade. They do poorly in hot, dry situations—especially if the soil dries out completely—and, in general, they don't succeed particularly well in hot-summer areas. In cool climates, though, they thrive even in full sun as long as you keep their soil moist. Deep shade is acceptable in both hot- and cool-summer climates, but the plants will most likely flower only lightly, if at all.

Where happy, hair grasses are virtually permanent landscape features and need little if any care, except for their annual haircut. Even in mild climates where the foliage is evergreen, it's best to cut hair grasses back to within 2 inches (5 cm) of the ground in late winter or early spring. This will help prevent the awkward stage in which the fresher green new leaves push up through the older ones, creating a decidedly unattractive appearance.

Division is the usual way of propagating hair grass cultivars because they don't come true from seed. It's possible to divide the dense clumps just about any time of the year the ground is not frozen. The species grow fine from seed sown indoors in late winter or outdoors in spring.

Good Neighbors

Masses of tufted hair grass (*Deschampsia caespitosa*) make a great background for lower-growing groundcovers, such as leadwort (*Ceratostigma plumbaginoides*).

Smaller crinkled hair grass (*Deschampsia flexuosa*) is suitable for rock gardens or for smaller-scale groundcover plantings.

Both species make a handsome contrast to perennials with bolder foliage, such as heartleaf bergenia (*Bergenia cordifolia*) and

'Herbstfreude' sedum (*Sedum* 'Herbstfreude', also called *S.* 'Autumn Joy').

Problems and Solutions

Rabbits are about the only enemies of hair grasses: They'll nibble these plants right down to the ground if given half a chance! Trapping or hunting the rabbits are the only effective, long-term solutions.

Top Performer

Deschampsia caespitosa (tufted hair grass): This is the most popular ornamental grass in the genus, with dark green, delicately pleated leaves. From late spring on, it's covered with taller, feathery, arching flower clusters that almost obscure the foliage. The flowers drop off by late summer, but the light, airy stems remain in place until winter. The remaining leaves turn yellow-green in the fall in mild climates but remain alive all winter. Elsewhere, they turn beige with the first hard frosts.

There are many cultivars of tufted hair grass, mostly differing by various flower colors and somewhat different heights. 'Bronzeschleier' (also called 'Bronze Veil') is probably the most popular, with green flowerstalks that turn bronze by midsummer and have better heat tolerance than most. 'Goldschleier' (also called 'Gold Veil') is similar but with golden yellow flowers eventually fading to silver. 'Schottland' (also called 'Scotland') is much taller than the others, growing to 4 to 6 feet (1.2 to 1.8 m). Height: 2 to 3 feet (60 to 90 cm). Spread: 1 to 3 feet (30 to 90 cm). USDA Plant Hardiness Zones 4 to 9; AHS Heat Zones 9 to 1.

More Recommended Hair Grasses

Deschampsia flexuosa (crinkled hair grass): This is a smaller grass forming dense tufts of narrow, wiry, very shiny green leaves. The purplish, slightly twisted bloom clusters appear from early summer to midsummer, somewhat later than those of tufted hair grass (*D. caespitosa*) but still earlier than those of most other ornamental grasses. They mature to yellowish brown. 'Tatra Gold', also called 'Aurea', with golden yellow foliage in the spring that turns a greener in the summer, is one of the rare cultivars offered. Height: 1 to 2 feet (30 to 60 cm). Spread: 1 to 2 feet (30 to 60 cm). USDA Plant Hardiness Zones 4 to 9; AHS Heat Zones 9 to 1.

With its threadlike leaves and wispy flowers, 'Goldschleier' tufted hair grass (*Deschampsia caespitosa* 'Goldschleier') works well as an accent plant for smaller groundcovers and perennials with bold, broad-leaved foliage. It's partial to moist, shady spots and sends up a profusion of delicate yellow flower spikes that fade to silver as they age.

Epimedium

Epimedium, barrenwort, bishop's hat

Like many other groundcovers, epimediums are almost two plants in one. The first is the beautiful foliage plant. The new leaves that first sprout in spring are pale, almost lime green, often with distinct red highlights. Their open clusters of flowers also make them stand out in the spring garden. In summer, the leaves turn a sober dark green, but their unusual form and great density still attract attention. They have a good fall color display, and because the foliage lasts through the winter, epimediums always have something to show.

Plant Profile

EPIMEDIUM
ep-ih-MEE-dee-um

- ■ Bloom Color: Pink, red, violet, white, or yellow

- ■ Bloom Time: Midspring to late spring

- ■ Length of Bloom: 2 or 3 weeks

- ■ Height: Varies by species; see individual listings

- ■ Spread: Varies by species; see individual listings

- ■ Garden Uses: Edging, groundcover, mass planting, mixed border, rock garden, woodland garden; attracts birds (including hummingbirds) and butterflies

- ■ Light Preference: Full sun to deep shade

- ■ Soil Preference: Moist but well-drained, acid to neutral soil

- ■ Best Way to Propagate: Divide in spring or fall

- ■ USDA Plant Hardiness Zones: 5 to 9

- ■ AHS Heat Zones: Varies by species; see individual listings

Growing Tips

Although these tough plants prefer light to partial shade and rich, moist soil, they'll also grow without complaint in full sun or deep shade and even very dry soil, seeming to shrug off the root competition of the most densely shallow-rooted trees. They'll even grow in the deep shade and dry, acid soil found under pines and other conifers. To really see them flourish, though, keep the plants cool and moist, covering their roots with a nice, thick mulch.

Epimediums are slow to establish, so mulch them well for the first few years to prevent weeds from getting any ideas. Once they're up and growing, though, epimediums need virtually no maintenance. On the downside, the plants are not any faster at reproduction than at growing. It can take several years before plants are well established enough to divide (in spring or fall), and don't even think of trying to grow the plants from seed: It's not only a slow, tedious process yielding limited success, but also most epimediums are hybrids that don't come true from seed.

Good Neighbors

Plant a grouping of epimediums under the shade of trees for a medium-height, undulating cover of good-quality foliage all summer and into the winter. Or mix them with astilbes, ferns, and other plants in a shade garden, preferably near a path so you can view the small but interesting flowers close up.

Problems and Solutions

Epimediums really have no major problems: Even deer and rabbits won't eat them.

Top Performer

Epimedium × youngianum (Young's barren-wort): This barrenwort is a hybrid of longspur barrenwort (*E. grandiflorum*) and a much rarer species, *E. diphyllum*. It's a low-growing plant with leaflets that are toothed and heavily marked with red in the spring, turning green in the summer and then deep crimson in the fall. The nodding, midspring to late spring flowers are tiny and range in color from white to deep pink. 'Niveum', called snowy epimedium, is the most common cultivar and one of the most widely available of all epimediums. As you'd expect from the name, its flowers are snow white. Height: 6 to 8 inches (15 to 20 cm). Spread: 8 inches (20 cm). USDA Plant Hardiness Zones 5 to 9; AHS Heat Zones 8 to 5.

Red barrenwort
(*Epimedium × rubrum*)

More Recommended Epimediums

Epimedium grandiflorum, also called *E. macranthum* (longspur barren-wort): The most commonly available of all the epimediums, longspur barrenwort is remarkable for its especially large, long-spurred flowers that grow 1 to 2 inches (2.5 to 5 cm) across. They bloom from mid-spring to late spring in various shades of white, pink, violet, and red. The margins of the deciduous leaflets are spiny. The foliage starts out a coppery brown color in spring, becomes green in summer, then turns red in the fall. The most popular cultivar is 'Rose Queen' with particularly large, deep pink flowers, sometimes with white spurs, over foliage that's distinctly reddish in the spring. 'White Queen' resembles 'Rose Queen' but has silvery white flowers. Height: 8 to 15 inches (20 to 38 cm). Spread: 15 to 18 inches (38 to 45 cm). USDA Plant Hardiness Zones 5 to 9; AHS Heat Zones 8 to 4.

E. × *rubrum* (red barrenwort): This popular cross between alpine bar-renwort (*E. alpinum*) and longspur barrenwort (*E. grandiflorum*) gets its name from its semievergreen foliage, which is red-tinged in both spring and fall and usually remains reddish all summer in cool climates. Its midspring to late spring blooms are bright crimson and creamy white in color. Red barrenwort spreads more quickly than most epimediums, so it's probably the best groundcover species, quickly giving a dense effect. Height: 8 to 12 inches (20 to 30 cm). Spread: 1 foot (30 cm). USDA Plant Hardiness Zones 5 to 9; AHS Heat Zones 8 to 5.

Larry's Garden Notes

Epimediums (*Epimedium* spp.) finally seem to be coming into their own—and its about time! For years they always seemed to be passed over in favor of more short-lived and temperamental plants with showier flowers. But epimediums have a quiet charm all their own that many show-off plants, for all their brash and brassy good looks, simply don't have. In fact, from my point of view, epimediums are nearly perfect groundcovers: not invasive, yet solid and permanent, firmly holding their own against the toughest weeds, and with some notably attractive features throughout the entire calendar year. To know them is to love them!

Fragaria

Strawberry

Although ornamental strawberries produce edible berries every now and again, you'll grow them strictly for their good looks. Strawberries are attractive plants in their own right, with lush, dark green, three-lobed evergreen leaves that are attractively toothed along the edges, not to mention their pretty and often numerous white, five-petaled flowers. They usually bloom profusely in the spring and early summer, then sporadically through the summer into fall.

Plant Profile

FRAGARIA
fra-GAH-ree-uh

- **Bloom Color:** Pink, rose, or white

- **Bloom Time:** Late spring to early fall

- **Length of Bloom:** 4 months or more

- **Height:** 6 to 10 inches (15 to 25 cm)

- **Spread:** 1 foot (30 cm)

- **Garden Uses:** Container planting, edging, groundcover, mass planting, mixed border, rock garden, wall planting, woodland garden; along paths, on slopes; attracts birds and wildlife

- **Light Preference:** Full sun to partial shade

- **Soil Preference:** Average to moist, well-drained soil

- **Best Way to Propagate:** Divide rooted plantlets in spring or fall

- **USDA Plant Hardiness Zones:** Varies by species; see individual listings

- **AHS Heat Zones:** 12 to 1

Growing Tips

Ornamental strawberries thrive in most sunny to partially shady spots in just about any kind of soil that's neither extremely dry nor soaking wet. They do wonderfully in areas that are wet spring through fall but need well-drained conditions in the winter. They're easy to transplant and fill in rapidly with long, thin reddish runners that reach out in all directions, producing plantlets that root wherever they touch the ground. Although these offsets are numerous, a single plant can take years to fill in entirely because the babies are produced haphazardly, many of them a long distance from the mother plant. For a nearly instant groundcover effect, plant strawberries in a 1-foot (30 cm) staggered pattern, then pinch off all the runners the first year: This helps create larger, sturdier mother plants that will fill in the gaps with their leaves alone. Or, for good results at less expense, plant strawberries 2 to 3 feet (60 to 90 cm) apart, then direct their first-year runners to fill in the gaps by moving plantlets to appropriate spots and pegging them into place with hairpins or coffee stirrers that have been bent in half.

Once established as a groundcover, strawberries don't need much maintenance. The evergreen leaves can look tired in spring, so you may want to cut them off at that time or trim them back with the lawn mower: Not only will the plants fill in again quickly, but this annual trim helps prevent disease.

If you need new strawberry plants, just dig up some of the rooted plantlets. You can also grow them from seed—just squish a ripe fruit, extract the seeds from along its outer skin, and sow in moist soil at any season—but there's no guarantee the offspring will be identical to the parents.

Good Neighbors

Bred more for a long season of bloom than for their small fruit, ornamental strawberries make good edging plants around white false indigo (*Baptisia alba*) and Siberian iris (*Iris sibirica*).

Alpine strawberry (*Fragaria vesca*) is a good choice for a wildlife-friendly garden: Birds and box turtles love the fruits! Use this plant in a partially shaded area as an edging plant around other seed- and fruit-bearing favorites, such as purple coneflower (*Echinacea purpurea*) and wintergreen (*Gaultheria procumbens*).

Problems and Solutions

Several leaf diseases can cause dieback or brown or black spots on leaves. Crown rot, in which the whole plant wilts and then dies, is also possible, especially in overly wet soil. Simply cut off any damaged leaves and cut out any dead or dying plants; new growth will fill in.

Top Peformer

Fragaria hybrids (pink strawberry, strawberry cinquefoil): Imagine, a strawberry with pink flowers! The pink strawberry is a cross between a strawberry of unknown origin and marsh cinquefoil (*Potentilla palustris*). The resulting plants are strawberry-like in form, growth habit, and flower—and even produce edible strawberries!

'Pink Panda' was the first hybrid to come along, with pink blooms and fuzzy centers. 'Shades of Pink' has flowers varying from palest pink to deep rose. 'Lipstick' is my favorite, with deep pink, almost rose, flowers. Height: 6 inches (15 cm). Spread: 1 foot (30 cm). USDA Plant Hardiness Zones 2 to 8; AHS Heat Zones 12 to 1.

More Recommended Strawberries

Fragaria vesca (alpine strawberry): Alpine strawberry is the typical wild European strawberry the French call *fraise des bois*. A natural everbloomer and everbearer, its white blooms produce tiny but sweet red fruits from late spring to fall. 'Alpine Yellow' is a selection with yellow fruit. 'Variegata' has green leaves heavily marbled with white. Height: 6 to 10 inches (15 to 25 cm). Spread: 1 foot (30 cm). USDA Plant Hardiness Zones 4 to 8; AHS Heat Zones 12 to 1.

'Pink Panda' strawberry (*Fragaria* 'Pink Panda')

Kissing Cousins

Think Twice: Barren strawberry (*Duchesnea indica*) plants look exactly like regular strawberries but with *yellow* flowers. The plants even produce bright red, long-lasting fruits that look just like small strawberries and are edible but not sugary. Mock strawberry is a tiny, low-growing plant that seems to thrive in deep shade as well as in full sun, but watch out! Its running stems are very quick to jump the fence and invade neighboring plantings. And the plant thrives in lawns! Height: 2 to 4 inches (5 to 10 cm). Spread: 6 inches (15 cm). USDA Plant Hardiness Zones 3 to 10; AHS Heat Zones 10 to 1.

Hakonechloa

Hakone grass, Japanese forest grass

Besides its ability to grow in shady spots, the main selling point of hakone grass is its beautiful, bamboolike appearance. Its relatively short stems grow upright, but the bright green, narrow, pointed leaves all arch to one side, creating a waterfall effect in the garden. The airy clusters of yellow-green flowers are mostly hidden by the foliage. In the fall, the leaves turn a beautiful pinkish red, then bronze, and remain through the winter.

Plant Profile

HAKONECHLOA
hah-koh-neh-KLOH-ah

■ **Bloom Color:** Yellowish green

■ **Bloom Time:** Late summer to early fall

■ **Length of Bloom:** 4 weeks or more

■ **Height:** 1 to 2 feet (30 to 60 cm)

■ **Spread:** 18 to 24 inches (45 to 60 cm)

■ **Garden Uses:** Container planting, edging, groundcover, mass planting, mixed border, rock garden, specimen plant, woodland garden; on slopes

■ **Light Preference:** Full sun to deep shade

■ **Soil Preference:** Humus-rich, moist but well-drained soil

■ **Best Way to Propagate:** Divide in spring or fall

■ **USDA Plant Hardiness Zones:** 4 to 9

■ **AHS Heat Zones:** 9 to 2

Growing Tips

One of the nicest things about this small deciduous grass is that it's so adaptable. It prefers light to partial shade, but it will also grow well in deep shade as long as it gets some morning sun. In cool-summer climates, it does fine in full sun as well, but partial shade is better in hot-summer areas. Although hakone grass thrives in evenly moist (but not waterlogged), humus-rich soil, it seems to adapt to most garden soil, except perhaps pure clay.

Hakone grass's only flaw is the slow to very slow speed at which it establishes itself. It is never invasive—in fact, it's a good substitute for pygmy dwarf bamboo (*Pleiablastus pygmaeus*), which can overrun your garden. Small divisions hardly seem to grow at all the first year and can take a good three to four years to form a decent-sized clump. Larger plants give a faster effect, but if you're using this plant as a groundcover, consider planting individual clumps about 1 foot (30 cm) apart or smaller divisions only 3 to 4 inches (8 to 10 cm) apart. Mulch abundantly between the plants to keep out any weeds until the various clumps join together to form a solid carpet.

Upkeep of hakone grass is minimal: Water during droughts, regularly apply fresh mulch, and give your plants an annual haircut in early spring if the faded leaves of the previous season bother you.

I'm not really sure what to say about this plant's hardiness rating: Most experts suggest a limited rating of only USDA Zones 6 to 9, yet it positively thrives in my Zone 3 garden. Friends in Minnesota's USDA Zone 4, who enjoy less snow cover, report that the plant is hardy, so I've suggested Zone 4 as a limit. To be safe, you might want to mulch in the winter.

Hakone grass seed sprouts easily, if you can find it, but the variegated cultivars don't come true from seed. Dividing a well-established clump will provide numerous offsets for you, although it does set the mother plant back a few years.

Good Neighbors

The most elegant of grasses, hakone grass adds a graceful touch to the shade garden. Combine green-and-gold *Hakonechloa macra* 'Aureola' with blue-leaved 'Halcyon' hosta and light green lady fern (*Athyrium filix-femina*) for a study of colors and textures. Planted in a mass as a groundcover or edging plant, hakone grass offers a soft-textured contrast to small shrubs or mass plantings of Japanese anemone (*Anemone* × *hybrida*) or bigleaf ligularia (*Ligularia dentata*). Hakone grass also works beautifully in gardens with an Asian theme.

Problems and Solutions

I have never seen any disease or insect problems with this plant.

Top Performer

Hakonechloa macra (hakone grass, Japanese forest grass): There's only one species of hakone grass, but you probably won't choose to grow the species form, which has all-green leaves. Instead, you'll want to pick one of the beautiful variegated cultivars. 'Aureola' is the most popular form, with golden yellow leaves that are lightly striped with green. The two colors in the leaves seem to melt together, at least from a short distance, giving the impression of a green plant hit by a ray of bright sunlight. 'Albo-aurea' is a collector's item, with leaves striped with yellow, white, and green. It isn't as striking in the garden as 'Aureola', but it's very nice in a container. 'Albo-striata' is a greener-looking plant than the others, with mostly green leaves with a white margin. Please note that although the species can tolerate full sun, the variegated cultivars may need some protection because they tend to burn in hot, sunny spots.

Golden variegated hakone grass (*Hakonechloa macra* 'Aureola')

Kissing Cousins

Looking for a grass that's similar to hakone grass (*Hakonechloa macra*) but grows quickly? Try yellow foxtail grass (*Alopecurus pratensis* var. *aureus*). It's a low-growing grass about 4 to 6 inches (10 to 15 cm) tall, with narrow, arching green leaves heavily striped with yellow. Unlike hakone grass, it does bloom fairly noticeably: a cylindrical, fuzzy "foxtail" held well above the foliage. It requires full sun to partial shade, and it prefers moist soil. Height (in bloom): 24 to 30 inches (60 to 75 cm). Spread: 16 inches (40 cm). USDA Plant Hardiness Zones 4 to 9; AHS Heat Zones 8 to 1.

Helianthemum

Sun rose, rock rose

Beautiful and long-blooming, sun rose is a low-growing, spreading perennial with nearly woody stems and a very shrublike appearance. Its small, evergreen leaves vary in shape from nearly round to thin and narrow and in color from glossy green to fuzzy gray. The leaves are always hairy and gray underneath. The five-petaled, 1- to 1½-inch (2.5- to 4-cm) flowers with clustered yellow stamens resemble wild roses, and they come in a wide range of colors.

Plant Profile

HELIANTHEMUM
hee-lee-AN-thuh-mum

- **Bloom Color:** Orange, pink, red, rose, white, or yellow

- **Bloom Time:** Late spring to early summer; some rebloom to early fall

- **Length of Bloom:** 6 weeks or more

- **Height:** 4 to 18 inches (10 to 45 cm)

- **Spread:** 2 to 3 feet (60 to 75 cm)

- **Garden Uses:** Container planting, edging, ground-cover, mass planting, mixed border, rock garden, wall planting; along paths, on slopes

- **Light Preference:** Full sun to light shade

- **Soil Preference:** Poor to average, very well-drained, alkaline to only slightly acid soil

- **Best Way to Propagate:** Take stem cuttings in summer

- **USDA Plant Hardiness Zones:** 4 to 9

- **AHS Heat Zones:** 10 to 3

Growing Tips

Except in the very hottest climates, where light shade is best, sun roses demand full sun and perfect drainage. Water should flow right through the soil, especially if you live in a climate where precipitation is abundant. Although drought-tolerant, the plants do enjoy a thorough drenching every now and then in dry-summer climates. In winter, though, they need to have their roots dry out somewhat.

If you supply good sun and excellent drainage, sun roses are a snap to grow, and their flowering season is very long. If you prune them back by about one-third when they stop flowering in mid-summer, the plants will bloom again, although more lightly and with smaller flowers, until late summer or early fall.

My best guess is that sun roses are hardy to USDA Zone 4 in dry climates as long as they have perfect drainage, but if your garden gets lots of rain, an airy winter mulch is a good idea in USDA Zone 6 and north. I have had great success with conifer branches as a mulch and know of others who do equally well with loose hay, both of which allow good air circulation.

Sun roses don't like their routine disrupted. You can divide sun roses, but it sets the plants back so much that it's best not to. In fact, if you have older sun roses that are beginning to look thin at the base, you'd do better to prune them back hard to rejuvenate them than try to divide them. Instead, if you want more plants, take tip cuttings. Even short pieces of stem, scarcely 1 to 2 inches (2.5 to 5 cm) long, root well but slowly.

You can also grow sun roses from seed. Sow the seed indoors about six to eight weeks before planting outdoors in early spring, when temperatures are still cool. It germinates readily and produces plants that bloom the following year.

Good Neighbors

Sun rose is a good groundcover to use on dry, sunny slopes where most other plants would not thrive. It requires well-drained, neutral soil and does poorly in fertile soil, making it ideal for the rock garden. For companions, choose plants that have similar requirements, including sea thrift (*Armeria maritima*), prickly pear (*Opuntia humifusa*), rock soapwort (*Saponaria ocymoides*), sedums, and yuccas. An interesting combination would be to pair a red-orange selection with late spring or summer-blooming 'Goodness Grows' veronica (*Veronica* 'Goodness Grows'), lavender (*Lavandula angustifolia* 'Hidicote'), or mountain bluet (*Centaurea montana*).

Problems and Solutions

Stem rot due to overly moist soil is the major killer of sun roses. There's little use trying to save a rotting plant: Start again with a new one under more appropriate conditions. Leaf spot can also occur in midsummer; prune off the offending branches.

Top Performer

Helianthemum hybrids (hybrid sun rose): Although most nurseries sell sun roses under the name *Helianthemum nummularium*, almost all sun roses are hybrids. There are hundreds of cultivars to choose from, so there's no way I can choose just one as the top performer. I've limited myself to describing a few of the widely available cultivars. 'Fire Dragon' has bright coppery red flowers and gray-green foliage. 'Fireball', also called 'Mrs. C. W. Earle', is similar, but with double blooms in a deeper red shade. 'Raspberry Ripple' is a more upright plant with gray-green leaves and crimson to deep pink flowers streaked with white. 'Wisley Pink', also called 'Rhodanthe Carneum', is perhaps the most popular of all, with soft pink flowers over grayish leaves and a nearly creeping habit. 'Wisley Primrose' and 'Wisley White' are similar, but with light yellow and pure white flowers, respectively. All the Wisley hybrids do particularly well in my USDA Zone 3 garden.

Common sun roses (*Helianthemum nummularium*) tend to spread out as they age, making them an ideal choice for edging flower beds and tumbling over rock gardens. Give them a sunny site with good drainage and they will be covered with masses of saucer-shaped flowers from late spring to mid-summer.

Lamium

Lamium, dead nettle

This perennial has all the qualities of an outstanding groundcover. Lamiums form a perfect mat of foliage that carpets even the most uneven terrain and is attractive right through the growing season—even all winter if you live in a climate where snow isn't an issue. Plus the semievergreen foliage isn't just green; it's almost always heavily marbled with silver. Lamiums also have attractive flowers, hooded and two-lipped, borne in clusters or whorls on upright stems.

Plant Profile

LAMIUM
LAY-mee-um

- **Bloom Color:** Lavender, pink, white, or yellow

- **Bloom Time:** Late spring to early summer

- **Length of Bloom:** 4 weeks or more

- **Height:** 6 to 12 inches (15 to 30 cm)

- **Spread:** 1 to 2 feet (30 to 60 cm)

- **Garden Uses:** Container planting, edging, groundcover, mass planting, mixed border, rock garden, wall planting, woodland garden; along paths, on slopes, in wet areas

- **Light Preference:** Full sun to deep shade

- **Soil Preference:** Average, well-drained soil

- **Best Way to Propagate:** Take stem cuttings at any time

- **USDA Plant Hardiness Zones:** 3 to 9

- **AHS Heat Zones:** 8 to 1

Growing Tips

Lamiums will grow just about anywhere, from full sun to deep shade, although partial shade is best in hot-summer climates. They'll likewise grow in just about any soil that's at least slightly moist at all times.

The very nature of lamiums is to creep, and all of them do so to some degree. And as they creep, they also root. This creeping, rooting habit means that you should only plant lamiums where you can control them. Root barriers, such as pails sunk into the garden, won't help because lamiums creep aboveground and will simply leap over the lip of the container and continue on their merry way. It's best to surround them with equally tough plants or with large barriers they can't easily creep across, like pavement or a wall. Where lamiums do get out of hand, at least you can pull them out easily.

Other than controlling their rampant growth, lamiums need little if any care. If you're a real stickler for perfection, just mow them once a year, after they bloom, to remove faded flower stems.

Multiplying lamiums is a snap: They provide ample offsets for division, and stem cuttings root in less than a week. You can also grow them from seed sown indoors or out in the spring. Some cultivars may seem to come true from seed but will slowly return to the wild type over time if you multiply them over and over from seed.

Good Neighbors

Spotted lamium (*Lamium maculatum*) is a handsome groundcover that makes an interesting complement to spring-flowering shrubs or trees. Cultivars with highly silver foliage (*L. maculatum* 'Silbergroschen' or

'White Nancy') are the least aggressive and can light up the shade garden. Combine them with spring bulbs or sturdy shade plants, such as hostas and ferns, for early to midseason color and all-season interest.

Problems and Solutions

Bare patches can occur if the soil dries out: Just keep your lamium moist and it will fill in again quickly. Some cultivars suffer from crown rot under hot, humid conditions. My suggestion? Don't plant them if they're likely to suffer from a problem in your area! Finally, slugs and snails can also cause some damage, but the plant is so prolific it usually repairs itself in no time.

Top Performer

Lamium maculatum (spotted lamium): Spotted lamium is definitely the lamium of choice, and the only one I recommend. It's a mounding, clump-forming plant that spreads outward relatively slowly. Please note that I did mention "relatively": It does spread, but at least you can control it. The species has pinkish or lavender flowers in late spring to early summer and grayish green leaves with slight silver mottling—but cultivars are the way to go because there are many exciting ones to choose from. Most popular is probably 'Silbergroschen', which is usually sold as 'Beacon Silver,' and may also be labeled as 'Silver Dollar'. Its leaves are almost entirely silver; only the margins remain green. The leaves turn bronzy in cold weather and often have a reddish tint even in summer. The pink to purplish flowers are an added treat. However, this formerly vigorous cultivar seems to have gone downhill in recent years, and I've heard gardeners—especially in hot, humid areas—complain that it's much more subject to crown rot and leaf spots than it used to be. 'White Nancy' is very similar, with white flowers and the same green-edged silver leaves as 'Silbergroschen', but it is still vigorous and disease-free; it does best in cool-summer areas. Think of 'Pink Pewter' as more of the same but with pink flowers. 'Aureum' is a golden yellow cultivar with a silver spot in the middle and light pink flowers.

'Pink Pewter' spotted lamium (*Lamium maculatum* 'Pink Pewter')

Larry's Garden Notes

The common name "dead nettle" is hardly auspicious—after all, who would want to grow a plant that looks like it's dead? Actually, though, the name dead nettle is quite appropriate for *Lamium*, but it doesn't describe the plant's looks. Instead, it refers to the fact that the stinging property of this nettle is "dead," meaning inactive. Lamiums are related to the true stinging nettles (*Urtica* spp.) and they looks like nettles, too, especially when the flowers drop off, leaving a bristly looking seed case. But while true nettles sting, dead nettle inflicts no pain at all.

Liriope

Liriope, lilyturf

With their tufted habit and narrow, strap-shaped, arching leaves, liriopes could easily pass for an ornamental grass—at least until they bloom! Then their dense, upright spikes of tiny lilac or white flowers leave no doubt that liriopes are more related to lily-of-the-valley (*Convallaria majalis*) than to grasses. That's why I just love the plant's other common name of "lilyturf": It really does express the plant's half-grass, half-lily appearance.

Plant Profile

LIRIOPE
lih-RYE-oh-pea

- **Bloom Color:** Lilac or white
- **Bloom Time:** Late summer to fall
- **Length of Bloom:** 3 weeks or more
- **Height:** 8 to 18 inches (20 to 45 cm)
- **Spread:** 1 foot (30 cm)
- **Garden Uses:** Container planting, cut flower garden, edging, groundcover, mass planting, rock garden, woodland garden; along paths, on slopes
- **Light Preference:** Full sun to deep shade
- **Soil Preference:** Average to moist, well-drained, neutral to acid soil
- **Best Way to Propagate:** Divide at any season
- **USDA Plant Hardiness Zones:** Varies by species; see individual listings
- **AHS Heat Zones:** Varies by species; see individual listings

Growing Tips

The ideal situation for liriopes is partial shade, but they thrive in full sun in cool-summer areas. They grow well enough in deep shade, but they take longer to fill in there and may produce taller leaves and flower spikes. Any well-drained, nonalkaline soil will do. Liriopes can tolerate even the driest locations once established, although an occasional watering during periods of drought will result in thicker, healthier-looking plants.

New plantings can be slow to fill in, so mulch well to keep weeds out. Maintenance is minimal for established plantings. Most gardeners mow the leaves down to about 1 inch (2.5 cm) in late winter or early spring because the leaves, although evergreen, are usually ratty by that time of year. Multiplying liriope is a snap: Just dig up and divide established plants any time the ground isn't frozen. You can also grow liriope from seed sown indoors in late winter or outdoors in fall or early spring, when the soil is still cool, although cultivars will not come true.

Good Neighbors

Use liriopes for edging paths, for massing under trees and shrubs, or at the front of a perennial border. For a stunning shade garden, try using them as edging for masses of caladiums (*Caladium* hybrids), ferns, and hostas.

Problems and Solutions

Slugs and snails can be an annoyance, but their damage is rarely noticeable among the dense foliage.

Top Performer

Liriope muscari (big blue lilyturf): This is the typical liriope, with wider and more evergreen leaves than creeping lilyturf (*L. spicata*). It spreads very slowly, so plant it rather densely—up to 4 inches (10 cm) apart if you have small plants and 1 foot (30 cm) or so if you have larger clumps.

There are more than 100 cultivars of this popular plant: I've listed just a few here. Unless otherwise noted, all have lilac-colored flowers in late summer to fall. 'Big Blue' isn't really much bluer than the others, but it does have wide, dark green leaves and better cold-hardiness than most (to USDA Zone 5). 'Majestic' is similar but has darker, almost purple flowers and is likewise very hardy. 'Munroe White' has white flowers that stand out from the dark foliage. It is *less* cold-hardy than most, scarcely more than Zone 8. 'Variegata' is the old-fashioned variegated form, with leaves brightly striped with green and cream. 'Silvery Sunproof' is one of the many more modern variegates and has leaves so heavily striped in white they seem almost silver. It does tend toward a greener coloration in shade, though. Height: 8 to 18 inches (20 to 45 cm). Spread: 1 foot (30 cm). USDA Plant Hardiness Zones 6 to 10; AHS Heat Zones 12 to 5.

Although you can grow big blue lilyturf (*Liriope muscari*) well beyond its usual USDA hardiness zones—I grow it with no problems in my Zone 3 garden—I've been quite conservative in my zone recommendations because you only get good groundcover use in areas where it's fully hardy.

More Recommended Liriopes

Liriope spicata (creeping lilyturf): This species is very similar to big blue lilyturf (*L. muscari*); careful inspection, however, will reveal its leaves are narrower and lined in tiny teeth. Also, creeping lilyturf leaves, although evergreen, turn yellowish at the first sign of winter, but big blue lilyturf retains its deep green coloration at least until spring.

Creeping lilyturf lives up to its name by spreading much more rapidly through much longer creeping roots. Narrow spikes of pale lavender (or sometimes white) flowers appear from late summer to fall. There are several cultivars, but only 'Silver Dragon', with white lengthwise stripes on dark green leaves, is really popular. Height: 8 to 12 inches (20 to 30 cm). Spread: 1 foot (30 cm). USDA Plant Hardiness Zones 5 to 10; AHS Heat Zones 12 to 1.

Pachysandra

Pachysandra, spurge

You just won't find a better groundcover for shady areas than pachysandra.
Slow-growing in the extreme, pachysandra eventually produces dense clumps
and creates a perfect carpet of greenery. Though deliciously scented, the spikes
of white flowers are neither striking nor long-lasting. White berries sometimes
follow the flowers, but they're not very noticeable, either. No, pachysandra can't
be considered anything but a foliage plant, but it fills that role wonderfully!

Plant Profile

PACHYSANDRA
pak-ih-SAN-druh

- **Bloom Color:** White
- **Bloom Time:** Spring
- **Length of Bloom:** 1 or 2 weeks
- **Height:** 6 to 12 inches (15 to 30 cm)
- **Spread:** 6 to 12 inches (15 to 30 cm)
- **Garden Uses:** Edging, groundcover, mass planting, rock garden, wall planting, woodland garden; along paths, on slopes, in wet areas
- **Light Preference:** Light to deep shade
- **Soil Preference:** Rich, moist soil
- **Best Way to Propagate:** Divide at any time
- **USDA Plant Hardiness Zones:** Varies by species; see individual listings
- **AHS Heat Zones:** Varies by species; see individual listings

Growing Tips

If pachysandras had their druthers, they would choose rich, moist soil
in the seasonal shade of deciduous forests, which is where they grow
in the wild. In gardens, though, we've discovered they will put up
with just about everything, even dry shade (with help from an occasional watering), at least once they're thoroughly established. Give
them your worst conditions and they will probably adapt perfectly
well. About the only thing they *won't* stand is full sun—at least some
shade from afternoon sun is needed, even in cool-summer areas.

Slow but steady wins the race, and that certainly is the case with
pachysandras. Plant them densely, on about 6-inch (15-cm) centers,
especially if you start out with small divisions, and mulch heavily to
prevent weeds from filling in the open spaces. Other than the occasional watering during periods of drought, pachysandras don't demand any care at all.

If you need more plants, division is the most obvious way to get
them. You can do this practically any time of the year when the
ground isn't frozen, although divisions made in summer will need
more careful watering than those taken during spring or fall. Stem
cuttings taken at any season are also an easy way to propagate.

Good Neighbors

Use evergreen Japanese pachysandra (*Pachysandra terminalis*) as a
groundcover in light to full shade, beneath and between trees and
shrubs. Excellent shrub companions for this vigorous spreader include azaleas (*Rhododendron* spp.) and rhododendrons (*Rhododendron*
spp.), Japanese pieris (*Pieris japonica*), and dwarf conifers.

Allegheny pachysandra (*Pachysandra procumbens*), on the other
hand, is a slow-spreading, deciduous clump-former appropriate for

use in the shade garden or in a woodland. Use it with other woodland plants, such as fringed bleeding heart (*Dicentra eximia*) and ferns, under the shade of deciduous trees.

Problems and Solutions

Leaf blight, which causes leaves to turn brown and die back, can be a serious problem with pachysandras grown in hot, humid conditions. Avoid overhead watering, thin out infected patches, and use an organic fungicide to control it—or tear out the patch and try something else.

Top Performer

Pachysandra terminalis (Japanese pachysandra, Japanese spurge): By far the most common species of pachysandra in home gardens, Japanese pachysandra is easy to tell from the only other cultivated species, Allegheny pachysandra (*P. procumbens*), by its shiny leaves and evergreen habit. Compact 'Green Carpet' grows only 6 to 8 inches (15 to 20 cm) tall with darker green leaves than the species. 'Green Sheen' has shiny, waxy, deep green leaves and excellent heat tolerance. 'Variegata' has creamy white edges on a green leaf. Beware that this plant, in spite of its slow start, is highly invasive in the long run. However, a lawn border sunk into the ground around the patch is sufficient to keep the shallow creeping roots within bounds. Height: 8 to 12 inches (20 to 30 cm). Spread: 6 to 12 inches (15 to 30 cm). USDA Plant Hardiness Zones 4 to 9; AHS Heat Zones 8 to 1.

More Recommended Pachysandras

Pachysandra procumbens (Allegheny pachysandra, Allegheny spurge): You'll never mistake the broader, deciduous leaves of this North American native for Japanese pachysandra (*P. terminalis*): They're velvety in texture and light green in color and turn bronzy in the fall. The spring flowers are generally similar. This pachysandra is naturally more of a clump-former than a spreader and is much less likely to escape from culture to become a weed than Japanese pachysandra. Some Allegheny pachysandras, such as 'Forest Green', have leaves attractively mottled with gray. Height: 8 to 12 inches (20 to 30 cm). Spread: 6 to 12 inches (15 to 30 cm). USDA Plant Hardiness Zones 5 to 9; AHS Heat Zones 9 to 5.

Japanese pachysandra
(*Pachysandra terminalis*)

Larry's Garden Notes

If you have only a small shade garden, you'll probably want to forego planting spreading groundcovers like Japanese spurge (*Pachysandra terminalis*) or common periwinkle (*Vinca minor*). Clump-forming Allegheny spurge (*P. procumbens*) is a perfect alternative. Not only is the foliage more attractive, but it's also a very refined neighbor and companion to other nonaggressive groundcovers such as ferns, gingers, hostas, and epimediums.

Prunella

Self-heal, heal-all

Pretty and easy to grow, ornamental self-heals make great groundcovers. They're mintlike, with square stems and deeply veined, oval leaves. And like mints, self-heals produce both aboveground and underground runners, but self-heal runners are short, meaning the plants aren't nearly as aggressive. The flowers are also mintlike, but much, much bigger, formed of tight spikes of large, wide-open, two-lipped flowers reaching out from among shorter petal-like leaves called bracts. Self-heal is evergreen in warm climates but tends to be deciduous in colder areas.

Plant Profile

PRUNELLA
proo-NEL-luh

- **Bloom Color:** Lavender, pink, purple, red, and white

- **Bloom Time:** Early summer to midsummer

- **Length of Bloom:** 4 weeks or more

- **Height:** 6 to 12 inches (15 to 30 cm)

- **Spread:** 1 foot (30 cm)

- **Garden Uses:** Edging, groundcover, mass planting, woodland garden; along paths

- **Light Preference:** Full sun to partial shade

- **Soil Preference:** Average to moist, well-drained soil

- **Best Way to Propagate:** Divide in spring

- **USDA Plant Hardiness Zones:** 4 to 9

- **AHS Heat Zones:** 8 to 5

Growing Tips

Self-heals prefer full sun to only light shade in the North but grow better in partial shade in the South because they prefer cool conditions. They adapt to a wide range of soil types but thrive in moist but well-drained, humus-rich conditions. They tolerate some drought once established but look much better if you water them regularly during dry periods.

Ornamental self-heals can spread out of bounds if you don't plan ahead to keep them in check. Surround them with equally vigorous companions or plant them in deep shade to control their creeping. Root barriers aren't effective because the aboveground runners will simply pole-vault over the barrier into the rest of your garden.

Self-heal can also spread by seed, although you may not want it to do that because it can invade through its seeds as well. Ideally, then, you should plant self-heal where the lawn mower can reach it: That way you can simply mow it down after it blooms, preventing any seed formation. To propagate the cultivars, just dig out and transplant some of the many offsets that the plants produce.

Good Neighbors

Enjoy self-heals as small-scale groundcovers under shrubs and trees or as front-of the-border plants in lightly shaded areas. The purple-flowered self-heals look particularly good with early-summer yellows: in front of shrubby cinquefoil (*Potentilla fruticosa*), for example, or combined with lady's-mantle (*Alchemilla mollis*) or yellow corydalis (*Corydalis lutea*).

Problems and Solutions

Self-heals are sometimes subject to leaf diseases such as leaf spot (brown marks on the leaves) and powdery mildew, especially in hot, humid conditions. Avoid overhead watering to prevent such problems, and try not to water in the evening because the plants stay wet, which encourages diseases to develop. If they do occur, chop the plants back to only 1 or 2 inches (2.5 or 5 cm) from the ground: They'll pop back up almost immediately.

Top Performer

Prunella grandiflora (large-flowered self-heal): By far the most common ornamental self-heal, this species produces dense spikes of short, colorful bracts that quickly burst into glorious bloom from early summer to midsummer. The species has purple flowers, but most cultivars tend toward pinks, reds, and whites. The Loveliness series is probably the most widely available and includes 'Loveliness', with lavender flowers, plus others whose names are self-descriptive: 'Pink Loveliness', 'Purple Loveliness', and 'White Loveliness'. 'Alba' is an old-fashioned but still popular white form, and 'Rotkäppchen' (also called 'Little Red Riding Hood') is a crimson red on a short plant, about 6 inches (15 cm). Height: 6 to 12 inches (15 to 30 cm). Spread: 1 foot (30 cm). USDA Plant Hardiness Zones 4 to 9; AHS Heat Zones 8 to 5.

More Recommended Self-Heals

Prunella × *webbiana* (Webb's self-heal): Some experts claim that Webb's self-heal is identical to large-flowered self-heal, but others say it's a hybrid form. Although Webb's self-heal is said to have shorter, less-pointed leaves and denser flower spikes than large-flowered self-heal, I suggest you not worry about the name of the self-heal you buy: Just pick one that looks pretty to you. Webb's self-heal has purple flowers, the cultivar 'Rosea' has pink blooms, and 'Alba' has white ones. Height: 6 to 12 inches (15 to 30 cm). Spread: 1 foot (30 cm). USDA Plant Hardiness Zones 4 to 9; AHS Heat Zones 8 to 5.

Large-flowered self-heal
(*Prunella grandiflora*)

Kissing Cousins

Big betony (*Stachys macrantha*, also called *S. grandiflora*) is actually more closely related to lamb's-ears (see page 370) than self-heal (*Prunella* spp.), yet you'd never guess from looking at it. In fact, I'd describe big betony as "self-heal on steroids," due to its similar but larger leaves and taller spikes of somewhat more open flowers of white, pink, or purple. The oval leaves are thick, grass green, and beautifully scalloped along the edges. 'Robusta' ('Superba') is the tallest of the cultivars, averaging 24 inches (60 cm). Height: 12 to 24 inches (30 to 60 cm). Spread: 12 inches (30 cm). USDA Plant Hardiness Zones 2 to 9; AHS Heat Zones 8 to 1.

Saxifraga

Saxifrage, rockfoil

Saxifrages are low-growing, mounding plants. Some form dense, rounded domes of foliage, and others form more spreading tufts. Closer inspection will reveal that the domes are formed of masses of densely packed individual rosettes. The leaves are highly variable, from rounded or heart-shaped to deeply cut and feathery, sometimes creating an almost mossy appearance. Five-petaled, cup- or star-shaped flowers in white or pink can be upright or drooping and are borne above the mounds of leaves, sometimes singly, other times in open clusters.

Plant Profile

SAXIFRAGA
saks-IHF-ruh-guh

- Bloom Color: Pink, red, or white
- Bloom Time: Varies by species; see individual listings
- Length of Bloom: 3 weeks or more
- Height: Varies by species; see individual listings
- Spread: Varies by species; see individual listings
- Garden Uses: Container planting, edging, groundcover, mass planting, mixed border, rock garden, wall planting, woodland garden; along paths, on slopes
- Light Preference: Light shade to deep shade
- Soil Preference: Varies by species; see individual listings
- Best Way to Propagate: Divide in spring
- USDA Plant Hardiness Zones: 4 to 9
- AHS Heat Zones: 9 to 6

Growing Tips

In the wild, saxifrages are mostly rock dwellers, and they maintain their need for good drainage when you grow them in a garden. Yet they don't really tolerate drought as well as you might expect. That's because they tend to stick to shady, moister sites in the wild, leaving the drier rock walls to more succulent plants. Most will require some soil moisture throughout the year and may require regular watering during periods of drought. The species described below generally prefer relatively rich, loamy soil that's neutral or slightly acidic.

Many saxifrages prefer at least light shade and all thrive in partial shade. Saxifrages tend to do best in cool-summer areas or, if the summers are hot, in climates that aren't too humid.

A light, airy winter mulch can be very helpful, not as much to protect saxifrages from the cold as to keep them dormant as long as possible in the spring so that early frosts won't nip their buds. Mulches will keep the soil frozen longer, preventing the plant from producing buds too early.

Maintenance of saxifrages is minimal: Cut back faded flower stems and occasionally divide the species that tend to fall apart in the center.

Multiplying saxifrages is a complex subject because different species have different needs. All those described here, though, are easy to multiply by division in spring.

Good Neighbors

Try saxifrages as small-scale groundcovers or as rock-garden accents in sites where they'll get adequate moisture and protection from afternoon sun. In the rock garden, good companions include rock cresses (*Arabis* spp.) and hens-and-chicks (*Sempervivum tectorum*).

Problems and Solutions

Other than a propensity for crown rot in wet soil (perfect drainage is always a must), saxifrages have very few insect and disease problems.

Top Performer

Saxifraga × arendsii (mossy saxifrage): The common name is well chosen: Mossy saxifrage produces extremely dense clumps of deeply cut, bright green leaves on short and well-hidden stems. The end result is a very mosslike dome of greenery. As the season progresses, the dome then spreads to become a carpet, making for a fine ground-cover appearance. Each plant produces dozens of short stems in late spring, each bearing a single, upward-facing, cup-shaped, red, pink, or white, 1-inch (2.5-cm) flower. Height: 4 to 8 inches (10 to 20 cm). Spread: 1 foot (30 cm). USDA Plant Hardiness Zones 4 to 9; AHS Heat Zones 9 to 6.

More Recommended Saxifrages

Saxifraga × urbium (London pride): Although this plant is often sold as *S. umbrosa*, the plant we know as London pride is usually the hybrid species. It produces open rosettes of dark green, spoon-shaped, toothed leaves with a lighter midrib and quickly forms dense carpets in light to deep shade. Tall stalks of white flowers with red centers bloom from late spring to early summer. There are many cultivars with other flower colors, such as 'Chambers Pink Pride', with pink flowers, and *S. × urbium* var. *primuloides*, with red flowers. 'Aureopunctata' has the same red-centered white flowers as the species, but its leaves are beautifully spotted with irregular yellow dots, as if fresh paint had been spilled on each leaf. This plant is more sun-tolerant than the others. Height: 18 to 24 inches (45 to 60 cm). Spread: 6 to 12 inches (15 to 30 cm). USDA Plant Hardiness Zones 4 to 9; AHS Heat Zones 9 to 6.

Mossy saxifrage
(*Saxifraga × arendsii*)

Around the World with Saxifrages

For the most part, saxifrages (*Saxifraga* spp.) are mountain plants, found on rock formations throughout the Northern Hemisphere. My most memorable encounters with wild saxifrages came only a short time apart. The first time I spied livelong saxifrage (*Saxifraga paniculata*), I was hiking high in the mountains of Switzerland where the plant's sparkling leaves and white flowers poked out of nearly every nook and cranny. Just a few weeks later I discovered the very same species on Mount Albert in Quebec, just above the treeline, sharing its mountain home with one of the rare troops of caribou still left in that area.

Sedum

Sedum, stonecrop

Creeping sedums are tough groundcovers that thrive in dry sites, thanks to their thick succulent leaves that store water and help the plants cope with drought. Although the leaves vary greatly in shape, the flowers of creeping sedums share some common traits: They tend to be clustered at the tips of the stems, and the individual blooms are made up of star-shaped petals.

Plant Profile

SEDUM
SEH-dum

- ■ **Bloom Color:** Pink, red, white, or yellow
- ■ **Bloom Time:** Summer
- ■ **Length of Bloom:** 3 weeks or more
- ■ **Height:** Varies by species; see individual listings
- ■ **Spread:** Varies by species; see individual listings
- ■ **Garden Uses:** Container planting, edging, groundcover, mass planting, mixed border, rock garden, wall planting; along paths, on slopes
- ■ **Light Preference:** Full sun to partial shade
- ■ **Soil Preference:** Average, well-drained soil
- ■ **Best Way to Propagate:** Take stem cuttings in spring or summer.
- ■ **USDA Plant Hardiness Zones:** 3 to 9
- ■ **AHS Heat Zones:** Varies by species; see individual listings

Growing Tips

Most sedums adapt well to anything from full sun to partial shade and will actually put up with—or even thrive in—moist soil, as long as it's well drained. All are, however, extremely drought-tolerant, looking cool and smug even as the garden's other plants are curling up from lack of moisture. And just about any kind of soil will do, from poor and stony to moderately rich. Maintenance of creeping sedums is essentially nil: Just plant them and ignore them.

Multiply creeping sedums by cutting off a short section of stem and pressing it into the soil elsewhere in the garden. Spring or summer is the best time for this. It's also easy to multiply sedums by division. Be forewarned that all creeping sedums are naturally invasive—thus the Think Twice logo.

Good Neighbors

Creeping sedums are well suited for use in rocky landscapes, on sunny banks, or in stone-wall crevices. Purple rock cress (*Aubrieta deltoidea*), yellow corydalis (*Corydalis lutea*), and evergreen candytuft (*Iberis sempervirens*) are suitable companions.

Problems and Solutions

Creeping sedums are generally free from insects and diseases.

Top Performer

Think Twice: *Sedum spurium* (two-row stonecrop): This creeping sedum forms low mats of dark green, oval leaves that are coarsely toothed at the tips, with a rough upper surface. As the common name suggests, the leaves are placed in two distinct rows along the stems. The older leaves are deciduous everywhere, but the younger leaves, those at the stem tips, are evergreen even in the coldest zones.

This sedum is arguably one of the least attractive creeping sedums as far as foliage is concerned, but it is one of the nicest in bloom. It produces dense clusters of numerous pink, star-shaped flowers at the tips of its stems in midsummer—truly remarkable in effect!

Green-foliage types that turn purplish only in the fall include, besides the pink-flowered species, 'Coccineum', with scarlet flowers, and 'Splendens', with deep carmine flowers. 'Schorbuser Blut' (also called 'Dragon's Blood') is renowned for its green and burgundy leaves that turn deep purplish bronze in the fall, not to mention its dark red flowers. 'Fuldaglut' is similar but with maroon leaves that change color in spring and remain that way all season; its flowers are burgundy. For an even deeper shade of purple leaves, try 'Purpurteppich' (also called 'Purple Carpet'). And then there's 'Tricolor', with green-centered leaves surrounded by a band of white with a pink border, and 'Variegatum', with

Two-row stonecrop
(*Sedum spurium*)

creamy pink margins on green leaves. Both variegated forms occasionally produce all-green stems. These should be removed or they'll come to dominate the less vigorous variegated sections. Both variegated cultivars have pink flowers. Height: 2 to 6 inches (5 to 15 cm). Spread: 8 to 18 inches (20 to 45 cm). USDA Plant Hardiness Zones 3 to 9; AHS Heat Zones 9 to 4.

More Recommended Creeping Sedums

Think Twice: *Sedum kamtschaticum* (Kamtschatka stonecrop): Kamtschatka stonecrop is prized for its attractive semievergreen, bright green, toothed leaves; its dense, creeping habit; and its bright yellow clusters of early summer flowers. After bloom, rusty red seed capsules form, so the plant adds color to the garden through the end of summer. *S. kamtschaticum* 'Weihenstephaner Gold', a cultivar that's also sold as *S. floriferum*, produces flowers prolifically and has red buds, to boot! The plant usually sold as *S. kamtschaticum* 'Variegatum' is now *S. middendorffianum* 'Variegatum', yet another Kamtschatka stonecrop look-alike but this time with a broad band of white around each leaf. It does tend to revert to all green; remove these sections. Height: 4 to 9 inches (10 to 36 cm). Spread: 15 inches (38 cm). USDA Plant Hardiness Zones 3 to 9; AHS Heat Zones 9 to 1.

Larry's Garden Notes

Most creeping sedums (*Sedum* spp.) can be somewhat invasive over time, but goldmoss stonecrop (*S. acre*) is so invasive that I recommend never planting it at all. As the name suggests, it truly is mosslike, with tiny ever-green leaves closely cloaking the stem and numerous little yellow flowers in spring. It's one tough cookie, even taking foot traffic. So far, so good, but goldmoss stonecrop also spreads incredibly quickly both by creeping, rooting stems and seed that's so tiny you don't even see it but that starts colonies throughout the entire neighborhood in no time.

Sempervivum

Hens-and-chicks, houseleek

You can grow hens-and-chicks in the worst soil imaginable. They'll even grow in gravel or in cracks between rocks where there seems to be no soil at all! So if you have a tough, rocky area that you'd like to dress up a bit, this is the groundcover to try. Hens-and-chicks form ground-hugging evergreen rosettes composed of thick, pointed, succulent leaves. In bloom, the rosettes transform into thick stems topped with clusters of starry flowers.

Plant Profile

SEMPERVIVUM
sehm-purr-VEE-vuhm

- **Bloom Color:** Green, pink, purple, red, white, or yellow
- **Bloom Time:** Summer
- **Length of Bloom:** 2 or 3 weeks
- **Height:** Varies by species; see individual listings
- **Spread:** Varies by species; see individual listings
- **Garden Uses:** Container planting, edging, groundcover, mass planting, rock garden, wall planting; along paths, on slopes
- **Light Preference:** Full sun to partial shade
- **Soil Preference:** Average, well-drained soil
- **Best Way to Propagate:** Divide at any season
- **USDA Plant Hardiness Zones:** Varies by species; see individual listings
- **AHS Heat Zones:** 8 to 1

Growing Tips

The thick, succulent leaves of hens-and-chicks seem to suggest that these perennials are ideal for sunny, dry locations. That's true to a certain degree, but these succulent plants also do surprisingly well in fairly shady conditions and relatively moist soil as long as it's well drained. In hot-summer areas, in fact, they actually *prefer* shade. Perfect drainage is even more critical in hot climates than in cool ones.

Hens-and-chicks are likewise very adaptable when it comes to soil. Although they're at their very best in gritty soils of average fertility, it's hard to imagine a soil condition they won't tolerate. Poor, stony or sandy soils suit them just fine. They do grow slowly, so plant them densely, 3 to 5 inches (8 to 12 cm) apart, if you want rapid cover. Or, to save on cash, just plant one hens-and-chicks, and then carefully dig up and replant all its "chicks" as they appear.

Once established, hens-and-chicks require practically no care other than carefully pulling out the fading rosettes of the "hens" after they finish blooming in order to leave space for the "chicks" to fill in.

With hens-and-chicks, an abundance of rooted secondary rosettes makes multiplication a snap. Just dig them up and replant as needed. Or don't even bother to wait until they root: Cut off small rosettes and simply press them into the soil as cuttings and they'll soon be growing on their way.

FUN FACTS

Although *Sempervivum* means "live forever," hens-and-chicks don't *really* live forever. The rosettes of hens-and-chicks are basically biennial, dying after blooming and producing seed. But secondary rosettes replace each generation as soon as it dies, and it's this constant renewal by younger rosettes that gives the plants their "live-forever" characteristic.

Good Neighbors

Grow hens-and-chicks in large patches on a dry sunny slope or as foreground plants for all kinds of sedums. Hens-and-chicks make interesting companions for small oreganos (such as *Origanum vulgare* 'Compactum') and creeping thymes as well as for small, grasslike plants, such as pinks (*Dianthus* spp.).

Problems and Solutions

Crown rot, in which the rosettes simply rot away, is the most common complaint. To avoid it, provide good drainage, and plant them in partial shade in hot, humid areas.

Top Performer

Sempervivum tectorum (hens-and-chicks): This old-fashioned favorite produces rosettes of gray-green leaves that are tipped in purple in full sun but are often all green in partial shade. The thick, hairy, leafy flowerstalk arises from the center of a mature rosette, producing dense clusters of purplish red, starry flowers in early summer to midsummer. There are hundreds of cultivars in a wide range of rosette sizes and leaf and flower colors. If you want more choice than your local garden center offers, visit a specialized nursery or shop by mail. I can't help mentioning, though, the decidedly weird 'Oddity' with leaves that are rolled up into hollow tubes. The species is quite hardy, to USDA Zone 3 or less, but hardiness varies for the cultivars: Some aren't trustworthy north of USDA Zone 5. Height in bloom: 8 to 12 inches (20 to 30 cm). Spread: 4 to 8 inches (10 to 20 cm). USDA Plant Hardiness Zones 3 to 9; AHS Heat Zones 8 to 1.

More Recommended Hens-and-Chicks

Sempervivum arachnoideum (cobweb houseleek): This is a much smaller plant with tiny, densely packed rosettes, many of them less than 1 inch (2.5 cm) across. The leaves are attractively draped in silky hairs that make them seem to be covered in a large spider web. Red flowers are produced in small clusters on short stems in midsummer, but cobweb houseleek doesn't flower all that regularly. Height in bloom: 4 inches (10 cm). Spread: 4 to 8 inches (10 to 20 cm). USDA Plant Hardiness Zones 2 to 9; AHS Heat Zones 8 to 1.

Hens-and-chicks
(*Sempervivum tectorum*)

Larry's Garden Notes

It was once believed that house leeks (*Sempervivum* spp.) prevented lightning and, indeed, Emperor Charlemagne ordered them planted on all rooftops in his empire. In fact, the very name "houseleek" comes from the fact that they were commonly grown on house rooftops. We know now that certain trees do indeed attract lightning more than others—but I have had no word on the current status of the houseleek. Who knows, maybe Charlemagne was right?

Thymus

Thyme

Ever popular in herb gardens, thymes have moved out into flower gardens and landscapes, too. Botanically speaking, thymes are shrubs, with woody stems and evergreen leaves, but they're so low-growing that gardeners think of them as perennials. Thymes produce tiny, narrowly oval leaves that are usually aromatic and often covered in fuzzy hairs. The red, pink, lavender, or white flowers are tiny, but thymes flower profusely, creating a lovely colorful carpet of bloom.

Plant Profile

THYMUS
TIME-us

- **Bloom Color:** Lavender, pink, purple, red, or white

- **Bloom Time:** Late spring to early summer

- **Length of Bloom:** Varies by species; see individual listings

- **Height:** Varies by species; see individual listings

- **Spread:** 1 foot (30 cm)

- **Garden Uses:** Container planting, edging, groundcover, mass planting, rock garden, wall planting; along paths, on slopes

- **Light Preference:** Full sun to partial shade

- **Soil Preference:** Average, well-drained soil

- **Best Way to Propagate:** Divide at any season

- **USDA Plant Hardiness Zones:** 3 to 9

- **AHS Heat Zones:** Varies by species; see individual listings

Growing Tips

Thymes need well-drained soil and will even grow in poor, sandy soil. Though they prefer full sun in most climates, thymes will tolerate partial shade without complaint, although the shadier the spot, the more important perfect drainage becomes. As with so many other plants, thymes prefer the most shade when they're growing in hot, humid climates. Elsewhere, morning sun is perfect, but a bit of protection against the hot afternoon sun is always appreciated.

Thymes are drought-resistant, at least when well established, but don't hesitate to water yours during severe drought.

About the only care thymes may need is the occasional mowing or shearing after the plants bloom, just to keep them looking tidy. In hot, humid climates, shearing the plants helps to keep them full and bushy. In all climates, the plants eventually become very woody at the base; just cut them back especially hard to rejuvenate them, and they'll sprout healthy young stems.

Thymes don't need division to stay healthy and happy, but it is a good way to multiply them any time the ground isn't frozen. It's also easy to multiply thymes by taking cuttings when the plants aren't in bloom. And you can also grow them from seed, although thymes cross easily with other species, so you're never sure what you're getting when you sow them. Start seed indoors or out in spring, without covering them: They need light to germinate.

Good Neighbors

The advantage that thymes have over most other groundcovers is that they can tolerate some foot traffic. Plant them between stepping stones and along paths. Pair them with contrasting colors and textures: pinks (*Dianthus* spp.), evergreen candytuft (*Iberis sempervirens*), and hens-and-chicks (*Sempervivum* spp.), for example.

Problems and Solutions

Slugs and snails love thyme, but these plants produce such abundant leaves the damage rarely shows. If wetter-than-usual weather causes shoots to die back, cut plants back harshly to stimulate healthy new growth.

Top Performer

Thymus serpyllum (mother-of-thyme): This is the most common ornamental thyme and has a whole list of common names, from wild thyme to creeping thyme to my favorite, mother-of-thyme. It's a beautiful, ground-hugging groundcover with slightly hairy, dark green leaves that smell much like common thyme (*T. vulgaris*). Mother-of-thyme is cloaked in purple to lavender flowers, borne mostly on dense spikes, in late spring to early summer. Some of the popular cultivars include the brilliant scarlet-flowered 'Coccineus' (also called *T. praecox* 'Coccineus'); 'Snowdrift' and 'Albus', both with pure white flowers; and 'Roseus', with pink flowers. 'Minor' (also called 'Minus') has lavender flowers and grows less than 1/2 inch (1.25 cm) tall. Height: 4 to 6 inches (10 to 15 cm). Spread: 1 foot (30 cm). USDA Plant Hardiness Zones 3 to 9; AHS Heat Zones 9 to 1.

More Recommended Thymes

Thymus pseudolanuginosus, also called *T. praecox* 'Pseudolanuginosus' or *T. lanuginosus* (woolly thyme): Woolly thyme has dense, narrow leaves heavily covered in soft hairs, giving the whole low-growing, creeping plant a distinctly woolly appearance. This is a top-performing groundcover, always attractive and especially resistant to foot traffic. On the downside, though, it needs dry conditions and won't thrive in rainy climates. And the short spikes of pale pink, midsummer flowers are few and far between. 'Hall's Variety', with lavender-pink flowers, is a better bloomer. Height: 3 to 4 inches (8 to 10 cm). Spread: 1 foot (30 cm). USDA Plant Hardiness Zones 3 to 9; AHS Heat Zones 9 to 4.

Mother-of-thyme
(*Thymus serpyllum*)

Larry's Garden Notes

If you have well-drained soil, then thymes (*Thymus* spp.) are the plants for you! One of their best uses is along a path where their soft, flowing foliage can soften the hard edges and add wonderful color and scent. What more could you want? Well, how about a choice of colors? How about a choice of scents? No problem. Thymes rank among the greatest of the olfactory pretenders. There are those that smell like lemon, like orange, like caraway, even like coconut. And, of course, there are those that just smell like thyme.

Vinca

Periwinkle, vinca

Periwinkles make great groundcovers around stepping stones and along woodland paths because they can withstand some foot traffic with no damage. Their shiny, dark green, evergreen leaves are evenly spaced along long, creeping or arching stems that root wherever they touch the ground. Periwinkles also produce elegant, funnel-shaped flowers, usually purple or blue, with five petals arrayed in a pinwheel pattern. The flowers are most abundant in spring, but the plants also bloom in summer and fall, especially when cooler weather returns.

Plant Profile

VINCA
VING-kuh

- **Bloom Color:** Blue, purple, or white
- **Bloom Time:** Varies by species; see individual listings
- **Length of Bloom:** 4 weeks or more
- **Height:** Varies by species; see individual listings
- **Spread:** Varies by species; see individual listings
- **Garden Uses:** Container planting, edging, groundcover, mass planting, rock garden, wall planting, woodland garden; along paths, on slopes
- **Light Preference:** Full sun to deep shade
- **Soil Preference:** Fertile, humus-rich, well-drained soil
- **Best Way to Propagate:** Divide at any time
- **USDA Plant Hardiness Zones:** Varies by species; see individual listings
- **AHS Heat Zones:** Varies by species; see individual listings

Growing Tips

One reason periwinkles are so popular is that they're so adaptable. Full sun suits them just fine in cool-summer areas, at least as long as you keep their soil moist, yet they do almost equally well in deep shade, although they don't bloom as heavily. In hot-summer climates, they'll need partial shade to grow, or, at least, protection from full afternoon sun. And though periwinkles prefer fertile, humus-rich soil, they also do fine in average garden soil. A generous layer of organic mulch will help keep the soil moist and cool in any climate.

It's best to plant periwinkles relatively thickly—about 1 foot (30 cm) apart—if you want a complete cover quickly. Mowing over young plantings in the fall helps to stimulate thicker growth, resulting in faster coverage.

Once established, periwinkles need little or no care. Some gardeners do, however, prefer to mow periwinkles down to half their height in the fall to stimulate thicker, more even growth.

Think Twice: Be aware that periwinkles are extremely invasive and get out of hand quickly. Root barriers are of no use in this case because periwinkles spread aboveground, not underneath. Plant periwinkles only where they're surrounded by natural barriers they can't possibly cross (such as paved areas).

The most obvious way to multiply periwinkles is by dividing the numerous offsets any time the ground isn't frozen. Periwinkles also root readily from stem cuttings taken from nonblooming stems.

Good Neighbors

A useful plant for covering large shaded areas, common periwinkle (*Vinca minor*) looks absolutely wonderful under spring-flowering trees and shrubs such as flowering cherries (*Prunus* spp.), magnolias, and viburnums.

Problems and Solutions

Periwinkles suffer from minor leaf diseases or insect infestations, but these problems usually clear up without help.

Top Performer

Vinca minor (common periwinkle): The best known and most widely grown species, common periwinkle produces pairs of smooth, shiny, dark green, oval or oblong leaves that are about 1½ inch (4 cm) long. Some stems produce only leaves and root as they grow; others produce 1-inch (2.5-cm) purplish blue flowers. The plant blooms heavily in spring, sporadically throughout the summer, then sometimes heavily again later in the season.

Cultivars include 'Atropurpurea' (also called 'Purpurea' or 'Rubra') has deep wine red flowers; 'Alba' has white flowers. 'La Grave' (also called 'Bowles' Variety') is a clump former with large, intense blue flowers. 'Aureovariegata' has pale blue flowers and yellow and green leaves, and 'Argenteovariegata' has the same flower color but leaves that are marbled with white and gray. Height: 4 to 10 inches (10 to 20 cm). Spread: 12 to 18 inches (30 to 45 cm). USDA Plant Hardiness Zones 4 to 9; AHS Heat Zones 9 to 1.

More Recommended Periwinkles

❚ **Think Twice:** *Vinca major* (greater periwinkle): The leaves of this aggressive species are larger than those of common periwinkle and have slightly hairy edges rather than smooth ones. Its nonflowering stems are long and creeping, rooting as they grow. The flowering stems are more upright and produce large, blue, funnel-shaped flowers near their tips. Like common periwinkle, greater periwinkle flowers most abundantly in spring but reblooms until fall. 'Variegata' (also called 'Elegantissima') is the most commonly available cultivar. Its green leaves blotched with creamy white are a common sight in flower boxes the world over. Height: 12 to 18 inches (30 to 45 cm). Spread: 2 feet (60 cm). USDA Plant Hardiness Zones 7 to 9; AHS Heat Zones 9 to 7.

'Burgundy' common periwinkle (*Vinca minor* 'Burgundy')

Larry's Garden Notes

Pretty as periwinkles (*Vinca* spp.) are in a woodland setting, they've caused immeasurable damage to North American forests by taking over natural habitats and driving out native plants. Don't hesitate to use them in areas where there is no danger they can escape into the wild, such as spots far from any natural forest. But if your garden is close to a natural woodland, avoid periwinkle, and use a groundcover that's native to your area instead and won't outcompete other local native plants.

PERENNIALS & GRASSES FOR
Dramatic Impact

Big, bold, and brash—that's what I had in mind when I selected the perennials and ornamental grasses for this chapter. While most perennials are modest plants that look best planted in groups, the plants you'll find here do just fine planted all by themselves. That doesn't necessarily mean that they blaze with color all summer or have the most fabulous foliage. No, these perennials have presence because of their sheer size. They're not just tall, not just wide—they're *both*. You'll want to be selective with these big beauties. By planting just one or two dramatic landscape perennials in the right spots, you can change the appearance of your whole yard.

Top Picks

◄ Tall and graceful, pampas grass (*Cortaderia selloana*) is eye-catching whether it's planted as a background in a large perennial bed or it's massed in groups. The plumed flower spikes appear in late summer and persist for months, lending interest to the winterscape.

One Is Enough

You're probably used to grouping perennials by threes or fives in your garden. But when you decide to plant a very large perennial, such as Joe-Pye weeds (*Eupatorium* spp.) or maiden grass (*Miscanthus sinensis*), restrain yourself. One is enough. Landscape and garden designers would say that the perennials and grasses in this chapter have "architectural impact." (That's a fancy way of saying they're big and look impressive.) The effect of using these plants rather than ordinary perennials is like putting a new couch in your living room instead of adding a few knickknacks to a shelf: It gives the setting a very new look. That's why I like to call these large perennials "landscape perennials"—when you plant them, you'll really notice the impact on your home landscape.

Using Perennials as Shrubs

When you're deciding how to use landscape perennials, think of them as shrubs. You'll probably plant them alone or in a row as a privacy screen. Or you might plant them to soften the effect of large trees. Landscape perennials can also serve as background plants in mixed perennial borders; their height and fullness set off the smaller perennials that grow at their base. Wherever you might want to use a shrub in your yard, you can probably use a landscape perennial in its place with the same effect.

You may be wondering, "Why shouldn't I just plant a shrub instead of a big perennial?" Well, you certainly can and should plant some shrubs in your yard. But dramatic-looking perennials can help round

Large ornamental grasses like miscanthus (*Miscanthus* spp.) have fountainlike foliage that is nothing short of majestic. The arching leaves can reach 5 feet tall (150 cm) and the flowery plumes, which usually appear very late in the season, dry to a pleasing cream color.

out the choice of shrubs for your garden. After all, you can never have too many choices when you're looking for just the right plant!

No Pruning Required

There are situations where big perennials beat shrubs at their own game. For one thing, unlike shrubs, landscape perennials don't need to be pruned to control their size. Landscape perennials have the good sense to die back to the ground annually and start anew each spring. They therefore take care of their own pruning, and once they're mature, they regrow to the same size and shape year after year. So if you don't enjoy pruning, landscape perennials could be a great shrub substitute for you. All you need to do is cut the plant back to its base each year to get rid of old stems.

A Bounty of Bloom

Another argument for dramatic perennials over shrubs is length of bloom. While there are a few long-blooming shrubs, like hydrangeas and shrubby cinquefoil (*Potentilla fruticosa*), most

flowering shrubs bloom for only a week or so. In contrast, many of the perennials in this chapter bloom for weeks and sometimes for much of the summer. Goat's beards (*Aruncus* spp.), Joe-Pye weeds (*Eupatorium* spp.), and most ornamental grasses are long-blooming substitutes for shrubs.

For a lacier, see-through look that few shrubs can offer, try Russian sages (*Perovskia* spp.) and white gaura (*Gaura lindheimeri*)—they soften the view without blocking it entirely.

A "Removable Screen"

When winter arrives, your seasonal hedge will die back to the ground, but that's not always a disadvantage. For example, you may want to screen your patio from your neighbor's backyard during the summer to reduce noise and provide privacy when you're sitting outdoors in your yard. But in the winter, when you aren't using your patio, it's nicer to have a larger vista to view through your windows. In the off-season, your yard and your neighbor's yard will blend together, especially when they're covered with snow, creating a pleasing view.

A seasonal screen also makes sense when you want to block out sun in the summer but not the winter. For example, you may want to keep the sun from overheating a south-facing room in summer but let the sun in for the winter. If so, the ideal choice is probably a deciduous shade tree, but if you don't have enough space for a shade tree, try planting a dramatic perennial. Even if you do decide a deciduous tree is the ideal solution in the long run, you still have to wait years for it to have an effect. In the meantime, use a fast-maturing landscape perennial like tall ornamental grasses or Joe-Pye weed (*Eupatorium* spp.) to block sun while the tree grows.

Safe from Snow Damage

Landscape perennials are great alternatives to shrubs in spots where plants might be damaged in winter, such as near roads, paths, or driveways. Snowplows and snowblowers hit the poor plants with blasts of heavy, icy snow, breaking their branches and tearing chunks out of their bark. And wind blowing over roads or highways can pick up salt spray from de-icing products, which burns tender buds. Even a heavy snowfall or, worse yet, mounds of icy snow slipping off a roof, can flatten shrubs and conifers. I know people who carefully board up their shrubs each winter, creating boxes around each one, to protect them from such dangers. Instead of going to such trouble, plant landscape perennials. Since perennials die back to soil level in winter, they're immune to damage from snow or snowplows. Any salt spray can be washed away before the plants sprout, yet they spring right up again with the first warm days of the new season.

In my Quebec climate, where snow is so abundant that meter readers go their rounds on snowshoes five months of the year, snow damage is such a problem that shrubby hedges are almost impossible to maintain. For us, landscape perennials are the plants of choice to accent our roadsides and driveways. If you've had problems with snow damage, I suggest you try a perennial hedge, too.

Ornamental Grasses with Pizzazz

Ornamental grasses described in other chapters are relatively modest in size and fit well in small-scale gardens or with smaller perennials in a border. Those described in this chapter are much more imposing plants. These plants attract attention in the fall and the winter. Though they may lose their bright green summer coloration, they stand tall and strong, resisting the winter winds and acting almost as much as a permanant feature as an evergreen. Their arching, fountainlike leaves topped by feathery plumes are nothing short of majestic—and they are just as capable of fitting into a larger border as of standing alone as a garden highlight in the lawn.

The larger ornamental grasses have the same architectural impact as any shrublike perennial, although their more narrow, upright habit puts them in a class all their own. Be daring and be bold, and most of all, be willing to experiment with these great plants.

12 More Dramatic Perennials

Looking for more perennials that make a statement? Take a look at these grand and gorgeous plants from other chapters:

Acanthus (Bear's breeches) . . .214	*Helianthus* (Sunflower) 178
Aconitum (Aconite) 192	*Lavatera* (Tree mallow) 89
Baptisia (Baptisia) 194	*Osmunda* (Flowering fern) 366
Darmera (Umbrella plant) 282	*Paeonia* (Peony) 206
Dictamnus (Gas plant) 198	*Rodgersia* (Rodgersia) 292
Helenium (Helenium) 176	*Yucca* (Yucca) 268

Aruncus

Goat's beard

Is it a shrub or a perennial? Goat's beard will keep 'em guessing! This very large, bushy perennial produces feathery plumes of creamy white flowers at the tips of its sturdy stems in summer. After the flowers fade, the dark green foliage takes over. Deeply cut, feathery, and quite dense, it creates an effect in the landscape every bit the equal of most shrubs. I suggest simply forgetting that it's a perennial and using it wherever you need a shrub in a somewhat shady environment. Goat's beard will never disappoint you.

Plant Profile

ARUNCUS
uh-RUN-kuss

- **Bloom Color:** White

- **Bloom Time:** Early summer to midsummer

- **Length of Bloom:** 4 weeks or more

- **Height:** 4 to 6 feet (1.2 to 1.8 m)

- **Spread:** 4 to 6 feet (1.2 to 1.8 m)

- **Garden Uses:** Cut flower garden, mixed border, seasonal hedge, specimen plant, woodland garden; at the back of beds and borders, in wet areas

- **Light Preference:** Full sun to partial shade

- **Soil Preference:** Rich, moist soil

- **Best Way to Propagate:** Sow seed in spring

- **USDA Plant Hardiness Zones:** 2 to 9

- **AHS Heat Zones:** 9 to 1

Growing Tips

Goat's beards have a tough, no-nonsense, I-can-survive-anything look about them—and they live up to that promise. The plants do well in full sun in cool-summer areas but appreciate partial shade, preferably with some morning sun, in other climates. Because they tolerate less than full sun, goat's beards are often promoted as shade lovers, but I find that reputation to be a bit exaggerated. Yes, goat's beards will grow in deep shade, but you couldn't say they thrive there, and the blooms will be few and far between.

Goat's beards prefer moist but well-drained soil and will even thrive under wet conditions, notably along streams and ponds. For plants native to moist conditions, though, they do amazingly well in dry shade—with the help of a little mulch, that is. They're adapted to growing in leaf litter in open forest locations in Europe, Asia, and North America, and a thick layer of organic mulch helps re-create those natural conditions. In dry conditions and poor soil, you'll have healthy foliage but very few flowers.

Once they're established, you can leave goat's beards alone. The plants don't appreciate being divided nor do they need it. Although some gardeners like to cut these plants back harshly after they bloom, claiming they look tidier that way, my opinion is that you miss half the fun by doing so. I suggest just leaving the flowerstalks standing after they bloom. They simply become thinner and browner in color but, like astilbes, remain attractive in a beige sort of way until fall.

Division, as mentioned, is never necessary, and that's fortunate because digging up the woody rootstock is as much work as digging out a tree stump! Instead, choose the slow but easy way: Sow seed indoors or out on top of a moist soil mix in spring. The seed may take a few weeks to germinate and will grow ever so slowly afterward, but it's still the simplest way of multiplying goat's beards yourself. Personally, if I want more plants, I just buy them.

Good Neighbors

The creamy white plumes of goat's beard look great with any color Siberian iris (*Iris sibirica*) in the spring border. Its good-quality foliage persists throughout the season, creating an excellent backdrop for later-blooming Japanese anemone (*Anemone × hybrida*), lilies (*Lilium* spp.), foxglove penstemon (*Penstemon digitalis*), and garden phlox (*Phlox paniculata*), all of which are adapted to the same partially shaded conditions. For a low-care planting in a moist woodland edge, surround goat's beard with a groundcover such as lady's-mantle (*Alchemilla mollis*), epimediums (*Epimedium* spp.), or Allegheny foamflower (*Tiarella cordifolia*).

Goat's beard
(*Aruncus dioicus*)

Problems and Solutions

Leaf spot can sometimes appear on the foliage, but it rarely causes problems worth treating.

Top Performer

Aruncus dioicus, also called *A. sylvester* or *Spiraea aruncus* (goat's beard): A monster of a plant and a true shrub impersonator, this is the best goat's beard to choose. It will eventually fill a space 6 feet (180 cm) across in the garden, so give it room to expand! The medium green leaves are up to 3 feet (90 cm) long with multiple, lance-shaped, pointed leaflets, and they form a very dense, bushy clump. The foamy, frothy, creamy white flower heads are spectacular, each one the size of a volleyball, and the display just keeps getting better and better as the plant matures. The species itself is spectacular, but there are a few cultivars, only one of which—'Kneiffii'—is commonly available. It has deeply incised leaves cut almost into threads, creating a look much like a Japanese maple, and it's smaller than the species, only about 3 feet (90 cm) tall and wide. 'Kneiffii' can only be multiplied by division; it doesn't come true from seed.

Larry's Garden Notes

If you enjoy arranging flowers and have a cut flower garden, be sure to plant this beautiful perennial. The sight of a full stem of goat's beard (*Aruncus dioicus*) in a vase stretching a good 4 feet (120 cm) into the air is quite remarkable. The stems also work well as an airy filler in large mixed arrangements. And as an added bonus, you can cut the flowers stems young, and they'll dry nicely to a yellowish beige for fall dried arrangements.

Cortaderia

Pampas grass

Pampas grasses are *the* most spectacular ornamental grasses for the home garden. These fast-growing plants produce dense, impenetrable, 4- to 5-foot (1.2- to 1.5-m)-wide evergreen fountains of saw-toothed, narrow, arching leaves. In late summer, the plants send up huge, dense, fluffy plumes of creamy white to pink flowers on tall, thick stems that usually reach more than 6 feet (1.8 m) tall—and sometimes two or three times that!

Plant Profile

CORTADERIA
kor-tah-DEER-ee-ah

- ■ **Bloom Color:** Pink or white

- ■ **Bloom Time:** Late summer to fall

- ■ **Length of Bloom:** 2 months or more

- ■ **Height:** 4 to 20 feet (1.2 to 6 m)

- ■ **Spread:** 4 to 5 feet (90 to 120 cm)

- ■ **Garden Uses:** Container planting, cut flower garden, mixed border, seasonal hedge, specimen plant; at the back of beds and borders

- ■ **Light Preference:** Full sun to partial shade

- ■ **Soil Preference:** Rich, moist but well-drained soil

- ■ **Best Way to Propagate:** Divide in spring

- ■ **USDA Plant Hardiness Zones:** 8 to 11

- ■ **AHS Heat Zones:** 12 to 7

Growing Tips

Pampas grasses may be big, imposing plants, but in the way of maintenance, they don't impose much on those who grow them. Simply plant them in full sun to partial shade and almost any well-drained soil, and they will do fine. Although they prefer rich soil that remains constantly moist, they will put up with drier conditions and even poor soil.

Upkeep of pampas grasses is minimal. Pampas grasses, in fact, really *need* no maintenance other than watering during times of drought and a regular topdressing of organic mulch. You may feel tempted to clean up the browned leaves in the spring (preferably not in the fall because the dead leaves make an excellent winter mulch). If you do, be very careful, because the leaves can injure you (see the "Warning" below). Unpruned pampas grasses will go through an ugly duckling stage in early spring when new leaves mingle with the old, but the new ones soon dominate. The plants look as fresh as daisies by midspring, whether you chop them back or not.

Pampas grasses don't need division, but that's the only way to multiply the cultivars. Divide clumps very early in the spring, after pruning the plants back harshly for the safety of your fingers. Don't try to dig up the whole rootball; just cut out a pie-shaped section from the back of the clump with a very sharp shovel.

If you live in a region where it's too cold to grow pampas grasses, maiden grasses (*Miscanthus* spp.) are good substitutes. To learn more about maiden grasses, turn to page 436.

Warning: Pampas grass leaves are covered with sharp teeth that catch onto clothing and rip into the skin. Approach them with extreme caution—and thick gloves, long sleeves and pants, boots, and goggles.

Although pampas grasses are widely grown in the same dry-season climates where brush fires can occur, you should know that their dead leaves are extremely flammable. Keep the plants away from other flammable materials (including your house and your deck!) and, in such areas, be sure you cut off the dead leaves and stems as soon as they occur rather than leaving them on the plants—it's just too risky.

Also, in some areas, environmental groups discourage growing any kind of pampas grasses because of their invasiveness. I find that a bit excessive, as ordinary pampas grass (*Cortaderia selloana*) is not very invasive and, indeed, seldom produces seed. (Most cultivars only produce female flowers, so there usually aren't males around for seed production.) An easy solution to preventing any spread is to cut off the flower-stalks of female cultivars before they produce any seed.

Pampas grass
(*Cortaderia selloana*)

Good Neighbors

Pampas grass is a huge ornamental grass that can easily look out of scale—and out of place. Give it a spot where you need a big, impressive accent, such as flanking an entrance or in a poolside setting. Surround it with mass plantings to balance its strong vertical form.

Problems and Solutions

The tough-as-nails constitution of this plant extends to its insect and disease resistance; it seems immune to just about everything.

Top Performer

Cortaderia selloana (pampas grass): This species deserves its ranking as Top Performer, but be careful when you buy it. Many plants sold under the name *C. selloana* may in fact be purple pampas grass (*C. jubata*), a much weedier plant that can be potentially invasive. Be sure you choose the true *C. selloana*. One way of making sure is to only choose named cultivars. 'Rosea', pale pink, and 'Carnea', darker pink, are two of the pink-flowered cultivars. Variegated cultivars include 'Aureolineata' (also called 'Gold Band'), with green leaves lined in yellow, and 'Albolineata' (also called 'Silver Stripe'), with white margins. Two handsome dwarf cultivars include 'Bertini', which grows 2 to 3 feet (60 to 90 cm) tall, and 'Pumila', which reaches 3 to 4 feet (90 to 120 cm) tall.

Larry's Garden Notes

Pampas grass (*Cortaderia selloana*) is so spectacular in the garden that it's very tempting to try growing it beyond its rather limited range. Although you'll note that I only rate it hardy to USDA Zone 8, you can grow it outdoors to Zone 6 if you carefully choose a well-protected spot for it. Mulch well around its base after the ground freezes, and certainly don't cut it back until spring because the dense clumps of foliage act like a nice, warm winter jacket. Further north than Zone 6, cut back the leaves in fall and dig up the plant. You can overwinter it, dormant, in a root cellar or other cool, frost-free spot. Or, for much less hassle, grow pampas grass in large pots like I do so you can bring them indoors for the winter.

Crambe

Sea kale, colewort

Think of a large cabbage crossed with baby's-breath, and you'll have a pretty good portrait of sea kales. Sea kales really *are* cabbage relatives, with huge, thick leaves and a silhouette like an overgrown, nonheading cabbage. Each of the creamy white, sweetly scented flowers has four petals and four sepals. But you're less likely to notice the individual flowers than the overall effect created by the masses of tiny blooms on branching stems that seem to hover over the heavy, mounded plant like clouds over a mountain.

Plant Profile

CRAMBE
KRAM-bee

■ **Bloom Color:** White

■ **Bloom Time:** Early summer to midsummer

■ **Length of Bloom:** 3 or 4 weeks

■ **Height:** Varies by species; see individual listings

■ **Spread:** Varies by species; see individual listings

■ **Garden Uses:** Cut flower garden, mixed border, seasonal hedge, specimen plant, wildflower meadow; at the back of beds and borders; attracts butterflies

■ **Light Preference:** Full sun to light shade

■ **Soil Preference:** Rich, well-drained, slightly alkaline soil

■ **Best Way to Propagate:** Sow seed in spring

■ **USDA Plant Hardiness Zones:** 4 to 9

■ **AHS Heat Zones:** 9 to 1

Growing Tips

Although tolerant of various conditions, sea kales prefer full sun and rich, moist soil. Constant moisture is especially important if you want the plants to look their best because, resilient as they appear, the huge leaves need lots of moisture to keep from wilting on hot days. In fact, sea kales can be a good choice for damp areas as long as the soil is well drained, especially in spring and winter.

Why aren't these plants more popular? It's probably because they're so slow to multiply. One option is to take root cuttings in fall or early spring by digging carefully at the plant's base and removing one or more of the thick side roots that run parallel to the ground. Cut them into 4- to 6-inch (10- to 15-cm) lengths and plant them on their sides, 1 inch (2.5 cm) deep. Or simply slice into the ground 1 to 2 inches (2.5 to 5 cm) from the plant's base with a sharp shovel. This inevitably severs a root or two, which then sends up plantlets that you can remove and replant in another spot.

If you need many new plants, seed is the way to go. Sow it outdoors in early spring before the ground has warmed up or in the fall, planting the seed about ½ inch (1.25 cm) deep. Germinating the seed indoors is much more difficult because the seed needs cool conditions—about 60° to 65°F (15° to 18°C)—to sprout. Sow the seed in peat pots, since the young plants quickly produce taproots and therefore transplant very poorly.

Sea kale also self-sows where conditions are to its liking and could possibly be invasive in coastal areas. If this worries you, simply cut back the flowerstalks after the last bloom fades to prevent seed production.

Good Neighbors

Careful companion selection is important because sea kales' large basal leaves will create a substantial hole when they die back in late summer. Try siting them behind 'Moonshine' yarrow, peach-leaved bellflower (*Campanula persicifolia*), or Siberian iris (*Iris sibirica*), and add some later-flowering asters to carry on the show.

Problems and Solutions

Sea kales don't seem to have any notable insect or disease problems.

Top Performer

Crambe cordifolia (colewort, heartleaf crambe, giant kale): This is easily the giant of the genus, a huge monster of a plant that fully merits a place among perennials with architectural presence. You rarely need more than one to create much of an impact. The leaves can be huge, up to 2 feet (60 cm) across, and are borne on long stalks. They're usually heart-shaped, especially the lower ones, and dark green in color. The early summer to midsummer flowers are tiny but abundant and generally white to creamy white in color. Height: 4 to 7 feet (1.2 to 2.1 m). Spread: 4 feet (1.2 m). USDA Plant Hardiness Zones 4 to 9; AHS Heat Zones 9 to 1.

More Recommended Sea Kales

Crambe maritima (sea kale): This plant is native to the windswept shores of the northern Atlantic and the Mediterranean Seas, so it shrugs off salt spray and the most wicked winds without any damage. Sea kale is therefore justly popular in seaside gardens, but it's also worth growing in gardens that are contaminated by road salt or ground salt. This species is a smaller plant than colewort (*C. cordifolia*) and has very different leaves, which are particularly thick and waxy, wavy at the edges, and the same blue-green shade as cabbage, making for a very handsome appearance. The early summer to midsummer flowers are similar to those of colewort, though on somewhat shorter stems and closer to creamy yellow in color than to pure white. Height: 2 to 4 feet (60 to 120 cm). Spread: 3 feet (90 cm). USDA Plant Hardiness Zones 4 to 9; AHS Heat Zones 9 to 1.

Colewort
(*Crambe cordifolia*)

Larry's Garden Notes

You can have your kale and eat it, too! The spring leaf stems of sea kale (*Crambe maritima*) have long been used as a vegetable. They soften up considerably as long as you blanch them. In spring, just as the plant begins to sprout, cover it up with a large inverted flowerpot, plugging its drainage holes. The plant will produce long, thick petioles (leaf stems) with a tiny leaf at the tip. Snap the petioles off at the base when they're about 6 to 9 inches (15 to 23 cm) long, and prepare them according to your favorite sea kale recipe. What? You don't have any sea kale recipes? Just choose one for asparagus and use sea kale petioles instead. After harvesting the first petioles, remove the blanching pot.

Eupatorium

Joe-Pye weed, boneset

Joe-Pye weeds are garden giants! While these thick, bushy plants die to the ground in the winter, as far as their appearance and use in the garden is concerned, they're shrubs. The individual flowers are tubular, but you'll scarcely notice that because they're grouped together in dense, flat to rounded clusters at the tips of the branches. The clusters have an appealingly fuzzy look.

Plant Profile

EUPATORIUM
you-puh-TOUR-ee-um

- **Bloom Color:** Pink, purple, or white

- **Bloom Time:** Late summer to fall

- **Length of Bloom:** 4 to 8 weeks or more

- **Height:** Varies by species; see individual listings

- **Spread:** Varies by species; see individual listings

- **Garden Uses:** Cut flower garden, meadow garden, mixed border, seasonal hedge, specimen plant; at the back of beds and borders, in wet areas; attracts butterflies

- **Light Preference:** Full sun to partial shade

- **Soil Preference:** Average, moist to wet soil

- **Best Way to Propagate:** Divide in spring or fall

- **USDA Plant Hardiness Zones:** Varies by species; see individual listings

- **AHS Heat Zones:** Varies by species; see individual listings

Growing Tips

Most Joe-Pye weeds grow in wet soil in the wild, yet are surprisingly adaptable to average garden conditions—although they definitely appreciate a generous layer of organic mulch. Just plant and water them, then let nature take care of the rest.

Because Joe-Pye weeds can spread through wayward seed, it's a good idea to deadhead after the last flower fades in fall.

Joe-Pye weeds don't need regular division to thrive, but that *is* the easiest way to multiply them. Just dig up a clump in early spring or autumn and cut the base into separate clumps, each with its share of roots. You can also raise Joe-Pye weeds from seed—at least the species (the cultivars don't always come true from seed). Sow the seed either in fall when it matures, directly outdoors, or indoors in late winter, just covering the seeds. Joe-pye weed can take anywhere from a few weeks to a few months to germinate.

Good Neighbors

Stately Joe-Pye weeds are a good choice for planting in low, moist areas. Or use them in a butterfly garden behind purple coneflower (*Echinacea purpurea*), garden phlox (*Phlox paniculata*), and shining coneflower (*Rudbeckia nitida*) for an end-of-summer flourish.

Problems and Solutions

Occasional outbreaks of aphids or caterpillars may feed on foliage (knock them off with a spray of water), and leaf miners may trace fine tunnels through their leaves (just remove the affected leaves). Powdery mildew can appear as gray patches on leaves in fall if the soil is too dry; just cut the plants back to the ground when this happens.

Top Performer

Eupatorium maculatum (spotted Joe-Pye weed). I rated this plant a Top Performer mostly because it's by far the most widely adapted of all the Joe-Pye weeds. It belongs to the North American group of whorled-leaved Joe-Pye weeds, including *E. maculatum, E. fistulosum,* and *E. purpureum,* all of which are very similar in appearance. All share gigantic, dense, domed clusters of pinkish to purplish flowers from mid-summer to fall, a shrublike appearance, sturdy stems, and rough-textured, lance-shaped whorled leaves.

Spotted Joe-Pye weed is, as you'd expect from the name, spotted. The stems are green mottled with purple, especially to-ward the tips. Other than that, the only really noticeable differences from the other species are that this one bears more flowers per cluster than the others (9 to 15), the clusters are more distinctly flat-topped, and it has the most fragrant flowers. By far the most commonly available cul-tivar is 'Atropurpureum' with purple flowers and purple-tinted leaves and upper stems. Height: 4 to 7 feet (1.2 to 2.1 m). Spread: 4 feet (1.2 m). USDA Plant Hardiness Zones 2 to 9; AHS Heat Zones 9 to 4.

More Recommended Joe-Pye Weeds

Eupatorium fistulosum (Joe-Pye weed): The best way of telling this plant from spotted Joe-Pye weed (*E. maculatum*) is to break a stem; it's hollow, while spotted Joe-Pye weed has solid stems. 'Bartered Bride' is a white-flowered form. 'Gateway' is more compact, a mere 4 to 5 feet (1.2 to 1.5 m) tall! Height: 4 to 7 feet (1.2 to 2.1 m). Spread: 3 feet (90 cm). USDA Plant Hardiness Zones 4 to 9; AHS Heat Zones 8 to 3.

E. purpureum (Joe-Pye weed): The hollow stems of this species are all green with just a hint of purple at the leaf joints, and the huge clusters of purple flowers are rounded rather than almost flat as in spotted Joe-Pye weed (*E. maculatum*). Also, the crushed leaves smell of vanilla. That may help you tell it from the others, but then, you really don't need to, as they can all be used pretty much interchange-ably. Height: 4 to 7 feet (1.2 to 2.1 m). Spread: 4 feet (1.2 m). USDA Plant Hardiness Zones 4 to 9; AHS Heat Zones 9 to 1.

'Atropurpureum' spotted Joe-Pye weed (*Eupatorium maculatum* 'Atropurpureum')

Larry's Garden Notes

Joe-Pye weeds (*Eupatorium* spp.) may be new perennials to you—they're just catching on with gar-deners in the United States and Canada. Long considered weeds, albeit very pretty ones, Joe-Pye weeds didn't really make much of a splash in their native land until North American gardeners began visiting the gardens of Europe. I must confess I was among those who had somehow managed to miss the potential of spotted Joe-Pye weed (*E. maculatum*) until I saw it in British gardens. I could kick myself now when I realize how blind I'd been. Let that be a lesson to us. Don't overlook the ornamental potential of our native plants!

Filipendula

Meadowsweet

If you're looking for a bold perennial for a wet site, look no further than meadowsweet. Like the other plants in this chapter, meadowsweets can make great shrub substitutes during the growing season; in the fall, they die back to ground level. These large, upright plants have jagged, feathery foliage, often with a network of deep veins. Their flowers are tiny and borne in dense heads at the ends of the stems. The billowy appearance comes from the numerous soft-looking stamens, which soften the cluster's silhouette.

Plant Profile

FILIPENDULA
fill-uh-PEN-djew-luh

- **Bloom Color:** Pink, red, or white
- **Bloom Time:** Varies by species; see individual listings
- **Length of Bloom:** 2 or 3 weeks or more
- **Height:** Varies by species; see individual listings
- **Spread:** Varies by species; see individual listings
- **Garden Uses:** Cut flower garden, mass planting, meadow garden, mixed border, seasonal hedge, specimen plant; at the back of beds and borders, in wet areas
- **Light Preference:** Varies by species; see individual listings
- **Soil Preference:** Varies by species; see individual listings
- **Best Way to Propagate:** Divide in spring or fall
- **USDA Plant Hardiness Zones:** 3 to 9
- **AHS Heat Zones:** 8 to 1

Growing Tips

In cool-summer areas, meadowsweets appreciate full sun; elsewhere, they prefer afternoon shade. Mulching is wise, as they do prefer keeping their roots cool. Wet is a key word in describing their needs. They do well enough in moist soil but prefer even soggier ones and will do well in those damp spots that so many other perennials dislike.

Division is required only if you want to multiply the plants. Using a very sharp shovel, cut the clumps into sections between any obvious divisions. You can also multiply the species by sowing fresh seed outdoors in fall or indoors under cool conditions—55° to 60°F (13° to 15°C)—about eight to ten weeks before the last frost. Barely cover the seed.

Good Neighbors

Try the soft pink flowers of queen-of-the-prairie (*Filipendula rubra*) with moisture-loving companions that have white, pale yellow, or deep purple flowers. Possible choices include daylilies, 'Blaustrumpf' bee balm (*Monarda* 'Blaustrumpf'), and great blue lobelia (*Lobelia siphilitica*).

The white blooms of queen-of-the-meadow (*F. ulmaria*) look great with almost anything, but make sure you choose equally vigorous companions, such as Siberian iris (*Iris sibirica*) or obedient plant (*Physostegia virginiana*).

Problems and Solutions

Meadowsweets are prone to powdery mildew during humid weather, especially if the soil is dry. Either use an organic fungicide as a preventive measure or grow them in the moist soil they prefer.

Top Performer

Filipendula rubra (queen-of-the-prairie): This is
one of the largest, shrubbiest, longest-
blooming, and easiest to grow of all the
meadowsweets. Its numerous dense leaves
are beautifully textured and featherlike, divided into varying numbers of leaflets. The
huge midsummer to late-summer flower head
is pink to peach in color. Queen-of-the-prairie
varies greatly in height, depending mostly on
the quantity of moisture available; it reaches
its tallest height in very moist soil. It seems to
have an even more definite preference for cool
conditions than the others. 'Venusta' (also
called 'Venusta Magnifica' and 'Magnifica') is
the usual cultivar, with brighter pink to almost
carmine-red flowers and a somewhat smaller
size than the species: only 4 to 6 feet (1.2 to
1.8 m) tall. Although the first generation
comes fairly true from seed, repeatedly growing it from seed generation
after generation tends to lead to taller, paler plants closer to the wild
species. Height: 6 to 8 feet (1.8 to 2.4 m). Spread: 3 to 4 feet (90 to 120
cm). USDA Plant Hardiness Zones 3 to 9; AHS Heat Zones 8 to 1.

Queen-of-the-prairie
(*Filipendula rubra*)

More Recommended Meadowsweets

Filipendula ulmaria (queen-of-the-meadow, meadowsweet): This popular species has a very shrubby appearance with numerous, fernlike
leaves that have 7 to 11 saw-toothed leaflets. The foliage is rough-
looking on top and felty white below. The early summer to midsummer flowers are white and sweetly scented. This species
self-sows, but the cultivars don't come true, so remove their flowers
before they go to seed. If you try growing queen-of-the-meadow from
seed indoors, make sure you start with fresh seed or give it alternating
periods of warm and cold temperatures. 'Flore Pleno' is the usual cultivar with very double, long-lasting flowers. 'Aurea' is a choice selection with beautiful golden yellow leaves. Its flowers are insignificant,
barely visible against the yellow background, and its seedlings won't
come true, so it's best to remove the blooms. Keep this one out of full
sun or it will burn. 'Variegata' (also called 'Aureo-Variegata') has dark
green leaves set off by a bright yellow to creamy yellow blotch in the
center. Height: 30 to 72 inches (75 to 180 cm). Spread: 3 feet (90 cm).
USDA Plant Hardiness Zones 3 to 9; AHS Heat Zones 8 to 1.

Larry's Garden Notes

Many meadowsweets have medicinal uses, but one meadowsweet
(*Filipendula ulmaria*), which is also
called queen-of-the-meadow, has
tremendous historical importance.
This meadowsweet, along with vervain (*Verbena officinalis*) and water-
mint (*Mentha aquatica*), were some
of the most sacred herbs of the
Druids. By the Middle Ages, it was a
popular herb to scatter on floors to
alleviate bad odors. In fact, the
name meadowsweet, commonly
used for the entire genus *Filipendula*, comes from this use. We can
enjoy queen-of-the-meadow and
other filipendulas in both formal
borders and naturalized plantings
instead of using them to sweeten
our paths.

Gaura

Gaura

Picture a large, vase-shaped clump of green stems with an airy, see-through appearance, and you'll understand the appeal of gaura. White gaura (*Gaura lindheimeri*) is the species that's commonly grown, and it has four-petaled flowers that are usually white with a pink tinge, becoming more pink as they age. The flowers are narrow at the base but broad closer to the tips of the petals, with prominent stamens. Each lasts only a few days, but new blooms open constantly from late spring until fall.

Plant Profile

GAURA
GAW-ruh

■ **Bloom Color:** Pink or white

■ **Bloom Time:** Late spring to fall

■ **Length of Bloom:** 3 months or more

■ **Height:** 2 to 5 feet (60 to 150 cm)

■ **Spread:** 2 to 3 feet (60 to 90 cm)

■ **Garden Uses:** Container planting, cut flower garden, mass planting, meadow garden, mixed border, specimen plant; at the back of beds and borders

■ **Light Preference:** Full to partial shade

■ **Soil Preference:** Average, well-drained soil

■ **Best Way to Propagate:** Divide in spring or fall

■ **USDA Plant Hardiness Zones:** 5 to 9

■ **AHS Heat Zones:** 9 to 2

Growing Tips

You can grow white gaura (*Gaura lindheimeri*) in any well-drained soil. In fact, it does better in average or even poor soil than in rich soil, where it tends to flop over by midsummer. While white gaura puts up with a considerable amount of drought, it also thrives in rainy climates as long as you provide a site with perfect drainage, such as a raised bed. (Otherwise, the plant can be short-lived.)

Although I've listed white gaura as hardy to USDA Zone 5, that's assuming good winter protection, such as snow cover, in Zones 5 and 6. (Excellent drainage is also a must.) Without cover, you can't expect survival much beyond Zone 7, although, to be quite honest, the plant simply thrives in my Zone 3 garden, perhaps due to the great snow cover.

Although native to hot-summer climates, white gaura actually makes a better garden plant in cool-summer areas, where it blooms nonstop all summer long. It tends to become leggy early in the season in hot-summer climates and also blooms less abundantly. In such cases, cut the flowerstalks back to just above the uppermost leaves, and they will quickly sprout new shoots that will carry on for the rest of the summer.

Division is never necessary, but it's one way to multiply your plants—especially the cultivars. Divide the clumps in spring or fall, being careful not to break the long taproot. Or dig out smaller offsets that haven't yet formed taproots.

Be aware that white gaura self-seeds abundantly. To keep it from becoming weedy, mulch the garden well each year, and also cut off the flowerstalks when they are forming more seed capsules than flower buds. Because pruning the stems back stimulates new stems and new blooms, it's something you'll want to do anyway.

On the other hand, if you want to multiply the species cheaply and in large quantities, let at least a few capsules mature. Collect the seed and sow it yourself, or leave a barren patch of garden nearby where the seed can sprout on its own. If you need to move any self-sown seedlings, do it while they're young because they quickly form long taproots and become more difficult to handle.

To grow white gaura from seed indoors, start it eight to ten weeks before the last frost, barely covering the seed. It will bloom right away the first year from seed sown indoors.

Good Neighbors

Exuberant, long-blooming white gaura is an excellent choice for a mass planting in a sunny, well-drained site. For a striking contrast, try it near a grouping of yuccas, against a backdrop of green shrubbery, or behind a carpet of mother-of-thyme (*Thymus serpyllum*).

White gaura's reseeding habit can cause a maintenance problem in a formal garden, but the flowers are a handsome addition if you prevent them from self-sowing. Try planting white gaura in front of lilies to hide their yellowing foliage after they bloom. Other good neighbors for white gaura include red valerian (*Centranthus ruber*), iris, and oriental poppy (*Papaver orientale*).

Problems and Solutions

White gaura doesn't seem to have any pest or disease problems.

Top Performer

Gaura lindheimeri (white gaura): The species is charming in its own right, but there are also some very nice cultivars. 'Corrie's Gold' is like the species but with cream and gold markings on the leaves. It tends to be less hardy than the species and may need winter protection even in USDA Zone 7. 'Siskiyou Pink' has flowers that start off pink and become even rosier as they age. 'Whirling Butterflies' is like the species, but it has a more compact habit—only 2 to 3 feet (60 to 90 cm) tall—and larger flowers. As with the species, the flowers start off white with only a faint pinkish tinge but turn a lovely rosy pink as they age.

White gaura
(*Gaura lindheimeri*)

Larry's Garden Notes

What we *really* need for this plant is a common name that would make it more acceptable to non-gardeners. Just try throwing "GAW-ruh" into a conversation with anyone but a gardener and you'll get totally blank stares. On the positive side, at least it has only two syllables, so it's easy to pronounce (unlike *przewalskii*, the tongue-twisting name of one species of *Ligularia*). Since the name, "Whirling Butterflies" is already taken (it's the name of a gaura cultivar), how about calling *Gaura* "dancing butterflies?" Well, it's just a thought!

Hibiscus

Hibiscus, rose mallow

The first thing to know about perennial hibiscus is that they're all *huge* plants. Their leaves are large and range in form from lance-shaped to heart-shaped to deeply lobed. The enormous flowers are saucer- or funnel-shaped with an extended column in the center formed of yellow anthers surrounding an even longer style. The individual flowers rarely live more than a few days, but the plants usually produce them prolifically over a very long season.

Plant Profile

HIBISCUS
hy-BISS-kus

- **Bloom Color:** Pink, red, or white
- **Bloom Time:** Usually late spring or early summer to fall
- **Length of Bloom:** 2 months or more
- **Height:** 2 to 8 feet (60 to 240 cm)
- **Spread:** 2 to 4 feet (60 to 120 cm)
- **Garden Uses:** Mass planting, meadow garden, mixed border, seasonal hedge, specimen plant; at the back of beds and borders, in wet areas
- **Light Preference:** Full sun to light shade
- **Soil Preference:** Rich, moist soil
- **Best Way to Propagate:** Take cuttings in summer or fall
- **USDA Plant Hardiness Zones:** 4 to 10
- **AHS Heat Zones:** 12 to 1

Growing Tips

Perennial hibiscus are "swamp things": In the wild, they grow in damp or even soggy soil. In the garden, they're much more accommodating, growing in average or even dry soil, but they'll still need regular watering during times of drought. When they're too dry, they quickly show it by wilting. Rich, humusy soil is a plus, but hibiscus will grow and bloom well in average or even poor soil.

Full sun or only light shade is a must. In shadier conditions, hibiscus will flower only lightly and their otherwise sturdy "no-need-to-stake-me!" stems may require support.

Southern plants par excellence, hibiscus are among the rare temperate perennials that seem totally immune to the heat and humidity of the Southeast. In fact, the hotter and more humid it is, the better they seem to bloom.

Prune hibiscus back lightly in the fall if their tall bare stems bother you, but leave at least 8 inches (20 cm) of stem at the base to help trap mulch, fallen leaves, and snow needed for their winter protection in colder climates. Prune off the dead growth entirely only after the plant has begun to sprout in spring.

Hibiscus don't like to be divided, nor do they need it. The best way to multiply your plants is by taking stem cuttings in the late summer or fall.

You can also grow perennial hibiscus from seed. Sow outdoors in spring for bloom the following year. You can also sow them indoors 12 to 14 weeks before the last frost date if you want to see them bloom the first season. Soak the seed in hot water for 24 hours before sowing to soften the hard seed coat, or chip it with a sharp knife. The seed sprouts best at warm temperatures: about 70° to 80°F (21° to 27°C).

Good Neighbors

Try combining perennial hibiscus with bluebells (*Mertensia virginica*), which will fill the space nicely in early spring to summer, then die back obligingly as the hibiscus gains momentum. Or accent the hibiscus with a moisture-loving groundcover, such as heartleaf bergenia (*Bergenia cordifolia*).

Problems and Solutions

Hibiscus often suffer from leaf diseases, including rust and leaf spots, but it's mainly the lower leaves that are infected, so the problems aren't too noticeable. Control aphids by spraying foliage with blasts of water, and treat scale insects with sprays of light horticultural oil. Whiteflies can really weaken the plant; you'll notice a yellowed appearance, listless growth, and reduced bloom. Try horticultural oil again, but spray at night, when whiteflies are sleeping, and repeat often, as whiteflies come back over and over. Japanese beetles can be devastating, leaving foliage so punctured with holes that it looks like you'd been using them for shotgun practice. See page 54 for some solutions to this problem.

Top Performer

Hibiscus moscheutos (common rose mallow, swamp rose mallow): While you'll have many choices of flower color and plant height with mallows, you'll find that most are sold as cultivars or strains of common rose mallow, so I've dubbed it the Top Performer. This species is so variable because the plants sold are probably some type of hybrid rather than the species form. Most are from mixed seed, including the popular Southern Belle strain, about 3 to 6 feet (90 to 180 cm) tall, and the dwarf Disco Belle series and Frisbee Hybrids, about 18 to 30 inches (45 to 75 cm) tall. All three will give flowers in pink, red, or white, often with a red center.

There also many cutting-grown cultivars, most growing 4 to 6 feet (1.2 to 1.8 m) tall. 'Anne Arundel' has pink flowers and deeply cut leaves. 'Blue River II' produces pure white blooms and blue-green leaves. 'Lady Baltimore' bears deep pink flowers with a red eye, while 'Lord Baltimore' has red blooms.

Common rose mallow
(*Hibiscus moscheutos*)

Larry's Garden Notes

Be careful that you got the right plant when you buy *Hibiscus!* There are more than 250 species, and most are native to tropical areas. They will not thrive in your garden unless you live in USDA Plant Hardiness Zone 10 or 11. Rose-of-China (*Hibiscus rosa-sinensis*) is sold in garden centers everywhere, but it is a houseplant. Put it outside for the summer by all means, but bring it indoors in the fall. The very popular shrub, rose-of-Sharon (*H. syriacus*) is every bit a hibiscus, but it is a deciduous shrub rather than a true perennial like the species described here.

Kirengeshoma

Kirengeshoma, yellow wax bells

Kirengeshomas are essentially foliage plants. Throughout the season, the plants sport slightly hairy, paired, broad, maplelike leaves that practically wrap around the stem at their base and always remind me of bat wings (I mean that in the nicest sense). At the end of the summer, however, these plants suddenly reveal a new side to their personality by producing clusters of bell- or trumpet-shaped, creamy yellow blooms that last into fall.

Plant Profile

KIRENGESHOMA
kih-reng-guh-SHOW-mah

- **Bloom Color:** Yellow
- **Bloom Time:** Late summer to fall
- **Length of Bloom:** 6 weeks or more
- **Height:** Varies by species; see individual listings
- **Spread:** 2 to 4 feet (60 to 120 cm)
- **Garden Uses:** Groundcover, hedge, mass planting, mixed border, specimen plant, woodland garden; at the back of beds and borders, in wet areas
- **Light Preference:** Partial shade
- **Soil Preference:** Rich, well-drained, acid soil
- **Best Way to Propagate:** Divide in spring or fall
- **USDA Plant Hardiness Zones:** Varies by species; see individual listings
- **AHS Heat Zones:** 8 to 1

Growing Tips

Kirengeshomas prefer partial shade, thriving in open woodlands and partially shaded borders. Their soil should be rich in organic matter, a bit on the acid side, and moist (water if necessary during times of drought). Cool-summer temperatures are best, although they can survive and even thrive in shady spots in the South, especially when planted near a cooling body of water, such as a stream or pond. Mulching with organic material helps re-create the leaf litter in which the plants naturally grow and also keep the soil cool and moist, which is very much to kirengeshomas' liking.

Avoid planting kirengeshomas in windy areas, as strong gusts can flatten the otherwise sturdy stems. These plants don't appreciate cold winter winds either, so planting them in a sheltered spot is always a wise decision.

Kirengeshomas spread, although slowly at first, by thick creeping roots. The plants never need division, and they look better when allowed to fill in. If they ever do spread beyond their boundaries, it's simple enough to control them; just dig out any sections that have gone too far. Kirengeshomas grow far too slowly to be called weedy.

If you want to multiply your plants, division in spring or fall is the best way to go. Seed is rarely available, but if your plants produce any, simply sow it outdoors after the last frost and cover it lightly. Germination is slow and irregular, taking from one to ten months, and is most successful in leaf litter under cool conditions. You can also sow the seed indoors at temperatures between 55° and 65°F (13° and 18°C).

Good Neighbors

With their purple-stemmed, maplelike leaves, kirengeshomas show up well against a background of tall ferns, such as ostrich fern

(*Matteuccia struthiopteris*) or royal fern (*Osmunda regalis*). Plants that hold their flowers well above their foliage look particularly handsome against the season-long green backdrop: Astilbes or one of the profusely flowering *Heuchera* × *brizoides* cultivars (such as 'Raspberry Regal' or 'June Bride') are just a few possible partners.

Problems and Solutions

Kirengeshoma has no major problems, but it can be subject to whiteflies on occasion. Spraying the undersides of the leaves with insecticidal soap or a light horticultural oil will help control whitefly problems; repeat as needed.

Yellow wax bells
(*Kirengeshoma palmata*)

Top Performer

Kirengeshoma palmata (yellow wax bells): The lower leaves of yellow wax bells are large, about 4 to 8 inches (10 to 20 cm) long. The upper leaves are smaller and spaced widely apart on thin, upright, deep purple stems that contrast nicely with the medium green of the leaves. The flowers droop slightly, and the flower stalks likewise arch somewhat, giving the whole plant a very elegant appearance.

By far the most commonly available species, *K. palmata* is more compact and has darker purple stems than *K. koreana* (see below). *K. palmata* is also slightly less hardy. However, the two plants are very similar, and you can use them interchangeably in your garden. They can bloom anytime from late summer to fall. Height: 3 to 4 feet (90 to 120 cm). Spread: 2 to 4 feet (60 to 120 cm). USDA Plant Hardiness Zones 4 to 9; AHS Heat Zones 8 to 1.

More Recommended Kirengeshomas

Kirengeshoma koreana: This is the taller and hardier of the two species. Its late-summer-to-fall flowers are perhaps slightly paler yellow, and the petals tend to curve upward at the tips. The stems are also more green than purple, but they're otherwise identical to those of *K. palmata*. Height: 5 to 7 feet (150 to 200 cm). Spread: 2 to 4 feet (60 to 120 cm). USDA Plant Hardiness Zones 3 to 9; AHS Heat Zones 8 to 1.

Around the World with Kirengeshoma

Although it may seem new to you, kirengeshoma is a very desirable plant that has long played a top role in Asian gardens. In Japan and Korea, it's found in temple and meditation gardens with its flowers modestly bowed as if in prayer. It's not really new, though—it was introduced to the West late in the nineteenth century. It's simply one of those perennials that has been slow to capture people's attention. Perhaps its lack of popularity is due to its rather slow-to-get-started habit. We Westerners tend to prefer instant results. Give your plant a few short years to settle in, though, and you'll be sure to agree it's a true charmer!

Miscanthus

Miscanthus, maiden grass

If you're looking for a landscape grass with natural impact, miscanthus is the choice for you! This tuft-forming, warm-season grass forms massive clumps of tightly packed stems. The stems and leaves reach upward at first, then arch over, giving miscanthus the fountainlike appearance for which it is so famous. And the towering, silvery, feathery, fan-shaped flower heads of miscanthus are almost as attractive as the foliage!

Plant Profile

MISCANTHUS
mis-KAN-thus

- **Bloom Color:** Reddish purple, silver, or tan
- **Bloom Time:** Midsummer or late summer to fall
- **Length of Bloom:** 2 months or more
- **Height:** 2 to 7 feet (60 to 210 cm)
- **Spread:** 3 to 4 feet (90 to 120 cm)
- **Garden Uses:** Container planting, cut flower garden, mass planting, mixed border, seasonal hedge, specimen plant, wildflower meadow; at the back of beds and borders, in wet areas
- **Light Preference:** Full sun to light shade
- **Soil Preference:** Average, moist but well-drained soil
- **Best Way to Propagate:** Divide in spring
- **USDA Plant Hardiness Zones:** 5 to 9
- **AHS Heat Zones:** 9 to 1

Growing Tips

Miscanthus thrive in rich, moist, well-drained soil in full sun but tolerate many other conditions as well. Light shade, for example, is perfectly fine, although the plants may tend to grow overly tall and then flop over if the conditions are too shady. While moist or even wet soil suits miscanthus to a T, the plants will put up with dry soil without much complaint, at least once they're well established.

The only maintenance miscanthus require is to be cut back to near ground level early each spring to leave room for the new season's growth.

Think Twice: One flaw with Japanese silver grass (*Miscanthus sinensis*) is that it can self-sow to the point of being invasive in mild-winter climates (south of Zone 6), so make sure you renew your mulch regularly so the plant can't reseed.

Be aware that miscanthus are essentially permanent plants. While not invasive, they cling tenaciously to the soil where they're planted, and moving them isn't easy. Fortunately, most kinds don't *need* dividing, but there are some cultivars that tend to die out in the middle over time, and you'll need to divide these to keep them in shape. I've suggested cultivars here that *don't* need division. Why choose a cultivar that's complicated to grow when there are so many easy ones?

Of course, division is the only method of multiplying cultivars, so if you need many plants and want to save money by buying only one and dividing it, I suggest lifting it and dividing it annually until you get the material you need. Young plants are easier to dig out and divide.

Good Neighbors

Use miscanthus (*Miscanthus sinensis*) as an accent, surrounded by massed plantings of lower-growing plants, such as leadwort (*Ceratostigma plumbaginoides*) or rose verbena (*Verbena canadensis*). Or try broad sweeps of a dwarf cultivar (such as *M. sinensis* 'Nippon') as a tall groundcover.

Problems and Solutions

Miscanthus is occasionally bothered by rust, which causes orange spots on leaves during periods of humid weather, but this usually disappears on its own.

Top Performer

Miscanthus sinensis (miscanthus, Japanese silver grass, maiden grass): Japanese silver grass is probably the most popular of all the ornamental grasses. It varies widely in size and color but always retains a similar form: a dense clump of arching leaves topped off in summer by tall, feathery, whisklike plumes in various shades of reddish purple, silver, or tan, fading to paler colors by fall. The foliage often turns a brilliant yellow or orange before fading to beige in winter.

Below are just a few of the dozens of choice cultivars. Unless otherwise mentioned, all are in the 4- to 6-foot (1.2- to 1.8-m) height category and hardy to USDA Zone 5 without winter protection.

'Cabaret' has green leaves with a broad white band down the middle. 'Nippon' combines a great red-bronze fall color with narrow leaves on 3- to 4-foot (90- to 120-cm) plants. 'Purpurascens' is one of the cultivars most appreciated for its fall color, as the foliage turns orange at first, then deep purple-red as the weather gets colder. It remains rust-colored through much of the winter. It's hardy to USDA Zone 4. 'Sarabande' is similar to 'Cabaret' but with narrower leaves and a more upright habit; use it to replace the popular but floppy all-green 'Gracillimus'. 'Strictus' (porcupine grass) is one of the better crossbanded cultivars—it has yellowish or creamy stripes that run horizontally across the leaves. Its narrow, upright, rigid habit makes it a better garden choice than the widely grown but floppy 'Zebrinus'.

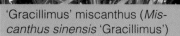

'Gracillimus' miscanthus (*Miscanthus sinensis* 'Gracillimus')

Larry's Garden Notes

I always feel sorry for gardeners who have no snow because miscanthus (*Miscanthus* spp.) are at their most beautiful in the winter. Not only is the beige winter appearance majestic with white powdery snow clinging to the feathery plumes, but the leaves also sing all winter long, rustling in the slightest breeze. One note of caution to these graceful and beautiful plants is that some native plant enthusiasts are concerned that miscanthus may be invasive. Environmental organizations are monitoring its spread, but let's hope this is a false alarm.

Panicum

Switch grass

Switch grasses are among the most delicate of all ornamental grasses. They grow in a dense, upright clump of narrow leaves that are green or gray-green in the summer, often turning yellow or red in the fall, then aging to beige and persisting all winter. The flowers are very light and airy, creating a delightful see-through haze a foot (30 cm) or so above the foliage. The flowers are generally pink, reddish, or silvery when they emerge, then fade to grayish white or brown in the fall.

Plant Profile

PANICUM
PAN-ih-kum

- **Bloom Color:** Brown, pink, red, silver, or white

- **Bloom Time:** Midsummer to fall

- **Length of Bloom:** 3 months or more

- **Height:** 3 to 6 feet (90 to 180 cm)

- **Spread:** 2 to 3 feet (60 to 90 cm)

- **Garden Uses:** Container planting, cut flower garden, hedge, mass planting, meadow garden, mixed border, specimen plant; at the back of beds and borders, in wet areas; attracts birds

- **Light Preference:** Full sun to light shade

- **Soil Preference:** Rich, moist soil

- **Best Way to Propagate:** Divide in spring

- **USDA Plant Hardiness Zones:** 3 to 9

- **AHS Heat Zones:** 9 to 1

Growing Tips

Switch grasses grow in soils ranging from very moist to very dry and acid to slightly alkaline and in anything from sand to heavy clay. They're highly tolerant of drought and howling winds and are immune to salt spray, making them a good choice for seaside gardens. For maximum flowering, full sun or light shade is best. In partial shade, switch grasses will grow without a problem but won't flower very much.

Annual maintenance for switch grasses consists mainly of cutting them back hard in the spring to allow room for new growth. But you don't even have to do that unless you want to because the new leaves simply push the old ones aside and take over. You may, however, need to divide the plants every four or five years if they open in the center.

Think Twice: Switch grasses produce abundant seed and self-sow readily—in fact, too readily under some circumstances. Mulching is the best way to keep them under control.

Of course, if you need to multiply the species, just leave a space free of mulch and let it self-sow. Or sow purchased seed outdoors after the last spring frost, covering it with about ⅛ inch (3 mm) of soil and keeping the spot moist until the young plants sprout. Division in spring is the way to go for propagating cultivars.

I've noticed that most experts suggest switch grass as hardy to only USDA Zone 5, which rather puzzles me. I've never had any

FUN FACTS

It may seem odd that many of the top cultivars of switch grass have German-sounding names because switch grass is a native North American species. But while we didn't realize the ornamental potential of our native prairie grass, the Germans certainly did, and they've been breeding ornamental forms for many years.

trouble growing it in Zone 3 and, in fact, the native species abounds in Zone 3 in the wild. I've therefore listed it under that zone but suggest using a winter mulch in areas of Zones 3 and 4 where the plant may be particularly exposed to winter winds

Good Neighbors

Switch grass is a natural choice for a meadow garden along with other meadow natives, such as butterfly weed (*Asclepias tuberosa*), purple coneflower (*Echinacea purpurea*), and goldenrods (*Solidago* spp.). Or enjoy it as a landscape accent, alone or with other grasses, for color and interest throughout the year.

Problems and Solutions

Leaf spot is an occasional problem but is never serious enough (or noticeable enough) to require treatment. And in gardens set near fields, grasshoppers can be an annoyance during periods of severe grasshopper infestations, but because grasshoppers are basically uncontrollable, just ignore them.

Top Performer

Panicum virgatum (switch grass): There are more than 600 species of *Panicum*, both annuals and perennials, but there's only one species that's been singled out as an ornamental perennial grass: switch grass. The species itself is attractive enough and is widely used in restoration and erosion control projects, but most ornamental kinds are cultivars specifically chosen for their summer or fall color.

'Haense Herms', also called 'Hänse Herms' (red switch grass), is a compact form, about 3 feet (90 cm) tall, with a beautiful orange-red fall color that contrasts beautifully with its whitish flowers. The cultivar 'Rotstrahlbusch' may be the same plant as 'Hänse Herms', but grass specialists often offer it separately. 'Heavy Metal' is perhaps the best of the blue switch grasses, with powder-blue leaves in summer turning bright yellow in fall. It's a nicer selection than the older 'Strictum', a more upright plant that's more blue-green than blue, although at least 'Strictum' comes true from seed. 'Rehbraun' (also called 'Rotbraun'), with reddish brown fall leaves, has been on the market for a while, but it has largely been replaced by other selections, such as 'Squaw', with redder fall color.

'Heavy Metal' switch grass (*Panicum virgatum* 'Heavy Metal')

Larry's Garden Notes

Switch grass (*Panicum virgatum*) is being used more and more often in erosion control throughout North America. Its dense roots help prevent slopes and banks from eroding away, and it tolerates road salts, making it a good choice along roads and highways. Since switch grass is native, there's no need to worry should it escape from culture: It's *supposed* to be there. Its "I-can-grow-anywhere" attitude and capacity to let native trees and shrubs seed into it further enhances its reputation as the perfect living erosion control.

Perovskia

Russian sage, perovskia

Russian sages produce clumps of attractive gray-white stems that arch outward at the base, then become upright toward the tips, creating a very neat "shrub" for the garden. Where the fuzzy gray-green leaves stop, the flowers begin! These tiny, two-lipped, tubular blooms appear in such profusion that the whole top of the plant is a haze of lavender-blue. Although Russian sages develop woody bases and are very shrublike in appearance, they die back nearly to the ground in the winter, as do most other perennials.

Plant Profile

PEROVSKIA
per-OFF-skee-uh

- **Bloom Color:** Light blue

- **Bloom Time:** Late spring or midsummer to fall

- **Length of Bloom:** 3 months or more

- **Height:** 3 to 5 feet (90 to 150 cm)

- **Spread:** 2 to 4 feet (60 to 120 cm)

- **Garden Uses:** Container planting, cut flower garden, groundcover, hedge, mass planting, mixed border, specimen plant; at the back of beds and borders

- **Light Preference:** Full sun

- **Soil Preference:** Average to poor, well-drained, even dry soil

- **Best Way to Propagate:** Take cuttings in summer

- **USDA Plant Hardiness Zones:** 3 to 9

- **AHS Heat Zones:** 9 to 1

Growing Tips

Russian sages do have their preferences but will grow under most conditions if you give them two things: good drainage and full sun. If your climate is naturally dry, you can plant them anywhere. Elsewhere, though, it's worth looking for a well-drained spot, perhaps in a raised bed, just to make sure Russian sages never sit in water. It's no use trying to grow these plants in shade or even partial shade; they simply won't perform.

The subshrubby nature of Russian sages means they need rather different treatment from other perennials. Don't cut the plants back to the base in spring because they normally sprout from above ground level. Instead, if you insist on early pruning, cut the plants back to about 1 foot (30 cm) from the ground. Otherwise, just wait until they start to sprout on their own, then cut them back to just above the lowest buds.

In mild-winter areas, Russian sages are up and blooming so early that they can peter out by late summer. If so, simply chop them back to just above the upper leaves and they will soon be blooming again. Elsewhere, summer pruning isn't necessary; Russian sages will bloom nonstop until the first hard frosts all on their own.

Mature Russian sage plants occasionally produce offsets that you can dig out and replant; otherwise, the plant's woody base makes regular division difficult. The main means of multiplication, therefore, is from cuttings. Just snip off a 3- to 5-inch (7.5- to 13-cm) piece of nonflowering stem, remove the lowest leaves, and dip the lower extremity of the cutting into a bit of rooting hormone that's been poured into a disposable container before inserting it into a pot of moist growing mix. Seal the container inside a plastic bag, and place in a warm, brightly lit spot with no direct sun. Cuttings root in two or three weeks. Water newly planted Russian sages for the first summer to help them settle in more comfortably. If you want to try seed, sow it indoors in early spring in a warm spot and be patient. It can take from one to five months to sprout.

Good Neighbors
Russian sage's light-colored, lacy foliage shows pinks, purples, pale yellows, whites, and greens to their best advantage. Use it among lower mounded perennials, such as asters and 'Moonbeam' threadleaf coreopsis (*Coreopsis verticillata* 'Moonbeam'), or contrast its airy form with daylilies or lilies.

Problems and Solutions
Russian sage has no significant problems.

Top Performer
Perovskia × *hybrida* (hybrid Russian sage): This group of plants of mixed parentage includes most of the currently available cultivars, including 'Blue Mist' with paler blue flowers and an early bloom, 'Blue Spire' with deeply cut foliage and deep violet flowers, and 'Filagran' with the most beautiful filigreed leaves of the group and light blue flowers. 'Longin' looks like 'Blue Spire' and may be the same plant. All bloom from late spring or midsummer to fall. Height: 3 to 5 feet (90 to 150 cm). Spread: 2 to 4 feet (60 to 120 cm). USDA Plant Hardiness Zones 3 to 9; AHS Heat Zones 9 to 1.

More Recommended Russian Sages
Perovskia atriplicifolia (Russian sage): Most Russian sages are sold under this name, but that's rarely what you get. *P. atriplicifolia* has leaves that range from large and oval at the base of the plant to small and narrow at the top of the plant. If your Russian sage has deeply cut leaves instead, you can bet you have a hybrid Russian sage. Height: 3 to 5 feet (90 to 150 cm). Spread: 2 to 4 feet (60 to 120 cm). USDA Plant Hardiness Zones 3 to 9; AHS Heat Zones 9 to 1.

Russian sage
(*Perovskia atriplicifolia*)

Larry's Garden Notes

Names often tell tales and so it is with *Perovskia*. It was named after the Russian general V. A. Perovsky (1794–1857) who was much admired in Russia when this plant was named. As for the common name, Russian sage, *Perovskia* species can be found on the steppes of Russia (although the species we usually grow, *P. atriplicifolia*, is actually found in Afghanistan and the Western Himalayas). The sage part of the common name is easier to explain—the silvery leaves and pungent mintlike scent are typical of sages, to which this plant is related.

Rheum

Rhubarb

No, it's not just for the vegetable garden! Rhubarb is a stately, decorative perennial that makes a dramatic addition to any planting. It's a giant of a plant, with huge, often wrinkled leaves and tall, branching flowerstalks with white to pink flowers. This description applies not only to the common garden rhubarb (*Rheum rhabarbarum*, also called *R. × cultorum*), but also to the strictly ornamental species. All create quite a splash in a border and are truly stand-alone plants; one is usually all you need.

Plant Profile

RHEUM
RAY-um

- **Bloom Color:** Pink, red, or white

- **Bloom Time:** Late spring to early summer

- **Length of Bloom:** 2 or 3 weeks

- **Height:** Varies by species; see individual listings

- **Spread:** Varies by species; see individual listings

- **Garden Uses:** Container planting, cut flower garden, hedge, mixed border, specimen plant; at the back of beds and borders

- **Light Preference:** Full sun to partial shade

- **Soil Preference:** Rich, deep, moist soil

- **Best Way to Propagate:** Divide in spring or fall

- **USDA Plant Hardiness Zones:** 3 to 9

- **AHS Heat Zones:** 9 to 1

Growing Tips

Garden rhubarb (*Rheum rhabarbarum*) will grow anywhere in full sun or partial shade as long as the soil is well drained. Most ornamental rhubarbs, on the other hand, need plenty of soil moisture and often do best in wet soil, although they will grow in average garden soil if you keep them mulched and water them occasionally. An annual top-dressing of compost or aged manure helps keep all rhubarbs happy.

Rhubarbs' origins are cold climates, and they seem to need some winter chill to survive. There's little use trying rhubarbs in the Deep South. They will grow fine for the first year, then they seem to hesitate about whether they should go dormant or not in fall. By the following summer, after a valiant attempt to resprout in the spring, they're usually dead or just barely alive.

Slow-growing but long-lived, rhubarbs need little care other than having their flowerstalks cut back after they bloom to prevent the plants from producing potentially invasive seeds.

The best way to multiply rhubarbs is by division in spring or fall. Dig up the massive rootball and wash away some of the soil so you can better see what you are doing; then cut the clump into sections with two or three crowns if you want fast results, or one single crown if you want a maximum number of plants. Plant the divisions with the buds about 1 to 2 inches (2.5 to 5 cm) below the soil line, mulch, then water well. Continue to water regularly the first year until the plants are well established.

Good Neighbors

With their massive leaves and statuesque habit, rhubarbs can't help but be a focal point in the garden. Try contrasting the broad foliage of rhubarb (*Rheum rhabarbarum*) with perennials that have finely cut leaves, such as yarrows.

Give ornamental rhubarb (*Rheum palmatum*) a moist, fertile site by a pond with companions that enjoy similar conditions; a few good candidates include sweet flag (*Acorus calamus*), Japanese iris (*Iris ensata*), and common globeflower (*Trollius europaeus*).

Problems and Solutions
Rhubarb rarely suffers from pests and diseases.

Top Performer
Rheum rhabarbarum, also called *Rheum* × *cultorum* (rhubarb, garden rhubarb). Yep, this is the old-fashioned garden vegetable that's so popular in cool-summer areas. Garden rhubarb produces huge, heart-shaped, somewhat wrinkled leaves with smooth edges and thick, green or red leaf stems. The tall, branching flowerstalks are made up of myriads of tiny white flowers and are spectacular from late spring to early summer. There are many cultivars of garden rhubarb and also a few seed strains. Tops in the ornamental department, though, are the red-stemmed cultivars, including 'Canada Red', 'Cherry Red', 'MacDonald', and 'Strawberry'. Height: 5 to 7 feet (150 to 210 cm). Spread: 3 to 4 feet (90 to 120 cm). USDA Plant Hardiness Zones 3 to 9; AHS Heat Zones 9 to 1.

More Recommended Rhubarbs
Rheum palmatum (ornamental rhubarb): This is by far the most popular of the ornamental rhubarbs. It produces huge, deeply lobed leaves and tall, narrowly upright, branching stalks of white or sometimes pink flowers from late spring to early summer. The leaves of the popular cultivar 'Atrosanguineum' (also called 'Atropurpureum') are a gorgeous deep red in the spring but turn medium green in the summer with only a slight reddish highlight. Its flowerstalks are a deep, purplish red and produce deep pink flowers. *R. palmatum* var. *tanguticum* likewise has reddish foliage in the spring, but its leaves are less deeply cut, and its flowers can be pink, red, or white. Height: 5 to 7 feet (1.5 to 2.1 m). Spread: 4 to 6 feet (1.2 to 1.8 m). USDA Plant Hardiness Zones 3 to 9; AHS Heat Zones 9 to 1.

Rhubarb
(*Rheum rhabarbarum*)

Larry's Garden Notes

Don't let the use of rhubarb (*Rheum rhabarbarum*) in the kitchen lull you into a sense of complacency. Only the petiole (leaf stem) is edible: Both foliage and roots are toxic. In fact, after the petioles are harvested, the leaves are often left to soak in water to create a very effective home-brewed insecticide!

So many garden plants, both edible and ornamental, have poisonous parts that kids should be trained not to eat *any* plant unless it has been OK'd by an adult.

Sanguisorba

Burnet

Long considered medicinal herbs, burnets are increasingly popular with flower gardeners—and with good reason. Burnets tend to be very shrublike, with leaves that arch outward from stiff stems to create a dense, bushy clump. Each leaf consists of many oblong leaflets delightfully crimped along the edges, as if they'd been carefully trimmed with pinking shears. The dense flower spikes have no petals but are instead densely covered in soft, fuzzy-looking stamens in a variety of colors.

Plant Profile

SANGUISORBA
sang-gwih-SORE-bah

- **Bloom Color:** Pink, purple, red, white

- **Bloom Time:** Summer

- **Length of Bloom:** 4 to 6 weeks

- **Height:** Varies by species; see individual listings

- **Spread:** 3 to 4 feet (90 to 120 cm)

- **Garden Uses:** Cut flower garden, mass planting, meadow garden, mixed border, seasonal hedge, specimen plant; at the back of beds and borders, in wet areas

- **Light Preference:** Full sun to light shade

- **Soil Preference:** Average, moist soil

- **Best Way to Propagate:** Divide in spring or fall

- **USDA Plant Hardiness Zones:** 3 to 9

- **AHS Heat Zones:** 8 to 1

Growing Tips

Burnets tend to grow in marshy settings in the wild and appreciate moist soil in the garden as well. You can even grow them in average garden soil—but give them a generous layer of mulch to keep their roots moist and cool. Burnets do best where the soil is poor to moderately fertile; rich soil tends to produce tall, floppy stems.

Full sun is ideal in most climates, but some protection from afternoon sun is preferable in areas where summers are hot. In truly hot-summer areas, make sure to combine partial shade with a thick layer of mulch to keep burnets cool.

Many burnets naturally bloom over a long period of time, but they'll flower even longer if you deadhead them regularly. Other than deadheading and possibly staking, maintenance is minimal.

Think Twice: Burnets can be very prolific under the right circumstances, so plant them within a root barrier, such as a bottomless plastic bucket, at the start or plan to divide them every few years. Deadheading will prevent self-sowing.

Division in early spring or fall is a good way to multiply burnets. You can grow burnets from seed as well; start it indoors in late winter or outdoors in early spring or late autumn without covering it. Seedlings appear within a month or two.

Good Neighbors

Burnets' attractive foliage and bottlebrush-like flowers look most natural in the wild garden, but they're also striking in more tended borders if you contain them with a root barrier. Pair them with other bold, moisture-tolerant late bloomers, such as azure monkshood (*Aconitum carmichaelii*).

Problems and Solutions
Burnets aren't particularly subject to pests or diseases.

Top Performer
Sanguisorba canadensis, also called *Poterium canadense* (Canadian burnet): This native burnet is a very tall, bushy plant with long leaves that have 7 to 15 oblong leaflets at the base. Toward the top of the stems, the leaves become smaller with fewer leaflets, and the stem ends in a tall, upright 6- to 8-inch (15- to 20-cm) green spike densely covered in buds. These burst open from the base upward over a long period of time, changing the green spike into a fuzzy white bottlebrush. The midsummer-to-fall show is absolutely delightful in the perennial border and perhaps even more extraordinary in wetter parts of a wild meadow garden.

Canadian burnet
(*Sanguisorba canadensis*)

Admittedly, Canadian burnet can be overly vigorous in moist, cool locations, but it's easy enough to check its spread by planting it within a root barrier and keeping it deadheaded. Height: 4 to 6 feet (1.2 to 1.8 m). Spread: 3 to 4 feet (90 to 120 cm). USDA Plant Hardiness Zones 3 to 9; AHS Heat Zones 8 to 1.

More Recommended Burnets
Sanguisorba officinalis, also called *Poterium officinale* (great burnet): Great burnet produces tall, upright stems, often with a reddish tinge, which are densely cloaked in large basal leaves with numerous leaflets. The leaves become progressively smaller, and the number of leaflets diminishes as they rise up the stem. The top part of the stiff stem has no leaves at all for 8 inches (20 cm) or so, then abruptly ends in a dense, stubby flower spike of fuzzy deep purple to blood red blooms from early summer to fall. The spikes are much shorter than those of the other burnets and don't create as much of a bottlebrush image, but what they lack in charm, they make up for in number and length of bloom. Control great burnet's creeping habit with a root barrier and keep it deadheaded to prevent self-sowing; well controlled, it's a handsome addition to the garden. Height: 3 to 4 feet (90 to 120 cm). Spread: 3 to 4 feet (90 to 120 cm). USDA Plant Hardiness Zones 3 to 9; AHS Heat Zones 8 to 1.

Larry's Garden Notes

Most burnets (*Sanguisorba* spp.) combine male and female flowers in the same flower spike, but if you grow Canadian burnet (*Sanguisorba canadensis*) from seed, you should know that individual plants can be either male, female, or hermaphrodite. Since female plants don't have the fuzzy white stamens that make the male and hermaphrodite flowers so attractive, consider planting them in out-of-the-way spots if you want to save your own seed or even eliminating them entirely if you don't. If you buy burnets in a nursery or by catalog, though, you needn't worry: They'll always sell male or hermaphrodite plants, never the females.

Spartina

Cord grass

You'll grow cord grass almost strictly for its handsome foliage because its comblike spikes of white to brownish flowers aren't nearly as attractive as its leaves. On the other hand, the foliage is something to behold. The bright, glossy green foliage is very upright, arching only at the tips, and is about ½ inch (1.25 cm) wide. And in the fall, the entire plant turns a beautiful golden yellow and remains an attractive pale beige through the winter.

Plant Profile

SPARTINA
spar-TEE-nah

- **Bloom Color:** Brown or white

- **Bloom Time:** Midsummer to late summer

- **Length of Bloom:** 6 weeks or more

- **Height:** 5 to 7 feet (150 to 210 cm)

- **Spread:** 3 feet (90 cm)

- **Garden Uses:** Groundcover, hedge, mass planting, meadow garden, mixed border, specimen plant; at the back of beds and borders, in wet areas

- **Light Preference:** Full sun to partial shade

- **Soil Preference:** Average to poor, wet to dry soil

- **Best Way to Propagate:** Divide in spring or summer

- **USDA Plant Hardiness Zones:** 3 to 9

- **AHS Heat Zones:** 7 to 1

Growing Tips

Cord grass is amazingly adaptable. Although most common in the wild in marshes and soggy spots, it's very drought-resistant when well established. It will grow in almost any soil in the garden, wet or dry, acid or neutral, and it even puts up with salty soil and salt spray, making it just as useful in arid regions (where soil is often salty) as along ocean coasts. Cord grass grows best in average to poor soil; in overly rich soil, it tends to grow too tall and become floppy.

Low-care grass par excellence, cord grass is best planted and left to grow on its own. Always plant this grass where you can contain the spreading roots, by surrounding the plant with equally tough plants like other grasses or shrubs or by planting it within a deep root barrier. About the only care it might need is cutting back in spring, but since the leaves fall to the ground on their own, forming their own layer of organic mulch, you don't even have to do that, unless you are feeling particularly meticulous!

Warning: If you do have to work with cord grass, either to divide it or move it, always wear goggles, long sleeves, long pants, and leather gloves because the leaf edges are incredibly sharp and cutting. Because of its knifelike blades, cord grass is *not* a good choice for planting along paths or in areas where there are small children.

You can simply let cord grass go its own way; division is simply never necessary. But if you want to propagate cord grass, division is the easiest method, and it's the only way to multiply cultivars because they don't come true from seed. Just dig up wayward plants in spring or early summer or even cut out a wedge from an established clump. If you fill in the resulting gap with fresh soil, cord grass will soon entirely fill in the empty space.

You can also grow the all-green form of cord grass from seed sown indoors in spring or outdoors in spring or fall. It sprouts quickly and is well established by the second year, sometimes even by the end of the first summer.

Good Neighbors

Cord grass isn't likely to be good company in the garden unless you control it, in which case it makes a delightful addition to the border. Try it as a backdrop for fall-flowering perennials, such as asters, common sneezeweed (*Helenium autumnale*), 'Herbstfreude' sedum (*Sedum* 'Herbstfreude', also called *S.* 'Autumn Joy'), and goldenrods (*Solidago* spp.). Cord grass also looks wonderful planted in a meadow garden, a situation that very much resembles the conditions under which it grows in the wild.

Problems and Solutions

Cord grass is essentially trouble-free.

Top Performer

Spartina pectinata, also called *S. michauxiana* (prairie cord grass): This is my choice for Top Performer because it's the only species commonly grown as an ornamental. In spite of its common name, prairie cord grass grows in a wide variety of environments. The all-green species is widely grown for erosion control purposes but it doesn't appear often in gardens. Instead, all eyes are on the pretty and easy-to-grow variegated cultivar 'Aureomarginata' (also called 'Variegata') with narrow, bright yellow margins surrounding a bright green center. The coloration is remarkable—just enough to highlight the leaf without dominating it—and this cultivar, all on its own, has led this otherwise rather obscure genus to prominence in the ornamental garden. Occasionally, 'Aureomarginata' does revert to the all-green species form, but the variegation usually returns on its own.

'Aureomarginata' prairie cord grass (*Spartina pectinata* 'Aureomarginata')

Larry's Garden Notes

The name *Spartina* derives from the word "esparto," as in esparto grass (*Stipa tenacissima*). Esparto grass was used to make cord in ancient Greece and was often called cord grass. *Spartina* resembles esparto grass, and so it came to have the common name of cord grass, too, even though it's never been used for making cord or cloth. As for the species name *pectinata*, it means comblike, referring to the one-sided flower spikes. A more contemporary use for *Spartina's* handsome foliage is for fresh or dried arrangements—just watch the sharp leaf edges when you handle it.

PERENNIALS FOR
Birds & Butterflies

One of the nicest things about a perennial garden is the life it brings to your yard. Not just the living plants, but birds, butterflies, bees—even toads and chipmunks—will be attracted. And once you start to see wildlife in your perennial garden, you may be inspired to turn your entire yard into a wildlife haven. It doesn't really require more work, only some special planning. You can and will attract birds and butterflies by just mixing different perennials together haphazardly, but your chances of success are even better if you set out purposefully to make your garden an ideal wildlife buffet, including seeds, nectar, berries, and more.

◄Put out the welcome mat for hummingbirds with generous clumps of summer-blooming bee balms, including *Monarda didyma*.

Creating a Backyard Wildlife Haven

Planting perennials that will provide food for birds and butterflies is a great first step in enticing them to visit your yard, and in this chapter, I've recommended some of the best wildlife-attracting perennials. But to create a site that's highly attractive to birds and butterflies requires a bit more than just planting some perennials. The real secret to attracting the widest selection and greatest number of birds and butterflies is to make your backyard environment as varied as possible. A wide variety of perching birds, from robins to house wrens, jays, sparrows, chickadees, and cardinals will frequent a well-planned wildlife garden, although the exact species will vary according to the region you live in.

Water, Food, and Shelter

Birds and butterflies need food, of course, but they also need water and places to take cover from predators and bad weather. Beds of nectar- and seed-producing perennials, such as columbines and purple coneflowers, are good food sources, and they provide some shelter for ground-nesting birds, such as sparrows and thrushes. Also, many kinds of birds and butterflies will take refuge from predators, rain, and cold winds by hiding in your garden.

Expanding the Menu

When you plant a perennial garden for birds and butterflies, mix in some annuals, too. The truth is, most perennials aren't at the top of birds' lists of favorite plants. Adding annuals like zinnias and

The trick to attracting beautiful butterflies of all kinds to your garden is to plant purple coneflower (*Echinacea purpurea*). Later in the season the ripe seedheads will beckon the finches and sparrows as well.

common sunflowers (*Helianthus annuus*) to a bird and butterfly garden will attract a wider variety of birds. And of course, you don't have to limit the food sources to your garden. You can also install bird feeders around your yard to attract more birds.

Adding shrubs and trees to your yard will greatly diversify the environment while supplying nesting and feeding material for an even wider variety of creatures. The ideal yard for birds and butterflies would contain a mix of shrubs, clusters of trees (both large and small), climbing plants, perennials, annuals, and bulbs.

When choosing shrubs, trees, and climbers, remember that many have attractive berries that birds love or will produce an abundance of seed that will attract birds like blue jays.

Water Is Welcoming

Adding a source of water may be the single best thing you can do to attract and keep birds in your yard. Just like us, birds need water every day, so if your yard doesn't supply it, they'll have to go elsewhere to find it. You can buy a traditional birdbath, but some birdbaths are too deep (birds prefer 1 to 2 inches of water). In this case, put a flat rock into the bath so it is just covered with water. You'll often attract more birds, though, with a water garden, especially if it has a shallow area, only about 1 inch (2.5 cm) deep, near the edge in a sunny spot. When you put in a birdbath or water garden, keep in mind that birds don't like to come down to ground level if there are shrubs and dense vegetation nearby: Predators could be hiding there and birds can sense this. If you're planning a bird bathing area, make sure it's in the open. A good spot would be in the middle of a modest-sized lawn that's edged by gardens, shrubs, and trees.

Dust Helps, Too

Many birds also like to take a dust bath: Provide them with a small area of fine sand and ash in a sunny place, and you'll have regular visitors. The rock garden, which is more open than other parts of the yard, is often the ideal spot for a dust bath.

Mud Puddles for Butterflies

Butterflies love mud puddles where they can soak up some water. You can attract them by leaving a small, shallow puddle of muddy water in the garden and even adding a bit of salt every now and then. Many butterflies "mud-puddle"—

gather in groups around a small pool of water—to drink; adding a bit of salt helps meet their need for sodium. In my neighborhood, butterflies often accumulate around puddles of moose urine . . . but if moose urine isn't widely available in your region, a mud puddle makes an excellent substitute!

Spots for Sunbathing

While birds and butterflies need shelter, they also like open areas. Butterflies need to gather heat from the sun to warm themselves up so they can fly, and birds like to alight. Open areas allow birds and butterflies the opportunity to keep a close eye on marauding predators as well. So you'll want to preserve some lawn in your yard or provide some flat rocks where birds and butterflies can perch. You may even find butterflies basking on your sunny patio.

Don't Tidy Up

If you want wildlife to feel at home in your yard, try not to be too picky about neatness. Many small creatures live, nest, feed, or overwinter in leaf litter or near dead branches and foliage. The less clean your garden is, the more wild visitors you'll have. Consider reserving a small section of your yard for weeds. Many of the plants we detest are favorite foods of birds and butterflies. Simply rake the surface of an out-of-the-way bed to turn up dormant weed seeds. When the weeds sprout, you'll have a new wildlife habitat!

By the way, in a "wild" garden, the number of insect pests usually decreases once the garden is established. The birds that visit your garden are voracious consumers of insects and can help keep marauding pests at bay.

Also, if you want to attract wildlife, always garden organically—never use pesticides. Even the mildest organic sprays, like insecticidal soap, can be toxic to butterfly larvae.

Hummingbirds in Your Garden

Hummingbirds are the smallest birds native to North America. Often brilliantly colored, hummingbirds have a long, pointed beak they can slip deep into flowers and an even longer tongue to slurp up insects and sugary substances. They feed mostly on nectar, although they eat insects as well (the ones in my garden just love the aphids on my lupines and roses). In fact, hummingbirds *must* eat insects: Nectar may be sugary and therefore energy-rich but supplies no protein. Insects are their protein source.

The secret to attracting hummers is to provide a season-long range of flowers, starting in the earliest spring and lasting until they migrate south for the winter. In warmer climates where they stay all winter, try for year-round bloom! And remember: Hummingbirds prefer tubular flowers, especially bright reds, oranges, and pinks. To draw hummingbirds to your yard, set up hummingbird feeders early in the season and maintain them throughout summer and into fall. Fill the feeders regularly with a sugar solution (one part white sugar to four parts water) or a commercially prepared "nectar." Clean the feeders regularly (every three days in hot weather) to prevent the nectar solution from spoiling.

13 More Bird and Butterfly Plants

Birds and butterflies will feed on many other perennials as well as the ones I've listed in this chapter. Here's the "supplemental menu" of perennials for birds and butterflies to try in your garden:

Aquilegia

Columbine

Columbines are a must for a hummingbird garden. Their flowers are perfectly designed to feed hummingbirds easily. Each columbine blossom consists of five petals, broad at the tip and narrow and tubular at the base, with backward-projecting spurs carefully designed to hold the nectar that hummingbirds—and butterflies—love. A collar of five larger petal-like leaves called sepals surround the flowers; the sepals are often pointed and are frequently of a different color. As a bonus, columbines have fan-shaped leaflets that are truly exquisite.

Plant Profile

AQUILEGIA
ack-wih-LEE-gee-uh

- **Bloom Color:** Blue, maroon, pink, purple, red, white, or yellow

- **Bloom Time:** Late spring to early summer

- **Length of Bloom:** Three to four weeks

- **Height:** Varies by species; see individual listings

- **Spread:** 1 foot (30 cm)

- **Garden Uses:** Cut flower garden, meadow garden, mixed border, rock garden, specimen plant, wall planting, woodland garden; attracts butterflies and hummingbirds

- **Light Preference:** Full sun to partial shade

- **Soil Preference:** Humus-rich, moist but well-drained soil

- **Best Way to Propagate:** Sow seed in late spring

- **USDA Plant Hardiness Zones:** 3 to 9

- **AHS Heat Zones:** 8 to 1

Growing Tips

Plant these easy-to-grow perennials in just about any well-drained soil that's not too dry and they will thrive. Although usually recommended as partial shade plants, columbines do perfectly well in full sun as long as the soil remains moist and temperatures are moderate. They don't like hot summers, so if you live in the Deep South, try fuller shade and an abundant organic mulch, or grow them as annuals.

The seed capsules of columbines are fairly attractive, but you'll often get repeat bloom if you deadhead at least the first flowers of the season. Leave a few in place, though, so the plants can self-sow.

Even under the best of circumstances, columbines are short-lived—three or four years is the average life span.

Division is possible with columbines, but almost nobody ever tries it: They're simply too easy to grow from seed. Many of the hybrid strains are practically identical from one generation to the next, making sowing them all that much more practical.

Good Neighbors

Ferns, hellebores (*Helleborus* spp.), small hostas, forget-me-nots (*Myosotis* spp.), taller blue star (*Amsonia hubrechtii*), and blue false indigo (*Baptisia australis*) all make pleasing companions.

Problems and Solutions

Think Twice: There's no use denying it: Columbines are *not* insect-resistant. Leaf miners are the most common problem. Removing the infected leaves will help slow the leaf miners' spread. But if leaf miners don't get the leaves, then caterpillars might; they can sometimes strip the plant totally clean almost overnight. And did I mention aphids? If by any chance your columbines get through the period of insect infestation just after bloom, remember there will now be a series of leaf diseases to deal with.

Before you give up in discouragement, though, learn to treat columbines as generations of gardeners have done: as one-season wonders. Cut them to the ground after bloom, just as the insect attacks begin or before they even start. The plants may produce a flush of new growth, or simply stay dormant until the following spring.

Top Performer

Aquilegia × *hybrida* (hybrid columbine): The vast majority of columbines sold today are complex hybrids, producing a highly variable group of plants that combine many different characteristics, sizes, and colors. Some popular strains are available as single colors, but most are sold in mixes. McKana Hybrids is the most widely available seed-grown strain, with large, long-spurred flowers in a full range of pastel shades. The plants measure 18 to 30 inches (45 to 75 cm) tall. The Songbird Series, including 'Robin', covers a range of plants of a similar size, but in brighter shades. Height: 9 to 30 inches (23 to 75 cm). Spread: 1 foot (30 cm). USDA Plant Hardiness Zones 3 to 9; AHS Heat Zones 8 to 1.

More Recommended Columbines

⭐ **Larry's Favorite:** *Aquilegia canadensis* (wild columbine): This is the native columbine of eastern North America. Its drooping flowers consist of yellow petals and blood red sepals and spurs. It's much less susceptible to leaf miners than any other columbine I have tried. 'Corbett' has all-yellow flowers. Height: 2 to 3 feet (60 to 90 cm). Spread: 1 foot (30 cm). USDA Plant Hardiness Zones 2 to 9; AHS Heat Zones 8 to 1.

❗ **Think Twice:** *A. chrysantha* (golden columbine): This columbine's yellow flowers are somewhat fragrant, rare for a columbine. It is mildew-resistant, but leaf miners devour it! Golden columbine will sometimes rebloom if cut back after flowering. Height: 2 to 3 feet (60 to 90 cm). Spread: 1 foot (30 cm). USDA Plant Hardiness Zones 3 to 9; AHS Heat Zones 8 to 1.

'Rocky Mountain' hybrid columbine (*Aquilegia* × *hybrida* 'Rocky Mountain')

Kissing Cousins

Semiaquilegia (*Semiaquilegia ecalcarata*, also called *S. simulatrix*) is so much like a columbine (*Aquilegia* sp.) that it's hard to tell the two apart. But the flowers of semiquilegia have no spurs and their petal-like sepals tend to open much wider. *S. ecalcarata* has pink to reddish purple flowers that seem to hang upside down and narrow, columbine-like foliage. This charming, easy-to-grow but short-lived plant self-seeds like a columbine and has the same insect problems. Height: 16 inches (40 cm). Spread: 1 foot (30 cm). USDA Plant Hardiness Zones 3 to 9; AHS Heat Zones 8 to 1.

Asclepias

Milkweed

Milkweeds are butterfly plants par excellence. Their flowers produce copious quantities of nectar for both day-flying butterflies and night-flying moths. These handsome perennials are generally clumping, upright plants with thick stems and leathery, smooth, shiny leaves. Break the stem, or a leaf or flower, and sticky white sap will flow out. The dense flower clusters are made up of star-shaped blooms. After the flowers fade, inflated seedpods filled with flat seeds, each equipped with a silky parachute, form.

Plant Profile

ASCLEPIAS
as-KLEE-pea-us

- **Bloom Color:** Orange, pink, red, or white
- **Bloom Time:** Late spring to late summer
- **Length of Bloom:** 6 weeks or more
- **Height:** Varies by species; see individual listings
- **Spread:** 2 feet (60 cm)
- **Garden Uses:** Container planting, cut flower garden, mass planting, meadow garden, mixed border, seasonal hedge, specimen plant; at the back of beds and borders, in wet areas; attracts butterflies
- **Light Preference:** Full sun or light shade
- **Soil Preference:** Varies by species; see individual listings
- **Best Way to Propagate:** Sow seed in spring or fall
- **USDA Plant Hardiness Zones:** Varies by species; see individual listings
- **AHS Heat Zones:** Varies by species; see individual listings

Growing Tips

These care tips are so easy, you can't forget them! Full sun or only light shade is a must for milkweed plants. They'll do fine in average or even poor soil. But be careful—too much shade or overly fertile conditions can lead to floppy stems.

Milkweeds usually have long, thick, carrotlike roots that are easily damaged during transplanting. Try to buy young plants and handle them with care; once they're in place, don't move or divide them.

If you don't want to collect seed, deadhead milkweeds to encourage rebloom. Fresh milkweed seed germinates readily. After the pods have split open, just sow the seeds directly outdoors, barely covering them, and they will germinate within a month.

Good Neighbors

Butterfly weed (*Asclepias tuberosa*) is a natural choice for a meadow garden. Pair it with native grasses and wildflowers, such as asters and purple coneflower (*Echinacea purpurea*), to create a butterfly-filled habitat. In the perennial border, pair butterfly weed with torch lilies (*Kniphofia* spp.) and other fiery flowers, or with cooler blues and purples, such as on 'Goodness Grows' veronica.

Combine swamp milkweed (*Asclepias incarnata*) with other moisture-tolerant plants, such as turtleheads (*Chelone* spp.) or Joe-Pye weeds (*Eupatorium* spp.).

FUN FACTS

Milkweed leaves are actually poisonous to most caterpillars, with one exception: The famous monarch butterfly lays its eggs on milkweed leaves and its multi-colored larvae eat the bitter leaves, absorbing the bitter taste of the plant. As a result, most birds and other predators will not eat monarchs—or if they do, then only once!

Problems and Solutions

The main pests of milkweeds are monarch butterfly larvae that eat away at the leaves and bright orange aphids that cluster at the top of the plant. If you find monarch butterfly caterpillars on your plants and just can't stand the thought of them eating the leaves off your milkweeds, delicately transport them to wild milkweeds in a nearby field. As for aphids, just knock them off with a strong spray of water. Repeat this every two or three days for a week.

Top Performer

Asclepias tuberosa (butterfly weed): This native of the West is by far the most popular of the ornamental milkweeds. It produces clusters of thick, upright stems with narrow, pointed, shiny green leaves. From late spring to late summer, each stem ends in a dense cluster of bright orange, or more rarely, yellow or red flowers. Butterfly weed can be tricky to grow in damp climates; it requires excellent drainage and won't stand winter wet. It's *very* slow to come up in the spring: Mark its spot so you don't dig into it by accident. 'Gay Butterflies', a seed-grown mix, is supposed to contain oranges, reds, and yellows, but I've only had the typical orange flowers of the species. 'Hello Yellow' is a yellow-flowered cultivar that does come true from seed. Height: 2 to 3 feet (60 to 90 cm). Spread: 2 feet (60 cm). USDA Plant Hardiness Zones 4 to 9; AHS Heat Zones 9 to 2.

More Recommended Milkweeds

⭐ **Larry's Favorite:** *Asclepias incarnata* (swamp milkweed): Swamp milkweed is bigger and denser than butterfly weed and produces similar dense clumps of thick stems, but the whorled leaves are a bit wider than those of its arid-climate cousin. Swamp milkweed produces numerous clusters of sweet-scented pink flowers from late spring to late summer, attracting butterflies from far and wide. Swamp milkweed is far easier to acclimate to the garden than butterfly weed (*A. tuberosa*), since it will grow in sites ranging from boggy to dry. 'Ice Ballet' is a white-flowered version of this species. Height: 30 to 60 inches (75 to 150 cm). Spread: 2 feet (60 cm). USDA Plant Hardiness Zones 3 to 9; AHS Heat Zones 8 to 1.

Butterfly weed
(*Asclepias tuberosa*)

Around the World with Milkweeds

Milkweeds are well known as the only hosts of the famous orange-and-black monarch butterfly. These butterflies, while spending their summers as far north as southern Canada, prefer to overwinter in the warmer climates of California and Mexico. I've had the pleasure of traveling to a monarch butterfly sanctuary in Angangueo, Mexico, one of the monarch's mountain nesting sites, and seeing millions of them covering native firs so thickly that, light as each butterfly is, their combined weight caused the branches to bend downward.

Centaurea

Centaurea, cornflower, knapweed

Centaureas are strictly for the birds—seed-eating birds, that is! The flower heads of centaureas may form a dense mop or look more like daisies, but birds love the seeds that form from all types of centaureas. The leaves vary between different species, from hairy to smooth in texture and green to silvery in color.

Plant Profile

CENTAUREA
sen-TOR-ee-uh

- **Bloom Color:** Pink or yellow

- **Bloom Time:** Varies by species; see individual listings

- **Length of Bloom:** 3 weeks or more

- **Height:** Varies by species; see individual listings

- **Spread:** Varies by species; see individual listings

- **Garden Uses:** Cut flower garden, mixed border, specimen plant, wildflower meadow; at the back of beds and borders; attracts birds

- **Light Preference:** Full sun to light shade

- **Soil Preference:** Average, well-drained soil

- **Best Way to Propagate:** Divide in spring or fall

- **USDA Plant Hardiness Zones:** Varies by species; see individual listings

- **AHS Heat Zones:** Varies by species; see individual listings

Growing Tips

Centaureas certainly aren't hard to grow. As long as you don't stick them in soggy soil or expose them to excessive heat or cold, they'll pretty much survive anything. They'll tolerate light shade without complaint, but even partial shade can lead to lanky, floppy growth that may need staking, so try to provide as much sun as possible. Any well-drained soil will do, even a poor one. All centaureas are drought-tolerant once established but will grow better if kept evenly moist.

Think Twice: All centaureas can self-seed enthusiastically, so consider deadheading as a means of control. On the other hand, if your main reason for growing centaureas is to attract seed-eating birds, deadheading will defeat your purpose. You'll have to decide which is in your garden's best interest: attracting birds or controlling spread. Personally, I vote for the birds and count on mulching to prevent unwanted seedlings from appearing.

Most centaureas don't require division, but you *can* divide them, preferably in early spring or fall, if you need more plants. Centaureas are also easy to grow from seed, often blooming the first year. Start them indoors in late winter or outdoors in spring or fall, barely covering the seed. Of course, as with most perennials, only the species reproduce dependably by seed: Most cultivars don't come true.

Good Neighbors

Try centaureas in a cottage garden or border with other old-fashioned favorites, such as lady's-mantle (*Alchemilla mollis*), coreopsis, foxgloves (*Digitalis* spp.), rudbeckias, and more.

Problems and Solutions

Under normal circumstances, centaureas aren't particularly subject to pests and diseases.

Top Performer

Centaurea dealbata (Persian cornflower): Persian cornflower is a full, leafy plant with deeply cut, fernlike leaves that are dark green above and hairy and silvery below. The leaves at the base of the plant are about 2 feet (60 cm) long, while those at the top are much shorter. The 2- to 3-inch (5- to 8-cm) flowers are made up of an outer ring of deeply fringed lavender to pink petals and paler central petals, looking like daisies. Persian cornflower blooms for about four weeks in early summer but will often bloom again if deadheaded. Height: 18 to 30 inches (45 to 75 cm). Spread: 18 to 24 inches (45 to 60 cm). USDA Plant Hardiness Zones 3 to 9; AHS Heat Zones 7 to 1.

More Recommended Centaureas

Centaurea hypoleuca 'John Coutts' ('John Coutts' centaurea): This plant is a dead ringer for Persian cornflower (*C. dealbata*) and may be sold as a Persian cornflower cultivar. The main difference is in the foliage, which is somewhat grayer overall, and the upper leaves of 'John Coutts' centaurea are lance-shaped. The flowers of 'John Coutts' are similar to those of Persian cornflower. Height: 18 to 30 inches (45 to 75 cm). Spread: 18 to 24 inches (45 to 60 cm). USDA Plant Hardiness Zones 4 to 9; AHS Heat Zones 9 to 1.

⭐ **Larry's Favorite:** *C. macrocephala* (globe centaurea): This distinctive centaurea is a massive plant that dominates the garden when in bloom. The deep green leaves are roughly textured and wavy. The huge flower buds, covered with papery metallic brown scales, look somewhat like artichokes. The buds burst into a fuzzy, moplike cluster of narrow yellow flowers from early to late summer, which last a long time but will not rebloom when deadheaded. Height: 2 to 4 feet (60 to 120 cm). Spread: 2 feet (60 cm). USDA Plant Hardiness Zones 2 to 9; AHS Heat Zones 7 to 1.

Persian cornflower
(*Centaurea dealbata*)

Kissing Cousins

Cupid's dart (*Catananche caerulea*) is an easy-to-grow relative that doesn't get the respect it deserves. The plant produces narrow, silvery, hairy leaves, mostly at the base of the plant; and many wiry upright stems, each bearing a single flower similar to that of a centaurea. It blooms almost continuously through the summer if deadheaded regularly. Cupid's dart rarely persists more than three years, although it self-sows readily. Height: 18 to 30 inches (45 to 75 cm). Spread: 1 foot (30 cm). USDA Plant Hardiness Zones 4 to 9; AHS Heat Zones 7 to 1.

Echinacea

Purple coneflower

Butterflies, birds, color, *and* drama? Run, don't walk, to the nearest nursery: You *need* this plant! Purple coneflowers produce large, daisylike blooms with a spiky central cone and slightly drooping petals. During the blooming season they're a favorite with butterflies, and the seedheads will attract seed-eating birds such as finches and sparrows well into winter. They have a long season of interest, from the pretty bloom in summer to the stiffly upright rounded cones in fall and winter.

Plant Profile

ECHINACEA
eck-in-AY-see-uh

- Bloom Color: Pink, purplish, white, or yellow
- Bloom Time: Midsummer to early fall
- Length of Bloom: 6 weeks or more
- Height: Varies by species; see individual listings
- Spread: Varies by species; see individual listings
- Garden Uses: Container planting, cut flower garden, mass planting, meadow garden, mixed border, specimen plant; attracts birds and butterflies
- Light Preference: Full sun to light shade
- Soil Preference: Average, well-drained soil
- Best Way to Propagate: Divide in spring or fall
- USDA Plant Hardiness Zones: 3 to 9
- AHS Heat Zones: 9 to 1

Growing Tips

You'd think that plants offering so many advantages would be hard to grow, but that's hardly the case. Purple coneflowers' two main requirements are good drainage and full sun; poor drainage leads to rot, and too much shade to floppiness. In hot-summer areas, however, light shade helps keep the bloom colors bright and vibrant. Average garden soil suits purple coneflowers just fine, though they will grow in both poor and rich soils. Steady soil moisture is best, especially to promote a long blooming season, but established purple coneflowers are quite drought-resistant.

My only complaint about purple coneflowers is that they are slow to multiply. Division is the best option for cultivars, though the plants will form dense clumps with plenty of material for division only after seven or eight years of growth. And while purple coneflowers grow moderately well from seed sown indoors or out, germination is irregular and seedlings grow slowly. Just barely cover the seeds, and if sowing indoors, provide darkness until germination occurs. Personally, I prefer to let the plants self-sow, and then I move the new plants wherever I want.

Good Neighbors

Make these fail-proof bloomers a focal point in the garden, surrounding them with yarrows, coreopsis, daylilies, spike gayfeather (*Liatris spicata*), and other colorful companions. Sow seeds of tall, multiheaded sunflowers (*Helianthus* spp.) between the perennials to attract even more feathered friends.

Problems and Solutions

Japanese beetles will feed on both the flowers and the leaves of purple coneflowers. Treating nearby lawns (where beetle larvae, or grubs, feed) with milky disease spores will help keep the population down to an acceptable level. I've also heard of problems with powdery mildew; to prevent it, keep the soil moist by watering at the base of the plant without getting the leaves wet.

Top Performer

Echinacea purpurea (purple coneflower): My principal gripe with this otherwise great plant is its name: *purple* coneflower. To my eyes, the flower of *E. purpurea* is pink! The sturdy plants produce coarse, toothed, dark green leaves and stiffly upright flowerstalks that are topped with huge pincushion-like coppery cones surrounded by usually drooping petals (known botanically as ray flowers).

'Magnus' purple coneflower
(*Echinacea purpurea* 'Magnus')

There are oodles of cultivars, most differing from the species in the ray flowers' colors, the droopiness of the ray flowers, and in relative size. Unfortunately, most don't come true from seed. The seedlings of 'Magnus', for instance, generally maintain the nondrooping habit of the original plant and exhibit a more compact form than the species, but the color range covers a wide array of pinks. 'White Swan', with drooping ray flowers, is the most common white-flowered strain and does come true colorwise; but the plants vary in height, leaf color, and other characteristics. 'White Lustre' is vegetatively produced and has horizontal white ray flowers around a bronze center. Height: 2 to 5 feet (60 to 150 cm). Spread: 18 to 24 inches (45 to 60 cm). USDA Plant Hardiness Zones 3 to 9; AHS Heat Zones 9 to 1.

More Recommended Purple Coneflowers

Echinacea angustifolia (narrow-leaved purple coneflower): This is one of the most popular purple coneflowers for medical purposes, and it's a terrific garden plant. Narrow-leaved purple coneflower bears narrow, drooping ray flowers in pink, rose, or white, and as the name suggests, narrow leaves. Try growing it in front of purple coneflower (*E. purpurea*): It will provide color from late spring to midsummer, when the purple coneflower will take over. Height: 1 to 3 feet (30 to 90 cm). Spread: 18 to 24 inches (45 to 60 cm). USDA Plant Hardiness Zones 3 to 9; AHS Heat Zones 9 to 1.

Larry's Garden Notes

Echinacea is one of three genera commonly called coneflowers, and telling them apart isn't easy. The cones at the center of the flower of praire coneflower (*Ratibida*) are long and narrow, and its leaves are deeply cut and fernlike. *Echinaea* and *Rudbeckia* aren't as easy to distinguish. *Rudbeckia* has green, purple, or dark brown cones, usually rather small, and yellow or orange petals. The cones may be firm, but not spiny. The most common purple coneflowers (*Echinacea* spp.) have pink or white ray petals.

Erigeron

Fleabane

These aster look-alikes are popular with both gardeners and butterflies. While fleabanes closely resemble asters, their petals form in two or more rows, while those of asters usually only have one single row. The foliage of fleabanes (and asters) is quite variable, with smooth-edged or lobed leaves that can be broad or narrow, rounded or pointed, smooth or hairy. Most fleabanes are clumping plants that produce upright or creeping stems with clustered blooms at the tops.

Plant Profile

ERIGERON
ee-RIJ-er-on

- **Bloom Color:** Lavender, pink, purple, or white

- **Bloom Time:** Early to late summer

- **Length of Bloom:** 6 to 8 weeks or more

- **Height:** 18 to 30 inches (45 to 75 cm)

- **Spread:** 1 to 2 feet (30 to 60 cm)

- **Garden Uses:** Container planting, cut flower garden, edging, groundcover, mass planting, meadow garden, mixed border, rock garden, specimen plant, wall planting; attracts butterflies

- **Light Preference:** Full sun to light shade

- **Soil Preference:** Average, well-drained soil

- **Best Way to Propagate:** Divide in spring or fall

- **USDA Plant Hardiness Zones:** Varies by species; see individual listings

- **AHS Heat Zones:** Varies by species; see individual listings

Growing Tips

Fleabanes need full sun or light shade, and good drainage is a must, but otherwise, they'll adapt to pretty much anything. To avoid the need for staking, plant fleabanes in poor to average soil, even dry, sandy sites (they're drought-tolerant), and don't fertilize or overwater.

Fleabanes flower for a particularly long period, but when they stop blooming, you can deadhead them and expect further bloom in the fall. If a clump dies out in the center, either dig up the mother plant and divide it, throwing away the dead core, or dig out the center and fill the empty spot with fresh soil. The plant will quickly fill in again.

Since fleabanes grow quickly, they produce ample material for division. They can be divided annually if many plants are desired, but most gardeners leave them alone for four or five years before chopping them into wedges and replanting them.

Good Neighbors

It's difficult to think of a plant that would not combine well with daisy fleabane (*Erigeron speciosus*). Combine it with coreopsis, irises, Shasta daisy (*Leucanthemum* × *superbum*), rudbeckias, or anything else that needs a friend.

Problems and Solutions

Fleabanes are almost too much like asters for their own good! They even share some of the same problems, most notably powdery mildew (well known to any gardener by the powdery look leaves take on in late summer). Another problem is aster yellows, which causes the plant to yellow and die. To prevent most diseases, including mildew, try to avoid moistening the leaves as you water fleabanes. But to control aster yellows, which is transported by aphids, you'll *need* to moisten the leaves. The best control for these pests is to treat infested plants with a strong spray of water, repeated every few days until the aphids are gone. Spray the plants in the early morning so they'll have time to dry off before evening: This will help prevent the development of other diseases.

Top Performer

Erigeron speciosus (daisy fleabane): The true daisy fleabane and its close cousin *E. speciosus* var. *macranthus* are almost never grown in gardens anymore. Modern plants are hybrids with a heavy dose of *E. speciosus* genes, but lots of input from other species, too.

Regardless of the name, these tall to medium-sized, clump-forming plants produce branching stems that end in clusters of daisylike blooms, each bearing more than 100 ray flowers. Top-notch perennials, they do best in average to cool-summer areas.

'Dunkelste Aller' (also called 'Darkest of All') is a 2-foot (60-cm) cultivar with violet-blue flowers. The true 'Rosa Juwel', about 30 inches (75 cm) tall with bright pink semi-double flowers, is one of the nicest cultivars. Long-blooming 'Prosperity' has semi-double lavender-blue flowers on a compact, solid, 18-inch (45-cm) plant. Height: 1 to 3 feet (30 to 90 cm). USDA Plant Hardiness Zones 2 to 9. AHS Heat Zones 8 to 1.

More Recommended Fleabanes

Think Twice: *Erigeron karvinskianus* (fleabane): This plant is so different from the usual hybrid fleabanes that it practically deserves its own category. It's a low-growing, trailing plant that's covered with ¾-inch (2-cm) daisylike flowers throughout the growing season. That can literally be 12 months out of 12 in totally frost-free areas or from the beginning to the end of summer toward the northern limits of its range. Watch out, though—it can be invasive. Height: 10 to 20 inches (25 to 50 cm). Spread: 14 to 20 inches (36 to 50 cm). USDA Plant Hardiness Zones 9 to 11. AHS Heat Zones 11 to 1.

Fleabane (*Erigeron karvinskianus*)

Larry's Garden Notes

The name "fleabane" (*Erigeron*) came from this plant's supposed ability to chase away fleas, but it's something of a misnomer. When beaver hats were all the rage, beaver pelts were shipped from Canada to Europe packed with branches of Canadian fleabane (originally *Erigeron canadensis*, now *Conyza canadensis*) to keep away clothes moths, not fleas. And since the original "clothes-moth-bane" has been moved to a new genus, there's no reason we should still be calling *Erigeron* fleabane. But names do stick, don't they?

Gaillardia

Blanket flower

No two ways about it—blanket flowers are daisies! They have the typical round center that's perfect as a butterfly feeding station and horizontal petals that make great landing platforms for tired gossamer wings. The centers of blanket flowers are burgundy red, and the petals are yellow, sometimes banded with red. Blanket flower foliage is nothing special, but with such brightly colored blooms, who cares?

Plant Profile

GAILLARDIA
gah-LARD-ee-uh

- **Bloom Color:** Orange, red, or yellow
- **Bloom Time:** Early summer to early fall
- **Length of Bloom:** 10 weeks or more
- **Height:** 1 to 3 feet (30 to 90 cm)
- **Spread:** 1 to 2 feet (30 to 60 cm)
- **Garden Uses:** Container planting, cut flower garden, edging, mass planting, meadow garden, mixed border, rock garden; attracts butterflies
- **Light Preference:** Full sun
- **Soil Preference:** Average, moist but well-drained soil
- **Best Way to Propagate:** Sow seed in spring
- **USDA Plant Hardiness Zones:** 2 to 9
- **AHS Heat Zones:** 12 to 1

Growing Tips

Blanket flowers need full sun or only light shade—otherwise they tend to flop—and good drainage is a must, but overall they're very adaptable. Although they do best in moist soil, blanket flowers are highly drought-tolerant. Like many daisies, they actually do *better* in somewhat poor soils than in rich ones. Heavy clay soils, though, don't suit them at all: A looser soil, even a sandy one, is much more likely to produce long-term success.

In my climate, blanket flowers just seem to bloom on and on with no intervention on my part. In other regions, you may need to either deadhead, or cut them back completely to about 6 inches (15 cm) from the ground in late summer. Don't worry: These plants will sprout again within a few weeks and will soon be blooming as heavily as ever.

Be aware that blanket flowers tend to be short-lived. Keep them going by letting them self-sow if they're not a cultivar (because the flowers probably won't come true); otherwise divide them every two or three years in spring or fall.

Good Neighbors

Bring out the gold rims of blanket flower blooms by mixing them with equally tolerant yellow-golds, such as 'Coronation Gold' yarrow, coreopsis, or 'Stella de Oro' daylily. Or use blanket flower as a companion to ornamental grasses.

FUN FACTS

The common name "blanket flower" reminds us that these flowers used to blanket the North American prairies with their bloom, creating a true blanket of color. Although fields of corn, oats, and soybeans have replaced the expanses of blanket flowers, you'll still see them popping up here and there in fields and along roadsides in the prairie region and into the Rockies.

Warning: Some people develop skin rashes after they have been in contact with the fuzzy hairs that cover blanket flowers. If you have ever developed rashes from touching fuzzy plants, wear gloves when you handle blanket flowers as a precaution.

Problems and Solutions

Blanket flowers don't have many serious problems, but aster yellows, a viruslike disease, can stunt growth and cause all flowers to remain green. Destroy infected plants: They will not recover. Since the disease is spread by insects, notably leafhoppers and aphids, the best control is a well-balanced, organic garden where predators abound. Otherwise, you can control leafhoppers with soap spray, and knock off aphids with a blast of water.

'Kobold' blanket flower
(*Gaillardia* × *grandiflora* 'Kobold')

Top Performer

Gaillardia × *grandiflora* (blanket flower): Rarely has a man-made hybrid known as much success as this hybrid blanket flower. It combines the fast-growing habit and continuous summer-long bloom of the annual species *G. pulchella* with the hardiness and perennial nature of *G. aristata*. There are a few chinks in its armor, though, notably where longevity is concerned: *G.* × *grandiflora* has inherited a short life span from its annual ancestor, so start it again from seed or division every two or three years or you may lose it.

This blanket flower is a variable plant, notably in its flowers, which range from the typical burgundy red with yellow tips to all sorts and shades of orange and red, often with three or more colors in the same flower. 'Monarch' is the most common seed-grown mixture and produces handsome plants. Seeds of many other "cultivars" are sold, but don't necessarily come true, resulting in considerable confusion. 'Burgundy' (also called 'Burgunder') is a full-sized pure burgundy red cultivar, while 'Tokajer' is similar, but with orange blossoms. 'Dazzler' is the most common yellow cultivar. 'Baby Cole' is one of the nicest dwarf strains, only about 1 foot (30 cm) tall, with yellow flowers banded red. 'Kobold' (also called 'Goblin'), with red flowers tipped in yellow, is another popular dwarf cultivar.

Larry's Garden Notes

You've just put in a huge bed but no longer have enough money to fill it with choice perennials? Start your own blanket flowers from seed. Start seed indoors about six to eight weeks before planting outside (after danger of frost is past) for bloom the first year. There's no need to cover the seeds—they need light to germinate. They give instant results by blooming abundantly in the first year, nicely filling in your garden. In future years, gradually replace the inexpensive blanket flowers with more expensive perennials, and you'll be able to watch your cheap and easy bed evolve bit by bit into the kind of garden you've always dreamed about!

Heuchera

Heuchera, alumroot, coral bells

Heucheras are a popular perennial for outlining the front of a bed or border. From late spring through much of the summer, their low, dense mounds of rounded or heart-shaped evergreen leaves are topped with wiry, branched stems covered on the upper reaches with beautiful bell-shaped flowers. The flowerstalks last for a long time, each stalk often blooming for six to eight weeks, and hummingbirds love the flowers—a real plus.

Plant Profile

HEUCHERA
HUE-ker-uh

- **Bloom Color:** Pink, red, or white
- **Bloom Time:** Late spring to late summer
- **Length of Bloom:** 6 weeks or more
- **Height:** 18 to 30 inches (45 to 75 cm)
- **Spread:** 1 foot (30 cm)
- **Garden Uses:** Container planting, cut flower garden, edging, groundcover, mass planting, mixed border, rock garden, specimen plant, woodland garden; attracts hummingbirds
- **Light Preference:** Full sun to partial shade
- **Soil Preference:** Average, moist but well-drained soil
- **Best Way to Propagate:** Divide in spring or fall
- **USDA Plant Hardiness Zones:** 3 to 9
- **AHS Heat Zones:** 8 to 1

Growing Tips

Heucheras are a snap to grow if you just meet their simple needs. In cool-summer climates, for example, they thrive in full sun but also tolerate partial shade. Since they don't like heat, partial shade produces the best results in hotter climates. While well-drained, crumbly, humus-rich soil is optimal and heavy clay is definitely a no-no, almost any other soil will do. Heucheras prefer regular watering but will tolerate drought reasonably well once established. In really cold climates, you might wish to protect your plants with a winter mulch.

To stimulate continuous bloom, prune out faded flowers at the base of their stems. Or, if the planting is large, simply use a string trimmer and hack the whole forest of stalks down when blooming begins to subside. The plants will soon be in full bloom once more.

Heucheras usually reach their full size in the second year and then stabilize, so they don't need regular division. The original rosette tends to get woody and die off over time: If possible, cut it out with a sharp pair of pruning shears, fill in the gap with fresh soil, and the plant will fill in nicely. If the base is too woody for the shears, dig up the whole plant and cut it into sections with a sharp shovel or an ax. Throw out the center and plant the resulting divisions.

If you need an extra plant or two for multiplication purposes, simply cut out the secondary rosettes that form around the out-

FUN FACTS

Hummingbirds prefer tubular flowers, which makes sense when you look at their long, thin, pointed beaks. But even though heucheras produce only tiny, bell-shaped blooms, that still doesn't stop hummingbirds from visiting these flowers. And heucheras don't even have to be red to attract them: White or pink-flowered ones bring hummingbirds in just as surely as honey attracts flies.

side of the main one, and plant them on their own. Heucheras are easy to grow from seed: Just start indoors in late winter or outdoors in early spring or early fall. Don't cover the seeds, as they need light to germinate.

Good Neighbors

Try heucheras as an edging plant against taller perennials with handsome green foliage, such as blue star (*Amsonia hubrectii*), blackberry lily (*Belamcanda chinensis*), daylilies, ferns, or Siberian iris (*Iris sibirica*).

Problems and Solutions

Heucheras have few serious pest or disease problems.

Top Performer

Heuchera × brizoides (hybrid coral bells): While many nurseries still sell coral bells as *H. sanguinea*, nearly all coral bells sold today are complex hybrids. There's such a vast array of cultivars that it's hard to recommend which to grow. Just pick and choose your plants according to color, height, and foliage color!

All coral bells are wonderful plants, but the following are some of the most widely available cultivars: 'Chatterbox', with bright pink flowers; 'Coral Cloud', with coral red ones; 'June Bride', with white flowers tinged pink; 'Leuchtkäfer' (also called 'Firefly'), with wine red blooms; and 'Pluie de Feu' (also called 'Feuerregen' or 'Rain of Fire'), with cherry red flowers. 'Snow Storm' has green leaves beautifully splashed with white and cream and reddish pink flowers. Bressingham Hybrids is a popular seed mixture giving a wide range of plants with coral, pink, red, rose, and white flowers. (Try growing these from seed for great results.) If you garden in the prairie region, try 'Brandon Pink', with light pink flowers, and 'Northern Fire', with scarlet red flowers and white variegated foliage. According to gardening friends in Manitoba and Minnesota, nothing can kill these plants, even the worst prairie weather.

Heucheras are also called coral bells or alumroots. The species called coral bells is grown for flowers, while alumroots are grown mostly for foliage. For more information on the alumroot tribe, with its gorgeous foliage, turn to page 364.

'Leuchtkäfer' hybrid coral bells (*Heuchera × brizoides* 'Leuchtkäfer')

Larry's Garden Notes

In my crystal ball, I see the current distinctions between the beautifully flowered coralbells (*Heuchera sanguinea* and relatives) and their gorgeous-leaved cousins, the alumroots (*H. micrantha, H. americana*, and others), gradually disappearing. After all, both do cross readily together. Why shouldn't gardeners be able to enjoy both beautiful foliage and attractive flowers on the same plant? I hold a lot of hope for the future of heucheras—although I can't predict into which chapter of future editions of this book I'll be able to place their hybrid offspring!

Kniphofia

Torch lily, red-hot poker

In their native South Africa, torch lily is visited by sugarbirds, but in North American backyards, hummingbirds very nicely take their place. The plant really does look like a burning poker or torch, with blooms that are orange-red on top and yellow or yellowish green below. The dense bottlebrush-like spikes are made up of many densely packed, tubular flowers on a stiff, upright stem. Each spike blooms for a long period over dense rosettes of narrow, arching leaves. This is one plant you just can't miss when it's in flower: It really stands out from the crowd.

Plant Profile

KNIPHOFIA
nee-FOFE-ee-uh

- **Bloom Color:** Cream, orange, red, or yellow
- **Bloom Time:** Spring through summer or fall; sometimes winter
- **Length of Bloom:** 6 weeks or more
- **Height:** 18 to 48 inches (45 to 120 cm)
- **Spread:** 18 to 48 inches (45 to 120 cm)
- **Garden Uses:** Container planting, cut flower garden, mixed border, rock garden, specimen plant; at the back of beds and borders; attracts hummingbirds
- **Light Preference:** Full sun to partial shade
- **Soil Preference:** Rich, well-drained soil
- **Best Way to Propagate:** Divide in spring
- **USDA Plant Hardiness Zones:** 5 to 9
- **AHS Heat Zones:** 9 to 1

Growing Tips

Waxing enthusiastic about the appearance of torch lilies is easy enough, but they can be tough plants to grow in many regions—they're not the hardiest of perennials. However, there has been considerable effort by breeders to select for improved hardiness, and modern hybrids will do well in climates with winter cold. With adequate protection I can grow them in my USDA Zone 3 climate, but I suggest taking special precautions even in Zones 5 and 6. Start by tying the leaves together over the top of the plants in the fall. And you might also cover the plants with Styrofoam rose cones or a thick, well-aerated mulch such as hay, pine needles, or evergreen boughs. In the spring, cut back the foliage (which will be mostly dead) to about 2 to 3 inches (5 to 8 cm) from the ground to give the plants a fresh start. In USDA Zones 7 to 9, plants don't need special winter protection, but many gardeners do choose to cut back the foliage in the fall, since the leaves tend to look ratty after bloom.

Torch lilies also have other special requirements, particularly moist—even boggy—conditions in the summer, yet perfect drainage in winter. That's easy enough to provide in the arid southwest United States; elsewhere, strive for perfectly well-drained soil with additional summer waterings.

Full sun is important in cool-summer areas, otherwise torch lilies barely begin to flower before the first fall frosts. In hot summer climates, however, partial shade is ideal. Torch lilies are quite adaptable as to soil, but they do grow best in rich, humusy soil.

Torch lilies do not like to be disturbed. Rather than dividing an adult plant and risking its bad humor, try carefully digging up one of the offsets that forms at its base. If you must divide torch lilies, do so in early spring. Sometimes torch lilies are also sold as bulbs, or to be more precise, as sections of rhizomes. Just plant these 2 to 3 inches (5 to 8 cm) deep in well-drained soil in early spring; they should flower the following year.

Good Neighbors

Position torch lily in the middle of the border, and surround it with soft-looking perennials, such as common baby's-breath (*Gypsophila paniculata*) or Russian sages (*Perovskia* hybrids). Echo their vivid colors in other parts of your garden with plants such as butterfly weed (*Asclepias tuberosa*), daylilies, and other brightly hued perennials.

Hybrid torch lily
(*Kniphofia* hybrid)

Problems and Solutions

Torch lilies suffer from no serious pests and diseases, but plants grown in overly moist winter conditions are likely to rot away before spring.

Top Performer

Kniphofia hybrids (hybrid torch lilies): Almost all the torch lilies currently sold are of this type, even many of those labeled *K. uvaria*. The result is an extremely varied group of plants, ranging from giant back-of-the-border skyrockets to neat little mounding border plants. 'Alcazar' has salmon-tinged red flowers, usually early in the season. 'Earliest of All' tends to be especially early, even in cold-winter areas. It's a dwarf selection with orange-red upper flowers and yellow lower ones, reaching 18 to 24 inches (45 to 60 cm) tall. 'Primrose Beauty' is long-blooming primrose yellow cultivar that seems hardier than many others. 'Shining Sceptre' is a striking golden orange cultivar.

   K. uvaria 'Flamenco' grows especially quickly from seed so can be treated as an annual. Start it indoors early, in January or February, for bloom the first year. It's a compact plant, only 30 inches (75 cm) tall, with narrow, grasslike leaves and slim 8-inch (20-cm) spikes of red, yellow, or orange blooms.

Around the World with Torch Lilies

Torch lilies attract attention wherever they grow. I've seen them by the thousands, in all sorts of shapes, sizes, and colors, in the moister parts of their native South African velds, where they dominate the landscape with burning colors during the late spring and summer (October through February). They're all the rage in European gardens, both on the continent and in Great Britain, and in southern Australia as well. But the most spectacular torch lilies I have ever seen are those that have escaped from gardens in New Zealand. There I saw dense clumps of them everywhere at higher altitudes.

Lobelia

Lobelia

In my neck of the woods, cardinal flower (*Lobelia cardinalis*) is the best flower for attracting hummingbirds—and the other lobelias don't trail far behind. But while we may think of lobelias as hummingbird flowers, the broad lower lip of the blossoms also provides a great landing platform for butterflies, notably the beautiful swallowtails. Most of the perennial lobelias produce upright stems covered with lance-shaped green leaves. Each stem ends in a spike of tubular, double-lipped flowers.

Plant Profile

LOBELIA
low-BEE-lee-uh

- **Bloom Color:** Blue, pink, red, or white
- **Bloom Time:** Varies by species; see individual listings
- **Length of Bloom:** 3 weeks or more
- **Height:** Varies by species; see individual listings
- **Spread:** 1 to 2 feet (30 to 60 cm)
- **Garden Uses:** Container planting, cut flower garden, mass planting, meadow garden, mixed border, specimen plant, woodland garden; at the back of beds and borders, in wet areas; attracts butterflies and hummingbirds
- **Light Preference:** Full sun or partial shade
- **Soil Preference:** Rich, moist but well-drained soil
- **Best Way to Propagate:** Divide in spring or fall
- **USDA Plant Hardiness Zones:** Varies by species; see individual listings
- **AHS Heat Zones:** 8 to 1

Growing Tips

While most perennial lobelias appreciate plenty of moisture and even soggy soil, they'll grow well in average garden conditions provided they are well watered during times of drought. Incorporating organic matter into the soil before planting and providing a generous layer of organic mulch will also help keep them moist.

Most perennial lobelias prefer full sun in cool-summer climates, but partial shade (at least protection from afternoon sun) is a necessity in hot-summer areas.

Lobelias tend to be short-lived, lasting only two or three years before going on to plant heaven. To extend their life span, either provide moist conditions under which the species can self-sow (they do so abundantly, yet never become weeds) or divide cultivars regularly (they'll also self-sow, but since they don't always come true from seed, that rather defeats the purpose). It's also easy to divide the clumps in either spring or fall, and this rejuvenates the plants enough to allow them to survive for another two or three years, until you divide them again. You can also multiply lobelias by taking stem cuttings in early summer from stems not yet showing any flower buds. These root readily under moist, humid conditions.

Lobelia seed is very fine and requires special attention. Sow it indoors in early winter, sprinkling the seed over a moist mix and sealing it in a plastic bag. Next, place the seed container in the refrigerator for three months. Then, move the containers to a warm, brightly lit spot, and look for seedlings in about two weeks. The tiny seedlings are fragile at first, so keep the bag on until they have at least seven or eight leaves, then gradually acclimate them to moving air by removing the plastic bag bit by bit, raising it higher each day until eventually the whole plant is exposed to air circulation.

Good Neighbors

Place lobelias with moisture-loving but not overly aggressive companions. Aconites (*Aconitum* spp.), white baneberry (*Actaea alba*), marsh marigold (*Caltha palustris*), and ferns are possible choices.

Problems and Solutions

Rust can be a problem on great blue lobelia (*Lobelia siphilitica*) but usually doesn't cause more damage than a few discolored lower leaves. If it recurs and if the damage is severe (which *can* happen in some climates), try growing new plants from seed and planting them elsewhere in the garden. Dividing rust-infested plants will simply spread the problem.

Top Performer

Lobelia cardinalis (cardinal flower): How could I not bestow Top Performer status on this gorgeous plant? This summer flower is a striking cardinal red in its normal form. The leaves are typical of most lobelias: long, medium green, lance-shaped, and slightly toothed. It is the most shade-loving of the lobelias, so avoid planting in full sun unless you live in a cool-summer climate. Hardiness and heat resistance vary according to the plant's origin, so it's best to grow from cuttings or seeds of local plants, or at least obtain plants from a climate similar to yours. Height: 2 to 4 feet (60 to 120 cm). Spread: 1 foot (30 cm). USDA Plant Hardiness Zones 2 to 9; AHS Heat Zones 8 to 1.

More Recommended Lobelias

Lobelia siphilitica (great blue lobelia): This eastern and midwestern native is a stately, upright plant with dense spikes of deep blue flowers in late summer, over bright green leaves. It makes a great cut flower and naturalizes through self-seeding where it's happy. Two cultivars of note are 'Alba', with white blooms, and 'Blue Select', which has brighter blue flowers. Height: 2 to 3 feet (60 to 90 cm). Spread: 1 to 2 feet (30 to 60 cm). USDA Plant Hardiness Zones 3 to 8; AHS Heat Zones 8 to 1.

Cardinal flower
(*Lobelia cardinalis*)

Larry's Garden Notes

Cardinal flower (*Lobelia cardinalis*) thrives in normal garden soils (especially with a bit of extra watering) but does even better in and around water gardens or natural bogs. In the wild, cardinal flower typically grows in soils that are entirely underwater in the spring and just barely emerges in the summer. It can even live as an entirely aquatic plant for years because it develops special leaves that float on the water's surface. Then, when one summer is drier than usual and the plant's base is above water, up it shoots to bloom!

Monarda

Bee balm

Bees love bee balm, but so do butterflies and hummingbirds—and people! On the other hand, deer don't like bee balm: If you have deer problems, try planting a screen of bee balm to discourage them. Bee balm forms upright, spreading clumps of four-sided stems with aromatic, toothed, pointed leaves. The flowers appear in whorls at the tips of the stems.

Plant Profile

MONARDA
mow-NAR-duh

- **Bloom Color:** Pink, purple, red, or white

- **Bloom Time:** Midsummer to late summer

- **Length of Bloom:** 8 weeks or more

- **Height:** Varies by species; see individual listings

- **Spread:** 3 feet (90 cm)

- **Garden Uses:** Cut flower garden, mass planting, meadow garden, mixed border, specimen plant, woodland garden; at the back of beds and borders, in wet areas; attracts butterflies and hummingbirds

- **Light Preference:** Full sun to partial shade

- **Soil Preference:** Varies by species; see individual listings

- **Best Way to Propagate:** Divide in spring

- **USDA Plant Hardiness Zones:** 3 to 7

- **AHS Heat Zones:** 9 to 1

Growing Tips

Different species of bee balms have different needs, but they can easily grow together in a typical flowerbed with well-drained but moderately moist soil. Full sun is ideal in cool-summer areas, although bee balms also do well in partial shade. In hot-summer climates, partial shade is best for most *Monarda* species; *Monarda didyma* will need partial shade and protection from burning afternoon sun as it simply does not like to dry out.

Think Twice: Be forewarned that *all* bee balms are aggressive plants, spreading rapidly by creeping stems. Grow them in a wild area or meadow garden where other equally pushy plants will keep them in check, or plant them in a root barrier, such as a bottomless bucket sunk into the soil.

Although bee balms spread in all directions quickly, they also tend to thin out in the middle, even dying back after a few years. Some gardeners divide them every year or two, keeping only healthy fresh stems from the outside of the clump. In my garden, though, I just dig out the dead spots, compost the dead plant material, and fill in the gap with fresh soil: Bee balms quickly grow back in to fill the gap.

If you want more bee balms without dragging out the shovel, consider stem cuttings: They root rapidly and, as with divisions, provide plants identical to the original plant. You can also grow the species bee balms from seed, which is widely available. They're a snap to grow—start them indoors or out, barely covering the seed.

Deadheading will prevent self-sowing and help prolong bloom.

Good Neighbors

Bee balms look great with lady's-mantle (*Alchemilla mollis*), Joe-Pye weeds (*Eupatorium* spp.), Shasta daisy (*Leucanthemum* × *superbum*), and other vigorous growers.

Problems and Solutions

Bee balms are terribly susceptible to powdery mildew, and by late summer all the lower leaves may seem dipped in white powder. This disease doesn't seem to bother the plants, which come up again and again even after a particularly hard hit the previous summer, but it sure does bother gardeners! The best approach is to grow only disease-resistant cultivars. In my experience, disease-resistant selections do sometimes get the disease, but the mildew tends to be limited to the lowest leaves and doesn't harm the display.

Top Performer

Monarda hybrids (hybrid bee balm): Most catalogs list this plant under the name *M. didyma*, but while the two look much alike, hybrid bee balm is less dependent on wet soil and has greater mildew resistance. It's a stunning plant because it just blooms and blooms and blooms from midsummer to late summer.

There may be disagreement about which cultivars are hybrids or not, but what matters most is how they perform in your garden. Mildew resistance is important, and mildew-resistant cultivars include 'Blaustrumpf' (also called 'Blue Stocking'), with deep violet-purple flowers; 'Jacob Cline', in deep red; 'Marshall's Delight', in bright pink; 'Pisces', in soft pink; 'Scorpion', with red flowers with green bracts; and 'Violet Queen', in deep purple. Popular and enduring (but not as mildew-resistant), 'Cambridge Scarlet' is a 3-foot (90-cm) cultivar with flaming red flowers. Spread: 3 feet (90 cm). USDA Plant Hardiness Zones 3 to 7; AHS Heat Zones 9 to 1.

More Recommended Bee Balms

Monarda didyma (bee balm): You may want to try growing the wild species in a wet part of the garden where the constantly damp soil will keep powdery mildew from becoming a problem. This looks just like the hybrid types but has beautiful scarlet red flowers and scarlet petal-like bracts. 'Alba' has white blooms. Height: 2 to 4 feet (60 to 120 cm). Spread: 3 feet (90 cm). USDA Plant Hardiness Zones 3 to 7; AHS Heat Zones 9 to 1.

'Cambridge Scarlet' hybrid bee balm (*Monarda* 'Cambridge Scarlet')

Larry's Garden Notes

Besides looking wonderful in the garden, bee balms are also useful: The leaves and flowers make a soothing herbal tea. Oswego tea, made from *Monarda didyma*, is the best known. The young leaves and flowers can add a citrusy zing to salads. The dried leaves and flowers are a nice addition to potpourris.

The Secret Meanings of Botanical Names

Almost every botanical name means *something*, and learning the meanings behind those megasyllablic monikers may help fix a name in your mind. Take small Solomon's seal, *Polygonatum biflorum*, as an example. *Polygonatum* derives from the Greek for many (*polys*) and knee (*gony*), and sure enough, the horizontal stems of *Polygonatum* have many "knees," or joints. The species name *biflorum* comes from the Latin prefix *bi-*, meaning two, and the suffix *-florum*, meaning flower. So *biflorum* means two-flowered—referring to the flowers that are often borne in pairs along the stem.

As you get to know plants better, you'll be able to understand many botanical names without help. For example, no one needs to tell you that *contortus* means twisted or that *americanus* indicates the plant is from the New World. Some botanical names (such as *thompsonii*) relate to the name of the person who discovered the plant. There are literally hundreds of species names that are easily understood by any English speaker. And if you studied French or Spanish in school, you can easily triple the number of words you understand, as both languages have many words based on Latin.

---

acaulis. Stemless, or with a very short stem.

alatus. Winged.

albus. White.

alpestris. Of lower mountains.

alpinus. Of higher mountains.

amabilis. Lovely.

-anthus. Suffix meaning flower, as in *macranthus*, large-flowered.

arborescens. Woody or becoming treelike.

arcticus. From the Arctic.

arendsii. In honor of Georg Arends, a German plant breeder.

argentus. Silvery.

arvensis. From cultivated fields.

aurantiacus. Orange.

aureo-, auri-. Prefixes meaning golden, as in *aureovariegata*, golden-variegated.

australis. Southern.

autumnalis. Pertaining to autumn.

azureum. Sky blue, azure.

barbatus. Bearded.

borealis. Northern.

bracteatus. Having bracts (bracts are petal-like leaves).

caeruleus. Dark blue.

campestris. From plains or fields.

candidus. Bright white.

capilliformis. Like a hair.

capitatus. Forming a head.

cardinalis. Scarlet.

carneus. Flesh-colored.

-carpus. Suffix meaning fruit or fruited, as in *melanocarpus*, black-fruited.

-caulis. Suffix meaning stemmed, as in *crassicaulis*, thick-stemmed.

-cephalus. Suffix meaning headed, as in *macrocephalus*, large-headed.

chinensis. From China.

chlor-, chloro-. Prefixes meaning green, as in *chlorophyllus*, green-leaved.

chrys-, chryso-. Prefixes meaning golden, as in *chrysanthus*, golden-flowered.

cinereus. Ash-colored, gray.

citrinus. Lemon-colored or lemonlike.

coccineus. Scarlet.

columnaris. Narrowly upright, columnar.

communis. Common, general.

cordi-. Prefix meaning heart, as in *cordiformis*, heart-shaped.

crassi-. Prefix meaning thick, as in *crassifolius*, thick-leaved.

cristatus. Crested.

cultorum. Of the garden, cultivated.

cyaneus. Blue.

dactyl-. Prefix meaning finger, as in *dactyloides*, fingerlike.

dasy-. Prefix meaning hairy, shaggy, or thick, as in *dasystemon*, with hairy stamens.

decumbens. Trailing but with upright tips.

deltoides. Triangular.

dentatus. Toothed.

depressus. Flattened.

di-. Prefix meaning two, as in *didymus*, twinned or double.

digitatus. Like an open hand.

dioicus. Having male and female reproductive organs on separate plants.

echinatus. Covered in prickles, like a hedgehog.

elatus. Tall.

ens-. Prefix meaning sword, as in *ensifolius*, with sword-shaped leaves.

eri-, erio-. Prefixes meaning woolly, as in *erianthus*, with woolly flowers.

falcatus. Sickle-shaped.

fastigiatus. Narrowly upright branches, columnar.

fili-. Prefix meaning thread, as in *filicaulis*, with a thin or threadlike stem.

fistulosus. Hollow.

flabellatus. Fanlike.

flav-, flavi-, flavo-. Prefixes meaning yellow, as in *flavispinus*, yellow-spined.

flore-pleno. With double flowers.

-florus. Suffix meaning flower, as in *biflorus*, with two flowers.

foetidus. Bad-smelling.

-folius. Suffix meaning leaved, as in *salicifolius*, willow-leaved.

formosus. Handsome.

fragarioides. Like a strawberry.

frutescens. Shrublike.

fulgens. Shiny.

fulvi-, fulvo-. Prefixes meaning tawny, as in *fulvidus*, somewhat tawny.

gigas. Giant.

glaber. Smooth.

gland-. Prefix meaning gland, as in *glandulifera*, gland-bearing.

glauci-, glauco-. Prefixes meaning glaucous or covered in powder; gray-green, as in *glaucifolius*, with gray-green or powder-covered leaves.

glob-, globi-. Prefixes meaning round or ball-shaped, as in *globularis*, globular.

glomeratus. Clustered into ball-shaped heads.

gracil-. Prefix meaning slender or graceful, as in *gracillimus*, very slender.

gramini-. Prefix meaning grass, as in *graminifolius*, grass-leaved.

graveolens. Heavily scented.

heli-, helio-. Prefixes meaning sun, as in *Helianthus*, sunflower.

heter-, hetero-. Prefixes meaning various, as in *heteranthus*, various-flowered.

hiemalis, hyemalis. Of winter.

hirtellus. Somewhat hairy.

hispidus. Bristly.

humilis. Low-growing.

hybridus. Of hybrid origin.

iber-. Prefix meaning from Iberia (Spain and Portugal), as in *Iberis*.

im-, in-. Prefixes meaning un- or without, as in *immaculatus*, without spots.

incanus. Hoary, gray, white.

incarnatus. Flesh-colored.

incisus. Deeply cut.

-issimus. Suffix indicating the superlative, as in *foetidissimus*, very bad-smelling.

labiatus. Lipped.

laciniatus. Deeply cut into tapered lobes.

lact-. Prefix meaning milky, as in *lactiflorus*, with milky white flowers.

laevigatus. Smooth.

lanatus. Woolly.

lanceolatus. Spear-shaped.

lasi-, lasio-. Prefixes meaning woolly, as in *lasiocarpus*, with woolly fruits.

lati-. Prefix meaning broad, as in *latifolius*, with broad leaves.

lept-, lepto-. Prefixes meaning slender, as in *leptopus*, thin stalked.

leuc-, leuco-. Prefixes meaning white, as in *leucanthus*, white-flowered.

liliflorus. Lily-flowered.

linearis. Linear.

lingu-. Prefix meaning tongue, as in *linguiformis*, tonguelike.

littoralis. Of the seashore.

lob-, lobo-. Prefixes meaning lobe, as in *lobatus*, lobed.

longi-. Prefix meaning long, as in *longicaulis*, long-stemmed.

luridus. Smoky yellow.

lutescens. Yellowish, or becoming yellow.

macr-, macro-. Prefixes meaning long or big, as in *macrorrhizus*, with large roots.

maculatus, maculosus. Spotted.

majalis. Of May.

marginalis. Marginal.

-marginatus. Suffix meaning margined, bordered, as in *aureomarginatus*, with a yellow edge.

marmoratus. Marbled, mottled.

medi-. Prefix meaning middle, center, as in *mediopictus*, striped down the middle.

mega-, megalo-. Prefixes meaning big, as in *megarrhizus*, with big roots.

mel-, melan-. Prefixes meaning black, as in *melananthus*, black-flowered.

meli-, mell-. Prefixes meaning honey, as in *melliodorus*, honey-scented.

melo-. Prefix meaning melonlike, as in *meloformis*, melon-shaped.

micro-. Prefix meaning small, as in *microdontus*, with small teeth.

mille-. Prefix literally meaning 1,000, but more generally, many, as in *millefolius*, many-leaved.

minimus. Smallest.

mollis. Soft or with soft hairs.

mon-, mono-. Prefixes meaning single, as in *monocephalus*, with one head.

monstrosus. Abnormal.

mont-, monti-. Prefixes meaning pertaining to mountains, as in *monticola*, mountain-dwelling.

moschatus. Musky.

mucosus. Slimy.

mucronatus. Pointed.

mult-, multi-. Prefixes meaning many, as in *multicaulis*, with many stems.

muralis. Of walls.

mutabilis. Changeable.

nanus. Dwarf.

napiformus. Turnip-shaped.

nemorosus. Growing in woodlands.

nero-, neuro-, nervi-, nervo-. Prefixes meaning "with nerves" (or leaf veins), as in *nervosus*, with conspicuous nerves (or leaf veins).

nidus, nitidi-. Prefixes meaning nestlike.

niger. Black.

nipponicus. Japanese.

novi-, novae-, novo-, neo-. Prefixes meaning new, as in *novae-angliae*, from New England; and *novi-belgii*, from New York (once called New Belgium).

nud-. Prefix meaning naked, as in *nudicaulis*, bare-stemmed.

nummularius. Resembling a coin, i.e., round.

obconicus. Shaped like an inverted cone.

obtus-. Prefix meaning blunt, as in *obtusifolius*, blunt-leaved.

occidentalis. Western.

ocellatus, oculatus. Having an eye or eyes.

ochr-. Prefix meaning ocher-colored or yellow, as in *ochroleucus*, yellowish white.

-odes, -oides. Suffixes meaning like, as in *agavaoides*, agave-like.

odoratus, odorifer, odorus. Scented.

officinalis, officinarum. Sold in shops: refers to plants that would have been sold by apothecaries.

oppositi-. Prefix meaning opposite, as in *oppositifolius*, with opposite leaves.

orbiculatus, orbicularis. Round and flat.

oreophilus. Mountain-loving.

orientalis. Eastern.

ornatus. Showy.

ovifer, oviger. Egg-bearing.

ovinus. Pertaining to sheep or pastures.

ox-, oxy-. Prefixes meaning sharp or acid, as in *oxylobus*, with sharply pointed lobes.

pachy-. Prefix meaning thick, as in *pachypodus*, with thick roots.

pallidus. Pale.

palmatus. Palmate, like an open hand.

paniculatus. With flowers arranged in a panicle (a branching flower cluster).

peduncularis. With a peduncle (a flowerstalk).

peltifolius. Shieldlike leaf; i.e., with the leaf stalk attached to the back of the leaf, not to the leaf margin.

penduli-. Prefix meaning hanging, pendulous, as in *penduliflorus*, with pendulous flowers.

peregrinus. Exotic, immigrant.

perfoliatus, perfossus. Perfoliate (with the leaf surrounding the stem).

petiolaris, petiolatus. With a petiole (a leaf stalk), especially a long one.

phae-, phaeo-. Prefixes meaning dark, as in *phaeus*, dark, dusky.

-phyllus. Suffix meaning leaved, as in *polyphyllus*, many-leaved.

pictus. Painted, colorful.

pilosus. Covered in long hairs.

pinnatus. Pinnate; with leaflets arranged on each side of a common stalk, like a feather.

plan-. Prefix meaning flat, as in *planiflorus*, with flat flowers.

plantagineus. Plantainlike.

platy-. Prefix meaning broad, as in *platyphyllus*, with broad leaves.

plen-. Prefix meaning double or full, as in *pleniflorus*, double-flowered.

plumarius, plumatus, plumosus. Feathery, featherlike.

poly-. Prefix meaning many, as in *polyanthus*, with many flowers.

praecox. Very early.

pratensis. Of the meadows.

primuli-. Prefix meaning pertaining to the primrose (*Primula*), as in *primulifolius*, primrose-leaved.

procumbens, prostratus. Prostrate.

pruinatus, pruinosus. With a frosted appearance.

pseud-, pseudo-. Prefixes meaning false, similar to, as in *pseudacorus*, similar to *Acorus*.

psil-, psilo-. Prefixes meaning smooth or hairless, as in *psilostemon*, with hairless stamens.

pter-. Prefix meaning winged, as in *pterospermus*, with winged seeds.

pubens, pubescens, pubigera. Downy, fuzzy.

pulchellus, pulcher. Pretty.

pumilus. Dwarf.

punctatus. Dotted.

pungens. Sharp-pointed.

purpuratus, purpureus, purpurascens. Purple.

pusillus. Very small.

pyramidalis. Pyramid-shaped.

pyri-. Prefix meaning pear, as in *pyrifolius*, pear-leaved.

querci-. Prefix meaning pertaining to oaks, as in *quercifolius*, oak-leaved.

racemosus. With flowers in racemes (an unbranched flower cluster with stalked flowers).

radiatus. With rays or radiating.

radicans. With rooting stems.

ramosus. Branched.

rectus. Upright.

reflexus. Bent backward.

regina. Of the queen.

reniformis. Kidney-shaped.

repens, reptans. Creeping.

reticulatus. With a netlike pattern.

retusus. With a rounded, slightly notched tip.

riparius. Of river banks.

rivalis, rivularis. Pertaining to brooks or streams.

roseus. Rosy.

rubens, ruber. Red.

rugosus. Wrinkled.

saccharoides. Like sugar.

sagittifolius. With arrow-shaped leaves.

salicifolius. Willow-leaved.

sangineus. Blood red.

sarmentosus. Bearing runners (a slender shoot rooting at the nodes).

sativus. Cultivated.

saxatilis, saxicolus. Found among rocks.

scaber. Rough.

scandens. Climbing.

schiz-, schizo-. Prefix meaning cut or divided, as in *schizopetalus*, with cut petals.

scoparius. Broomlike.

scopulorum. Of cliffs or rocks.

scorpioides. Resembling a scorpion.

semi-. Prefix meaning half, as in *semialatus*, semi-winged.

semper-. Prefix meaning always, as in *semperflorens*, always in flower, everblooming; and *sempervirens*, evergreen.

septentrionalis. Northern.

serpens. Creeping.

serratus, serrulatus. Saw-toothed.

sessil-, sessili-. Prefixes meaning stalkless, as in *sessiliflorus*, flowers without a stalk.

silvaticus, sylvaticus, silvestris, sylvestris, silvicola, sylvicola. Of the woods.

simplici-. Prefix meaning simple, unbranched, as in *simplicfolius*, with simple leaves.

sinensis, sinicus. Chinese.

spathuli-. Prefix meaning like a spatula, as in *spathulifolius*, with spatulate leaves.

speciosus, spectabilis. Showy.

-spermus. Suffix meaning seeded, as in *megaspermus*, large-seeded.

sphaero-. Prefix meaning spherical, as in *spaherocephalus*, with a rounded head.

spinifera, spinosus. Spiny.

stellaris, stellatus. Starlike, starry.

-stemon. Suffix meaning stamen, as in *dasystemon*, with hairy stamens.

steno-. Prefix meaning narrow, as in *stenopetalus*, with narrow petals.

strepto-. Prefix meaning twisted, as in *streptophyllus*, twisted leaf.

striatus. Striped.

strictus. Upright.

suaveolens. Sweet-scented.

suavis. Sweet, pleasant.

sub-, sur-. Prefixes meaning under, almost, slightly, etc., as in *subdentatus*, nearly toothless; and *subhirtellus*, slightly hairy.

suffrutescens, suffruticosus. Somewhat shrubby or woody.

sulphureus. Sulfur yellow.

syriacus. Syrian.

tabularis, tabuliformis. Flat and tablelike.

tardi-. Suffix meaning late, as in *tardiflorus*, late-blooming.

tartaricus. Of Central Asia (Tartary).

tectorum. Of rooftops.

tenui-. Prefix meaning slender, as in *tenuifolius*, with slender leaves.

terminalis. Terminal.

textilis. Used in weaving, woven.

tinctorius. Used in dyes.

tomentosus. Densely woolly.

trich-, tricho-. Prefixes meaning hairy, as in *trichophyllus*, hairy-leaved.

tristis. Sad, dull.

truncatus. Cut off square, truncate.

tuberosus. Tuberous.

tubi-. Prefix meaning tubular, as in *tubiflorus*, tubular-flowered.

ulm-. Prefix meaning like an elm, as in *ulmifolius*, elm-leaved.

umbellatus. With an umbel (a flower cluster where all flowerstalks arise from one point).

umbrosus. Liking shade.

undatus, undulatus. Wavy.

usitatissimus. Most useful.

variegatus. Irregularly colored, variegated.

velutinus. Velvety.

ventricosus. Swollen on one side, pot-bellied.

venustus. Charming.

veris, vernalis, vernus. Of the spring.

verrucosus, verruculosus. Warty.

versicolor. Variously colored.

verticillaris, verticillatus. Growing in whorls.

villosus. Covered with down.

violaceus. Violet-colored.

virens. Green.

virescens. Becoming green.

virginalis, virgineus. White, virginal.

virginianus, virginicus, virginiensis. Specifically, of Virginia, but often used to mean North American.

vulgaris. Common.

xanth-, xantho-. Prefixes meaning yellow, as in *xanthocalyx*, yellow calyx (outer part of a flower).

zebrina. Striped.

zonalis. Banded.

Acknowledgments

I would like to thank the team at Rodale Organic Gardening Books for having made this book possible, with special thanks to Karen Bolesta and Fern Bradley for delicately prodding me to get things done, to Heidi Stonehill for her impeccable attention to detail with plant nomenclature, and to Pam Ruch for her assistance with the Good Neighbors research. I'd also like to sincerely thank Pam Baggett, Beverly Fitts, Joanne Kostecky, Pam Ruch, and Barbara Wilde for creating the beautiful perennial garden designs that appear in Chapter 3.

Special thanks also to my wife, Marie, who put up with months of spousal neglect while I locked myself in the basement to write (she did get a great meal at the best restaurant in town for all her troubles, I do hasten to add), and my assistant, Susanne, for keeping the office running all on her lonesome while "big boss" tried to concentrate on writing, writing, and more writing.

Photo Credits

© C. Colston Burrell 275, 416, 423

© Karen Bussolini 65, 318

© David Cavagnaro vii, x, 1, 129, 295, 381, 411, 448, 471, back cover

© R. Todd Davis 8, 17, 93, 113, 133, 143, 147, 188, 195, 281, 341, 353, 387, 393, 441

© Alan & Linda Detrick ii, 13, 19, 24, 27 (blue), 27 (yellow), 31, 51, 54, 55, 59 (both), 106, 139, 187, 201, 203, 209 (right), 217, 241, 450, back cover

© Ken Druse 133, 187, 190, 240

© Derek Fell 105, 185, 233, 443

© Garden Picture Library (Mark Bolton) 169, 447, back cover

© Garden Picture Library (Philippe Bonduel) 208 (left)

© Garden Picture Library (John Glover) 313

© Garden Picture Library (Gary Rogers) 107

© Garden Picture Library (Didier Willery) 291

© Galen Gates 20, 23, 32, 63, 85, 97, 101, 103, 151, 159, 207, 219, 225, 240, 249, 259, 269, 303, 315, 363, 395, 415, 431, 445, back cover

© John Glover vii, 26, 70, 121, 166, 242, 247, 272, 289, 316, 329, 389, 391, 461

© Pamela Harper 27 (green), 115, 117, 145, 173, 177, 193, 293, 321, 331, 355, 361, 365, 421, 457, back cover

© Larry Hodgson 75, 83, 175, 205, 215, 231, 287, 403, 427, 435, 437

© Bill Johnson 106, 251, 447

© Dwight R. Kuhn 54, 55

© Janet Loughrey 227, 261, 409, back cover

© Charles Mann v, vi, 48, 81, 87, 91, 123, 125, 141, 153, 163, 171, 181, 210, 221, 229, 237, 239, 253, 267, 277, 285, 296, 307, 309, 311, 327, 346, 351, 357, 359, 371, 383, 405, 413, 425, 437, 439, 457, 463, 467, back cover

© David McDonald 2, 7, 27 (red), back cover

© Allen McInnis/Liaison Agency ix

© Clive Nichols 27 (orange), 28, 66, 67

© Robin Orans 208 (right)

© Jerry Pavia 16, 127, 164, 183, 335, 337, 401, 433, 459

© Susan A. Roth 4, 14, 19, 27 (violet), 29, 61, 68, 73, 77, 79, 89, 95, 108, 110, 119, 131, 134, 136, 149, 157, 161, 179, 199, 223, 235, 255, 257, 270, 283, 298, 305, 323, 325, 339, 343, 345, 348, 353, 367, 369, 377, 379, 385, 399, 418, 429, 453, 455, 469, back cover

© Barry Runk/Grant Heilman Photography 56

© Richard Shiell 99, 107, 155, 197, 241, 263, 265, 279, 333, 372, 397, 407, 465, back cover

© Mark Turner 209 (left), 301

Sources

The catalogs I have listed here are well known to plant nuts like myself for their excellent selection and great service. Many of these mail-order sources are small family-run businesses and may charge a fee for their catalog (usually refundable with a purchase) to keep costs down.

UNITED STATES

1800Daylily.com
15528 Aiken Road
Louisville, KY 40245
Phone: (800) 329-5459
Fax: (502) 245-7008
Web site: www.1800
  daylily.com

A & D Nursery
P.O. Box 2338
Snohomish, WA 98291
Phone: (360) 668-9690
Web site: www.adpeonies.com

American Daylily & Perennials
P.O. Box 210
Grain Valley, MO 64029
Phone: (800) 770-2777
Fax: (816) 443-2849
Web site: www.american
  daylily.com

André Viette Farm & Nursery
P.O. Box 1109, State Route 608
Fishersville, VA 22939
Phone: (800) 575-5538
Fax: (540) 943-0782
Web site: www.viette.com

Bluestone Perennials
7211 Middle Ridge Road
Madison, OH 44057
Phone: (800) 852-5243
Web site: www.blue
  stoneperennials.com

Busse Gardens
17160 245th Avenue
Big Lake, MN 55309
Phone: (800) 544-3192
Fax: (763) 263-1473
Web site: www.busse
  gardens.com

Canyon Creek Nursery
3527 Dry Creek Road
Oroville, CA 95965
Phone: (530) 533-2166
E-mail: johnccn@sunset.net

Carroll Gardens
444 East Main Street
Westminster, MD 21157
Phone: (800) 638-6334
Fax: (410) 857-4112
Web site: www.carroll
  gardens.com

Cordon Bleu Daylilies
P.O. Box 2033
San Marcos, CA 92079-2033
Phone: (760) 744-8367
Fax: (760) 744-0510
Web site: www.buenacreek
  gardens.com

Dabney Herbs
P.O. Box 22061
Louisville, KY 40252
Phone/fax: (502) 893-5198
Web site: www.dabney
  herbs.com

Forestfarm
990 Tetherow Road
Williams, OR 97544-9599
Phone: (541) 846-7269
Fax: (541) 846-6963
Web site: www.forestfarm.com

Heronswood Nursery Ltd.
7530 NE 288th Street
Kingston, WA 98346-9502
Phone: (360) 297-4172
Fax: (360) 297-8321
Web site: www.herons
  wood.com

High Country Gardens
2902 Rufina Street
Santa Fe, NM 87507-2929
Phone: (800) 925-9387
Fax: (800) 925-0097
Web site: www.highcountry
  gardens.com

Klehm's Song Sparrow Perennial Farm
13101 East Rye Road
Avalon, WI 53505
Phone: (800) 553-3715
Web site: www.klehm.com

Kurt Bluemel, Inc.
2740 Greene Lane
Baldwin, MD 21013-9523
Phone: (800) 498-1560
Fax: (410) 557-9785
Web site: www.kurt
  bluemel.com

Louisiana Nursery
5853 Highway 182
Opelousas, LA 70570
Phone: (337) 948-3696
Fax: (337) 942-6404

Milaeger's Gardens
4838 Douglas Avenue
Racine, WI 53402-2498
Phone: (800) 669-9956
Fax: (262) 639-1855

Niche Gardens
1111 Dawson Road
Chapel Hill, NC 27516
Phone: (919) 967-0078
Fax: (919) 967-4026
Web site: www.nichegdn.com

Paradise Water Gardens
14 May Street
Whitman, MA 02382
Phone: (800) 955-0161
Fax: (781) 447-4591
Web site: www.paradise
  watergardens.com

Park Seed Company
1 Parkton Avenue
Greenwood, SC 29647-0001
Phone: (800) 845-3369
Web site: www.parkseed.com

Plant Delights Nursery
9241 Sauls Road
Raleigh, NC 27603
Phone: (919) 772-4794
Fax: (919) 662-0370
Web site: www.plantdel.com

Plants of the Southwest
3095 Agua Fria Road
Santa Fe, NM 87507
Phone: (800) 788-7333
Fax: (505) 438-8800
Web site: www.plantsofthe
  southwest.com

Shady Oaks Nursery
1601 5th Street
P.O. Box 708
Waseca, MN 56093
Phone: (800) 504-8006
Fax: (888) 735-4531
Web site: www.shadyoaks.com

Siskiyou Rare Plant Nursery
2825 Cummings Road
Medford, OR 97501
Phone: (541) 772-6846
Fax: (541) 772-4917
Web site: www.srpn.net

Thompson & Morgan Inc.
P.O. Box 1308
Jackson, NJ 08527-0308
Phone: (800) 274-7333
Fax: (888) 466-4769
Web site: www.thompson-
  morgan.com

Wayside Gardens
1 Garden Lane
Hodges, SC 29695-0001
Phone: (800) 845-1124
Fax: (800) 817-1124
Web site: www.wayside
  gardens.com

Weiss Brothers Nursery
11690 Colfax Highway
Grass Valley, CA 95945
Phone: (530) 272-7657
Fax: (530) 272-3578

White Flower Farm
P.O. Box 50
Litchfield, CT 06759-0050
Phone: (800) 503-9624
Fax: (860) 482-0532
Web site: www.whiteflower
  farm.com

William Tricker, Inc.
7125 Tanglewood Drive
Independence, OH 44131
Phone: (800) 524-3492
Fax: (216) 524-6688
Web site: www.tricker.com

CANADA
Fraser's Thimble Farms
175 Arbutus Road
Salt Spring Island, British
  Columbia
V8K 1A3
Phone/fax: (250) 537-5788
Web site: www.thimble
  farms.com

Gardens North
5984 Third Line Road North
R.R. #3
North Gower, Ontario
K0A 2T0
Phone: (613) 489-0065
Fax: (613) 489-1208
Web site: www.gardens
  north.com

**Hole's Greenhouses and
Gardens Ltd.**
101 Bellerose Drive
St. Albert, Alberta
T8N 8N8
Phone: (780) 419-6800
Fax: (780) 459-6042
Web site: www.holes
  online.com

Lost Horizons
R.R. #1
Acton, Ontario
L7J 2L7
Phone: (519) 853-3085
Fax: (519) 853-2279
Web site: www.eridani.com/
  losthorizons

Mason Hogue Gardens
3520 Durham Road #1, R.R. #4
Uxbridge, Ontario
L9P 1R4
Phone/fax: (905) 649-3532
Web site: www.mason
  hogue.com

The Perennial Gardens
13139 224th Street
Maple Ridge, British Columbia
V4R 2P6
Phone: (604) 467-4218
Fax: (604) 467-3181
Web site: www.perennial
  gardener.com

Wrightman Alpines
1503 Napperton Drive, R.R. #3
Kerwood, Ontario
N0M 2B0
Phone/fax: (519) 247-3751
Web site: www.wrightman
  alpines.com

Recommended Reading

When it comes to growing plants, you can never have enough knowledge. If half of the secret of growing great perennials comes from trial and error, the other half comes from learning all you can about the plants you're trying to grow. I hope you find that this book is a great source of information about perennial gardening and tells it like it is with popular perennials, but you may want to find out even more about the plants I've featured or others that I mentioned. Here are some of my favorite books that I turn to again and again for information and inspiration.

Armitage, Allan M. *Herbaceous Perennial Plants*. 2nd ed. Champaign, IL: Stipes Publishing, 1997.

Art, Henry W. *The Wildflower Gardener's Guide: Pacific Northwest, Rocky Mountain, and Western Canada Edition*. Pownal, VT: Storey Communications, 1990.

Brickell, Christopher, and Judith D. Zuk, eds. *The American Horticultural Society A–Z Encyclopedia of Garden Plants*. New York: DK Publishing, 1996.

Burrell, C. Colston. *Perennial Combinations*. Emmaus, PA: Rodale Press, 1999.

Cox, Jeff. *Perennial All-Stars*. Emmaus, PA: Rodale Press, 1998.

Garden Way Publishing Editors. *Perennials: 1,001 Gardening Questions Answered*. Pownal, VT: Storey Communications, 1989.

Greenlee, John. *The Encyclopedia of Ornamental Grasses*. Emmaus, PA: Rodale Press, 1992.

Heriteau, Jacqueline, and André Viette. *The American Horticultural Society Flower Finder*. New York: Simon & Schuster, 1992.

Hill, Lewis, and Nancy Hill. *Successful Perennial Gardening*. Pownal, VT: Storey Communications, 1988.

Hole, Lois, and Jill Fallis. *Lois Hole's Perennial Favorites*. Renton, WA: Lone Pine Publishing, 1995.

MacKenzie, David S. *Perennial Ground Covers*. Portland, OR: Timber Press, 1997.

McClure, Susan. *Easy-Care Perennial Gardens*. Emmaus, PA: Rodale Press, Inc., 1997.

McGourty, Frederick. *The Perennial Gardener*. Boston: Houghton Mifflin Co., 1991.

Meyer, M. Hockenberry, D. B. White, and H. Pellett. *Ornamental Grasses for Cold Climates*. St. Paul, MN: Department of Horticultural Science, University of Minnesota Extension Service, 1996.

Ondra, Nancy J. *Easy Plant Propagation*. (Taylor's Weekend Gardening Guides Series.) Boston: Houghton Mifflin Co., 1998.

Phillips, Ellen, and C. Colston Burrell. *Rodale's Illustrated Encyclopedia of Perennials*. Emmaus, PA: Rodale Press, 1993.

Powell, Eileen. *From Seed to Bloom: How to Grow over 500 Annuals, Perennials & Herbs*. Pownal, VT: Storey Communications, 1995.

Robinson, Peter. *The American Horticultural Society Complete Guide to Water Gardening*. New York: DK Publishing, 1997.

Rumary, Mark. *The Dry Garden: A Practical Guide to Planning & Planting*. New York: Sterling Publishing Company, 1995.

Sinnes, A. Cort, and Larry Hodgson. *All about Perennials*. rev. ed. San Francisco, CA: Ortho Books, 1996.

Still, Steven M. *Manual of Herbaceous Ornamental Plants*. 4th ed. Champaign, IL: Stipes Publishing Company, 1993.

Sunset Books and *Sunset* Magazine editors. *Sunset Western Garden Book*. Menlo Park, CA: Sunset Books, 1995.

Tatroe, Marcia. *Perennials for Dummies*. Indianapolis, IN: IDG Books Worldwide, 1997.

Taylor's Guide Staff. *Taylor's Guide to Ground Covers, Vines & Grasses*. Boston: Houghton Mifflin Co., 1987.

Taylor, Norman. *Taylor's Guide to Perennials*. Rev. ed. Boston: Houghton Mifflin Co., 1986.

Thomas, Charles B. *Water Gardens*. (Taylor's Weekend Gardening Guides Series.) Boston: Houghton Mifflin Co., 1997.

Valleau, John M. *Perennial Gardening Guide*. Abbotsford, British Columbia, Canada: Valleybrook Gardens Ltd., 1995.

Index

Note: Page references in **boldface** indicate photographs or illustrations.

B

Rudbeckia fulgida var. *sullivantii*, 94
    'Goldsturm', **68**, 69, 95, **95**
Rudbeckia hirta, 95
Rudbeckia laciniata 'Goldquelle' ('Gold
    Fountain', 'Gold Drop'), 107
Rudbeckia maxima, 107
Rush, common (soft), 275
    'Spiralis', 275
Russian sage, 29, 56, 70, 111, 418,
    440–41, **441**
    hybrid
        'Blue Mist', 441
        'Blue Spire', 441
        'Filagran', 441
        'Longin', 441
Rust, 59, **59**

S

Sage, 96–97, **97**
    azure, 97
    blue, 97
    blue anise, 107
    garden, 97
    lilac, 'Purple Rain', 97
    meadow, 107
    violet, 97, **97**
        'Mainacht' ('May Night'),
           97
        'Ostfriesland' ('East
           Friesland'), 97
        'Rose Queen', 97
    white, 351, **351**
        'Silver King', 351
        'Silver Queen', **346**, 347,
           351, **351**
        'Valerie Finnis', 351
Sagebrush, 350–51, **351**
Salix species, 273
Salvia (*Salvia*), 31, **31**, 56, 96–97, **97**
    blue (annual), 8, **8**
Salvia azurea, 97
Salvia guaranitica, 107
Salvia nemorosa, 97, **97**
    'Mainacht' ('May Night'), 97
    'Ostfriesland' ('East
        Friesland'), 97
    'Rose Queen', 97
Salvia officinalis, 97
Salvia pratensis, 107
Salvia verticillata 'Purple Rain', 97
Sanguisorba, 444–45, **445**

Sanguisorba canadensis, 445, **445**
Sanguisorba officinalis, 445
Saponaria, 83
Saponaria ocymoides, 83
Saponaria officinalis, 83
Sarracenia, 294–95, **295**
Sarracenia leucophylla, 295
Sarracenia purpurea, 295, **295**
Saxifraga, 406–7, **407**
Saxifraga × *arendsii*, 407, **407**
Saxifraga paniculata, 407
Saxifraga umbrosa, 407
Saxifraga × *urbium*, 407
    'Aureopunctata', 407
    'Chambers Pink Pride', 407
Saxifraga × *urbium* var. *primuloides*,
    407
Saxifrage, 406–7, **407**
    livelong, 407
    mossy, 407, **407**
Scabiosa caucasica, 99
    'Fama', 99
    House Hybrids (Isaac House
        Hybrids), 99
Scabiosa columbaria, 99
    'Butterfly Blue', 98, 99, **99**
    'Pink Mist', 99
Scabiosa ochroleuca, 99
Scabious (*Scabiosa*), 98–99, **99**
    small, 99
    yellow, 99
Sea holly, 23, **23**, 70, 256–57,
    257
    alpine, 257, **257**
    amethyst, 257
    flat, 257
Sea kale, 424–25, **425**
Sea lavender, 232–33, **233**
    'Blue Cloud', 233
    'Violetta', 233
Sea pink, 220–21, **221**
Sedge, 358–59, **359**
    Bowles' golden ('Aurea'), 358,
        359
    Japanese, 359
        'Variegata,' 349, 359
    leatherleaf, 358, 359, **359**
Sedum (*Sedum*), 4, **4**, 166, 182–83,
    183, 187, 408–9, **409**
    'Herbstfreude' ('Autumn Joy'),
        164, 165, 182–83, **183**
    'Mohrchen', 183

    'Ruby Glow', 186, 187, **187**
    'Vera Jameson', 182, 183
Sedum acre, 22, 409
Sedum alboroseum, 186
Sedum floriferum 'Weihenstephaner
    Gold', 409
Sedum kamtschaticum, 409
    'Variegatum', 409
    'Weihenstephaner Gold', 409
Sedum middendorffianum
    'Variegatum', 409
Sedum sieboldii, 186
Sedum spectabile, 183
    'Brilliant', 183
    'Carmen', 183
    'Iceberg', 183
Sedum spurium, 408–9, **409**
    'Coccineum', 409
    'Fuldaglut', 409
    'Purpurteppich' ('Purple
        Carpet'), 409
    'Schorbuser Blut' ('Dragon's
        Blood'), 409
    'Splendens', 409
    'Tricolor', 409
    'Variegatum', 409
Sedum telephium, 183
Sedum telephium subsp. *maximum*
    'Atropurpureum', 183
Self-heal, 404–5, **405**
    large-flowered, 405, **405**
        'Alba', 405
        'Loveliness', 405
        Loveliness series, 405
        'Pink Loveliness', 405
        'Purple Loveliness', 405
    large-flowered
        'Rotkäppchen' ('Little Red
           Riding Hood'), 405
        'White Loveliness', 405
    Webb's
        'Alba', 405
        'Rosea', 405
Semiaquilegia, 453
Semiaquilegia ecalcarata, 453
Semiaquilegia simulatrix, 453
Sempervivum, 410–11, **411**
Sempervivum arachnoideum, 411
Sempervivum tectorum, 411, **411**
    'Oddity', 411
Setcreasea, purple-leaved, 101
Shade, 6–7, 10, 317

USDA Plant Hardiness Zone Map

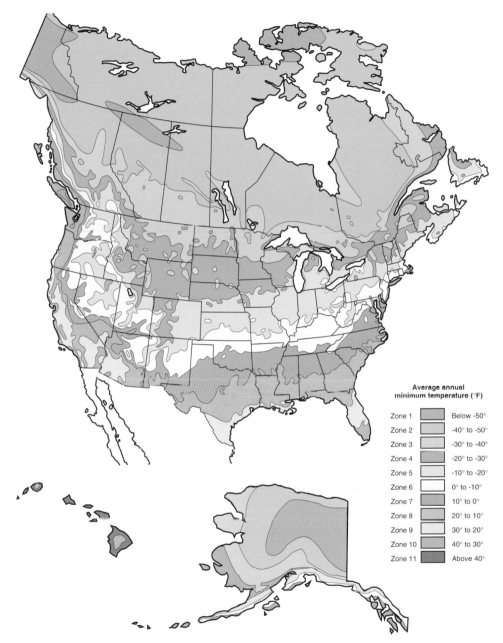

Average annual minimum temperature (°F)

Zone 1		Below -50°
Zone 2		-40° to -50°
Zone 3		-30° to -40°
Zone 4		-20° to -30°
Zone 5		-10° to -20°
Zone 6		0° to -10°
Zone 7		10° to 0°
Zone 8		20° to 10°
Zone 9		30° to 20°
Zone 10		40° to 30°
Zone 11		Above 40°

Revised in 1990, this map is recognized as the best indicator of minimum temperatures available. Look at the map to find your area, then match its color to the key at the right. When you've found your color, the key will tell you what hardiness zone you live in. Remember that the map is a general guide; your particular conditions may vary.

American Horticultural Society Heat Zone Map

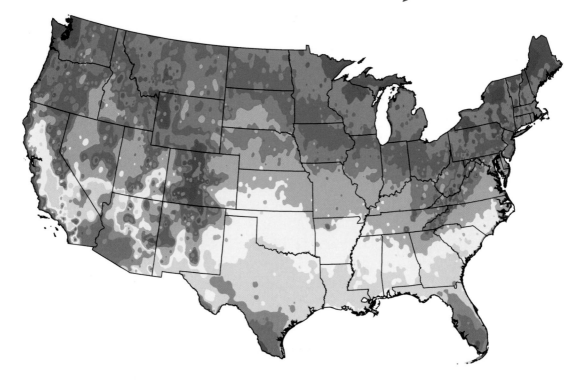

AMERICAN HORTICULTURAL SOCIETY

7931 East Boulevard Drive
Alexandria, VA 22308 U.S.A.
(703) 768-5700 Fax (703) 768-8700

Coordinated by:
Dr. H. Marc Cathey, President Emeritus

Compiled by:
Meteorological Evaluation Services Co., Inc.

Underwriting by:
American Horticultural Society
Goldsmith Seed Company
Horticultural Research Institute of the
American Nursery and Landscape Association
Monrovia
Time Life Inc.

Average Number of Days per Year Above 86°F (30°C)	Zone
< 1	1
1 to 7	2
> 7 to 14	3
> 14 to 30	4
> 30 to 45	5
> 45 to 60	6
> 60 to 90	7
> 90 to 120	8
> 120 to 150	9
> 150 to 180	10
> 180 to 210	11
> 210	12